European Journalism Education

European Journalism Education

European Journalism Education

Edited by Georgios Terzis

intellect Bristol, UK / Chicago, USA

First published in the UK in 2009 by
Intellect, The Mill, Parnall Road, Fishponds, Bristol, BS16 3JG, UK

First published in the USA in 2009 by
Intellect, The University of Chicago Press, 1427 E. 60th Street,
Chicago, IL 60637, USA

A catalogue record for this book is available from the
British Library.

Cover designer: Holly Rose
Copy-editor: Jessica Mitchell
Typesetting: Mac Style, Beverley, E. Yorkshire

ISBN 978-1-84150-235-9

Printed and bound by Gutenberg Press, Malta.

To Melina

Contents

Foreword

Hugh Stephenson

The landscape of journalism has changed beyond all recognition in the two decades since Pierre Mory of the Institut des Hautes Études des Communications Sociales in Belgium and I researched and wrote our 1990 report, *Journalism Training in Europe*.[1] We did so at the request of the European Commission and the European Journalism Training Association in response to the view that journalism and journalists performed (or should perform) a powerful and positive role in the social and political development of Europe and that, consequently, it was important to identify and then spread 'best practice' in the training of journalists as widely as possible.

What has changed so fundamentally in these last twenty years? First, of course, is the political context. In 1990 there seemed no point in even bothering to include a survey of journalism training in East and Central Europe. It was assumed that, in these parts of Europe, most journalists working in mainstream media were either witting or unwitting agents of the state; while those who so bravely worked for the underground media also tended to behave more as propagandists for their cause than as 'objective' journalists.

When all that changed with the unexpected collapse of the Soviet Union, there followed a period of excessive hope that journalists, free at last to perform in a professional manner, would be key agents in the building of new civil societies in their countries, perhaps even in Russia. Also, in the years since 1990, the 'European project' itself has greatly lost its sense of direction and impetus and with that has come a lowering of the expectations, in that respect, that were once loaded on the shoulders of journalists.

Second, these two decades have seen journalism transformed by technological change, including particularly the changes associated with the Internet and the World Wide Web. The revolution was, of course, already under way in 1990 and those with foresight were making predictions as to where things were going. Media organizations and journalists in 1990 were trying as fast as they could to come to terms with the brave new world that was engulfing them, but the underlying structure of the media business was still entirely traditional. Journalists (in the print media or in broadcasting) produced material for newspapers, or magazines, or radio, or television. Alongside this activity, a few journalism-based websites were experimenting with the new possibilities available and were, in general, losing significant sums of money in the process.

However in 1990 none of the current preoccupations of the media were at the centre of the stage. Media convergence was still a vague idea, not the reality that it has become in the meantime. The subsequent requirement for media organizations to forget their original position in the traditional scheme of things and to deliver their 'product' across the whole range of available media outlets has had (and continues to have) a profound effect on the job descriptions of journalists. In this process of 'media convergence' the organizations involved, both for reasons of flexibility and in order to save money, have begun to rely to a greater extent on casual labour or to take on (usually younger and cheaper) staff to work in the new production processes, who have little or no previous experience of the traditions and requirements of journalism. With the partial exceptions of Italy and Greece, journalism in Europe has never been a 'profession' in the narrow sense of an activity to which entry is regulated by some governing body requiring proof of competence and from which a person can be excluded for improper conduct. In talking about 'professional standards' in journalism, one is referring to the recognition of and adherence to standards of technical competence, of ways of working and of codes of ethics that are generally accepted in the business. The main purpose of formal journalism education has been to convey such professional standards to those who wish to work in the media in a more systematic, efficient and rapid way than would be the case just by learning 'on the job'.

A by-product of the new working patterns introduced to meet the requirement of the new technology, however, is that journalistic professionalism in this sense risks being significantly diluted. All of this has profound implications for those involved in the training of journalists. On the positive side, the liberating power of the new technology provides previously undreamed of journalistic possibilities. On the negative side, the same new technology has promoted the requirements of 'production' at the expense of time spent on original research, investigation and reporting.

Third, in 1990, though the gradual decline in the fortunes of traditional print media was evident in most European countries, the fragmentation of readerships that have since been brought about by the new technology was still something for the future. Since 1990, too, the widespread deregulation of radio and television throughout Europe has similarly fragmented viewing and listening audiences. In addition, large segments of our populations now no longer rely on the traditional media as their main source of news, having turned instead to the Web, to the Internet, to mobile telephones or to free newspapers. The loss of revenue to the individual media organizations affected by all this has created acute commercial pressures to make media 'output' more attractive, particularly to younger people who have been turning away from traditional media forms in large numbers. This is sometimes called the move towards 'infotainment'.

All of these trends have tended to dilute the idealized role assigned to journalists in the traditional liberal model of journalism: that of professional actors with a moral purpose to serve the truth and to expose wickedness in the interests of a better society. They are clearly trends that need to be analysed and reacted to by those involved in the training of journalists.

Fourth, nothing, however, has diluted this traditional model of the journalist's role more than the current world financial crash and global recession. Almost all sections of the media, including those that rely mainly on state funding, are faced with sharply reduced revenues and the need to cut costs. This is not a climate in which media organizations feel themselves able to afford the undoubted expense involved in providing high levels of professional education, nor the resources required to support high quality journalism. The first pressure is inevitably resulting in staff reductions on a significant scale and in the cutting back on the more expensive elements of journalistic output. Whole sections of the media in the United States appear to be in meltdown and though, apart from private broadcasting, the media situation in general across Europe appears, for the moment, to not be as bad, the trend is clear. As there is little hope of substantial economic recovery for several years, the trend can only intensify.

It is pointless to indulge in nostalgia about the journalism of yesteryear. The changes in the patterns of both the production and the consumption of media brought about in the last twenty years by the application of new technologies and by economic circumstance have been profound. By contrast, debate about how the media should or can continue to play a positive social role in these changed circumstance has been curiously muted.

So, too, it has to be said, has any discussion about how journalism training should adjust to this totally different environment. Journalism training has, of course, more than kept pace with the changes in media technology and production techniques. But, to a surprising extent, on the side of content, rather than production, most journalism training seems to be strikingly similar to that being provided twenty years ago. It is to be hoped that this survey of the current state of affairs will provoke more of a debate about where this aspect of journalism education should be aiming to go in the next twenty years.

The Author

Hugh Stephenson is Emeritus Professor of Journalism at City University, London. He was a member of the European Journalism Centre's board from its formation in 1993 until 2007 and was its chairman from 1995 until 2002.

Note

1. Stephenson, H., and Mory, P. (1990), Journalism training in Europe, Brussels: Commission of the European Communities.

Introduction

European Journalism Education in a Mess Media World

Georgios Terzis

Twenty years have passed since Hugh Stephenson, the director of City University Journalism School at the time, asked me, as one of his students, to help him find data about journalism education in Greece in order to compile the first ever study of the topic at a European level.[1] At that time there were very few UK universities where you could study journalism, while no such universities existed in Greece. Today there are approximately 100 in these two countries and more than 500 such institutions in Europe.

This book aims at, first, mapping this amazing sea of change of the past twenty years by providing an extensive review of the national journalism education landscapes of 33 European counties. Second, as noted by Paolo Mancini during the European Communication Research and Education Association conference in Barcelona last year that 'comparative analysis makes the invisible visible', it attempts to make these European trends in journalism education visible by providing not only a comparative review of 33 national education landscapes but also four regional introductory chapters as well as conclusions and an epilogue at the crossroads of journalism education at a European level and beyond.

Despite the fact that these national chapters have certain 'unique characteristics', all of them provide a brief history of journalism education in the country and a review of the organizations which provide journalism education. Such organizations include state universities and polytechnics, private universities, national unions of journalists, employers associations, private media companies (in-house training) and the church.[2] The chapters extend their analysis to describing the type of faculty/instructors that these institutions use, the content of the education they provide, i.e. theory vs. practice, communication or journalism studies or a mixed system, the impact of new media in the content of the curriculum, the level of specialization according to fields (science, sports, international journalism etc), the level of specialization according to medium (print, broadcast, etc.), the percentage of journalism education courses in their curricula vs. general education, the role of internships, the level of different degrees offered (Diploma, Bachelor's, Master's, Ph.D.) and exchange programmes with other institutions (bilateral or participation in the EU Erasmus, Erasmus Mundus, etc.).

Moreover the 33 national chapters discuss the issue of the duration of studies in different countries, and the type of students or professionals attending their mainstream or continuing education programmes. Some chapters also provide data on the number of students/professionals that are involved in such trainings every year, as well as a gender breakdown of these data.

Further, the authors of the national chapters discuss the mechanisms of accreditation of such organizations, their participation to the Bologna Process and the European Transfer Credit System (ECTS), the connection of the training institutions with the industry (funding, mutual accreditation and involvement on hiring practices), and the participation of the journalism education institutions to national or international associations/networks.

Finally, the chapters conclude with an analysis of the place in history and current situation of journalism education in the political, economic and social frame of each country and the authors present their views on the future of journalism education.

During the course of the exercise described above, which involved no less than 60 authors, a number of definitional problems came to fore which mainly had to do with the three words that are used in the title of this book: European, journalism and education.

Since the geographic definition of Europe is highly contested, the term 'European' could have been defined politically by the membership to the Council of Europe [47 members] or educationally by the membership to the Bologna Process [46 members]. Both definitions would have made the publication of this book almost impossible due to the large memberships of these organizations. Therefore, it was necessary to adopt a more 'pragmatic' approach and it was finally decided to include in our analysis the 27 member states of the EU and the three candidates Croatia, F.Y.R.O. Macedonia, and Turkey, as well as the three EFTA countries Iceland, Norway and Switzerland.[3]

The second term, 'journalism' is also becoming elusive in recent times as a result of the introduction of new technologies that created a very 'messy' situation in the 'mass' media world. Without claiming it as a term that should be used for research purposes, it would be possible to describe the current situation as a mess media one, where senders, channels and receivers interchange roles constantly and the basic characteristics of mass media organizations as taught in an COMM 101/Introduction to Mass Communication course do not apply any more. The boundaries of journalism have been constantly eroded by new forms of media/journalism such as blogs, citizen journalism, gossip, lifestyle and tabloid journalism, multimedia journalism, and public relations practitioners who, given the economic pressures on the media, have ended up 'writing' a number of stories on behalf of journalists who are constantly under pressure to produce more with less. For this, it was decided to allow the authors of the national chapters to include in their analysis institutions that, according to their judgement, 'train journalists', irrespective of the titles and content of such training programmes.

Finally, the third term, 'education', is constantly defined and redefined due to the current technological as well as political and financial developments. One can log on to the US Ivy League schools today and find out that the top-tier universities are racing to give the public online access to their best lecturers, while more and more universities around the world are offering on-line degrees. Moreover, journalists from the world's leading media organisations give professional tips on YouTube with tens of thousands of views every month. At the same time, two professors from the University of Minnesota took the frontiers of journalism education to new lengths when they used the new video game *Neverwinter Nights* to provide their students with interactive lessons in journalism. Two more developments, the dominance of the free market ideals in European education which accentuated the presence of private universities in the field of journalism education across the continent, and the Bologna process which made comparisons, as well as competition among some institutions more prevalent were also considered. Again here it was decided to allow the authors of the national chapters to exercise their discretion and include the institutions and programmes that 'train journalists' according to local characteristics.

In conclusion, this book hopes to provide a basic examination of the philosophy of journalism education and address questions regarding education policy, human development, and curriculum theory and study the purpose, process, nature and ideals of journalism education in Europe. Within this context, this book attempts to analyse the way in which European journalism education fits in the 'media governance' patterns [the interrelationships between the market, the state and the civil society which affect the media] in every country, as well as at the regional and European levels. It aims to use a two-dimensional or 'bifocal approach' (both micro and macro) in order to show how the commercialization, concentration, convergence and globalization of the media have affected the journalism education landscapes in Europe both at an institutional as well as at an individual level.

At an institutional level it analyzes the ways in which the 'normless' scene (McQuail 2007, 24) of today's mess media environment creates and reproduces itself by a 'normless' reflection in the journalism education landscape. The shattering of the national public spheres brought by the technological change in the media sector and the reduced possibilities for social engineering are also reflected in the European journalism education landscape where issues such as pluralism and diversity have to be redefined constantly in the education policy and curriculum theory, as well as human development, where universal access to both education and media are now 'defined' by pleonastic excommunication.

While at an individual level it focuses on how journalism education institutions in most European countries today are producing a plethora of graduates with diminished professional accountability and a 'proactive obedience'[4] to their employers, due to their bureaucratic 'reactive obedience' to political and market forces.

The Author

Georgios Terzis is associate professor at Vesalius College, Vrije Universiteit Brussel and the chair of the Journalism Studies Section of the European Communication Research and Education Association.

Notes

1. Stephenson, H., and Mory, P. (1990), Journalism training in Europe, Brussels: Commission of the European Communities.
2. The complete directory of all the institutions providing journalism training in Europe compiled by the authors of this book is published and regularly updated at http://www.ejc.net <http://www.ejc.net/> as well as http://wjec.ou.edu/selectcountry.php. More information about these institutions and other academic resources related to journalism in Europe is also available at http://www.journalismstudies. eu/directory.htm.
3. Liechtenstein was not included because there are no institutions providing journalism education in this country.
4. *Vorauseilender Gehorsam* is the more accurate German term.

References

McQuail, D. (2007), The Current State of Media Governance in Europe, in Terzis, G., *European Media Governance: National and Regional Dimensions*, Intellect: Bristol.

Part I

The North Atlantic/Liberal Media Model Countries

Introduction

Michael Bromley

In comparing media systems Hallin and Mancini (2006: 296) identify 'the development of journalistic professionalism' as one of four chief factors in the structuring of media ecologies. They contend that 'journalists' conceptions of their own role in society, the professional values and representational practices, and so on' are cultivated within the wider (political) context (297). The people, who manage, and are contracted to and employed by the media, tend to embrace and sustain the underlying rationales of the systems with which they are associated, whether or not these foreground the broader political-economy or socio-culture. For their part, as they have standardized (Woolf 2008: 48) the media have sought primarily to reproduce themselves not least through the deployment of human resource (for the extreme example of News Corp, see Osnos 2008). Becker (2008) states matter-of-factly that, 'Journalism education is instruction for work in the news departments of media organizations […reflecting…] the control from, and involvement of, media businesses'. In this context, 'business' does not necessarily mean commerce (although the commercialization of the press is a chief characteristic of the liberal model) but more generically 'activity', including statal and not-for-profit public service. In summary, the media system, politics, economics, culture and society – including journalism and its educational processes – are closely bound together (Hujanen, Lehtniemi and Virranta 2008, xx). Therefore, the professional ideal in journalism both helps shape, and is shaped by, liberal concepts of the media as political-economy and socio-cultural entities (Lauk 2008: 194).

One outstanding feature of journalistic professionalism in liberal (sometimes called North Atlantic or even Anglo-Saxon) countries has been the progressive reliance over the twentieth century for its formation on higher education (Deuze 2006). Given that, like the media and journalists, universities and educators make their own claims to professionalism and autonomy, this arrangement can be seen as being either mutually supportive or laden with tension between academe and journalism (Deuze 2005). Formal journalism education may be viewed as being 'only a step away from the licensing of journalists' (Raudsepp 1989: 5) or as a form of domestication of an otherwise 'unruly class' of radical 'itinerant scribblers' (Carey 2000: 16). Education can either uphold journalism as a relatively autonomous activity, or disempower it in the interests of the state or media institutions. Not surprisingly, then, formal journalism education developed relatively hesitantly in liberal systems – earlier, more rapidly and more comprehensively in the United States; later, more slowly and more patchily in Canada, Ireland and the United Kingdom (French 2007: 41; Hallin and Mancini 2006: 222; Johansen, Weaver and Dornan 2001: 471). Paradoxically, the idea of professionalization through education – the global diffusion of the US model (Hallin and Mancini 2006, 257) – began to gain close to full acceptance among journalists in the United Kingdom at the moment when, from the 1980s, the drift to neo-liberalism (and away from democratic corporatism) actually weakened such structures (Aldridge and Evetts 2003).

At the beginning of the twenty-first century even the typical American journalist, although a graduate, has not majored in journalism in college (Weaver et al. 2007: 1). In Canada, hostility to journalism graduates is widespread and persistent (Edge 2004: 173–4). The United Kingdom demonstrates the characteristics of both – four out of five journalists are graduates, but academic journalism qualifications are discounted (Delano 2000: 267–8). Kenny suggests in this volume that higher education journalism qualifications are more acceptable in Ireland. However, all the authors acknowledge the pervasive influence of, and in many cases the intention to replicate, the workplace in journalism education which leads to an emphasis on vocationalism (see also Cushion 2007). Consequently, it is plausible to argue that any disempowering of journalists results primarily from journalism education being a site principally of institutional enforcement and compliance (Hanada 2007: 135). Even before they begin formal education in journalism, for students:

> shared understandings of journalism's roles and practices are already significantly influential […] The effects of these cultural understandings of journalism, together with real-life experience of the media, may in fact be far more powerful in shaping attitudes and aspirations of future journalists than journalism education. (Sanders et al. 2008: 137)

Any attempts at 'bottom-up' change have to negotiate inhospitable conditions (Freedman 2007: 3) which are routinely determined by states or corporations seeking to impinge, both directly and indirectly, on the education and training of journalists (Botha and de Beer 2006: 2; Mai, Ilisei and Hoffman 2007: 1). Moreover, control of the education system itself occurs through 'regulatory surveillance' representing a combination of statal and market imperatives (King 2006: 2). Consequently, the main endeavour to address what are perceived to be systemic failures in liberal journalism's performance in the late twentieth and early twenty-first centuries (exemplified by Kovach and Rosenstiel 2001) constitute a reformism which seeks to re-institute 'professional' values through formal instruction without challenging the hegemony of either the state or the corporate media (Macdonald 2006: 746). At the other end of the spectrum, as it were, journalism education is also construed as a function of a residual collectivism. In both the United Kingdom and Ireland, the National Union of Journalists (NUJ) extends its interest beyond training (http: //www.nujtraining.org.uk/) to approving some education courses (National Union of Journalists 2007: 24). In the archetypal liberal arrangement, in which 'quality journalism degree programs' can – but do not always – foster the wider acceptance of 'editorial independence' as a media characteristic (IREX 2007), education at best promotes a journalistic professionalism to counterbalance statal and corporate control with editorial legitimacy (Bennett, Gressett and Haltom 1985: 51).

Frohlich and Holtz-Bacha (1994) suggested that the influence of media systems, and particularly the political-economy of the media, was mitigated by the role and function allocated to journalists by society, and the structures of the field of journalism itself. Of course, the relationships of these elements are not always antagonistic, and the boundaries between them are often poorly maintained; for example, a recent history of the NUJ pays little attention to training and less to education (Gopsill and Neale 2007). Deuze (2007: 106) noted that the characteristics of professional service (collegiality, collaboration, etc.) (Goffee and Scase 1995: 137–57; Scarborough and Corbett 1992: 103–9) were largely absent from media organizations. A standard criticism of liberal journalism is that it has progressively become less pluralistic and is representative of a narrow, chiefly middle-class and still predominantly white, culture (Beckett 2008: 149). Hallin and Mancini (2004: 271–3) observed that the relatively autonomous 'critical expertise' which underpinned the role of journalism in liberal systems (incorporating higher levels of education; greater specialization and access to more resources; professionalization; availability of enabling technologies, and enhanced prestige) was undermined by both the internal weaknesses of liberal forms of journalism and the external strength of media commercialization.

In short, the liberal model of journalism education, while retaining the potential for resistance, opposition and negotiation, and for cultivating alternatives in practice, nevertheless is chiefly concerned with the unproblematic reproduction of the existing labour force. On the other hand, there is little uniformity in liberal systems (Hujanen, Lehtniemi and Virranta 2008, xx). Exceptionalism is well established (and freely acknowledged by Hallin and Mancini; for example, see pp.198–9). Furthermore, the liberal model has been exported, in whole or part and more or less successfully, through Anglo-Saxon (US and British) imperialism and colonialism (utilizing international news agencies such as Reuters and the Associated Press and broadcasters such as CNN and the BBC), beyond Canada and Ireland to Australia, New Zealand, South Africa, parts of Asia, such as the Philippines (Coronel 2000) and Hong Kong (Lee, Man Chan and Lee 1997: 5), Africa (Mwesige 2004) and Latin America (Waisbord 2000: 3–4) – and after the end of the Cold War, to central and eastern Europe (as noted by Jakubowicz in this volume). Hallin and Mancini (2004) 294) summarized that 'A global media culture is emerging, one that closely resembles the Liberal Model [...]'. A parallel homogenized journalism education system has evolved, too.

This seemed to be confirmed in practice when, in 2007, the first World Journalism Education Congress adopted a declaration of principles, which stressed that 'Journalism is a global endeavour; journalism students should learn that despite political and cultural differences, they share important values and professional goals with peers in other nations' (Principle 10) and that 'graduates should be prepared to work as highly informed, strongly committed practitioners who have high ethical principles and are able to fulfill (*sic*) the public interest obligations that are central to their work' (Principle 6). The declaration accompanied the publication of model curricula for journalism education intended for developing countries and emerging democracies (Unesco 2007). These appeared to conform to the diffusion of the 'news paradigm' (based on the event, news values, the interview, the inverted pyramid narrative structure and objectivity) from the United States and, later, Britain, beginning in the nineteenth century (Høyer and Pöttker 2005: 7).

The characteristics of the liberal model are well enough known: the Fourth Estate with its ideal of the separation of journalism from political partisanship (Høyer 2005: 75–6), the watchdog role (McNair 2005: 37), objectivity (Hanitzsch 2008: 419) and reporting (Chalaby 1996). In summary, journalists act on behalf of the public at large ('in the public interest'), monitoring power through the reporting of 'facts'. Nevertheless, there is little uniformity in the ways in which these ideals are configured, even within liberal domains (Weaver 2005: 49–54). Indeed, differences between US and British journalism provoke much comment (for a recent example, see Riemer 2003). Moreover, underpinning the liberal model is an adherence to commercialization (on the grounds that in turn this underwrites journalistic autonomy, status and values), the primacy of meeting audience demands, and the development of journalistic status and competence (Splichal and Sparks 1994: 184–5). Thus, in the liberal model, those who both organize and process (make accessible and meaningful to audiences) and comment (engage audiences in debate) on material gathered by reporters are considered to be journalists, too. This caused Splichal and Sparks (1994: 177) to argue that the liberal model of journalism was focused not only on power (politics, democracy) but also on entertainment (selling itself).

Traditionally, curricula have far from fully recognized this. As both Kenny and Bromley note in the chapters in this section, journalism education in Ireland and the United Kingdom continues to privilege the study of politics, administration and law. However, it also remains anchored in the technical, scientific and professional domain, as Kenny puts it. Consequently, none of the ancient universities – Oxford, Cambridge, St. Andrews, Glasgow, Aberdeen, Edinburgh and Dublin – offers journalism, although the Thomson Reuters Foundation offering fellowships to journalists from around the world has been based at Green College, Oxford, since 1983, and the Reuters Institute for the Study of Journalism, a university research centre opened in 2006, is located in the university's Department of Politics and International Relations. Indeed, of the second wave of universities founded in the United Kingdom in the nineteenth century (the so-called civic or red-brick institutions) only Leeds, Sheffield and constituent colleges of the former National University of Wales (Cardiff, Swansea and Bangor) and the University of London (Birkbeck and Goldsmiths)[1] do. Journalism found its way into the academy after 1970 chiefly through universities established in the 1960s, many of them with origins as technical colleges, including Brunel, City, Kent, Salford, Strathclyde, Surrey and Ulster. The related field of media studies began in earnest in English polytechnics in the 1970s, and journalism programmes are now largely provided by these institutions which were granted university status after 1989. The pattern is similar in Ireland, where only one college (Galway) of the National University offers journalism. The three other public providers are a 'new' university (Limerick), a former college (Dublin City) and an institute of technology (DIT). Such has been the growth in journalism programmes that the editor of *Journalism Training* could state that 'degrees and diplomas in media studies and especially journalism courses are now the most sought-after by students in the UK (Bennett-England nd).'

This arrangement reflects a contextual factor which is distinctive of the liberal model: rising general affluence and the emergence of new patterns of consumption after 1945 leading to demands for higher levels of technical, scientific and professional capacity, in which the media played important political, economic, social and cultural roles. The media expanded as commercial entities (driven by more advertising); provided more employment (more journalists), and greatly increased their popularity (more readers, listeners, viewers) making them less dependent on any remaining vestiges of political patronage (Bromley 2003; Horgan 2005: 17). This was achieved against a backdrop of strong state sponsorship of public service in broadcasting (O'Malley 2001: 29) which served to strike a balance by offering some protection of culture and fostering of social cohesion (Bromley 2003: 215–16). In 2009, however, journalism in liberal countries is beset by job losses, employer bankruptcies, disaffected and fragmented audiences, media hyper-commercialism, changing standards and challenges from citizen journalists. Newspapers like *The Irish Press* decline from national institutions with large readerships to oblivion (Burke 2005). Commentators like Roy Greenslade (2007) argue that 'Journalistic skills are not entirely wiped out [...] but they are eroded and, most importantly, they cannot be confined any longer to an exclusive élite group. [...] The top is crumbling and the bottom – individual citizens, but working together in loosely-knit collaborative communities – is rising'. The question is whether the liberal model of journalism education can respond adequately to the changes which have overtaken journalism in its domains since the late 1970s (Bromley 2006: 54–5, 59; Tumber and Prentoulis 2005: 71).

The Author

Michael Bromley is the Head of the School of Journalism and Communication, University of Queensland.

Note

1. Queen Mary College, University of London, collaborates with City University in offering an undergraduate programme in Journalism and Contemporary History. Queen Mary delivers the Contemporary History element, and City –the Journalism.

References

Aldridge, M. and Evetts, J. (2003), 'Rethinking the concept of professionalism: the case of journalism', *British Journal of Sociology*, 54(4), pp. 547–64.
Becker, L.B. (2008), 'Journalism education,' In W. Donsbach (ed.) *The International Encyclopedia of Communication*, Oxford: Blackwell.
Beckett, C. (2008), *SuperMedia: Saving Journalism So It Can Save the World*, Oxford: Blackwell.

Bennett, W.L., Gressett, L.A. and Haltom, W. (1985), 'Repairing the news: a case study of the news paradigm', *Journal of Communication*, 35(2), pp. 50–68.

Bennett-England, R. (nd), 'Journalism courses in the UK', Courses and Careers, http: //www. he.courses-careers.com/journalism.htm. Accessed 8 April 2009.

Botha, N. and de Beer, A. (2006), 'Revisiting South African journalism education in the post-apartheid era', *Global Media Journal* (Polish edn), 1, pp.1–8.

Bromley, M. (2003), 'The media', In J. Hollowell (ed.) *Britain Since 1945*, Oxford: Blackwell, pp. 211–37.

Bromley, M. (2006), 'One journalism or many? Confronting the contradictions in the education and training of journalists in the United Kingdom', In K.W.Y. Leung, J. Kenny and P.S.N. Lee (eds.), *Global Trends in Communication Education and Research*, Cresskill, NJ: Hampton Press, pp. 53–71.

Burke, R. (2005), *Press Delete: The Decline and Fall of 'The Irish Press'*, Blackrock, Co. Dublin: Curach Press.

Carey, J.W. (2000), 'Some personal notes on US journalism education', *Journalism*, 1(1), pp. 12–23.

Chalaby, J.K, (1996), 'Journalism as Anglo-American invention', *European Journal of Communication*, 11(3), pp. 303–26.

Coronel, S.S. (2000), 'Philippines: free as a mocking bird', In L. Williams and R. Rich (eds.), *Losing Control: Freedom of the Press in Asia*, Australian National University, Asia Pacific Press, pp. 147–68.

Cushion, S. (2007), '"On the beat" or in the classroom?', *Journalism Practice*, 1(3), pp. 421–34.

Delano, A. (2000), 'No sign of a better job: 100 years of British journalism', *Journalism Studies*, 1(2), pp. 261–72.

Deuze, M. (2007), *Media Work*, Cambridge: Polity.

Deuze, M. (2006), 'Global journalism education', *Journalism Studies*, 7(1), pp. 19–34.

Deuze, M. (2005), 'What is journalism? Professional identity and ideology of journalists reconsidered', *Journalism*, 6(4), pp. 442–64.

Edge. M. (2004), 'Balancing academic and corporate interests in Canadian journalism education', *Journalism & Mass Communication Educator*, 59(2), pp. 172–85.

Freedman, E. (2007), 'After the Tulip revolution: press freedoms, constraints and competition in Kyrgyzstan', http: //www.irex.org/programs/stg/research/06/freedman.pdf. Accessed 18 December 2008.

French, N. (2007), 'Journalism education in Ireland', *Irish Communications Review*, 10, pp. 41–9.

Frohlich, R. and Holtz–Bacha, C. (1994), 'Structures of inhomogeneity – dilemmas of journalism training in Europe', In the *International Association of Mass Communication Research Conference*, Seoul, South Korea.

Goffee, R. and Scase, R. (1995), *Corporate Realities: The Dynamics of Large and Small Organisations*, London: Routledge.

Gopsill, T. and Neale, G. (2007), *Journalists: 100 Years of the NUJ*, London: Profile.

Greenslade, R. (2007), 'Why I am saying farewell to the NUJ' (25 October), http: //blogs.guardian. co.uk/greenslade/. Accessed 5 November 2007.

Horgan, J. (2005), 'Foreword', In R. Burke, *Press Delete: The Decline and Fall of 'The Irish Press'*, Blackrock, Co. Dublin: Curach Press, pp. 17–19.

Høyer, S. (2005), 'The rise and fall of the Scandanavian partisan press', In S. Høyer and H. Pöttker (eds.), *Diffusion of the News Paradigm 1850-2000*, Göteborg: Nordicom, pp. 75–91.

Hujanen, J., Lehtniemi, N. and Virranta, R. (2008), *Mapping Communication and Media Research in the UK*, Department of Communication, University of Jyväskylä.

Hallin, D.C. and Mancini, P. (2006), *Comparing Media Systems: Three Models of Media and Politics*, Cambridge: Cambridge University Press.

Hanada, T. (2007), 'Returning to journalism in the post-mass-media age in Japan: how the field of study and interest of a research unit changed over time', Proceedings of the *B K21 conference*, Seoul National University, 19–20 November, pp. 134–42.

Hanitzsch, T. (2008), 'Comparative journalism studies', In K. Wahl-Jorgensen and T. Hanitzsch (eds.), *The Handbook of Journalism Studies*, London: Routledge, pp. 413–27.

Høyer, S. and Pöttker, H. (eds.) (2005), *Diffusion of the News Paradigm 1850–2000*, Göteborg: Nordicom.

IREX (2007), 'Quality journalism education urged for media success across the Arab world', http://www2.gsu.edu/~wwwaus/current_event/2007/IREXStory.htm. Accessed 18 December 2008.

Johansen, P., Weaver, D.H. and Dornan, C. (2001), 'Journalism education in the United States and Canada: not merely clones', *Journalism Studies*, 2(4), pp. 469–83.

King, R. (2006), *Analysing the Higher Education Regulatory State*, Discussion Paper 38, The Centre for Analysis of Risk and Regulation, London School of Economics and Political Science.

Kovach, B. and Rosentstiel, T. (2001), *The Elements of Journalism: What Newspeople Should Know and the Public Should Expect*, New York: Crown.

Lauk, E. (2008), 'How will it all unfold? Media systems and journalism cultures in post-Communist countries', In K. Jakubowicz and M. Sükösd (eds.), *Finding the Right Place on the Map: Central and Eastern European Media Change in Global Perspective*, Bristol: Intellect, pp. 193–212.

Lee, C-C., Man Chan, J. and Lee, P.S.N. (1997), *Professionalism Among Hong Kong Journalists in Comparative Perspective*, http: //dr.ntu.edu.sg/bitstream/10220/1287/1/AMIC_1995_08_14.pdf. Accessed 5 March 2009.

Macdonald, I. (2006), 'Teaching journalists to save the profession: a critical assessment of recent debates on the future of US and Canadian journalism education', *Journalism Studies*, 7(5), pp. 745–64.

McNair, B. (2005), 'What is journalism?', In H. de Burgh (ed.), *Making Journalists*, London: Routledge, pp. 25–43.

Mai, K., Ilisei, I. and Hoffmann, D. (2007), 'The media system of Portugal: status of media professionalism', 3rd Report, Institute of Media and Communication Science, Technische Universität Ilmenau.

Mwesige, P.G. (2004), 'Disseminators, advocates and watchdogs: a profile of Ugandan journalists in the new millennium', *Journalism*, 5(1), pp. 69–96.

National Union of Journalists (2007), *Shaping the Future*, London: NUJ Commission on Multi-Media Working.

O'Malley, T. (2001), 'The decline of public service broadcasting in the UK 1979–2000', In M. Bromley (ed.), *No News is Bad News: Radio, Television and the Public*, Harlow, Essex: Longman, pp. 28–45.

Osnos, P. (2008), 'The platform: the Murdoch way', The Century Foundation (June 17), http: //www.tcf.org/print.asp?type=NC&pubid=1939. Accessed 18 December 2008.

Raudsepp, E. (1989), 'Reinventing journalism education', *Canadian Journal of Communication*, 14(2), pp. 1–14.

Riemer, M. (2003), 'American journalism: objectivity and reverence', *Yellow Times* (26 June), http://www.globalpolicy.org. Accessed 4 April 2009.

Sanders, K, Hanna, M., Berganza, M.R. and Aranda, J.J.S. (2008), 'Becoming journalists: a comparison of the professional attitudes and values of British and Spanish journalism students', *European Journal of Communication*, 23(2), pp. 133–52.

Scarborough, H. and Corbett, J.M. (1992), *Technology and Organization: Power, Meaning, Design*, London: Routledge.

Splichal, S. and Sparks, C. (1994), *Journalists for the 21st Century*, Norwood, NJ, Ablex.

Tumber, H. and Prentoulis, M. (2005), 'Journalism and the making of a profession', In H. de Burgh (ed.), *Making Journalists*, London: Routledge, pp. 58–74.

Unesco (2007), *Model Curricula for Journalism Education for Developing Countries and Emerging Democracies*, Paris, Unesco Communication and Information Sector.

Waisbord, S. (2000), *Watchdog Journalism in South America: News, Accountability and Democracy*, New York, Columbia University Press.

Weaver, D.H. (2005), 'Who are journalists?', In H. de Burgh (ed.), *Making Journalists*, London: Routledge, pp. 44–57.

Woolf, M. (2008), *The Man Who Owns the News: Inside the Secret World of Rupert Murdoch*, New York: Knopf.

The Republic of Ireland Journalism Education Landscape

Colum Kenny

Introduction

During the last 40 years, in the Republic of Ireland, third-level education in general has developed at an unprecedented rate. Its development has included the creation of journalism courses. Previously, journalists had received their professional education almost entirely 'on the job', while employed as researchers or as trainee or junior journalists. If they had a degree it was likely to be in an area of the humanities such as English, history, law or economics. A few sputtering attempts to generate interest in journalism studies at university level, including by means of a series of lectures at Trinity College Dublin in 1908–9, had come to nothing. Not only was journalism regarded by some academics as unworthy of serious consideration, many journalists themselves thought that journalism could only be learnt in 'the University of Life' and that the primary requirement for it was a certain aptitude associated with an individual's personality. One contemporary correspondent scoffed at the Trinity experiment as follows ([Lawrence]),

> It seems to me that they are setting out to prove the truth of a quaint contention I heard uttered by a certain Dublin editor not long after their scheme was formulated. 'The whole mistake', he said, 'arises from the gratuitous assumption that journalism is a profession. As a matter of fact, it is not so much a profession as a disease. It can be caught – not taught. Knack presses the button and experience does the rest. The great *desideratium* is aptitude, and that is precisely the one thing that cannot be evolved.'

During the first 40 years of the independent state, following British withdrawal from most of Ireland in 1921, the Irish economy was weak and little thought was given to expanding education in radical new directions. However, innovative programmes of national development, adopted from the late 1950s, began to bear fruit in the 1960s. The Republic of Ireland's first television service was launched in 1961 and this highlighted the need for journalists who were well equipped to deal with the complexities of modern society. The National Union of Journalists lobbied the government to provide appropriate training and, by the end of the decade, a one-year full-time journalism course was being offered at a college of commerce in Rathmines, Dublin. It was partly modelled on courses at British colleges and even obtained accreditation from the British National Council for the Training of Journalists.

Economic expansion within the Republic, an international media focus on 'The Troubles' in Northern Ireland and a growing appreciation of the benefits of journalism education all prompted consideration of the need for new media courses. However, existing universities had been founded prior to the creation of an independent Irish state and were slow to respond to some emerging technical, scientific and professional challenges. In the late 1970s, the government decided to create two new third-level institutions in Dublin and Limerick to fill some of the educational gaps. The two new institutions are now known as Dublin City University (DCU) and the University of Limerick (UL). When the former institution came into existence, (as the National Institute for Higher Education until 1989), its courses included journalism. Today, a journalism degree is generally regarded by those recruiting journalists as a definite advantage, although it is still not an essential prerequisite for employment.

Organizations providing courses

Five publicly-funded institutions offer a variety of journalism programmes. These institutions are Dublin City University (DCU), Dublin Institute of Technology (DIT), the National University of Ireland, Galway (UCG), the University of Limerick (UL) and Coláiste Dhúlaigh, Dublin. Two privately-funded institutions offer undergraduate degree programmes, these being the Dublin Business School (DBS) and Griffith College. Finally, various privately-owned institutions offer certificate and diploma courses in journalism. Some media organisations provide in-house training for employees.

(1) Publicly-funded institutions offering Degree programmes

(a) Dublin City University:
The DCU BA (Hons) in Journalism course is a blend of practical and theoretical subjects. Students gain a wide range of skills in print and broadcast journalism. They also take modules which encourage them to look critically and theoretically at the significance of the media in society, and at society itself. There are also modules in Law and Politics, and a distinct BA in the Irish Language and Journalism. A core and vital element of the course is an eight-week placement in a media organisation. The duration of this course has been reduced to three years in line with the Bologna Process.

The DCU Master's in Journalism course is Ireland's oldest Master's in Journalism programme and is designed to provide wide-ranging training and education for twenty to 25 prospective entrants to the profession. It balances practical, theoretical, technical and analytical elements in the context of a changing media environment and the new, and increasingly diverse, demands being made on entrants to journalism. The core modules are news reporting, newspaper editing, radio journalism, newsdays (real-time news assignments), media law, feature writing, research methods and communication ethics. It is an intensive, full-time programme, of which a work placement in a media organization is an integral part. Students must also complete a substantial practical project or academic dissertation.

During 2008, DCU launched a new, three-semester, full-time or part-time Master's in International Journalism Studies degree programme. It is targeted mainly at Irish graduates of journalism degree programmes, who wish to deepen their understanding of the media's role in international society and to develop their capacity to operate professionally in international contexts. Entrants may be recent graduates or may have worked for some years in media practice. The programme facilitates analysis of how journalism performs. It provides for journalism graduates a structured environment in which to develop their skills through international study and working experience. A dissertation or project forms part of the programme.

(b) Dublin Institute of Technology (DIT):
On the DIT BA Journalism course, students study journalistic practice, seek an understanding of the importance of journalism in democratic society and of key domains relevant to journalism such as politics and economics: they may also chose to gain relevant linguistic skills, together with a knowledge of the media, culture and literature of a language if chosen. Students are encouraged to publish and broadcast their work throughout the year in the School of Media publications. Subjects such as law and business enhance the students' journalistic ability.

The DIT Master's in Journalism one-year programme covers the practice and theory of journalism. It is designed for about twenty prospective entrants to the profession and ranges from the basics of the journalistic craft to a consideration of the part that journalists play in society. A fundamental principle behind the course is the belief that good journalism, produced by reflective, critical practitioners, is crucial in a democracy. The programme seeks to produce journalists who are multi-skilled and critically aware, and have a good understanding of the social role of journalism.

The new DIT Master's in International Journalism is a three semester, full-time programme, covering both the practice and the theory of journalism in an international context. Aimed primarily, although not exclusively, at international students, the programme is intended to enable them to gain a high level of professional competence, a systematic knowledge and understanding of the theory and practice of journalism, and a reflexive awareness of the role of journalism in society world-wide. The programme is divided into three strands: journalism practice, context and content. Modules include sub-editing, layout, international media law, reporting international business and journalism in a globalized world. Students will also complete a dissertation (journalism-related) during the third semester. Non-native speakers of English must have an IELT score of 7.5 overall in each component, or equivalent.

(c) National University of Ireland, University College Galway:
The NUI Galway one-year Master's in Journalism course aims to combine the practical, analytical, theoretical, and technical skills necessary to the practice of journalism in contemporary media. It offers places for up to sixteen prospective entrants to the

profession. The programme consists of taught courses over two semesters and a final project (dissertation) which is a major piece of journalistic writing, of 10,000–12,000 words in length. Students also participate in a placement in a relevant working environment. Tuition is carried out in a dedicated newsroom and radio studio environment. The core courses are news writing and reporting, feature writing, broadcast journalism, sub-editing, media law, media ethics, government and politics, photojournalism.

(d) University of Limerick (UL):

During 2008, the University of Limerick commenced a print-journalism programme. This four-year B.A. in Journalism and New Media is one of a number of two-subject degrees designed for students who wish to undertake specialised study in two subjects in the arts, humanities or social sciences, to degree level. It is intended to enable students to develop skills required of print journalists and to understand the role played in contemporary society by the media. Work placements are planned, and students will have an opportunity to develop a portfolio of their work for presentation to potential employers.

Also during 2008 the University on Limerick unveiled plans for a Graduate Diploma/ Master's course in print journalism, which is intended for up to fifteen students. To progress from the Graduate Diploma to Master's level, students must achieve a second class honours (grade one) overall.

(2) Publicly-funded institutions offering a Higher Diploma

Coláiste Dhúlaigh College of Further Education:

The main focus of Colaiste Dhúlaigh's Higher National Diploma in Journalism (Hons) is good writing, but skills such as word processing, web design and desktop publishing are also taught. Additionally, students are introduced to contemporary media issues, theories and debates. Successful students may transfer to the final year of certain degree programmes in Britain and Ireland.

(3) Privately-funded institutions offering Degree programmes

(a) Dublin Business School (DBS):

The BA (Hons) Journalism at DBS features practical, theoretical and professional subjects that are explored and developed over three levels, with integral opportunities for the cultivation of personal and intellectual skills. It offers a range of transferable skills including computing, communication, writing and editing skills. DBS also offers a one-year Diploma in Journalism and Media Studies.

(b) Griffith College Dublin:

The Griffith College BA (Hons) in Journalism and Visual Media honours degree programme aims to inspire an intellectual capacity for self-expression and objective enquiry, while developing practical skills necessary for media production. Writing, design, presentation, production, layout and publishing for newspaper, radio, video, photography and the Internet are covered.

On the Griffith College BA in Journalism course students learn a range of media production and academic skills. Print and broadcast media production is catered for, alongside learning about society. Further study is an option for students who successfully complete this course and the progression suggested by the college is to take the final year of its BA in Journalism and New Media.

Griffith College also offers, both in Dublin and in Cork, a one-year Higher Diploma in Journalism and Media Communications, as well as a one-year Certificate in Journalism or Radio Production.

(4) Privately-funded institutions offering Certificates and Diplomas

Other institutions offering diploma or certificate courses in journalism include the Communications and Management Institute, European Institute of Communications, Independent Colleges (a recent initiative supported by Ireland's leading newspaper group, INM), Kilroy's College and The Irish Academy.

Faculty and instructors

From the outset, it has been common to find professional journalists teaching on journalism courses in Ireland, with the greatest numbers being at DCU and DIT. Some are staffed as academics, while others are recruited part-time to deliver specific modules.

Irish degree programmes in journalism offer a mix of subjects that are by no means all professional or 'practical'. Courses of a general theoretical nature relating to social, economic, legal or political matters of relevance to journalists may be offered by academics who have not worked as journalists. The balance between instructors with working experience of journalism and those without it varies considerably from programme to programme, course to course.

As courses have become more established, and as universities tend to assert their standing by reference to lists of academic publications, the recruitment of media professionals who do not have a Master's degree or even a doctorate has become less common. Those who helped to build the reputation of existing journalism courses, and who only completed higher degrees after being employed by a university, are not convinced that insistence on a doctorate as a condition of employment is necessarily in the best interests of journalism education.

Duration

Degree courses range from one-year Master's programmes to three or four-year undergraduate programmes. There is some confusion in Ireland about the appropriate length of undergraduate programmes in general at present. The European principles of accord agreed at Bologna inspired DCU to reduce its undergraduate journalism degree course from four to three years, yet the new degree programme in journalism and new media at the University of Limerick will be four years long and that at DIT has not been reduced. Moreover, while two years is in principle the desirable duration for a contemporary Master's courses, all Master's in journalism courses currently on offer are of a shorter duration.

Applicants

Most applicants for undergraduate degree courses are school-leavers. Most applicants for Master's courses have a primary honours degree but exceptions include people with adequate or equivalent experience in journalism. Anyone hoping to secure a place on a Master's course is likely to benefit if he or she can produce some evidence of an active interest in or of experience of journalism.

Fewer women than men are employed at the top level in media and journalism in Ireland. However, girls are performing better than boys in secondary level examinations and this means that they are better placed than boys to achieve the points needed to secure places on college courses. Gender bias is not evident in the selection of candidates for journalism courses. It may be noted that special efforts are made to assist people with disabilities who wish to take courses.

Continuing education for journalists in employment has not been a priority for the industry, and few working journalists have taken time off to pursue college courses in journalism.

Accreditation

The chief accreditation body for university degrees in the Republic of Ireland is the Higher Education Authority. Other courses may be accredited by the Higher Education and Training Awards Council. Prospective students of journalism courses are well-advised to check that any course in which they are interested has been validated by one of these bodies.

Prospective students may also wish to check if a course is recognized and approved by The National Union of Journalists. There is no formal mechanism whereby the media industry or professional journalists either determine the content of courses or are required to approve them before they may be offered. However, approval by the NUJ leads to the issuing of temporary union cards to students and this facilitates the creation of those placements for work experience that form an important part of some courses.

Some third-level institutions have taken an active interest in the Bologna Process, while the European Transfer Credit System is being gradually developed in practice. If either Bologna or the ETCS are of relevance to an applicant then he or she should ascertain carefully from the relevant institution what is the precise position is in respect of any particular course.

Industry connections

The media industry as a body has not played a very active role in the development of journalism training in Ireland but has benefited greatly from having trained graduates available for employment. While individual media practitioners have agreed to advise on course design or to participate in course boards or to support programmes in other ways, the sector generally has been slow to provide much funding.

Occasional and limited funding to support a few media or journalism students has been provided by, for example, RTE (the state-owned broadcaster), Independent News and Media and *The Irish Times*. However, the vast majority of funding for journalism training comes from the state and is supplemented by the fees of individual postgraduates. The media industry does provide opportunities for work experience, which is an important part of some journalism courses on offer, although these placements are frequently either unpaid or poorly paid and are not all equally well structured or supervised. They are, nevertheless, a valuable opportunity for learning and are much appreciated by third-level institutions and their students.

The media industry in general in not involved in accreditation of courses and some academics regard this as a beneficial consequence of the industry's failure to become significantly involved in educational funding. Recently, Independent News and Media has launched a private educational initiative that offers courses in law and journalism to the public, although it is too early to gauge the significance of this particular venture and its implications if any for established third-level courses in journalism.

Associations

There is no national association for the training of journalists in Ireland. The School of Communications, which delivers journalism courses at DCU, and the School of Media, which delivers journalism courses at DIT, are both institutional members of the International Association for Media and Communication Research. Journalism educators at both institutions are also listed members of the European Communication Research and Education Association, and the chairperson of the Master's in Journalism course at DCU is currently also Vice-Chair, ECREA Journalism Studies Section. Staff at DCU have also played an active role in the European Journalism Training Association, including holding its offices of president and general-secretary, and in the Association for Journalism Education.

Concluding Remarks

Journalism education is continuing to expand in the Republic of Ireland. This partly reflects the unprecedented prosperity of the state, which has been called by some 'The Celtic Tiger' because of an economic boom that lasted from the 1990s until recently. Shortly before that boom became established, the present author commented upon the fact that the economy was then 'reeling' and suggested (Kenny: 47–8) that, 'Perhaps we need a College of Communications similar to the College of Physicians, where resources could be centralised more fruitfully'. Today, three Irish universities are offering a range of degrees in journalism. Moreover, the college of commerce in Rathmines, which had launched the first full-time course, has also grown into the Dublin Institute of Technology (DIT) and there is a brisk trade in other journalism courses and in journalism qualifications at private colleges. While 'recognition' of courses by the National Union of Journalists is sought and welcomed, not least because of the benefits for students who are issued with temporary NUJ membership cards, the precedent of seeking recognition by British bodies such as the NCTJ has not generally been followed and there is no system of close industrial monitoring or approval of courses. Institutions take their own initiatives to ensure that practitioners in the field of journalism, both employers and working journalists, respect the quality of courses on offer.

The head of the Department of Communications and Journalism at DIT has recently written (French: 47) that,

> At present, DCU and DIT are recognised as the primary centres for journalism education. They both run highly sought after courses at undergraduate and Master's level, courses that are aimed at the teaching of professional practice as well as more theoretical approaches to journalism. Both also are involved in research and have students taking research degrees up to doctoral level [...].Whereas DIT has a longer tradition, DCU has currently somewhat of a lead in journalism education [...]

Growth in the field is continuing, with both DIT and DCU now offering new Master's programmes that specifically address international aspects of journalism and with the University of Limerick about to commence print-journalism degree courses. Institutions, including the National University of Ireland at Maynooth, also offer general media degrees that may help students to find work later as journalists.

A number of institutions are currently considering new ways of responding to the continuing growth of online journalism, and to its implications for traditional divisions between the teaching of print, radio and television. While eager to preserve standards in each distinct area, staff appreciate that a level of convergence requires flexibility in respect to the overall framework within which such skills are taught and that existing multimedia programmes may be developed to facilitate journalism training. The international aspects of journalism are also receiving greater attention than they did previously.

The future of journalism education in Ireland is closely related to the funding of university education and the fate of the media industry. Ireland has been hit hard by the current international recession and there is unlikely to be any further expansion of graduate programmes during 2009. However, the principle that those entering journalism in Ireland can benefit from formal graduate training in the subject is now securely established and most existing graduate programmes are likely to survive.

The Author

Prof. Colum Kenny BCL, BL, Ph.D., is chairman of the Masters in Journalism course board at the School of Communications, Dublin City University, a board member of the EU MEDIA Desk in Ireland, a columnist with the *Sunday Independent* and a regular contributor to public debates on the future of the media.

References

French, Nora (2007), 'Journalism education in Ireland', *Irish Communications Review*, 10, pp. 41–9.

Kenny, C. (1993), 'A decade of broadcasting research', *Teaglaim*, 1, pp. 46–8.

Lawrence, W.J. (1908), *Dublin Evening Mail*, 15 December (where the author of the letter is identified only as 'A Dublin freelance'. Press cutting found in the scrapbooks of part-time journalist W.J. Lawrence (Personal Cuttings Book, National Library of Ireland Manuscript 4296)) – I am grateful to my colleague Martin Molony for drawing this letter to my attention.

The United Kingdom Journalism Education Landscape

Michael Bromley

Introduction

What might be called 'the British system' of journalism education and training has undergone a quite extraordinary transformation in the last 35 years. This was comprised of three interrelated facets. First of all, journalism education primarily involved university graduates. Second, growing numbers of those graduates were enrolled in dedicated journalism programmes and, third, most of these courses of study were located in higher education institutions (Frith and Meech 2007: 138). In 1970, none of these factors applied (Sanders et al. 2008: 135). As recently as 1980, they were only rarely applicable. In the mid-1970s it was commonplace to enter journalism as an occupation direct from secondary school: the editorial training scheme of Thomson Regional Newspapers (TRN), then the largest provincial publisher in the United Kingdom, enrolled equal numbers of school leavers and university graduates.[1] This was the model established following the report of the Royal Commission on the Press (1947–49). The Commission criticized journalism as a 'ramshackle' occupation with few, if any, discernible and enforceable standards (Bromley 1997: 333; O'Malley 1997: 150–1).

Although standards had emerged by 2008, the overall situation was no less clear: the National Union of Journalists (NUJ) said that journalism training was in 'disarray' (NUJ, 2006). Education and training are offered in two main modes: prior to employment (called 'pre-entry') and following employment (mid-career and professional development) (Spilsbury Research 2006, i). In the pre-entry realm universities award a range of degrees, diplomas and certificates at undergraduate and postgraduate levels. Colleges offer pre-graduate qualifications, although they sometimes also deliver university degrees as franchisees (Bromley 1995: 142–3). Many of these awards are accredited by industry bodies, which simultaneously provide their own courses and qualifications. Cutting across all of these are national schemes for key skills, occupational standards, vocational qualifications, foundation degrees (Fdg), and qualifications validated under the City & Guilds and Business and Technology Education (BTEC) systems, as well as emerging European standards under the Bologna Declaration. Attempts were made to codify them all under a National Qualifications Framework. Finally, a number of commercial providers both participate in these arrangements to varying degrees and develop their own programmes, principally of short courses. These include media companies whose internal training schemes are also sometimes available to non-employees. In many instances, these latter examples constitute continuing professional development.

There is not even much consensus over how many institutions are involved in journalism education and training, and there are many overlaps. At the time of writing, the National Council for the Training of Journalists (NCTJ), a newspaper body, both accredited 70 courses in 40 institutions – 22 universities, twelve colleges, four commercial organisations and two media companies – and offered its own programme. The Broadcast Journalism Training Council (BJTC) had accreditation arrangements with 23 universities and five colleges. The Periodicals Training Council (PTC) accredited fourteen programmes and ran its own short courses for employees of member companies. The NUJ approved a small number as well, and offered its own skills development courses to members. Skillset, a peak training body in the audio-visual area which collated an 'academy' of seventeen universities and colleges, was also involved in journalism training (Phillips 2005: 238–9). Moreover, not all programmes containing elements of journalism were labelled as such, and journalism might be included in courses with titles such as 'writing for media'. The research undertaken for this chapter identifies 113 organisations which were delivering, validating and accrediting in one form or another education and training formally labelled 'journalism' in 2008 (see also Gibson 2008: 380–406).

Through these it was possible to study not just journalism generically but also the following:

- newspaper/print journalism
- news journalism
- magazine/periodical journalism
- multimedia/online/digital/web/internet/new media journalism
- digital journalism production/digital photo journalism
- press photography/photojournalism
- television/radio/broadcast journalism
- television current affairs journalism
- international journalism/international broadcast journalism/international media journalism
- sports journalism
- business journalism
- theatre journalism
- travel journalism
- automotive journalism
- arts journalism
- science journalism
- investigative journalism
- fashion/fashion and lifestyle journalism
- freelance journalism
- comparative journalism

– and a range of more specific skills, such as reporting, feature writing and sub-editing.

The most common qualification is the three-year BA with Honours (in Scotland, three years without Honours; four years with). Many courses link journalism with other disciplines and fields of study, sometimes in multiple combinations. There are also a small number of undergraduate certificates (one year) and diplomas (two years). Colleges offer Fdgs, and Edexcel (the successor to BTEC) qualifications which range over six levels, from 'entry' to 'advanced professional' and which can be used to qualify for entry to degree programmes. The centralized higher education admissions service, UCAS, listed 733 possibilities to study journalism below graduate level in colleges and universities in 2008 (http: //www.ucas. ac.uk). The second most popular programmes are MAs, usually nested with postgraduate certificates (PGCert) and diplomas (PGDip). The PGDip is also a relatively common terminal award. Research degrees (MPhil, Ph.D.) are offered but the number of students is usually small. Only one university out of 55 noted their availability in one list of providers (Gibson 2008: 380–406).

Journalism programmes are available throughout the United Kingdom – in England, Scotland, Wales and Northern Ireland – although they are concentrated in England. Accurate national statistics are not kept, so it is impossible to determine how many students are enrolled in all of these programmes. In 2007, nearly 2,400 applications for places in undergraduate and pre-graduate journalism programmes at universities and colleges were received by UCAS, however. Cole (nd) estimated that in a decade the number of enrolments on the broad spectrum of media-related courses, including journalism, had risen from 3,000 to more than 40,000. By 2005, 95 per cent of journalists held degrees, of whom 61 per cent were graduates of journalism, and 43 per cent held postgraduate qualifications (Phillips 2005: 232–4).

A very peculiar British system

Prior to this flurry of activity there were very few attempts to provide systematic education and training in journalism. The first was initiated by the University of London in 1919 for non-matriculated students. It existed intermittently and with varying degrees of success until 1939. The Kemsley newspaper group introduced a company-based scheme, the Kemsley Editorial Plan, after 1945 'to help equip young men and women for the profession of journalism'. It was based on the perceived failure of the University of London diploma to focus on 'practical instruction' (Bromley 1997: 334; Kemsley 1952, v). The third effort arose as a consequence of the first of three Royal Commissions on the Press. The National Advisory Council for the Training and Education of Junior Journalists (NACTEJJ) oversaw from the 1950s a system whereby all trainees entered journalism *via* local newspapers and sat for a qualifying certificate (Bromley 1997: 334–5; Stephenson and Mory 1990: 193). In 1963, the director of the NCTJ, which had succeeded the NACTEJJ, and the education officer of the NUJ could write: 'More attention is now being given to the training of journalists in the United Kingdom than ever before' (Dodge and Viner 1963: 9).

The educational apparatus was weak, however, reflecting the non-university and training orientation of the only programmes available until 1970 (Sanders et al. 2008: 135). The NCTJ and NUJ co-operated in publishing a series of texts coinciding with the roll-out of the national training scheme (Dodge and Viner 1963; Goulden 1967; Harris and Spark 1966). In the early 1970s the NCTJ sponsored publication of a five-volume 'manual of English, typography and layout' written by the distinguished newspaper editor Harold Evans (Evans 1972, 1973, 1974a, 1974b, 1978). While British journalism schools were early participants in the European Journalism Training Association (EJTA) and sponsors of the European Journalism Centre in Maastricht, no formal national association existed until the formation of the Association for Journalism Education (AEJ) in 1997. In 2008, AEJ membership was drawn from 41 universities and one college: five universities were members of EJTA.

The amount of mid-career education and training encompassed by these arrangements is small and provided particularly by private suppliers, the NUJ, the PTC and the NCTJ (Hollege 2008). Universities and colleges are not seen by employers as major sources of continuing professional development (Spilsbury Research 2006: 31). The Thomson Foundation, based in Cardiff, offers training in media development, including courses in investigative journalism, news and current affairs reporting, feature writing and web publishing: 90 per cent of its work is conducted overseas (http: //www.thomsonfoundation.org). From the mid-1990s to 2001, when it was closed, the Freedom Forum's European Centre in London provided a discursive space for journalists especially those covering war and conflict. In 2006 the Reuters Foundation donated £1.75million to establish an international research centre in the comparative study of journalism at Oxford University. This was in addition to the Foundation fellowship programme which has been running at Oxford since 1983 (http: //reutersinstitute.politics. ox.ac.uk/). This is the first initiative of its kind in the United Kingdom.

What militated against the development of the systemic operationalisation of a universal structure of education and training was a strong belief that journalism was best learnt 'on a weekly or small evening paper where there is more time to supervise the work of the inexperienced' (Andrews 1962: 27–8, 68). This notion persisted into the twenty-first century: the editor of a national daily broadsheet, *The Independent*, who began work as a journalist with the weekly *Neath Guardian* newspaper straight from school, argued in 2004, 'I think it still holds true that the best training is to be had on a local paper' (cited in Brown 2004). Yet when he joined the *Middlesbrough Gazette* in the heyday of this approach, Dennis Hamilton, who later became editor-in-chief of *The Times* and *Sunday Times* and chairman of Reuters, found 'there were no training sessions or anything at all formal in the way of advice' (Hamilton 1989: 3). An 'apprenticeship' in journalism involved a range of activities from volunteering for assignments to making tea (Orr 1989: 13). James Cameron (1980: 28) 'entered the back door of journalism' in the Manchester office of the *Weekly News* 'filling paste-pots and impaling the other daily newspapers on the files'. James Kelly (1995: 35–6), who was taken on as a triallist by the [Belfast] *Irish News* as an 18-year-old in 1929, received 'no advice, no instruction […] It was a brutal case of the survival of the fittest.'

What a junior reporter could aspire to within journalism was limited. Mr. Farr, the senior reporter on the fictional *Tawe News* in Dylan Thomas's (1965) *Portrait of the Artist as a Young Dog* (Thomas joined *the South Wales Evening Post* in Swansea as a copy boy in 1931) was 'a great shorthand writer, a chain-smoker, a bitter drinker, very humorous' who was assigned to all the big stories, but whose life was essentially a disappointment (95). Another of the paper's journalists, Ted Williams, rather pathetically 'dreamed of Fleet Street and spent his summer fortnight [holiday] walking up and down past the *Daily Express* office and looking for celebrities in the pubs' (99).

There were others, of course, who revelled in the opportunities offered by this kind of ground-floor journalism. As a young reporter, Hugh Cudlipp (1995: 11), who was appointed features editor of the national *Sunday Chronicle* at age 19, regarded his posting to Blackpool for the *Manchester Evening Chronicle* as 'El Dorado for a young newshound': 'It was in Blackpool at 17 that I took my degree in street wisdom, with Honours in creative journalism' (10). Roy Greenslade, who later became editor of the *Mirror*, professed

> In […] three and a half years at the *Barking Advertiser* I learned more about newspapers than I have done in the 35 years since. I didn't realise it at the time, of course. Like all young people in a hurry, I was desperate to escape from the parochialism of my local weekly to get to Fleet Street. Over time, I have come to understand the value of those years. I'm not talking about the formal training […] What really counted was the education by osmosis […]. (Greenslade 2001)

Day-to-day supervision came chiefly from experienced reporters, although editors were nominally in charge (Andrews 1962: 27–8, 68). Cox and Morgan (1973: 117) observed 'a tiny handful of middle aged senior journalists supervising and directing assistants twenty years their junior'. In this way, Nick Pollard (by 2004 the head of Sky News), who started on the *Birkenhead News* in 1968, recalled, young people 'stumbled into journalism' (quoted in Brown 2004).

In the 1960s a first job as a (copy-) runner still provided a recognised route into journalism (Conroy 1997: 9), and could do so occasionally even in the 1990s (Harris 2004). It was also widely believed that journalism was an alternative to university (Barber 2003; Kenny 1990: 227). In the 1980s it was still possible to enter journalism without first going to university: among the more prominent journalists who did so was the editor of the BBC Television's *Breakfast* show. The editor-in-chief of the magazine *Elle* did not even sit for A-levels (high school graduation), but took a job as an editorial assistant before advancing to a traineeship in journalism (Brown 2004).

Training was largely a hit-and-miss affair at least until 1961 when enrolment in the formalised national training scheme became notionally compulsory (Andrews 1962: 72, 79). Even then, what constituted 'training' continued to vary widely (Harris 2004), and some journalists avoided any form of training at least up to the end of the century (Harris 2005). Originally, the NACTEJJ merely offered guidelines rather than a prescribed curriculum

(Bromley and Purdey 1998: 81). The idea of competitive entry gained ground only slowly, too (Gailey 1995: 5). Roger Alton found an entrée into *The Observer*, a national Sunday title which he later edited, through his parents' connections: 'nepotism,' he argued in the twenty-first century, 'is a bloody good way of getting in' (quoted in Brown 2004).

As the NCTJ took over in the 1960s, recruitment increased until by the end of that decade up to two-fifths of journalists on local weekly newspapers were in training (Boyd-Barrett 1980: 315; Cox and Morgan 1973: 7; Tunstall 1971: 60). In 1960–61, seven out of ten trainees possessed only the supposed minimum educational entry requirement, formally introduced in 1965, of O-levels (awarded at age 16). 12 per cent held no qualifications at all (Andrews 1962: 78; Stephenson and Mory 1990: 194). Journalism was a divided occupation: Franklin (1997: 40) called it 'the upstairs, downstairs profession'. As well as those who left school at as young an age as 14 to work in a local newspaper office, a minority went directly to Fleet Street from university (commonly but not exclusively, Oxford or Cambridge). The editorial staffs of even so-called popular newspapers were often made up primarily of middle-class public schoolboys and/or graduates (Bromley 1997: 332; Bromley 2003b: 130).

The 'one journalism' model

The 'one journalism' model, cultivated under the aegis of the NACTEJJ from the 1950s, continued by the NCTJ, and based on all trainees entering journalism *via* local newspapers, was no substitute for higher education, and led in many cases to only relatively mundane white collar work (Cox and Morgan 1973: 117; Keeble 1994: 5; Tunstall 1983: 191). Graduate recruits in particular sometimes found the requirement to work a period of indenture of up to three years stifling. What they had learnt at university commonly bore no relationship to what a local newspaper reporter did. For example, Tom Evans, a CNN producer, joined the TRN editorial training scheme in the early 1980s after graduating from Aberdeen University with a master's degree.

> A career in journalism seemed like a splendid idea after four years studying international politics and strategic issues. […] I went into the world of journalism thinking that in a matter of months, if not weeks, I would be able to apply all this great knowledge in my new career. Reality soon set in […] local newspaper journalism provided few opportunities to discuss the global issues that were shaping our planet. (Evans 2003)

The 1960s brought not only an expansion in numbers (by the end of the decade by possibly by as many as 1,000 local journalists a year) but also the wholesale 'gentrification' of journalism (Bromley 1997: 338; Franklin 1997: 50). The number of registered trainees doubled during the 1990s to 900 a year (Stephenson and Mory 1990: 196). These trends coincided with the rapid graduatization of journalism, reflecting both wider, social trends (Bromley 1997: 339) and the presence of conglomerate newspaper ownerships. In the mid-1970s almost a half of the trainee journalists recruited by the large local press groups were graduates (Boyd-Barrett 1980: 317). In 1967–8 the proportion of graduate recruits to journalism was double the 1960–61 figure (at 12 per cent) (Tunstall 1971: 60). It had doubled again (to 25 per cent) by 1977 (Boyd-Barrett 1980: 317), but graduates were not exempted from the tradition of initial training on a local paper (Boyd-Barrett 1980: 317–8). A decade later, many graduates sought to avoid, or at least foreshorten, the local newspaper 'apprenticeship' by studying for a PGDip in journalism at university.

The first authentic higher education course – a PGDip – in journalism began at University College Cardiff (subsequently, Cardiff University) in 1970. Similar courses at City University, London, and the Lancashire Polytechnic (later the University of Central Lancashire) followed (Bromley 2006: 57; Tunstall 1971: 60). The idea that such courses were not a substitute for but a precursor to a local newspaper 'apprenticeship' was kept alive for at least 25 years. The graduate journalist was still in a small minority. In the mid-1970s the most common experience was to have started in journalism before the age of 25 on a weekly newspaper but outside a formal training scheme (Social and Community Planning Research 1977, 282). Fewer than one in five newspaper editors held degrees (Delano and Henningham 1995: 13). Weaver (2005: 47) reported that at the end of the twentieth century only 4 per cent of all British journalists held journalism degrees.

An education 'revolution'

The proportion of graduates starting on local newspapers grew more than six-fold between the late 1960s and 1980 (from 5 per cent to 31 per cent), and then rose again by almost another three-quarters in nine years to 53 per cent (Bromley 1997: 339; Tunstall 1983: 190). By 1990, 45 per cent of trainees entered journalism through PGDip courses (Stephenson and Mory 1990: 194). The 'one journalism' model began to fragment with the introduction of separate training (including PGDip courses) in broadcast and periodical journalism, and a move away from shopfloor 'apprenticeships' (Bromley 1997: 338). At the same time, journalists trained on the local press found it more difficult to move into other more rapidly expanding – and better paying – media, such as broadcasting (Tunstall 1971: 58; Tunstall 1983: 195).

The profile of the trainee journalist also changed. The director of the NCTJ estimated in 1967 that about a quarter of new entrants into journalism were women (Dodge 1967: 70). This figure had doubled by 1989 (Stephenson and Mory 1990: 194). By 2008 up to 75% of students enrolled in many journalism programmes in higher education were women. Precise figures were not collated (Chambers, Steiner and Fleming 2004: 70), but in 2008 the group Women in Journalism started a student section (http://www.womeninjournalism.co.uk). While the increased recruitment of graduates favoured women because of the greater equity practised in admissions to higher education, the hidden costs of studying journalism worked against those from poorer backgrounds and so-called ethnic minorities (categories which often overlapped)

(Aldridge 2007: 148–9; Beckett 2008: 149). To a perhaps surprising degree, journalism remained stubbornly white, male, middle-class, metropolitan and middle-aged (Aldridge 2007: 76, 145–6). Notwithstanding the influx of new generations of (mainly female) graduates (Chambers, Steiner and Fleming, 2004: 2; van Zoonen, 2004: 38), the median age of journalists actually rose between the early 1980s and the end of the century (Delano 2000: 267). Furthermore, the idea that it was preferable to hire 'local talent' declined markedly (Guild of Editors 1996: 2; Keeble 1994: 7; Tunstall 1977: 335). Ray (1995: 360) concluded, after interviewing 55 local editors, that any inclination to favour local hirings had dissipated by the early 1990s.

By the mid-1990s it was also no longer as necessary to endure a number of years in a local newsroom in order to claim credentials as a newspaper journalist. National newspapers, including *The Independent*, *Sunday Times*, *Daily Express* and *Mirror*, as well as more traditional employers of graduates, such as *The Times* and *Financial Times*, sought recruits directly from university, often using postgraduate courses for initial training. Students on these courses began eschewing the local 'apprenticeship' and seeking first jobs in the national press. Individual newspapers and groups initiated their own training schemes more or less independently of the NCTJ, culminating in the (ultimately failed) *Daily Mirror* 'academy of excellence' in the 1990s (Hagerty 2003: 204; Stephenson and Mory 1990: 196). A number of journalism schools, including Cardiff and City, withdrew from the NCTJ accreditation scheme. Delano and Henningham (1995: 4) argued that there had been a veritable revolution in recruitment and training.

The debate over J-schools

Not surprisingly, the role of education and training attracted a large amount of attention from the mid-1990s continuing into the following century (Cole 1996; Tumber and Prentoulis 2005: 66). It was significant, therefore, that for twenty years the only approved higher education courses in journalism were for postgraduates (the first undergraduate programme started in 1991). In some journalism schools the students were more educationally qualified than the instructional staff, encouraging trade-offs between 'intellectual development' (the student's domain) and 'employability' (the mission of the journalism school). How the latter was defined was not always formally regulated, however, and thus difficult, if not impossible, to prescribe in curricula (Hartley 1996: 35–6; Purdey 2001: 162). The main function of journalism schools was role socialisation – the translation of *ad hoc* workplace practices and learning schema into a curriculum in order to supply newsrooms with a controlled supply of cheap but effective labour (Boyd-Barrett 1980: 309–10, 316; Bromley and Purdey 2001: 111). The 'sub-culture of the local newspaper office' prevailed (Boyd-Barrett 1980: 320; Hartley 1996: 36).

Boyd-Barrett (1980) argued that, expressed through the NCTJ, the skills requirements which formed the basis of the curriculum were kept purposely low and uncomplex (318); that entry qualifications were artificially deflated (317); that a rhetorical assault was kept up on the latent alternative influence of an educational sub-culture which was routinely decried as being 'too academic' (311), and that graduates were denounced both as 'potential subversives' in the newsroom, and as carpet-baggers interested only in exploiting local newspaper training in order to prepare themselves for more lucrative and glamorous careers elsewhere, particularly in television (316). Hartley's (1996) critique of journalism training and education was that the centrality of journalism to modern societies as 'a product and promoter of modern life' (33), not least in diffusing popular democracy, and its 'salient features' (society, knowledge, politics, capitalist-culture) (34), was not simply missing from the orthodox training and education of journalists but was deliberately excluded from it, 'reducing news to a set of technical operations' (39).

Delano and Henningham (1995: 4) argued that changes in training and in 'the nature of recruits' underlying journalism's status in the 1990s had not been fully accommodated. Although two-thirds of practising news journalists had received some form of 'apprenticeship' training (invariably in a local newsroom), only two-fifths had successfully completed the formal NCTJ qualification (15). Nearly 70 per cent had some experience of higher education (3), and 15 per cent were graduates of Oxford and Cambridge (14). The researchers concluded that 'the fast-rising educational as opposed to training standards displayed by British journalists [...] must be seen as the most significant element in the profile of the present-day British news journalist'. Moreover, they projected that

As on-the-job training become[s] less available, formation will increasingly be sited outside the arena of professional practice[.] [J]ournalists of the future are less likely to [be] socialised within their occupation and to retain their middle-class values, attitudes and expectations. (20)

Accommodating new factors

The Guild of Editors (1995: 8) suggested that 'changing culture and technology has (*sic*) underlined the need for a more formal training structure'. The observation was no doubt driven by the opening statement of its report of a survey of editorial training needs: 'Entry into journalism is in danger of becoming dominated by middle-class graduates' (1995: 2). The Guild's prescription was to accommodate both the 'six GCSE school leaver' and 'the high-flying graduate' (8) with a differentiated, multi-tiered training programme (9). TRN proposed a pre-training induction programme for school-leavers to counteract the trend to graduatization (Slattery 1995). The chief executive of the NCTJ argued that the admission criteria set by colleges and universities for courses were unsatisfactory and served the purposes of the institutions rather than the press, and the head of a private training centre said that academics and retired journalists were not best placed to make crucial selection decisions about entry into journalism (Cullum 1996). The consultant placed in charge of the TRN scheme bemoaned the demise of 'the route from copy boy to editor' and the requirement for 'qualifications' (Geere 1995; Slattery 1995). Nevertheless, more than 90 per cent of trainees chosen for the TRN course by the group's editors were graduates; many others were mature entrants with qualifications in other occupations: in early 1996, only two out of eighteen trainees (11 per cent) enrolled were school leavers (Johnston 1996).

Others pointed out that training in local journalism had not progressed much since the 1930s, and was unattractive to graduate entrants. The press officer for the University of Wolverhampton argued,

> I meet many young people who get their baptism on the student newspaper and the university magazine. They become stringers for the press office, unpaid I might add, and their enthusiasm is impressive. Meet them after a year in a reporters' room and they are disillusioned, depressed and ready to leave. They cite penny-pinching, mind-numbing routine, petty bureaucracy, tired old writing styles and being anchored to their work stations. It isn't just the money. [...] There used to be an allure, an excitement, almost a vocation for journalism. That image has worn so thin that even a journalist could see through it, never mind a graduate. (Branton 1995)

Beginning journalists voted with their feet. In the three years prior to 1989, two-thirds (48 out of 73) of those leaving City University with a PGDip in newspaper journalism took first jobs in the local press: only two (less than 3 per cent) went directly to national newspapers. In the three years following 1989, the proportion entering the local press fell by nearly two-thirds to 28 per cent (23 out of 82), while the number going to national newspapers increased to an almost equal figure of eighteen (22 per cent). The proportion of diplomates taking first jobs outside these two newspaper sectors (including national media such as the BBC, ITN, Reuters and the Press Association) also rose by a third (from 30 per cent to 40 per cent: 22 out of 73 to 33 out of 82). Of those entering either local or national newspapers only, the proportion taking the former option fell by more than a third (from 96 per cent to 61 per cent) over the period. In 1990–91, only a fifth of diplomates (six out of 29) graduated into jobs in the local press.[2]

Journalism education and training fragmented further with the institution of separate programmes across media platforms, practices, sectors and specialisms, and the participation of more universities and colleges (Bell and Alden 2003: 281–5; Bromley 1997: 336; Purdey 2001). From within the European journalism training community questions were asked about the appropriateness of 'a single curriculum [...] address[ing] the needs of such a functionally differentiated workforce' (Bierhoff, Deuze and de Vreese 2000: 11). Surveying journalism education, Hartley (1996: 33) argued

> it can be persuasively argued that there's no such thing as journalism in the singular; nothing that unites all the things that may be associated with the term 'journalism' except the term itself. It seems to exceed any category that might be used to encompass it – it is found in so many different forms, media, times, places, contexts, genres and industries,

with so many different styles of writing and representation, so many ways of presenting itself as true, addressing so many different types of reader, that any suggestion that something called 'journalism' even exists would be foolhardy, a totalizing projection of the false unity of a word.

The primacy of news

The NCTJ offers a generic 'basic training', which sets benchmarks for and is reproduced in the majority of programmes, in reporting, news values, newsroom practices, current affairs, sub-editing, feature writing, pertinent elements of law and public administration, and ethics (Herbert 2001: 70–1; National Council for the Training of Journalists 1989a, 1). The scope of the curriculum is national insofar as the public administration curriculum includes central government, the British constitution and 'economic literacy' (National Council for the Training of Journalists 1992b); but specifically local activities are also stressed (for example, reporting the magistrates' courts, councils and committee meetings, etc.) (National Council for the Training of Journalists 1992a). The aims of the newspaper journalism syllabus are

To recognise, obtain and select important, relevant and newsworthy facts from either written or verbal sources, using appropriate skills or techniques.

To write clear, vigorous and balanced reports in a form that will attract and interest the reader.

To gain a general knowledge of the departments of a newspaper (for instance production, advertising, circulation and finance, etc. as well as editorial), and an understanding of the industry's structure and economics. (National Council for the Training of Journalists 1989a)

The connections between newsrooms and educational institutions delivering a growing proportion of the syllabus are built around instructional staff. At first, in the 1950s, the scheme was dependent on local journalists taking time out from work to contribute casually in the classroom on a sessional basis. Colleges began appointing journalists as full-time staff instructors in 1965 (National Council for the Training of Journalists 1989b, 4). The NCTJ maintains a requirement that instructors on accredited courses ought to have substantial experience as journalists. Pressures from within the university sector, particularly following the introduction of the Research Assessment Exercise, resulted in the strengthening of the academic robustness of journalism schools through mergers (at Cardiff into a school with media and cultural studies), loss of independence (the Department of Journalism at City University was folded into a Faculty of Arts) and the hiring of staff with Ph.D.s (Bromley 2006: 57–8).

Drawing up a postgraduate scheme for the Scottish Centre for Journalism Studies (1991), the University of Strathclyde and Glasgow Polytechnic argued that journalists' education should develop 'a professionally critical understanding of their role in the industry and of the industry's role in the European and global information economies' (3–4). Quite unusually, a textbook published in 2004 unapologetically articulated vocational training in journalism with 'critical reflection and understanding', introducing 'some of the more academic analysis that aids our understanding of how journalism works', as constituting journalism 'education' (Harcup 2004: 8). Even the NCTJ's Oxdown, which was created as a 'mythical, but typical, English town served by a truly local weekly newspaper', was dropped from the curriculum in 2006 (Anon 2006).

This seemed to clash with the simple centrality of news in the training curriculum. Keeble (1994: 343) advised the student readers of his textbook, which was still in print in 2008, that 'the dominant view in the industry' remained largely that,

> You may have great ideas about the nature of reporting, you may know all about ideology and the history of the press in 18th century Britain. But if you can't bash out a quick story on a murder you're useless.

Traditionally, all trainees began as 'reporters' and aspirants were told that the job entailed 'reporting the news and commenting upon it' (Dodge 1967: 70–1). The NCTJ curriculum (fundamentally unchanged for 40 years, according to the Guild of Editors (1996: 3)) includes 'accurate reporting [...] the precise and cogent use of language and [...] essential background knowledge of such fields as government, law and current affairs'. A 'nose for news' is *de rigeur*, and progression is achieved through being given 'more important assignments'. This 'training in reporting' is based on the accepted view that 'basic experience as a reporter is the best foundation for other newspaper work, either as a specialist, feature-writer or sub-editor' (Dodge 1967: 72–3).

Programmes tend to be strongly vocational. One estimate was that at least 50 per cent of undergraduate programmes, and 80 per cent of post-graduate programmes, are based on practice (Cole nd). Many see this as serving to distinguish journalism programmes from those in the more academic fields of media, cultural and communication studies. In the mid-1990s, the British and Irish section of EJTA attempted to establish a scheme whereby programmes were classified in relation to the amount of journalism practice they contained.

Claims are made for extremely high employment rates for graduates: one institution said its data showed that over ten years the figures fluctuated between 92 per cent and 100 per cent, while another put its graduate employment level at 83.5 per cent.[3] Accreditation by the NCTJ is believed to lead to successful employment outcomes for graduates. One educator said: 'Evidence of our own research among local editors has established that most are reluctant to hire any candidate who has not completed the NCTJ syllabus successfully'. Another observed: 'We concentrate on helping students acquire the skills required by a trainee on a provincial newspaper'. The data support these views: the majority of employers (70 per cent) recruit directly from education, and 73 per cent look for applicants with an industry accredited qualification (Spilsbury Research 2006: 25–6). Overwhelmingly, for newspaper journalism students the model remains that of the local press (weekly, daily, or evening). Alternatives (tabloid national daily journalism as practised at *The Sun*) are routinely held up as abhorrent. Many journalism programmes maintain close ties with local newspaper journalists and editors; but few are involved, through consultancy activities, in development work.

Not surprisingly, then, the overarching source of modelling for journalism into the twenty-first century is the NCTJ syllabus. It is said to be 'both a constant and a "gold standard"' which editors recognise and trust'. 82 percent of newspaper employers seek recruits who hold a recognised industry qualification, of which the NCTJ awards are the primary example (Spilsbury Research 2006: 26). Nevertheless, the Guild, principally representing local newspaper editors, broke ranks when, in drafting a proposed revised training programme in the mid-1990s, it adopted a different focus on news. The tests of newsgathering and news writing (an interview, a report of a speech, a news story written from a handout), on which the NCTJ placed so much emphasis that they formed the basis of qualification in journalism, were excluded from the first level, at which some trainees could exit the programme. Instead, this stage, while acknowledging the presence of 'newsgathering and the role of the news desk', broadened both the scope of the curriculum (to include photography, sub-editing, design and broadcasting) and the definition of 'news' to incorporate 'customer care and grass roots news' which it assessed as 'the invaluable commodity' (Guild of Editors 1996: 12–3). Yet education and training remain primarily shaped by the NCTJ apparatus which culminates in examinations in news writing, and leads to emphases on simulated news activities, coursework exercises, and the use of practice papers in the classroom based on the syllabus.

All the same, there is some unease with the NCTJ, as has already been noted. This mirrors wider debates about the purpose of journalism, and revolves around potential distinctions between 'news value' (as taught through the syllabus) and 'reader interest' (as discerned by interaction with audiences). Some journalism educators began to question whether there are 'basic rules', and if there are, how to apply them. Others adhere to what are believed to be journalism's unchanging virtues – 'professional' attributes, such as being objective, exerting influence, reporting on the activities of authorities and elites, and concentrating on news; rather than publishing 'publicity material dressed up as news [...] just to whip up a decent crowd'. On the other hand, some believe that news is indefinable, and news values 'very individualistic'. They encourage students to abandon the formulaic approach embedded in the NCTJ syllabus which is condemned as a form of arranging facts in hierarchical order without reference to 'the imagined audience'. Furthermore, while employment opportunities in newspapers declined, the magazine sector seemed to thrive, and magazines are less likely to seek graduates holding industry accredited qualifications (Spilsbury Research 2006: 25–6).

As journalism migrated into higher education in undergraduate programmes, it was compelled to adopt the forms of universities. Courses in PGDip programmes, which had previously been only loosely constructed under portmanteau descriptions, such as 'practical journalism', which were believed to be reflective of actual practice, have to be made to conform to the structures of degrees with modules and units measured in terms of study hours, learning outcomes, assessment regimes, progression, etc., which are often seen as alien to practice. These arrangements have to be reconciled with the NCTJ's less modular approach, and the availability of alternatively structured journalism training opportunities. Journalism schools are pulled in several directions by several forces (Bromley 2006).

Concluding Remarks

In sum, there is evidence of a degree of confusion endemic in journalism schools (Bromley 2006). Students rightly single out their success in NCTJ examinations as a decisive aid in landing first jobs, particularly in newspapers. The link between accredited education and first jobs is even stronger in broadcasting (Spilsbury Research 2006, 25–6). Second, functional skills are also highly valued: many graduates (43 per cent of a sample surveyed) rate shorthand instruction as one of the most important parts of their programme. A debate about the utility of shorthand re-surfaced in the trade periodical *Press Gazette* in 2008 (http://blogs.pressgazette.co.uk). At the same time, the NCTJ attempted to assert its authority by announcing its intention to compile a 'league table' of j-schools (McNally 2008). On the other hand, a number of students want 'more imagination and creativity'. One practitioner-lecturer proposed a curriculum focused on creativity, innovation, media literacy and social networking skills (McClellan 2007). What seems to be concentrating minds most is the march of so-called 'new media'. The Saturday editor of *The Times* noted: 'there is a very big disconnection between that [optimistic] way of thinking about the future newsroom and the preparation, training and resources that editorial organisations seem to be giving to it' (cited Luft 2008).

The approach of journalism programmes, while perhaps not fixed in the 1950s, is nonetheless largely uninformed by journalism's own history of dynamic development (Frith and Meech 2006, 142–3). Debates over the theory-practice dichotomy, heightened by digitisation, continue into the twenty-first century (Tumber and Prentoulis 2005: 66, 70–1). The basic textbook on newspaper reporting, first published in 1967, was reissued in a second edition in 1993, a third in 1997 and was still available in 2008 (Harris and Spark 1966). To stray too far from the industry model epitomised by the NCTJ can be viewed as an abrogation of professional duty. It is tempting, therefore, to dismiss journalism schools as out of touch, and their programmes of declining relevance to journalism at it is practised. Yet they have to negotiate what is happening on a wider canvass and the inability of journalism as a whole to understand its own changing contexts, practices and processes. One observer argued that 'newspaper journalists have difficulty imagining non-traditional, even bold answers' to their own problems. These included 'the vocabulary of newspapers', such as what constitutes 'a story' (Porter 2005) or, in broadcasting, 'the way we tell it' (Damazer cited Bromley 2003a, 13–4).

Journalism in the United Kingdom, it seems, gets the education and training it deserves.

The Author

Michael Bromley is the Head of the School of Journalism and Communication, University of Queensland.

Notes

1. Author's personal experience.
2. Data taken from *Newsletter* no.5 (pp. 20–8) and *Newsletter 94* no.8 (pp. 38–42), the annual magazine of the Department of Journalism, City University.
3. Material in this and the following sections is drawn from a series of interviews with journalism educators conducted in 2001–2.

References

Aldridge, M. (2007), *Understanding the Local Media*, Maidenhead, Berks: Open University Press.

Andrews, L. (1962), *Problems of an Editor: A Study in Newspaper Trends*, London: Oxford University Press.

Anon (2006), 'Farewell then, Oxdown', *Press Gazette* (11 August), http: //www.pressgazette.co.uk. Accessed 30 June 2008.

Barber, L. (2003), 'Liddle at large', *The Observer* (5 October), http: //observer.guardian.co.uk. Accessed 17 September 2004.

Beckett, C. (2008), *SuperMedia: Saving Journalism so it can Save the World*, Oxford, Blackwell.

Bell, E. and Alden, C. (eds.) (2003), *'MediaGuardian' Media Directory 2004*, London: Guardian Books.

Bierhoff, J., Deuze, M. and de Vreese, C. (2000), *Media Innovation, Professional Debate and Media Training*, Maastricht, European Journalism Centre.

Boyd-Barrett. O. (1980), 'The politics of socialization: recruitment and training for journalism', In H. Christian (ed.), *The Sociology of Journalism and the Press*, Monograph 29, Staffordshire: University of Keele, pp. 307–40.

Branton, R. (1995), 'Newspapers are driving away the best potential', Letter to the editor, *UK Press Gazette* (13 March), p. 19.

Bromley, M. (1995), *Media Studies: An Introduction to Journalism*, London: Hodder and Stoughton.

Bromley, M. (1997), 'The end of journalism? Changes in workplace practices in the press and broadcasting in the 1990s,' In M. Bromley and T. O'Malley (eds.), *A Journalism Reader*, London: Routledge, pp. 330–50.

Bromley, M. (2003a), 'A sham renaissance? 9/11 and the authority of newspaper journalism', *Australian Journalism Review*, 25(1), pp. 3–31.

Bromley, M. (2003b), 'Objectivity and the other Orwell: the tabloidism of the *Daily Mirror* and journalistic authenticity', *Media History*, 9(2), pp. 123–35.

Bromley, M. (2006), 'One journalism or many? Confronting the contradictions in the education and training of journalists in the United Kingdom' in Leung et al. (eds.), *Global Trends in Communication Education and Research*, Cresskill, NJ, Hampton Press, pp. 53–71.

Bromley, M. and Purdey, H. (2001), 'Chilling out – but not yet "cool": new media training in a UK journalism school: a further report on 'journomorphosis', *Convergence*, 7(3), pp. 104–15.

Bromley, M. and Purdey, H. (1998), 'Journo-morphosis: today's new media and the education and training of tomorrow's "cool" journalists', *Convergence*, 4(4), pp. 77–93.

Brown, M. (2004), 'Learning curve', *The Guardian* (23 August), http: //media.guardian.co.uk. Accessed 24 August 2004.

Cameron, J. (1980), *Point of Departure: Experiment in Biography*, London: Granada.

Chambers, D., Steiner, L. and Fleming, C. (2004), *Women and Journalism*, London: Routledge.

Cole, P. (1996), 'Are journalists born – or trained?', *British Journalism Review*, 7(2), pp. 42–8.

Cole, P (nd), 'Study journalism in the UK', http: //www.instudy.com. Accessed 29 June 2008.

Conroy, H. (1997), *Off the Record: A Life in Journalism*, Argyll: Argyll Publishing.

Cox, H. and Morgan, D. (1973), *City Politics and the Press: Journalists and the Governing of Merseyside*, London: Cambridge.

Cudlipp, H. (1995), 'For Balliol read Blackpool', *British Journalism Review*, 6(2), pp. 9–18.

Cullum, G. (1996), 'Editors unite to apply standards', *Press Gazette* (14 June), p. 16.

Delano, A. and Henningham, J. (1995), *The News Breed: British Journalists in the 1990s*, London: The London College of Printing and Distributive Trades.

Delano, A. (2000), 'No sign of a better job: 100 years of British journalism', *Journalism Studies* 1(2), pp. 261–72.

Dodge, J. (1967), 'Training to become a journalist', In R. Bennett-England (ed.), *Inside Journalism*, London: Peter Owen, pp. 69–77.

Dodge, J. and Viner, G. (eds.) (1963), *The Practice of Journalism*, London: Heinemann.

Evans, H. (1978), *Pictures on a Page*, London: Heinemann.

Evans, H. (1974b), *News Headlines: An Illustrated Guide*, London: Heinemann.

Evans, H. (1974a), *Handling Newspaper Text*, London: Heinemann.

Evans, H. (1973), *Newspaper Design*, London: Heinemann.

Evans, H. (1972), *Newsman's English*, London: Heinemann.

Evans, T. (2003), 'Making the news', *Gaudeamus*, 18 (June), http: //www.abdn.ac.uk/alumni_relations/gaudeamus. Accessed 11 February 2004.

Franklin, B. (1997), *Newszak and News Media*, London: Arnold.

Frith, S. and Meech, P. (2007), 'Becoming a journalist: journalism education and journalism culture', *Journalism*, 8(2), pp. 137–64.

Gailey, A. (1995), *Crying in the Wilderness. Jack Sayers: A Liberal Editor in Ulster, 1939–69*, Belfast, The Institute of Irish Studies, The Queen's University of Belfast.

Geere, A. (1995), 'Shooting ourselves in the foot', *UK Press Gazette* (13 March), p. 2.

Gibson, J. (2008), *media 08:* , London: Guardian Books.

Goulden, J.F. (1967), *Newspaper Management*, London: Heinemann.

Greenslade, R. (2001), 'Let's hear it for the rag trade', *The Guardian* (21 May), http: //www.mediaguardian.co.uk. Accessed 22 May 2001.

Guild of Editors (1995), *Survey of Editorial Training Needs: Summary of Findings*, London: Guild of Editors.

Guild of Editors (1996), *Tomorrow's Journalist: A 'Green Paper' on Editorial Training*, London: Guild of Editors.

Hagerty, B. (2003), *Read All About It! 100 Sensational Years of the 'Daily Mirror'*, Lydney, Gloucs: First Stone.

Hamilton, D. (1989), *Editor-in-Chief: The Fleet Street Memoirs of Sir Denis Hamilton*, London: Hamish Hamilton.

Harcup, T. (2004), *Journalism Principles and Practice*, London: Sage.

Harris, G. and Spark, D. (1966), *Practical Newspaper Reporting*, London: Heinemann.

Harris, R. (2004), 'How to be… Natasha Kaplinsky', *The Guardian* (1 November), http://mediaguardian. co.uk. Accessed 8 March 2005.

Harris, R. (2005), 'How to be… Louise Chunn', *The Guardian* (7 March), http://mediaguardian.co.uk. Accessed 8 March 2005.

Hartley, J. (1996), *Popular Reality: Journalism, Modernity, Popular Culture*, London: Arnold.

Herbert, J. (2001), 'Educating the friend of the family: the local journalist', *AsiaPacific Media Educator*, 10, pp. 68–74.

Hollege, R. (2008), 'Seen it all? Well, get ready to learn it all over again', *The Guardian* (7 April), p. 5.

Johnston, T. (1996), 'Trinity editorial training', In *Turning 21: Journalists for the New Century*, London, 7 March.

Keeble, R. (1994), *The Newspapers Handbook*, London: Routledge.

Kelly, J. (1995), *Bonfires on the Hillside: An Eyewitness Account of Political Upheaval in Northern Ireland*, Belfast: Fountain.

Kemsley, Viscount (1952), 'Introduction', In *The Kemsley Manual of Journalism*, 2nd edn, London: Cassell, pp. v–viii.

Kenny, M. (1990), untitled contribution to T. Gray (ed.), *Fleet Street Remembered*, London: Heinemann, pp. 227–9.

Luft, O. (2008), 'Future of newsrooms is integrated, claims editors survey' (6 May), http://www. journalism.co.uk. Accessed 30 June 2008.

McNally, P. (2008), 'NCTJ to offer "transparency" through courses league table', *Press Gazette* (16 April), http://www.pressgazette.co.uk. Accessed 29 June 2008.

National Council for the Training of Journalists (1989a), Newspaper journalism syllabus – aims (August), copy held by author.

National Council for the Training of Journalists (1989b), *How Journalists are Trained*, Epping: NCTJ.

National Council for the Training of Journalists (1992a), Accreditation checklist (November), copy held by author.

National Council for the Training of Journalists (1992b), Public Affairs course: aims and objectives (August), copy held by author.

NUJ (2006), 'Training policy', National Union of Journalists, http://www.nujtraining.org.uk/. Accessed 2 September 2009.

O'Malley, T. (1997), 'Labour and the 1947–9 Royal Commission on the Press', In M. Bromley and T. O'Malley (eds.), *A Journalism Reader*, London: Routledge, pp. 126–58.

Orr, C. (1989), *Splash! Drama and Comedy in a Newspaperman's Career*, Braunton, Devon: Merlin Books.

Phillips, A. (2005), 'Who's to make journalists?' in H. de Burgh (ed.), *Making Journalists*, London, Routledge, pp. 227–44.

Porter, T. (2005), 'Redefining the language of journalism', *First Draft* (29 January), http: //www. timporter.com. Accessed 1 April 2005.

Purdey, H. (2001), 'How broadcast journalism training in the UK is adapting to industry changes', In M. Bromley (ed.), *No News is Bad News: Radio, Television and the Public*, Harlow: Longman, pp. 157–74.

Ray, G.W. (1995), 'The future of "parish pump" newspapers: how editors of British local newspapers view their work and communities', Ph.D., University of Wales Cardiff.

Sanders, K, Hanna, M., Berganza, M.R. and Aranda, J.J.S. (2008), 'Becoming journalists: a comparison of the professional attitudes and values of British and Spanish journalism students', *European Journal of Communication*, 23(2), pp. 133–52.

Scottish Centre for Journalism Studies (1991), Post-graduate Diploma in Journalism: Course Documentation, Glasgow, Strathclyde University and Glasgow Polytechnic, copy held by author.

Slattery, J. (1995), 'TRN to restore local touch with school leaver plan', *UK Press Gazette* (13 March), p. 5.

Social and Community Planning Research (1977), *Attitudes to the Press*, Royal Commission on the Press (Command 6810–3), London: HMSO.

Spilsbury Research (2006), *An Audit of Training Arrangements for New Entrants into Journalism*, London: Skillset.

Stephenson, H. and Mory, P. (1990), *Journalism Training in Europe*, Brussels: European Commission.

Thomas, D. (1965), *Portrait of the Artist as a Young Dog*, London: J.M. Dent.

Tumber, H. and Prentoulis, M. (2005), 'Journalism and the making of a profession', In H. de Burgh (ed.), *Making Journalists*, London: Routledge, pp. 58–74.

Tunstall, J. (1971), *Journalists at Work. Specialist Correspondents: Their News Organisations, News Sources, and Competitor-Colleagues*, London: Constable.

Tunstall, J. (1977), '"Editorial sovereignty" in the British press: its past and present', In O. Boyd-Barrett, C. Seymour-Ure and J. Tunstall, *Studies on the Press*, Working Paper Number 3, Royal Commission on the Press, London: HMSO, pp. 249–341.

Tunstall, J. (1983), *The Media in Britain*, London: Constable.

van Zoonen, L. (2004 edn), 'One of the girls? The changing gender of journalism', In C. Carter, G. Branston and S. Allan (eds), *News, gender and power*, London: Routledge, pp. 33–46.

Weaver, D. (2005), 'Who are journalists?', In H. de Burgh (ed.), *Making Journalists*, London: Routledge, pp. 44–57.

Part II

The Northern European/Democratic Corporatist Media Model
Countries

Introduction

Lennart Weibull

C an journalism really be taught? If so, who shall teach it? And what shall be taught? These are three questions that have dominated the debate on journalism education in Northern Europe since its beginning. Answers to them have been different over the years and between actors, but inside the individual countries the discussions have been remarkably similar, which is demonstrated by the following country overviews. In the following I shall develop these three basic questions by trying to point out some general patterns for the development of journalism education in the Northern European countries. The overview is made on the premise that there is a common ground for media and journalism in Northern Europe as presented by Daniel Hallin and Paolo Mancini (2004: 143ff; cf. Weibull 2007) in the Democratic Corporatist media model. However, I will also approach the question of validity in their perspective.

Eleven countries are selected for the overview. They are countries of Northern and, to some extent, Central Europe: the Nordic countries Denmark, Finland, Iceland, Norway and Sweden, Germany, Austria and Switzerland as well as Belgium, Luxembourg and the Netherlands. They are all strongly urbanized and most of them have a long industrial tradition. However, they differ significantly in size – from more than 80 million inhabitants in Germany to less than half a million in Iceland – and in their cultural and political heritage.

The cultural and political tradition

To a large extent the eleven countries are part of a common history and culture. Germanic languages – German, Dutch, Swedish, Danish, Norwegian and Icelandic – are spoken in most of the countries, denoting the common roots. However, Roman languages – French and Italian – coexist in the south as the national languages in Belgium and Switzerland; and Finnish, the national language of Finland, is part of the Fenno-Ugrian language family with no relation to most other European languages.

Probably the single most important factor in bringing the northern countries together and also stressing the language per se was the Lutheran challenge to the Roman Catholic Church in the early sixteenth century. Also in countries where the Roman Catholic Church came back to power, like in Austria, Belgium and southern Germany, the new ideas had challenged the authoritarian power structure.

The common Northern European tradition is also present in politics and the economy. Political democracy was established in most countries in the early twentieth century.

A majority of the countries are oriented to consensus politics, based on what Hallin and Mancini call a moderate pluralism (2004: 68), which in practice means a high level of political stability based on strong parties with long traditions. In most countries there is a clear left-right dimension in party structure, but even though political majorities may change large differences in actual politics are less frequent.

The legislative and governmental bodies are generally respected by the citizens, expressing the strength of the rational-legal authority: the state is normally regarded as the guardian of freedom and justice as well a guarantor of the welfare state, even though public trust has gradually declined in the latest decades in almost all Democratic Corporatist countries. There are obvious differences within some of the countries but in most of the areas presented above they represent a common perspective, which makes them different from countries in Eastern and Southern Europe, but also from the United Kingdom.

The common tradition of the Northern European countries both in politics, economy and culture is also reflected in the development of their media systems. Daniel Hallin and Paolo Mancini (2004: 144f) point out three 'coexistences' between media and politics, which they regard as distinctive to the Democratic Corporatist countries: (1) The high degree of political parallelism between the growth of the mass press and party political development, (2) The political parallelism in media development has coexisted with a high degree of journalistic professionalization, meaning the existence of independent media and (3) The paradox of, on the one hand, the early introduction of press freedom (from the state) in most of the countries, and on the other hand a high level of acceptance of state activities in the media sphere.

The media industries

The cradle of the world's newspaper industry stood within the Democratic Corporatist countries. The roots of the modern mass press can also be found in the same area. The mass press developed during the mid-nineteenth and the early-twentieth centuries; the first wave of the modern commercial press was aimed at industrialists, merchants and intellectuals who were the main actors of the developing industrial society. Today we find that citizens in most countries of the Democratic Corporatist media tradition buy far more newspapers than the average European. Norway, Finland and Sweden show the highest figures. The basic pattern is the same for regular newspaper reading.

The expansion of the daily press coincided, in most countries, with increased democracy. The liberals especially played an important role in pushing political liberties forward. Most newspapers became gradually affiliated to political parties. There are reasons to believe that this presence of a broad partisan press or 'segmented pluralism' (Hallin and Mancini 2004: 152f), was important to educate citizens as newspaper readers and seems to have contributed to the high prestige of the press. Later dictatorship in some of the countries, however, may have changed this pattern.

One reason for the general acceptance of the party political press in the Democratic Corporatist countries was, to a large extent, a general trust in politics and political bodies. Direct state subsidies to the press exist in all of the countries, with the exception of Germany and Austria.

The strong presence of the state in the Democratic Corporatist countries is most obvious in the areas of radio and television. In all the countries public service television is very strong. As is pointed out by Hallin and Mancini (2004: 164) public service radio was developed almost as a parallel to the extension of the welfare state, as *res publica*, almost as a social enlightening programme. Most of the public service organizations were modelled on the BBC, but the organizational structures differed a lot between the countries.

During the 1980s the Democratic Corporatist countries were gradually opened up for competition from private broadcasters, mostly both in radio and television. The private television sector has gradually expanded in most of the countries and public service television has gradually lost market shares.

However, considering the long-term trends of the media industry, it is obvious that the late 1990s prompted a gradual change to the traditional Northern European media system. The increasing role of the Internet – which had an especially rapid development in the Democratic Corporatist countries, probably reinforced by the strong reading tradition – opened up a totally new market, where both traditional and new media engaged. One important consequence has been the increasing segmentation of the media audience – this fragmentation leaves less room for public sphere journalism, traditionally guaranteed by the main newspapers and public service broadcasting.

Perspectives on journalism education

Along with the expansion of the press industry, newspapers and editors formed their own associations across the borders of the party political press. In most countries it had already taken place during the early twentieth century. At approximately the same time journalists had organized themselves into professional organizations or unions, as in The Netherlands and Sweden. Most of these organizations became very strong, not least because of their high membership numbers. Further, the organizations had close contact with one another and in some countries there were professional press clubs, which both editors and journalists could join.

One consequence of the organizational activities was the work on principles of good journalistic practice. In most countries this soon developed into formalized systems of self-regulation of the press. Press Councils were established, normally by the newspaper industry and the journalist associations, to handle readers' complaints against the rules of good practice. The rules and the councils are normally well anchored in the media culture of the Democratic Corporatist countries. These professional organizations formed the basis of a journalistic autonomy that is normally called professionalization, which meant a striving for an independent, unpartisan journalism. This striving is also one of the most common points of departure for the ideas of journalism education.

However, when comparing the development of journalist education it is important also to consider the differences between the countries of the Democratic Corporate Media Model. The Scandinavian group of countries shows great similarities in media and education traditions, but is very different from the development in The Netherlands and Belgium, where religion has had a greater influence on social and cultural development.

The roots of journalism education: Can journalism be taught outside the media?

Modern journalism developed during the first decades of the twentieth century. It was mostly the main city newspaper that introduced new models of political and cultural coverage; especially in Scandinavia, where the Copenhagen paper *Politiken* is a prominent example. However, these new trends did not mean very much in terms of journalism education. In-house schooling was still the only way for a person to get into a career in journalism – if it was not possible to establish a newspaper of one's own.

However, this lack of formal journalism education did not prevent the development of journalism as an area for academic scrutiny. The German *Zeitungswissenschaft* represented the new field and soon had followers in Scandinavia, especially in Finland where the subject was introduced at a Civic College in Helsinki in 1925. The introduction of journalism as a field of study meant an increased awareness of its importance. Even though the new subject was mainly based in departments of political or economic studies, these also sometimes offered specialized courses aimed at students interested in the field. But there were also, in this period, some initiatives from journalist associations, e.g. in Austria, Belgium and Sweden, to start vocational courses, but those were not part of a formal education.

In Northern Europe, formal journalism education in most countries is a product of the post-war era, especially of the 1950s and 1960s, when there was an explosion of new departments or schools: Denmark and the Netherlands in 1957, Sweden in 1959, Switzerland 1960, Norway 1965 and Austria 1969 – and in Finland the early initiative was upgraded to a school in 1960. In most of those countries there had been minor post-war initiatives, often lasting only a few years like in Austria, but the journalism education establishment in the 1960s meant the final advent of a formal educational structure, although differently organized in individual countries.

The expansion of journalism education in the 1960s seems to have at least two reasons. The first and most obvious was the expansion of European mass media. The rise of radio and television and the expansion of the modern press meant a development of journalism that required educated journalists. The traditional way of in-house training was not enough. The second, closely related, reason was that, as a consequence of the increased social and political importance of the media, journalism gradually began to be perceived as a profession – and for a profession it was important to relate to a formal education structure (cf. Djerf-Pierre and Weibull 2008).

Having said this it is necessary to stress that, even if academic programmes and professional schools expanded, the traditional in-house route into journalism remained. Actually, a large portion of journalists in the Northern European countries have such a background. Especially notable is the situation in Germany where the figure is more than 60 per cent. In the Scandinavian countries the percentage is much smaller but often sports writing is a typical way into the local press. In Sweden the percentage of journalists with no formal journalism education is stable, or has even increased somewhat as a consequence of the expansion of different types of new media.

Organizing journalism education: Who should be responsible?

Looking into the rise of journalism education in Northern Europe it is obvious that in most countries there are at least three main actors: (1) media organizations or Journalist Unions, (2) public institutions like universities or other schools, and (3) political and religious organizations. Whereas media organizations, Journalist Unions and public institutions have been active in almost all countries, the role of political and religious organizations reflects the character of the national system. Thus, in the Netherlands the so-called 'pillarized politics', including religious organizations, have influenced journalism education.

In most countries initiatives to establish formal journalism education mainly originated from journalist organizations, while media employers were less active. The general tendency, however, was that public institutions gradually increased their importance. Still the educational model could differ, especially between traditional university studies and vocational programmes, based for example in new university colleges of applied science like in Finland or Switzerland, or in professional schools like in Denmark. In Sweden the development is typical of the Scandinavian approach, starting as an initiative from media organizations to establish a national journalism school, later taken over by the public college system; this can be interpreted as a typical reflection of the Democratic Corporatist model where government institutions are accepted by most groups of society.

Even if the main platform of higher journalism education in Northern Europe is public education programmes, there are a lot of other alternatives in all countries; these alternatives mirror the different ways to get into professional journalism. Also media organizations, journalist unions and political, religious or social groups are still active in offering education. This is especially true for Belgium, Switzerland and Germany but plays a somewhat minor role in the Scandinavian countries; it is mainly a matter of course programmes in specialized fields.

It has to be added that the 1980s meant the advent of a new type of private journalism school. Private schools are no novelty in journalism education – actually there are one or two commercial schools in most Northern European countries – but what was new in the 1980s was that they were established by big media conglomerates, like Springer in Germany or Sanoma in Finland. One of the stated reasons for the existence of such schools is increasing competition for the best journalists, but another might be a criticism of the curricula of the public programmes or schools.

Types of journalism education: What is the relevant content?

During the expansion of journalism education since the 1950s and 1960s, there has been an ongoing debate about what is relevant curriculum for a professional journalist. The early university programmes were often regarded as too theoretical, not focusing on the practical needs of the craft. On the other hand the development of post-war societies meant that media and journalism organizations also pointed out the increasing need for political and economic knowledge amongst journalists. The ideal stated, but seldom agreed upon in practice, was an integrated model. However, within an integrated programme the same discussion continued on the proportion of courses and their differing characteristics.

In the Scandinavian countries, the integrated model is the principle that is guiding public journalism education. It means journalism programmes organized by universities or university colleges contain both academic courses and practical applications like writing, radio and television production as well as internships. Another model can be found in Germany. Here in-house training – *volontariat* – is dominant, but most of the students admitted have a solid academic background. Between these two extreme models of integration, we can find a lot of education with very different foci. Educations established by media organizations generally tend to be more vocational. This is also true for most private schools.

It is very difficult to point out any trends in terms of curriculum development. However, the increased role of universities of applied science in many Northern European countries indicates that the role of craft is increasing within the public educational institutions. In many countries this development reflects the expansion of radio and television. This area was, for a long time, a matter of inside training though the public service companies, but since the 1980s it is found in all curricula and requires more practical training. The challenge for journalism education in the last decade has been the Internet, which has gradually been introduced into the curricula.

Concluding Remarks

The increasing role of radio and television production in the curricula illustrates how journalism education depends upon media development. Education is not only a matter of professional skill but also a means of understanding how individual media function. Similarly the increased computerization of the editorial process and the expansion of online journalism means that more practical training, including further education, including leadership training, is needed to understand these new contexts. These are tendencies that can be found in most countries; however, the main characteristic of the Northern European media model is the pluralism of both media and education.

Typical for most countries of the Northern European Democratic Corporate media model are strong public service radio and television, as well as a strong daily press with many small local newspapers. Thus, journalism education in these countries has to cover a broad spectrum of journalistic platforms, which influences both the character of the educational system and the curricula. The needs of small local newspapers are very different from those of the news desk of a huge public service TV channel. The former, with their small organizations, very often ask for journalists who can handle the craft, whereas the latter normally needs specialized competence.

Even if public institutions form the basis for education in most countries, this means that there is also room for other alternatives in smaller countries. Similarly, there is a continuous need for further education and so-called lifelong learning to keep up with changes in the media system. It is also important to add that formal journalism education is just the start for young journalists. Where students finally land is less influenced by their education per se, than by what they do with their education when in practice.

The Author

Lennart Weibull is the chair of Mass Media Research at the Department of Journalism and Mass Communication, University of Gothenburg, and pro vice-chancellor of the university.

References

Djerf-Pierre, Monika and Weibull, Lennart (2008), 'From Public Educator to Interpreting Ombudsman. Regimes of Political Journalism in Swedish Public Service Television 1925–2005', In J. Strömbäck, M. Örsten and T. Aalberg (eds.), *Communicating Politics. Political Communication in the Nordic Countries*, Göteborg: Nordicom.

Hallin, Daniel C. and Paolo Mancini (2004), *Comparing Media Systems. Three Models of Media and Politics*, Cambridge: Cambridge University Press.

Weibull, Lennart (2007), The Northern European/Democratic Corporatist Model Countries, Introduction, In G. Terzis (ed.), *European Media Governance. National and Regional Dimensions*, Bristol/Chicago 2007: Intellect Books.

The Austrian Journalism Education Landscape

Johanna Dorer, Gerit Götzenbrucker and Roman Hummel

Introduction

Efforts in journalism educational training have been made in Austria since the beginning of the twentieth century; this has led to a diversity of education and training possibilities for beginners as well as for journalists. But as of yet, journalism is a non-regulated profession.

Journalism education and training in Austria depends on three important characteristics: Firstly the increasing interest of young people to get a job in the limited media market of a small state; secondly on the development of a competitive educational market since the mid 1990s; and thirdly on the widely shared belief that formal education as a prerequisite for journalism might impede the independence of media. Therefore, the access to journalism as a profession is free and unbound by educational requirements.

However, while specific educational requirements are not necessary to become a journalist, most of the incoming young journalists (predominantly female) in newspapers, radio and TV stations have enrolled in a kind of formal education or training due to the heavy competition in this field: But all in all, no more than 150 job offers per year are available in Austrian journalism. On the one hand about seven academic training-programmes attract high-potential students (in an intellectual as well as economic sense) with a capacity of approximately 180 students. On the other hand, three public universities give more or less open access to all applicants and serve more than 7600 enrolled students – mostly in Vienna (more than 5400). These institutes offer a more theoretically-based education for a full spectrum of communication and media professions (not only journalism) as well as academic careers. The graduates are also potential candidates for entering the journalistic profession. Additionally, further education for professional journalists is offered.

The proportion of women working in all media rose up to 34 per cent in the last decade (Hummel 2008). While a strong increase of female students in all kinds of media-educational programs has been noticed in the last 10 years, female journalists hold lower career expectations than their male counterparts (Dorer 2008).

The historical development journalism training programmes in Austria[1]

The discussion of journalistic training in Austria has been influenced equally by both technological developments in the media and by the political decisions in media policy and educational policy.

At the beginning of the twentieth century, the development of the mass press created a situation where the media consisted of a large number of badly trained and equally badly paid journalists. Both politicians and journalist organizations felt the situation had to be improved. Those discussions were not followed by concrete measures. However, they did result in several lectures being offered on the subject of journalism at the University of Vienna.

In the 1920s, a successful initiative for the improvement of journalistic training was started by the workers' movement, which was to have a widespread effect on the profession. Politicians and journalists associated with the workers' movement worked towards an improvement in education and training for Austria's working class and, after several years of preparation, opened a so-called *Arbeiterhochschule* (High School for the Working Class).

The journalism courses organized by the Worker's Union were short-lived. In February 1934, the socialist press, the socialist trade union, and every other part of the workers' movement were outlawed under the authoritarian regime (1934–38).

During the Nazi regime, Austrian journalism training fell under German law. As Austria no longer had its own training programme, trainee journalists were sent to Berlin for three months to attend the German Press School. As of 1943, a year after a 'Department of Press Studies' had been officially established at the University of Vienna, journalists' training recommenced in Austria. The head of this department was a German National Socialist who abided strictly to the party line.

In 1946, courses recommenced at the Department of Press Studies at the University of Vienna. Naturally, this department wished to distinguish itself from the old department. So for many years, study was limited to historical and theoretical approaches to print media. During the Allied Occupation (1945–1955), the Americans ran a programme whereby young journalists were trained on the job at newspaper editorial offices. There was also an exchange programme ('Exchange of Persons Program') that enabled Austrian journalists to travel to the United States to spend a month at various American newspapers and also to study at American universities. As a result of the strong direction of journalism during the Nazi regime, media professionals were firmly opposed to any form of structured education for journalists. 'Training on the job' was seen as the only guarantee for a free press. The first Vienna School of Journalism, founded in 1948 by the director of a private school, closed down some years later and had no lasting effect (cf. Dorer 2003: 244).

It was not until the end of the late 1960s that the issue of implementing journalistic training re-emerged in Austria. The main reasons can be seen on the one hand in the growing interest of young people for a job in the media and on the other in the technological and economical change in the media industry itself (increased competition by press-concentration and overall supply of TV programmes). In 1968, for the first time, a three-year traineeship was introduced in the collective agreement for dailies and weeklies – but without any further specification regarding goals or circumstances.

In 1969 the Department of Communication was founded at the University of Salzburg. At first, the proportion of practical training to theory was very small. In 1971, in response to a Press Council initiative, the department began preparations for the establishment of an extra university course for journalists. But it was not until 1974 until the first 'basic course for journalism education' could be held in cooperation with the Editor's Association of Austrian Newspapers (Pürer 1980: 13). The range of courses offered continued to grow and in 1978 the Austrian Media Academy was established under a 'Board of Trustees for journalistic education (KfJ)'. Members of this board were officials of the Editor's Association, the Journalist's Union and the public broadcasting company ORF, advized by scientists of the departments of communication in Vienna and Salzburg. Today this media academy is one of the most important training institutions for journalism in the country: The collective agreement for dailies and weeklies demands the passing of the Austrian Media Academy as a prerequisite for employment at the rank of an editor or reporter. An additional media academy – the Catholic Media Academy – was founded by the Catholic Church in 1977. It offers basic courses for journalists who wish to work in areas of the catholic press. Other ideologically earmarked institutions followed (party- and union-affiliated), partly also because, since 1979, state subsidies were granted to all institutions providing accompanying vocational training for journalists (this means training is subsidized only for professional journalists. In 1982 the public broadcaster ORF established a training department (*Berufs- Aus und Fortbildungssystem, BAF*) for all its employees and also its freelancers. (ORF Almanach 1983: 301))

A blooming educational market soon emerged for the growing number of people not actively working with media but nonetheless attracted by the idea of working in the field of media – in 1984 the number of applicants was already 15 times higher than the labour market could offer positions for (Pürer 1984: 334). At the University of Graz, a committed professor began offering a two-year journalism course (*Medienkundlicher Lehrgang*) in 1974. This course was privately organized and financed partly by the university, partly by the students. Throughout the 1980s, two departments of communication at the Universities of Vienna and Salzburg changed their curricula to reflect this trend. In 1983 the University of Klagenfurt established a course of studies in media and communication.

From the early 1990s on, the universities began offering privately organized one-year training courses for journalists-to-be. In the mid 1990s, the government passed a significant reform in the education system, introducing on the one hand 'private universities' and on the other hand 'universities for applied sciences' (*Fachhochschulen*) in Austria. Shortly thereafter, a highly professional, costly two-year university course in journalism for print and broadcast media was established at the Danube University of Krems. Then the universities for applied sciences began offering four-year programmes that concentrated on the technological developments within the media industry as well as in journalism and public relations.

The present state of journalistic training in Austria

The present situation for beginner journalists is remarkable for its diversity of training possibilities. The length and quality of the various programmes varies greatly. Training programmes that lead to journalistic qualifications claim to provide a good balance between theoretical and practical knowledge, as well as some practical experience. This balance, however, is seldom achieved (Fabris 1996: 10).

The training programmes and courses offered by the universities and schools of journalism vary widely. From March until June of 2008, a thorough survey of the training possibilities for journalists in Austria was carried out.[2] The following data concern the number of training programmes, students and teachers for the year 2007. A clear distinction can be made between non-academic and academic programmes (university and university-style training). A further distinction can be made between different target groups: (a) general communication education curricula not specifically intended for journalistic education; (b) specific journalistic education intended solely for persons wishing to become journalists; (c) accompanying vocational training for journalists.

(a) Non-academic programmes

Non-academic programmes are offered by four media academies (Österreichisches Journalisten Kolleg, Katholische Medien Akademie, Oberösterreichische Medienakademie, Journalismus & Medien Akademie des ÖCJ), three adult education centres (Polycollege, Wifi Tirol, Wifi Burgenland), three training institutions owned by the Conservative Party, the Socialist Party and the Austrian Journalist's Association respectively (Friedrich Funder Institut, Friedrich Austerlitz Institut, Gesellschaft für Publizistik und Medienforschung) and two further media institutions, the public broadcasting ORF and a non-commercial radio (ORF, Radio Orange).

The non-academic institutions are notably led mainly by political parties, industrial lobbies and the Catholic Church. Often, these serve the purpose of educating the organizations' own members. The quality and scope of education offered by these institutions varies greatly, as does their cost. What is commonly noted about these institutions is the emphasis on job-oriented practical education, while theoretical education largely assumes more of a background role. In the foundation courses, students are taught in small groups of approximately fifteen people, of which 36–64 per cent are female. The teachers are experienced local and foreign journalists, as well as experts in the fields of politics and economics. These foundation courses conclude with a certificate confirming the student's participation in the course. This certificate is accepted as practical education by media establishments.

The most important and prestigious educational establishment is the Austrian College of Journalism (Österreichisches Journalisten Kolleg) of the board of trustees for journalistic education (Kuratorium für Journalistenausbildung). The board is responsible to the Associations of Austrian Newspapers and Magazines (Verband österreichischer Zeitungen, Österreichischer Zeitschriftenverband), and the trade union. The foundation courses are targeted at young journalists who already have some work experience. In addition to the foundation course, with a duration of 480 hours, one- and two-day seminars are offered for further education. These seminars have an average intake of 400 participants each year.

The foundation courses of the Catholic Media Academy (Katholische Medien Akademie) have a similar scope. In addition to the foundation course, seminars spanning several days are offered, with a yearly intake of around 120 participants (50 per cent female). The Upper-Austrian Media Academy (Oberösterreichische Medienakademie) was founded in 1990 by the upper-Austrian print media conglomerate and press club, and offers several foundation courses each year, for both print and radio journalism. Additionally, multiple-day seminars are offered with an average yearly intake of 400 participants (65 per cent female).

The Journalism and Media Academy (Journalismus & Medien Akademie) of the Club of Austrian Journalists (Österreichischer Journalisten Club) offers occasional foundation courses at irregular intervals. In 2007, of a total of two planned courses, only one course, pertaining to press photography, took place.

As a result of the foreseeable privatization of the public broadcast sector in the 1990s, institutes of further education started offering foundation courses for journalism. The Polycollege (affiliated to interests of employees) has been offering foundation courses for radio and online journalism several times per year since 1992. These courses are predominantly finished by women. Additionally, a variety of seminars on journalistic methods are offered. Wifi Tirol and Wifi Burgenland, institutes of further education (both affiliated to interests of the chamber of commerce), offer foundation courses in both e-journalism and journalism in general, in collaboration with local press businesses and local studios of the ORF (Österreichischer Rundfunk). While the scope of these courses is significantly larger, the cost is also markedly higher.

Table 1: Foundation courses in journalism offered by four media academies in 2007.

Organization	Established	Foundation Course	Duration (in h)	Fees (in euro)	Participants (N)	Female (in %)	Trainers (N)	Female (in %)
Österr. Journalisten-Kolleg	1978	journalism	480	(2.910*) 3.420	23	52	79	18
Katholische Medien Akademie	1978	journalism	500**	1.390	11	36	22	40
Oberösterr. Medienakademie	1990	press journalism	110	450	46	70	17	6
		radio journalism	70	450	15	60	7	5
Journalismus & Medien Akademie	1995	press-photography	400***	(3.450*) 4.600	14	64	12	17

(*) for members only

(**) excluding 12 weeks (480 hours) practice in newsrooms

(***) including several days practice in newsrooms

Table 2: Foundation courses in journalism offered by three adult education centres in 2007.

Organization	Established	Foundation Course	Duration (in h)	Fees (in euro)	Participants (N)	Female (in %)	Trainers (N)	Female (in %)
Polycollege	1992	radio journalism	46	745	24	65	5	60
		online-journalism	37	562	11	78	2	0
Wifi Tirol	1999	e-journalism	450	5.030	16	60	9	33
Wifi Burgenland	2004	journalism	480	3.380	15	44	40	n/a

Neither the two media institutions associated with the main political parties, nor the one linked to the trade union, offer courses in basic journalism-education. The Friedrich Funder Institut of the Austrian Conservative Party (ÖVP) limit themselves to awarding grants for internships in press offices and organizing one- to three-day seminars on the topic of school newspapers, aimed at high-school students. The Friedrich Austerlitz Institut of the Social Democratic Party (SPÖ) is also limited to awarding subsidies and, like the Society for Communication and Media Studies (Gesellschaft für Publizistik und Medienforschung), organizing lectures and discussions.

Two additional educational institutions, led by the media establishments themselves, must be noted: The ORF (Österreichischer Rundfunk) presides over the ORF-human resources, an educational centre offering an extensive educational programme for its own employees. Those new to the job are offered a foundation course spanning 40 days (320 hours). Furthermore, a wide range of multiple-day seminars and trainings for radio and TV production, speech training, etc. are offered as further education. Employees of non-commercial media may take advantage of several seminars offered by the Freies Radio Orange Wien on the topics of media production, media technology, ethics of journalism, copyright, etc. In 2007, these courses had 537 participants, of which 70 per cent were female.

In 2007, the total number of individuals participating in foundation courses offered by non-academic educational institutions was 175. Of these, the proportion of women was 57 per cent. This figure has not changed since the same study was conducted ten years ago. (Dorer 2003: 248).

(b) Academic programmes

The academic journalistic education and training programmes offered by the universities are much more theoretical. Thus, the universities prepare their students for a much wider range of career possibilities in the more general field of media and communication.

Public universities

Unlike other institutions the departments of communication at the Universities of Vienna, Salzburg and Klagenfurt do not provide a specific journalism education, but rather a social-scientific curriculum which also includes specialized courses related to applied journalism. Most of the undergraduates, after having finished a three-year BA, continue with a two-year MA-study. Subsequently, doctoral studies (which only public universities are entitled to provide) may also be attained. All in all, around 1500 students (current in 2009 there are 2100) begin their studies in one of the three sites each year (two thirds of them in Vienna). About 75 per cent are female.

Estimations on the basis of the decisions of the students in Salzburg (where one has to choose a specialisation, amongst them journalism) indicate that about 25 per cent of students intend a journalistic career, in other words about 375 or nearly three times the amount of

Table 3: Journalism-related curricula at three public universities in 2007.

Name of Institution	Universität Wien	Paris-Lodron-Universität Salzburg	Alpen-Adria Universität Klagenfurt
Department	Publizistik- und Kommunikationswissenschaft	Kommunikationswissenschaft	Medien und Kommunikationswissenschaft
Established in	1941	1969	1996
Leaving Certificate	BA, MA, Dr.	BA, MA, Dr.	Mag., Dr.
Workload in ECTS	180 BA, 120 MA	180 BA, 120 MA	not applicable
Curriculum's Main Topics	– journalism – organizational communication and PR – communication theories – media economy – media politics – media psychology	– journalism – PR and organisational communication – communication theories – media systems – cultural communication – media economy – audiovisual communication	– organisational communication – computer aided communication – culture and media
Economic Partnerships	Donated professorship by the Austrian PR Association	none	none
Number of Students (N)	3730 in BA; 522 in MA; still 1211 in the yet terminated Diploma	708 in BA, 535 in MA	972 in MA-study
Female (in %)	70 BA; 79 MA; 64 Diploma	68 BA; 77 MA	69 MA
Number of Graduates (N)	741	257 BA; 104 MA	94 MA
Female (in %)	75	74 BA; 84 MA	72
Number of teaching staff (N)	181	68	61
Female (in %)	45	28	49

positions the labour market can offer per year. Therefore the curricula of all departments is not closely focused on journalism, but gives a social-scientific education enabling graduates to apply for a wide range of positions within the field of communication – no more than one third of the classes are dedicated to media practice.

Two universities for applied sciences

In contrast to public universities, the universities for applied sciences are authorized by law to restrict access by testing the students' qualifications. According to this restriction, only a small number of students – based on the college's capacities – are enrolled. Similar to the public universities, the universities for applied sciences rearranged their academic programmes in the course of the EU Bologna process. In actual fact, two programmes in the academic field of 'journalism' are offered in two Austrian universities for applied sciences, located in Vienna and Graz.

The academic programme 'journalism and media management' at the University for Applied Science Vienna was formally established in 2004 as a full diploma study. Since 2007 this programme was restructured for a BA comprising 180 ECTS points within six semesters. The institution responsible for this programme, which costs €363 per semester, is the Chamber of Commerce in Vienna. The academic schedule in detail comprises both theoretical and practical education in lectures, workshops and exercises mainly in the journalistic field, focusing on journalistic education and media management skills. The MA programme is scheduled to start in 2011. In 2007, 34 students were on the BA. In total, the programme has 170 students (amongst them 51% female) and 49 (60% female) graduated as Mag. (FH) or Bachelor of Arts, which is a primary academic degree. The teaching staff at this University of Applied Science Vienna is mainly male (75%), which highlights a generally discussed problem of gender disproportion within journalism education.

In Graz, the former full-time diploma studies 'journalism and organizational communication' at the Joanneum Graz was recently restructured to a BA named 'journalism and public relations' that encompasses an all-round education in a mixed field of journalism and PR. The Styrian provincial government operating authority of this university of applied science enables cost-free access (no study fees) for the 101 students. The MA study is scheduled to start in 2011. The BA programme, which is limited to 25 students a year, comprises 199 ECTS points and offers theoretical and practical education consisting of exercises and workshops. 69% of the 22 graduates (Mag. (FH) and BA of Art and Business) were female, while the proportion of female teachers is below 22%.

In total, 271 students were enrolled in 2007 in the two universities for applied sciences (60% female) that have 47 graduates a year (64% female). The staff lacks female teachers, as only 23% of female staff educate the predominantly female students.

Additionally, it must be mentioned that several universities for applied sciences in Austria are related to the fields of new media, telecommunication, information science and technology, which might have intersections with journalism. But these educational programmes mostly neglect explicit journalism education.

Two private universities

Journalism education at the private universities is much more expensive than the state-run programmes.

The Centre for International Journalism at the Danube University Krems, which is a public university with private organization and funding, has offered two academic programmes, one MA programme in 'quality journalism' (90 ECTS) and a course in 'TV-journalism' (60 ECTS). The MA was established in 1995 as a course for 'print-, radio- and TV-journalism' and restructured in 2007 to be theoretically-based but mainly oriented on practical contents, as well as 'trimedial' (radio, TV and online) education and further development for journalists. The total cost of the vocational training is €11,690. The yearly student capacity is restricted to 20: in 2007 only eleven students were enrolled (73% female) and fifteen graduated in MA (60% female). Only 13% of the 53 journalism experts in the teaching staff are female. The MA expanded in autumn 2008 to a 120 ECTS programme in 'quality journalism and new technologies' in co-operation with the Institute for Language and Speech Processing in Athens, Greece.

Additionally, the Danube University Krems frequently offers short two-day courses in health communication. The course 'TV Journalism' is certified as 'academic expert in TV-journalism' and costs about €5,700 for an explicit practical and vocational training in TV-production, TV-trends and format-development. Eleven students (82% female) joined the course in 2007, and ten graduated (90% female). The 30% female share of the teaching staff is somewhat high compared to that of other institutions.

The private Webster University Vienna offers a BA programme in 'media communications major; certificate for advanced training in selected areas', which are related to the American educational system and taught in English. The education is based on professional training for journalists: topics are journalism, video/film, new media, media research and -analysis. The total cost of this three to four year BA programme is €59,520. In 2007 there were 37 students enrolled in the major-stream (65% female) and seventeen in the minor-stream (69% female), giving a total of 54. The share of women within the graduates is very high at about 72% – as well as within the female teaching staff (41%).

In total, 59 students a year are enrolled at the private universities' BA/MA programmes and courses, with a female percentage of 75%. In total, 42 students passed these programmes/courses annually (78% female).

Academic courses at the public universities

Universities are entitled to offer 'academic courses' to the general public apart from their general education programs. Such journalism-related courses are offered by the University of Klagenfurt (*'SciMedia Universitätslehrgang für Wissenschaftskommunikation'* – Academic Course for Science-Communication), and the University of Salzburg (*'Universitätslehrgang für Sportjournalismus'* – Academic Course for Sports-Journalism). These courses are targeted at beginners in journalism as well as for media professionals intending to extend their professional skills and knowledge. The syllabus is balanced between theoretical and practical training.

All these courses are with costs and accept a limited number of students only. All in all, 37 people – three-quarters of them female – passed one of these academic courses in 2007. The courses' workload fluctuates between 400 and 600 hours while the grades vary between an MA and becoming a so-called 'academic expert'.

Concluding Remarks

In Austria, the profession of journalism is accessible in several ways – with and without a specific education or training. There are also a variety of institutions providing theoretically and practically oriented curricula on media and journalism, which can help entry into a journalistic career but do not serve as a prerequisite for it.

In general, schools and courses can be distinguished in pre-professional study-offers (and here again between generally media-related and specifically media-oriented) and vocational trainings for working journalists. Most of these institutions are financed or at least co-financed by the public.

Curricula with a workload of more than 1000 hours are provided by academic institutions only and certified by an academic degree. In 2007, 1322 students graduated from these schools. All of these educations are pre-professional and not only targeted at a career in journalism, but also at a wide range of professions related to public communication. Pre-professionals as well as professional journalists frequent academic courses dealing with specific sectors of journalism.

Non-academic institutions provide, on the one hand, vocational training for professional journalists only and journalism-related education within the framework of adult education on the other. Because a non-specifiable number of participants frequent more than one course per year, a reliable figure of students cannot be given. The course's workload varies between half a day and a few weeks. Institutions of adult education offer training programmes in media and journalism, mostly with a duration of less than 500 hours per course, and were passed by about 175 people in 2007.

The output of all these schools and courses was roughly ten times higher in 2007 than the need of the labour market in journalism (Hummel 2008: 12). In spite of increasing competition within the Austrian media market, a heavily growing attraction of media-related jobs amongst young people and a rising importance of technical skills in journalism, the ways into this profession are neither formally nor informally regulated – and all indicators show that this will remain the status quo for the years to come. To work in the media sector was a strong desire for an increasing number of young Austrians within the last few years and it still will be in the future, despite the fact that the attempts of the majority are not really successful. But in reverse this demand is the factor of success for a mushrooming sector of journalism and media education. The present situation described in this article, showing a huge diversity in curricula, duration, costs and levels of excellence of courses, will also characterize the near future.

The Authors

Johanna Dorer is an Assistant Professor at the Department of Communication/University of Vienna, and Equal rights representative at the University of Vienna.

Gerit Bettina Götzenbrucker is an Associate Professor at the Department of Communication/University of Vienna.

Roman Hummel is a Professor at the Department of Communication/University of Salzburg, and Head of Journalism Studies.

Notes

1. For a detailed description see: Dorer, 2003, 232–246, following Bettel 1991; Pürer 1974/75; Institut für Publizistik 1986.
2. The authors did parts of this survey on the phone and via email. It also involved internet research. The survey covered 21 institutions: twelve non-academic institutions, five universities (three public and two private universities), two privately organized certificate programmes on journalism (universitäre Lehrgänge) and two universities for applied sciences (Fachhochschulen).

References

Bettel, S. (1991), 'Aus- und Weiterbildung für Journalisten in Österreich: eine historische und kommunikationstheoretische Analyse der Defizite. /Education and vocational training for journalists in Austria: a historical and theoretical analysis of shortcomings', Dissertation, Wien.

Dorer, J. (2003), The historical development and present state of journalism training in Austria, In Romy Fröhlich and Christina Holtz-Bacha, (eds.) *Journalism education in Europe and North America. An international comparison*, Cresskill/N.J.: Hampton, pp. 237–253.

Dorer, Johanna (2008), Status quo and development of the professional situation of women in Autrian journalism. In Romy Fröhlich and Sue Lafky (eds.), *Women journalists in the western world*, Cresskill/N.J.: Hampton, pp. 101–122.

Fabris, Hanz-Heinz (1996): Arbeitsfelder im Journalismus und in anderen Informations- und Kommunikationsberufen. /Fields of journalism and other information and communication jobs. In: Heinz Pürer. (ed.): *Praktischer Journalismus in Zeitung, Radio und Fernsehen. /Journalism practice in newspaper, radio and television*. Salzburg: Kuratorium für Journalistenausbildung, pp. 393–400.

Hummel, R. (2008), Strukturdaten zum österreichischen Journalismus /Structure of the Austrian journalism, In *Journalismus in Österreich. Bericht der Abteilung Journalistik des Fachbereichs Kommunikationswissenschaft Salzburg /Journalism in Austria*, Report of the Department of Communication at the University of Salzburg, Salzburg.

Institut für Publizistik- und Kommunikationswissenschaft der Universität Salzburg (ed.) (1986), *Massenmedien in Österreich. Medienbericht 3 /Mass media in Austria. Handbook 3*, Wien: Buchkultur.

ORF (1983), *ORF Almanach 1983*, Wien: Verlag des Österreichischen Rundfunks.

Pürer, H. (1974/1975), Journalistenausbildung in Österreich /Journalism education in Austria, In *Publizistik*, 19/20, pp. 524–529.

Pürer, H. (1980), *Aus- und Fortbildung für Journalisten in Österreich. /Journalism education and training in Austria*, Salzburg: Kuratorium für Journalistenausbildung.

Pürer, H. (ed.) (1984), *Praktischer Journalismus in Zeitung, Radio und Fernsehen. /Journalism practice in newspaper, radio and television*, Salzburg: Kuratorium für Journalistenausbildung.

The Belgian Journalism Education Landscape

Nico Carpentier and François Heinderyckx

Introduction

The Belgian political realities and its series of state reforms unavoidably affect the worlds of media, journalism and journalism education. Without spending too much effort on explaining Belgium's institutional structures, we need to at least mention the existence of three so-called Communities (the Dutch-speaking, the French-speaking and the German-speaking[1] Communities) and three Regions (the Flemish and the Walloon Regions, and the Brussels-Capital Region). The Belgian state structures play a vital role in the debate on journalism education, as both the educational system and the media system are now (with the usual exceptions) the competences of the language-based Communities. At the educational level this means that the Belgian schools, polytechnics and universities each resort to one of the country's Communities, resulting in a diversity of policies and educational practices. At the level of the media system, the effect is similar. With the exception of the national news agency Belga, Belgian (i.e. national) media organizations have ceased to exist and have now almost completely been replaced by regional media. In addition, media consumption patterns are dramatically different. For example, newspaper readership and penetration is significantly higher among the Dutch-speaking population in the North (62% versus 54% [CIM, 2009])[2] while the average television viewing time is higher among the French-speaking population in the South (225 versus 180 minutes [IP International Marketing Committee, 2009]).[3] These structural differences of course interconnect with the cultural-linguistic differences, as the North and South of the country have each developed into their own imagined communities (Anderson 1983). This in practice means that the countries' regional media focus on their 'own' community, and only report on the 'other' community in a limited way. Similarly, the regionalized educational organizations (including those involved in journalism education) also focus on their own communities.

This does not imply that some of the debates on journalism education cannot be found in both the Dutch-speaking and French-speaking part of Belgium, as our analysis of the situation in June 2008 shows. One crucial debate on the relationship between the universities and the polytechnics is strongly related to the Bologna process, as this process not only lead to a restructuring of the entire higher educational landscape (moving from a Candidate/Licentiate model to a Bachelor/Master model) but also to a repositioning of universities and polytechnics. In the Dutch-speaking part of Belgium, universities became responsible for the so-called 'academization' of the polytechnics, through the establishment of all-encompassing associations (incorporating a university and several polytechnics). In practice, this implies that polytechnics are forced to do research and increase the research-based nature of their teaching. Similar regroupings are underway among French-speaking institutions, although at a slower pace. On the other hand, these regroupings and repositionings are not isolated incidents, but build on a long history of 'rationalizing' the educational landscape by merging educational institutions and/or creating superstructures (as for instance with the decree of 13 July 1994 grouping the Dutch-speaking polytechnics, and the decree of 5 August 1995 for French-speaking side of things).

The debate on the relationship between polytechnics and universities, and on the 'academization' of the polytechnics touches upon another key debate, which deals with the focus on the academic or the practice-based and vocational nature of journalism training. This debate raises the question of whether journalism education requires a more academic focus, either on Journalism Studies (or Communication and Media Studies), or on more topical fields like Political Studies, History or Literature, resulting in journalist-experts that are knowledgeable about either the social phenomenon of journalism (or communication), or the societal field they have studied. On the other side, advocates of the practice-based nature of journalism training insist that journalism is a profession, which requires the skills to use specific tools. As Stovall puts it, these more academic approaches risk producing 'second-class academic citizens' (1993: 26), which are seen as distinct from 'real' journalists. One can also wonder about the impact of the more academic critical approaches; for instance Frith and Meech conclude the following on the basis of their survey of 50 young British journalists:

[...] we found no evidence whatsoever that graduate journalists brought anything of the critical 'media studies' approach to their activities; their accounts of the value and meaning of journalism replicated those of journalism tradition (which is why they discounted the significance of classroom journalism education). Going by these findings the occupational culture of the newsroom does not seem to be under any threat from the intellectual culture of the academy. (2007: 158)

They nevertheless add a word of warning, saying that this conclusion could be 'misleading', as '[t]his is a snapshot of an occupational cohort at a particular, rather satisfactory moment in their careers,' (Frith and Meech 2007: 158) and these young journalists might reconsider later. Frith and Meech also add (based on informal contacts with their formal students) that the 'newsroom disdain for academic training' is 'vastly overstated' (Frith and Meech 2007: 159).

This debate about the academic or vocational focus is very much related to the university-polytechnics debate, as universities (not surprisingly) privilege the more academic focus, and the polytechnics are defending a more practice-based type of training, although at the same time being forced into a more research-supported model. The debate is also related to what Deuze (2006) calls the choice between the follower mode or the innovator mode. Here the question is whether journalism education should follow the journalistic practices and cultures that now dominate the media industry, preparing future journalists for what they will undoubtedly have to face, or whether they will train new generations of journalists that will be able to improve the social and democratic quality of the contemporary journalistic practices and cultures. Clearly, the presence of a follower or innovator mode is not necessarily linked to a more academic or vocational approach, but a very strict focus on journalism education as teaching the tools of the trade would be difficult to combine with a more critical approach towards the structural problems and limitations of the journalistic profession.

The final debate deals with the formal nature of journalism education. In the above-discussed configuration, the focus was placed on formal training by polytechnics and universities, which is often aimed at producing professional journalists for the mainstream media system. Interestingly, even the journalist union that is active in the Dutch-speaking part of Belgium (the so-called Flemish Organisation of Journalists – VVJ) distinguishes (albeit implicitly) between journalists and professional journalists in one of their press documents:

> It speaks for itself that each individual is keeper of the press freedom, but that doesn't entitle everybody the right to access the press tribune of a parliament or a football stadium. Would one blame professional journalists that they have access to a number of specific facilities allowing them to do their job? That is why the legislator, in a law of 30 December 1963, created the title of 'professional' journalist. (VVJ, 2006)

Similarly, a number of civil society organizations have initiated journalistic training projects, which are more linked to alternative media (like Indymedia or some of the Brussels' radio stations), with the aim of providing (critical) hands-on training for people that are now frequently termed citizen journalists. However informal these training projects are, they will still be included in this article.

Journalism education in the Dutch-speaking part of Belgium: A brief and recent history

The Dutch-speaking polytechnics have a complicated history, which transcends the ambition of this article.[4] Two important moments need to be mentioned: the decree of 1994, which led to the merger of many of the polytechnics and decided on the present-day structure of the higher (non-university) education landscape, and the introduction of the Bachelor/Master structure, which led (among many other things) to the introduction of most of the Bachelors in Journalism in 2004–2005.[5] Before 2004–2005, most polytechnics offered Bachelors or Bachelor profiles[6] in Communication Management, Corporate Communication, Marketing Communication, Applied Communication, Public Relations, or Press and Education. These polytechnics used the introduction of the Bachelor/Master structure to transform one of their Bachelors in these fields into a Bachelor of Journalism.

The current Master programmes at the polytechnics have an even more recent origin. The Masters at the Lessiushogeschool, Erasmushogeschool Brussel and Vlekho only started in 2007–2008. Both the Masters at the Lessiushogeschool and Vlekho are supported by the Catholic University of Leuven (KUL). Before 2007, these two polytechnics already had postgraduate programmes in Journalism, which in the case of Vlekho started in 1995–1996, and in 2002–2003 for the Lessiushogeschool. The Erasmushogeschool Brussel had originally two postgraduate training programmes, one on print media, which started in 2000–2001, and one on radio and television, which started in 2001–2002. Both postgraduate training programmes were integrated into the new Master in 2007.[7]

Also the explicit emphasis on journalism training at university level was introduced recently. At the University of Ghent (UGent), the postgraduate degree in Media and Communication was changed into a so-called 'Master after Master in Journalism', which was offered for the first time in 2004–2005 (VLIR 2007: 266). After the 2006 VLIR-review of this Journalism programme and of the Communication Studies programmes in the Dutch-speaking part of Belgium, the UGent Master after Master in Journalism was incorporated into the 'regular' Communication Studies Master in Ghent, as one of its four profiles. At the Free University of Brussels (VUB) the VLIR-review lead to a change of one of the profiles offered in the Communication Studies Master (and the third Bachelor year). The Media, Politics and Citizenship profile was changed into a Media, Democracy and Journalism profile, which was organized for the first time in 2007–2008.

Belgian institutions and structures in the Dutch-speaking part of Belgium

The educational landscape in the Dutch-speaking part of Belgium is characterized by a diversity of institutions and types of trainings. A first cluster is constituted by the three year journalism Bachelors organized by Dutch-speaking polytechnics (180 ECTS). They tend to emphasize the vocational nature of the training, which combines (training in) journalistic skills, traineeships, project work and language skills. As the website of the Arteveldehogeschool puts it: 'Journalism is a profession, a métier. The professional bachelor is completely focused on acquiring these skills. This makes the training different from the academic education' (Arteveldehogeschool 2009).[8] The Hogeschool West-Vlaanderen formulates their perspective on journalism education as follows: 'You become a journalist by being a journalist,' and they add 'experienced journalists don't give any boring theoretical lectures' (Howest 2009).

This nevertheless does not imply that the curricula of these journalism schools do not include more knowledge-focused components. Most of the curricula include courses that allow students to frame and contextualize events and that provide them with insights in media law, media structures and/or media ethics. At the same time it should be added that the VLHORA (2007: 16) review of the six Bachelor programmes concluded that: '[p]robably because of the strong professional orientation and the focus on competence-oriented learning established [by the review committee], the attention for the general competences threatens to be weakened.' The review committee advized all six polytechnics that: '[t]he theoretical

Table 1: Bachelors in journalism at the Dutch-speaking polytechnics.

Polytechnic	Department
Arteveldehogeschool	Trade and corporate sciences
Erasmushogeschool Brussel	Campus Dansaert (Communication Department)
Xios Hogeschool Limburg	Trade and corporate sciences
Hogeschool West-Vlaanderen	Trade and corporate sciences
Katholieke Hogeschool Mechelen	Trade and corporate sciences
Plantijn Hogeschool Antwerpen	Corporate Management

and academic basis of the course material requires more attention in all programmes."
(VLHORA 2007: 16 – our translation)

Most of the polytechnics focus their (online) promotional texts on the practice-based experience and celebrity-status of their teaching staff. This is sometimes combined with the opportunities of students to 'actually' publish or broadcast their material (also on websites like http://www.supo.be (Supo, 2009)), or with the prizes they have won. On this website, the Katholieke Hogeschool Mechelen for instance refers to one of its student's documentaries, entitled *Cow Hugging*, that won the 2007 prize of the digital news broadcaster Actua-TV (Howest, 2009). Arguably the main difference among the journalism training programmes at bachelor level is between a focus on an all-round / multimedia training (e.g. the Arteveldehogeschool) and a training programme that allows students to specialize in one type of media (e.g. the choice between radio, print, mixed media and online in the third bachelor year at the Katholieke Hogeschool Mechelen).

A second cluster consists of the one-year Masters in journalism, which is being offered by both polytechnics and universities (60 ECTS). Both types of institutions combine an emphasis on vocational training with a more academic approach, claiming to educate 'critical journalists', albeit the balance differs. As the website of the Lessiushogeschool Antwerpen puts it:

This programme aims to build critical journalists. General education, journalistic skills, case studies and writing the master thesis constitute the programme. You'll get courses on the media world, like Research, or Ethics, or Critical analyses of images, but also communication courses like Writing skills, Interviewing techniques, Visual language, etc. (Lessius, 2009)

The presence of an academic focus in the Masters of two of the three polytechnics (Lessiushogeschool and Vlekho) is further enhanced by stressing the corporation with two universities (KUL and KUB). Still, the 'academic' focus has a different weight in the three polytechnics with 12 ECTS of 'academic' courses (out of 60 ECTS) in the Erasmushogeschool Brussel, 18 ECTS in the Vlekho Brussel and 24 ECTS in the Lessiushogeschool Antwerpen.

Table 2: Masters in journalism at the Dutch-speaking polytechnics and universities.

Institution	Department
Erasmushogeschool Brussel	Applied Linguistics
Lessiushogeschool Antwerpen	Applied Linguistics
Vlekho Brussel	Languages and Literature
Universiteit Gent (UGent)	Communication Studies
Vrije Universiteit Brussel (VUB)	Communication Studies

Specific for the polytechnics that offer a Master degree in journalism is that all three of them are based in Linguistics departments. This firstly implies that the Journalism Master degrees are structurally detached from the professional Bachelors in Journalism. This embeddedness in Linguistics departments also has implications for the (direct) access of students, as in a number of cases (e.g. the Lessiushogeschool Antwerpen) Bachelors in Applied Linguistics (or Literature) have privileged access to the Master degree, while students with other Bachelor or Master degrees need to follow a (limited) number of additional courses in order to gain access.

Not surprisingly, the balance of academic and vocational courses at the two universities is the inverse in comparison to the polytechnics. In the case of the Ugent Communication Studies Master (profile Journalism), the practice-based part of the curriculum consists out of a 7 ECTS journalistic practice course, two optional courses (a second journalistic practice course and a Dutch language skills course [both 7 ECTS]) and the traineeship (14 ECTS). In the case of the VUB Communication Studies Master (profile Media, Democracy and Journalism), the practice-based courses are the Seminar on Media, Democracy and Journalism (6 ECTS) and the traineeship (12 ECTS).

The third cluster consists of a number of additional Bachelors or postgraduate courses. In two cases these programmes are so-called 'Bachelor-after-Bachelor' programmes, aimed at people who already have a Bachelor degree. Similar to the 'ordinary' Bachelor programmes in journalism, these Bachelor-after-Bachelor programmes have a vocational focus. The same applies to the other programmes, which are smaller postgraduate courses, more focused on a specific aspect of journalism (namely Research Journalism or Video Journalism). One special case is the 'Flemish Journalism Course' and the 'Advanced Flemish Journalism Course' of the Dutch Fontyshogeschool, which both consist of an eight-week course.

The last example of the Dutch Fontyshogeschool could also be seen as part of the fourth cluster, focusing on non-formal journalism training programmes. But the most important example here is the Institute for Journalism, which was originally established in 1922 by the Belgian union of journalists. While this Institute had French-speaking and Dutch-speaking departments from the start, two new (and mutually independent) organizations were established in 1995.[9] The Dutch-speaking Institute for Journalism is now linked to the Flemish Organisation of Journalists (VVJ), and provides a training programme combining

Table 3: Additional bachelors in journalism at the Dutch-speaking polytechnics.

Institution	Name	Department	ECTS
Campus De Ham Mechelen	Postgraduate International Research journalism	Trade and corporate sciences	27
Xios Hogeschool Limburg	Bachelor in the Advanced Study of Journalism	Trade and corporate sciences	60
Xios Hogeschool Limburg	Postgraduate Video Journalism	Trade and corporate sciences	20
Hogeschool West-Vlaanderen	Professional masterclass (Bachelor)	Hiepso (former Institute for Economic, Paramedia and Social Education)	60
Fontyshogeschool (NL)	Course Flemish Journalism (& Advanced Course Flemish Journalism)	–	–

courses on the legal and professional position of the journalist, media law and ethics, and a series of more skills-oriented courses. Currently, the Institute of Journalism is negotiating with the Dutch-speaking polytechnics to exchange courses and/or to provide access to each others' programmes.

One other example is the 'videoreporter' training course organized by OFF TV for unemployed youngsters, in collaboration with the unemployment office that operates in the Dutch-speaking part of the country (The Flemish Public Employment and Vocational Training Service – VDAB). Even more linked to civil society are the training courses of Getbasic and Kif kif, which aim to support forms of citizen journalism. Getbasic is an NGO which has a close relationship with the Belgian Indymedia, while Kif kif is an NGO that aims to give voice to ethnic minorities. Both NGOs stress the importance of citizen journalism and media participation, and aim to contribute to these forms of empowerment by organizing journalism training courses.

Table 4: Non-formal courses in journalism in the Dutch-speaking part of Belgium.

Institution	Name
Institute for Journalism	Journalist training
OFF TV	Videoreporter
Getbasic	Making Media
Kif Kif	Basic journalism training for allochteneous youngsters

A brief comment on the educational situation of journalists in the Dutch-speaking part of Belgium

Paulussen and De Clercq published in 2006 an analysis of the educational situation of journalists in the Dutch-speaking part of Belgium, based on a survey of 1026 journalists in 2003. According to their data, 57.5% had a university degree, and 32.5% had a degree from a polytechnic. Half of the respondents had a Communication or Journalism related education, but only 29% studied Communication Studies or Journalism as their main degree. They provide more detailed data:

> 17% of the 1026 respondents studied Communication Studies, and 12% got a degree in Journalism. Moreover, a third of the respondents followed one or more additional training programmes at a university, at a polytechnic, at the Institute for Journalism or at work. (Paulussen and De Clercq, 2006: 78)

The considerable number of journalism training programmes in the Dutch-speaking part of Belgium also has consequences for the number of potential journalists entering the job market. Exact numbers are difficult to trace, but the two journalism profiles of the university programmes generated around 70 Masters in 2008. The number of Masters at the polytechnics in 2008 is estimated at around 80.[10]

Finally, at the professional bachelor level, the Vlhora (2007) review report offers some (limited) inflow data: the professional Journalism bachelor of the Erasmus Hogeschool had 141 students at the time of the review (Vlhora 2007: 79), and during the first year the Plantijnhogeschool offered the journalism bachelor, 190 students entered the programme (Vlhora 2007: 176). When combining these inflow data with the success rates, one can only conclude that the outflow is substantial. One indication of the problems caused by this large outflow can again be found in the Vlhora (2007: 23) review report: "The students that graduate seem to have little difficulties finding work, although only rarely at the level of employment they expect."

Journalism education in French-speaking Belgium: A brief and not so recent history

As mentioned before, the earliest journalism education initiative is of an informal nature and was initiated in 1922 by the journalists themselves, as the Belgian union of journalists ('Association des journalistes professionnels de Belgique') created 'L'Institut de journalisme (IDJ)'. After the establishment of two separate institutes in 1995, the IDJ still operates today in French-speaking Belgium, in total independence from public authorities as well as from any sponsors. Students are selected – no specific diploma is required – and courses are taught by volunteer professional journalists in the form of evening classes. The curriculum evolved gradually over the years to follow the evolution of the media and the emergence of new media. Web journalism was introduced as of 2000. To this day, their programme is the only significant of non-formal programmes (without an official diploma) specialized in journalism training.

Formal journalism education made its way very early in French-speaking universities. In 1946, the Université Libre de Bruxelles (ULB) was the first to offer an ad hoc second cycle programme in the form of a two-year 'Licence en journalisme' which, from the start, included a mandatory professional traineeship and required students to demonstrate their command of at least one foreign language. The ULB has offered a programme explicitly in Journalism ever since and expanded it to a first cycle programme as of 1971 (first in the form of 'Sciences Humaines préparatoires à la Licence en Journalisme et Communication Sociale').

The Université Catholique de Louvain (UCL) started a 'Séminaire pratique de journalisme' in 1947 within the programme in Political and Social Sciences where a 'Groupe Journalisme' appeared in 1952. The programme was renamed 'Techniques de diffusion et relations publiques' in 1963, with the start of a major in 'Information' in 1976. An orientation of UCL's 'Licence en Communication' was more explicitly named 'Journalism' as of 1991. The Université de Liège (ULg) also offers a branch in 'Presse écrite et audiovisuelle' aimed at students preparing a career in journalism. In all three universities, the organization of specific curricula in journalism was at first met with scepticism, if not fierce resistance.

French-speaking Belgian institutions and structures

The higher education system was thoroughly restructured starting in 2004. It now distinguishes 'universities' from 'higher education outside of universities' (polytechnics as grouped in 1995, i.e. essentially 'hautes écoles' and 'écoles supérieures des arts'). Universities organize 1st (Bachelor), 2nd (Master) and 3rd (Doctorate) cycle studies, with the Bachelors being conceived as a preparation for the Masters. Higher education establishments outside of the universities provide a mixed offer of 'long' studies (two cycles, minimum 240 ECTS) leading to Master diplomas 'of university level', and 'short' studies (first cycle only, minimum 180 ECTS) leading to Bachelor diplomas preparing for specific professions.

At the level of universities, a Decree of 31 March 2004 reorganized all recognized diplomas, which were harmonized and limited to a fixed list, each associated with a defined list of universities that are accredited for each diploma. An 'Information and Communication' domain was defined with accreditation limited to five universities for the Bachelor degree (ULB, UCL, ULg, Facultés Universitaires Notre-Dame de la Paix de Namur and Facultés Universitaires Saint-Louis) and to only three universities for the Master degree (the three full universities ULB, UCL and ULg). Because journalism is offered as a profile ('finalité spécialisée') within that domain, journalism-oriented Masters are exclusively offered in those three universities.

Table 5: Masters in Journalism (within the domain 'Information and Communication') in Belgian French-speaking universities.

University	Faculty	Profile name
Université Libre de Bruxelles	Philosophy and Letters	Journalisme
Université Catholique de Louvain	Economics, Social and Political Sciences	Ecole de journalisme de Louvain
Université de Liège	Philosophy and Letters	Presse écrite et audiovisuelle

Note that all three journalism programmes in these universities share a number of characteristics. First, they are offered as a specific profile within larger communication programmes. In the case of ULB and ULg, communication is anchored to the Faculty of Philosophy and Letters (or Humanities) while at UCL it is anchored to the Faculty of Economics, Social and Political sciences. Secondly, their approach to journalism combines the academic curriculum one would expect from a university with a significant amount of practical, vocational courses and one or more traineeships in news media. Vocational courses rely heavily on high profile professional journalists (from radio and television – mostly public service – and from the press) for teaching and training, with the use of high-end equipment where needed. UCL and ULB have formally identified the structures in charge of journalism programmes as 'Schools of Journalism' (respectively 'Ecole de journalisme de Louvain' and 'Ecole universitaire de journalisme de Bruxelles'), with an implicit reference to renowned journalism schools in neighbouring France.

For higher education outside of universities, another Decree (2 June 2006 amended by Decree of 2 July 2007) lists diplomas along with the required courses and the corresponding number of hours in. Interestingly, journalism as such is absent from the short professional Bachelors (three years), unlike other communication-related fields such as advertising, marketing or simply communication, which are each offered as a specific programme. Some courses of journalism do exist within programmes with a broader scope, even though journalism might be advertized as a possible career prospect.

Among long programmes, the Decree lists a Bachelor and Master in Applied Communication which includes a sub-section 'Presse et Information' (along with one

Table 6: Bachelor in Communication with at least one vocational course in journalism.

Institution	Diploma
Haute Ecole Libre du Hainaut Occidental	Communication
Institut Supérieur de Formation Sociale et de Communication	Communication
Haute Ecole de la Province de Liège	Communication

Table 7: Master in Journalism outside of Belgian French-speaking universities.

Institution	Diploma
Institut des Hautes Etudes en Communication Sociale (IHECS)	Presse et information

on Advertising and Commercial Communication and another on Public Relations). This programme in Applied Communication is only organized in one such school, namely the Institut des Hautes Etudes en Communication Sociale (IHECS).

Note that IHECS, now based in Brussels, is gradually integrating into the Académie de Louvain, allowing shared activities or even some level of integration within the UCL.

Universities have consistently kept their journalism programmes somewhat accessible to students having earned a degree in another discipline and willing to orient their career towards journalism or communication within the area of their initial field of study. Likewise, universities have made the necessary investments to keep equipments and vocational courses in tune with the evolution of technologies used in newsrooms. The ULB and the UCL offer some form of activities oriented towards online and multimedia journalism.

Journalism education remains very attractive to students, in spite of bleak prospects on the job market (few positions available and precarious wages). Because journalism education is virtually unbound by any quotas on the number of students or graduates, the number of students earning a degree in journalism exceeds the needs of the market. An estimate made by the union of journalists in 2006 reckoned over 300 graduates that year alone (Dumont 2006: 20). Although no systematic study has examined the careers of graduates in journalism, their number alone indicates that many will work, at best, in the broader field of communication, if not in a completely different line of work. As a very vague indication of the job market, the 'Association des Journalistes Professionnels', which delivers the official press card, issues about 80 new cards a year.[11]

Concluding Remarks

Despite some of the shared problems and debates, the situation in the Dutch- and French-speaking parts of Belgium is structurally different, because of the lack of a long tradition of (explicit) journalism training in the North of the country. Looking at the future of journalism education, there are a number of reasons to expect changes. In North Belgium, given the high number of (relatively) new journalism training programmes at the Bachelor level, and the official discourse on 'rationalisation', one can wonder if this high number will be sustained in the future, also because the process of the 'academization' of the polytechnics is planned to be finalized in 2012, and a further regrouping of the higher education institutions after that date is likely. Second, one can question the desirability to embed journalism training programmes almost exclusively in Communication Management departments (at the Bachelor level) and in Applied Linguistics departments (at the Master level). Although these programmes have a certain degree of independence, broadening their habitats remains an important requirement. A related problem is that this structural embeddedness (at the Master level) also generates unnecessary barriers for students with a Bachelor degree from other disciplines, sometimes even including communication-related disciplines.

The novelty of journalism training in the Dutch-speaking part of Belgium, and the already-existing collaborations between universities and polytechnics also generates a number of opportunities for improving the quality of journalism education. Both the academic and vocational components of journalism education are necessary and inseparable. Attempts to organize these mixed models do exist, such as the master thesis model at the Journalism Master of the Erasmushogeschool Brussel and the Lessius Hogeschool. In this model, a journalistic project is combined with an academic reflection on the journalistic project. Behind these kinds of mixed models is the recognition that journalists need to know the tools of the trade, but as a 21st century class of intellectuals, they also need to receive a substantial intellectual training. In other words, a radical focus on practice needs to be combined with radical focus on reflection.

In French-speaking Belgium, the long standing tradition to organize journalism curricula in universities is not challenged by the reorganisation of the higher education system. It was in a way reinforced as a journalism-oriented Master now requires five years.[12] The extension enhances the academic grounding of the curricula, but in most cases also increases the vocational activities with a view to optimize the graduates' employability. The ULB even allows the master's thesis to result into the making of a significant journalistic product.

The contrast between the journalism education provisions in both parts of Belgium is striking and intriguing. It does not entail a discrepancy in the quality of journalism, but makes Belgium a promising field for analysing how different approaches to journalism training affects the work and production in the newsrooms.

The Author

Nico Carpentier is an assistant professor working at the Communication Studies Department of the Vrije Universiteit Brussel (VUB – Free University of Brussels). He is co-director of the VUB research centre CEMESO and vice-president of the European Communication Research and Education Association (ECREA).

François Heinderyckx is Professor at the Université Libre de Bruxelles (ULB) and director of the Department of information and communication sciences. He is president of the European Communication Research and Education Association (ECREA).

Notes

1. This article will not include the German-speaking Community in the discussion.
2. Based on dailies readership surveys (universe: residents aged 12 and over) of the 'Media Surveys Press and Cinema 08–09' (CIM 2009).
3. Average viewing time per individual for adults (age 15 and over) for 2008, published by IP International Marketing Committee (2009: 41).
4. This article also only focuses on the still-existing programmes.
5. 2005–2006 in the case of the Katholieke Hogeschool Mechelen.
6. These Bachelors were then called 'graduate degrees'.
7. Based on personal (email) communications with Jacky Stijven (Lessius), Lut Lams (HUB), Annemarie Bernaerts (HUB), Martina Temmerman (EhB) and Herman Duponcheel (KHM).
8. All citations from Belgian authors and websites were translated from French and Dutch into English by the authors of this chapter.
9. Based on personal (email) communication with Marc van Impe (Instituut voor Journalistiek).
10. Based on personal (email) communications with Jacky Stijven (Lessius), Lut Lams (HUB), and Martina Temmerman (EhB).
11. Average of yearly figures between 1994 and 2007, not counting foreign journalists (Dumont 2008: 5).
12. A 'Licence' previously required only four years, and the master's track in North Belgium is at this point in time still at four years as well.

References

Anderson, B. (1983), *Imagined Communities: Reflections on the Origin and Spread of Nationalism*, New York: Verso.
Arteveldehogeschool (2009), *Bachelor in de journalistiek*, http://www.arteveldehs.be/emc.asp?pageId=1953. Accessed 21 March 2009.
CIM (2009), *Media Surveys Press and Cinema 08–09*, http://www.cim.be. Accessed 20 Oct. 2009.
Deuze, M. (2006), 'Global journalism education: a conceptual approach', *Journalism Studies*, 7(1), pp. 144–156.
Dumont, J.-F. (2006), *Le livre noir des journalistes indépendants*, Brussels: Luc Pire.
Dumont, J.-F. (2008), *Le dossier: la commission d'agréation, Journalistes – Le Lettre de l'AJP*, n°94, pp. 4–5.
Frith, S. and Meech, P. (2007), 'Becoming a journalist: journalism education and journalistic culture', *Journalism*, 8(2), pp. 137–164.
Howest (2009), *Bachelor journalistiek*, http://www.howest.be/Default.aspx?target=hiepso&lan=nl&item=130. Accessed 1 June 2009.
IP International Marketing Committee (2009), *Television 2009, International Key Facts*, Luxembourg: IP Network and RTL Group.
Lessius (2009), *Master in de journalistiek*, http://www.lessius-ho.be/tt/stk/masterjournalistiek/default.aspx. Accessed 1 June 2009.
Paulussen, S. and De Clercq, M. (2005), 'Eigen berichtgeving. Bevindingen en beperkingen van sociologische enquêtes bij journalisten', In F. Saeys and H. Verstraeten (eds.), *De media in maatschappelijk perspectief*, Gent: Academia press, pp. 69–90.

Stovall, J. (1993), 'The practitioners', In D. Sloan (ed.), *Makers of the media mind. Journalism educators and their ideas*, New Jersey: Lawrence Erlbaum, pp. 25–58.

Supo (2009), *Home*, http: //www.supo.be/. Accessed 1 June 2009.

VLHORA (2007), *Onderwijsvisitatie Journalistiek. Een onderzoek naar de kwaliteit van de professioneel gerichte bacheloropleiding Journalistiek aan de Vlaamse hogescholen*, Brussels: VLHORA.

VLIR (2007), *De onderwijsvisitatie Communicatiewetenschappen. Een evaluatie van de kwaliteit van de bachelor- en masteropleidingen Communicatiewetenschappen, de masteropleiding Informatie- en Bibliotheekwetenschap en de master na masteropleiding Journalistiek aan de Vlaamse universiteiten*, Brussels: VLIR.

VVJ (2006), *Erkenning als beroepsjournalist*, Brussels: VVJ, http://www.agjpb.be/vvj/beroepsjournalist_erkenning.php. Accessed 1 June 2008.

The Danish Journalism Education Landscape

Kim Minke

Introduction

Journalism training in Denmark was on-the-job until 1946. Right after the Second World War a group of editors and journalists and professors from the University of Aarhus joined forces and began to offer a three-month course in journalism or rather in a compilation of subjects making up what a journalist should minimally know in areas such as law, economics and public administration. The course was non-compulsory for journalism trainees, but proved a success and to some degree it helped in abating the incessant journalist bashing and the claim that journalists knew nothing about anything.

In the following years the organizers and fiery souls who started the course worked hard to get it formalized and institutionalized so that journalism could become a subject for study and so that entrance to the 'profession' would require also some formal education. Negotiations took place both with the educational authorities and the organizations representing employers and employees. From the outset the goal was to secure a place for journalism within the university curriculum, however, opposition to having journalism academized was strong on the part of powerful segments of the profession. The following decades were characterized by efforts to balance the two opposite positions and find solutions that would accommodate the range of interests involved.

Aarhus hub

By 1957 the emerging institution for journalism training had its own facilities on the university campus including a dormitory designed to house the trainees, who came to Aarhus from all over Denmark to take part in the course. At the same time a mid-career training centre formed jointly by the Nordic countries was in place on the premises. Aarhus was about to become a hub of Northern European journalism education. In 1962 the institution was officially named The Danish School of Journalism and appeared for the first time in the Danish Finance Bill. The course requirements were extended to six months and participation became mandatory.

The school persisted in trying to extend its reach and volume, and its leadership clearly saw the need to prolong the education and move away from its rooting in on-the-job training. Negotiations took place in the late 1960s with the Prime Minister's office as the PM was 'Minister of the Press'. The PM may have felt somewhat annoyed by the minuscule scale of the problem – he was at the time also working on bringing Denmark into the European Union – and the story goes that he caved in to the requests by curtly stating, 'Alright then, but costs must not exceed those of a provincial high school.' The law setting out the new parameters for the Danish School of Journalism was passed in 1970. The school would offer a four-year basic education and move to a separate location in a new building outside the university campus.

Negotiated compromises

The design of the new curriculum and the institutional set-up were the result of a compromise between the professional hands-on supporters and the educational reformists. The compromise could be seen on four points: The new school was untied from its origin as an initiative to which the University of Aarhus was a partner and became a stand-alone institution. Entrance to the school would be based on a specially designed range of tests and not on high-school diploma results. The school would be governed with the participation of a board made up of people from the profession. And finally the four-year programme would contain an eighteen-month trainee period in the middle of the programme, in which the students would work as paid interns in various media companies. These were the concessions made to the sceptics who feared that real talent and a true understanding of ordinary people would not be appreciated in a formal educational system.

The first classes under the new system started in 1971. The education quickly became popular, and the entrance test used to screen applicants earned a reputation for being both tough and fair. It even grew to be seen as a yardstick of knowledge about culture and society and language skills, which could be of use in other contexts as well. After some years the intake stabilized at 250 students per year, which was a lot when compared to the number of journalistic jobs in the old media. But the Government was expanding further education and had asked for a high intake, and luckily most graduates got jobs if not in old media then in PR and communications.

In 1996 a new law provided the school with the obligation and finances to develop and run a mid-career training and competence centre. The law was a follow-up to the reports of a Danish Media Commission and politicians' abiding feeling that journalists did not know enough. Aarhus already housed the Nordic mid-career training centre and a big mid-career training centre run by the media organizations and the trade union and financed by money set aside in negotiated agreements. After ten years of friendly competition the three centres merged into a new centre called 'Update' in 2006 and located on new premises at the School of Journalism.

The school expanded its range of offers to students by tailoring semester-long courses to academics and advanced university students. The first course of this sort ran in 1984. Over the next twenty-five years collaboration with universities and especially the University of Aarhus grew steadily, and the school offered components to be integrated into the various fields of study of university students. By the year 2000 the new activities of the school – apart from the four-year programme – was the better part of the budget. However, the four-year programme remained in high demand and was still seen as the flagship. Graduates from the programme seemed to hold their own against increasing competition for jobs in the media sector.

In parallel with the journalism programme the school established a four-year programme in photojournalism from 1992. Storytelling skills and classic journalistic awareness and know-how formed part of the programme and set it apart from many previous courses in press photography. The curriculum expanded into video and new media after a few years.

Two new university programmes

The late nineties also saw the birth of two university-based education programmes in journalism, in Roskilde and Odense. The initiative was political and again partly based on the feeling of leading politicians that Danish journalism was not as well-informed and shrewd as they would wish. Also the Aarhus school's virtual monopoly of supplying the Danish media with their employees gave cause for concern. More diversity was called for. The design of the two new curricula, however, took after the model from Aarhus with entrance tests (in Odense) and a long trainee period of one year quite unusual for university programmes. An official quality evaluation report by the Danish Evaluation Institute in 2004 expressed disappointment that the break up of the monopoly of the Danish School of Journalism had not resulted in more diversity and more scope and urged the institutions to aim for different profiles. However, the criterion for success in all three places has been to see graduates get jobs, and the demands from the job market have been pretty uniform and have exerted a homogenising influence on curricula and teaching methods. The wish for more diversity has not been met in the years since the 2004 report as far as the basic bachelor programmes go. However, the media's possibilities of recruiting staff with combined journalistic and academic training have increased considerably.

In 2006 when the Danish sector for further education was reformed, the Aarhus school's board of directors opted for a continued stand-alone position albeit amalgamating with a small graphic arts institute in Copenhagen. The alternative option would have been integration into the University of Aarhus and becoming part of a large consolidation process in the Danish university sector. In the two-tier system resulting from the overall reform process the Danish School of Journalism is now in the jurisdiction of the Ministry of Education, whereas the two university-based programmes are in the jurisdiction of the Ministry of Science.

State influence

Today, basic journalism education is provided by the state through the three designated journalism programmes. The media, of course, also sometimes recruit journalistic staff with other backgrounds although it seems to happen only rarely. In general, further education in Denmark is state-financed, although the country may be heading for more paid-for education, foreign private universities setting up campus in Denmark and so forth. So far this is only a possible prospect.

One of the Danish tabloids in the nineties played with the thought of recruiting and training their own journalists in order to get a wilder, more unorthodox less white-collar kind of reporter. However, the initiative died in its infancy.

Until the mid-nineties mid-career training was mostly financed by agreements between trade unions and employers' organizations. Employment prompted a capitation charge, which was paid into a foundation, which ran a mid-career training system. On top of that and just as importantly, most union agreements ensured the employee mid-career training one week a year. As a result the format of mid-career training had gravitated towards one-week tailored courses for journalists. In the new millennium training courses on the job and integrated into the development plans of the company grew in importance. The newly established state-funded institute at the Danish School of Journalism had seen this tendency coming and was asked to incorporate the private institution and the privately generated funds into its system. Also the growing importance of formally recognized educational programmes, which was the result of a globalized educational market, favoured the state-run institution as the continuing entity. Today mid-career training, in-house training and competence development will most likely enjoy some state subsidy, receive funds from the private foundation, and a sum will be paid by the company in question.

Mixed curricula

The Danish journalism training system has sprung from a mixed professional-academic initiative, but has had a leaning towards a professional, practical approach. The major part of the teaching staff, both at the Danish School of Journalism and in the two university programmes, have been professional journalists recruited into teaching after working some years in the profession. A workshop-based, hands-on approach to teaching has been the norm supplemented by a curriculum of academic subjects. The challenge has been to integrate the two components. The evaluation report mentioned above concluded that all three programmes should work harder at trying to do just that. The ambition is to avoid allowing the students to short-circuit ordinary academic knowledge even though they may arrive at passable journalistic results at a realistic pace by doing just that.

The content of the programmes in all three places has been centred on journalism. In Aarhus at an early stage all media were included: print, radio, TV and later on internet media. In the beginning radio and TV, however, did not quite get the emphasis they should have, given the growing importance especially of TV. This was mainly due to reasons of cost. In the new millennium the digitalization of TV production has sunk the cost of teaching TV and the school has upped its offers to students. To some degree the school allows students to specialize in TV, radio, print media or internet-journalism. However, with media-integrated newsrooms winning over the need is increasingly that graduates must master all media, at least to some degree. The curriculum at the University of Southern Denmark in Odense has taken much the same road. The Roskilde University curriculum until reform plans in 2008 has mainly focused on print. At Roskilde the curriculum is influenced by the university's unique two-year basic-study structure, which students must pass before specializing. As a consequence a degree in journalism from Roskilde has been a master's degree from the start, whereas master's degrees have been offered from Odense and Aarhus only in the last three years.

The curriculum in Roskilde allows the students a second subject studied with the same weight as journalism. A graduate from Roskilde is already a specialized journalist. However, the career patterns of graduates from Roskilde seem to mirror this only to a slight degree. The impression is that journalism as such is invasive and takes over the graduates' professional identity leaving very little space for their specialist subject field.

An inclusive concept of journalism

Unlike the situation in for example Norway, the Danish journalistic environment has included journalists in PR and communications. There has not been any split and in general it is accepted that a professional career may see a journalist move back and forth between the two sides. The Aarhus School introduced a semester-long specialization in communications some ten years ago, realising that so many of its graduates ended up in jobs in communications anyhow. Mid-career training offers in communications have been extensive as the long-term trend has been stagnation in the number of jobs in independent media and ever increasing job numbers in communications and PR. Recruitment to communications and PR jobs is sourced from journalism graduates and business-school graduates. It is a contest, but somewhat ameliorated by the fact that many communications departments opt for a mix of backgrounds in their staff.

The intake into the three specialized journalism programmes is impressively high for a small country of 5 million inhabitants. All three programmes have many more applicants than places and so can be highly selective in their intake. This probably supports a kind of upward spiral, so that good-quality students and graduates attract ever more good students and secure more jobs than the naked odds would suggest.

Roskilde takes in about 50 students a year for a six-year long programme including the one-year internship. Odense, after the establishment of their master's programme, takes in 75 students on their bachelor programme and twenty five on their master's programme (three-and-a-half years and five years respectively). Aarhus takes in about 250 a year including a small batch of photo-journalism students (sixteen). Male and female students are about the same number.

Large numbers in a small country

Continuing education programmes are centred in Aarhus. In 2007 the programmes enrolled 490 open university students taking 10–20 ECTS courses, 335 taking one-year 60 ECTS courses, about 2000 taking the specially designed traditional one-week courses, 262 participants in media in-house training courses, and 3–400 seminar and conference participants including 57 participants in the yearly joint Poynter-Update summer school. From 2005–2007, 210 journalists and media-workers took part in a special qualification-development programme sponsored by the European Social Fund and run by Update. Sixteen Nordic journalists took part in two-month journalism programme offered by the Nordic Journalism Centre at present located at and managed by Update.

The Erasmus Mundus 'Journalism and Media within Globalization – The European Perspective' programme has the Danish School of Journalism and the University of Aarhus as lead partners and includes the universities of Hamburg, Swansea and Amsterdam as well as City University (London). The 2007–09 Masters group includes 41 participants from all over the world: Australia, Belarus, Bhutan, Canada, China, Denmark, El Salvador, Germany, India, Italy, Kenya, Lebanon, New Zealand, the Netherlands, Norway, Serbia, Turkey, Ukraine, the USA, and Zimbabwe.

The Aarhus School runs four other one-semester or two-semester programmes in English in order to be able to take in international students: Journalism and Multimedia, Europe in the World (together with Hogeschool Utrecht, The Netherlands), TV Journalism in Denmark and Photo Journalism in Denmark

Accreditation and professional credibility

Accreditation of educational programmes in Denmark is governed by the state. Denmark participates in the Bologna process and the European Credit Transfer System and so do the journalism programmes. However, it would be correct to say that there is also a tight connection to the industry. This is based on the historical origin of journalism education in Denmark, on the highly regulated internship system – which has always had the full support of the Journalists' Union and the Employers' organization – and on the substantial amount of money set aside by the industry for mid-career training – money at present entrusted to the state-initiated mid-career institution in Aarhus and managed in a mixed economy. So although the accreditation process is formal and government-run, the informal relationship of trust between the two university departments and the School of Journalism on the one side and the industry on the other is just as important. In practical terms, it is probably the more important part for the students.

Concluding Remarks

Independent media and journalism are under increasing pressure. Newspapers are downsizing at the same time as they are expanding their activities into other media. Historically, newspapers were the cradle of journalism, and they also played a major part in establishing journalism education as a field. For decades they have been seen as institutions, which have provided a public service for private money. Today necessity pushes them to be more market driven. Public-service radio and TV are under increasing pressure from private competitors, who do not provide the same amount and quality of journalistic service, but usurp money and consumer interest from traditional players. More and more journalism is produced as a service sponsored by corporations, organisations and government institutions. This shift is impacting on the educational institutions. The one-to-one relationship between journalism programmes, their ideals and practices, and the demands from the industry, is no longer a given.

It seems difficult to solve the increasing mismatch. Educating journalists is still a matter of public trust, and the ideals handed down from the evolving democracies of eighteenth and nineteenth-century Europe and the United States are not easily abandoned. The reality is, however, that more and more journalists are using their professional toolbox in the service of particular interests and not in the service of an ideal democracy. So far the journalism programmes mirror this only to a very minor degree. It will take some spectacular adjustments of ideals to realign the programmes with the realities of today's media world. Perhaps that cannot be done. The educational programmes may have to live with an increasing tension between practical reality 'out there' and the good practice and idealistic morals 'in here.'

The Author

Kim Minke is a lecturer at the Danish School of Journalism.

References

Betænkning om udbygning af journalistuddannelsen i Danmark (1968), *Betænkning 474*, Medieudvalget: Statsministeriet.

Betænkning om Danmarks Journalisthøjskole (1978), *Betænkning 851*, Undervisningsministeriet, København.

Betænkning om journalistisk efter- og videreuddannelse (1995), *Betænkning nr. 1294*, Medieudvalget: Statsministeriet.

The Danish Evaluation Institute (EVA) (2004), *Evaluering af journalistuddannelserne i Danmark*, http://www.eva.dk/projekter/2003/evaluering-af-journalistuddannelserne-i-danmark/projektprodukter/evaluering-af-journalistuddannelserne-i-danmark. Accessed 2 September 2009.

The Finnish Journalism Education Landscape[1]

Raimo Salokangas

Introduction

Formal journalism education was already established in Finland in 1925, when the new 'Civic College' (Kansalaiskorkeakoulu) was founded in Helsinki. The main task of the college was to provide civil servants for fields that were neglected by universities, but as also journalism was regarded an important and influential factor in society, a 'newspaper examination' became one of the college's degrees. Previously newspapers and journalists had themselves arranged some ad hoc courses for practising journalists.

The college, later renamed 'College for Social Affairs' (Yhteiskunnallinen korkeakoulu), did not require a high school final examination as a term of admission, and thus it was not a university. However, the college had professors, and a chair in Journalism was, in principle, established in 1947, the first in the Nordic countries, but because of the lack of competent applicants it took nine years to nominate a permanent holder. In the first decades the journalism degree was rather insignificant and had a low status among employers. The number of enrolled students was relatively high, but only rarely more that half a dozen students of a year's cohort completed the examination.

In 1960 the status of the college was upgraded: it became the University of Tampere, as it was also moved from Helsinki to that industrial city about 170 kilometres north of the capital. With the professorship getting a new holder in 1961, the tradition of German *Zeitungswissenschaft* and *Publizistik* was denounced, and the American mass communication research approach took over. The new university status brought about a division that was later to cause plenty of internal trouble at Tampere: the practically oriented journalist degree was administratively placed in the 'Education Division' granting bachelor's level degrees (*sosionomi*), while the professorship was in the Faculty of Social Sciences, where studies were leading to a master's degree. The faculty track developed into a Department of Journalism and Mass Communication, and in the mid-1970s the journalist degree became part of it, but at the same time preserved its administrative ties to the Education Division. It was only in the mid-1990s that the vocational track was totally incorporated into the academic department.

The constitution of Finland states that the country has two national languages: Finnish and Swedish. Presently (2008) the Swedish language minority is about 290,000 in number, comprising 5.5 per cent of the country's population. The public service broadcasting company YLE has two radio channels (Radio Vega and Radio X3M/ 'Extrem') and a television channel (FST5) in Swedish (Svenska YLE 2009) and there are eight Swedish language dailies and four non-dailies, with a total circulation of 154,000 copies (Suomen Lehdistö 2008: 10; Jyrkiäinen 2008). Journalism education in Swedish was started in a small scale in 1962 in the Helsinki-based Swedish School of Social Sciences (Svenska social- och kommunalhögskolan, SSKH), and in the mid-1960s a journalism programme was established, with journalism as a major in a bachelor's level degree (*socionom*). With its vocational emphasis the programme resembled the Education Division track at Tampere.

As SSKH was incorporated in the University of Helsinki in 1984, bachelors that graduated from the journalism programme gained the right to continue studies for a master's degree in the Department of Communication at the bilingual University; the SSKH can only grant bachelor's degrees.

In 1987 a second academic Finnish language journalism education programme was established in the University of Jyväskylä in Central Finland, 270 kilometres north of Helsinki. After that, Tampere, Jyväskylä and SSKH comprised the academic journalism education system in the country. The Jyväskylä programme was founded by suggestion of a state committee on 'the education demand of journalists'. Between 1969 and 1984 no less than four committees submitted their report on journalism education. It was a heated political issue in late 1960s and the 1970s, but not anymore as the Jyväskylä programme actually started. The deal also included an increase of resources for the Tampere department.

One significant question in the discussions and committee reports of the 1960s and 1970s was the relation between the 'academic' and the 'vocational', and whether a bachelor's degree was enough, or whether a master's degree was preferable. (The degree system is described later.) A broad generalization might be that historically the employers tend to have given less emphasis to academic studies than the other actors. In 1974 the union of journalists changed its opinion in favour of the longer university education, and later in the decade finally it was the employers' organization that took the initiative to work out an education structure based on the existing two lanes at Tampere. So, by the late-1970s there was a broad consensus on keeping journalism education in the universities, and of preserving, and preferring, the master's level (Salokangas 2003).

There was one exception to this academic structure, the private journalism school of Sanoma Company, the biggest newspaper publisher in Finland, with Helsingin Sanomat as its flagship. A new generation of the owner family took over in the mid-1960s, and the new leadership founded the journalism school in 1967 as part of an overall renovation and development plan for the company's newspapers. Sanomat's school selected fifteen to twenty-five students every third year for a very practical course lasting one and a half year. The purpose of the school was to provide journalists for the company's own papers, and the students were paid a trainee's salary. The last general course ended in 1990, by which time the school had educated about 250 journalists. After that there were only small-scale mid-career courses to the company's own journalists, until in 1997 the school enrolled a full length course in economic journalism, and later a course in new media. In 2007 another new group of students was taken in. (Ritvos 2008; Sanoma 2009.)

Ferment in the field

Still in 1997 an exploratory committee on communication education, with representatives from the Ministry of Education, the universities, the union of journalists, and the employers' organizations, confirmed that the universities of Tampere and Jyväskylä, and SSKH were the proper places for journalism education. There was also a consensus on the preferability of a master's degree, with the employers' remark that a bachelor's degree in journalism would still be regarded as the formal criterion of an 'educated' journalist. (Salokangas 2003: 14).

On the other hand, in the 1990s the Ministry of Education allowed and encouraged the establishment of a totally new section of higher education which expanded, if not exploded, the supply of various communication-related programmes. The Finnish word for these colleges, *ammattikorkeakoulu*, corresponds with the German *Fachhochschule*, and there is also certain correspondence with the former British polytechnics. A deeply symbolic identification question emerged soon: how to translate the word *ammattikorkeakoulu* into English. The universities would claim exclusive rights to 'university' and translate the new establishments as 'polytechnics' (which is also suggested by the Ministry of Education), while the *Fachhochschulen* themselves prefer to be presented as 'Universities of Applied Sciences'. In this article they are mostly referred to with the neutral 'college'.

According to the Act (Ammattikorkeakoululaki 9 May 2003: 351) their core task is to provide higher education fitting the needs of the labour market. They are supposed to be vocational and practical in their education, as well as in their applied development and research activities. The Ministry introduced the concept of a 'dual model' with two 'pillars' or 'columns' of higher education, urging the universities to concentrate on research, while the polytechnics were expected to be close to the actual, explicitly regional, market. As academic journalism education already was close enough to the labour market, the policy caused some tensions both within universities and between the universities and the new college system.

A thorough report on the wide area of communication-related education in Finland was compiled in 2004–2006, financed by the European Social Fund. The researcher's conclusion was that whichever development scenario the field of communication and the Finnish society follows, there is too much communication related education. Another conclusion was: 'Repeatedly throughout this report the research result has emerged that communication education is too much oriented to occupations of traditional media industry.' (Raittila et al. 2006: 102, 105.)

After first having allowed the polytechnics sector to grow beyond its resources and, in many areas, its demand, the ministry is now urging the colleges to cut down their programmes in some fields, also in the communication area. But significantly, journalism education is not among the fields that need to be diminished. The three academic institutions are planned to preserve their volume, and some of the colleges are offering journalism education within their own specialisation areas. Those colleges are Haaga-Helia University of Applied Sciences in Helsinki, the Turku Campus of Diaconia University of Applied Sciences (Diak), and Oulu University of Applied Sciences.

The structure of the degrees

Until the full introduction of the Bologna process, academic studies in Finland were based on a five-year structure, and the point of departure was that in the fields where a bachelor's degree was in use, it was only a halfway station, and the actual and 'real' one was the master's degree; a bachelor's holder had not really finished his/her studies. Journalism studies made an exception in two cases: the final examinations at the Swedish language SSKH and the Education Division at Tampere were also bachelor's level, and neither of the institutions was allowed to offer master's studies. The faculty track at Tampere and the Jyväskylä programme were based on the assumption of a 'full length' (theoretically five years) master's degree.

Initially faculties of social sciences where among those that did not have a bachelor's degree at all, only a full five year's master's degree, while faculties of humanities also had the 'intermediate' bachelor's degree. At Tampere the Department of Journalism and Mass Communication is in the Faculty of Social Sciences, and it was only in 1996 that the bachelor's degree was established there. At Jyväskylä the journalism programme is in the Faculty of Humanities, and thus the faculty from the start granted both bachelor's and master's degrees. At Tampere the programme is also a department of its own, but at Jyväskylä journalism is part of the Department of Communication which consists of four independent majors: Journalism, Speech communication, Organizational communication and PR, and Intercultural communication. The fact that the two Finnish language academic journalism education units are located in different faculties is not significant in terms of study substances; the Jyväskylä programme is 'humanities' mainly because in the late-1980s that faculty showed more interest in taking the newcomer than the faculty of social sciences.

The strength of the former Finnish university degrees was their wide scope: they consisted of a major and several minors. This is still the case in the Bologna era, but the role of minors is smaller. In the old system for which the transition period ended in the summer of 2008, the bachelor's degree consisted of 120 'study weeks' (a concept theoretically corresponding to 40 hours of work), and the master's degree 160 (including the 'interim' bachelor's degree).

Probably the most important consequence of the Bologna model is the abolition of the connection between bachelor's and master's degrees. Earlier the major in the bachelor's degree was almost always the same as the major in the master's degree. The subjects were divided into three levels: basic, intermediate, and advanced, and the two first levels of the major were included in the bachelor's degree. Then the bachelor's studies were included in the master's degree, and the major was expanded with advanced level studies. In the Bologna-era bachelor and master are two different degrees, and it is possible to take a bachelor with, say, theoretical physics as the major, and take a master with, say, journalism as the major. A Finnish bachelor's degree is 180 ECTS credits and a master's degree 120 ECTS credits, while the former five year master's degree was 300 credits.

According to 2008 curricula the bachelor's degrees consist of the following parts (in ECTS credits) in the three academic units:

	general	major	minors
Tampere	42	85	53
Jyväskylä	15	80	85
SSKH	41	85	54

In the colleges (or polytechnics, or universities of applied sciences) the four year bachelor's degree consists of 240 ECTS credits which all can be regarded as 'major'; the term in use is 'study programme'. However, the 'major' also includes 'basic studies' comparable to 'general studies' at universities (e.g. languages), as well as some optional studies.

Contrary to the Ministry of Education's initial intentions about the 'dual model', the college degree is in many cases becoming a potential ticket to master's studies in universities. Interviewed for the ESF study, representatives of academic journalism education units at Tampere and Jyväskylä already had positive experiences of having accepted bachelors graduated from colleges. In both universities, however, a varying amount of supplementary studies were required, particularly regarding research methods and communication theory. Contrary to these two rather practical and vocationally-oriented units, the more theoretical, or solely research-oriented communication departments required one or even two years' 'bridge studies' for students coming from the colleges (Raittila et al. 2006: 112–113).

Universities: Journalism, research, minors

The objectives of the three academic units can best be chrystallized by quoting the introductory statements of their curricula. They are freely translated from the Finnish/ Swedish language websites, addresses of which are in the bibliography. (Tampere 2009; Jyväskylä 2009; SSKH 2009.)

Tampere:

Journalism and mass communication has developed from earlier Newspaper studies and Radio and Television studies into a communication research subject, especially researching mediated public communication. Theory and practice of journalism are emphasized in the studies. Professional skills in journalism are developed by combining those two. In addition, the studies prepare for research and doctoral studies in the field. Thus, Journalism and mass communication is a programme aiming not only at professional skills but also at wide knowledge of society and culture.

Jyväskylä:

The vocational task of the programme is to educate journalists for the media. The programme emphasizes factual journalism solid in content and rich in form. In the education, journalistic content is regarded as primary, and technical skills are seen as instruments to produce and mediate the content. The scholarly objective of the education is to introduce the students to scientific theories and research methods of media and communication. Academic journalism education is based on the conviction that journalism and research are on the same continuum of acquiring, interpreting and presenting information, and support each other.

SSKH:

The major is Journalism and media knowledge and media language. The major contains communication theory, media knowledge, journalistic work, and research in journalism and communication. The studies lead to the degree of bachelor in social sciences and give competence to work as a journalist in the press, radio and television. The studies also give competence to studies for a degree of master in social sciences.

Below the major is roughly divided into 'journalism' and 'theory and research' (in ECTS credits) as follows. It should yet be reminded that because of the integrative approach, the division is often factitious and only shows the emphasis in individual courses.

	bachelor		master	
	jour	th & r	jour	th & r
Tampere	44	41	18	102
Jyväskylä	35	45	25	55
SSKH	44	41		

All three programmes have both basic and advanced courses in print journalism, radio and television, and to a growing extent pay attention to the multimedial digital world. There is also an internship period – normally in the form of a summer job with a trainee's salary. There is also a built-in assumption that the students work as journalists every summer during their studies.

The three programmes encourage their students to participate in the Erasmus exchange programme and study for a semester in a foreign university or college. The programmes are also members in the cooperation committee of Nordic (Denmark, Finland, Greenland, Iceland, Norway, Sweden) journalism education units, and have established a Nordplus exchange network financed by the Nordic council of ministers.

Colleges: practical media skills

Diak/Turku describes its programme:

> We educate skilled journalists primarily for broadcast media. During the studies you can orientate to studies in multimedia or community journalism. [...] Journalistic skills are central in the education. We initiate you into the special features of journalistic work in radio, the net and television. The media-specific skills are deepened in multimedia journalism, and new working forms of journalism are developed in community journalism. Internships and working projects are part of the education. (Diak 2009)

Haaga-Helia:

> The objective of Haaga-Helia's economy-oriented journalism education is to gain the broad professional competence needed in a print journalist's work. [...] Core skills are the ability to write good journalistic texts, as well as to acquire information. In addition, the journalism student acquires the basic information about communication, journalism, economy, structures of society and the media branch, necessary for a print journalist. The student develops facilities to work as a print journalist even in an international and digitalized world. (Haaga-Helia 2009)

Oulu:

> We educate communication professionals for expert tasks and content production in traditional and new media. The objective is to educate professionals who integrate communication skills with an understanding of the human being and society, and who are able to use the developing communication techniques. The journalism programme gives basic skills for work as a journalist, and a producer of journalistic content, in press, radio, television and the net. [...] As a journalist a medianomi is at ease with multimedial tasks in which he/she must master expression forms of several media, and make versions of stories for different media. In addition to media skills, knowledge of society is in the core of a journalist's education. (Oulu 2009)

The curricula of the colleges include plenty of practical hands-on courses on a wide range of media-related areas. The compulsory internship period (or 'practical training') is 30 ECTS credits, while in the universities it is 6 ECTS credits. The role of theory and research is rather small in the colleges: about 20 ECTS credits (or in some colleges even up to 40 credits, depending on which elements are counted in this section).

Concluding Remarks

Journalism education in Finland started in a semi-academic environment that eventually became academic. But it must be borne in mind that journalism has always been a 'free trade' without any formal requirements for those whom the employers have wanted to hire. Consequently the academic journalism education units have only supplied part of the new labour force. At least since the 1984 committee on journalism education the universally acknowledged thumb rule has been that roughly half of the new recruits have been educated in the academic journalism programmes, and the rest come from elsewhere, mainly with a university degree from some other field.

This was the case from late 1980s (when the Jyväskylä unit was established) till the turn of the millennium. The calculations of various committees showed that the demand of new journalists was about 250 per year, and the number of students taken in by the three academic programmes was roughly half of that. The proportions changed when the new colleges were introduced, and some of them started programmes that more or less were dealing with journalism education; the total supply of young journalists educated in journalism studies is growing, as the universities are providing the same amount as before, or more, and the three colleges have their own journalism programmes. The 'or more' at the universities refers to new openings like education in visual journalism located at Tampere, in cooperation with the two other academic units, and a programme on magazine journalism at the University of Industrial Arts (Helsinki).

A prominent feature of the journalist profession is its feminization. In the spring of 1998 the number of women exceeded the number of men among the members of The Union of Journalists in Finland. In early 2008 women comprised 56 per cent of members, and a total of almost 70 per cent of student members were female.

In the autumn of 2008 the future of the abundant communication related programmes in the colleges is under scrutiny: the Ministry of Education requires cuts in the intake and abolition or mergers of programmes, but this does not seem to apply to the actual journalism programmes. No cuts have been suggested to the universities. In the light of current wisdom it seems that the colleges are to stay in the journalism education market (in the present atmosphere of university system reform it seems appropriate to use the word 'market'), and from the university point of view it is also possible (or even probable) that the colleges are becoming one of the sources to recruit students to master's studies.

The Author

Raimo Salokangas is professor in Media and Journalism at the University of Jyväskylä, Finland.

Note

1. The author would like to thank Ph.D. Pirita Juppi and Professor Heikki Luostarinen for their valuable comments on the manuscript.

References

Diak (2009), http://www.diak.fi/viestinnnkoulutu (website of Diaconia University of Applied Sciences / communication programme).

Haaga-Helia (2009), http://www.haaga-helia.fi/fi/hakeminen/amk-tutkinto/journalismin-ko (website of Haaga-Helia University of Applied Sciences / journalism programme).

Jyrkiäinen, J. (2008), *The Finnish Media: Internet Moves Media Plates*, http: //finland.fi/Public/default, aspx?contentid=162833&nodeid=41808&culture=en-US. Accessed 2 September 2009.

Jyväskylä (2009), https: //www.jyu.fi/hum/laitokset/viesti/Opiskelijalle/Opetussuunnitelmat/jou. Accessed 2 September 2009.

Oulu (2009), http://www.oamk.fi/opiskelijalle/rakenne/opinto-opas/koulutusohjelmat/?sivu=k_kuvaus &lv=s2008&id=54 (website of Oulu University of Applied Sciences / journalism programme).

Raittila, P., Olin, N. and Stenvall-Virtanen, S. (2006), *Viestintäkoulutuksen nousukäyrä. Monta tietä unelma-ammattiin ja suuriin pettymyksiin*, Tampere: University of Tampere, Department of Journalism and Mass Communication. http: //www.uta.fi/laitokset/tiedotus/viest_ammatit/loprapverkkoversio.pdf. Accessed 2 September 2009.

Ritvos, K. (2008), *Toimittajakoulu 1967–2007*, Helsinki: SanomaWSOY.

Salokangas, R. (2003), 'Finland: The Road to Consensus in Journalism Education', In R. Fröhlic and C. Holtz-Bacha (eds.), *Journalism Education in Europe and North America: An International Comparison*, Creskill, NJ: Hampton Press.

Sanoma (2009), http: //www.sanoma.com/content.aspx?f=2797. Accessed 2 September 2009.

SSKH (2009), https: //oodi-www.it.helsinki.fi/hy/vl_kehys.jsp?Kieli=2&MD5avain=&vl_tila=1&Opa s=1533&Org=1000003029. Accessed 2 September 2009.

Suomen Lehdistö (2008), *Suomen Lehdistö 6–7/2008*, Helsinki: Finnish Newspapers' Association.

Svenska YLE (2009), http: //svenska.yle.fi. Accessed 2 September 2009.

Tampere (2009), http: //www.uta.fi/laitokset/tiedotus/opiskelu/arkisto/Tiedotusoppi_tutkintovaa timukset_2006-08-2.pdf. Accessed 2 September 2009.

The German Journalism Education Landscape

Romy Fröhlich and Christina Holtz-Bacha

Introduction

Discussions about the necessity and the best way of journalism education have accompanied the development of the profession for a long time in Germany. As early as 1899, the first private journalism school was founded by Richard Wrede in Berlin. It existed for only seven years (Müller 2005: 25) because it was disputed whether journalism could be learned or rather was a vocation (Brückmann 1997: 114–115). However, the discussion about the need for formalized and academic education of journalists continued which was caused by the decline in the share of academic graduates in the profession. In the middle of the nineteenth century, 87.5 per cent of journalists had studied at a university (any subject, due to missing journalism programmes). In 1900, the number had fallen to 78.5 per cent (Requate 1995: 143).

The increased influx of non-academics to the profession at that time followed far-reaching changes of the newspaper market as well as within the press. During the last two decades of the nineteenth century, the introduction of the rotary press and the typesetting machine accelerated the production of newspapers and fostered the development of the mass press. Other than the political newspapers that dominated the market before, the new type newspapers were financed by advertising to a great extent and therefore could be offered at a low price. These newspapers were 'unpolitical' which also allowed them to reach a wider audience. This development led to criticism about the quality of the press which was also extended to the reputation of journalists. At the same time, the shift from serious reporting to lighter contents allowed non-academics to enter the profession. The development of the mass press was paralleled by a differentiation within the press. New sections were introduced in addition to the classical newspaper sections which led to an increased demand for personnel, and the addition of women's pages opened the way for female journalists to join the editorial staff (Requate 1995: 149–154).

The increased importance of newspapers in general and the growing share of non-academics in journalism followed by concern about the quality of the press kept the discussion about the right way of educating journalists alive. Around the turn of the century, universities and business schools started to offer courses dealing with newspapers as economic and cultural factors (Bruch 1980). Finally, in 1916, the first institute for the 'science of the press' was founded at the University of Leipzig. Better than anything else, the establishment of the institute in Leipzig shows that two currents came together here and fostered the development of the new academic discipline. One was a growing awareness of the public relevance of the press by academics from different disciplines, particularly from political economy and history. The other pillar was an interest of publishers, journalists and their professional associations in journalism education at the universities. This was to provide some basic knowledge for journalists and thought to be a preparatory training only, because the professional qualifications were still to be acquired on the job. In fact, the director of the institute, Karl Bücher, represented both currents: He was a professor in political economy and also had some journalistic experience which had brought him to study the press and make it a subject of his teaching (cf. Fischer and Minte 1980; Straetz 1986).

Soon after the establishment of the institute in Leipzig, similar institutions emerged at colleges and universities in other German cities and in Switzerland. However, the need for systematic journalism education remained disputed. There were many, particularly among journalists themselves, who regarded journalism as a vocation rather than a job to be learned at university. At the same time, many people from the field feared that the state would gain more influence on the press with a somehow regulated access to journalism. During World War I and the following years, criticism of the press grew and thus supported those who argued for the systematic training of journalists. So, all in all, the establishment of a new academic discipline rested on two pillars, the scientification of the study of the press and the professionalization of journalism through academic education which was also supposed to lead to an improvement of the image of journalists and to increasing salaries.

When the Nazis came to power in January 1933, the whole media system was restructured in order to serve their ideology. The academic discipline mostly yielded to instrumentalization. Several measures were taken to control the journalistic profession. With the *Schriftleitergesetz*, released in October 1933, for the first time in Germany a law prescribed a professional education of journalists. The regulation required at least a one-year training which made training-on-the-job obligatory. Training contracts had to be approved by the *Reichsverband der Deutschen Presse* which was the professional association of journalists incorporated in the institutional system through which the Ministry of Propaganda controlled the media. In 1935, the Nazis also set up a school that offered quarterly courses to supplement the training-on-the-job in the publishing houses. The school was closed in 1939 with the beginning of World War II (Müsse 1995).

The experiences from the Nazi regime and its tight control of the media not only affected the discussion about new structures right after the war and in the early years of the Federal Republic of Germany, but has remained a general liability of German history that is still present today. For instance, access to the profession is completely open and there are no prescribed requirements for becoming a journalist or any other regulation. The freedom of the press and of journalism is assured through the German constitution which does not allow any official regulatory procedures, even if it concerns journalism education only. While this explains the persistent scepticism towards regulated journalism education, the fact that everybody can work as a journalist sometimes nurtures debates about the legitimacy and the quality of journalism.

The trauma of the Nazi years met with widespread doubts about the need for formalized journalism education and many people's conviction that journalism is a vocation and cannot be learned. This thinking prevailed until the end of the 1960s when a new discussion about some kind of formalized education for journalists started. In 1969, the process was initiated by an agreement of the journalists' unions and the newspaper publishers' federation upon a treaty that defined basic conditions for the in-house training of journalists at daily newspapers. Even more important was a memorandum that was passed by the German Press Council (Deutscher Presserat) in 1971 and confirmed by a similar memorandum two years later. These statements acknowledged the increasing relevance of the communication professions and therefore called for a university education of journalists while at the same time emphasizing that access to journalism should remain open with respect to the press freedom article of the constitution. The contradictory nature of the two demands may be the reason for the fact that the demand for an academic education of journalists has not been officially repeated by any professional association since then. Already existing academic journalism programmes, however, are strongly defended by the journalism associations. Their motivation, mainly, is to ensure higher salaries; at least for those colleagues who had the opportunity to gain one of the rare and specific journalistic academic titles.

However, since the early 1970s, different models of journalism programmes were introduced at German universities. Often these programmes developed out of or in the neighbourhood of existing programmes in communication. Whereas the latter were dominantly theory-oriented, the journalism programmes were conceived as combinations of practical training, usually in the field, and the acquisition of knowledge relating to the profession (e.g. media law, media economics, ethics).

It is not by coincidence that the debate of journalism education and the establishment of the first academic programmes started at about the same time when a wave of mergers swept over the newspaper market. Increasing concentration, and the gradual recognition of the fact that the media are not as powerless as they were for a long time conceived to be, led to a discussion of how diversity of media content could be best guaranteed. In this context, the systematic education of journalists was regarded as a means of safeguarding content diversity and thus the quality of media content. In a similar way, whenever the discussion about the training of journalists came up again in later years, it was usually provoked by public concern and discontent with the performance of the media and a systematic education of journalists was seen as a response to those problems.

University education

When the Kölner Schule/Institut für Publizistik (today Kölner Journalistenschule für Politik und Wirtschaft) started its four-year journalism programme in 1968, it was the first of a new model that combined practical training outside the university with an academic education. Parallel to academic studies in macroeconomics and political science at the University of Cologne, this school until today offers a solid practical journalism training. Quite similar was a journalism programme started by the University of Munich (LMU) in 1973 which also combined an academic education (communication science, political science and sociology; diploma degree comparable to a master's degree) with practical training outside the university. In this case, the journalism programme was offered in cooperation of the Institute for Communication Science at the LMU and the private journalism school Deutsche Journalistenschule (DJS) which was founded in 1949 and since then offers so called 'compact courses' – a two-year full-time practical journalism training programme with integrated internships in renowned TV, radio and print media organizations. The academic diploma programme in cooperation with LMU is a stand-alone programme with its own study and examination regulations and thus completely different and separated from the non-academic compact courses. By the end of 2008 the traditional diploma programme will be changed into a journalism master programme.

In 1976, the University of Dortmund established a four-year journalism programme that included a one-year internship at a newspaper or a broadcasting station. Also in 1976, the University of Hohenheim established a two-year graduate programme. Until today, it is the only journalism programme which explicitly favours graduates from natural sciences, economics, law and social sciences over graduates from the humanities. Soon, other German universities followed these models and, over the years, journalism programmes sprouted all over the country.

Today, journalism is offered in different varieties at universities and so-called 'universities of applied sciences'. The latter are special institutions of higher education in Germany which have more in common with the Anglo-Saxon type of 'advanced technical colleges' or 'polytechnics' than with classical universities. Universities of applied sciences cannot award doctoral degrees. With the Bologna process, however, the differences between the two types of academic institutions could disappear. Another particularity complicates matters in Germany: Undergraduate programs (Bachelor) have been unknown so far. Full-time four-year graduate programs instead directly lead to a master's degree or diploma, which allow for admission to a doctoral programme. According to the Bologna agreements, the whole system is currently reconstructed. This applies to universities as well as to universities of applied sciences. As a consequence, the old and the new system will exist side-by-side at least for another decade thus providing for a complex situation in Germany. Therefore, the following description of the current status of academic journalism programmes will try to keep things as simple as possible.

For this contribution, different sources and directories for relevant programmes at universities *and* universities of applied sciences (private and public) were analysed.[1] According to our findings, Germany counts twenty five academic journalism programs (undergraduate/new B.A. system) and graduate (old master and diploma system), eight journalism master programs (new system; two-, three- or four-semester programs), and eleven continuing/further education programs (including part-time continuing programs for professionals).[2] No reliable data on the number of participants are available for continuing education programmes at the university/university of applied sciences level.

In addition to journalism programmes which usually have former practitioners among their teaching staff, there are almost 40 programmes in communication at universities. Here it is rather uncommon that former journalists belong to the teaching staff.[3] A generous count of all media-related programs[4] at university/university of applied sciences level yields an even broader choice: While in 2000, 64 German universities and universities of applied sciences offered 131 different academic courses and subjects (Wirth 2002: 40), the web portal *Medienstudienführer* (see footnote 1) currently lists approximately 400 different university programmes. Although these programmes do not claim to educate for journalism, there are usually many students in these programmes who nevertheless hope for a future in journalism.

Due to a variety of part-time and full-time programs, specialized courses, university and college level programmes, undergraduate and graduate as well as continuing programmes, technical-oriented versus content-oriented programs etc.[5] offered by a big variety of different disciplines at private and public institutions of higher education, it has become very difficult to exactly sort out the whole range of possibilities. A recent survey of human resource managers at media organizations shows, that even these specialists are not familiar with the educational situation for media professions at German universities and universities of applied sciences. The vast majority of the respondents stated that they cannot keep up with the confusing state (Siegmund 2006: 181).

The inhomogeneous nature and particularly the part played by practical training in these academic programmes must also be regarded as the reason why graduates usually cannot start as journalists right away but have to go through additional training at the media companies. In fact, about 60 per cent of the German journalists have undergone traditional vocational training, many of them after they have graduated from one of the university (of applied sciences) programmes (or journalism schools) (Table 1).

Table 1: Education of journalists 1993 and 2005.

	1993 in %*	2005 in %*
Internship	32	69
Vocational training (at media companies)	61	62
Journalism School	10	14
Journalism programme/university	21	14
Communication, media programme/university	18	17
Other education or further education	47	14
N	1.498	1.636

* Adding up to more than 100% because multiple responses were possible.
Source: Weischenberg, Malik and Scholl 2006: 265

Journalism programmes at universities usually combine theoretical knowledge about the media system, media law, content, audience and effects research with practically-oriented training in journalism. Practical training is provided in courses at the university, taught by former journalists who have become university teachers or by journalists who are still active in their profession. Journalism programmes as well as many programmes in communication mostly have their own technical equipment. Some of them run their own radio station or produce for television and often reach an audience beyond the campus.

In addition, students acquire practical experiences during internships in media companies. These are usually obligatory and can be completed before, during or after the university programme – depending on the respective programme and its study guidelines and examination regulations. The internships differ in their length and there may be specific requirements with regard to the medium.

Journalists in East Germany (German Democratic Republic, until 1989/90) got their education either at the Faculty of Journalism (nicknamed 'The Red Monastery') that was part of the University of Leipzig since 1954, or a college of journalism which was also situated in Leipzig. Since the education of journalists was deemed crucial by the socialist regime, it was under the jurisdiction of the propaganda unit of the state party's Central Committee and entry to the profession was strongly regulated. The two only GDR institutions providing journalism education were closed down with the unification process. Since then, several communication departments were established at East German universities but only Leipzig offers a journalism programme at the university level.

Journalism schools

Journalism schools in Germany are non-academic (private) institutions; their teaching staff comprises almost exclusively former professionals. The first and still existing stand-alone journalism school,[6] the Deutsche Journalistenschule (DJS) in Munich, was founded in 1949 under the name of Werner-Friedmann-Institut. Friedmann was editor-in-chief of the *Süddeutsche Zeitung* and also the publisher of the Munich tabloid paper *Abendzeitung*. The school is financed by publishers, broadcasting stations, unions and political parties. Not least because of its supporters, the school soon gained a high reputation but for a long time did not win any imitators. Only in the 1970s and 1980s, were three more journalism schools established, all of them owned by major German publishing houses: The Henri-Nannen-Schule was founded in 1978 by Gruner + Jahr, which is part of Bertelsmann, Germany's biggest media company, and one of the most important journal publishers in the country. The Axel-Springer-Schule followed in 1986. It was established by the Axel Springer media company which is a heavyweight on Germany's newspaper market. In 1988, the Holtzbrinck group, owner of the business paper *Handelsblatt* and the renowned weekly *Die Zeit*, founded the Georg von Holtzbrinck-Schule that specializes in business and finance journalism. With this specialization, the Holtzbrinck School was a harbinger of a differentiation process that characterized the further development of the journalism schools.

Today, Germany counts seventeen journalism schools (Deutscher Journalistenverband 2008: 28–32). While ten offer an all-round programme, five specialize on a medium (e.g., television, newspaper), and another three offer a specialized training for the different editorial departments of the media. Among the seventeen journalism schools owned by media organizations there are two journalism schools run and organized by the two main religious communities, the catholic and the protestant churches: (1) The Evangelische Medienakademie (founded 1949 by Christian-minded journalists and since 1973 owned by the 'Protestant Church in Germany' (EKD)) offers further/continuing education for print, radio and TV journalists, is engaged in off-the-job training programmes for trainees of the media's in-house training programmes (so-called Volontariat; see next section) and also offers further/continuing education in PR. The participants have not necessarily to be protestant. (2) The ifp – Institut zur Förderung publizistischen Nachwuchses e.V. is a programme founded in 1968 by order of the German Conference of Catholic Bishops and offers attendant-study journalism courses for (catholic) students (whichever subject), off-the-job training programmes for trainees of in-house training programmes of newspapers (mainly but not exclusively catholic press) and private radio stations, and finally so-called media trainings for theologians (including an introduction into PR).

In addition to the seventeen journalism schools, twelve different institutions are specialized on 'interplant' courses for *Volontäre* of media organizations (Deutscher Journalistenverband 2008: 27–28). Within an off-the-job scenario they offer additional journalistic training through (partly highly) specialized seminars.

According to Table 1, the number of journalists who attended a journalism school has slightly increased between the years 1993–2005. However, their share stays comparatively low which is due to the small number of students who are admitted every year. The selection procedures for the journalism schools differ but usually applicants have to go through a multistage entrance exam where they have to demonstrate their general knowledge, give an impression of their journalistic talents and prove their motivation for the journalistic profession. The journalism schools enjoy a high number of applications and thus can choose from several hundreds or even thousands of young people who try to get into journalism this way.

In addition to the journalism schools, a variety of academies offer different kinds of advanced training and further education for journalists. These academies are mostly supported by private sponsors. Their courses usually concentrate on special skills and topics or are provided for those who undergo in-house training who, according to a collective agreement, have to participate in a certain amount of external courses (see below).

In-house on-the-job-training: *The Volontariat* and continuing in-house education

In spite of the trend towards an academization of journalism education and the still increasing number of university- and, in particular, college-level programmes (at universities of applied sciences) and journalism schools, the so-called *Volontariat* remains the most important entry to journalism. *Volontariat* is the German special term for the media's traditional in-house training programmes. The regular length of these programs is two years but may be reduced to 18 or 15 months for those who have graduated from university or went to journalism school. As Table 1 demonstrates, the in-house training programmes have not lost their relevance over the years. According to the most recent 2005 journalism survey (Weischenberg et al. 2006) slightly more than 60 per cent of the German journalists went through in-house-training, other sources even speak of an 80 per cent intake (Deutscher Journalistenverband 2008: 16). However, only a small percentage of beginners enter the profession after having gone through a *Volontariat* only. Instead, it is frequently combined with an academic (but mainly non-journalistic) education.

When the journalism programmes at university-level were introduced, those, as well as the journalism schools, were supposed to replace the traditional in-house programmes at the media companies. Nevertheless, the *Volontariat* still seems to be key for a career in journalism. Several factors may have contributed to this situation. First of all, practitioners usually are convinced that some professional skills can only be acquired by training-on-the-job although many of today's journalists have themselves undergone some academic education (whichever subject). In addition, the *Volontäre* (the participants of an in-house programme) are low-cost employees who are not necessarily hired at the end of the training programme. The increasingly difficult situation of the newspaper market since 2001 has probably made the employment of *Volontäre* even more attractive.

Until not so long ago, the *Volontariat* was not really regulated and sometimes work of the apprentices was similar to that of a fully employed journalist while apprentices did not get any further education. Since the early 1970s, the German journalists' unions fought for binding regulations at newspaper companies but could not reach an agreement with the publishers. In 1982, the Publishers' Federation BDZV (Bundesverband Deutscher Zeitungs- und Zeitschriftenverleger) laid down unilateral regulations for the journalistic in-house training. It took until 1990, when the publishers and the unions finally reached a collective agreement on the *Volontariat*. The agreement, which is still in effect,[7] offers guidelines for a comprehensive programme that integrates theoretical and practical parts. Regulations refer to the length of the Volontariat (maximum two years, which may be reduced to a minimum of fifteen months), the objectives and the breadth of the programme that includes in-house training and courses offered by other institutions. Mentors from the editorial staff make sure that the training programmes comply with the regulations of the collective agreement. In 2005, the unions reached a similar agreement with the private broadcasting companies.

Newspaper companies offer the most chances for young journalists. Of about 2600 offers for in-house training, about 1100 are provided by daily newspapers, 800 by journals, more than 400 by regional and local private radio stations, about 200 by the big broadcasting companies and 100 by freesheets (ad-papers). Only about one-third of those who complete the in-house training programmes get employed on a regular basis by the same company where they were educated (Deutscher Journalistenverband 2008: 18).

Again, no reliable data on the number or gender of the participants of in-house continuing education programmes are available. The only data available concern the continuing education seminars of the German public service broadcasting stations. In 1978, they established the Zentrale Fortbildung der Programm-Mitarbeiter/Gemeinschaftseinrichtung ARD/ZDF (ZFP) as a central institution for the continuing education of their journalistic and editorial staff. ARD[8] and ZDF[9] once a year publish a detailed report on their education and further/continuing education programmes and courses. According to the most recent report, they offered 631 continuing education seminars in 2006 with 5542 participants in total. In comparison to 2005, this is an increase in seminars of 8 per cent and in participants of 14 per cent. (Hessischer Rundfunk 2007: 5)

Journalism education and gender

The majority of students at academic communication and media programmes in Germany are female (cf. Fröhlich and Holtz-Bacha 2008). Already, since the beginning of the 1990s,

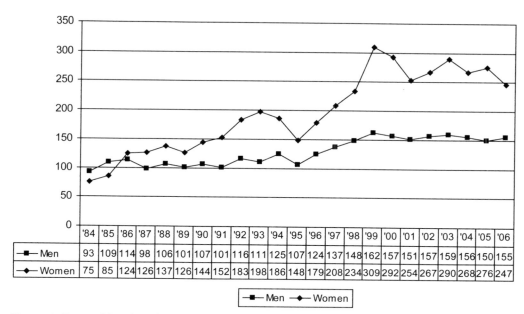

	'84	'85	'86	'87	'88	'89	'90	'91	'92	'93	'94	'95	'96	'97	'98	'99	'00	'01	'02	'03	'04	'05	'06
Men	93	109	114	98	106	101	107	101	116	111	125	107	124	137	148	162	157	151	157	159	156	150	155
Women	75	85	124	126	137	126	144	152	183	198	186	148	179	208	234	309	292	254	267	290	268	276	247

Figure 1: Share of female *Volontäre* (in-house trainees) at public broadcasting stations 1984 to 2006 (by percentage). *Source:* Hessischer Rundfunk 1985–2007.

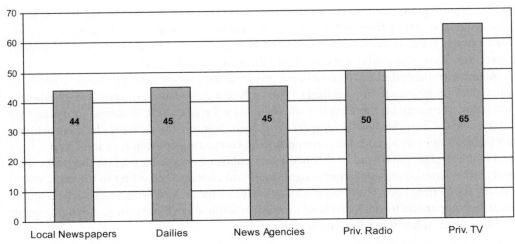

Figure 2: Share of female *Volontäre* (in-house trainees) according to type of media (by percentage). *Source:* Weischenberg, Keuneke, Löffelholz and Scholl 1994.

the majority of students who study public relations, journalism, communications, and media studies are women. On the other hand, the share of women at academic journalism programmes on average is about 45 per cent. Public broadcasting companies in Germany – the most common training ground for broadcast journalism – have also long since experienced the gender-switch within their training programmes. It can be clearly seen that since the mid-1980s ARD and ZDF educate more young female than male journalists (Figure 1).

The figures from other media fields also clearly show that women have almost equal accessibility to all media types in Germany (Figure 2).

For many years now, we observe a clear feminisation of the journalistic educational sector in Germany. Current data, however, allows for the conclusion that in relation to their number in journalism education women are still extremely underrepresented in the German profession itself: With a female share of currently 37 per cent of journalists overall (Weischenberg, Malik and Scholl 2006), the feminisation of German journalism still falls far short of expectations.[10]

Concluding Remarks

The development of academic journalism education in Germany has undergone three stages of institutionalisation (Hömberg 2002: 18–20). The 1970s saw the discussion about the need for a systematic education of journalists and the start of pilot projects in Munich, Dortmund and Hohenheim. In the early 1980s, these programmes got permanently established and served as models for similar programmes at other universities. At the same time, this was also the start of the emergence of the new academic discipline which provided a theoretical basis for journalism education and the profession in general. The 1990s can be characterized as a period of expansion and differentiation. In the mid-1990s, more than 40 institutions (academic and non-academic), focusing on communication and journalism, existed and offered about 60 programmes with different profiles; in addition, another 109 institutions offered all sorts of (specialized) training in journalism. By now, almost 200 universities, universities of applied sciences, academies, journalism schools, associations and foundations engage in some kind of journalism education (Hömberg 2002: 20).

The expansion went hand in hand with differentiation processes on four levels that also reflect the changes and thus the demand of the media market (Hömberg 2002: 22):

1. More and more programmes offer specialized training for the different editorial departments of the media (e.g., economics, sports, science).
2. In addition to traditional journalism, training for and job offers in strategic and corporate communication (PR) are on the rise.
3. Job profiles are changing as a consequence of commercialization (e.g., programmes in media management) and the growing relevance of online communication.
4. Universities of applied sciences have increasingly engaged in journalism education which again tips the balance of theoretical and practical education to practical training.

Concerning point (2), it is interesting to note that specialized non-academic educational programmes for Public Relations are no longer exclusively offered by special PR institutions but instead more and more traditionally journalistic educators integrate PR education into their portfolio.[11] While this development is highly questioned by the journalism associations which fear a growing blurring of the professional and ethically relevant boundaries between journalism and PR, the meanwhile rather problematic labour market for journalists clearly rises the demand for PR education.

Today, the German average journalist is male (63%), almost 41 years old, comes from a middle class background, has graduated from a university (69%) (whichever subject), and has gone through an in-house training programme at a media company (63%; Weischenberg, Malik and Scholl 2006: 186). These figures show that journalism is an academic profession although only 14 per cent of the German journalists have explicitly studied journalism at a university (of applied sciences) (Weischenberg, Malik and Scholl 2006: 67, 265, 266). Thus, a comparatively high percentage of journalists have graduated from other programmes and therefore usually do not have any practical knowledge in journalism if not from internships. This may be one explanation for the fact that most journalists also undergo extensive in-house training (*Volontariat*) at the media companies. Another factor is the attitude of practitioners – publishers, journalists – who are still convinced that the practical training in journalism programmes at universities or in journalism schools cannot replace the experiences made on the job.

Finally, as was mentioned above, young journalists who still go through in-house training are low-cost employees. In fact, the latest journalism survey revealed a considerable increase in the number of journalists who have completed an internship. Between 1993 and 2005 the percentage of those who did an internship more than doubled (Weischenberg, Malik and Scholl 2006: 67). In the youngest age group, among the journalists who are less than 36 years old, the figure even rises to more than 90 per cent. These findings cause Weischenberg et al. to speak of a 'Generation Praktikum' (literally: generation internship; Weischenberg, Malik and Scholl 2006: 67) that is capturing the profession.

Since the so-called media crisis in 2001, the journalistic labour market in Germany is experiencing a rather problematic development and still suffers from major challenges. Job security is declining dramatically, contracts on the basis of a full-time permanent employment are increasingly hard to get. The job-related degradations within the journalistic job market partly result from structural and technical developments: (1) the economic crisis of the traditional media market (general decline of newspaper circulation and declining gains of the publishers from traditional advertising etc.),[12] (2) the digitalization of media (for example online papers) and with it the rising need for online-skills and multi-media expertise, (4) the increasing cross-media development which forces journalists to be more flexible than previously and to produce for different media types (TV, radio, print and online).

This of course had and still has consequences for the educational sector: Between 2000 and 2004, in-house-training places (*Volontariate*) at newspapers decreased by 22 per cent (Nicolini 2005: 199). In 2001, the amount of *Volontäre* (in-house trainees) in Germany declined to 2400 and reached its lowest level since 1991 (DJV 2001/02: 55; DJV 2003/04: 57). And there is more evidence that the crisis hit the educational market: A survey of the German journalism association showed that at the end of 2003, 40 per cent of the editorial departments did not offer a *Volontariat* anymore; the rest reduced its supply of places by 30 per cent (Hausmann 2003: 35). Parallel to this, the supply of journalistic internships is rising since 2004 and the average duration of internships is extended (Lungmus 2006: 18). Finally, between 2003 and 2005, the share of freelancers among journalists increased by 11 per cent (DJV 2005/06: 55). Thus, the most recent developments in the job and educational market can be regarded as an indicator for a proceeding economic struggle.

Despite this rather unpleasant development, journalism is still highly attractive for young people in Germany. This applies to media professions in general. According to the most recent study (Wirth 2000: 37), the number of graduates of respective academic subjects and programmes doubled during the 1990s and reached 55000 in the year 2000. As has been shown here, however, the number of young applicants for the respective programmes is much higher. An exemplary count of the numbers of applicants[13] for six academic journalism programmes, eight academic communication programmes and four journalism schools shows an average ratio of 1: 25 for academic journalism programmes. For academic communication programmes the ratio ranges from 1: 9 to 1: 62, and at journalism schools the average ratio is about 1: 29.

It is a long and thorny way into the profession and it has become even more difficult during the last decade or so – characterized by the emergence of online communication, the commercialization of broadcasting and, recently, a newspaper crisis. The imponderability of the whole media sector had consequences for journalism education; this makes it a dubious matter to come up with a prognosis for its future.

The Authors

Romy Fröhlich is a full professor at Ludwig-Maximilians-University Munich (Germany), a Member of the Associate Editorial Boards of *Feminist Media Studies, Communication, Culture & Critique* and *Journalism & Mass Communication Editor.*
  Christina Holtz-Bacha holds the chair in communication at the University of Erlangen-Nuremberg, Germany.

Notes

1. http: //www.medienstudienfuehrer.de/; http: //www.journalismstudies.eu/germany.htm; http://careerservice-konstanz.de/cs/content/view/95/136/. All websites accessed 1 September 2009. Hömberg and Hackel-de Latour 2005 ; Basel 2006.
2. All three types of programmes included highly specialized programmes (TV journalism for example) or a particular news department (music journalism at the University of Music in Karlsruhe for example or science journalism at the University of Dortmund).
3. Conservative counting with concentration on the more narrowly defined programmes of communication. However, the respective course/subject names are different which makes it very difficult to compare the diverse programmes ('Publizistik', Communication Science, Media Science, Media Research, Media & Communication, Media Management, Information & Communication Management, Communication Research etc.)
4. Including Media Design, Media Culture, Multi Media, Media Economy, Media & Music, Media & Fashion (etc.), Corporate Communication, Public Relations, Media Technology, Media Pedagogy etc.
5. For a good systematic overview of different orientations and emphases, see Basel 2006.
6. The first non-academic journalism school, the Deutsche Journalistenschule Aachen e.V., was founded in 1946 but closed down a couple of years later.
7. For the original text see Deutscher Journalistenverband 2008: 83–115.
8. Arbeitsgemeinschaft der öffentlich-rechtlichen Rundfunkanstalten Deutschlands /Working Group of the German Public Broadcasting Stations, founded in 1950 and thus Germany's oldest public broadcasting station.
9. Zweites Deutsches Fernsehen /Second German Television] founded in 1963.
10. For a possible explanation for this strange 'loss' of women between journalistic education and the profession itself, see Fröhlich 2004.
11. Since 2005, the University of Applied Sciences in Gelsenkirchen offers a B.A. programme that combines journalism and PR.

12. In Germany, the newspaper market traditionally is the biggest job market for journalists.
13. According to self-disclosure of the institutions. Within the respective groups of programmes, the selected institutions belong to the well-established ones.

References

Basel, N. (2006), 'Das Aus- und Weiterbildungsangebot für den Mediensektor in Nordrhein-Westfalen. Eine Studie im Auftrag des Medienrats von Nordrhein-Westfalen und der Landesanstalt für Medien Nordrhein-Westfalen (LfM)', In LfM (ed.), *Dokumenten-Band zum zweiten Bericht des Medienrates*, Düsseldorf: LFM, pp. 5–44. Unpublished Report; available at http://www.lfm-nrw.de/downloads/medienrat_bericht2006_2.pdf. Accessed 1 September 2009.

Bruch, R. vom (1980), 'Zeitungswissenschaft zwischen Historie und Nationalökonomie', *Publizistik,* 25, pp. 579–607.

Brückmann, A. (1997), *Journalistische Berufsorganisationen in Deutschland. Von den Anfängen bis zur Gründung des Berufsverbandes der Deutschen Presse*, Köln: Böhlau.

DJV (Deutscher Journalisten-Verband) (ed.) (2008), *Journalist/in werden? Ausbildungsstudiengänge und Berufschancen im Journalismus 2008/2009*, Berlin: DJV.

DJV (Deutscher Journalisten-Verband) (ed.) (2005/06), *Journalist/in werden? Ausbildungsgänge und Berufschancen im Journalismus 2005/*, Bonn: DJV.

DJV (Deutscher Journalisten-Verband) (ed.) (2003/04), *Journalist/in werden? Ausbildungsgänge und Berufschancen im Journalismus 2003/2004*, Bonn: DJV.

DJV (Deutscher Journalisten-Verband) (ed.) (2001/02), *Journalist/in werden? Ausbildungsgänge und Berufschancen im Journalismus 2001/2002*, Bonn: DJV.

DJV (Deutscher Journalisten-Verband) (ed.) (1993), *Journalist/in werden? Ausbildungsgänge und Berufschancen im Journalismus 1993*, Bonn: DJV-Verlags und Service GmbH.

Deutscher Presserat (1974), 'Neues Memorandum für einen Rahmenplan zur Journalistenausbildung', In *Deutscher Presserat, Tätigkeitsbericht 1973*, Bad Godesberg: Zeitungs- und Zeitschriften-Verlag, pp. 93–111.

Deutscher Presserat (1972), 'Memorandum zur Journalistenausbildung', In *Deutscher Presserat, Tätigkeitsbericht 1971*, Bad Godesberg: Zeitungs- und Zeitschriften-Verlag, pp. 20–63.

Fischer, H.-D., and Minte, H. (1980), 'Karl Bücher – Leben und Schriften', In H.-D. Fischer and H. Minte (eds.), *Karl Bücher. Auswahl der publizistikwissenschaftlichen Schriften*, Bochum: Studienverlag Dr. N. Brockmeyer, pp. V-XLIII.

Fröhlich, R. (2004), 'Feminine and feminist values in communication professions: Exceptional skills and expertise or 'friendliness trap'?' In M. de Bruin and K. Ross (eds.), *Gender and Newsroom Cultures. Identities at work*, Cresskill, NJ: Hampton Press, pp. 65–77.

Fröhlich, R. And Holtz-Bacha, C. (2008), Gender and German journalism: Where do all the women go? In R. Fröhlich and S. Lafky (eds.), *Women journalists in the Western world: Equal opportunities and what surveys tell us*, Cresskill, NJ: Hampton Press, pp. 81–97.

Hamann, Götz (20 September 2007), 'Sparen, bis die Leser gehen?', *Die Zeit*, pp. 25–26.

Hausmann, L. (December 2003), 'Umfrage Zeitschriften: Krasse Wirklichkeit', *Journalist*, pp. 34–36.

Hessischer Rundfunk (ed.) (1985–2007), *Bericht über die Aus- und Fortbildung im öffentlich-rechtlichen Rundfunk der Bundesrepublik Deutschland (ARD/ZDF) (1984 – 2006)* (unpublished annual reports), Frankfurt: Hessischer Rundfunk.

Hömberg, W. (2002), 'Expansion und Differenzierung. Journalismus und Journalistenausbildung in den vergangenen drei Jahrzehnten', In K.-D. Altmeppen and W. Hömberg (eds.), *Jour-*

nalistenausbildung für eine veränderte Medienwelt. Diagnosen, Institutionen, Projekte, Wiesbaden: Westdeutscher Verlag, pp. 17–30.

Hömberg, W. and Hackel-de Latour, R. (Hrsg.) (2005), *Studienführer Journalismus, Medien, Kommunikation* (3rd., completely revised edition), Konstanz: UVK/UTB.

Kaube, J. (2004), 'Ihr geht alle in die Medien. Die deutschen Universitäten basteln an Berufsattrappen', *Frankfurter Allgemeine Zeitung*, 8 May, p. 35.

Kloft, J. (2007), 'Berufschancen in der Medienkrise. Eine Befragung von Absolventinnen und Absolventen der Kommunikationswissenschaft München (Abschlussjahrgänge 2000 bis 2006)', unpublished Master Thesis, München: Ludwig-Maximilians-Universität, Institut für Kommunikationswissenschaft und Medienforschung.

Lungmus, M. (2006), 'Sparpolitik: Die rote Gefahr', *Journalist*, September, pp. 10–18.

Müller, D. (2005), 'Richard Wredes Schule – das ausgeschlagene Erbe. Wissenschaftliche Journalistenausbildung um 1900', *Journalistik Journal*, 2, pp. 24–25.

Müsse, W. (1995), *Die Reichspresseschule – Journalisten für die Diktatur? Ein Beitrag zur Geschichte des Journalismus im Dritten Reich*, München: K. G. Saur.

Nicolini, M. (2005), 'Nadelöhr journalistischer Berufseinstieg. Gute Chancen für Stipendiaten des Instituts zur Förderung publizistischen Nachwuchses', *Communicatio Socialis*, 38, pp. 198–212.

Requate, J. (1995), *Journalismus als Beruf. Entstehung und Entwicklung des Journalistenberufs im 19. Jahrhundert. Deutschland im internationalen Vergleich*, Göttingen: Vandenhoeck & Ruprecht.

Siegmund, I. (2006), 'Ausbildung für die Medienwirtschaft', In K.-D. Altmeppen and M. Karmasin (eds.), *Medien und Ökonomie 3*, Wiesbaden: Westdeutscher Verlag, pp. 169–192.

Straetz, S. (1986), 'Das Institut für Zeitungskunde in Leipzig bis 1945', In R. vom Bruch and O. B. Roegele (eds.), *Von der Zeitungskunde zur Publizistik. Biographisch-institutionelle Stationen der deutschen Zeitungswissenschaft in der ersten Hälfte des 20. Jahrhunderts*, Frankfurt a. M.: Haag und Herchen. pp. 75–103.

Weischenberg, S., Keuneke, S., Löffelholz, M. and Scholl, A. (1994), *Frauen im Journalismus. Gutachten über die Geschlechterverhältnisse bei den Medien in Deutschland* (im Auftrag der Industriegewerkschaft Medien), Stuttgart: IG Medien, Fachgruppe Journalismus (dju/SWJV).

Weischenberg, S., Malik, M., and Scholl, A. (2006), *Die Souffleure der Mediengesellschaft. Report über die Journalisten in Deutschland*, Konstanz: UVK.

Wirth, W. (2000), 'Wachstum bei zunehmender Unübersichtlichkeit. Institutionelle Strukturen und Ausbildungssituation in der Kommunikations- und Medienwissenschaft in Deutschland', *Medien Journal*, 24 (2), pp. 36–46.

The Icelandic Journalism Education Landscape

Birgir Guðmundsson

Introduction

Journalism qualifications are a relatively new phenomenon in the Icelandic media world. The concept of formal education in the field of journalism is closely linked to the concept of journalism as a profession; this is an idea that was not generally accepted in Iceland until late in the twentieth century. The history of the media in Iceland from the middle of the nineteenth century up to the present day can be divided into six periods, each with its own particular characteristics. The boundaries between these periods is sometimes unclear, and putting an exact date on the transition between periods is not always possible (Gudmundsson, 2007). The periods are:

1. Post and Tidings (1773–1848)
2. Editorial Sheets and the Struggle for Independence (1848–1910)
3. The Early Years of the Newspaper – the *Cavling* Period (1910–16)
4. The All-embracing Political Party Press (1916–60)
5. Decline of the Political Party Press (1960–2000)
6. The Market Media (2000–)

The demand for professionalism among journalists emerged first during the period when the influence of the political parties was receding, although several decades passed before the concept of a professionally-educated media corps became a priority for those involved in journalism.

How could it be? The story

The emergence of professionalism reflects the maturity and diligence of the Icelandic Union of Journalists (Bladamannafelag Islands), a group that was once regarded as being just some sort of discussion club for media men rather than a respectable professional institution. The association changed considerably from the 1970s on, and the call for qualifications and professionalism, free of political connections, became gradually stronger. As the new millennium dawned, bringing to an end the period of the Decline of the Political Party Press here in Iceland, the market media period got underway; professional working methods achieved through education and preparation are now a priority for everyone involved in the field (Haraldsson 1987; Gudmundsson 2007).

The spotlight did not fall on journalist education issues until changes were made to the organization and staffing of the Icelandic Union of Journalists in 1978. The years immediately following this restructuring saw limited progress. The association assisted its members in attending language courses and other training that might help them in their work. There was no systematic move towards continuing education training courses. Journalists could attend courses that might help them in their work, but the available teaching was conceived for use in a wider context (Haraldsson 1987). An important exception was the Nordic Journalist Centre (NJC) in the Danish city of Aarhus, which was part of a joint Nordic effort. Many Icelandic journalists have attended the centre, which for many years has held an eight-week course covering subjects connected to journalism. One or two Icelandic journalists have attended this course each year since the 1970s. Support for continuing education for journalists was not formalized by the Icelandic Union of Journalists until the late 1980s, when new rules were drawn up. This step was partly due to developments in the public education system, both in upper secondary schools and especially in the University of Iceland, where preparations had been made for courses in practical media studies in partnership with the Union of Journalists and certain newspaper publishers (Jonsson 2008).

Upper secondary schools (high schools)[1] in Iceland began teaching media-related material during the second half of the 1960s. Teaching was mainly aimed at giving students an insight into the media world and improving their media literacy. Communication Studies has been defined as an area of specialization in sociology courses for those aiming to pass matriculation examinations in upper secondary schools. In addition, some high schools began to offer courses connected to the technical aspects of media work and media-related information technology (Ministry of Education 1999, 2004).

In 1987–88, a short time before these educational developments, the University of Iceland began teaching a one-year postgraduate diploma course entitled 'Practical Communication Studies'. This course, as mentioned earlier, was the result of a joint operation involving the University of Iceland, the Icelandic Union of Journalists and a group of leading newspaper publishers. Few working journalists attended the course, but a compulsory part of the curriculum expected students to receive vocational training in media companies, and ties evolved between the course and working editors (Stefansdottir 2008). Communication Studies has been part of the University of Iceland's social studies programme since 1970–71. In 1984, Communications Studies was specified as an optional module for sociology undergraduates. This arrangement remained unchanged until 2004, when Practical Communication Studies was changed somewhat, the programme renamed and became a two-year master's degree in journalism (Broddason 2008). A year earlier, in 2003, the University of Akureyri had introduced a degree course in Media Studies, which was intended to be a mixture of journalism and traditional academic Communication Studies. It is also worth mentioning that a third institution, Reykjavik University, embraced journalism in 2006 when RU's Continuing Education department, in partnership with media company 365 Media, offered

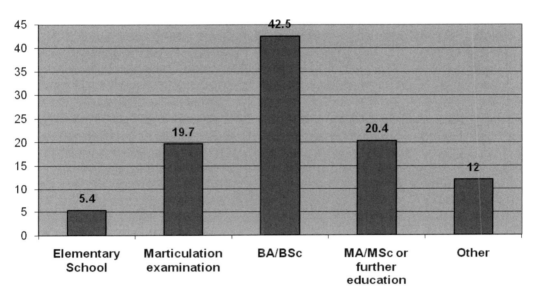

Figure 1: The level of education of members of the Icelandic Union of Journalists, from a survey carried out in September 2005 for the union. *Source:* Bladamadurinn, February 2006.

some journalism courses giving ECTS credits. However, these courses were not part of a wider programme (Kristjansson 2008).

Journalist education courses in Iceland might thus be said to fall into three categories:

1. University degree courses that are a regular part of the curriculum in two universities.
2. Continuing education courses that are held intermittently, sponsored either by journalist associations or media companies. The most highly respected courses are run by the NJC in Aarhus and at Reykjavik University.
3. Courses in communications studies and communications technology, taught as options in upper secondary schools.

Who are the educators? – Training for journalists today

Of the three types of media course mentioned above, the university course and the continuing education teaching carry more weight than the upper secondary school course, although the latter can also be significant sometimes. However, statistics indicate that fewer than 20 per cent of journalists have only an upper secondary school matriculation certificate, while almost 63 per cent have a university degree of some sort (Figure 1.) The secondary school course may be regarded as important preparation for a course in journalism or a university degree course rather than being a professional qualification in itself for Icelandic journalists.

As stated above, two universities include degree courses in journalism in their curricula: the University of Iceland, located in Reykjavik, in the southwest of the country, and the University of Akureyri, in the north. The courses offered by these two state universities are somewhat dissimilar.

The University of Iceland

The University of Iceland offers two study programmes. The first is a one-year theoretical foundation course in Communications Studies. It is a module that yields 60 ECTS credits, and it can be taken alongside the principal programmes worth 120 credits. Candidates must gain 180 ECTS credits to graduate with a BA. The course is academic and closely linked to sociology teaching. It covers social science theories and the results of research into the role of the media, its power and its influence (Broddason 2008).

The second study programme is a two-year vocational and theoretical second degree leading to an MA in journalism and news editing, requiring 120 ECTS credits. This course concentrates primarily on issues that directly concern journalists, both in theory and in practice. The subjects covered on the course include news editing, print media and broadcast media. An important element of the course is a work-placement within a media company. In the past few years, part of the course has been a 30-credit master's project in two parts: a theoretical section and some sort of media production, which could be a television programme, a series, or a collection of articles made up of published media items.

Communications Studies teachers are primarily academic staff, but part-time lecturers who are professional journalists working in the field of media are responsible for the practical side of the course. The master's course is supervised by a highly experienced journalist who also has an academic background (University of Iceland 2008).

University of Akureyri

The University of Akureyri offers a three-year BA degree. It covers general Social Science theory as well as allowing students to acquaint themselves with current media practices. During their first year, students follow a general academic foundation programme in Social Sciences. In addition, they take an introductory module in Media Studies (University of Akureyri 2008a).

The latter course is closely linked to working media, especially local media. In their second and third years, students are introduced to the infrastructures of a range of media types, and they familiarize themselves with the technology necessary for working in those fields. Students also take courses in print media, broadcasting and new media techniques. All these courses are taught by experienced media professionals. A number of compulsory courses are taught concurrently. They include media reporting, a history of the media, and legal and ethical frameworks. In addition, first and second-year students contribute to a special internet publication, which is part of the course curriculum. Teaching on the reporting courses is handled both by full-time lecturers and part-time staff who have experience in journalism along with an academic background. Other theory courses are taught by teachers from the Humanities and Social Sciences departments (University of Akureyri 2008b). The University of Akureyri complies with the requirements of the European Credit Transfer System.

Continuing education

Unlike the systems that are in place in other Nordic countries, there are no special provisions for continuing education for media professionals in Iceland, and no institution specialises in this field. The continuing education system has been built up in a different manner. Funds give journalists the capability to attend courses that are generally available in the public market or within the education system, both in Iceland and in other countries. Continuing education is like a box of chocolates: with the assistance of union funds, journalists can choose a tasty-looking morsel that fits their interests and abilities.

However, two interesting possibilities worth mentioning do exist: a course provided by Reykjavik University and another at the Journalist School in Aarhus. Since 2006, Reykjavik University has worked with 365 Media, a media company based in Reykjavik, to offer a number of courses that are taught by nationally-recognized journalists and which give ECTS credits. The courses constitute a series of independent lectures rather that a unified programme and they do not lead to any particular qualification. The most noteworthy choice of course is strictly speaking not an Icelandic solution. It is the result of Nordic co-operation. The Nordic Journalist Centre in Aarhus has run an eight-week course for many years. It covers a wide range of subjects, and many Icelandic journalists have received grants from the Icelandic Union of Journalists to attend these classes. This is further facilitated by a clause in Icelandic journalists' contracts that gives them paid leave for almost three months when they have completed five years in a professional position. They receive similar leave after ten years and then at four-year intervals. The Icelandic Union of Journalists also allocates grants from its cultural fund, that individuals may use in any way they see fit, including to fund trips abroad.

However, the union's principal support mechanism is the Journalists' Continuing Education and University Fund, which was established at the end of the 1980s. Publishers contribute to the fund in line with contractual agreements with journalists. Grants are then made available to those who want to attend continuing education courses of some type. The fund's regulations allow grants for a range of courses, both long (more than one week) and short.

The union also sponsors its members to attend short courses in Iceland and abroad. There is no requirement for the courses to be directly connected to journalism; the objective is that the individuals in question improve their ability, for example by attending a language course (Icelandic Union of Journalists 2008; Jonsson 2008).

Concluding Remarks

One of the peculiarities of journalist training in Iceland is its short history and the extent to which interest in professionalism and education in the media has awakened during the last ten years or so. The reasons are first and foremost rooted in the unique history of the Icelandic media and the fact that the period of political party influence lasted almost until the turn of the century. For much of the 20th century, politics governed the press in this country. Political parties directly controlled the newspapers, most of which were little more than mouthpieces for political views (Fridriksson 1998). The airwaves were controlled exclusively by the Icelandic National Broadcasting Service (RUV) from 1930–86. RUV itself was held hostage by the political parties for most of that period; all discussions were carefully steered so that nothing of political weight was ever transmitted. In these circumstances, politics and political views were an important indicator of a person's ability to work in the media, while professionalism was not held in particularly high regard in the field. This changed rapidly as the politicians' hold on the media began to weaken and market views superseded political evangelism. The political standpoint shifted as the parties recognized the importance of a free press and sought new ways to communicate with the media. The privatization of mass media posed new questions about editorial independence in relationship to owner influence and advertizing power. A revolution in media markets swept across Iceland in 2001 when the first free daily newspaper was delivered to every household. The print market was transformed, while the rapid development of the Internet and digital techniques had a huge effect on the broadcasting sector (Gudmundsson 2007). A shrinking party-political press on the one hand, and growing market media on the other, combined to underline the importance of professional discussions about mass media at a national level; their independence had to be increased, as did the education of journalists. Another ingredient was added to this melting pot when an acrimonious political dispute emerged concerning the framework within which the media would operate in Iceland. The clashes reached a peak when the President of the Republic, Olafur Ragnar Grimsson, blocked new media legislation in June 2004 (Gudmundsson, B. and Eliasdottir, I., 2004). This issue remains unresolved five years later, although most of the heat has dissipated. The press and professionalism in journalism have been in the spotlight in Iceland for the last ten years, and this is reflected by the increasing number of graduates entering the profession. A university education in journalism is becoming far more important for entrants to the press corps than was previously the case and most graduates from courses of this type take up positions in the media (University of Akureyri 2008c).

Although the structure of continuing education courses has not changed during this period, there are clear indications of attempts to bridge the gap between the continuing education system and the universities. One example is the course offered by Reykjavik University. In this case, the union of journalists is using its fund in partnership with 365 Media and the university to provide a choice at degree level for working journalists. There is every reason to believe that these developments will continue, and that more bridges will be built between the two camps. The University of Akureyri, for instance, has announced that it will run a distance learning course worth up to 60 ECTS credits in the near future leading to a Diploma in Communication Studies. The course will be suitable for people in full-time employment. This will clearly become part of the continuing education system for journalists. Professional training for journalists in Iceland can be expected to strengthen during the next few years. Existing options in the country's schools and available continuing education will grow, as links with the universities improve.

The Author

Birgir Guðmundsson is an assistant professor of Media Studies at the University of Akureyri, Iceland.

Note

1. The school system in Iceland is divided into the following four stages: Play school up to six years old; elementary school for students ages 6–16 years; upper secondary school or high school, 16–20 years, which ends with a marticulation exam; and finally university.

References

Broddason, Thorbjorn (2008), 'A senior professor´s view on the history and content of media and communication studies at the University of Iceland', Personal communication (31 May).

Friðriksson, Guðjón (1998), 'Tímabil flokksfjölmiðla', In I. Guðmundur, J. Guðmundsson and Eiríkur K. Björnsson (eds.), Íslenska söguþingið, May 1997, Reykjavík: Sagnfræðistofnun Háskóla Íslands, pp. 28–31.

Friðriksson, Gudjón (2000), Nýjustu fréttir! Saga fjölmiðlunar á Íslandi frá upphafi til vorra daga, Reykjavík: Iðunn.

Gislason, Vilhjalmur Þ. (1948), 'Blaðamannafjelagið', In Vilhjálmur S. Vilhjálmsson (ed.) Blaðamannabókin 1948, Reykjavík: Bókfellsútgáfan.

Gudmundsson, Birgir and Eliasdottir, Ingibjorg (2004) "Fjölmiðlalög – góð eða vond?", In Úlfar Hauksson (ed.), Rannsóknir í félagsvísindum V, Félagsvísindadeild Háskóla Íslands, Háskólaútgáfan.

Gudmundsson, Birgir (2006), 'Fréttir ljósvakans í gíslingu flokksblaðamennsku', In *Þverfagleg ráðstefa í Háskóla Íslands í tilefni af útvarpi á Íslandi í 80 ár 11. Nóvember,* an interdisiplinary conference at the University of Iceland to commemorate 80 years of broadcasting in Iceland, 11 November, unpublished paper.

Gudmundsson, Birgir (2007), 'Inngangur – *Í spegli Tímans*', In Birgir Guðmundsson (ed.), *Íslenskir blaðamenn*, Reykjavík, Blaðamannafélag Íslands.

Haraldsson, Throstur (1987), 'Grúskað á safni. Slitrur úr sögu BÍ fram á sjötta áratuginn', *Blaðamaðurinn (Journal of the Union of Icelandic Journalists)*, 9(4).

Icelandic Union of Journalists (No date), Official website, 'Endurmenntun og styrkir', http: //press.is/page/styrkir. Accessed 18 June 2008.

Jonsson, Elías Snæland and Valdimarsson, Ómar (1987), 'Að efla faglegan metnað', *Blaðamaðurinn (Journal of the Union of Icelandic Journalists)*, 9(4).

Jonsson, Hjalmar (2008), 'The view of the manager and formert president of the Icelandic Journalist Union on the rules, regulations and history of education supportfunds of the Icelandic Union of Journalists', Interview (19 June).

Kristjánsson, Jonas (2008), 'The view of former Newspaper editor and chief organizer and instructor of journalism continuous education at the University of Reykjavík', E-mail (10 June).

Menntamálaráðuneytið /Ministry of Education (1999), 'Aðalnámskrá framhaldsskóla, almennur hluti, 1999', http: //bella.mrn.stjr.is/utgafur/AFalmennurhluti.pdf. Accessed 26 May 2008.

Menntamálaráðuneytið/ Ministry of Education (2004), 'Aðalnámskrá framhaldsskóla, almennur hluti, 2004', http: //bella.mrn.stjr.is/utgafur/Mmal.pdf. Accessed 26 May 2008.

Menntamálaráðuneytið /Ministry of Education (2008), 'Viðurkenning menntamálaráðherra á fræðasviðum háskóla', http: //www.menntamalaraduneyti.is/visindamal/vidurkenning/. Accessed 28 May 2008.

Stefánsdóttir, Sigrún (2008), 'The view of former professor and chief instructor and organizer of the Practical Journalism programme at the University of Iceland on the history and content of the programme', E-mail (3 July).

University of Akureyri (2008a), 'Social Sciences – Media studies', http: //english.unak.is/?d=5&m=page&f=viewPage&id=4. Accessed 15 June 2008.

University of Akureyri (2008b), 'Social Sciences – Media studies, staff members', http: //english.unak.is/?d=5&m=page&f=viewPage&id=100. Accessed 15 June 2008.

University of Akureyri (2008c), 'Fjölmiðlafræði', http://unak.is/skrar/File/Kynningarefni/fjolmidlafradi 2008.pdf. Accessed 15 June 2008.

University of Iceland (2008), 'Blaða– og fréttamennska', http: //www.hi.is/is/felagsvisindasvid_deildir/felags_og_mannvisindadeild/nam/framhaldsnam/11179. Accessed 16 June 2008.

The Luxembourgian Journalism Education Landscape

Mario Hirsch

There is neither formal nor institutionalized journalism education in Luxembourg. The formation of journalists is done on the spot in the various media. Among the 500 professional journalists recognized by the Press Council who are ipso facto holders of a professional card delivered by this institution, less than one-third have a university education and about 80 have followed studies in journalism and communication at foreign universities or specialized schools abroad.

There are no formal educational requirements to become a professional journalist for the time being. The main reason for the lack of formal education for journalists in the country has to do with the fact that until three years ago there was no university in Luxembourg. The University of Luxembourg does not offer as yet courses in journalism or communication. No plans exist in the foreseeable future to complete that gap.

For the past ten years the Press Council has been offering vocational training courses for aspiring journalists. The course is not compulsory and on average about ten young journalists make use of it every year. The courses on offer deal primarily with the institutional set-up of Luxembourg's political system, the judicial system and Luxembourg's foreign relations. After completion of these courses, a diploma is delivered by the Press Council.

The Press Council is eager to protect the title of professional journalist established by the 8 June 2004 Press Law and it is aware that something must be done to ensure proper qualifications and some kind of a minimal formation for journalists. It is of the opinion that an educational profile is required if one wants to protect the professional title of journalists, increasingly undermined by all kinds of people from freelance collaborators of the media and people working in the advertising sector.

The Press Council has published a 'Yearbook' of all the recognized journalists, which also contains the relevant legislation governing the profession.

The Author

Mario Hirsch is the director of the Institut Pierre Werner, a trinational cultural institute supported by France, Germany and Luxembourg.

References

Conseil de Presse (2008), *Annuaire des journalists*, Luxembourg: The Press Council.

The Netherlands Journalism Education Landscape

Gabriëlla Meerbach

Introduction

Twenty-first century Dutch journalists are no longer top-down oriented independent watchdogs who, by and large, dictate news and opinion or truth and morality to the public. Rather, they have become consumer-oriented marketers who invite citizens not only to participate but also to contribute professionally.

According to observations culled from actual curricula used by Dutch vocational journalism schools, their Anglo-Saxon journalism inspired breed are like spiders caught within a web of the many complexities of target groups in a multicultural/multiracial society. They keep an eye open for new trends occurring in all these diverse areas, track societal issues, act locally and, if not too Eurocentric, make an effort to be globally focused.

The new journalists keep in mind, more than ever, the commercial interests of their employers. While on management level white Caucasian male journalists still rule the roost, many more white Caucasian female journalists are to be found in the lower ranks. This breed of technological marvels in the flesh knows how to handle audio, visual or virtual equipment, preferably all at the same time, and has therefore become a really cost-effective vehicle for conveying news, information and entertainment or rather: infotainment.

In terms of education or training for their profession, where do these journalists originally come from and where are they likely to end up?

The origins of an academic versus a non-academic tradition

A curriculum for journalists? As Gods come to life, or at least seeing themselves as such, were journalists not justly empowered to rule unchecked over the destiny of their own craft? One typical and revealing classical line making the rounds in the Netherlands from the mid-nineteenth to mid-twentieth century indeed pitted beleaguered dug-in, die-hard practitioners against entrenched, dogged pro-education trailblazers. A curriculum for journalists? Don't make me laugh.

For worse rather than for better, journalists and poets in the nineteenth century were lumped together. Although notoriously lacking in basic creative literary skills, journalists were branded 'artists'. Perversely enough, they also role-modelled as educators and members of society, a popular saying even purporting that, 'Once a teacher, a priest, or a social worker, next a journalist'. An all-male craft during that era, journalism was also characterized as a badly paid sector, befitting a bachelor's lifestyle only. The upgrading of working conditions in the 1880s and 1890s led to the improvement of professional quality and social empowerment. Consequently, educational issues cropped up on the agenda of newspapers, unions and universities as early as 1900. So very much in tune were press and political party then that any editor-in-chief anywhere in the country would automatically become a political leader in his own right and ipso facto a potential member of parliament or the First Chamber.

The most emblematic and frequently cited example of this phenomenon was the journalist and Anti-Revolutionary Party (ARP) card-holder Abraham Kuyper, editor-in-chief of his own newspaper *De Standaard*, who would later become Minister of the Interior. Kuyper 'the journalist' also had tenure at Amsterdam's Free University (VU), argued in favor of an academic path to journalism and advocated for the granting of a press-related doctoral degree. Nonetheless it took more than half a century before the same VU finally hosted a Press Science chair in 1957. Charles Boissevain, a self-educated man and chief editor of the daily *Algemeen Handelsblad*, was Kuyper's greatest adversary. Taking up arms against exams and diplomas in journalism, Boissevain instead promoted learning by doing, in other words, beginning as a reporter at a small newspaper and rising through the ranks. The true journalist, in his view, was born, not educated.

Kuyper's academic views had been challenged, notably in 1903 with the first attempt by the Dutch Journalism Circle (*Nederlandsche Journalistenkring* <NJK>)[1] to set up a non-academic path to the profession. Addressing the needs of the print press only, this initiative resulted in the launching of a two-pronged programme combining one practical on-the-job training programme and one theory-supported scientific programme.

Societal roots: Segmented pluralism or 'pillarization'

The media industry in all its aspects was part and parcel of Dutch society. This sector and its multiple-track evolution reflected the political developments of twentieth century society. To quote Brants and McQuail,

> The recent history of press and broadcasting is closely intertwined with the socio-political developments of the past 90 years, summarized in that one word for the kind of social system almost unique in the Netherlands: 'pillarization'. Dutch society between the beginning of the twentieth century and the mid-1960s (especially the first 20 years after the Second World War) was a principal example of 'segmented pluralism', with social movements, educational and communication systems, voluntary associations and political parties organized vertically (and often cutting through social strata) along the lines of religious and ideological cleavages. Unlike the two religious groups, Calvinists and Catholics, the Socialists incorporated only one class on the basis of a clearly class-bound ideology. From a social-economic point of view, the liberal 'pillar' was the mirror-image of the socialist one. (1997: 154)

Within this societal context, the first half of the twentieth century was, to a certain extent, dominated by a tireless three-directional battle to shape, institutionalize and systemize journalism education. It was waged against the proponents of the vision of journalism as a God-given vocation. Heated debates about these issues occurred during:

- 'Union-driven', in-house practical discussions at regional and national levels on issues such as upgrading print press professionals, starting as early as 1910.
- 'University-driven', out-of trade-based theoretical discussions on issues such as academic and non-academic approaches to training and the question of backdoor, religion-related university education held by the University of Amsterdam and Nijmegen. Battles over the relevance of journalism education remained notably confined to the realm of print. All the way up to World War II, discussions focused more on scientific education, while practical training was simply dropped from the agenda (Hemels 1972). There was a simple reason for this. 'Supermen', as the Dutch journalists were in their own eyes, did not need practical training. In their essays they loved to define their own qualities in terms of such characteristics as intuition and high-standing moral principles, in conjunction with dynamic feelings, and a sense of rhythm. Alongside the male journalists writing about themselves, there was a lone female voice, which belonged to a journalist named Emmy Belinfante. She stood for a more progressive approach, even suggesting that all graduate schools should have a department of journalism and offer a doctoral course in print media (Belinfante 1931).
- 'Interest group-driven' discussions on Roman Catholic-, Calvinist-, Liberal-, or Socialist-linked 'pillarization' and ecclesiastical confessionalization of society and the media.
- The arrival on stage of 'new media' such as radio in the 1920s through the convergence of radio amateurs and the telecommunication industry (Philips) resulted in quite a different media landscape from the 1930s on. As described by Brants and McQuail,

In 1930 the government made special rules for radio in which only broadcasting corporations with strong ties to [set] targeted streams in society were allowed on the air: the VARA for the Socialists, the KRO for the Catholics, the NCRV and the VPRO for the Protestants. The AVRO, originally born out of commercial interests, aspired to be a national broadcasting corporation, but in reality had strong links with the bourgeois-liberal sphere. (1997: 154)

This media landscape was to undergo an even more dramatic change when the cinema came on the scene as yet another competitor for the press to face.
- 'Nazi-Germany's' unprecedented direct interference from 1940–1945.
A 1941 Journalism Decree issued by the Nazi rulers officially profiled journalists in the Netherlands in reference to education, experience, accountability to 'His Master's Voice', age and native cultural background. Narrowly circumscribed, the term 'journalists'

instantly surfaced in a *Berufsverbot* tightly worded in order to explicitly exclude Jews and keep out other 'non-native' elements.

Post-war developments

A spate of post-war purges rid newsrooms of generations of journalists who had sided with the enemy. Started in August 1945, post-war discussions about creating schools continued. Once again, ideas emerged around connecting practical training and back-door religion-related university education. They fizzled, as did many other initiatives.

Whilst prior to World War II it was seen as rather unbecoming to combine professional education with university mass communication studies, this idea resurfaced as an imperative from 1945-onward and even featured within the curricula at Amsterdam, Groningen, Nijmegen and Utrecht universities.

From 1945 onwards the pattern in journalism education evolved as follows:

1. Extension of education from print media to the fields of now institutionalized electronic media (radio and television), cutting-edge computer-based new media, and communication;
2. Initiatives to formalize journalism education taken by the Federation of Dutch Journalists (FNJ), later renamed the Dutch Union of Journalists (NVJ);
3. Introduction of university curricula and mass communication-focused journalism education;
4. Introduction of a higher level strictly vocational BA followed by a post BA based MA in journalism education;
5. Renewed discussions about academic versus non-academic training;
6. 'Depillarization' (*ontzuiling*) and ecclesiastical 'deconfessionalization' of both media and education and a new need: developing a multicultural profile;
7. Demonstration of a trade-led need to reorient journalism education in light of significant changes affecting different tasks for journalists that now include new media, a multimedia approach and internationalization as well as civic and citizen journalism.

Democratization, depillarization and the union's role in setting up the first school

During the fifties, professional institutions were still very much organized along the same 'pillarized' lines: Catholics had their Catholic Dutch Journalism Circle (KNJK) and Protestants their Protestant Christian Journalism Circle (PCJK) whilst the *Dutch* Journalism Circle (NJK) catered to a reputedly neutral national constituency. NJK's report about creating a joint institution was only endorsed by the others to the extent that their own religious outlook on life (theological and church history for Catholics) found expression within it.

The end of the 1950s and the beginning of the 1960s were characterized by the implementation of several versions of a report initiated by the neutral Federation of Dutch Journalists (FNJ). In 1965, FNJ joined hands with the *National Daily Press* employers' organization (NDP) to create the first ever extra-academic School of Journalism in the Netherlands in Utrecht. However, as the so-called roaring sixties heralded a democratization process in education, the first ten years were tumultuous. Former colleague Marianne Peters (and former EJTA President) reminisces jokingly, 'It would be hard today to trace back any student file of that era it being considered undemocratic at the time to keep such a file.' The process of democratization was felt in all sectors of the society.

Thanks to the loosening of religious and ideological ties, the confessional pillar-based polarized architecture of journalism changed dramatically towards the end of the 1960s. Party press and broadcasting systems were consequently 'de-pillarized'. National dailies such as *De Volkskrant, Trouw, Het Vrije Volk, De Tijd* all ended narrow ties to a given political party or church. The 'old' broadcasting corporations (NCRV, KRO, VARA) followed suit, albeit with a ten-year delay.

The profession's profile was also changing, with those who had no prior education in the field calling themselves journalists. Bakker and Scholten (1997) find a perfect fit in the fact that the first regular educational institution was founded around that time. Journalism changed from a calling into a profession. Journalists therefore had to be highly educated and no longer just party-people. However, parallel to that development, the complaints around issues of quality have increased. Across the spectrum this was an opportune call for democratization and it was heeded, as Brants and McQuail write,

> While political parties had to change their campaign politics, press and broadcasting engaged in a struggle for as large a public as possible, while radio and TV pirates disturbed the tenuous balance of the system by broadcasting from the North Sea. (1997: 154)

Dutch society itself was implicated in these changes. Culture became more international, the churches grew empty. Mass media adopted an informative function, rather than an ideological and socialising one. In 1965, the confessional Liberal Government stumbled over its own conservative approach and licensed new non-confessional broadcasting corporations, allowed the introduction of commercials and permitted co-operation amongst broadcasting license-holders. In that year, On Air Publicity Foundation (STER) became a fact of life, although the first commercial was only broadcast on television in 1967 and on radio in 1968, as J. H. J. van den Heuvel (1995) described those events. The same year witnessed the renaming of the Dutch Journalism Circle into 'Dutch Union of Journalists' (Nederlandse Vereniging van Journalisten, NVJ).

The 1970s were characterized by an increasing openness that translated into an internal competition within the media sector. Government became more actively involved in policy making. Pluralism and diversity – more the unintentional side-effect than the preliminary goal of the 'pillarized' system – became the buzzwords of the day. These pivotal years were marked by concentration within the media. In broadcasting, it was sandwich-formula time – infotainment in its foetal form. As far as education was concerned, the (neutral) Utrecht school occupied a unique position, trying hard to be taken seriously by a business sector itself trying hard to wean itself away from its long-held and deeply rooted conviction that only those 'born-journalists' still ruling the newsrooms were worthy of being named journalists of quality. Once again, some voices raised the question of freedom of education and religion. It was in fact on that very basis that two new schools were designed and established, the south-based Catholic 'Academy of Journalism' in Tilburg (its current full name being: 'Fontys Hogeschool Journalistiek') opened in 1980 and, in 1981, a north-based Protestant one started in Kampen as well before resettling in Zwolle. In addition to Zwolle the Evangelic Broadcasting Corporation, or EO felt a need to create yet another Bible-inspired institution, first located in Amersfoort and then since 1995 a part of the Christelijke Hogeschool Ede.

The Dutch vocational schools in today's media landscape

A mind-boggling proliferation of new technology, information and communication tools has been brought to the audiences: web-based newspapers, (interactive) radio and television, broadcast and narrowcast, blogging and vlogging, social networks and community sites. In other words: globalization through the Internet.

An increasing orientation towards the interests and participation of target groups (civic journalism) has had an immense impact on the form and content of all journalistic media. Developments such as growing commercialization, technological innovations, decline of traditional newspaper-readership, free media, lifestyle media, web-based journalism and the pro-active access of citizens (Citizen Journalism) to new media impose on the professional journalist of today and tomorrow the need for yet other different, basic, ethical, analytical and technical skills.

How do the Dutch schools deal with this reality? Today in The Netherlands one could enroll in a complete Bachelor's (BA) programme offered by four different public vocational schools, where the oldest 'neutral' School voor de Journalistiek is still located in Utrecht (1965). The Fontys Hogeschool Journalistiek Tilburg and the Hogeschool Windesheim in Zwolle schools still bear the imprint of their respective original religious legacies. Tilburg does not promote any catholic identity, and instead questions the journalist's role, place, accountability and responsibilities within a multicultural society. It has also created a chair called: 'Interculturality and quality of journalism' (comp. Evers 2005).

Zwolle's original protestant colors shine through the school's vision in matters such as societal responsibility, training in civic journalism and institutionalized cooperation with the protestant university Free University of Amsterdam (VU). The most recent and numerically smallest institution, Christelijke Hogeschool Ede, chooses to be explicitly different by remaining strongly connected to its Christian protestant identity in content and pedagogical approach, as well as explicitly addressing the journalistic responsibility of its graduates to contribute in building a different, more humane society.

(2008) Utrecht seats about 360 first-year students, Zwolle 325, Tilburg 285 and Ede 65, the four sites totaling 1035 places (with numerus clausus, or a 'closed number' of students being admitted, apart from Ede). About 60% of the students are female. Tilburg also runs a four-year evening BA diploma programme attended mainly by active professionals or working enrollees from other sectors of the marketplace (50 places per year). Up to 60% of the students pass their first year. On average, the output of the larger schools is 120 to 150 students graduating with diplomas per year.

All the schools cited above reflect the newsrooms of the nation where a predominantly white Caucasian profile is a fact of life. When the schools introduced affirmative action, that initiative failed. In addition, the so-called 5% norm (allowing direct admission of 5% of students from minority groups without numerus clausus) no longer exists.

Why are there not more non-native Dutch citizens choosing a future in the media? Is it a matter of identity and language skills and just a matter of time before they opt for their own media and schools? Is it a question of low earnings? Do they think this sector lacks authority? Far more young lawyers than journalists (especially women), who come from a Moroccan or Turkish background, seem to be graduating.

Some freshly minted 'not to miss or misconstrue' buzzwords within the vocational schools of today are both media and didactics oriented: 'new media', 'convergence', 'cross-media newsroom', 'multicultural journalism' in conjunction with 'competence directed learning', 'extensive teaching,' and 'tutoring'. Based on the shared approach of learning-by-doing, project-, theme- or problem-based training is more or less carried out much the same way in all four polytechnics. Overall focus (basic, medium, beginners levels) is on professional competence and directed learning under headings such as choosing, organizing, collecting, selecting, evaluating, reflecting (upon the métier and societal developments) and working in a team/newsroom. Theory is taught in political science, history, law, sociology, economics, philosophy, psychology, human sciences and languages alongside journalistic skills such as news gathering and reporting, interviewing techniques and feature writing.

Traditionally, during the first year, emphasis in most schools is placed on all the basic professional skills needed, followed by a broadening of the lens in the post introductory year with more emphasis placed on embracing all media (print; electronic; new media). The third and fourth years are reserved for in-depth theoretical and medium-specific specialization courses. Currently every institution's attention is focused on integrating computer-based media in its journalism curriculum through a 'multimedia' or 'cross media newsroom' approach. Professional education is completed subject to one or two internships.

The differences between these institutions lie in their didactic structuring, extensive or intensive teaching, tutoring, theoretical approach and thematic choices. Other differences include the choices they make in explicitly or implicitly profiling their identity in terms of content, research purposes or in their selection of a Scientific Chair. The latter is also a relatively new phenomenon and illustrates a new kind of synergy between non-academic and academic education. Utrecht, the oldest, remains the biggest institution and also claims to be the only one out of the four that offers specializations in photography and editorial design.

Educational reform and economic measures or simple cuts by the Ministry of Education have put unbearable pressure on both lecturers and administrators. Nico Drok (lecturer at Zwolle): 'Within 27 years I saw the lecturer-student ratio changing from 1–12 to 1–36.' Nevertheless Zwolle is able to project yet a broader market profile for itself as a School of Media, emphasizing an innovative time-effective student-friendly routing for either HAVO and VWO students or journalism and communication professionals. It has also created a full-fledged BA (Bachelor's) + MA (Master's) programme in collaboration with the Free University of Amsterdam.

Tilburg was one of the earliest to master labour intensive modular and project education. Nowadays its innovations are in the didactics of extensive teaching and it has also invested in the developing of tools for a (self-) learning community within an electronic cross medial newsroom, as director Wiel Schmetz points out.

According to the personal testimony of Bartho de Looij, coordinator of education in Ede, he counts its being 'convincingly different' and remaining a small-scale Christian operation with a profitable lecturer-student ratio among Ede's blessings (1–22).

The four vocational schools work together with the Department of Journalism in the University of Groningen (Masters or MA programme) to spread internships across the Industry (TUZEG).

Who's getting the job?

Significantly, the traditional, century-old discussion on education-based and theoretical knowledge versus practical training is still very much alive. According to the latest Dutch Union's survey (NVJ 2008), carried out among 140 alumni from TUZEG institutions (the four vocational schools and the University of Groningen), employers prefer novices with an academic background to those with a background in vocational training, but they also consider practical experience more important than a diploma. However their first choice would be a beginner with both a journalistic educational background and working experience with a local newspaper or broadcasting corporation. Students often start their first job at a local or regional broadcasting station even before they graduate. While job opportunities with dailies have declined dramatically, the new media niche has opened up more promising territory for young journalists.

With just any degree – whether it is in history, politics or sociology – considered enough to enter the trade, and even no degree at all being acceptable, one might well ask why there are so many institutions. The reason is that graduates, wherever they land, generally arrive well prepared for the challenges they might face and are usually capable of doing much more than pass the proverbial pot of glue. What do these graduates really think, though, about the quality of their former schools, and how prepared do they feel for their future jobs?

Among journalism graduates, according to the same survey by NVJ, 13 per cent are jobless or studying again. Also according to those alumni, schools still concentrate too much on traditional newspaper journalism and too little on a multimedia approach. They consider their education as 'okay', but feel that sometimes it is not up-to-date enough, because their teachers either are not working in media or are no longer working with the media.

The staff in all schools consists of an assortment of (former) journalists, academics and technical workers. Within schools the following basic questions still remain: Should we put more into in-depth theory or practice? Should staff members take refresher courses or pursue internships so that they can keep up both with the rapid changes in their discipline and students who are increasingly knowledgeable about the world?

The profession tomorrow: Educational issues

As Irene Costera Meijer (University of Amsterdam) puts it,

In a world of abundance of it, information itself loses importance. While inspiration, the feeling to belong and lead a meaningful life become more important. We evaluate to an economy of experience or perception. Media will have to master the art of creating appealing perceptions of the environment. Not only to reach young people, but everybody. If they do not, they will be doomed to die. (free translation from Drok 2007: 131)

Citizenship is changing. As more mature consumers, citizens are developing new information needs and are dealing differently with the institutional world of traditional media. Apart from that, not only do they have proactive access to technology, they are also becoming influential producers themselves: for example, citizen journalists are becoming a significant source of information and might even be considered competition for mainstream journalism.

The job itself has become more and more individualized, as journalists are held more and more individually accountable both for the production process and for providing their own technological support. Employers (NVJ 2008) explicitly value alumni who improve on their language and presentation skills, have specialized knowledge, show a capacity for building and extending networks and also demonstrate knowledge of Content Management Systems (CMS) as well as evidence of target group oriented thinking.

New citizens and new technology demand new professional standards for gathering, selecting, writing and producing as a whole. Given that reality, the way journalists are trained, of necessity, has to undergo similar changes. The relevance of the curriculum became a prime issue. The norm is for vocational schools to have up to a 25 per cent margin of freedom to invest in theory or particularities (called 'minors') of their choosing into their curricula. The remaining 75 per cent covers the obligatory programmes ('majors').

Narrowly concentrated vocational schools or Institutions of Higher Professional Education (HBO) should slowly change into business-oriented enterprises with a healthy commercial, partly privatized base and focus more on the national or world market. Choices can be driven either by economic cycles or defined by effect finance. That scenario, however, raises new dilemmas about preserving standards. Those opposing change fear that too much market orientation could easily prostitute the profession. For example, does the market prefer lifestyle magazines rather than institutional life-oriented traditional dailies? Very well, we will deliver lifestyle specialists. Then the question arises again, what does that do to quality journalism?

Quality control: The role of the union, the employers and accreditation for Higher Education

Whilst few may consider traditional journalists an endangered species (comp. Gillmor 2006), the majority simply pleads for a reliable selection and control mechanism to uphold the quality of 'traditional institutional life journalism'.

To assure quality-control within the Netherlands and beyond, in alliance with other organizations, the Dutch Union of Journalists NVJ concentrates mostly on matters related to employment, in-house newsroom rules, ethics and juridical as well as financial or other support for freelance journalists. The union attaches great importance to in-house rules as the best means of protecting both professional integrity and journalistic independence.

In fact, the processing of in-house rules had already started in the 1960s and had become the norm within dailies as well as many magazines, with broadcasting corporations following suit at a much later date. VPRO was the first big corporation with a full-fledged newsroom or programme charter in 1994. Soon IKON, RTL4-News, the World Broadcasting Corporation and NOVA also joined in, as did the Daily Planet Edition of Internet provider Planet Internet (Bakker and Scholten 1997).

Although it prescribed no particular code of ethics, NVJ deferred to the internationally accepted Code of Bordeaux. For the sake of quality control, however, it joined hands with other national organizations such as the publishers of dailies the NDP, the Dutch magazine publishers NOTU, the Dutch Broadcasting Corporation's NOS, the Dutch National News Press NNP and the Union of Dutch Chief-Editors to create a Council for Journalism (Raad voor de Journalistiek), an independent complaint commission that hears the general public's grievances against the media, albeit without any power at all to pass sentence.

As regards freelancers, the title only designates practitioners who log a minimum of 20 hours a week and earn no less than 50% of an adult minimum wage. Some alumni (NVJ 2008) have pleaded for more information about how to run a freelance practice and more knowledge about the juridical implications (rights and obligations) of their métier. Criteria applicable to their status in terms of quality or for the purposes of educational references are generally not yet available or they are not open either to information officers working for non-profit outfits and the public sector. Though not yet eligible for union membership, journalism students are already reaping some union benefits.

NVJ and employers' organizations work closely together with the Dutch schools of Journalism as attested by a joint production for the HBO Raad (Council for Higher Learning) (2004). The synergy in the educational approach of the four schools (Tilburg, Utrecht, Zwolle, Ede: TUZE) is found in the description of a Professional Competence Profile. In this document they have formulated standards for a professional profile as well as basic curriculum and a joint educational approach. Both NVJ and employers have agreed on the content.

As far as the quality of their education is concerned, the schools have been certified by the 'Nederlands-Vlaamse Accreditatie Organisatie' (NVAO). The NVAO is an independent bi-national public institution that judges and guarantees the quality of Higher Education in the Netherlands and Dutch-speaking institutions in Belgium and promotes Higher Education in both national and international circles.

New markets and providers for education and retention in journalism and communication

New services are being developed for diversified groups at the postgraduate or extra graduate level. New clients are now to be found among alumni who enrol in: refresher courses or mid-career and journalism management courses. Courses for different professional groups such as police or politicians have already been a reality for almost two decades. Nowadays, clients of the schools can be journalists and communications specialists or, in fact, anyone who is expected to know how to deal with journalists and communicate with the public.

According to a publication on the Internet by the NVJ (webadress: http: //www. villamedia.nl/opleidingenkaart), journalism education in The Netherlands now has many interconnecting and intersecting strands. Apart from the four vocational schools of Journalism and The University of Groningen (TUZEG), the publication includes the Erasmus University of Rotterdam and the University of Amsterdam which offer MA journalism courses. Windesheim Zwolle has come together with the Free University of Amsterdam (VU) to offer a joint BA and MA programme. The University of Leiden offers a practical study programme in journalism and the Centre for Communication and Journalism of the Polytechnic of Utrecht offers academic courses as well. The School of Journalism in Utrecht offers 'minors' to students of the University of Utrecht.

Many public schools and individuals, as well as privately-run organizations, offer commercial courses, workshops such as journalistic writing skills, interviewing, writing for the Internet and photography. The Media Academy in Hilversum is the one with the longest experience in this field. A new commercial initiative, a three-year BA programme, is being implemented by INHOLLAND Select Studies in Rotterdam (ISS).

Local and global

Internationalization is now one of the buzzwords in all the schools. Tilburg, Utrecht and Zwolle are but three out of 48 member-institutions belonging to The European Journalism Training Association (EJTA). From the start they have cultivated a special relationship with the association, which was established in Brussels in 1990. They nurtured and raised it and currently preside over it. The Association is a non-profit organization and a legal body under Dutch Law. EJTA's Tartu declaration (2006) defines a common ground for member institutions and, in its appendix presents a professional competence profile, which in many ways is an elaboration of the professional competence profile developed by Dutch Schools and employers in 2004 (HBO Raad).

Running a school in the Netherlands without an international curriculum has simply become impossible under the justified imperative of educating students for the world at large rather than the home market alone. Although, originally, journalism education was Europe-centered, due to the mere fact that funding had always come first and foremost from the Ministry of Education and the European Union, heeding globalization's call, the sole alternative route to survival remains an escape through and beyond the walls of the European fortress. Some schools already offer a comprehensive international programme, while others are expanding on a 'cafeteria model' (fast food approach, pick some ingredients of your liking and go), depending on their bilateral connections with media and educational institutions scattered here and there around the world.

Some highlights: Ede has begun to collaborate with Hungary (radio) and with the Potchefstroom University in South Africa. In addition to a City Trips and European Programme, the Tilburg-based School runs an Africa-focused Programme and facilitates internships in Indonesia. Zwolle provides study and exchange programmes with a European perspective in the United States, Egypt, South Africa and Namibia and has prospects for including other world regions and countries. Utrecht has a specialization programme in European Culture and European Journalism and together with the Danish School of Journalism hosts an international programme for foreign students called: Europe in the World.

Concluding Remarks

This chapter[2] examined various facets and phases of a more than a century-long development of academic and non-academic journalism education in The Netherlands. It is a development at all times deeply steeped in and watermarked by three all-encompassing phenomena: 'perceived democratic identity, (de)pillarization, and new media'.

Pillarization or segmented pluralism marks twentieth century Dutch perceptions of democratic identity through the society's adhesion to egalitarianism by way of inclusively extending equal rights, equal societal freedoms and the freedom of expression to every individual and all groups. For instance, each ideological or religious group is granted full and unabridged rights and the freedom to form a political party of its own, run a newspaper of its own and create schools of its own, thus laying a foundation for home-grown sectarianism or compartmentalization.

From the 1960s on, both society and the media depillarized and deconfessionalized. The educational system followed suit, during the same period that The Netherlands was developing from a mono-cultural to a multi-cultural society searching for new parameters to mark its political and social identity.

If the twentieth century was marked by the shaping, institutionalizing and systemizing of academic and non-academic journalism education for print media as well as new media like radio, television and cinema respectively, the priority of the late-twentieth and early-twenty-first century lies instead in dealing with making changes that can accommodate both citizen participation and other citizen initiatives, given prospects for the imminent arrival of even more cutting-edge virtual media and technology on the scene. Although 'multimedia' skills are now demanded by business, creating a need for technical answers from the educational system, there is a risk of overlooking the very real changes inherent in having to deal with diversified interest groups and a mobilized public which pro-actively creates its own (citizen) media.

The Author

Gabriella Meerbach is an independent researcher and international consultant. She taught for almost 20 years at Fontys Hogeschool Journalistiek (Tilburg), was member of the Board of the Professional Education Section of the IAMCR in the nineties; next worked for Radio Netherlands Training Centre as coordinator of training projects; currently she manages Media on the Spot (MOS). MOS fosters bottom-up communication for participatory democracy through innovative use of both traditional and new media, within young democracies and countries in development. She is a member of the International Editorial Advisory Board of AEJMC's Journalism & Mass Communication Educator.

Notes

1. NJK was founded in 1884 as a club and developed in few decades into a professional organization. It suspended its activities in 1940, resuming them in 1945. In 1968 it took its present name of Nederlandse Vereniging voor Journalisten (NVJ).
2. This chapter is both a summary and an update of 'The Development of Journalism in The Netherlands: A Century- Long Duel Pitting Beleaguered "Rejectionists" Against Pro-Education Proponents', In R. Fröhlich and C. Holtz-Bacha (2003).

References

Bakker, P., and Scholten, O. (1997), *Communicatiekaart van Nederland*, Houten/Diegem, Netherlands: Bohn Stafleu Van Loghum.

Belinfante, E.J. (1930), *De vrouw als journaliste*, Netherlands: Morks' Beroepenbibliotheek nr, 48, p.5, In Hemels (1972), p. 54.

Belinfante, E.J. (1931), *Holland, let op uw pers! Degelijke vorming van den journalist: een eisch van den tijd*, In Haagsch Maandblad, September 1931, pp. 266–277, in Hemels (1972), p.55.

Bierhoff, J., and Schmidt, M. (1996), *European journalism training in transition: the inside view*, Maastricht, Netherlands: European Journalism Centre.

Brants, K., and McQuail, D. (1997), 'The Netherlands', In Euromedia Research Group (ed.), *The Media in Western Europe. The Euromedia Handbook*, London: Sage, pp. 153–167.

Drok, N. (ed.) (2007), *De toekomst van de journalistiek*, Amsterdam, The Netherlands: Boom.

Evers, H. (2005), *Over interculturaliteit en kwaliteit van de journalistiek*, Tilburg: Fontys Hogescholen.

Evers, H. and Rennen, T. (ed.) (2005), *Journalistiek moet verder. Tien beschouwingen over journalistiek*, Nijmegen, The Netherlands: Valhof Pers.

Gillmor, D. (2006), *We the media. Grassroots journalism by the people, for the people.* California, USA: OReilly.

HBO Raad (2004), *Beroeps- en opleidingsprofiel Journalistiek*, The Hague, The Netherlands: HBO Raad.

Hemels, J. (1972), *De journalistieke eierdans*, Assen, Netherlands: Van Gorcum & Comp, N.V.

Meerbach, G. (2003), 'The Development of Journalism in The Netherlands: A Century- Long Duel Pitting Beleaugured "Rejectionists" Against Pro-Education Proponents', In Fröhlich, R. and Holtz-Bacha, C. (2003), *Journalism Education in Europe and North America. An international Comparison*, New Jersey, USA: Creskill.

NVJ, *Journalistieke Opleidingen/ Journalism Education in The Netherlands*, http: //www.villamedia.nl/opleidingenkaart/opleidingen-hbo.

NVJ (2008), *Startbekwaamheden van journalisten. Onderzoek onder alumni van de journalistieke opleidingen en werkgevers/ Skills for starting journalists. A survey among alumni from the journalism vocational schools and employers.* NVJ publication.

Rathenau Instituut, (1995), *Toeval of Noodzaak? Geschiedenis van de overheidsbemoeienis met de informatievoorziening/ Coincidence or necessity? History of government's interference with the provision of information*, Amsterdam, Netherlands: Otto Cramwinckel Uitgever.

The Norwegian Journalism Education Landscape

Gunn Bjørnsen, Jan Fredrik Hovden and Rune Ottosen

Introduction

Journalism is one of the most popular study programmes in Norway. There are several pathways into the Norwegian news industry for young people seeking a career in journalism, but it is increasingly common for aspiring journalists to start off with a journalism education. The trade union for journalists in Norway (NJ) organizes more than 90% of all working journalists. In 1992, only 19% of NJ members had journalism education, whereas by 1999 the number had increased to 30% (NJ/NR 1999: 9) and 48% in 2002 (Sørensen 2005). Even if there are still many journalists who come to the profession through other kinds of education and news room experience, the study of journalism has become an increasingly important pathway to the profession, especially to the national and larger regional media. The journalism schools (J-schools) evidently play a more and more significant role in the shaping of the Norwegian journalists of tomorrow.

In this chapter we will present the landscape of Norwegian journalism education, including a closer look at the content of the studies, the connection to the industry and the students of journalism themselves. The description of the students is based on a dataset from a series of questionnaires administered between 2000 and 2004 to three complete cohorts of Norwegian journalism students at Oslo University College and Volda University College, the largest and oldest J-schools in Norway.[1]

The past and present of Norwegian journalism education

Prior to the formal start of the first J-school in Oslo several shorter courses for journalists had been offered, organized by the industry itself from 1951 under the name of the Journalist Academy (*Journalistakademiet*). The first J-school, with duration of one year, was established in 1965. If relatively synchronous with the development in other Nordic countries, this is still quite late compared to many other western countries. Australia, for example, established their first journalism school in 1921. Both the journalism trade union and engaged editors and journalists played a central role in starting up and running the first state run school. The establishment of the first journalism school in Oslo was seen as an important step in the professionalization of journalists (Ottosen 1996).

The second J-school was established in the rural small town Volda in 1971 after a lot of discussion about both the content and the placement of the school (Alme et al. 1997). From this year on the state-run schools offered a two-year programme. It has been argued that the political focus on regional development in deciding the placement of this school weakened the possibility for the academic development of journalism and set the research at risk of being fragmented and little coordinated in a small country like Norway (Bjørnsen et. al 2007a, Ottosen 1997).

In 1987, the coastal towns of Bodø and Stavanger followed suit. In 2000 a separate journalism education was established for the indigenous Sami people at the Sami College in Kautokeino, recruiting Finnish and Swedish students as well. Finally, the University in Bergen established its own journalism programme in 2005, representing a more 'pure academic' flavour to the variety of journalism programmes.

Several private journalism programmes offering a bachelor-degree in journalism have also been established. The Christian institution Gimlekollen in Kristiansand established its own J-school, Gimlekollen School of Journalism and Communication, in 1981 and was approved as a credit point-giving private university college in 1996. This J-school is extraordinary in the way that it is run within a Christian framework. In 2000 an internationally oriented journalism programme started up at Bjørknes International College in Oslo. This was a joint venture between Bjørknes and The University of Queensland in Australia, where the students attended the first year in Norway and then completed the bachelor-degree with two following years of study in Australia.[2] In 2002 a journalism bachelor programme was founded at the Norwegian School of Management in Oslo. The profile of this study programme is an evident specialization; approximately half of the curriculum consists of economic and management topics.[3]

Cooperation between public and private actors should also be mentioned; e.g. a cooperation between Oslo University College and a private college (NKS) and a joint venture between Bodø University College and Folkeuniversitetet ('The people's college'). The division between public and private is thus to some extent blurred, also as the government encourages public institutions to offer journalism courses with a course fee.

The main institution for further education offering short courses for practising journalists is the Norwegian Institute of Journalism; 'a knowledge and resource centre for media practitioners' (The Norwegian Institute of Journalism 2008). The centre was established in 1975 by the principal media associations: The Norwegian Union of Journalists, The Association of Norwegian Editors and The Norwegian Newspaper Publisher's Association.

All the public J-schools in the Norwegian system had by around 2005 established a three year bachelor programme in line with the so called Bologna process.

A major (extended, two years duration; 'hovedfag') in journalism was established in 2000 as a joint venture between Oslo University College and Oslo University (Department of Media and Communication). As part of the agreement both institutions established one professor position each. The first professor in journalism in Norway was appointed in 1999 at Oslo University College. As a part of the Bologna process the major ('hovedfag') was renamed master in journalism as from 2003. The master programme is a two year programme with 60 ECTS points obtained through four courses and 60 ECTS points in writing the master thesis. The master programme qualifies as further higher education for journalists, a scientific career as media researcher and as teachers in the journalism educations.

In cooperation with University of Helsinki, University of Tampere in Finland and University in Örebro in Sweden, Oslo University College offers a programme in Global Journalism as a two year programme for journalists wanting to further their journalistic knowledge and skills focusing on international news reporting. The programme has a global focus and brings together professional journalists from Africa, Asia, North and South America, and North and Eastern Europe. The student's varying experience from different countries, cultures and media provide the basis for a discussion on differences in work practice and ethics, and shared problems and challenges for the journalistic profession.

Political regulations in the organization of Norwegian journalism education have been few except for the geographical placement of the teaching institutions. Regarding the content of the J-schools there is a high degree of autonomy and the government has had scarce impact compared with other vocational educations, as teachers and social workers (having quite detailed instructions about content through so called 'frame plans'). This may reflect that the strong idea of the free and independent press in Norway is valid in the education of journalists as well. There exist few regulations and a large degree of freedom from governmental control. This also strengthens the understanding of journalism as a semi-profession (Ottosen 2004).

Curricula between practice and theory

All the study programmes leading to a bachelor degree have a duration of three years of study, each year consisting of 60 ECTS points (total of 180 points). It has also, until 2009, been possible to complete only two years of study and achieve the degree 'University College graduate of journalism' ('høgskolekandidat').

The content of the education of journalists in Norway can largely be said to be characterized by being practically oriented with much weight on journalism as a craft. Theoretical and factual topics are taught mainly integrated with a journalistic perspective and seldom in academic depth.

In general the journalism training favours a so-called all round model. The young journalists mainly become generalists, not specialists. Nevertheless, the different journalism educations obviously also are diverse both regarding types of topics and subjects taught, teaching methods and medium specialization. One example of this is that the second largest journalism education in Volda offers more specialization in broadcasting, while in Oslo the largest J-school's main strength is in newspaper journalism.

The required readings in the different schools' study curricula are largely similar. The same basic book of journalism is mainly used throughout. There is also a common emphasis on training of ethical awareness. When it comes to other topics, and the weighing between them, the variety is larger. For instance there is more focus on scientific methods in Bergen, international affairs in Oslo and civic journalism in Volda.

Most of the J-schools put a lot of weight on the production side of the education with the aim to resemble the real life of the newsrooms. At the same time there has been a drive towards more research-based and academic content in the curriculum, especially in the last decade, from 'craft' to 'academic discipline'. To some extent, one might say that this doubleness represents a kind of 'schizophrenia' in the Norwegian journalism education of today. There is a challenge to balance the demands of the industry with the driving forces in the academic world.

The internship period is a vital part of the programme and lasts for two months. Many students consider the internship period to be the most important part of their studies, and experience also shows that it is often a gateway to the first job after completed studies.

Journalism education in Norway places heavy emphasis on preparing students to become critical watchdogs, and to adopt this function as part of their role as a journalist. In the curriculum and course literature, this watchdog function is underlined to such an extent that it is likely to affect students' attitudes, drilling into them the view that journalists should make a difference in society even though they may have other personal priorities. A strict demarcation is marked vis-a-vis media and communication studies in general and PR and information topics in particular.

When students are asked what 'they' believe are the important qualities for a journalist and a journalistic education, we can observe some patterns. At the beginning of their studies the students emphasize personal traits and professional knowledge. During their studies, they appear to substitute their initially more charismatic and professional ideals of the good journalist with a more practical, skills-based ideal. Also, press ethics appear increasingly important to them. When asked three years after graduation about how they retrospectively evaluate their education, 65% of the students express satisfaction. This is an increase of 15% from when they ended their studies (Bjørnsen, Hovden and Ottosen 2007).

The students: Middle class, ethnic homogenous and female

In Norway, the recruiting bias of the journalism profession – especially the predominance of middle- and upper-class socioeconomic backgrounds and left of centre political leanings – has been well-known for decades (Høyer 1982), and still persists today (Hovden 2008). Such bias in the social recruitment of journalists has, not surprisingly, been perceived as problematic, especially in the eyes of other elites. It is potentially compromising because it threatens journalists' public legitimacy, not only as 'objective' reporters of events – by the possibility of others linking social bias to a real or perceived 'journalistic bias' ('of course the leftist press will try to discredit conservative political parties') – but also through journalists' frequent claim of representing and defending 'the common people' against social elites (Petersson 1994).

We can summarize some of the social characteristics of journalism students from Volda and Oslo who started their studies in the years 1999–2001. So far as the 'basic demographics' are concerned, students of journalism in Norway are predominantly female, relatively young and ethnic Norwegians. While journalism education in Norway was male-dominated until the early 1980s, the proportion of women has been steadily rising. In the 1970s, only one in three Norwegian journalism students was female. In the 1980s, male and female students were roughly equal in numbers, but in the last fifteen years female students have been clearly in the majority. In 2001, they outnumbered male students by two to one.[4] This seems to be in line with international trends (cf. Splichal and Sparks 1994: 110).[5]

The mean age for new journalism students in 2000–2001 was 23–24 years, which is about average for students at universities and colleges. The students of journalism, however, appear particularly homogenous regarding age, as more than two-thirds were between 21 and 24 years (Bjørnsen 2003b: 31).

Journalism students are still an ethnically homogenous group: less than 3% says 'both' their parents were born abroad (quite low, compared both to the 6% national average for Norwegian students and to the proportion with a non-western minority background in the population as a whole – 19% in Oslo and 6% nationally (SSB 2006)). This skewed representation is perceived as a challenge, in parts of the education system, in some newsrooms and in the journalists' union (Bjørnsen 2003a).

Geographically, students appear to be fairly representative of the Norwegian population, both regionally (by county) and in term of city-peripheries, with a slight over-representation from the capital and the regions closest to the schools.

Regarding students' 'previous experience', findings illustrate the problems of a clear division between 'students' and 'professionals': more than half of the Norwegian students of journalism have undertaken paid journalistic work before starting their studies (predominantly in local and regional newspapers), and almost a third had worked for at least a year as a journalist.[6] These numbers are decreasing after the new system of intake to the J-schools was implemented. Now a special quota of 50% of the students' are being recruited almost directly from high school. This intake rule implies that half of the students are only 21 years old or younger when they start their studies.

Seventy-five per cent have completed some kind of university education before starting their journalism training. Of these, the large majority has completed only shorter studies (less than two years), mostly in the humanities (media and communication, history and languages being popular subjects) or – somewhat fewer – in the social sciences (political science or sociology) or psychology. Subjects from the natural sciences, or vocational subjects, are very rare.

Politically, students of journalism are more likely to vote for a radical socialist party than professional journalists are (and again, much more so than the general population), but not more than university students in the social sciences and humanities (Hovden 2002). Only 13% said they were 'very interested' in politics, indicating that political activism is not important to most Norwegian journalism students' choice of a journalistic career.

Even so, most journalism students appear to come from relatively privileged social backgrounds. If less a social elite than students of medicine and of the Norwegian School of Economics and Business Administration (NHH), their backgrounds appear markedly more privileged than those of other student groups at the university colleges (teaching, engineering, health/social studies). Compared to students in the social sciences and arts faculties, which are quite similar to journalism students in their social background, journalism students appear to have parents with somewhat more economic capital but less political capital.

Eighteen per cent of the students of journalism have a father or mother 'with journalistic experience'.[7] Even if this survey question is rather vague, the number still appears large compared to the 1 per cent of university students who have a father working in journalism or information. This suggests a tendency towards a direct social reproduction of the journalistic profession by the way of journalism studies.

Cooperation with the industry

All the established J-schools have established a system with training and internship in newsrooms. Both the schools and the industry support the idea that internship is an important contribution to the education. This is supported by the pedagogical notion in the schools that the importance of learning through practical work as a journalist is an important element in the education. It varies from school to school at what stage in the education the internship takes place. For example, at Oslo University College the internship is placed in the summer between the first and second year in the bachelor degree whilst in Volda the internship is placed in the last term in the third year in the curriculum.

Another important contact between the education field and the industry is that active journalists and editors regularly teach as guest lecturers at the campuses and also function as examiners during exams. The majority of the staff in the J-schools has a background as journalists themselves.

Many newsrooms also use students as extra staff while they study. Sometimes this can be a challenge for their education since the risk is always that when they get a chance to work as journalists their attention will be as much in the newsroom as the classroom. It could be discussed whether the relation between the industry and the J-school is asymmetrical. Since the J-schools are dependent on the industry to have agreements on internship there is always the danger that the industry decides the terms and wants to pick the candidates for internship themselves. Here is a potential conflict of interest since the J-schools try to implement the principle that all students have an equal right to internship whilst many newsrooms tend to look for the best students to get as much as possible out of the trainee period.

The possible asymmetry in the relation between the J-schools and the industry is also manifested in the challenge of balancing the aim to 'produce' journalists for the newsrooms and at the same time represent a critical correction to the news industry. This can also be seen as a version of the market vs. ideals dilemma in journalism (Ottosen 2004).

Another potential problem for the J-schools is in recruiting teachers from the industry. The teaching institutions can seldom compete with the industry on the wage level.

Networking among the J-schools

There is an active network between the established J-schools both at a national Norwegian level and at a Nordic level. The most important part of the networking is a biannual joint conference where the institutions meet and exchange experiences on teaching and curriculum issues. The institutions take turns in hosting the conference and the network is called 'Nordic journalism education'. Since the end of the cold war the Baltic countries to a certain degree have been included in the network (Hovden et al. 2009).

To some extent there is also student exchange where the Nordic J-schools open their courses for students from other countries. Through the Interlinks cooperation there is a programme for student exchange on master level between some Baltic and Nordic institutions. On the same level there is also a development in the direction of joint degrees. As an example University in Örebro, Sweden, Tampere and Helsinki in Finland and Oslo University College have a joint Global Master in Journalism mainly recruiting students from developing countries.

There are also several examples of joint research with the staff between Nordic institutions.

The Nordic Council has established a financial support system where they support research, student exchange, teacher exchange and joint meetings and seminars through a system called Nordplus.

Most J-schools in Norway are also members of the European Journalism Training Association (EJTA) and take part in annual meetings and conferences there.

Concluding Remarks

Summing up, Norwegian journalism education can be described as working quite well as measured by both the students' success in the job market and their expressed satisfaction with their studies (Bjørnsen, Hovden and Ottosen 2007b). The fact that the application rate for several years has been among the very highest compared with other university programmes also validates this point.

From the high percentage of the recently educated journalists who are able to get relevant – and in many cases permanent – jobs, there is also reason to be slightly optimistic about the future for young, newly educated journalists. However, there is obviously a discrepancy between where the newly educated end up, and what their first preference in the job market was. Those who preferred jobs in newsrooms in highly profiled newspapers and the larger broadcasting companies, sometimes have to settle for part-time jobs or less popular permanent jobs in local newspapers, professional magazines or online newspapers. But it is reasonable to believe that this might be the first step towards a career in their preferred jobs at a later stage.

It is fairly safe to say that the J-schools understand themselves to play an important role as a knowledge base and a critical corrective for the industry through publishing and participation in the public debate on issues related to journalism and through critical analyses of certain development trends in the industry such as commercialism and concentration of ownership, ethical issues etc. (Ottosen 2004).

The tendency is clearly that journalists are increasingly recruited to the industry through the J-schools (*Kunnskapsløftet*). This has the positive factor that it strengthens the professional identity and ethical level in the journalist community as a whole. A potential danger could be that the journalist profession as a whole becomes too conform and in the long run loses the individualists and nonconformists that have always provided the spice in the profession as a whole. It could also be argued that there is a potential danger that the education system as a whole educates generalists while a broader recruitment from other educations, professions and walks of life could secure a broader and more varied journalism community. Even though the J-schools appreciate that the level of education is rising, there is a general support of the idea that the journalist profession should be open and recruit staff with varied backgrounds.

There is a growing awareness that the journalism community and the J-schools should reflect the multicultural society. At the same time there is a long way to go before the recruitment of journalists with an ethnic minority background reaches a satisfactory level. This counts for both the J-schools and the newsrooms. Oslo University College has established an experiment with a quota system where five study places each year are earmarked for qualified minorities. This is a controversial system and is just a very small step on the road to a multicultural journalist community.

The trend is that the J-schools become more international to the extent that journalism students are now encouraged to take parts of their education abroad. To a certain extent the schools also receive exchange students, but mostly on a master level since most of the teaching is in Norwegian at the bachelor level. The increased level of internationalization is obviously an effect of the Bologna process which in itself stimulates internationalization.

The Norwegian J-schools have become what they are through a historical process where the struggle for academic independence has developed hand in hand with a will to be relevant and attractive for the industry. The process of change from the 1960s, when the education level was low and the available education weak, has been quite significant. The present development of academization (Zelizer 2004) of journalism as a trade and J-schools as institutions have given the J-schools self-confidence and autonomy, even though the power of the industry and the commercialism of the media sector with increased concentration of ownership causes concern and challenges for the future.

The Authors

Gunn Bjørnsen is a Ph.D. scholar at the Faculty of Media and Journalism at Volda University College.

Jan Fredrik Hovden is an associate professor at the Department of Information and Media Science at the University of Bergen and researcher II at the Department of Media and Journalism at Volda University College.

Rune Ottosen is a professor of journalism at Oslo University College.

Notes

1. This chapter is to some degree based on the article 'Journalists in the Making' where we discuss some major findings from these longitudinal surveys (in Journalism Practice, 2007, 1: 3). The surveys were answered at the start and end of studies and three years after study completion. The surveys were conducted in cooperation with The Centre for the Studies of Professions at Oslo University College.
2. In 2007 this vocational journalism programme was converted into a part of the media studies programme (60 credit points) at Bjørknes College, still qualifying for pursuing journalism bachelor studies abroad.
3. This programme was not offered in 2009 because of reduction in the number of applicants.
4. The estimates are based on data from 1971–2003 for students at Volda University College (Alme, Vestad et al. 1997), and data from 1993–2003 for Oslo University College (Bjørnsen 2003b: 30). It should, however, be noted that these changes are not confined to journalism studies, but follow quite closely the changing male-female ratio in the Norwegian student population in general over the last 35 years (SSB 2000: table 192).
5. David Weaver also documents the gender composition in journalism internationally. Ten years ago Finland (49%), New Zealand (45%) and Germany (41%) had the highest proportion of women in the journalism work force. At the bottom of the list was Korea (14%) and Algeria (24%). In England, Spain, Equador and Mexico around every fourth journalist was a women around ten years ago (Weaver 1998: 457).
6. An interesting trend in this regard is that the number of journalism students who have some form of previous journalistic experience has been increasing, but the average length is declining (Bjørnsen 2003b: 40).
7. Two per cent have both parents in this category, eleven per cent only their father and five per cent only their mother.

References

Alme, Bjarte (1997), 'Utdanning mot alle vindar', In Alme, Sande og Vestad (eds.), *Mot alle vindar? Mediefag i Volda 1971 – 96*, Jubileumsskrift: Høgskulen i Volda.

Bjørnsen, Gunn (2003a), *Flerkulturell bakgrunn som journalistisk kompetanse?* Report, Nordisk Journalistcenter, http: //www.njc.dk/farver. Accessed 15 April 2008.

Bjørnsen, Gunn (2003b), *Journalister i støpeskjeen? Yrkesholdninger blant journaliststudenter i Volda og Oslo*, HiO-rapport 23: Høgskolen i Oslo.

Bjørnsen, Gunn; Hovden, Jan Fredrik and Ottosen, Rune (2007a), 'Journalists in the Making. Findings from a longitudinal study of Norwegian journalism students', *Journalism Practice*, 1(2), pp. 383–403.

Bjørnsen, Gunn; Hovden, Jan Fredrik and Ottosen, Rune (2007b), 'Fra valp til vaktbikkje. En longitudinell studie av norske journaliststudenter', *Nordicom information*, 29 (4), pp. 57–70.

Hovden, Jan Fredrik; Bjørnsen, Gunn; Ottosen, Rune; Willig, Ida and Zilliacus-Tikkanen, Henrika (2009), 'The Nordic Journalists of Tomorrow. An exploration of First Year Journalism Students in Denmark, Finland, Norway and Sweden, *Nordicom Review*, 30.

Hovden, Jan Fredrik (2008), 'Profane and Sacred. A Study of the Norwegian Journalistic Field', Ph.D. thesis, Bergen: University of Bergen. http: //hdl.handle.net/1956/2724. Accessed 8 September 2009.

Hovden, Jan Fredrik (2002), 'Arvingane: Studentar og kulturinstitusjonene' in Bjørkås (ed.), *Individ, identitet og kulturell erfaring*, Oslo: Høyskoleforlaget/NFR.

Ottosen, Rune (1996), *Fra fjærpenn til Internett. Journalister i organisasjon og samfunn*, Oslo: Aschehoug.

Ottosen, Rune (1997), 'Akademisk, kommersiell eller distriktspolitisk. Journalistutdanningens jakt på identitet', *Norsk medietidsskrift*, pp. 83–107.

Ottosen, Rune (2004), 'I journalistikkens grenseland: journalistrollen mellom marked og idealer', IJ-forlaget: Kristiansand.

Petersson, Olof (1994), 'Journalistene som klass, journalismen som ideology', in T.S. Edvardsen (ed.), *Media og samfunnsstyring*, Oslo: Fagbokforlaget.

Splichal, Slavko and Colin Sparks (1994), *Journalists for the 21st century*, New Jersey: Ablex.

Sørensen, Bjørg Aase (2005), *Tatt av ordet. Medienes forspill til framtidens arbeidsliv*, AFI-rapport no 4, Oslo: Arbeidsforskningsinstituttet.

Zelizer, Barbie (2004), *Taking journalism seriously. News and the Academy*, Thousand Oaks: Sage Publications.

Weaver, David H. (1998), *The Global Journalist. News people around the world*, IAMCR, Inc. Cresskill, New Jersey: Hampton Press.

The Norwegian Institute of journalism, http: //www.ij.no. Accessed 15 April 2008.

The Norwegian Union of Journalists and The Association of Norwegian Editors (1999), *Kunnskapsløftet*, Report, Oslo.

The Swedish Journalism Education Landscape

Marina Ghersetti and Lennart Weibull

Introduction

In the fall semester of 1905 professor Otto Sylwan, holding the chair of literature, held a series of lectures on journalism at the University of Gothenburg, analysing American journalistic writing.[1] It was no journalism education per se, but it reflected the interest in increasing knowledge of the field. Two years later the board of the Swedish Union of Journalists, founded in 1901, discussed a proposal to initiate formal training of journalists (Petersson 2006). The union board argued that formal education was an important means in increasing the status of journalism as a profession.

The two initiatives, however, did not result in either academic courses or schools of journalism. It took more than five decades until journalism education was formally established in Sweden. However, these early initiatives show the two main actors in proposals on journalism education in the coming years: the academics of the higher education institutions and the representatives of the media practice, both interested in contributing to professionalism of journalism.

In Sweden today there are about 17000 journalists. Of those two-thirds have a formal journalism education and more than three-fourths a university level education. How did it come about?

In the following we shall first try to map the discussion on journalism education until its establishment as a university study in the late 1970s, and then present an overview of the situation as it looks today.[2]

The origins of journalism education

In the beginning of the twentieth century learning of the journalism craft was defined as two years of non-salaried work in a newspaper (Petersson 2006). The leading body in terms of professional conduct, at least in the early twentieth century, was the Publicists' Club (PK), founded in 1874. The PK was not a press organisation in the traditional sense but an association of leading journalists and publishers, interested in standards for good journalism, including ethics. In 1900 a first code of conduct was decided on by Stockholm journalists. In 1916 an honorary court was established to solve conflicts between journalists, and in 1923 PK approved a national code of conduct (Weibull and Börjesson 1991).

The initiatives of the PK to increase the quality of journalism were backed up by both the Swedish Union of Journalists (SJF) and the Association of Newspapers Publishers (TU), founded in 1898. SJF took some new education initiatives in the 1910s – one of them resulted in a handbook for self-studies of journalism – but little happened (Petersson 206). In 1921 the TU, together with the PK and the SJF, took the initiative of a joint commission that would look into the need for journalism education. The commission recommended that an education should be set up, focusing on social and political issues, and organized in cooperation with the Swedish School of Social Policy, a public institution established in 1920 for the education of local civil servants. The proposal did not meet great enthusiasm. Sceptics were afraid that such an education would be too long, probably also too academic, and thus make young people less interested in journalism practice (Petersson 2006). The proposal was not implemented, but inspired the establishment of annual Nordic courses for journalists.

During the years until the Second World War we can identify a lot of initiatives, which were either academic or vocational. In the early 1930s a private school was founded in Stockholm with a focus on journalistic writing. The most interesting initiative was a Bachelor of Journalism starting at the University of Gothenburg in 1938. It was a programme, where students were offered courses relevant for journalism, supplemented by seminars with leading journalists and a possibility for internships. Similar bachelor programmes were proposed at other universities, but the idea was met with criticism from the press organizations because of their academic focus. Thus, the courses did not materialize, and for newspapers the traditional way of recruitment by in-house training remained, whereas the radio, having started in 1925, began recruiting academics and testing them on speech competence (Engblom 1998).[3]

New initiatives focus on the profession

Looking at the demands of the post-war world the two main organizations, the TU and the SJF, again raised the issue of formal education. It was thought that journalists did not always understand their responsibilities, especially in a situation where the newspapers became more and more important. The discussion coincided with the work of the PK to broaden the journalist code of conduct. In 1944 a new joint commission was set up.

Its report offered some basic ideas on what should be required of a journalist, stressing that theoretical knowledge now was important as a consequence of the increasing level of education in the population. Thus, it recommended that journalists should have at least secondary school background, but at the same time added that it was important to recruit persons with practical work experience if they had a talent for journalistic writing. The commission proposed a bachelor education, but at the same time added that academic studies were not necessary to work as a journalist (Petersson 2006). The conclusion was that it was still too early to start journalism schools. Instead all three press organizations began to organize courses, mostly as further education, and in 1947 the well known journalist Set Poppius started the private 'Poppius journalistskola' (Poppius' Journalism School), stressing the practice but not excluding theory. In 2008 this school was still the main private journalism school in Sweden (Larsson 1997).

The final model

The rapid expansion of the newspaper market in the 1950s and the introduction of a newsroom in the Swedish Radio in 1956 were signs indicating the need for a formally educated journalist generation. SJF took the final initiative in 1955. A commission with representatives from PK, SJF and TU presented its report in 1957. It stressed that a formal journalism education would lead to an increased status for journalists and therefore facilitate recruitment. It pointed out that the field of journalism had broadened considerably during the post-war era and now new types of knowledge were needed. Inside journalism training was simply not enough. To increase journalism quality a formal professional education of journalists was now necessary.

The commission argued that the new education should not be organized by an academic institution but by the media organizations themselves. The result was the Journalist Institute (Journalistinstitutet). It was organized as an independent foundation, financed by the press organizations, individual media companies and some Government grants, situated in Stockholm. It was inaugurated in January 1960 with the minister of education attending the ceremony and in his speech stressing the importance of professional journalism for a democratic society.

In its first year 30 students attended the Journalist Institute. It offered a one-year programme combining studies of politics, government and economy (40%) with practical training in editing and writing (60%).[4] The financing soon turned out to be a heavy burden for the media organizations. It was the argued that it should be part of the public education system and in 1962 the Government took over the responsibility and established a national board for the coordination of curricula, and also established a second institute in Gothenburg.[5]

Now forming a part of the higher school system in Sweden, the Journalism Institutes developed their curricula. The national board proposed a two-year programme with a one-year basic course, six-month internship and six-month specialization. The proposal was approved by the Government and the two-year studies started in the fall of 1967. The number of students also increased to 120 new beginners each year.

The model, developed by the rector of the Stockholm institute Lars Furhoff, meant an integration of theory and practice. It is the same basic model that is still guiding Swedish journalism education. In 1977 the schools were integrated in the university system as academic departments, which meant that the media organizations lost their formal influence. Instead a strengthening of a research-based education followed, and both schools, in 1989 and 1990, merged with departments specializing in media research and thus opened for a Ph.D. in journalism. At the same time a third journalism programme was established and located to the University College of Mid-Sweden, later the Mid-Sweden University, in Sundsvall.

Swedish journalists

The three departments in Stockholm, Gothenburg and Sundsvall by tradition dominate the Swedish journalism education, including postgraduate studies, even though the character of the programmes today vary somewhat. However, their dominance does not preclude the existence of other schools and institutions. Eventually, the 1980s meant an increase of new journalism education institutions, not least as a consequence of the strong increase in the number of applicants to the traditional studies, reflecting the expansion of Swedish journalism. Thus the SJF almost doubled its membership between 1980 and 2000 (Engblom 2001, Djerf-Pierre and Weibull 2001).

The expansion has meant that Swedish journalists today form a heterogeneous group, but its members still have quite a few characteristics in common. In 2005 half of all the Swedish journalists are women (Djerf-Pierre 2007). A little less than one-third (29%) are under 35 years of age and one fifth is 55 years or older. More than half of all journalists (55%) have a middle-class or academic family background, one-third (33%) comes from the working class. Whereas gender and age of journalists are similar to the general population in Sweden this is not true for their socio-economic background, where middle-class and academic background is strongly over-represented, and even over-represented in relation to the average of university students. Also journalists strongly differ in ethnic background from the general population: 5% are born abroad to be compared with 15% among all Swedes. In spite of intense discussions about how to change the situation, there has been almost no increase in the percentage of journalists with non-Swedish backgrounds in the last decade.

Swedish journalists work over a broad range of media, from the traditional press to the web. More than two-thirds have an ongoing position, but a rapidly changing media market has brought an increasing percentage of journalists with temporary employment or journalists working as freelancers. The latter group is especially increasing in the area of television and radio. Sweden is known for its strong press, especially the local press, and the newspaper industry is still the biggest employer, where almost 50 per cent of Swedish journalists work, but it has to be reminded that the newspaper sector in the late 1980s employed almost two-thirds of the journalists.[6] During the same period the percentage working in radio and television has increased from 15% in 1989 to 27% in 2005, mainly reflecting the new private radio and TV sector developing in Sweden since the early 1990s (Hadenius, Weibull and Wadbring 2008).

More than one-third of the Swedish journalists work mainly as general reporters. Also politics and social issues is an increasingly important area with more that one-fourth having it as their main field of coverage. Also reporters in areas like culture, entertainment, crime and features have increased their shares, reflecting changes in journalistic trends, especially during the 1990s. The main tendency is that general reporters are replaced with specialized ones.

Current state of academic journalism education...

Changes in both media industry and in journalistic trends have influenced the landscape of Swedish journalism education. In the 1980s and 1990s new, often specialized, journalism programmes were set up at other universities and university colleges, adding special profiles to the three general departments. At the University College of Kalmar there is a one-year programme focused on media production and at the university college of Södertörn there is one specializing in web journalism. Also the universities of Lund and Umeå have established journalism courses, even though they are not regarded as general journalism programmes. In total, however, it is estimated that about 800 students initiate some sort of academic journalism course each year (Högskoleverket 2006).

A report from the Swedish National Agency for Higher Education in 2007 states that there are many ways to become a journalist in Sweden, but that the development within media and society increases the need of academic journalism education. Academic degrees have so far had low status within the media trade, but according to the report a change is on its way (Högskoleverket 2007).

By tradition, and by sharing a common background from the journalism schools, the three main journalism departments at the universities of Stockholm, Gothenburg and Mid-Sweden in Sundsvall, have a similar character. Besides the journalism programme they also have media programmes and courses in public relations on the undergraduate level and offer postgraduate education. The size of the departments is comparable both regarding numbers of students and teachers. All three of them have somewhere between 220 and 250 journalism students per term and between twenty three and thirty members of staff – both journalists and senior lecturers.

There are some basic parallels between the three programmes. First, the programmes are between three and five years long, leading to bachelor or master degrees in journalism. Second, the focus of the studies is on news reporting in newspapers, radio, television and the Web, although there are also special courses in features journalism. Third, the programme courses mix theory and practice, and try to include results from journalism research. The students also have to carry out a minor scientific project. Fourth, all programme students have to complete an internship of between sixteen and twenty two weeks, mainly in newspapers, radio and television. The latter is regularly discussed with representatives of the media organizations, which underlines the close relationship between the three programmes and the Swedish media industry. Fifth, all three schools offer several exchange programmes, mainly with other universities in the Nordic as well as other European countries, both on bachelor and master levels.

Table 1: Three major schools of journalism studies in Sweden.

	University of Stockholm	University of Gothenburg	Mid-Sweden University of Sundsvall
Faculty:	Fine Arts	Social sciences	Science, Technology and Media
Journalist students per term:	217	255	250
Number of teachers:	28	23	30
Professors	2	2	3
Senior lecturers	10	8	6
Journalists	8	11	13
Internship:	16–18 weeks	22 weeks	6–20 weeks
Admission requirements:	Upper secondary school Swedish Scholastic Aptitude Test (SweSAT) Entrance tests	Upper secondary school Swedish Scholastic Aptitude Test (SweSAT) Entrance tests	Upper secondary school
Undergraduate studies:	Science of Journalism, 60 ECTS Journalistic production, 60 ECTS Journalistic writing, 7.5 ECTS	Journalist Programme, 180 ECTS	Journalist Programme, 180 ECTS Photojournalism, 180 ECTS Journalism for postgraduate students, 60 ECTS
Postgraduate studies:	MA Programme in Journalism, 120 ECTS Ph.D. Programme in Journalism, Media and Communication, 240 ECTS	Ph.D Programme in Journalism, Media and Communication, 240 ECTS	International MA Programme in Journalism, Media and Democracy, 120 ECTS
Exchange programmes with universities in:	Nordic countries, Estonia, France, Italy, Lithuania, Portugal, Spain, Switzerland, Czech Republic, Germany	Nordic countries, Germany, England, Austria, Spain, Scotland, Netherlands, Poland, Belgium, Italy, Bulgaria	Nordic countries, Austria, Belgium

However, during the last two decades, the three programmes in Stockholm, Gothenburg and Sundsvall have gradually developed somewhat different profiles, partly as a consequence of trends within the Swedish university system (Högskoleverket 2007). The programme at the University of Stockholm has stressed a research profile and developed courses in the science of journalism, which the student has to pass before being admitted to the more practical courses that are offered on a postgraduate level. The University of Gothenburg and the Mid-Sweden University in Sundsvall both have focused on the professional character of the programmes by integration of theory and practice from the start and throughout the whole education. The Gothenburg programme has a little more focus on writing and on multimedia journalism, whereas photojournalism has been a strong feature of the Sundsvall programme. All three schools offer more or less a whole term of internship.

Follow-ups at the Gothenburg programme show that the students have established themselves on the Swedish labour market fairly soon after finishing their studies. The results for 2008 show that 88% work as journalists after their graduation. After two years 77% are still holding an occupation in journalism or communications, dropping to 67% after five years (Ghersetti 2009).

Despite somewhat different profiles the three main programmes still recruit students from quite homogeneous social-economic and ethnic backgrounds (Kjellson and Ottsson 2007, Grehn, Kruse and Larsson 2008, Björnsen, Hovden et alt 2007). The majority are born in Sweden from Swedish parents, come from families of salaried employees and academics, have grown up and are living in major cities and are between twenty two and twenty four years old when beginning their studies. This also applies to other academic journalism courses and is partly reflected in the studies of Swedish journalists. Only when it comes to sex is there a notable difference between the students and the journalists. While the female first-term students amount to 60–70 per cent, the women only reach 50 per cent among professional journalists, although increasing their share.

It is generally considered as a problem, both by the profession and the education institutions, that large groups in Swedish society are under-represented among journalism students, and among active journalists. As employment in the media today normally requires an academic exam, editors and media directors tend to hold the journalism educations responsible for the uneven recruitment to the profession. A significantly different recruitment of journalist students would demand revised admission requirements as well as extensive information campaigns pointed directly to the wanted groups, efforts that the university educations so far have not been able to do.

... and Folk High Schools

Also the private journalism education sector in Sweden has expanded over the last decades. Besides the private Poppius School, many so-called Folk High Schools have started journalism programmes. The first Folk High Schools (FHS) in Sweden were established in

Table 2: Folk High Schools (FHS) with journalism courses, 2009.

Schools	Courses	Length	Admission requirements	Coordinates
Bona FHS	Journalism	2 years	Upper secondary school	www.bona.nu
Bollnäs FHS	Radio-journalism	1 year	Interview	www.bolnas.lg.se
Jakobsberg FHS	Feature	1 year (+ internship 6 months)	Personal letter	www.jakan.nu
	Web-TV	1 year	Personal letter	
Kaggeholms FHS	Journalism	2 years	Upper secondary school	www.kaggeholm.nu
	TV-journalism	2 years	Upper secondary school	
Kalix FHS	Journalism	2 years	Upper secondary school	www.kalix.fhsk.se
	Web-editing	6 months	Upper secondary school	
	TV-journalism	2 years	Upper secondary school	
	Multi Media-journalism	6 months	Journalistic experience	
Ljungskile FHS	Journalism	2 years	Upper secondary school	www.ljungskile.fhsk.se
	Journalistic writing	3 months	-	
Molkom FHS	Journalism	1 year	Upper secondary school	www.molkom.nu
Nordens FHS Biskops-Arnö	Freelance in Latin America (Feature in Chile)	1 year	Personal letter, Spanish language	www.biskopsarno.se
	Nordic countries in Chile – documentary video and radio production	1 year	Personal letter, Spanish language	
Nordiska FHS	Journalism	1 year	Upper secondary school	www.nordiska.fhsk.se
Skurups FHS	Journalism	1 year	Upper secondary school, entrance test, interview	www.fhsk.skurup.se
Strömbäck FHS	Journalism	2 years	Upper secondary school	www.stromback.fhsk.se
Södra Stockholms FHS	Film/video, photo and radio	1 year	–	www.sodrastockholm.se
Södra Vätterbygdens FHS	Journalism	2 years	Upper secondary school	www.svf.fhsk.se
Tollare FHS	Feature (Basic)	1 year	Upper secondary school	www.tollare.org
	Feature (Advanced)	1 year	Upper secondary school, Media education or journalistic experience	
	Web-journalism	1 year	–	
Vara FHS	Radio-journalism	2 years	Upper secondary school	www.vara.fhsk.se
Ålsta FHS	Journalism	1 year	-	www.alsta.fhsk.se
Ädelfors FHS	Journalism	2 years	Upper secondary school	www.adelfors.nu

Source: www.folkhögskola.nu (March 2009).

1868 offering education to the working class and people of small means. There are today 148 FHSs in Sweden and they constitute an established part of the Swedish education system. A majority are run and financed by political, religious or social movements (NGOs).

The overall objective of the Swedish FHSs is to offer general civic education, but over the years a number of special courses have been established, such as journalism. In the early 1980s, when the number of applicants to the journalism schools outnumbered the available seats many times, several FHSs set up journalism education. Today seventeen FHSs give courses in journalism, each for approximately twenty pupils per year. Many of the courses are specialized, e.g. on writing, Web-journalism, radio or television production. The minimum age for admission to the general courses is eighteen years. There is no upper age limit.

A BA thesis from 2008 comparing students at the university programmes in journalism with pupils at the FHS courses shows that the recruitment base differs between the two types of education (Grehn, Kruse and Larsson 2008). A higher percentage of the pupils have grown up in working class families and have a non-Swedish ethnical background. They also to a lager extent have grown up in smaller towns or in the countryside. Many of the FHS courses, especially the longer ones, are well reputed in the media business and their pupils compete with university students for employment after graduation.

Professionalizing journalism

One of the main aims when formal journalism education was initiated in the early 1960s, and expanded during the 1970s, was to develop a journalistic profession in Sweden. Educated journalists were important for increasing the quality of journalism and hence for the trust in media news. Even though some critical voices questioned the value of academically educated journalists, it is quite clear that since the late 1980s journalists with a university background dominate the profession. In 2005 it was true for four out of five Swedish journalists (Edström 2007).

Looking more closely into the statistics we find that there are some important differences in educational background. As expected the percentage of academically educated journalists is smaller in the oldest generation – 71 per cent among journalists over 60, to be compared with 78 per cent among those less than 35 years of age. The difference was, however, much larger in the late 1980s when only 45 per cent of the oldest had academic education while the youngest already reached 78 per cent. Further, academic education was much more frequent two decades ago by journalists of the national public service radio and television (78 per cent) than in the regional press (50 per cent), whereas comparable figures today are 80 per cent and 81 per cent. Thus, the expansion of academic education can be regarded as a traditional diffusion process, where the young of the main cities were the first to try it.

But there is another important feature to this: the expansion of academic education has been a very important means for the increase in the number of female journalists. When the old internship model of journalism education dominated, it was often difficult for

Table 3: Educational level of Swedish journalists 1989–2005 (per cent).

	1989	1995	1999	2005
Compulsory school	9	5	5	2
Secondary school/Folk High Schools	20	20	18	19
College/University	71	75	77	79
Total	100	100	100	100
Number of respondents	826	1050	1070	1025

Source: Surveys of Swedish Journalists. Department of Journalism and Mass Communication, University of Gothenburg.

women to be admitted. With the introduction of formal education it turned out that women outnumbered the male applicants, which opened their way to journalism. In the late 1980s, 86% of the female journalists had university education compared to only 62% among the males. Since then there has been a gradual convergence; this is due to increasingly higher education among male journalists, although the percentage of female journalists with an academic education is still higher than that of the men (Edström 2007).

However, it is important to note that all academic education does not necessarily mean a full university programme of journalism. Actually, about 40 per cent of the Swedish journalists in 2005 had their exams from one of the three main academic programmes, and the percentage has been quite stable since the mid 1990s. The percentage of journalists with no journalism education has declined during the same period, but instead combinations of traditional academic studies and non-academic journalism education have increased. Eventually, the percentage of Swedish journalists with some type of formal journalism education has increased from 42 per cent to 67 per cent between 1989 and 2005. In this percentage all types of courses are included. But even if there are big differences in scope and character between different schools and institutes, education per se is important and will influence the profession.

Journalism education and journalistic ideals

The introduction of formal journalism education in the 1960s and early 1970s coincided with a general increase in the importance of the media as an independent social institution. The first rector of the Stockholm School of Journalism, Lars Furhoff, was an outspoken critic to the traditional role of the Swedish newspapers. He meant that the party political connection of the press should be replaced by an independent press, focusing on an investigative journalism (Furhoff 1963). This perspective, already developing in radio and television, also influenced the curriculum and became gradually associated with Swedish professional journalism, not least by journalists educated at the two main schools in

Stockholm, Gothenburg and Sundsvall during the 1970s (Cf. Engblom 1998, Petersson 2006, Hadenius, Weibull and Wadbring 2008).

Since the professional ideals of Swedish journalism are closely associated with the main academic programmes it is interesting to analyse what a long-term change in recruitment means for the journalistic profession. Table 4 is based on the Swedish national journalist surveys and shows how journalists with and without formal journalism education evaluate

Table 4: Swedish journalists' views on professional ideals 1989 and 2005, related to education (percentage that totally agree).

Journalists should...	Journalism education	No journalism education	Balance of percentage
Examine those in power			
1989	78	65	+13
2005	83	78	+5
Simplify complicated events			
1989	71	61	+10
2005	77	76	+1
Stimulate new thoughts and ideas			
1989	49	46	+3
2005	53	48	+5
Criticize injustice in society			
1989	51	41	+10
2005	47	44	+3
Give people new experiences			
1989	47	43	+4
2005	43	41	+3
Report what happens in a neutral way			
1989	22	35	−13
2005	31	37	−6
Reflect general opinion			
1989	16	28	−12
2005	17	24	−7
Number of respondents			
1989	351	468	
2005	694	340	

Source: Surveys of Swedish Journalists. Department of Journalism and Mass Communication, University of Gothenburg.

different journalistic ideals in 1989 and in 2005. It is clearly demonstrated that journalists with formal education in journalism have a stronger preference for investigative and critical reporting, whereas journalists without formal journalism are less negative concerning neutral reporting. If we consider investigative reporting as an indicator of professional journalism we can conclude that it is correlated with education in journalism.

A second observation is that the difference between educated and non-educated journalists declines from 1989 to 2005. It seems that the professional ideals that were connected to formal education now are more generally accepted. The establishment of the journalism schools in the 1960s meant that there was a platform for professional discussions, reinforced by the opinion climate of the time. Later the ideals are generally accepted. It also means that the similarities between academic journalist programmes and academic studies in general are less today than a decade ago.

A third observation based on a separate analysis is that the socialization in the newsroom also is very important for the journalistic ideals. Young, newly educated journalists are often more critical to how news is handled in the media, pointing at routines and market concerns as strong factors behind the daily journalistic work. After just a few years they have changed their views, meaning that professional news reporting is a much more complex phenomenon than they had understood from the text books during their studies (Ghersetti 2007).

Concluding Remarks

To get back to the initial question: has formal education meant professionalizing of Swedish journalism? The question has often been debated. On one hand it is fully clear that the education has contributed to the articulation of professional values in journalism. Independence, autonomy, strong ethics and investigative reporting are values strongly focused in education. On the other hand, the Furhoffian idea of formal requirements to have the right to work as a journalist did not materialize. Today, less than half of the Swedish journalists have a formal academic journalism education, however this is higher among the youngest workers but with only a slow progression. Thus, journalism in Sweden does not meet the traditional criteria of a profession.

It is reasonable to conclude that journalism education reflects the developmental trends in the media industry. Therefore, it is not to expect that the academic journalism programmes will play a more important role in the future. With the ongoing changes in the media industry and the increasing heterogeneity of the Swedish media market there will always be a need for specialized education. Today, as we have observed, a lot more journalists than before have some type of journalism education. More education means a possibility to articulate journalistic ideals and thereby stimulate reflection on journalism development. In this process it is probable that the academic journalism programmes of today will function also in the future as a sort of spearhead of professional discussions, contributing to the craft by developing the ideas of high quality journalism.

The Authors

Marina Ghersetti, is a Senior Lecturer at the Department of Journalism and Mass Communication at the University of Gothenburg.

Lennart Weibull is the chair of Mass Media Research at the Department of Journalism and Mass Communication, University of Gothenburg.

Notes

1. For a detailed overview see Den svenska pressens historia III (2001: 79).
2. For the historical overview we are in great debt to Britt Hultén, the late chairwoman of the Department of Journalism, Media and Communication at the University of Stockholm, who has written a well-researched overview of the history of Swedish journalism education (Hultén 2001) and the historian Birgit Petersson who has researched the professionalization process of Swedish journalists (Petersson 2006). Also Lindskog (1997) presents basic facts on journalism education in Sweden.
3. It is also important to note, that the Swedish radio did not have a newsroom of its own until the mid 1950s and that programmes to a large extent were educational (Nordberg 1998).
4. The majority of the applicants were women, but the media organizations had decided that only one third of those admitted should be women (Petersson 2006: 333f).
5. It might be noted that the new model was met with criticism from some newspapers, arguing that media should not be dependent of Government decisions (Petersson 2006: 330).
6. All comparisons are taken from surveys of Swedish journalists carried out by the Department of Journalism and Mass Communication, University of Gothenburg 1989, 1994, 1999 and 2005. (cf. Weibull 1971 and Asp 2007).

References

Asp, Kent (ed.) (2007), *Den svenska journalistkåren*, Institutionen för journalistik och masskommunikation: Göteborgs universitet.

Björnsen, Gunn; Hovden, Jan Fredrik; Ottosen, Rune; Schultz, Ida and Zilliacus-Tikkanen, Henrika (2007), 'The Nordic Journalism Student: A Cross-National Study', In IAMCR Conference, 2007, UNESCO: Paris.

Djerf-Pierre, Monika (2007), 'Journalisterna sociala bakgrund', In Kent Asp (ed.), *Den svenska journalistkåren*, Institutionen för journalistik och masskommunikation: Göteborgs universitet.

Djerf-Pierre, Monika and Weibull, Lennart (2001), *Spegla, granska, tolka: Aktualitetsjournalistik i svensk radio och tv 1925–1995*, Stockholm: Prisma.

Edström, Maria (2007), 'Journalisters arbete och utbildning', In Kent Asp (ed.), *Den svenska journalistkåren*, Institutionen för journalistik och masskommunikation: Göteborgs universitet.

Engblom, Lars-Åke (1998), *Radio- och TV-folket: rekryteringen av programmedarbetare till radion och televisionen i Sverige 1925–1995*, Stockholm: Stiftelsen Etermedierna i Sverige.

Engblom, Lars-Åke (2001), 'Varför professionalizering?' In Kent Asp (ed.), *Den svenska journalistkåren*, Institutionen för journalistik och masskommunikation: Göteborgs universitet.

Furhoff, Lars (1963), *Pressens förräderi*, Stockholm: Bonniers.

Ghersetti, Marina (2007), 'Vad bestämmer nyhetsvärdet?', In Kent Asp (ed.), *Den svenska journalistkåren*, Institutionen för journalistik och masskommunikation: Göteborgs universitet.

Ghersetti, Marina (2009), 'Vad gör journalisterna efter utbildningen', http: //www.jmg.gu.se/ Utbildning/Journalistutbildningen/Journalisternas+arbetsmarknad/. Accessed 6 September 2009.

Gustafsson, Karl-Erik and Rydén, Per (eds.) (2001), *Den svenska pressens historia III*, Stockholm: Ekerlids.

Hadenius, Stig; Weibull, Lennart and Wadbring, Ingela (2008), *Massmedier: Press, radio och tv i den digitala tidsåldern*, Stockholm: Ekerlids.

Hultén, Britt (2001), 'Utbildning – behövs det?', In Agneta Lindblom Hultén (ed.), *Journalisternas bok 1901–2001*, Stockholm: Scvenska Journalistförbundet.

Högskoleverket (2007), *Uppföljande utvärdering av utbildning i journalistik vid universitet och högskolor i Sverige*, Rapport 2007: 4 R.

Högskoleverket (2006), *Arbetsmarknad och högskoleutbildning 2006*, Rapport 2006: 28 R.

Kjellson, Cajsa and Ottosson, Jennica (2007), 'Framtidens journalist – vem är du?', BA thesis in journalism, Program for Media Production and Journalism, University of Kalmar.

Kruse, Filip; Larsson, Andreas and Grehn, Per (2008), 'Vem är den svenska journaliststudenten?', BA thesis in journalism, Department of Journalism and Mass Communication, University of Gotheburg.

Larsson, Sören (1997), 'Poppius journalistskolan', In S. Larsson (ed.), *Poppius. Journalisternas skola*, Stockholm: Poppius Kunsult AB.

Lindskog, Thorbjörn (1997), 'Några viktiga årtal i journalistutbildningens historia', In S. Larssson (ed.), *Poppius. Journalisternas skola*, Stockholm: Poppius Kunsult AB.

Löfgren-Nilsson, Monica (2007), Journalistiken – ett könsmärkt fält?, In Kent Asp (ed.), *Den svenska journalistkåren*, Institutionen för journalistik och masskommunikation: Göteborgs universitet.

Nordberg, Karin (1998), *Folkhemmets röst. Radion som folkbildare 1925–1950*, Eslöv: Symposion.

Petersson, Birgit (2006), *Från journalist till murvel: journalistyrkets professionalisering från 1900 till 1960-talet*, Göteborg: Nordicom-Sverige.

Weibull, Lennart (1971), *Svenska journalister. Ett grupporträtt*, Stockholm: Tiden/SJF.

Weibull, Lennart and Börjesson, Britt (1991), *Publicistiska seder*, Stockholm: Tiden/SJF.

The Swiss Journalism Education Landscape

Thomas Hanitzsch and Annette Müller

Introduction

Switzerland is a small country with a relatively high number of media organizations operating in small markets. Organized into 26 mostly rather small cantons, a key feature of the country is its cultural diversity. Switzerland accommodates four culturally somewhat different geographical areas which are defined by the language spoken by the majority of the people: the German-speaking part in the north and northeast, the French-speaking part in the southwest, the Italian-speaking part in the southeast, as well as a small area in the east inhabited by a small Romansh-speaking minority. Altogether, foreigners make up more than 20 per cent of Switzerland's total population of about 7.5 million inhabitants (Bundesamt für Statistik 2008), and it is estimated that some ten per cent of all Swiss citizens have a migration background.

This cultural diversity has not only translated into a unique political system that stresses the principles of federalism and concordance, but it has also deeply shaped Switzerland's mediascape. The Swiss Broadcasting Corporation (SRG), founded in 1931 and modelled after the BBC, produces and broadcasts not less than twenty three radio and television programmes in all four official languages (Meier 2002). The creation of a public monopoly that is mainly financed by license fees has helped to prevent excessive economic competition between print and broadcasting media and 'brought about a financially healthy private and a viable public system' (Meier 2004: 250). In addition to the SRG, there are about 50 local and regional radio stations operating in Switzerland.

Newspapers and magazines are still the most important sector of the Swiss mediascape. Of all advertising revenues, 63 per cent goes to print media and 45 per cent to newspapers alone (WARC 2007). Although the consumption of paid-for dailies has been gradually declining over the years, Switzerland was able to retain its very tradition of newspaper reading until today. With the introduction of daily free sheets such as *20 Minuten*, however, the newspaper market has profoundly shifted, putting traditional and prestigious titles such as the *Neue Zürcher Zeitung* and the *Tages-Anzeiger* under heavy economic pressure. The Swiss print media sector is nevertheless one of the most saturated markets in the world, with about 100 daily and another 200 weekly newspapers, as well as more than 1000 magazines struggling for readership (WAN 2007; Schweizer PR- und Medienverzeichnis 2007).

History

Journalism education in Switzerland has, as noted by Blum (2002), three distinctive features: Firstly, due to the geographic and cultural diversity, the country's press system is characterized by rather small media companies. Most of the media organizations do simply not have the resources necessary for a systematic and professional in-house training and education programme. Only the Swiss Broadcasting Corporation and the publishing house Ringier have an internal system for further education and professional updating in place. Furthermore, the division of the country into language areas has resulted in different and often even incompatible traditions of doing and going about journalism education. Secondly, with an average population of 129 journalists per 100,000 inhabitants, Switzerland has an exceptionally large number of journalists in proportion to the overall population (as of 2000; Marr et al. 2001). Given the above mentioned lack of resources, it becomes difficult to educate such a large number of journalists by media organizations alone.

Thirdly, and probably most importantly, journalism in Switzerland has traditionally been substantially interlocked with the political system. Up until the end of the 1960s, Swiss newspapers were mostly affiliated with political parties. Furthermore, a special feature of the Swiss political system is the principle of 'militia democracy' which entails involvement of the citizenry in political decision making. The citizens' political involvement was usually carried out on a voluntary basis, and the necessary skills were acquired 'on the job'. Both principles, the relatively strong party-press parallelism and the voluntary civic involvement, translated into a press environment where journalism was considered an essentially political activity for which a specialized education was seen as detrimental.

Under these circumstances it is hardly surprising that journalism education in Switzerland has been called a 'jungle' (Szer 2007: 7) and a 'diversified late starter' (Blum 2002: 49). The first professional school for journalists, the Centre romand de formation des journalistes (CRFJ) in the French-speaking city of Lausanne, was founded in 1965 by the Swiss Broadcasting Corporation and several newspaper publishers. In the German-speaking part of Switzerland, private institutions took the lead when the School for Applied Linguistics (Schule für angewandte Linguistik, SAL) was established in 1969 in Zurich and a journalism school was set up in Zofingen in 1974 by the publishing house Ringier. The year 1984 eventually gave birth to today's most influential professional school for journalists, the Media Education Center (Medienausbildungszentrum, MAZ), located in Lucerne. The MAZ is run as a foundation and financed by the Swiss Broadcasting Corporation, the Swiss Press Association (VSP), associations of Swiss journalists, as well as the city and canton of Lucerne.

In a similar vein, Swiss universities have long marginalized journalism education and research. It was not before 1996 that mass communication and media studies could be studied as a major (Gysin et al. 2004). In general, the cultural diversity of Switzerland has generated very different traditions of going about communications and media studies, with approaches broadly stretching between the social sciences and linguistics. Although most universities run study programmes in the field of communications and media studies, there is no particular specialization in journalism. Since the late 1960s, communication schools have moved closer to the social sciences and humanities – and further away from a more practical orientation (Blum 2002). Only the University of Fribourg had offered a diploma in journalism and communication studies, from 1966 to 1998, but today journalism can only be studied as a minor. With the creation of universities of applied sciences ('Fachhochschulen'), such as the Zürcher Hochschule für Angewandte Wissenschaften Winterthur, which are more oriented towards teaching practical skills and professional knowledge, journalism education in Switzerland seems to be on a shift, away from research-oriented universities to the universities of applied sciences.

Despite the late introduction of formalized journalism education in Switzerland, studies have indicated a remarkably high level of professionalization among journalists. According to a representative survey of 2020 journalists in Switzerland conducted in 2000, about 44 per cent of all journalists have acquired a university degree, though mostly not in journalism, communications, media studies or in other related fields. Overall, there seem to be multiple pathways into journalism in Switzerland: Only one out of four journalists has studied communications and/or media studies, and about 26 per cent of the journalists went through a non-academic journalism school, such as MAZ and CRFJ.

The most common way of recruitment is the so called *Volontariat*, completed by half of all journalists, and internships (34 per cent). The *Volontariat* is a kind of semi-formalized professional traineeship that usually involves a period of between one and two years. The different ways of entering the world of journalism are not mutually exclusive, however. Many journalists, for instance, have completed their studies in mass communication and media studies before they entered the *Volontariat*. Only 15 per cent of all Swiss journalists do not have any professional education (Marr et al. 2001).

Institutions and Programs

Blum (2002: 53) distinguishes between four basic types of journalism education in Switzerland: (1) 'Preparatory journalism education' includes all kinds of education that is to be completed before junior journalists start their professional careers. Study programmes in (mass) communications and media studies fall within this category, as well as journalism programmes at the School of Applied Linguistics and the Migros Media School. (2) 'Continuing journalism education' includes professional courses offered by the Media Education Center in Lucerne, Centre romand de formation des journalistes in Lausanne, Corso di giornalismo della Svizzera italiana, and the Media School Northwest Switzerland. Here, as well as in the next category, (3) 'postgraduate journalism education', professional expertise and previous employment as a journalist is mostly a requirement. The Media Education Center and the University of Geneva are currently the only institutions that offer postgraduate journalism education. (4) In-house continuing journalism education mainly refers to internal structures of formalized professional education set up by large media companies, such as the Swiss Broadcasting Corporation and Ringier. In the following, however, we will use a simpler typology, consisting of three basic types of journalism education: university-based, college-based and professional. Due to the limited space, we will provide details only for the most significant institutions.

University-based journalism education

As of today, most universities in Switzerland offer programs in (mass) communication and media studies, at both the bachelor and master levels. Communication and media studies can be studied at the universities of Bern (BA, only as minor), Fribourg (BA and MA) and Geneva (MA). In 2008, the University of Geneva also introduced an MA in Journalism as an attempt to bridge theory and practice in academic journalism education. Study programmes in the field of communications and media studies are also offered by the universities of Zurich (Mass Communication and Media Research, BA and MA), Basel (Media Studies, BA and MA), Lugano (Communication Science, BA and MA), Lucerne (Social and Communication Sciences, BA; Comparative Media Research, MA), Neuenburg (Linguistics and Communication Studies, BA and MA), and St. Gallen (Corporate Communication, BA and MA).

College-based journalism education

Probably the most significant college-based institution of journalism education in Switzerland is the Institute of Applied Media Studies (IAM) in Winterthur, nearby Zurich. Since 1998, the school belongs to a larger network of colleges united under the umbrella Zürcher Hochschule für Angewandte Wissenschaften. The IAM, which tries to balance aspects of theory and professional practice in its curricula, offers a Bachelor degree in Journalism and Organizational Communication and a Master degree in Publishing. Another important college-based institution is the School of Applied Linguistics (SAL) in Zurich. The school, which is especially targeted at individuals who intend to pursue a career in language-related professions, offers a skills-based programme in Journalism that can be studied either full-time or part-time. Students earn their diploma degrees after four to five years, which includes an introductory study period of one or two semesters.

Less central but still noteworthy is the College of Technology and Economy (Hochschule für Technik und Wirtschaft, HTW) in Chur which is part of the University of Applied Sciences East Switzerland. The college offers a BA programme in Multimedia Production from which students can directly proceed to the consecutive Master of Information and Communication Science. The master's programme is run by the HTW in collaboration with the German University of Applied Sciences Mittweida. In addition, the college also offers a part-time programme in Journalism in cooperation with the School of Applied Linguistics. Different from HTW, the Lucerne University of Applied Sciences and Arts (Hochschule Luzern) positions itself as an educational institution especially devoted to management-related teaching. The college offers a Bachelor of Science in Business Administration with a special focus on communication and marketing that also includes many aspects of journalistic work and media-related knowledge.

Professional journalism education

Among the professional schools, the Media Education Center (MAZ) in Lucerne is clearly regarded as the leading institution in the field of journalism education in the German-speaking part of Switzerland. The MAZ offers a diploma and a master's programme in journalism. The part-time diploma programme includes 90 days of teaching over a period of two years. About 60 per cent of all classes are elective, which enables students to choose subjects and classes that fit their needs best. Students are required to be employed by a media organization prior to and during their enrolment, and they have to pass an entrance test. The full-time Master in Journalism has been introduced in 2006 and is offered in collaboration with the Hamburg Media School and the University of Hamburg. Two-thirds of the curriculum are devoted to professional practice and skills, the remaining one-third includes theory and reflection. Students receive a double degree, an MA in Journalism from the University of Hamburg and a diploma issued by MAZ. The list of instructors at the MAZ is long and impressive, one finds enlisted the names of several distinguished professors in journalism, communications and media studies, prominent journalists and presenters, professionals working in public relations and even experts from the Federal Statistical Office.

Another important professional institution in journalism education is the Centre romand de formation des journalistes (CRFJ) in Lausanne. Founded in 1965 as the first journalism school in Switzerland, the CRFJ offers a skills-based course for journalists working for French-speaking media. The course which takes between 45 and 50 days obliges the students to work, either as employee or a freelancer, for a recognized media organization. After finishing their training, students will receive a certificate.

In addition to the MAZ and CRFJ, there are a few institutions that also provide professional education pertinent to the field, but they are not nearly as significant as the two mentioned above. The Media School (Medienschule) St. Gallen, belonging to the larger networks of Migros Klubschule, offers part-time courses of 30 days over a period of eight months which are designed for both experienced journalists and beginners. The Media School Northwest Switzerland (Medienschule Nordwestschweiz, MSN) has been founded in 2001 by Lexpress, a small group of freelance journalists, and provides further education for only five journalists per semester. The MSN also cooperates with the School of Applied Linguistics in Zurich and the Media School Klara in Berlin. The last institution mentioned here is the EB Zurich which offers a skills-based course in Journalism for part-time journalists who receive a certificate after three semesters.

Only a few media companies have embarked on a more structured in-house journalism education so far. The Swiss Broadcasting Corporation, for instance, offers formal traineeships and some systematic further training to its employees especially in the fields of television journalism, TV direction and radio journalism. More formalized is the Ringier Journalism School, founded in 1974 by Ringier, one of Switzerland's largest media companies. For 30 years, the Ringier Journalism School provided courses and internships to trainees while also offering basic knowledge about media history, media law and other areas of interest. Due to the job crisis in the media industry, the school had suspended its service, but it resumed its activities in 2007 after the job situation had improved. Today, the education offered by the Ringier Journalism School is strongly based on practical skills and 'more suited to the needs of newsrooms'.[1] The fourteen trainees attend classes on four days each month over the duration of one year, but they spend most of their time with working in a Ringier-owned newsroom. There is no guarantee for a permanent employment by Ringier after completion of the trainee stage, however.

Concluding Remarks

One of the major obstacles to further professionalization of Switzerland's journalism education is the widespread cultural resistance to academic journalism teaching and research (Saxer 1979). Not only do senior journalists tend to regard academic journalism education as being overly theoretical (which it certainly is), they also believe that journalistic qualification mostly stems from talent and an individual's 'nose for news', while everything else can easily be learnt on the job. Opposition can be found even at universities which tend to see journalism merely as an area of vocational education and often deny it the status of an academic field in its own right.

The cultural resistance to academism notwithstanding, there are a few indications of a trend towards more academic journalism education in Switzerland. One recent example is the launch of two master's programmes at the Media Education Center in Lucerne: An MA in Journalism was introduced in 2006 and is run in close cooperation with the Hamburg Media School and the University of Hamburg, while an MA in New Media Journalism started in 2008 in collaboration with the University of Leipzig, the College of Mass Communication (AfP) in Hamburg and the College for Journalism Education (KfJ) in Salzburg. Another MA in Journalism started recently at the University of Geneva. As part of a general movement within the Swiss system of higher education, the Bologna process has been implemented in all institutions that offer academic journalism education.

A second major trend is indicated by the ongoing debate about the need for further formalization, standardization and country-wide harmonization of journalism education. In a widely discussed policy paper, Marek Szer (2007), secretary of the journalists union 'impressum', has proposed a radical reform of Switzerland's system of journalism education. At the core of his suggestion are standardized means of quality control and an official recognition of journalism as a true profession by awarding professional certificates to those who have completed journalism education. In a nutshell, the proposed reform aims at a journalism education that is (a) tailored to the needs of the markets, (b) suited to professional practice, (c) transparent, (d) standardized in terms of quality controls, (e) compatible to the European job market, (f) timely in terms of professional know-how and (g) open for lateral entrants. It should also (h) recognize equivalent expertise, (i) upvalue the professional register, (k) allow mobility across similar programmes and institutions, and (l) guarantee every journalist a professional degree that is officially recognized.

Szer's suggestion for a more formalized and standardized journalism education has been greeted with mixed reactions. While it was welcomed by most journalists unions, critical voices dominate in the Swiss Association of Publishers and the establishment of Swiss journalism schools. The Swiss Association of Publishers seems to worry about a potentially greater influence of employees' associations, whereas the hesitation of the Media Education Center (MAZ) and the Centre romand de formation des journalistes (CRFJ) may be seen as an attempt to secure their unique position in Switzerland's journalism education and, therefore, to safeguard their legitimacy (Brügger 2007). The reputation of both journalism schools stems from the fact that they are, until today, the only providers of professional journalism education that award widely recognized certificates, and hence, the proposed professional certificate or diploma degree might undermine their exclusive position in the market.

The Authors

Thomas Hanitzsch is an assistant professor at the Institute of Mass Communication and Media Research, University of Zurich, Switzerland. He founded the ICA Journalism Division and co-edited the *Handbook of Journalism Studies* (Routledge 2009).

Annette Müller is research associate at the Institute of Mass Communication and Media Research, University of Zurich, Switzerland.

Note

1. Personal communication with Fridolin Luchsinger, 17 June 2008.

References

Blum, R. (2002), 'Die Schweiz als diversifizierter Spätzünder', In K.-D. Altmeppen and Walter Hömberg (eds.), *Journalisten-Ausbildung für eine veränderte Medienwelt*, Diagnosen, Institutionen, Projekte, Wiesbaden: Westdeutscher Verlag, pp. 49–57.

Brügger, H. (2007), 'Eidg. Dipl. Journalist Klartext.ch', http: //www.klartext.ch/detail.php?&id= KT2007-12-10-001755. Accessed 2 April 2009.

Bundesamt für Statistik (ed.) (2008), *Statistisches Jahrbuch der Schweiz 2008*, Neuchâtel: Verlag NZZ.

Gysin, N; Meier, P; Blum, R; Häussler and Süss, D. (2004), *Evaluation der Kommunikations- und Medienwissenschaft in der Schweiz: Selbstevaluationsbericht*, Bern: SGKM.

Marr, M; Wyss, V; Blum, R. and Bonfadelli, H. (2001), J*ournalisten in der Schweiz: Eigenschaften, Einstellungen*, Einflüsse, Konstanz: UVK Medien.

Meier, W. A. (2002), 'Das Mediensystem in der Schweiz', In Hans-Bredow-Institut (ed.), *Internationales Handbuch Medien*, Baden-Baden: Nomos, pp. 548–558.

Meier, W. A. (2004), 'Switzerland', In M. Kelly; G. Mazzoleni and D. McQuail (eds.), *The Media in Europe*, London: Sage, 3, pp. 249–261.

Saxer, U. (1979), 'Journalistische Aus- und Fortbildung – Der Beitrag des Publizistischen Seminars der Universitaet Zuerich', In SGKM (ed.), *Journalistenausbildung in der Schweiz*, special issue of *Bulletin/ Schweizerische Gesellschaft für Kommunikations- und Medienwissenschaft*, Bern: SGKM, pp. 43–48.

Schweizer PR- und Medienverzeichnis (2007), Zürich: Edition Renteria SA.

Szer, M. (2007), *Journalismus Schweiz. Strategiekonzept zur Vereinheitlichung der Berufsbildung*, Fribourg: Impressum.

Part III

The Mediterranean/Polarized Pluralist Media Model Countries

Introduction

Stylianos Papathanassopoulos

J ournalism is generally regarded 'as an activity of gathering and presenting information and commentary about current events for public discussion' (Hallin 2004: 7995). Journalism as Paolo Mancini has argued 'does not grow in a vacuum: it is the fruit of the interaction between different actors and systems and such differences in social structure and context have to be taken in to account even when theorizing models of journalism' (Mancini 2000: 267). Therefore, journalism is also affected by the political, social and economic conditions, population, cultural and consumption traits, physical and geographical characteristics in the countries in which it operates (Papathanassopoulos 2004). It is not therefore a coincidence that there exists a variety of approaches to the study of journalism (education and studies) (Deuze 2005). According to Hallin and Mancini (2004) and Hallin and Papathanassopoulos (2002), the media in Southern Europe share some major characteristics such as low levels of newspaper circulation, a tradition of advocacy reporting, instrumentalization of privately owned media, politicization of public broadcasting and broadcast regulation and limited development of journalism as an autonomous profession.

Journalism in Southern Europe

In many ways these conditions reflect the development of journalism in Southern Europe, and most importantly the history of journalism in the region is closely parallel to the political history of the media. To a certain extent, journalism in Southern Europe resembles the journalism once characterized by Max Weber as a 'type of professional politician' since journalists are often advocates of the world of politics and for political causes (in Hallin 2004: 7996). Journalists in theory state that they adopt the neutral and objective model of journalism, which performs a watchdog function, but in practice facts and comments are freely intermixed in news reporting (Papathanassopoulos 2004). On the other hand, state intervention, particularly in periods of repression of the democracy, interrupted the development of journalism as a profession. The level of professionalisation in journalism thus has remained lower in Southern Europe, although it increased in important ways in the last couple of decades of the twentieth century (Hallin and Papathanassopoulos 2002), especially with the intense commercialization of the media sector.

The notion of journalistic professionalism, which forms the basis for journalists' claims of autonomy, is connected with the idea that journalists serve a public interest that transcends the interests of particular parties, owners or social groups (Hallin 2004). To some extent this situation applies to many countries, although this is more apparent in the media of Southern Europe (Mancini 2000: 266). One can say that due to the political particularities of Southern European societies, it has been difficult to develop a culture of journalistic professionalism faithful to the Anglo-American liberal model. This is because journalism always reflects and embodies the historical processes within which it has developed and the contemporary social conditions within which it is created (McNair 1998: 64). One has to note that western democratic practices and functions in Spain, Portugal and Greece, especially since the restoration of the Parliament in mid 1970s have influenced the performance of the news media. At the same time, there are some persistent particularities of Southern European societies and, consequently, of the mass media, which indicate that journalism does not grow in a vacuum. On the contrary it is the fruit of the interaction between different actors and systems and differences in social structure and historical and political context. For example, interpretative reporting remains the dominant model of news coverage and sets the journalist at the centre of the story, regardless the commercialization of the media and market-driven orientation of the news media. At the same time, the interests of their news organizations influence journalists heavily. This was (and still is) the basic framework of today's journalism in most parts of Southern Europe.

On the other hand, when we say that the level of professionalization is lower, it does not mean that journalists in Southern Europe are less educated than their European colleagues. Journalists in the region are more likely to have university degrees today than those in major European countries (Weaver 1998). The close connection of journalism with the political world and the orientation of newspapers to educated elites have meant that journalism has in some sense been a more elite occupation in Southern Europe than in other European countries (Hallin and Mancini 2004). Besides, it is a tradition that even though the media in Southern Europe operate in a market framework, the press and subsequently newspaper journalism offers information, analysis and comments produced by a few elite groups, which address other political, cultural and economic elites in order to send messages and start up negotiations. As for television, it has adopted a rather infotainment journalistic approach, but still is coloured by politics (see also Papathanassopoulos 2001; Mancini 2000).

As noted above certain things have changed in the last decades. The intense competition caused by the electronic media, the new entrants in the press market, and the increasing importance of the regional papers have made the elite newspapers less unique, and the prestige of the media as a social actor has surely increased.

Professional associations and journalists' unions are not as strong as their counterparts in Northern European countries. Moreover, formal accountability systems are essentially absent. Attempts to establish codes of ethics have certainly occurred, but it is questionable whether and to what extent they are applied in practice. Probably the most significant form of this has been the use of media by commercial owners to wield influence in the political world. In effect, it seems that journalists have realized that there in a new era of 'interplay' between media owners and political power. In general, journalism in these countries tends to emphasize opinion and commentary and newspapers to represent distinct political tendencies. This characteristic, however, is not distinct to Southern Europe, but is also characteristic of most of continental Europe, though over the last decade or so the movement away from advocacy journalism has probably been faster in northern than southern Europe.

The instrumentalization of the news media is also related to prevalence of clientelism in the Southern Europe. Clientelism has also affected the content of the media, especially newspapers, as means of negotiation among conflicting elites rather than means for the information of the public and, therefore, mass circulation. More precisely, clientelism forces the logic of journalism to merge with other social logics – of party politics and family privilege, for instance. And it breaks down the horizontal solidarity of journalists as it does the solidarity of other social groups. Thus the journalistic culture of the Northern, corporatist countries that is manifested both in relatively strong journalistic autonomy and in highly developed systems of ethical self-regulation is absent in countries with a stronger history of clientelism because of the overriding importance of political interests. A sense of a public interest transcending particular interests has been more difficult to achieve in societies where political clientelism is historically strong, and this contributes to the difficulty of developing a culture of journalistic professionalism.

The role of the state

The interplay between the state and the media has largely arisen from the political tensions in the history of most Southern European societies. These tensions, combined with the absence of a strong civil society, have made the state an autonomous and dominant factor. The over-extended character of the state has coincided, as noted above, with the underdevelopment of capitalism. This makes the Southern European systems less self-regulatory than developed capitalist systems such as in the Liberal model. The lack of self-regulation is also noticeable at the level of politico-ideological superstructure, because with a weak civil society, even the economically dominant classes do not manage to form well-organized and cohesive pressure groups. As Hallin and Mancini (2004: 119) note: 'the state's grasp often exceeds its reach: the capacity of the state to intervene effectively is often limited by lack of resources, lack of political consensus, and clientelist relationships which diminish the capacity of the state for unified action.'

In the case of the media, the state's intervention can be seen in various aspects (Hallin and Mancini 2004: 119–121). First, the state has played the role of censor. The direct authoritarian control of the years of dictatorship is presumably a thing of the past, but some remnants have carried over into the democratic period. Second, the state has also played an important role as an owner of media enterprises. The electronic media have traditionally been under the total and tight control of the state, but apart from the state-owned electronic media, the state has also had significant ownership in commercial media in the Mediterranean countries, including in the print press (for example, the Franco regime in Spain often had state-owned newspapers) and, of course, in news agencies (Agence France Presse, the Italian Agency AGI, EFE in Spain, ANA in Greece, Anadolu Ajansi in Turkey, Agência Lusa in Portugal). Publicly-funded news agencies function both to maintain the presence of the national press on the world scene and as a subsidy to domestic news media which use the service. Thirdly, in a more indirect but more effective way, the state acts to support its policies on ownership as well as to enforce the unwritten rules of power politics by using a wide range of means of intervention which are at its disposal. These means include sizable financial aid to the press, on which individual enterprises become dependent because they cannot cover their production costs. For example, as Hallin and Mancini (2004: 121) note, extensive indirect subsidies have been provided to the press as a whole in the form of tax breaks, reduced utility rates and the like. As the press have entered a recession period due to the increasing uses of the internet and the subsequent decrease in sales, more and more newspapers will ask for new public subsidies and this may affect a new spiral of clientelism affecting journalism as well.

Journalism training

National systems of journalism education are also closely related to or are the outcome of the role and function a society attributes to its journalists. Hallin and Mancini (2004) note the socioeconomic and political differences between Northern and Southern European countries have strongly affected their respective media cultures. Moreover, the structures in the areas of journalism and the media systems also strongly affect journalism training (Fröhlich and Holtz-Bacha, 1994). Fröhlich and Holtz-Bacha (1994) also note that there are two different ways of entering the profession: (a) direct entry though the media companies, such as 'on-the-job' training or 'undergoing training which is formalized in some way for a fixed period of time', and (b) training outside the media which is either provided in 'the form of vocational training by stand-alone schools of journalism or as journalism studies at the university'. Journalism training in Southern Europe, as in other countries, follows a mixed system of university level education, stand-alone schools and on-the-job training. However, on-the-job training remains as somewhat of a prerequisite for becoming a journalist. This is not a particularity of the Southern European societies, since in most countries the academy and the media industry 'employ criteria for accessing success in journalism education which are currently too divergent' (Bromley, Tumber and Zelizer 2001: 252). Nevertheless, Sanders et al. (2008) show in their study that although British and Spanish students exhibit similar views on journalism ethics, distinct, national journalistic 'cultures' have influenced students before they arrive at university.

The history of journalism education in Southern Europe, as the relevant chapters in this volume indicate, is characterized by a series of attempts that aimed at the creation of a professional school of journalism. These attempts began, as early as the 1920s in Spain and in Greece, with the formation of 'schools' of journalism with a semi-academic character, and lasted until the restoration of the parliamentary democracy. By and large, until the late 1980s few university departments offered curricula to train students in the practice of journalism. Usually instruction came from other institutions of higher education focused on specialized trades and occupations. In most cases universities offered courses to examine critically how journalism operates, often from the point of view of sociology or political science. As Hallin and Mancini (2004: 112) note formal education in journalism in Southern European countries developed relatively late since in most cases the access to the 'profession' was rather through families or friendship ties. This changed to a certain extent in the mid 1980s, when University Faculties and Departments were established in most countries.

Moreover, the rise of formal journalism education in the region is also related to the historical absence of education and training in the field of journalism, since the role of education is of central importance in establishing and maintaining professional status, as well as to the weakening of clientelism due to European integration (Hallin and Mancini 2004: 136). It is also related to the important changes that took place in the wider field of communications and the formation of a new media market in the beginning of the 1990s. This new market demanded specialized personnel with basic education, which could have been done in university departments of communications and mass media studies. In effect, although the demand of university journalism education can be seen in most Southern European countries in the past, the need for a combination of university theory and vocational practice is evident in the late 1980s. So the historical demand for the creation of a school of journalism, but also the modern demand of a new developing media market led to the creation of these new departments. Needless to say, the number of journalism education programmes and institutions, both private and public, has grown rapidly since the mid-1980s, and more and more young journalists nowadays are graduates from the media programmes at the universities.

However, there is not much in the way of practical training since in most cases it is a recent subject of study. Would-be journalists typically enter their faculties and study communications or media studies and are strongly focused on theory and research. This is because the tendency in Southern Europe, as in many other European countries, is to believe that journalists must also be well-acquainted with theory because without it they cannot become good journalists. However in most of the cases, practical skills training is less prominent than theoretical analysis of the role of journalism in society, reflecting the countries' strong literary and humanistic traditions. In a number of cases such as Portugal, Greece and to a certain extent Spain, journalism faculties are overwhelmed by academics coming mainly from other disciplines such as Sociology, Law, History, Philosophy, Political Science and even Arts, while there is an increasing number of on-the-job journalists participating as teachers in laboratories and practical courses. On the other hand, the prevailing attitude in the media industry, as in other Northern European countries, is that editors are content to hire political science and sociology graduates with passable writing styles. They believe that whatever polishing these graduates need can be done on the job.

Development trends

In the countries covered in this section, significant changes in the media sector have affected the development of journalism education. Although the developments in the media sector may not entirely respond to the needs of their industry, both their media systems and subsequently journalism have been surprisingly adaptable and flexible in the face of new developments. The commercialization of the media systems and the multiplication of media outlets have increased the demand for journalists who had to be better trained and to have an academic background. Thus, all Southern European countries have introduced journalism education on a university level. Regardless of the heterogeneity of journalism education in Southern Europe countries, the market seems to demand, in most cases, additional 'on-the-job' training. This is probably because the media industry and professionals consider university education as too theoretical. However, this is not a Southern European anomaly. As Simon Frith and Peter Meech (2007) inform us the steady growth of journalism in the UK has been greeted with both scepticism and anxiety by already established journalists, who argue that universities are unsuited to prepare new entrants for the 'realities' of journalism as an occupation.

On the other hand, it is not a coincidence that the overwhelming majority of journalists in Southern Europe are university graduates but not necessarily journalism graduates. In countries like Greece and Italy, for example, all young journalists, regardless of their university qualification, have to be registered with the professional associations and follow their registration requirements (such as exams, professional experience, etc.). Perhaps this echoes an earlier conclusion by Romy Fröhlich and Christina Holtz-Bacha (2003: 319) that 'the way journalists are educated influences their perception. Their self-perception and their role in society lead to differences in journalistic practice'.

To a certain extent this has changed the 'classical' notion of what a journalist is in these countries, although education has not reflected this change adequately. In the age of digitalization and media convergence, Europeanization and globalization, journalism education in Southern Europe must also take into account the changes in society (e.g. multiculturalism), in the economy as well as in the journalism profession too, with the rise of online news, internet and citizen-journalism (see also Holm 2002).

Since the differences among the media systems have weakened due to the prevalent logic of media markets (Hallin and Mancini 2004: 211) we can assume that journalism as a component of the media systems has started a similar homogenization process. And to extend this, under certain circumstances it may encourage a subsequent process in journalism education as well. On the other hand, as Henrik Örnebring (2009: 12) notes 'the prognosis for the emergence of a "European journalism" or pan-European journalistic culture is poor'. We may have a growing but small elite European journalism, focused on and around issues about the EU and addressed to a relevant elite audience, but this will probably not lead to a homogenization of European journalism and certainly not the homogenization of journalism education regardless of any Bologna agreement. On a critical basis, it might be argued that homogenization of journalism education in Europe could be seen as a part of a wider 'McDonaldization' of journalism education, which is also a part of a wider globalization of the present communications systems.

Technological advances may also 'challenge the traditional understanding of journalism' (Josephi 2005: 588–89). Internet, citizen journalism and bloggers on the one hand question journalism (Karam 2009), and on the other challenge traditional journalism education. As we have entered the age of convergence, digitalization and user-generated content, journalism education may need another evaluation and understanding.

The Author

Stylianos Papathanassopoulos is a professor and Head of the Faculty of Communication and Media Studies, National & Kapodistrian University of Athens.

References

Bromley, Michael; Tumber, Howard and Zelizer, Barbie (2001), 'Journalism Education', *Journalism*, 2(3), pp. 251–254.

Deuze, Mark (2005), 'What's journalism?', *Journalism*, 6(4), pp. 442–464.

Frith, Simon and Meech, Peter (2007), 'Becoming a journalist: Journalism education and journalism culture', *Journalism*, 8(2), pp. 137–164.

Fröhlich, Romy and Holtz-Bacha, Christina (eds.) (2003), *Journalism Education in Europe and North America: An International Comparison*, Cresskill, NJ: Hampton Press.

Fröhlich, Romy and Holtz-Bacha, Christina (1994), 'Structures of Inhomogeneity- Dilemmas of Journalism Training in Europe', the International Association of Mass Communication Research, July 1994, Seoul, Korea.

Hallin, C. Daniel and Mancini, Paolo (2004), *Comparing Media Systems; Three Models of Media and Politics*, Cambridge: Cambridge University Press.

Hallin, Daniel and Papathanassopoulos, Stylianos (2002), 'Political Clientelism and the Media: Southern Europe and Latin America in Comparative Perspective', *Media, Culture & Society*, 24(2), pp. 175–195.

Hallin, Daniel (2004), 'Journalism', *International Encyclopaedia of the Social & Behavioral Sciences*, pp. 7995–8000.

Holm, Hans-Hnrik (2002), 'The Forgotten globalization of journalism education', *Journalism and Mass Communication Educator*, 56(2), pp. 67–71.

Josephim Beate (2005), 'Journalism in the Global Age: Between Normative and Empirical', *Gazette: The International Journal for Communication Studies*, 67(6), pp. 575–590.

Karam, Francisco José Castilhos (2009), 'Journalism in the age of the information society, technological convergence, and editorial segmentation. Preliminary observations', *Journalism*, 10(1), pp. 109–125.

Mancini, Paolo (2000), 'Political Complexity and Alternative Models of Journalism, The Italian Case', In J. Curran and M.J. Park (eds), *De-Westernizing Media Studies*, London: Routledge, pp. 264–278.

McNair, B. (1998), *The Sociology of Journalism*, London: Arnold.

Örnebring, Henrik (2009), *Comparative European journalism: the state of current research*, Working Paper, Oxford: Reuters, Institute for the Study of Journalism/Oxford University.

Papathanassopoulos, Stylianos (2004), *Media and Politics; the case of Southern Europe*, Athens: Kastaniotis (in Greek).

Papathanassopoulos, Stylianos (2001), 'Media Commercialization and Journalism in Greece', *European Journal of Communication,* 16(4), pp. 505–521.

Sanders, Karen; Hanna, Mark; Berganza, María Rosa and Aranda, José Javier Sánchez (2008), 'Becoming Journalists: A Comparison of the Professional Attitudes and Values of British and Spanish Journalism Students', *European Journal of Communication,* 23 (2), pp. 133–152.

The Cypriot Journalism Education Landscape

The Greek Cypriot

Nayia Roussou

Introduction

The practice of journalism in Cyprus began as early as the nineteenth century, with the establishment and circulation of the first bilingual newspaper in the Island, *Cyprus* launched by Theodoulos Constantinides in Larnaca, on 29 August 1878. The town of Limassol followed suit and for ten years the two towns pioneered in press journalism, with Nicosia joining them in 1890, partly with fresh newspapers and partly with newspapers like *Neon Kition* and *Phoni tis Kiprou* which had first circulated in Larnaca. (Sophocleous, An.: 1997)

During these years, however and for a long time to come, many forerunners in journalism were self-taught, applying themselves to newswriting, mainly because of their literary talents. Many of them were indeed well-known and well-respected poets and prose writers, often publishing their literary writings in the Cyprus press, alongside their journalistic articles, commentaries and critiques.

Education in journalism by academic institutions

During the first half of the twentieth century the number of newspapers was on the increase in Cyprus and with the proclamation of independence in the Island in 1960, strong moves were made by both Government bodies and by private organizations for the promotion of arts and letters in different areas. The first private tertiary education institutions in the Island began functioning in the 1970's and it was in the context of their programmes of study that journalism education first began. So in 1972–1973 KES, a private tertiary education college, began offering a journalism programme, with courses taught by professional journalists, aiming mainly at familiarization of the students with journalism as a professional occupation, enriched by Public Relations, sports, as well as subjects on international journalism. The main scope of lessons covered Press and Radio journalism, the terminal degree being a three-year diploma. The average number of students yearly has since been ten to fifteen, mostly young women, with numbers of young men being on the increase in recent years. The programme is registered with the Cyprus Ministry of Education and Culture but does not participate in the European policies, like the Bologna Process, any exchange programmes, or the ECTS. Several students are funded however for their studies with KES, by different commercial organizations in the Island. (Stylianou, Th: April 17, 2008)

In 1977 the Europa Mass Communication Centre ('Europa College' in 1987) was founded and for about two and a half decades became a pioneering school in teaching journalistic courses. In 1999 the Europa College merged with the Cyprus College, established in 1961 and from 1977 to 2004 it was one of the leading schools in journalism with subjects taught by highly qualified academics as well as professional journalists, leading to a two-year college diploma. Adjunct subjects like Public Relations, Advertising and Marketing were offered with great success, preparing students for the LCCI (London Chamber of Commerce and Industry) exams. The journalistic courses were both theoretical and practical and the students were given the opportunity of practical training in the Cyprus media, including press and radio-television. About twenty to twenty-five students attended the College yearly, the practical subjects being conducted in the workshops and studios of the Europa College and after 1999, the Cyprus College. Many graduates of the College were employed not only by the Cyprus Media of communication but also by the National Greek Radio (ERT), the London Greek Radio (LGR), the Cyprus News Agency and the Cyprus Broadcasting Corporation, as well as the Cyprus Embassy in Mexico and the French Embassy in Nicosia.

After 2004 the collaboration with the Cyprus College was interrupted and as the Europa College degree was only of a two-year duration it did not participate in the Bologna Process or the ECTS, and neither did the College apply to the Cyprus Ministry of Education and Culture for accreditation. (Georgiades, G: May 30, 2008).

In 1980 the Philips College began offering a BA in Journalism under the Faculty of Languages and Communication. The programme which is registered with the Cyprus Ministry of Education and Culture and supported by an adjunct BA in Public Relations is accredited by the Ministry and has the following objectives:

- To provide a practical education in journalism and proficiency in journalism skills
- To develop communication skills
- To develop awareness of the ethical issues facing journalism

The duration of the studies is four years and the programme offers practical training in print, broadcasting and online journalism, underpinned by the study of communication, law, ethics and politics. It is addressed to both students aspiring to become professional journalists, as well as to practitioners, desiring higher qualifications. It is part of the Bologna Process and the ECTS system. (Journalism Faculty, in http: //www.philips.ac.cy/cgibin/hweb?-A=1259&-V=degrees, accessed on 5 March, 2008)

With the further explosion of the Media in Cyprus in the decade of the 90's and the beginning of private broadcasting, more emphasis was given to journalism education.

A major landmark towards this increased emphasis was the crucial change that marked the fates of the private tertiary colleges in 2007. A new Law licensed three Colleges to function as private Universities, with Intercollege becoming the University of Nicosia Cyprus College, the European University and the Frederick Polytechnic, Frederick University. Not all of their programmes were accepted to be included in the University curricula, however.

The Journalism Programme of Frederick University and the three media programmes of the University of Nicosia were accepted as university programmes.

The University of Nicosia (Intercollege up to 2007) launched a two-year communications diploma in 1991, under the Communications Department, with a concentration on journalism, attracting both aspiring students and practitioners wishing for academic learning and qualifications. In 1993 the two-year diploma was extended into a four-year B.Sc. in Communications, the programme still offering a concentration in journalism, consisting of both theoretical and practical courses in both Press and Electronic media. The lecturers included both highly qualified academics as well as established professionals with a reputable career in the Cyprus Media. The University afforded the students the opportunity to do their practical exercise in the Radio-TV Unit of the institution, which Unit has recently been upgraded to a 'Mediazone' Centre. The BSc in Communications offered the students a triple choice for a major concentration:

- Journalism
- Radio/TV Production
- Corporate Communication (Public Relations, Advertising, Marketing).

The programme continued to grow and to flourish with its graduates pursuing professional careers in the Cyprus media, or continuing their media studies abroad. In the year 2000 both the Diploma and the BSc were accredited by the Ministry. In 2005 an MA in Media and Communication was introduced with theoretical and practical courses in communication, like Newspaper Production and Management, Public Relations Theory and Advertising and Research topics.

All of the programmes are attended by both students and practicing journalists who seek to upgrade their qualifications. The latter attend mainly the evening courses which are offered in Greek and all the two-year diploma courses are offered in Greek in the evening. The courses in English are attended by both Greek Cypriots and international students and many communication courses including journalism are also attended inter-departmentally, with students that are from different departments in the University, aside from the Department of Communications. Some of the students are given the chance to work in the Mediazone Center and to get practical experience in the different newspapers published by the students, either in the context of their coursework, or by different student groups working in the context of the Student Affairs Department.

Besides their practical work on the grounds of the Nicosia University, the students are also given the opportunity to work in Radio/TV channels and in the newspapers of the Island, as well as to take part in different research projects conducted by the faculty in the courses they teach. Further to this extramural experience, the Department, like the rest of the University is networked with different European exchange programmes like Erasmus and parallel to this, the whole university is also moving currently from the American credit system to the Bologna process and the ECTS.

A considerable number of graduates are pursuing careers in newspapers and Radio/TV channels or media research and market communication offices. The subjects offered in the programme range all the way from introductory subjects, to Press and Radio/TV production in conventional journalism and newswriting, sports journalism, photo-journalism, as well as Ethics and Law. In the past academic year, 2007–08, 221 students were registered – 86 men and 135 women.

The Department is also currently processing a BA in Journalism in Greek, as this was considered to be an imperative response to the demand from high school graduates who want to acquire journalism qualifications in Greek and also from experiential journalists who consider that their practical experience is not enough and they should obtain academic qualifications to face competition in the market. Some of the new courses envisaged to complete the new BA in Journalism are on Research in Journalism and European and International Journalism, as well as Online journalism subjects. (Roussou.N: 2008)

Frederick University (Polytechnic, before 2007) began offering a four-year programme of journalism studies leading to a BA in Journalism, in 1993 with a faculty body consisting of 90% academics and 10% professional journalists. The main aims of the programme were as follows:

- To offer students the professional training in the skills and techniques needed to practice journalism in all its forms.
- To familiarize students with the cultural, political and economic tendencies which shape the world and train them in the use of the analytic models of the social and historical sciences as interpretative tools in organizing and analyzing information.
- To guide students to examine critically the realm of publicity with a special focus on public discourse, public relations and the laws and ethics of the journalistic profession.
- To provide students with an understanding of the processes of development and change in the increasingly complex world of mass communication and encourage the development of the necessary skills for working and creating in this context.
- To help students develop personal qualities that contribute to social responsibility, cultural interest and successful careers in a democratic society by taking into consideration both the needs of their own society and the condition and needs of the global human community.

In the light of the above, new technologies like Internet Journalism have been incorporated in the programme, which offers Investigative Journalism, Sports Journalism and International Journalism. Emphasis with practical exercises in the second and fourth years of study is distributed among the different Media as follows:

- Press: 25%
- Radio: 25%
- TV: 25%
- Internet: 15%

The programme carries 130 credits or 240 ECTS and it is networked with European exchange programmes like ERASMUS. There are about 30 students aspiring to become professional journalists every academic year, with 60% men and 40% women. The programme is accredited by the Cyprus Ministry of Education and Culture and many graduates are absorbed by the Cyprus media.

The university has its own Radio/TV station licensed to broadcast on a national level, in which station the students have the opportunity to do their practical work in a professional context. (Theocharidis, S., May 5, 2008)

Journalism education by public bodies

As the media explosion spread in Cyprus and private broadcasting also began in the early 1990s, deregulation and re-regulation finally settled down with the passing, in 1998 of the Law for Private Broadcasting. The law also established the Cyprus Broadcasting Authority and it was natural that the Authority would also, at some stage of its function, become interested in the education of Cyprus journalists. The Broadcasting Authority organized its first seminar for journalists in 2000, with the participation of about 60 people. The purpose of the seminar was the acquaintance with the philosophy and the legal provisions which regulate private radio/television stations, especially the contents of news bulletins. The participants were not directly involved with the preparation of the news bulletins and even though the audio-visual materials shown were very relevant to the chosen topics of human rights and the protection of minors, the general conclusion of the Authority from the seminar was that in future it would be more useful and effective to organize such seminars for the electronic media journalists who are directly involved in journalistic practices.

In the year 2002 the Cyprus Broadcasting Authority additionally organized, in collaboration with the Ministry of Education and Culture, a special seminar for journalists on 'The Correct Use of the Greek Language in the Electronic Media of Communication.' A certificate was awarded at the end of the seminar and materials about correct linguistic expression prepared by the Ministry of Education and Culture were distributed to the participants. (Aletrari, M. & Peristiani: 2002)

The Union of Cyprus Journalists, ever since its establishment in 1960, has been actively involved in the professional education and further training of its members, especially the younger professionals. So from time to time the Union organizes seminars which are practically oriented, on language issues and Press Law and Ethics. It is worth mentioning, that emphasis on language use in Cyprus is much more necessary, perhaps, than in many other countries, as Greek-Cypriots use the Cypriot Dialect in their everyday life and in their family and peer context, but the official language of the country, the formal education language and the media language is the Demotic or Panhellenic Greek. This discrepancy sometimes creates a diglossic canvas against which professionals have to work. In order to improve the language abilities of its members, the Union of Cyprus Journalists organized in the 1990s a series of lectures by the Department of Communication of the Panteion University of Athens. The seminar was also attended by officers of the Press and Information Office and official certificates by the Panteion University were given to all participants.

The Union of Cyprus Writers have organized seminars in collaboration with the Cyprus Press and Information Office, the Association of Newspaper and Magazine Publishers, the Cyprus Broadcasting Authority, as mentioned earlier, the European Journalism Centre, as well as non-Cypriot Journalistic Organizations. They have also subsidized Radio/TV presentation courses for their members. The different seminars were taught by academics and experienced professional journalists and did not involve public relations and advertising topics. The seminars did not include topics on new technologies and the number of journalists attending, even though subsidized by both the State and the Association of Newspaper and Magazine Publishers, has been comparatively small. The seminars are not accredited by the Ministry of Education but the latter collaborates in the organization of such seminars, as we saw earlier.

The Union also organizes lectures on journalism topics by the members of the Union's Board, to high school students who are members of journalism clubs, a practice which is becoming popular in Cypriot high schools, of recent years.

The Union of Cyprus journalists envisages the creation of an Institute of Mass Media and Communication, which will aim at offering a programme of about 8 to 10 months to young journalists embarking on their professional career. To this end they are working together with the Cyprus University, the Technological University of Cyprus (TEPAK) and the Cyprus Press and Information Office. (Kannaouros, A., May 8, 2008)

Finally in 1999 the Institute for Mass Media of Communication was established as a non-profit, scientific research and academic organization affiliated with the University of Nicosia. Its main objectives are oriented towards upgrading the journalism profession and organizing seminars on journalism and communication. It has also been building a valuable archive on journalists and print media. (Lambidonitis,D. in http: //www.immecy. org/achievements.htm, accessed on 16 June, 2008)

Concluding Remarks

In spite of its small size Cyprus has been modernizing in the area of the media, not only on the practical, production level, but in the sphere of academic education as well. The emphasis given to media teaching and to the education of journalists in particular, has been an ongoing process during the last three decades, developing from early non-accredited college diplomas to accredited bachelor's and master's programmes, functioning in the context of European policies. Much has yet to be done with regard to the transition of journalism from conventional forms to online practices and the training and preparation of journalists to that effect is not on a desirable or effective level. A fact which is not particular to Cyprus alone as the domestication of new technologies is still in process in many European countries. In research conducted by nine researchers among newsrooms in eleven countries

(Cyprus, Estonia, Finland, Greece, Ireland, Italy, Lithuania, United Kingdom, Slovenia, Spain and Sweden) in 2005/6, about how journalists perceive the changes introduced by the Internet in the functions, practices and ethics of the profession, a general note of scepticism by respondent journalists themselves, about the domestication of the internet was noted in the conclusion by the writers. (Fortunati, L. et al., 2008)

According to our respondents, the great value of the internet is to be a vast deposit of information that they can search to retrieve, when needed, information to enrich their articles. However, journalists do not think that web or multimedia publishing is in itself a way to write more interestingly or with greater satisfaction. Moreover they do seem to consider print and web journalism as two distinct jobs: a good print journalist is not necessarily also a good web journalist, and vice versa.

New forms and opportunities for the profession are, however, constantly developing in cyber journalism and technology is, after all, scarcely ever adopted through a flash of lightning but through long and laborious practices.

The Author

Nayia Roussou is a Media Professor and Chair of the Communications Department in the University of Nicosia, Cyprus.

References

Aletrari, Marianna and Persiani, Loukia, Officers of the Cyprus Broadcasting Authority (2002), Memo to the President and Members of the Cyprus Broadcasting Authority,

Fortunati, L.; Sarrica, M.; Balcityene, A.; Harro-Loit, Halliki; Macgregor, Ph.; Roussou, N.; Salaverria, R.;O'Sullivan, J. and de Luca, F., 'The Influence of the Internet on European Journalism', in "Journal of Computer-Mediated Communication" 14 (2009) 928–963.

Georgiades, G. former owner of EUROPA College, in personal interview, 30 May, 2008.

Journalism Faculty, "Bachelor in Journalism", in http: //www.philips.ac.cy/cgibin/hweb?-A=1259&-V=degrees, accessed on 5 March, 2008)

Kannaouros, Andreas, President of the Union of Cyprus Journalists, E-mail interview, May 2008.

Lambidonitis, D. (2008), "Profile" in IMME Website, http: //www.immecy.org/achievements.htm, accessed on 16 June, 2008

Roussou, Nayia (2008), Records of UNIC and of Department of Communications, UNIC.

Sophocleous, Andreas (1997), "Οι Πρώτες Ελληνικες Εφημερίδες της Λευκωσίας» (The First Greek Newspapers of Nicosia), Nicosia, Intercollege Press.

Stylianou, Th., (2008), Owner/Director of KES, E-mail interview , 17 April , 2008.

Theocharidis, Sotiris , Chair of Journalism Programme, Frederick University, E-mail interview 5 May, 2008.

Turkish Cypriot

Bekir Azgin and Mashoed Bailie

Introduction

Turkish Cypriot journalism education is a relatively new phenomenon. Until the 1970s, anyone (usually male) with an interest in newspapers, could either work for a newspaper or, in rarer cases, start a newspaper of their own. Newspapers proliferated in the Turkish Cypriot community although many of them were short-lived due to economic strain or simply loss of interest in the enterprise (Azgin 1998). Beginning in the early 1970s the Turkish Cypriot newspaper industry saw the first graduates from universities in Turkey although the majority of journalists without a university education remained high. It was not until the mid-1990s that Turkish Cypriot universities began offering four-year journalism degrees. The first programme was offered at European University of Lefke in 1994 followed by Eastern Mediterranean University in 1996, Near East University and Girne American University in 1997 and Cyprus International University in 1998. Today, five Turkish Cypriot universities grant Bachelor of Arts Degrees in Journalism. While this has lead to an increase in the number of women entering the field of journalism (over fifty per cent of the workforce in 2008), the so-called 'glass ceiling' persists with a complete absence of women in upper decision-making positions and with no women owning a newspaper or radio or television station.

All five programmes offer a selection of Faculty core courses in communication and media studies (including communication history, theory and research), Department core courses in journalism theory, history and practice, and departmental elective courses that have strong practical applications. Only the Eastern Mediterranean University offers a programme with a liberal-arts orientation where students take university-wide compulsory courses in areas that include physics, math, psychology, sociology, anthropology, philosophy and the arts.

Turkish Cypriot journalism education today.[1]

	Turkish	Turkish Cypriot	Other Countries	Female	Male	Total Currently Enrolled
EMU	45%	50%	05%	55%	45%	108
CIU	98%	02%	0%	35%	65%	131
EUL	93%	06%	01%	40%	60%	59
NEU	73%	27%	0%	40%	60%	180
GAU	No Data	No Data	No Data	40%	60%	200

Four-year Turkish Cypriot university journalism programmes: Area focus percentages.

	Liberal Arts	Faculty Core	Department Core	Department Electives	Internship
EMU	25%	25%	30%	20%	Yes
CIU	n/a	50%	30%	20%	Yes
EUL	n/a	65%	35%	n/a	Non-compulsory
NEU	n/a	50%	30%	20%	Yes
GAU	n/a	50%	30%	20%	Yes

With the exception of EMU, all other Journalism programmes include compulsory courses in public relations and advertising.

Journalism education departments and faculty

Turkish Cypriot journalism education is conducted at the five Turkish Cypriot universities. There are no pre-university or technical school training courses available. Turkish Cypriot journalism programmes have been historically housed in faculties of communication and media studies. Faculties house departments of journalism, radio-television and film, public relations and advertising, and visual arts and communication. While CIU, LAU, NEU, and GAU offer programmes that consist of a mixture of faculty and department courses (that include courses in public relations and advertising as part of their required courses), EMU has opted for a mix between general education (including sciences, math, liberal arts), faculty core courses, departmental courses and electives. EMU journalism students are not required to take courses in public relations and advertising although they may choose to broaden their understanding of the market-orientation of their profession through the elective track. While core faculty members hold doctoral degrees, there has been a history of inviting professionals from the industry to share knowledge and experience with journalism students. EMU, for example, has invited journalists concerned with the promotion of peace communication to offer specialized courses to journalism students and to promote awareness of the process of investigative journalism (this is especially important on an island where the tendency is to rely too heavily, perhaps, on 'official sources' comprising of government press releases and the semi-official TAK news agency).

Internships of between six and eight weeks are required of all journalism students (with the exception of LAU where internship is voluntary) and must be completed prior to graduation. The goal of the internship programme is to give students opportunities to experience current practices in newspapers and other news media, to enhance their chances of making contacts in the field, and to assist them in gaining the knowledge they will need to secure positions within the industry. The programme also provides a space for probing the differences between theory and practice as students encounter the limitations and possibilities of working in commercial, non-profit and public media outlets. All of the Turkish Cypriot faculties of communication and media studies have in-house student newspapers that are usually published bi-monthly and radio stations where journalism students can practice both print and broadcast journalism. EMU, NEU and GAU also have television stations that provide journalism students with additional opportunities to practice their art. A unique aspect of EMU's department of journalism is that students are required to take courses in online journalism and to produce an online faculty newspaper.

EMU's liberal-arts orientation reflects its interest in joining the Bologna process. EMU has been engaged in a three-year bid for acceptance into the process although at the time of writing EMU has yet to succeed in gaining entrance. Ironically, while Turkish Cypriot students are recognized as EU citizens, Turkish Cypriot universities are not eligible for membership. Furthermore, Turkish Cypriot students are excluded from participation in ERASMUS and other EU institutional educational programmes. Importantly, the International Crisis Group report (2008) has recognized this problem and included in its report a recommendation that 'Greek Cypriot embargoes on Turkish Cypriot involvement in international sporting activities, cultural exchanges and adhesion to European University programmes like the Bologna process could be lifted' (9).

The emphasis in Turkish Cypriot journalism education is on combining journalism theory, professional practices and engagement with new technologies of communication although at the Faculty core level, courses tend to focus on theories of media and society with an emphasis on understanding the relationship between media, images, words and the production and circulation of information in shaping cultural, social, political and economic environments. Due to the specific historical and political circumstances that confront Turkish Cypriot students and potential journalists, there is an overt attempt to sensitize journalism students to the importance of language as a tool for promoting understanding, empathy and cooperation – juxtaposed to the 'reactionary' and 'sensational' emphasis that can often be found in mainstream reporting.

Currently degrees in journalism are offered at the BA level in all five universities and students may continue in their studies to the MA and Ph.D. level at EMU and NEU. At EMU, the MA and Ph.D. are research-oriented thesis and dissertation programmes in communication and media studies and may have an emphasis in journalism depending upon the student's area of focus. At NEU the MA programme is housed in the department of journalism whereas the doctoral programme is faculty-wide. The MA and Doctoral level tend to be more theoretical and focused on examining the relationship between journalists and journalism at the local, national and international/global level.

BA programmes in Journalism are conducted over a four-year (eight semesters) period, MA programmes generally consist of one year of coursework with between one and three years for the completion of the thesis. Ph.D. programmes include one year of coursework with from three to five years of supervision to complete the dissertation. At EMU doctoral candidates are required to publish at least one article in a social science indexed journal prior to defending their doctoral dissertation.

Turkish Cypriot university journalism programmes are accredited by YODAK (The Turkish Cypriot Local Higher Education Accreditation Institute) and YOK (Turkish Higher Education Institution).

Associations

EMU's Faculty of Communication and Media Studies is a member of the European Communication Research and Education Association (ECREA) listed under the category of 'Turkey' and EMU and NEU are members of the European University Association (EUA) under the category of 'Other'. All Turkish Cypriot journalism departments are members of the Turkish Cypriot Journalists Union and/or the Turkish Cypriot Journalists Association.

Concluding Remarks

Little systematic investigative scholarship has been conducted on the role of the Turkish Cypriot media. Without a clearer understanding of exactly how the Turkish Cypriot press currently operates, it is difficult to ascertain the current strengths and weaknesses of journalism on the island or to prescribe pedagogical interventions that might increase the capacity of journalists to intervene as social actors in promoting more democratic society.

In one recent study (Bailie and Azgin 2008), a picture emerges of an antagonistic Turkish and Greek Cypriot media landscape where contemporary journalistic routines and practices discourage journalists from broaching the divided Cypriot community and establishing dialogue with their 'other'. Furthermore, sensationalism as a priority 'news value' (Wolfsfeld, 2004) is the norm in Turkish Cypriot journalism. It is rare to find stories that encourage empathy with the Greek Cypriot community or that increase understanding in the Turkish Cypriot community of the complex problems that have to be faced if resolution to the division of the island is to be found.

This journalistic unwillingness to empathetically seek out the stories of the 'other' – giving voice to the Greek Cypriot partner community – is something that Turkish Cypriot journalism education will have to take seriously. The point is made succinctly in the recent (2008) International Crisis Group (ICG) report entitled 'Best chance for a solution since 1974'. The ICG report insists that 'due to total lack of communication and media vilification', Cypriots 'have hostile, outdated and misleading images of each other' (8). The report also makes a connection between lack of communication and over-reliance on media as vehicles for information when it argues that: 'These two parties barely know each other, having not talked for 40 years, and are all too ready to believe extremist rhetoric in nationalist media' (i). Communication scholars Morley and Robins (1995) have argued similarly and in a global context insisting that '[…] the further the "event" from our own direct experience, the more we depend on media images for the totality of our knowledge' (133).

Turkish Cypriot journalism education has to engage this problem seriously and work with the premise that change is not only possible, but inevitable if journalists are to play a productive and pro-reconciliation role in Cyprus. As accented by Manoff (1998): '[...] journalism is a specific social practice that has a history, and [...] this history is one of unending social invention. In other words, in discussing "media and conflict" issues, it is important not to fall prey to an ahistorical essentialism that presumes that today's form of journalism is, or ought to be, tomorrow's'. (Manoff, 2009)

Turkish Cypriot journalism education, as with its Greek Cypriot counterpart, cannot escape the complexities of life in the Cypriot communities and is, to a large extent, held hostage to the ever shifting boundaries that make up each sides 'national struggle' as expressed in the political spheres of each community. This is a broad cross-community concern that university journalism curricula must highlight in order to encourage an increase in the range or scope of journalistic critical thought – to be able to 'think outside the box'. McChesney (2008) makes this point well when arguing that 'Journalism today has much more in common with the elites it supposedly regulates than with the public on whose behalf it supposedly speaks' (71).

Overcoming this tendency in professional journalism is not an easy task and ultimately means learning to challenge the mundane, taken-for-granted routines that limit both the journalist's world-view and her sources; encouraging journalists to seek information from beyond the 'usual suspects' which includes entrenched political parties and their leaders, government officials and other elites; to accentuate the many-sidedness of each issue; to encourage deeper understanding of the historical context within which contemporary dramas are enacted daily; and to act as a vehicle for the sharing of concerns from a much broader base of respondents.

One such group is Women who are severely under-represented both in the content of daily news stories and at the highest levels of media management. Gender sensitization is thus another crucial area that needs to be further encouraged in journalism education both in terms of scholarship and in terms of media practices. Certainly developments in feminist media theory (Riordan 2004; Roach 1993; Sreberny 2005) highlight the importance of recognizing the value of women as producers of knowledge that partially shapes the social, political and economic spheres and it is here that journalism education might play a significant role in preparing a new generation of Cypriot women who might take up and challenge the conventional, hierarchical, and all-too-often conflict oriented structures and practices of the Cypriot press.

The Authors

Bekir Azgin is Chair of the Department of Journalism at Eastern Mediterranean University where he teaches in journalism and communication and is a regular contributor to the Turkish Cypriot press.

Mashoed Bailie is Chair of the Department of Radio-TV-Film Studies at Eastern Mediterranean University and Editor of the *Global Media Journal: Mediterranean Edition*.

Note

1. Data provided by the respective Journalism Departments.

References

Azgin, B. (1998), 'The Turkish Cypriot Mass Media', In K.D. Grothusen, W. Steffani, and P. Zervakis (eds.), *ZYPERN*, Vandenhoeck & Ruprecht: Göttingen/Zürich.

Bailie, M. and Azgin, B. (2008), 'A barricade, a bridge and a wall: Cypriot journalism and the mediation of conflict in Cyprus', *Cyprus Review*, 20(1), pp. 57–92.

Evripidou, S. (2008), 'Best chance for a solution since 1974', *Cyprus Mail*, http: //www.cyprus-mail. com/news, 24 June. Accessed 15 July 2008.

International Crisis Group (2008), 'Reunifying Cyprus: The best chance yet', Europe Report No. 194, 23 June, pp. 1–34, http: //www.crisisgroup.org/home/index.cfm?id=5502&l=1. Accessed 25 June 2008.

Manoff, R. (1998), '"Role plays": Potential media roles in conflict prevention and management', *Track Two*, 7(4), http: //www.ccr.uct.ac.za/archive/two/7_4/p11_roleplays.html. Accessed 25 February 2009.

McChesney, R. W. (2008), *The political economy of media: Enduring issues, emerging dilemmas*, New York: Monthly Review Press.

Morley, D. and Robins, K. (1995), *Spaces of identity: Global media, electronic landscapes and cultural boundaries*, New York: Routledge.

Roach, C. (1993), 'Feminist peace researchers, culture, and communication', In Colleen Roach (ed.), *Communication and culture in war and peace*, London: Sage, pp. 175–191.

Reordan, E. (2004), 'Feminist theory and the political economy of communication', In Andrew Calabrese and Colin Sparks (eds.), *Toward a political economy of culture: Capitalism and communication in the Twenty-First Century*, New York: Rowman and Littlefield, pp. 342–356.

Sreberny, A. (2005), 'Globalization, Communication, democratization: Toward gender equality', In Robert A. Hackett and Yuezhi Zhao (eds.), *Democratizing global media: One world, many struggles*, New York: Rowman and Littlefield.

Sunday Mail (2008), 'Tales from the Coffee Shop. The alley-cat who loves a public spat' http: //www. cyprus-mail.com/news, 22 June. Accessed 15 July 2008.

Wolfsfeld, G. (2004), *Media and the path to peace*, UK: Cambridge University.

The French Journalism Education Landscape

Jacques Le Bohec

Introduction

The situation of journalism education in France is rather complex. While writing this text even I, as the author, am realizing the difficulty in expressing peculiar and quite untranslatable details and structures. To describe the situation we could use words like anarchical, controversial, fragmented, paradoxical, etc. For instance students, parents, guidance counsellors and ordinary people believe very strongly that having a journalism degree is mandatory to becoming a journalist. Actually, if not, why do these journalism schools exist? In fact the individual routes are very heterogeneous. In order to clarify progressively the situation, this first section deals with seven issues about journalism education in France. They compose a useful code to understand what really occurs.

Distanced teaching or technical training?

This question is about divergent goals of teaching. On the one hand some think a professor's role consists in passing on accepted scientific knowledge, a knowledge discovered by researchers controlled and ratified by colleagues in a perspective of social sciences (sociology, history, political science, ethnology, demography, economy, geography, communication). On the other hand some consider their work consists primarily in helping students to find a job. So there is a distinction between the teaching of journalism and teaching on journalism. In theory, technical training is the goal of post-baccalauréat schools (A-level, at 17 years old) while the goal of universities is research and distanced teaching (at least until the 2007 Pécresse Act on Universities 'autonomy'). In recent years political pressures on universities push them towards formal training. Implicitly and sometimes explicitly they are strangely accused of being responsible for unemployment levels. It is the reason why there are many diplomas of master's 'professionnels' (formerly DESS, diplôme d'études spécialisées supérieures) proposed in journalism with a technical goal.

Weak or strong ties with employers?

The question here is about money but not only that. A weak tie means more autonomy in teaching content. Teachers are not obliged to promote professional myths for instance. But how is it possible to learn some audiovisual and expensive techniques without up to date facilities?

The French government never financed these expensive facilities by a sufficient subvention. The annual necessary amount to train a journalist was evaluated at €12,000 in 2007. Consequently all schools and universities must find other resources or abandon some specific paths. There are three other possible resources: tuition and entrance examination fees, professional tax and education tax (5 per cent of media companies total salary expenses for basic training). In theory accredited schools tuition fees must be reasonable, but the precise 'reasonable' amount appears rather vague. Only schools (private companies and association status) can demand high tuition fees of students and parents (around €6000). We also have to clarify that basic and continuous training are legally separate in France. Moreover employers are not obliged to pay the professional tax to formal training in journalism. Many feel reluctance towards a school system suspected of producing employees who are intellectually too intellectually pretentious and not flexible enough. They prefer controlling the training directly. For instance, Prisma group (Bertelsmann) created its own technical training for future magazine press journalists and executives (which the students are paid a salary for while attending).

School or on-the-job training?

Historically there is a debate about the utility of schools in journalism. Some people think schools are not necessary at all. They prefer on-the-job ('*sur le tas*') mimesis. Very often we observe there is a continuity between the curriculum of a journalist and his/her point of view about usefulness of schools dedicated to journalistic know-how. When one is an autodidact one will be very cautious with schools, and vice-versa. That explains also the co-opting phenomenon: editors and journalists who teach in schools will have a tendency to help younger graduates from their former schools. With narcissistic nostalgia, hiring a young journalist from these schools is a means to remember their youth. For students, formal schools are the best way to touch flesh and blood journalists and the real job thanks to internships. Many of them have a dialectical relationship with the school system. They are not the best students who prefer the '*Grandes écoles*' or a career in teaching and research. They do not really like the intellectual work (reading, concepts, dissertations, etc.). They are bored and fed up by traditional courses. Their main purpose is only to find a job as journalist. They do not care about research on journalists. All that is considered as 'too theoretical' (or 'abstract') even if courses describe social reality and use empirical inquiries. According to them, technical trainings and unpaid internships seem the best exit out of the school system.

Generalist or specialist?

Opinions about this aspect are also controversial. Some assess that journalism education should be broader, more general, that it is better if the journalist in question is not familiar with what he is reporting (see 'parachute journalism' model). In this way the papers or reports will be understandable by a major part of the whole population. In this perspective, the training aims to produce polyvalent journalists able to deal with a large range of subjects. In fact journalism training is focused on apprenticeship of genres and technical expertise. Other people think in a different way. Polyvalent journalists risk committing many factual errors because of their ignorance and numerous gaps (grammar rules in French included). It is the reason why, in this conception, formal training has to prepare applicants to a journalistic speciality (politics, religion, science, law, local, international affairs, business, sports, culture, etc.), or knowhow in one specific technical skill (anchorman, cameraman, investigation, photography, documentary, sub-editor, local affairs, web, radio, etc.). But another danger then appears: lack of adaptation abilities in case of technical changes, unemployment, bankruptcy, transfer and lack of knowledge and weak credibility.

Malthusianism or opening?

In 2008, the commission which delivers the official identity press cards in France (CCIJP: *Commission de la carte d'identité des journalistes professionnels*) has given out 37,000 cards for a total population of 65 million people. During the last decade the CCIJP has delivered an average of 1,000 additional cards each year (more arrivals than departures). But among all card-carrying (called '*encartés*') people only 20 per cent hold a diploma from a journalism school in France (registered or not). We thus observe that a large part of *encartés* have another school path. From where do they come? A small percentage have bypassed initial training and have followed a continuous training programme (at the CFPJ, *Centre de formation professionnelle des journalistes*, for example) instead. Actually, it is very

Table 1: Recently attributed press cards to registered graduates.

Schools	2002	2003	2004	2005	2006
EJCM	15	16	18	15	24
IJBA	43	19	37	33	37
CELSA	7	7	8	11	13
CFJ	39	36	35	43	54
EJT	14	16	27	24	21
ICM	–	–	–	–	6
IPJ	28	36	43	42	43
IUT-L	–	–	–	3	13
ESJ	41	36	43	42	43
CUEJ	33	27	37	37	29
IUT-T	45	24	30	35	28
Total	265	217	294	303	322

difficult to pass the entrance test of registered journalism schools. There are a large number of candidates for very few places inside. Moreover, the ad hoc Commission which gives accreditation to diplomas in journalism has a Malthusian policy. There are less registered than non-registered diplomas (see Table 4). Why? It is difficult to explain. Perhaps it is in correspondence with the traditional elitist conception of journalism: a prestigious, noble and intellectual 'profession' rather than a simple and manual 'occupation'. Table 1 above shows figures about attributed press cards to registered graduates from 2002 to 2006.

Deontology or not?

This issue deals with training content. The question of the ethical rules imposed on journalists appears in France during the last decades of the nineteenth century and after. It is a reaction to what has been called the 'venal press' ('*presse vénale*') namely the tendency to accept money in exchange for printing articles with hidden advertising and deliberate lies. The First World War was a period of military propaganda (lies, censorship); so, after 1918, some journalists attempted to moralize and organize the 'profession', notably Georges Bourdon, who created the first union. The idea is that a professional deontology must be inculcated or imposed in order to avoid these scandals in the future. It is also a question of credibility for journalists.

Given that the respect of ethical rules does not belong to criteria taken into account by the Commission which delivers press cards, some thought deontology must be learnt inside schools. But very few schools really attribute a great importance to this. Johanna Siméant thus showed that at the CFJ teachers' conception of deontology consists in an early and progressive adjustment of relationships with three types of social agents: colleagues, sources and public. In fact this ethical question very often concerns journalists with religious mental structures (or ethos), who tend to express value judgments. Actually, the recall of moral rules is a modern way to impose their views. It is not a coincidence if the first journalism school (ESJ) was created in 1924 by the Catholic University of Lille and that the courses on ethics are still made in collaboration with it.

Information vs. communication?

In the French language, information and communication can be defined thanks to a Saussurian perspective, especially about journalism. 'Information' supposes independence and objectivity whereas 'communication' implies propaganda and advertising. It is the reason why the commission which delivers official labels to schools requires the communication path to be parallel with the journalism (not mixed up) within each school or university department. Journalists are supposed to be independent authors using free speech without any hindrance except truth and law. Journalists who fight for a political cause or work in an opinion or party newspaper-media are often condemned by their peers; by the transnational association 'Reporters sans frontières' or their colleagues who play the role of moral judges, for example.

These involved journalists are not considered as 'true' journalists but as activists. We observe the same reactions when famous journalists do what jargon designates as '*ménages*'. Originally this word means 'cleaners' work', therefore a manual job, dirty and humiliating. In journalism, it means well-paid animation performances; see for instance the accusations against a dominant journalist, Christine Ockrent, both wife of current Foreign Affairs Minister Bernard Kouchner and president of the holding France-Monde (France24, RFI and TV5), because she made such lucrative '*ménages*'.

These seven recurrent issues converge to explain the current situation, which is a social product of opposite conceptions and divergent interests between various social groups (governments, union, employers lobbies, scholars, dominant journalists, associations of journalists). There is an absence of a coherent schedule or national policy concerning journalism education in France.

Some features of French journalism

There are other relevant elements to introduce, which deal with five important characteristics of 'journalism' in France.

What does 'journalism' mean?

Behind a word like 'journalism' many denotations may be hidden in the same country, *a fortiori* among different countries, with the methodological risk consisting in an artificial homogenization of realities and meanings under the same wor(l)d. Consequently we have to be very cautious towards the risk of fallacious similarity due to the apparently similar semantic and social uses. These are the CCIJP figures about press card owners:

Table 2: All attributed press cards in 2008.

	Men	Women	Total
Incumbents:			
Salaried employees	15,500	10,645	26,145
Freelancers	2,795	2,806	5,601
Unemployed	668	644	1,312
Directors (former journalists)	439	82	521
Trainees:			
Salaried employees	1,150	1,313	2,463
Freelancers	579	680	1,259
General total:	21,131	16,170	37,301

'Real' and 'fake' journalists

Officially only the *'encartés'* may be called journalists, that is 37300 in 2008. But there are other people who could claim to belong to the category. First, there are journalists who work for private companies and local governments' newspapers. Secondly, there are local correspondents of regional weekly and daily newspapers (around 50,000), which have a special status. Thirdly, we have to mention journalists who earn more money from freelance articles and reports paid by copyright and communication jobs than from the usual journalistic jobs. Fourthly, many young journalists do not earn enough to be officially considered as journalists. Paradoxically, these four groups are much more numerous than 'real' journalists...The distinction between real and fake journalists is also subjective and tactical.

Criteria of school agreement

The competent commission to give the official agreement to schools is the CNPEJ: *Commission nationale paritaire de l'emploi des journalistes*. Translation: 'joint national commission of journalists' employment'. The word 'joint' (*'paritaire'*) means there are elected representatives of both journalists unions and employers lobbies. The French word for agreement of initial training is *reconnaissance* (recognition). Since 2001, it is rather clear: there are three recommendations and ten criteria. Instead of examining all the details, we selected and summarized the more important aspects. First of all, communication and journalism school paths must be clearly split: one does not educate a journalist as press attachés, public relations employees, heads of communications or spin doctors. Besides, journalists must be implicated in educational methods as council members and teachers for technical training. Tuition fees must be 'reasonable' but no maximum amount is indicated. The content has to last three six-month periods at least and include: general knowledge courses, specific knowledge lectures (about media law, economy, history, deontology, etc.), gaining perfect oral and writing skills in French and training of various technical skills. The last aspect is that the school must have up-to-date equipment in correspondence with the courses it provides. In theory, the accreditation is controlled every five years but, in fact, it has never been taken away. We also observed that general and specific knowledge is often neglected by schools.

Recruitment of journalists

In a ritual (recurrent and inevitable), performative (which contributes to create reality) and auto-suggestion discourse, French journalism is often declared 'open' (*'ouvert'*). The advanced reasons are philosophical principles of press and speech freedoms, as it is written for example in the articles 10 and 11 of Declaration of Human and Citizen Rights (adopted on 26 August 1789). In concrete terms the hiring of journalists is not conditioned by a registered journalism school degree. Contrary to engineers, there is no national commission which grants to selected schools the authorization to give out titles of 'journalist for life'. No minimum school level or specific diploma is required by employers. After two years of unemployment one loses the press card. Strangely, only 15% of new press cards are delivered to people who have a registered journalism school degree (12% ten years ago). If we take all dedicated schools into account, we arrive at the level of 20%. Nevertheless, most new press cards are given to people who have passed the *baccalauréat* and followed courses at the university. But for them it is more difficult to find internships in dominant media and secure work contracts. Surprisingly, Infocom University Departments with a large numbers of students provide more journalists than journalism schools themselves (registered or not). The neologism *infocom* is an abbreviation of the phrase *information et communication*. Students with a degree in History or in Political Science also have good chances to obtain the mythical press card seen as a talisman (Ruellan, 1993). In fact there are various watertight segments (sub-markets) inside the journalistic job market. Co-optation, nepotism, high positioned relations, high social origins (bourgeoisie), *promotion canapé* (sexual relations), conformist opinions and old France rooted patronymics are more effective than degrees, merit, competence, alternative ideas and vocation.

Obviously this situation makes relative the interest of focusing attention only on official journalism schools. It also brings to light the question of the nature of journalism in general. Is this occupation (or 'profession') a manual or an intellectual activity? According to the answer one gives, the content of formal training will either emphasize on general knowledge or on technical skills.

Structures of formal journalism training

Here are the various school paths frequently used to become journalist. They depend on ten main distinctions.

Accredited or not?

Not all schools are accredited by the Ministry of National Education (at state level). In journalism training, some schools actually exist that are not very reliable (mainly private without state accreditation). The directors and executive staff goal is more about business than education. Their advertizements sometimes announce false information (such as famous instructors and high rates of graduate employment). On the job market, their non-accredited diplomas have a low value for media managers (see appendix table 9).

Table 3: Disciplinary origins of new press cards owners.

	1990 (%)	1998 (%)
Civil service	2.1	0.3
Arts	3.5	3.4
Trade	3.5	2.7
Law	6.6	8.8
Economy	6.3	4.0
Education	0.5	0.5
Geography	2.1	1.3
Management	4.0	3.7
History	7.7	10.1
Infocom	19.7	24.1
Languages	7.7	5.8
Litterature	14.8	12.5
Philosophy	1.9	1.3
Health	2.3	1.3
Political science	6.1	5.3
Social sciences	2.8	2.9
Physics	3.5	6.6
Technique	4.7	5.3
Total (known)	100.0	100.0

About European integration, a large proportion of public schools and University departments are involved in the Bologna process and ECTS credits whereas private schools, even those accredited and registered (the best in theory), deliver their specific diplomas. They are focused on their own partnerships with national and foreign institutions. As mentioned on Table 7 (appendix), those who participate in the Erasmus programme are few; their functioning is rather autarchic. Only ESJ-Lille is apparently interested in a European validation. Far from this international dimension, school managers are principally focused on the French context (students' employment, financial questions and competition between schools). Nevertheless, most of public journalism schools which deliver formal masters (see appendix, Table 8) are involved in the Bologna process.

Registered-accredited

There is a great semantic confusion in French about the word 'reconnaissance' and its declension 'reconnu' (past participle of the verb 'reconnaître'). This substantive means both accreditation by the State and registration with the Commission (CNPEJ). Many schools are accredited but only a few schools have the Commission label (twelve). Opposite, Table 4 shows the three categories (I, II and III) of diplomas/schools which come from these

Table 4: The three categories of diplomas/schools.

	Registered (by the Commission CNPEJ):	Non Registered (by the Commission CNPEJ):
Accredited (by the National State):	[I] Very sought-after (private or more theoretical than practical)	[II] Average sought-after (public or private, some cheap, some costly, not all good)
Non Accredited (by the National State):	(None)	[III] Low sought-after (private, costly, quite all second-rate)

different certifications. Warnings: the Commission gives its label to a diploma, not to an entire school or department. Tables 8 and 9 do not correspond to catégories II and III.

Thus, we observe that some private schools are 'accredited' by the State but not 'registered' by the *profession* (namely the CNPEJ). But no doubt some of them will get the CNPEJ label in the future. They have enough money to have up-to-date facilities, to pay famous journalists and to find internships within major media companies. Nevertheless some of them, the worst ones, play in their ads with the word *reconnaissance* to attract naive students and parents. Using the same word (past participle *reconnu*) they may think their school is registered (*reconnu*) by the CNPEJ whereas it has only been accredited (*reconnu*) by the state. The registered schools produce 450–500 graduates a year (calculations by M. Mathien).

Private-public

There is a classic and simple distinction between private schools and public schools (IUT, Universities). The word 'private' here means they are accredited by state but must find their resources by themselves (see above). If we only observe the current twelve registred schools, we notice there are four private (CFJ, EJT, ESJ, IPJ) and eight public (CELSA, CUEJ, EJCM, ICM, IFP, IJBA, IUT Tours, IUT Lannion) (see Table 7). There are also several Infocom Departments inside Universities: Bordeaux III, Grenoble III, Nice, Paris III, Paris VIII, Paris X, Lille III, Lyon II, Lyon III, Rennes II, Toulouse III, etc. But there does exist other departments offering a. specialization in journalism at a general and formal BA ('*licence professionnelle*') or master ('*mastère*') level (see appendix Table 8).

Long-short curriculum

From the *baccalauréat* to the *licence professionnelle*, three years are necessary (two years for the DUT, *diplôme universitaire de technologie*, a degree only prepared in IUT). On the contrary, one year suffices if you are enrolled in a DU (University Diploma), a formal Master 2 (*professionnel*) or in continuous training over several weeks. The trend is to begin the first half-year period with general courses, and then go towards a more technical and practical training (with group simulation and long internships). But some schools are testing out a new method introducing practical exercises each week (reports, school-papers, radio-flashes, rewriting, dispatches synthesis, etc.) in order to satisfy students who are bored and fed up by lectures that are 'too theoretical' and non-interactive.

Certificate-degree

Finally, the registered schools which accept students with the *baccalauréat* are rather rare (only the two 'colleges' with the initials 'IUT'). For instance, a former IUT, at Bordeaux, re-named IJBA, henceforth requires a '*licence*'. The IUT of Lannion, in Northern Brittany, allows students to enter without the *baccalauréat*; it is a sort of affirmative action against socio-economic discriminations explicated by Pierre Bourdieu. For all other registered school students, the entrance test is difficult because of the high number of competitors (more than 1,000). Very often, only one class is accepted each year (20–30 students) (see Table 7 in appendix). Logically, a great part of those who succeed get a master (five years after the *baccalauréat*). In this case, school managers think that general knowledge is now learnt and then prefer to focus courses on technical matters. The more 'recent' statistics (ten years ago…) show that the medium level of studies was 'Bac + 2.6 (years)' in 1990 and 'Bac + 2.9' in 1998 ('Bac' is an abbreviation of *baccalauréat*):

Table 5: Degrees of press cards owners (1990–98).

	1990 (%)	1998 (%)
Without Bac	12	5.8
Only Bac	14.4	11.8
Bac + 1	2.9	2.8
Bac + 2	17.3	18.6
Bac + 3	15.5	18.1
Bac + 4	21	23.4
Bac + 5	13.8	15.9
Over Bac + 5	3.1	3.5
Total (known)	100.0	100.0

Unique-multi paths

Schools may offer a unique path with a common training for all students. They also may offer various specialized paths during the last or a supplementary year. For instance, ESJ-Lille offers various paths in journalism. The more frequent specializations are audio-visual and cameraman (officially called JRI). We can also notice that the majority of schools propose a basic training programme in various media (press, radio, television, Internet) in order to prepare future journalists to 'polyvalence', namely the ability to work simultaneously for different media in the same newsroom.

Initial-continuous-alternance

It is important to specify that the relevant Commission gives agreement only to initial training. Nevertheless some registered schools offer opportunities for continuous education (courses reserved for already employed people) and 'alternance' (training which combines successive courses and internships) paths (see Table 6). But it is rather rare: ESJ Lille and IUT Tours for example. But there is a school fully dedicated to continuous training: the CFPJ (*Centre de formation et de perfectionnement des journalistes*), located in the centre of Paris (near the CFJ and Le Figaro, rue du Louvre). This choice can be a good idea for students who failed the competition examinations for initial training. The CFPJ thus offers several technical training programmes (layout, photo, oral skill, editing, DTP, etc.) which allow not only discovery and improvement of skills but also the obtaining of a formal certificate that is close to registered school diplomas in terms of peer esteem and employability.

Table 6: Origins of new press cards in 1999.

Types of journalism training	Total
All sorts of training	31.7
Various short training	6.8
Short Journalism training	8.3
Unregistered schools and short training	1.6
Registered schools	14.5
Qualification contract	0.4
Without journalism training	68.3
Total	100.0

Outside-corporate

Some formal training is provided outside media firms; during the 1980s, some tried to train their own future employees but these initiatives are now over. Schools in the classic definition and organization seem to keep their utility and their prestige. The 'Académie Prisma', a corporate school launched by the eponymous media group which mainly publishes magazines, continues its curriculum to train future journalists with a managerial mentality. We can also notice that internships are really appreciated by students because they often have an inferiority complex and a magic vision; they actually think that working as a journalist is a very difficult and an improbable task. So the main effect of these internships is to reassure them. Nevertheless, quite all internships are not in accordance with their official goal: students are scarcely helped by their tutors inside newsrooms. They also provide an unpaid manpower and hold regular jobs.

Expensive-cheap

The scale of tuition fees is rather large. The cheaper schools are public because the Ministry of National Education and the Law require a low level of fees. The goal is to open colleges and universities up to all young people, not only rich people from the bourgeoisie.[1] In these public schools the tuition fees are more or less €300 all included (before probable effects of the 2007 Act). This low level does not mean that their formal training is mediocre. That chiefly depends on technical equipment, teachers' contribution, a research department and available space. Except for public schools (low tuition fees), the social selection by money is manifest. In the four registered private schools: examination and fees are more expensive (around €3,500 for tuition fees). Among private schools some have state agreement and can receive professional taxes but a large majority of schools impose very high tuition fees (from €5,000 – €7,000 a year).

Paris-province

Are Parisian schools better than provincial schools? It all depends. If the specialization and the projects of students aim for local press and media, it is a disadvantage to be located in the suburb of Paris. But there is a structural aspect: France is a very centralized country. Thus, in 2000, 60.3% of journalists live and work in the urban area of Paris (only 18% of the whole population). Moreover, almost all French media companies are settled there (except local media and a scarce few magazines such as *Sciences Humaines* and *Golias*). But as one can see in Table 7 (appendix), only four of the registered schools are Parisian: CFJ, CELSA, IPJ and IFP. On the contrary, many private school managers understood the strategic interest to be in the bourgeois urban area of Paris. Actually it is easier to find available and prestigious teachers (during their holidays) and to find stimulating internships and future jobs for students.

The entrance tests are not unfavourable to female candidates. Statistically speaking, they are very effective because female candidates are generally hardworking and obedient during their time in the school system. Moreover, for them, passing diplomas is very important, as it allows them to be personally independent in the future. Aside from following careers as camera operators (too heavy in spite of miniaturization and digital cameras), female candidates are very numerous, and this corresponds with the general increase of women among '*encartés*' journalists: 33% in 1990, 39% in 2000. But female journalists are often obliged to accept subaltern positions and insecure jobs, except in some specific magazines (health, women, children, fashion) where subjects correspond with the traditional sexual division of work. Among freelancers (called '*pigistes*'), 45% are female and 55% male. Among salaried employees, 37.5% are female and 62.5% male.

It is rather clear that the selection criteria to enter in registered journalism schools are very close to the real corporate practice. The required knowledge is journalistic and directly linked to the daily routines: review of the press, work under emergency pressure, enterprising ('*débrouillardise*'), intellectual modesty, technical expertise, fluent English, submission to the editor (see the saying 'the boss is always right even when he's wrong'), broad general and current affairs knowledge, linguistic expertise in French, capability in order to sell his/her ideas of reportage or broadcast.

Concluding Remarks

Finally, there are two important paradoxes about journalism training in France. First, there is a huge gap between, on the one hand, the candidates coming from university and *Grandes écoles* and, on the other hand, technical exercises during formal training, namely between professional myths and prosaic practices. Logically, many disappointments arise from this situation among the – young – people coming in: 'The gap between initial formal training and ordinary destiny of intellectuals is rather problematic. *Tout ça pour ça?*' ('All these efforts and dreams for arriving at a so deceiving result') (Rambach 2001). It is exactly what P. Bourdieu and A. Accardo have named as the '*misère de position*': journalists belong to a professional group which has a prestigious social image and is situated among elites, whereas a large majority of journalists are over-qualified and occupy subaltern and insecure jobs.

The second paradox is as follows; given the great selectivity and the technical nature of registered schools' entry tests applicants are obliged to master skills beforehand. Many of them have followed a specific and costly preparation (IPÉSUP, ESJ-Lille telepreparation, Paris 8, EFFICOM, etc.). Many students have also completed simulations internships and summer jobs before entry tests. Consequently, one may wonder what can be the pedagogical contribution of formal training in these conditions… Schools are thus in a double-bind situation: how is it possible to occupy successful students during two years when, (1) technical training requires eight weeks, (2) employers expects journalists not to be too intellectually ambitious and (3) students are fed up by traditional courses and dream of money, historical role and contacts with celebs.

The Author

Jacques Le Bohec is Professor at the University of Lyon 2.

Note

1. Warning: the French word '*collège*' is a *faux-ami* because it means 'secondary school' (UK) or 'junior high school' (US).

References

Accardo, Alain et al. (1998), *Journalistes précaires*, Bordeaux : Le Mascaret, p. 414.

Agnès, Yves (2008), *Manuel de journalisme*, Paris: La Découverte, p. 448.

Albert, Pierre (2008), *La presse française*, Paris: La documentation française, p. 216.

Allemand, Sylvain (ed.) (2008), *Comment je suis devenu journaliste*, Paris: Le cavalier bleu, p. 222.

Bourdieu, Pierre (1998), *La domination masculine*, Paris: Minuit, p. 148.

Carlo, Anne-Lise and Sultant-R'bibo (2007), *Journaliste. Concours d'entrée en école de journalisme*, Paris: Foucher, p. 224.

Charon, Jean-Marie (1993), *Cartes de presse. Enquête sur les journalistes*, Paris: Stock, p. 356.

Civard-Racinais, Alexandrine and Rieubon, Édith (2008), *Les métiers du journalisme*, Paris: L'étudiant ed., p. 224.

Colo, Olivia et al. (2005), *Photojournalisme à la croisée des chemins*, Marval et CFD, p. 222.

Delporte, Christian (1995), *Histoire du journalisme et des journalistes en France*, Paris: PUF, p. 126.

Devillard, Valérie et al. (2001), *Les journalistes français à l'aube de l'an 2000. Profils et parcours*, Paris: LCDJ, p. 170.

Feyel, Gilles (2007), *La presse en France des origines à 1944*, Paris: Ellipses, p. 192.

Gaudin Philippe (2007), *Préparer les concours des écoles de journalisme*, Paris: PUF, p. 118.

Lacan, Jean-François et al. (1994), *Stars, scribes et scribouillards*, Paris: Syros, p. 280.

Le Bohec, Jacques (2000), *Les mythes professionnels des journalistes*, Paris: L'Harmattan, p. 398.

Marchetti, Dominique and Ruellan, Denis (2001), *Devenir journalistes. Sociologie de l'entrée sur le marché du travail*, Paris: La documentation française, p. 166.

Mathien, Michel, (2007), *Les journalistes. Histoire, pratiques et enjeux*, Paris: Ellipses, p. 270.

Neveu, Érik (2001), *Sociologie du journalisme*, Paris: La Découverte, p.124.

Pinçon, Michel and Pinçon-Charlot, Monique (2008), *Sociologie de Paris*, La Découverte, p.124.

Rambach, Anne and Marine (2001), *Les intellos précaires*, Fayard, p. 256.

Rieffel, Rémy (1984), *L'élite des journalistes*, Paris: PUF, p. 222.

Ruffin, François (2003), *Les petits soldats du journalisme*, Paris: Les arènes, p. 276.

Ruellan, Denis (1993), *Le professionnalisme du flou*, Grenoble: PUG, p. 240.

Sales, Claude (1998), *La formation des journalistes*, Paris: Rapport Ronéo.

Siméant, Johanna, 1992, 'Déontologie et crédibilité: le réglage des relations professionnelles au CFJ', *Politix. Travaux de science politique*, 19, pp. 37–55.

Vistel, Jacques (1993), *Qu'est-ce qu'un journaliste?*, Paris: La documentation française.

Appendices

Table 7: The 12 French journalism schools with agreement (2008).

Initials	Official name	City	Status	Tuition Fees (Euro)	Places	Creation date	Agreement date	Duration (months)	Delivered certificate	Paths	Partnerships with foreign universities
ESJ	École supérieure de journalisme	Lille, Montpellier	Private (with Catholic Uni.)	3500	56	1924	1956	24	School diploma	General + special. (scientific, local weekly, farming, cameraman)	(Laval (Canada), Louvain (Belgium), City University of London
CFJ	Centre de formation des journalistes	Paris	private	3000	40	1946	1960	20	School diploma	General training + specialization (cameraman)	Erasmus, special examination for foreign students
CUEJ	Centre universitaire d'enseignement du journalisme	Strasbourg	Public (Strasbourg 3)	300	40	1958	1968	24	Master	General training	Double german-french path Relocated school week abroad
IJBA	Institut de journalisme de Bordeaux Aquitaine	Bordeaux	Public (Bordeaux 3)	300	34	1967 (IUT-B)	1975	24	Master	General training + specialization (cameraman, radio)	[almost vague]
IUT	Institut universitaire de technologie	Tours	Public (Tours)	300	30	1968	1980	24	formal BA (licence)	General training (local press and other media)	Erasmus, passible BA abroad
CELSA	Centre d'études littéraires et scientifiques appliquées	Neuilly sur Seine	Public (Paris 4)	300	20	1979	1981	24	master	General training (audio-visual) + communication path	Possible one abroad school year
EJCM	École de journalisme et de communication de M.	Marseille	Public (Aix-Marseille 2)	1000	20–25	1982	1984	20	DU + Formal master	General (local press), spécializations (magazine, cameraman)	Maghreb and Canada
IPJ	Institut pratique du journalisme	Paris	private	4370	40	1978	1991	24	School diploma	General training + specialization (radio)	Erasmus, Dublin Institute of Tehcnology, Louvain (Belgium)

Table 7: *Cont.*

Initials	Official name	City	Status	Tuition Fees (Euro)	Places	Creation date	Agreement date	Duration (months)	Delivered certificate	Paths	Partnerships with foreign universities
EJT	École de journalisme de Toulouse	Toulouse	private	3500	30	1996	2001	36	School diploma	General training (local press, audio-visual)	Ties with Spain, Maghreb [only in project]
IUT	Institut universitaire de technologie	Lannion	Public (Rennes 1)	300	30	1996	2003	24	BA (licence)	General training (local press and media)	(Laval) Canada, (Louvain) Belgium, Brazil, Mexico, (Carlos 3, Madrid) Spain, Eire, UK
IFP	Institut français de presse	Paris	Public (Paris 2)	300	23	1937 (1951)	2004	24	Master	General training (press and audio-visual)	Reserved places to 5 foreign students + Carleton, Ottawa (Canada), Berkeley (USA)
ICM	Institut de la communication et des médias	Échirolles	Public (Grenoble 3)	300	60	1997	2005	24	master	General training	Socrates + Erasmus, Québec, Ontario

Table 8: Unregistered public journalism schools.

Official name	Content	Level	City
Univ. Aix-Marseille 2	Economic journalism	Master	Aix-en-provence
Institut d'études politiques	International journalism	Master	Aix-en provence
Univ. Aix-Marseille 3	Juridical journalism	master	Aix-en provence
Univ. Aix-Marseille 3	Economic journalism	Master	Aix-en provence
Univ. Nice (IUT)	Audio-visual journalism	BA (licence)	Cannes
Univ. La Rochelle	Culture and new media	BA (licence)	La Rochelle
Univ. Lille 1 (with ESJ)	Scientific journalism	Master	Lille
Univ. Lille 3	Local weekly journalism	BA (licence)	Roubaix
Univ. Lyon 3 – IUP	General training	Master	Lyon
Institut d'études politiques	Local journalism	Master	Lyon
Univ. Montpellier 1	General training	Master	Montpellier
CFPJ	Continuous training + spécializations	Certificate	Paris
Institut d'études politiques	Audio-visual journalism	Master	Paris
Univ. Paris 1	Economic journalism	Master	Paris
Univ. Paris 3	Bilingual journalism	Master	Paris
Univ. Paris 3	Cultural journalism	Master	Paris
Univ. Paris 3	German-French journalism	Master	Paris
Univ. Paris 5	Medical journalism	DU	Paris
Univ. Paris 5 (IUT)	Webmaster	BA (licence)	Paris
Univ. Paris 7	Scientific and technical journalism	Master	Paris
Univ. Paris 12	Medical journalism	DU	Créteil
Univ. Paris-est	European journalism	Master	Champs sur Marne
IEP de Rennes	Journalism and Public sphere	Master	Rennes
Univ. Strasbourg 1	Scientific and technical journalism	Master	Strasbourg
Univ. Toulon	Magazine, multimedia journalism	DU	Toulon
Institut d'études politiques	Examination preparation	Master	Bordeaux
Univ. Valenciennes	Radio and cameraman	BA (licence)	Valenciennes
Univ. Lille 3	Newsroom jobs	Master	Villeneuve d'Asq

Table 9: Unregistred private journalism schools.

Initials	Official Name	Content	City
APP	Académie Prisma-Press	Web and magazine press	Paris
EFJ	École française de journalisme	General training	Levallois-Perret
EICAR	École internationale de création audiovisuelle et de réalisation	Audio-visual journalism	Saint-Denis
EDJ	L'école de journalisme Nouvelles	General + Sport journalism	Nice
EDM	École des médias	Audio-visual journalism and animation	Paris
EFAP	École française des attachés de presse	Public relations, Press attaché, advertising	Paris, Bordeaux, Lille, Lyon
EFDJ	École française de journalisme	General training	Levallois-Perret
efficom	École française de formation à l'information communication	General training + preparation	Paris
EJC (isfp)	École de journalisme et de communication	General training	Paris, Blagnac
EJO	École de journalisme de l'ouest	Press, cameraman, radio	Luçon
ESJ-Paris	École supérieure de journalisme	General training	Paris
HEJ	Hautes études de journalisme	General training	Lyon, Marseille, Montpellier
IFT	Institut de formation technique	General training	Paris
IICP	Institut international de communication de Paris	General training	Paris
ISCOM	Institut supérieur de communication et de publicité	Audio-visual and multimedia	Paris
ISCPA	Institut des médias	General training	Paris, Lyon
ISFJ	Institut supérieur de formation au journalisme	General training + cameraman	Paris
ITAIM	Institut des techniques avancées de l'information et des médias	General training	Levallois-Perret
Studec	Studio école de France	Radio journalism	Boulogne-Billancourt

The Greek Journalism Education Landscape

Thomas Siomos

Introduction

In Greece, journalists' education exhibits vagueness, immaturity and institutional limitations to an extent similar to that of the rest of the mass media field, i.e. of the journalists' unions and the General Secretariat of Communication, and the qualified state officer for mass media functioning.

In the following review, in order for the reader to understand the scenery in journalism education, we begin with specifying what the meaning of university for the Greek society is and what role the post-high-school studies hold for young people in this country. Afterwards, we describe the situation in the field of journalism education. A thorough presentation of the three university departments of mass communication and journalism follows. Then, the following section presents other forms of journalism education such as private colleges, technical schools, etc. The last section notes sociological extensions of the journalist's profession and the problems in mass media functioning in order for the reader to realize the irrationality and vagueness of journalism education and training.

Education, markets and journalists, consist of the three 'pillars' of the mass media; they interact to form an unpleasant environment – one that is difficult to analyse in the confines of the present text. They provide, however, a good starting point to explore, in general, the issues of journalism education in Greece.

What is the meaning of 'university studies' in Greece?

Greece has maintained a stable political system since 1974, after the end of the dictatorship period. Since 1980, entering the then-called EEC, it has been trying to obtain European characteristics as a state and as a society. In this effort, university studies comprised a main vehicle of social upward mobility and progress, mainly made by rural families of low-income background, who aimed to climb up the social hierarchy and gain a medium or an even higher civil status. Thus, university education, from a Greek families' viewpoint, is always obliged to offer a pragmatic and realistic perspective and connect with what Greek families call a 'settle down' condition for their children. For this reason, very often there are surges of students towards university schools with social status and a promise for future career paths (e.g. in the 1970s civil engineering due to mass building constructions, in the 1980s education/pedagogic due to the openings in state schools, in the 1990s doctors due to positions in the National Health System programme, etc.) as the sole criterion. Due to the constitution and the lack of legitimation of private universities, many young Greeks are leaving to study what they wish abroad, worried that they might fail the very difficult Pan-Hellenic admission exams for state universities at home. In such an atmosphere it is natural that journalism schools were the first choice of Greek students for only a short period of time. This happened when these schools were initially founded and the electronic mass media were deregulated, being transformed from state to private, in the beginning of the 1990s. What followed frustrated the first students of these schools and today the area of journalism education mirrors all the problems of mass media in Greece.

Journalism education and training

The first university schools of communication science in Greece were founded in 1990 at the National and Kapodistrian University of Athens and at Panteion University both in Athens and in 1991 at the Aristotle University of Thessaloniki. These schools were mainly staffed with university faculty members, teaching theoretical courses, from already existent schools and departments of humanity studies for two reasons: (1) The legal framework in Greece imposes every new school or department to function with already-elected teachers from other schools' hierarchy until it creates its own hierarchy. (2) Up to then professional journalists in Greece acquired no university degree since they were either studying at private journalism schools or studying something entirely different, such as law, mathematics or dentistry, and leapt into the journalism profession acquiring journalistic experience and proficiency from old professionals. Therefore, since their foundation, these schools have refrained from the market and the practices of the journalistic profession. This gap is expanded on the issue of the students' practical training, which exists only in a procedural form as a prerequisite for their graduation.

For many years and up until today, young journalists, who are taught how to do the job from older 'wise elders' of journalism are called 'birdies', they do the so-called 'wash-up', i.e. they write about the pharmacies' duty chart and horoscopes, are obliged to respect hierarchy and are submitted to many insults for their possible technical or spelling mistakes.

On the other hand, university school graduates rarely work as journalists after their graduation; according to rough statistics, obtained by journalist unions, maybe less than 10 per cent of graduates of these schools will eventually become professional journalists. It is also important to underline that, although these schools offer an uncertain professional occupation, they require a rather high admission grade from the Pan-Hellenic exams, taking place every year, in order for the students to be selected and, then, admitted into state universities, where studies are offered free of charge and are legitimized by the Greek state.

From the opposite point of view, the few foreign university schools, which function as Liberal Studies Colleges due to a constitutional prohibition to function as private universities and offer a degree, similar to that of technical schools – which also need to be qualified via

Pan-Hellenic qualification exams – are no longer in demand and are closing one after the other. In these foreign university branches, tuition fees range from €2500 to €6000 per year and studies last for three years. State schools offer a career opportunity, mostly in marketing or communication but not in journalism, and it is for this reason they are so popular.

There are also schools which belong to media groups, like ANT1 TV or Channel 10 TV in Athens and Politis Tileorasi in Thessaloniki; these schools make use of the students by asking them to produce parts of the channel's programme. There are also technical journalism schools (at the level of technical high school) – Professional Proficiency Institutes – which function under the aegis of the Ministry of Education and the PTPO, the Professional Training and Proficiency Organisation; this organization is also responsible for certifying the Journalism Degrees acquired from all the non-state schools in Greece. This certification takes places once a year in the beginning of summer via a large examination with nearly 200 questions, regarding politics, history, the European Union, etc.

University schools

Panteion University of Athens: Department of Communications, Media and Culture

The Department of Communications, Media and Culture offers a systematic university teaching, so that its graduates acquire scientific knowledge and essential technical skills for their further career. The Department argues that it is aware of the difficulties, encountered by its graduates in the business market and that the best way to face these difficulties is neither adaptation to financial reality nor recourse to superficial specialization models, but training of critical thinking, structured knowledge and substantial improvement of spoken and written language.

Accordingly, the ICT competence of students is highly regarded. Their methodical avocation with English language, especially in fields like journalist reportage, cultural reportage, political remarks and book reviews, is also deemed as important. The opportunity for as many students as possible to accomplish one part of their studies in other European universities has also been provided.

Students of the institution auditing a course for free, which allows young journalists and cultural administrators, who fulfil the relevant prerequisites, to attend courses of the study curriculum, is very significant. Participation of students in the practical training plays a crucial role in the educating procedure, along side the attendance of fieldwork courses. The Department offers the opportunity to accomplish paid practical training in various businesses, state organizations and research centres to almost all senior undergraduate students.[1]

National and Kapodestrian University of Athens: Department of Communication and Media Studies

The Department of Communication and Media Studies was founded in 1990 and offers undergraduate and postgraduate study programs, focusing in three domains: Division of Psychology of Communication, Division of Social and Political Analysis of Communication and Division of Culture, Environment, Communication Applications and Technology.

It also acquired five laboratories: New Technologies in Communication, Administration and Promotion of Cultural Environment, Psychological Applications and Communication Planning, Social Research in Mass Media and Audio-Visual Media. The department also owns a Research University Institute of Applied Communication – RUIAC, founded in 1996. It offers two postgraduate study programmes in Political communication and New media.[2]

Aristotle University of Thessaloniki: Department of Journalism and Mass Communication

Since September 2005 the Department of Journalism and Mass Communication has acquired a new Curriculum according to which two main study divisions function: division of Journalism and division of Mass Communication.

According to their content, courses are divided into three categories: Theoretical Courses, Fieldwork Courses, Theoretical-Practice Courses, which combine elements of the above-mentioned two divisions, i.e. they combine learning of theoretical concepts and analytic methods by conducting practical exercises and activities. Attendance of these courses is optional for Theoretical Courses and mandatory for Fieldwork and Theoretical-Practice Courses. Completion of studies in the Department of Journalism and Mass Communication is achieved after submission of a thesis.

Also, the department participates in an Inter-university Interdepartmental Postgraduate Programme, entitled 'Advanced Computer and Communication Systems' and offers two postgraduate study programs: New media and journalism and Culture and journalism.[3]

Private and State colleges and Professional Proficiency Institutes

For many years before the establishment of the above mentioned State schools, the only available journalism education in Greece was offered by private journalism schools, with 'Ergastiri' in Athens and EKES in Thessaloniki being the most well-known. A majority of journalists, who now occupy important positions in news production in all media (TV, radio, newspapers), have come from these specialized schools. A large portion of press workers also come from journalism schools which functioned in the framework of private education organizations, usually representing a foreign university as well, without, however, being able to offer degrees legitimized by the state, since the constitution prohibits the operation of private universities.

The in-house journalism schools of TV channels, such as ANT1 and Channel 10, have a significant number of students; these schools lure students in by promising immediate practical training at the channel (which owns the school), and the promise of a potential collaboration in the future. In reality, these channels only ever employed a minimal number of these graduates; instead these graduates moved into other provinces of the country and took part in the professional culture there.

Journalism education (technical knowledge and news production skills) is also offered by private and state Professional Proficiency Institutes in the form of Liberal Studies Colleges. Each graduate of these schools is obliged to take Pan-Hellenic exams, common for all private colleges' graduates, after the completion of studies in order to qualify.[4]

Concluding Remarks

In order to better comprehend the irrationality in the field of journalism education in Greece, the reader should know the following in relation to mass media in Greece: The journalist's profession is unarmored and not professionally authorized. It is indicative that there is no qualified authority to map the journalist's profession and present demographic and other statistical evidence, describing the situation. In the past there were only two efforts of charting the journalism scenery by VPRC survey company on behalf of the Women Journalists' Union, which, although emphasizing distribution of problems based on gender, highlighted some of the other problems. It is, thus, characteristic that only 5 per cent of journalists who participated in the research, named poor or non-existent education as one of this field's problems.

The total estimated journalists' positions today are almost 18.960 with a mean total work hours per week of 55.5. Both male and female Greek journalists experience an alienation from their job. It is observed that they are in an extensive or even complete contradiction to the product of their work while presenting low self-esteem for their field as well. Journalist's employed relations are characterized by irrationality. All possible forms of payment and extremely loose forms of employment in terms of time shifts have been noticed. Also, several forms of multi-employment have been adopted. In accordance with the research evidence, the journalist's profession continues to be conducted mostly by men (58%) and less by women (42%).

Furthermore, private electronic mass media are still functioning with temporary licenses, issued by local authorities and never by the Ministries of Press or Communications, nearly twenty years since their foundations have passed. During all these years the license issuance is utilized as a means to put pressure on media owners and, consequently, on journalists for self-censorship. The prerequisites, occasionally published, for a potential future license issuance of electronic mass media do not incorporate any education regulation-prerequisite, relevant to the employment of people at them as journalists; therefore it is not necessary for somebody who wishes to work in the media field to acquire a degree (from a university or other institute).

Additionally, Journalists' Unions and not the Ministry of Press are the responsible commissioned service for qualification of a journalist identification card for professionals in the media. In order to register in these unions, there is also no specification for education of higher or highest level as a prerequisite. Many of the members are high-school graduates and those who have a university journalism degree represent less than 10 per cent in each union from a total of almost 3000 journalists-union members (there is an estimate of 18960 journalists, employed in communication media, but they do not fulfil insurance and salary prerequisites in order to register in a union). These unions, which have geographic distribution, did not accept journalists of broadcast media until ten years ago, and some of them still do not accept online journalists.

Finally, the issue of depreciation of the journalists' employment field and of low appreciation by the society is expressed via the popular slogans such as 'Bums Snitches Journalists', which affects journalists' self-esteem and indeed TV crews usually comprise targets for demonstrators while newspapers or TV channels are the targets of terrorist attacks. During the past ten years this issue has intensified; this is due to the information that there are 150 journalists who are regarded as hired by the Ministry of Press to support the policies of government in the media. This ambience discourages young people from choosing to work in the mass media field and, moreover, to study in order to achieve that. Those who really wish to become journalists attempt to find a job as trainees straight off. Hence, only those who are willing to work in the field of communication, culture, public relations and marketing, study journalism, since there are no relevant university departments which would be able to offer pertinent knowledge.[5]

Evaluating all the above, it is a logical conclusion to think that any effort for coordination, planning and rationalization of journalism education and training in Greece stumbles on the 'pathogenesis' of the mass media field, the public sphere's quality and the unionist obstacles, put forth by academic teachers as well as by journalists' unions.

It is obvious that any effort of regulating the Mass Media field cannot be fragmented and concern only one domain, such as education for instance, at a time but instead asks for aggregate treatment and reformation. The state, which qualifies for university education, as well as for media functioning, along with journalists' unions, should proceed in an open deliberation with all involved parties before creating a precise legal framework for media functioning, in which education and the job market will be interconnected and counter-supplied areas, something obviously absent nowadays. The segregation of studies into studies in communication-culture and studies in journalism as two different and distinct branches should be performed through study curricula and divisions of university schools, as well as via available postgraduate programmes. European experience would be particularly useful in changing the situation in Greek university journalism education, and adoption of good practices can redefine the role of journalism schools. However, current signs do not seem promising and do not leave us much room for optimism.

The Author

Thomas Siomos is a journalist working for *Eleftherotypia* newspaper and the Greek State Radio, and a Master's student at the Political Science Department of Aristotle University.

Notes

1. http://cmc.panteion.gr
2. http: //www.media.uoa.gr
3. http: //www.jour.auth.gr
4. www.minpress.gr
5. http: //www.eurofound.europa.eu/eiro/2005/02/word/gr0502103fel.doc

References

National and Kapodestrian University of Athens: www.media.uoa.gr
Panteion Univeristy of Athens: http: //panteion.criticalpublics.com/cmc
Aristotle University of Thessaloniki: www.jour.auth.gr

The Italian Journalism Education Landscape

Angelo Agostini

Introduction

Italy is a strange country indeed. 74 years ago, it showed Europe and the rest of the world the first true dictatorship in modern times. Italy taught Nazi Germany various techniques for the strategic use of mass media: radio, cinema, newspapers, publishing, commercial design, architecture, town planning, monuments, and city furniture. It was the Italy of the denied political rights, the inexistent civil rights. It was the Italy of jail and political confinement, torture and death for those who opposed the regime. It was the Italy of Fascism.

Yet, in that year, 1934, three men were thinking the very same thing. Those three men could not be any different. One was holding power. His name was Ermanno Amicucci and he had founded the first Italian school of journalism in Perugia. He was a Mussolini man and obviously, his was a school of fascist journalism, a school of propaganda. The other man was Alcide De Gasperi. From the region of Trentino, already representative at the Diet of the Austro-Hungarian Empire, De Gasperi was living those years protected by the friendly walls of the Vatican State. A little over ten years later, with the end of World War II, he would become the artificer of the Italian reconstruction, President of the Council and Secretary of Christian Democracy. In 1934, he was taking care of the World Exhibit Book List for the catholic press that would be published two years later. Taking steps from the School of Journalism in Lille, France, initially a catholic school founded ten years before, in 1924, De Gasperi theorized the requirement for reporters of a free and democratic society to be formed in schools. The idea he had in mind was very similar to what we call a bachelor degree in current days: three years of theoretical and practical training after high school.

In that very same year of 1934, the third man mentioned above was being transferred from the prison of Turi to the sickroom of the forensic hospital in Formia. He already suffered from a disease that would, eventually, kill him. He was Antonio Gramsci, already representative in Parliament, founder (in 1921) of the Italian Communist Party. He was a powerful Marxist thinker, not properly orthodox. In those months, he wrote, 'the principle that Journalism should be taught and it is not rational to leave the reporter free to learn by himself through experience, is vital and will prevail more and more as journalism in Italy becomes a more complex field and a more responsible civil organism'.

With regard to the propaganda purposes of the fascist Amicucci and the strong catholic determination of Alcide De Gasperi, still today it is surprising that the Marxist Gramsci combines the need for the training of the reporter with the growth of the media as industry and the articulated civil responsibility of the mass media.

It is surprising that fascists, catholics and communists had a vision that in the mid-thirties belonged only to the United States: journalism is a job that can and must be taught: only education allows the reporter to work consciously, controlling what – at the time – was just the beginning of mass media.

Today: 21 journalism schools

Astuteness, tricks, or deceit of history? The schools of journalism thought or hoped for by De Gasperi and Gramsci would never become reality; they would only be a precursor idea. The fascist idea of Amicucci soon died because a school is a source of critical thoughts and free minds, thus fascism soon got rid of them.

Only in 1977 in Italy, the first School of Journalism is established almost clandestinely and with a 40-year delay. It happened in Milan thanks to one of the corporate laws that democratic Italy revived from the old fascism regime. From 1963, in fact, in Italy journalism has been protected by law. Only those who are listed on the Registry are allowed to perform this job (the equivalent of the Doctors, Architects, Engineers, and Attorneys Registry). Before journalists are able to enrol in the Registery they must first complete an 18-month apprenticeship with an editorial staff and successfully pass a National Exam held by reporters and judges. Regional committees are in charge of the registries' bookkeeping; the regional committees will be in charge of the first degree of ethical assessment. The National Council of the Association of Reporters (Consiglio nazionale dell'Ordine dei giornalisti), the national body, is a simple Appeal Application for ethical trials and a general cultural body for the profession.

On this basis, and anticipating facts that would happen ten years later, the President of the Association of Reporters of Lombardy, Carlo De Martino, opened in 1977 in Milan the first School of Journalism. It was the Institute for Journalism Studies (Ifg) in Milan; a two-year school with a limited number of students who were admitted after a general and practical examination. In theory, a high school degree was the only prerequisite. In practice, the majority of students could attend the school only after college (at the time four or five years). The law allowed Mr. Martino (with his Registry's regional Committee) to decide where and how the apprenticeship could be carried on. He decided that the apprenticeship could not be performed in a publishing company but rather in a school. The school should not merely be academic; it should also have been a newspaper, agency, radio and, with time, television. The first example of a School of Journalism was born in Italy.

Several directors, many managing editors, tons of correspondents, and many columnists graduated from the Ifg of Milan. They were the precursors. The quality of their work as reporters opened the door to many young reporters that were formed in schools and joined the editorial industry from the beginning of the 1990s.

Today Italy has twenty-one schools officially recognized. Each of them is allowed to have twenty or thirty students and a two-year course, producing 500–600 new graduates every two years. There are too many graduates and too many schools for a profession that has already (according to various surveys) 12–16,000 full-time professionals. Not to mention that the country has a population of 58 million people, little less than 6 million papers are sold, and each family has a TV and more than 30 per cent of the population has regular access to the Internet.

We need to tell another story now, and, in order to do so, we need to take a step back.

A Historical Delay

The Chambers of Journalists and the law that founded, recognized, and sorted the profession are not a corporative insanity nor do they mean to show how powerful the association is. The Association was founded about twenty years after WWII and the dictatorship. It was intended as an instrument to protect the autonomy and the independence of the reporters from the industrial and political interests present in the Italian media. Those interests were (and are today, 45 years later) strongly influenced by the fascist heritage and the scarce power with which they worked and made profit in the new and weak democracy.

The professional mobility from the fascism to the democracy in Italy was weak, limited, and not incisive. Most of the reporters who were working under Fascism continue their work in the new democracy without many problems. For several years that affected personal relations, relations between teachers and students, cultural models and hierarchies, and staff relations, even after the democracy was unquestionable and successful.

The media industry that survived during twenty years of dictatorship did not have an easy time after WWII. In a country with a democracy blocked by international balances, publishing entrepreneurs grew their interests for almost 40 years in other economic fields. Automobile, oil, construction, sugar, chemical tycoons, or small local economic powers strongly held the ownership of newspapers and magazines, exchanging favors with political power. Papers were not made to be sold, but to exchange favours between economic and political powers through the mass media. In the 1950s, the powerful director of the first newspaper in Italy, Mario Missiroli who directed the *Corriere della Sera*, used to say, 'Newspapers are the passive voices of credit income statements'. In other words, it was not important that newspapers sold, captured readers, or created profits. Their mission, in the editors' mind, was the exchange of favours with the existing political powers.

As a natural and appropriate consequence, the reporters tried to protect the small margins of their autonomy through a legislation that would seem obsolete to the rest of the European Countries. The first step was the legislation that found the Association of Reporters in 1963. The reporters had granted the legal status of liberal professions with a shorter training. The training was given by the simple acknowledgment of the profession; it was not tied to any educational institution, much less a college. To be a reporter it was necessary to study as a reporter, but a person studied as reporter by being a reporter, by learning the job in the editorial office. The training of new reporters was delegated to reporters themselves, who represented the only self-control and self-governing of the profession.

Inversely, from a cultural standpoint, Italian journalism kept for more than forty years after the Liberation the perspective of an artisan profession, where the job was passed by word of mouth from the master to the apprentice in the small shop. From an economical standpoint, the media industry was also anchored to the vision of a craft shop. It was a paradox, but that was reality. The Country who first experimented with the dimension of mass culture and production fell, after the war, in a pre-industrial dimension. In the meantime, Catholics and communists, the Christian Democratic and the Communist Party became more and more suspicious of the media that pervaded everything and everywhere. The Christian Democratic and the Communist Party organized their office with a widespread network of personal communications to use as direct contacts with people, individuals, or groups while in the rest of the world television, cinema, radio, and music created a network that would be called mass society at first, and mass media later. Journalism and mass media were still anchored to the patterns of the early-twentieth century even in the sixties, when Italy, with many difficulties, was going through a hardy industrialization and modernization period.

Journalism did not follow the same path. For many and various reasons that the author of this chapter cannot list here, journalism remained attached to uses and procedures typical of the first half of the century. Training in journalism also did not make an exception to the general rule.

A concrete model for the future

With regard to the long chain of historical facts I mentioned above, the concepts of Carlo De Martino worked well and quickly. The pattern of the School of Journalism in Milan was simple: academic knowledge and professional knowledge. Sociology, Economics, Law, Geography, and History were combined with writing, editing, and newspaper preparation techniques. Theoretical classes were alternated with real-life situations, in which students practiced working in newspapers, agencies, news radio, and TV news. It represented the model to follow and, still today, it challenges the structures of the best journalism schools, especially those established at the most prestigious universities.

De Martino had an easy time in 1977. He was in Milan, the capital of Italian publishing world. Soon the first commercial TV station would be founded. He was a precursor of the times and he was able to understand what the 1980s would finally bring to Italy: the rise of publishing entrepreneurs who would pay attention to the monetary profits that would be gained from mass media, more than the political profits. The time came for the rise of a publishing class that needed skilled professionals, who would be able to manage the news and the productive and industrial process at the same time.

After a little more than ten years, in accordance with a process that normally takes place in all corporate organisms, the balance and the domestic political situations influenced the internal balance (with more or less synchrony, with more or less delay). The same happened in the Association of the Reporters that survived decades of critiques and attempts at reform. A very well culturally organized leadership in 1989 with Giuseppe Morello as President and Gianni Faustini as Secretary, gained the power of the Association. The new leadership made the professional experiment going on in Milan the main path for the Nation. They created a framework of common rules and authorized the establishment of a limited number of schools all over Italy. Other Schools of Journalism were established in other cities and towns. In Urbino and Bologna, two schools were opened within private colleges. One was the Luiss in Rome, managed by Confindustria, the Italian Manufacturers' Association and the second was Università Cattolica in Milan, the most prestigious Catholic College in Italy. In Perugia, Rai (Italian PBS) entered into an agreement with the local university and established the first school with strong corporate ties.

The centralized organization, guaranteed and consolidated by law with a sort of regulatory power granted to the Association on formation and training patterns, worked well at first. There were very few rules clear to everyone. Schools would have the number of students decided nationwide, based on the absorption ability of the market. Classes would last two years, with enrollment requirements that preferred candidates with a college degree to those without a college degree. Schools would prefer professional training and use academics to implement and improve the profession of a reporter. Institutional and training models spread into different directions over a common theme.

Nationally a few well-distributed schools (two in Milan, one in Bologna, Urbino, Perugia, and Rome) assured an enrollment that was almost rational. Teachers would choose among the best that the profession and the academia could offer; while exchange student and cooperation programmes were also developed.

In the early 1990s exchange opportunities were widely possible and at hand. Milan, Bologna, and Perugia joined the European Journalism Training Association shortly after their establishment. They hosted the annual general meeting and some seminars; they even held important corporate offices (Angelo Agostini was first secretary and the President of Ejta). In 1995, Milan, Bologna, and Perugia achieved the first attempt in Europe of multimedia production, made of three training levels of cooperation in TV, radio, Web and CD-ROM. With the help of Indaco, an Institute established by Renato Porro in the Department of Sociology at the University of Trento, national and international workshops were held for students and teachers.

In the mid-1990s, the model of training for journalism became solid throughout Italy. There were a small number of schools, six of which were ruled by a central body (the Association of Reporters); various institutional and economical models were managed locally (university's schools and schools managed by trade associations; schools based on tuitions and others that received local and /or EU funds). The educational system was almost the same everywhere. All the schools featured a two-year course with workshops for students who already had a college degree, a highly specialized teaching body made up of mostly reporters, an academic body that through time learned the difference between teaching in college and teaching in a professional School of Journalism. This model was the one widely tested and used by the Journalism School at Columbia University in New York, obviously adapted to the unique needs of the Italian profession.

The professional industry answered to all these solicitations fairly quickly. Reporters welcomed the interns from the schools. Some reporters were welcomed with more enthusiasm, some others with less enthusiasm. The personality and the training which the interns received from their respective schools caused these varied feelings of enthusiasm. The initial wariness against interns led to an increased selection by newsrooms between schools who provided a better training and those to set aside.

Between academy and corporation

Italy is a strange country indeed. After the mid-1990s, three processes developed at about the same time, colliding as crazy meteors on the young journalism education institutions.

First, there was a change in the leadership of the Association of Reporters. The leadership that impressively led to a careful and organized opening to the college training abdicated for internal reasons in favour of a completely different leadership that was more sensitive to local needs. The new leadership listened to the many cultural, political, and professional movements, even though it did not have a real plan and did not consider that all the movements required a profound renovation of the corporate legislation that ruled the journalism profession. The new leadership did not obtain from the Parliament liberalization and new rules for the profession. Journalism remained tied to the legislation of 1963. However, the new leadership started a process that would lead to the establishment of twenty-one schools of journalism by 2006 compared to the initial six. Any university which wanted a school of journalism could open one. Training to become a journalist became one of the easiest and most glamorous tricks to attract a student.

The Italian Parliament started a long and difficult process to restructure the academic education world through the autonomy of the universities and the renovation of educational programmes. Each university was free to offer all the Bachelor programmes they wanted to, including Master's and Ph.D.s. This lead to an explosion of BA programmes in Communication Science with more than 70 on offer. Each Italian student could count on a Major in Communication Science within 50 kilometres or less from his or her hometown or municipality. Communication Science, in the fantasies of the Italian youth of the nineties or early noughties, meant a career as a reporter or TV host, with no difference between them.

The Chamber of Journalists reacted like a fish out of water to the changes that took place in the academic world over these years. It authorized schools even in the most remote towns, then decided that the Ph.D.s were a prerequisite for the profession, and then again wisely went back to the Master's as a requirement. In the meantime, the confusion was already established in the system. Twenty schools, without common ground could only create confusion in a field where excellence is duly recognized.

The deep restructuring that affected the mass media industry created problems with the unions and contractual obligations with the reporters who; in the summer of 2008, did not have a national labour agreement. The last agreement was signed three years before. The unions had a logical and consequential reaction (even though it was short-sighted). For more than two years, the reporters' union (in Italy there is only one: the National Federation of Press) fought the Schools of Journalism. The reason was simple and straightforward. Internships were hosted in editorial offices, radio and TV stations, and websites only during the summer months. Interns did not cost anything and companies that hosted them were able to cover the vacancies caused by the vacations they had granted to hired reporters. The result was that unemployed reporters, who were usually given the opportunity to take home a minimum wage and benefits in these months, were left without a part-time job. It was a paradox: the union insisted with its requests, the Association acknowledged the union's requests and prohibited the internships during the summertime. It was a pure act of madness, of course. Formation, culture (and even union's commitment) of future generations of reporters went down the drain for a few Euros gained with small salaries or social security benefits. It became a war between the poor. The same thing had happened twenty years before in Fleet Street, in London.

In 2007, the Chambers of Journalists had another change of leadership and another consequential renovation of the politics that affected the Schools of Journalism. All the attempts to create an organized relationship between universities and the journalists failed, causing an absurd paradox that still dominates Italy today. The Association of Reporters, the only professional journalistic body recognized by law in Europe, has full legal rights to choose the framework of the training in journalism. The Association is the only one in charge with deciding if a body can be designated as a school that qualifies for professional training.

All schools of journalism became academic bodies; but because of the lack of agreement between the Ministry of Education and the Association itself, the only authority, in the end, is in the Association. The Association is the only one entitled to decide if a student, after two years of school of journalism may take the National Exam or not. It is understood that if a school were not recognized, no student would attend it, otherwise that student would not be allowed to work as a reporter after two years spent studying to become a reporter.

Since 2007, the Association has made new rules. Internships during summer were abolished. A lot of bureaucracy for a single matter: schools, (universities or other, it does not matter) invest money, programmes, teachers, and creativity: at the end, it is only the Association that decides if that school qualifies its students for the National Test. The Association of Reporters prevails on universities. Italian universities establish, manage, and pay for Schools of Journalism. The Association of Reporters writes the rules and the school must comply with such rules, regardless of the university's autonomy as declared by a national Legislation.

It is a war for power, of course. There is a corporate body that does not count in the profession (mass media have no respect for codes of ethics, and the Chambers does not have real power to have those codes of ethics respected. The Chambers itself is made mostly of retired reporters or reporters outside the main journalism areas). The university took the formation of young reporters to heart but it could not count on real cooperation with the journalism or the media industry.

Just for the record, we will describe how young reporters are really trained in Italy. One thing is the institutional, juridical, and legislative framework. Another thing is the experience that the schools gained – for good and for worse – in the last twenty years they spent working at the training of many new reporters, growing a capital of knowledge and skills.

New schools after new rules

For the first ten years, few institutes followed one didactic pattern. During the second decade more and more schools joined the first pioneers.

Some schools were able to succeed because they could count on a heritage, a teaching body and professional environment that was more favorable. Some schools did much worse, for the opposite reasons. Yet, all Schools of Journalism in Italy moved their steps on the same path: training institutions that were open to college graduates, trying to offer the practical and academic knowledge that was necessary to work in the journalism industry.

The student of an Italian School of Journalism has already achieved the first level of education. It is a given that graduates have some basic knowledge since Philosophy, Sociology, Political Science, Literature, History, and, sometimes, Economics are very common choices. This is the base to start from, trying to combine the skills acquired on two fronts: basic technical knowledge of journalism and specific academic knowledge that are necessary for a professional specialization.

The techniques of research, control, and elaboration of the news are oriented to the various fields, which the reporter may work in: first the media then several opportunities of specialization. Education is still based on two years of study. Usually the first year is spent studying the basic techniques, the second learning the profession along with one or two Majors. Each school outlines its vocational fields on a common journalistic ground (basic knowledge is taken for granted).

Among the best and most known schools, some are traditionally dedicated to the training of reporters, other have a media vocation, such as TV and radio or press or another type of broadcasting. Of course, the geographic location and the opportunity to hire reporters from the best national media both play an important role in the selection of the school and its offerings. The institutional framework of schools and their relation with publishing companies makes the same selection. Among the major publishing companies, two have relations recognized by political institutions: Rai, with its School of Journalism in Perugia and Mediaset with its Master at the University of Iulm in Milano. The relations between other companies are less clear but with the same essence. Other schools have a good fame and tradition and do not need specific relations with other publishing companies. The author here refers to the school of the Università Statale in Milan, the Università Cattolica and Istituto per la formazione al giornalismo in Milan, the Ifg of Urbino, the Luiss University in Rome.

In all these cases, the teaching body became more and more skilled, both academically and journalistically, developing a common ground upon different skills and styles. Each Institute participated in the same training and publishing project. For example, we could report the case of the Ifg of Urbino, established twenty years ago by Silvano Rizza, then by Giovanni Mantovani, and now by Raffaele Fiengo. In that small town of the Marche region, without a local newspaper, the fortnightly magazine issued by the School of Journalism became the town paper, a true training for the young reporters who worked at it (and the cause of some problems for the directors). Otherwise I could explain about my school; the Masters in Journalism at the Iulm University in Milan was developed through cooperation with Mediaset, the work of our Managing Director Ivan Berni, along with the Director of TgCom Paolo Liguori. Those are only two examples among many others that could prove that the Director, the teachers, the students are those who actually 'make' the school, just like a good paper, a good radio station, a good TV news programme or a good website is made. The best schools of journalism in Italy were founded and grew on this basis, and then each of them added a touch of its own style.

Concluding Remarks

It is hard to analyse the single pieces that form this mosaic; they cannot be dismantled according to specific and fixed elements. We could say that the best schools in Italy moulded themselves to a very unusual scenario; they added the best reporters-teachers to their teaching body, moulding the academics to the journalism while meeting the labour market's demands, anticipating the skills required by publishing companies.

Schools were able to reach this goal working within a legislative framework that would be considered crazy by any other European country. They were able to achieve their goal because journalism in Italy, as in any other country of the European Union, is certainly a job, but it is also a passion and vocation. It is this passion that allows us to balance various laws with the need to teach, and gives us the courage to imagine how the journalism of tomorrow will look.

The Author

Angelo Agostini is Professor of Journalism at the University of Iulm in Milan, where he directs the Masters in Journalism. He is Director of the scientific quarterly *Problemi dell'informazione*.

References

Agostini, Angelo (1999), 'Accesso alla professione e formazione professionale nel giornalismo italiano', *Trattato di diritto amministrativo, XXVIII, Informazione e telecomunicazione*, (a cura di Roberto Zaccaria), Padova: Cedam.

Agostini, Angelo (ed.) (1996), *New Media New Journalism. Journalism Education in the Information Society*, Bologna-Maastricht, Ejta-Reports, 1, European Journalism Training Association.

Agostini, Angelo (1995), 'Le scuole di giornalismo. Una sfida per la professione', *Problemi dell'informazione*, 4.

Faustini, Gianni (2008), '1934, De Gasperi (anche lui): serve una scuola di giornalismo', *Problemi dell'informazione*, 2.

Gallavotti, Eugenio (1982), 'Come nacque e presto fallì la scuola fascista di giornalismo', *Problemi dell'informazione*, 1.

Tonelli Giorgio (2007), '1934, Antonio Gramsci: per diventare giornalisti servono scuole', *Problemi dell'informazione*, 1.

The Maltese Journalism Education Landscape

Joseph Borg

I joined the *Times of Malta* as a cub reporter on January 7, 1963, when I was not even 15. I had done my GCE O-levels and two Matriculation exams, but I failed my Physics O-level, so I could not enter University. Like other reporters at the time, I had no formal training and was almost immediately thrown in at the deep end – sink or swim. But the experience was useful and after a few months I was promoted to law reporter, reporting from the Lower Courts. In December of 1963 I was asked to fill a temporary vacancy in *The Sunday Times of Malta* as a junior sub-editor. That vacancy, originally meant to last three months, turned out to be open-ended. I ended up spending 44 years at *The Sunday Times*, the last 17 of which as editor. (Grech 2008)

Introduction

Malta is the smallest member state of the European Union but one of the most densely populated countries in the world with 400,000 inhabitants occupying a surface area of 316 km. sq. The service industries, tourism and IT are among the biggest employers on the Island. Catholicism is the religion of well over 97 per cent of the population. Two parties are represented in Parliament: the Partit Nazzjonalista (a member of the European People's Party is in government) and the Partit Laburista (a member of the Socialist European Party). There is also a very small Green Party called Alternattiva Demokratika (Democratic Alternative) and a small right-wing party called Azzjoni Nazzjonali (National Action Party).

Malta is a bilingual country. While Maltese is the national language, English is the second official language. Maltese is a synthesis of the Semitic and the romance strands of languages. This language hails from the period when Malta was dominated by the Arabs and reflects the chequered history of Malta which saw the presence of many occupying European countries.

Malta is a media-rich country. There are seven national TV stations, thirteen national radio stations, four daily newspapers and twelve weekly papers besides hundreds of magazine titles and over twenty community radio stations. In fact, Malta has a national television and radio station for every 16 km sq. and a daily or weekly newspaper for every 27,000 persons. Over 99% of households have at least one TV set while more than half have an Internet connection; the majority of which are broadband subscriptions. In spite of its small size, it rates among the best countries in the EU for e-government services.

Short history of journalism education

The introductory quote from Mr Laurence Grech, former editor of *The Sunday Times* – the newspaper with the largest circulation in Malta – was made while speaking during the celebration of the Eight Anniversary of the Fundazzjoni Tumas Fenech ghall-Edukazzjoni fil-Gurnalizmu (Tumas Fenech Foundation for Education in Journalism or FTFEFG). This quote epitomizes the history of journalism education in Malta for several decades. Journalists were trained on the job by their seniors. The occasions for formal education, generally in the form of overseas scholarships were few and far between. The United Kingdom based Thompson Foundation was a well sought after prestigious training centre. Many journalists considered this situation of lack of formal training organized locally as inadequate and consequently continued to harbour the desire for the organization of such training.

In 1969 and 1971 the Malta College of Arts, Science and Technology (MCAST) organized a two-year training course in journalism studies. Both were evening courses giving six hours of tuition every week. The course, which was co-ordinated by the veteran journalist Joe Felice Pace was generally given by practicing journalists and experts in different fields e.g. politics, economy, writing in English and Maltese (Felice Pace 26 June 2008 interview).

In 1976 Felice Pace organized a two-year course through the Extension Studies Board of the University of Malta. This was an evening course leading to a certificate in journalism and like the MCAST courses provided six hours of tuition every week with an emphasis on practical training (Felice Pace 26 June 2008 interview).

In the middle of the Eighties the University of Malta organized a ten-day hands-on course in journalism, led by Ms Val Clarke, a Senior Lecturer from the London College of Printing. This idea developed further and the University organized a year and half-long evening diploma course in journalism. It planned to hold three consecutive 'diploma' courses; one building on the other in such a way that the third diploma would be equivalent to a degree. The initiator and administrator of this seminal course in journalism was Professor Dominic Fenech, Rector's Delegate, while Ms Val Clark was again responsible for the course design and for its academic content, as well as teaching its core elements. The course, which had a strong component of practical journalistic work, was very well subscribed by both working journalists and others aspiring to be journalists. Many of the students finally graduated, mostly with a BA in Communication Studies and Contemporary Mediterranean Studies (Fenech 30 June 2008 interview).

This and similar courses prepared the way for the eventual setting up of a department of communication studies which later on developed into the Centre for Communication Technology (CCT) as part of the University of Malta.

Besides courses organized by the CCT , training in journalism is today also provided on informal level by the Institute of Maltese Journalists, the Tumas Fenech Foundation for Education in Journalism, the Strickland Foundation and some of the media houses themselves.

Courses provided by the CCT

The Centre for Communication Technology was set up by the University Council in 1991 to complement the University Library by providing computer support and audiovisual services. Under the direction of Professor Saviour Chircop the Centre expanded its services in other areas and became the university's communication teaching centre. Originally, its communication programme was academically placed under the Faculty of Arts and then the Faculty of Education. Since 2000, the awarding of degrees became part of the formal remit of CCT. The formation of personnel capable of understanding the media context and creating media products is part of the remit of CCT (CCT Website 2008a).

Three divisions make up the CCT: Communications and Instructional Design; Library and Information Studies; and Law and Information Technology. The journalism courses are part of the first division.

The CCT is not and does not pretend to be a school of journalism; however, it is undoubtedly the main provider of journalistic training on the Island. The number of students following the courses offered by CCT during the academic year 2008/2009 was just over 200, two-thirds of which are female students. The number of students following the specifically journalistic courses varies from seven studying 'In-depth reporting' to 108 following 'Journalism 1'. Both courses are electives. Roughly, one-third of the students following these courses are male. Most of these courses are taught by part-timers, the vast majority of whom are professional journalists. Probably because of these reasons, the research component of CCT in directly journalistic issues is not very vast.

During March 2009, the author conducted an e-mail survey among the Maltese students who graduated from CCT from 2005/2006 to 2007/2008. An e-mail was sent to the University e-mail address of students. When one takes into account the probability that several graduates no longer access their University e-mail account, one can consider as reasonable the survey's response rate of seventeen per cent. From these answers, it transpired that just over half the students are doing work related to the media industry which varies from journalism to web advertising. One fifth of the respondents are working in journalism, while another fifth work in public relations.

Undergraduate courses

CCT offers two courses at the undergraduate level. The Bachelor's in Communication is a three-year, full-time degree programme offering a theoretical approach to media and its interaction with society and contemporary culture. The Bachelor's in Communication (Honours) is a four-year, full-time programme focusing on both the theory of communications and practical media production (CCT Website 2008b).

Both are courses in communication studies not in journalism *per se* though both courses have a considerable component of direct journalism studies.

Diploma in Journalism

A Diploma in Journalism is offered at the undergraduate level. This 'is a two-year (part-time, day) course, for persons in the field who would like to acquire a conceptual framework and, guidance in the creation, and dissemination of effective news delivery' (CCT Website 2008b). The programme was set up to encourage working journalists to continue their education. The number of professional journalists profiting from this initiative is minimal. In fact, during the 2008/2009 academic year, there were no students following the course.

Students following the diploma have to complete 30 ECTS courses each year. A number are compulsory courses while others are electives. All courses offered as part of the diploma course are also offered as part of the undergraduate courses. Students, for the successful completion of the diploma, are expected to write a long essay (between 5000 and 7000 words) which has a value of 6 ECTS and undergo a placement with a journalistic organization (2 ECTS).

MA in Journalism

CCT also provides for a Master's programme which allows specialization in specific areas enabling students to take up middle-management positions in their chosen field. The areas include a Master's in Journalism available on a part-time basis during the evenings (CCT Website 2008c). This course is not on offer for the time being.

Courses closely related to journalism

The courses – diploma and undergraduate – provide a mixture of practical and theoretical courses as well as general communication and directly journalistic courses, though the distinction is not always easy to make. Credit courses such as 'Basic Reporting', 'Journalism I and II', 'Meet the Press', 'In-Depth Reporting' – each is a 4 ECTS course – are mainly practical courses. During these courses, students are introduced to the concept of news value and taught the basic skills of interviewing and writing news stories.

As multi-tasking is increasingly becoming the order of the day in this sector, the centre also offers courses in desktop publishing, printing processes, video production and scripting. Practical placements with a number of different media organizations are also on offer. These practical courses are accompanied by several theoretical courses on research methods, gender, content analysis, economic principles, media law and ethics. Students are situated in the local scene by taking the course 'Media in Maltese Society' and on the international level by credits such as 'Issues in Journalism' (4 ECTS).

Courses offered by IMJ and FTFEG

The Institute of Maltese Journalists (formerly The Malta Press Club) from its beginning in 1989 actively worked to further journalism education and training. In 2000, it teamed up with the Board of Directors of Tumas Group to set up the Tumas Fenech Foundation for Education in Journalism – FTFEG (Press Release 1 February 2001). The alliance between the Group and the Institute provided the latter with the necessary funds to hold journalistic training courses even with the participation of foreign professionals.

Since then courses in different aspects of journalistic training have been organized every year. Giving a few examples would not be amiss here: a seminar in newsroom management in 2001; a seminar on e-communication for journalists in 2002; a one-week course in journalistic photography in 2004, sports journalism in 2005, journalism and irregular migration in 2006; and a course on the interpretation of statistics in 2007 (Mr Mario Schiavone, Administrator of Foundation, 30 June 2008 interview).

The Foundation set up a Board of Studies composed of academics and members of the profession who are responsible for proposing courses that can be organized by the Foundation. These courses are led by foreign trainers, local academics or local professionals. During these courses, practice and theory are mixed together but there is a predominance of practice. The courses vary from weeklong full-time courses to others taking up only a few hours.

Courses organized by The Strickland Foundation

The Strickland Foundation was set up by the Hon. Mabel Strickland and is the beneficiary of the majority shareholding in Allied Newspapers Ltd, publishers of *The Times* and *The Sunday Times*.[1] Among the objectives of the Foundation one finds the following: 'to help improve the standard of Maltese journalism and the preservation of its freedom and independence' (Montanaro 1996: 1).

In the beginning of the 1990s the Foundation organized a three-week course on 'the editor as manager and journalist' and a two-week course for broadcast journalists. The Thompson Foundation provided lecturers for both courses. Since then the contribution of the Foundation to journalism training takes the form of periodic holding of conferences given by high profile overseas personalities (Frank Bonello, Secretary, The Strickland Foundation, 18 June 2008 interview). The Foundation has also helped finance in-house training courses organized by Allied Newspapers for their own staff.

In-house national and international training

Several media organizations from time to time organize in-house training for their journalists or use the services of other organizations, including foreign ones. Some examples of particular interest can give an indication of this process.

PBS Ltd (Public Broadcasting Services Ltd.) is a member of CIRCOM which is an international audio-visual network in Europe comprising 376 regional television stations from 38 countries. Since 2005, six PBS journalists participated in CIRCOM courses in journalism, new technology, management and production (Anna Dalli, Administration Coordinator, PBS, 21 June 2008 interview).

Some journalists participate in courses organized by the European Journalism Centre based in the Netherlands. Sometimes journalists are helped by their employers to attend such courses but at other times no help is forthcoming and journalists have to cover the participation in the course from their own leave allotment. This attitude discourages several journalists from furthering their professional training.

In recent years there were a number of occasions when foreign tutors were invited to Malta by particular media organizations to train their journalists. RTK, Radio 101, and PBS are among the broadcast organizations that held such courses. These courses were hands-on ones and generally including tutorial sessions held during normal working hours.

Above I referred to the new face of journalism as a result of multi-tasking. This is also evidenced in the type of training that is being offered. For example, PBS decided to send a number of its journalists for training in Avid editing at the Malta College of Arts, Science and Technology. This training coincided with the newsroom turning digital. In fact, whenever the newsroom goes through a period of technological change this is always accompanied by some kind of training (Dalli 21 June 2008 interview).

Several media houses do no formal in-house training while others only organize the occasional short course. The Allied Newspapers group have taken a different option. They have decided to organize in-house journalistic training in a systematic way. Through the Press Association of England they identified a professional trainer and commissioned him to plan a training module for the staff of Allied Newspapers.

Once we have the training module we will then nominate a number of mentors who, basing themselves on criteria set by the Press Association, will evaluate the work of trainees. The idea is to have the course at diploma standard. We are also complementing this by sending people to PA courses in the UK. (Mr Ray Bugeja, Editor *The Times*, 30 June 2008 interview)

Largely one can say that the main in-house training is still on the job training, by practice much more than training by formal courses. Owners still find it hard to find enough money for investment in the formal training of their staff.

Concluding Remarks

The above description and analysis leads to a number of comments, conclusions and considerations.

1. The seminal courses of the mid-1980s would not have developed into the present variety of university courses had there not been a number of important political, economic and educational developments that radically changed the University of Malta and the local mediascape thus creating a need for such courses.

   The University of Malta was re-founded in the late-1980s, several faculties were re-instated while new centres and programmes were set up. The Centre for Communication Technology is a case in point. Besides, the number of university students today is more than ten times as much as it was at the end of the 1980s.

   Changes in the local mediascape were similarly very great. The beginning of the 1990s saw the advent of pluralism in broadcasting. As a result, today's mediascape is varied as well as crowded. A digital radio platform was inaugurated in mid-2008 and the switch over to full digital TV coverage will happen by the end of 2010.

   Economic expansion and the concomitant increase of the expenditure on advertising encouraged entrepreneurs to enter the newspaper market. This resulted in the publication of seven new newspapers (six of them published in English) totally owned by commercial interests. Broadband penetration has rapidly increased in the last couple of years thus increasing the possibility of new journalistic initiatives and other media-related projects.

   This new media environment increased the employment opportunities and, consequently, students' interest in communication courses. Quite naturally, journalism is just part of this complex media environment. It is not even the most lucrative part. Jobs in advertising and public relations generally pay much more and tend to be less demanding. This reality is reflected in the fact that the journalism component is just one of the many facets of the communication courses at the University of Malta and it has to compete with the rest for the attention of the students.

2. Graduates from the University of Malta communication courses and graduates from other departments and faculties are today well placed in several newsrooms of Malta's broadcasting and print media organizations. Their presence is, though, larger in the broadcasting media than in the print media. For example, the editors and/or news editors of the three main TV stations are communication graduates and two of them are females. Half of the journalists in the newsroom at PBS Ltd are communication graduates. The newsrooms of the radio stations that give a lot of importance to news are managed by communication graduates. On the other hand, only one newspaper editor is a communication graduate, though a number of others are graduates in other areas.

   This difference between the print and the broadcasting media can be due to the fact that there was already a large pool of experience-based print journalists to choose from for the position of newspaper editors. On the other hand, there was a void in the case of the newly created posts for editors in the nascent broadcasting media organizations.

3. Does the increased presence of so many communication graduates bring with it an increase in the quality of journalism? How are communication graduates perceived by the other journalists?

The former editor of *The Sunday Times*, Laurence Grech (2008), had this comment on the subject in question:

> What I am worried about, however, is the danger of falling standards both in English and Maltese writing, and a lack of general knowledge and of Maltese politics, history and culture displayed by the younger generation of journalists, reporters, sub-editors and editors. This, I feel, is an essential part of a media person's background and it pains me when I see grammatical and orthographic mistakes and, worse, wrong information. Obviously, a university degree is not enough.

Mr Ray Bugeja, the present editor of *The Times* says that 'those graduating from the University of Malta leave a lot to be desired' and that 'it is evident that the University is not adequately preparing students to the real world of newsroom work' (Bugeja 30 June 2008 interview).

However, it seems that not all is negative. According to the same journalists, university training could have brought some improvements.

Grech (2008) continues saying:

> On the other hand, young journalists today are more adventurous. They work harder to dig out news stories, seek out exclusive interviews and give their newspapers a breezier, more reader-friendly look. Naturally, the growing competition is at the back of their minds, and we have seen this especially in the English-language newspapers.

Even Bugeja sees a silver lining. 'This time we were luckier and we did manage to identify three or four graduates who seem to have what it takes' (Bugeja 30 June 2008 interview).

This perception of University of Malta communication graduates is shared by several full-timers working in the area especially those who built their skills over the years through experience but have not had any formal academic training. In fact, in several newsrooms there is a kind of tension between the graduates and the experience-based journalists.

It seems that working journalists expect graduates to have more proficiency in what can be called 'tricks of the trade' i.e. the practical side of the profession. The University courses are communication more than journalism courses and as such do not aim at developing fully-fledged journalists. My reaction, as someone who lectures in the CCT, is that in the rapidly changing media environment even a generalist first degree in communication is of value to those who want to work in one aspect of the area. On the other hand, these general courses give the opportunity for a fair amount of practice to those students who opt for the practical credits. Quite naturally, on the job experience should then exploit the potential created by the training given at the University.

4. While would-be university students show enthusiasm for communication courses it seems that established journalists do not show a lot of interest for the furthering of their formal journalistic education. The Diploma and the MA in Journalism have been minimally supported by full-time working journalists. The same can be said for several

of the courses that are organized by IMG and FTFEG. There are a number of structural reasons that best explain this attitude. Generally journalists are expected to do this training over and above their normal workload. Besides, journalists tend to work long, as well as odd hours. These two factors tend to make many courses that are organized over-and-above their workload unattractive.

5. Suggestions for the future,

i. The degree courses at the University of Malta are a mixture of different aspects of communication studies. This is to be expected of general courses. On the other hand, the University can study the possibility of having a stronger journalistic component during its honours course in communication so that students can opt to have more specialization in journalism and a recognized degree in the area.

ii. Organizations providing ad hoc courses can consider shifting the emphasis from organizing courses for which full-time journalists attend to organizing newsroom-based courses. In this scenario, the course goes to the students and not the students go to the course. Such courses can have a short theoretical component which different journalists will go to, but the main thrust of the course will be in the form of on-the-job tutorials. This training would be tailor-made to the needs of different newsrooms and can be done during normal working hours without disrupting the flow of work.

iii. An effort should be made to bring together the institutions involved in some form of training. Each can keep its own identity and autonomy but different areas of specialization can be mutually agreed to. This synergy should be to the benefit of all. Courses can, for example, be organized in such a way that they fit in the ECTS system and reach a level set and recognized by the University. Such courses can then be followed by students and working journalists alike and will be credited by the University. Such a system of accreditation could make these courses more attractive.

iv. It is important that the industry becomes an eager participant in the training process. There is already an element of interest and co-operation. BPC and the Tumas Group work with the Institute of Maltese Journalists. On the other hand, hardly any of the owners of the broadcasting stations or newspapers make any substantial contribution to the training of their journalists. Unless the other owners are involved, future developments will be limited. Such rapprochement can clarify the aims and needs of both parties and perhaps lead to more understanding and the development of new products that would answer the needs the industry feels it has. Probably the University can play an important role due to its recognized prestige and expertise.

6. In the last two decades the change from experience-based journalists to formally and academically trained journalists has been gathering momentum. This direction is expected to be strengthened in the future. It will succeed more if the training institutions synergize their efforts preferably under the aegis of the University and employers consider money spent on training as an investment more than a burden.

The Author

Fr Joseph Borg lectures in communication studies at the University of Malta. He is the Editor of Campus FM and member of the Management Board of the TV station E22.

Note

1. The Hon. Mabel Strickland was a Maltese politician and leader of the Progressive Constitutional Party. She was also the owner of *The Times* and *The Sunday Times*, Malta's largest daily and weekly newspapers.

References

CCT Website (2008a), *History of CCT*, http://www.cct.um.edu.mt/html/m03-00-00.html. Accessed 10 May 2008. Centre for Communication Technology, University of Malta.

CCT Website (2008b), *Programmes: Undergraduate Level*, http://www.cct.um.edu.mt/html/m01-02-00.htm. Accessed 10 May 2008. Centre for Communication Technology, University of Malta.

CCT Website (2008c), *Postgraduate programme*, http://www.cct.um.edu.mt/html/m01-03-00.htm. Accessed 20 May 2008. Centre for Communication Technology, University of Malta.

Grech, Laurence (2008), *The Maltese Newspaper scene*, Speech delivered during the celebration of the Eighth Anniversary of the Tumas Fenech Foundation for Education in Journalism, 2 May.

Il-Fundazzjoni Tumas Fenech ghall-Edukazzjoni fil-Gurnalizmu (2008), official website, http://www.maltapressclub.org.mt/tumas.html. Accessed 2 May 2008.

Institute of Maltese Journalists (2008), official website, http://www.maltapressclub.org.mt. Accessed 2 May 2008.

Legal Notice 13 (2005), *Malta Government Gazette*, 25 January 2005, No. 17,712.

EDUCATION ACT (CAP. 327) (2005), *Bye-Laws of 2005 in terms of the General Regulations for University Undergraduate Awards, 2004 for the Diploma in Journalism – Dip. Journalism – under the auspices of the Centre for Communication Technology.*

Montanaro, A. (ed.) (1996), *The Strickland Foundation*, Malta: Progress Press.

The Malta Press Club (1998), *Five Year Plan (1998–2003)*, http://www.maltapressclub.org.mt/5yearc.htm. Accessed 1 May 2008.

Tumas Fenech Foundation for Education in Journalism (FTFEG) (2001), 'Press Release 1 February 2001', *Fondazzjoni Tumas Fenech ghall-Edukazzjoni fil-Gurnalizmu celebrates first anniversary,* http://www.maltapressclub.org.mt/tumas.html. Accessed 2 May 2008.

The Portuguese Journalism Education Landscape

Manuel Pinto and Sandra Marinho

Introduction

The path and evolution of Journalism Education in Portugal cannot be dissociated from the country's economic, social and political development, which explains, amongst other aspects, its late start: the first Journalism Education university programme only began in 1979 and served as a model for subsequent projects. As a result of almost 30 years of expansion, reorganization and search for consistency, higher education, through state and private polytechnics and universities, is today the major player in the journalism education system.

This is still a field crossed by tensions and dichotomies (academia vs. newsroom; theory vs. practice) and the impact of recent transformations is yet to be fully understood. Ongoing reforms in the higher education system; the implementation of Bologna Declaration and changes that have been occurring in journalism and in the way journalists work, especially the ones caused by new media and digitization, these are all adjustments whose effects and developments should be attentively followed.

A historical overview of journalism education in Portugal constitutes an interesting case, for two interconnected circumstances: the non-existence of programmes during the longest-running European authoritarian regime (all attempts to develop them were either avoided or pre-empted); and, consequently, the still-recent appearance of journalism education in the Portuguese higher education system, which makes Portugal the last European country to provide academic journalism schooling (Ferreira 2005).

In fact, in Portugal, the first university programme (in Communication Sciences) that explicitly claimed the purpose of training journalists appeared only in 1979, at Universidade Nova de Lisboa (Social Sciences and Humanities School), influenced by Portuguese professors educated abroad, particularly at the Catholic University of Louvain. The first programme exclusively centered on journalism in Portugal only started in 1991, at Universidade de Coimbra (Humanities School).

Today, the country has a number and variety of programmes, which has actually been considered by some observers as excessive, due to an 'explosion' of new curricula. A researcher on this subject called it 'the miracle of programs' multiplication' (Mesquita 1995).

But, if journalism as a matter for higher education is recent, debates on the pertinence and configuration of this type of instruction are very old. The first documented reference goes back to 1898, when the 4th International Press Conference[1] took place in Lisbon, where the need and timing for the creation of journalism schools was debated. This discussion lasted until the 25th of April [1974] revolution, sometimes only in terms of maintaining a dialogue, and other times resulting in actual proposals and accomplished projects.

Generally speaking, one might say that the social actors involved in this debate were professional journalists, 'newsroom educated', which could explain the fact that most of them advocate, more or less intensely, the idea that journalism, at its core, cannot be learned at school. In other words, if you're not born with it, you will never be a true journalist. As an example, Bento Carqueja, a former director of one of the greatest Oporto's daily newspapers, claimed that 'such as there are no schools for poetry, there can't be also schools for training journalists' (cit. in Cunha 1941: 30–31).

A sign that reflects the fact that the topic of journalism education wasn't on the agenda can be drawn from research (Sousa et al. 2007). When analysing intellectual production in the field of journalism, in Portugal, until 1974 – the year when the 25th of April revolution took place and democracy was installed – researchers identified and examined 357 texts, and found out that only 3 (0.8 per cent) could be classified as 'journalism education', all of them published between 1930 and 1960.

We may, so, establish that, in regard to both crucial issues recognized by these researchers as subjects for debate in the last century (Can journalism be learned or are people born journalists? Is there a point on having journalism schools? If so, which type of schools should be created and which type of curricula should be implemented?), we can observe three different approaches, the first gathering the majority of supporters:

- Newsrooms are the main schools
- Specialized education is useful, but not essential
- It is necessary to have a school to train journalists

Another noticeable aspect, when it comes to movements towards the institutionalization of journalism education, has to do with the involvement of professional elites. The first initiative clearly oriented towards this course occurs in 1941, by the hand of the National Journalists' Union (Sindicato Nacional dos Jornalistas), formed a few years earlier.[2] Earlier still, back in 1926, the Lisbon Press Workers Union had already taken a stand on the same issue, but with no consequences (Sobreira 2003).

In the proposal of 1941 a two-year programme was advanced; classes would take place at the Union's facilities and applicants should be journalists with at least one year of professional experience, or candidates with at least nine years of formal education. The project was grounded on the need to 'professionally value journalists and to uplift their cultural level to the standards required by the mission they carry out in Portuguese society' (Boletim Informativo do SNJ 1941, cit in Sobreira 2003). It intended to gather academics and journalists around the idea of what a journalist should know to perform the job: solid general knowledge; and skills on newsgathering, writing printing techniques (Correia and Baptista 2005). This proposal was presented to the Government and ended up forgotten, although Sousa et al. (2007) believe that lack of consensus among the journalistic class may also have contributed to the failure of the project.

In 1966, a Portuguese newspaper called *Diário Popular* organized the *I Diário Popular's* Introduction to Journalism Program (I Curso de Iniciação Jornalística do *Diário Popular*), the first project of the kind ever carried out in Portugal (Correia and Baptista 2005).

Later, in 1968, the National Journalists' Union, after twenty-eight years of claims, got to organize and implement, on its own, the I Journalism Program, attended by 160 applicants (48 of them were journalists), which was considered a very successful initiative (Correia and Baptista 2005). Teachers were both journalists and academics.

But the project of involving public authorities was taken once more 30 years later, in a more open political context. Salazar had died and its successor at the head of the Executive initially gave some reasons (feeble) to believe that change was on the way. The authoritarian regime had weakened, especially because of the maintenance of three war fronts in Africa, since the early 1960s, against independence movements in Angola, Guinea-Bissau and Mozambique, then Portuguese colonies. The National Journalists' Union's Board, presided by a prestigious professional, took advantage of the fact that a major reform of the national education system had been proposed, coordinated by a reformist minister, to present, in 1971, a 'Project for Journalism Education'. This time, nevertheless, as claimed by the Union itself, the failure of the proposal was due to the fact that 'too many people were interested in the tutelage of journalism education' in Portugal.

Even if the National Journalists' Union was the first to propose a university journalism degree, another institution, ISLA – Languages and Administration Institute (Instituto Superior de Línguas e Administração, the first private higher education institution in Portugal, ended up achieving this goal. ISLA's proposal was very well accepted by the Government, and ESMC – Social Communication Media Higher School (Escola Superior de Meios de Comunicação Social) opened in 1971/72, providing a three-year Journalism programme. The project was financed by a private bank (Banco Borges & Irmão), but was compromised by the 25th of April (1974). As a result of the revolution, banking and insurance activities were nationalized and the School was extinguished in the 1980s (Correia and Baptista 2005). This initiative is not considered as a reference for the establishment of journalism higher education in Portugal because, as stated above, it was terminated shortly after it started and we can't even account for the existence of any graduates.

Journalism education at universities and polytechnics: The most relevant model

If it is true, in fact, that journalists were the ones that supported and carried out the debate and efforts for the institutionalization of journalism education in Portugal, it is also true that, despite some training initiatives carried out in the 1960s (Correia and Baptista 2005), this goal ended up being achieved by the academia. And, in fact, higher education has been and still is the main "provider" of journalism education in Portugal. State and private universities and polytechnics can be viewed as the main newsroom 'suppliers', if we consider that there is a considerable growth of journalists with higher education degrees as well as degrees in the areas of communication and journalism (Fidalgo 2004), a very different reality from the one of less than ten years ago (Pinto and Sousa 2003). This happens regardless of the fact that a higher education degree is not a legal requirement to be a journalist in Portugal.

Journalism higher education follows the same structure as others areas of knowledge and research: private and state universities and polytechnics co-exist; and programmes are organized according to three cycles, as proposed by Bologna Declaration (the first cycle is equivalent to a first degree and lasts six semesters; the second is a master's degree and can be concluded in four semesters; and the third is a Ph.D.). In 2007/2008 all journalism education programmes had completed their adaptation to the Bologna Process requirements and all of them participated in the European Credit Transfer System (ECTS). Exchange programmes are widespread, especially the EU Erasmus. All of this represents a contribution to national and international mobility of students and staff, which could be enhanced, especially at the national level, if the necessary conditions could be met. Mobility was actually one of the goals clearly expressed by Bologna Declaration.

At this point we must recognize a methodological difficulty while gathering and analysing data on journalism education programmes: the lack of available information, especially in formats that allow comparisons.[3] There is not a national database on this subject and most of the available information only covers the public sector. As for online information, it is very scarce on some subjects, such as the type of faculty and students, and, in some circumstances, curricula were not available online. As for syllabi, the task revealed itself as even harder. Because of this, our analysis will be resumed to available information and, in some cases, hard data will not be presented, but, instead, we shall discuss overall tendencies.

In 2007, 34 journalism higher education programmes existed in Portugal.[4] If we consider that in 1996 there were twenty three programmes (Mesquita and Ponte 1997), this represents a significant growth. Actually, it is fair to say that, through the years, there has been a consistent growing of the courses on offer. The public sector offers nineteen programmes, most of them (eleven) at universities; and the private sector has fifteen programmes, almost

Table 1: evolution of the number of Journalism Education Programs (1996–2007),

	1996/1997			2007/2008		
	Bach./Lic.	Master	PhD	1st Cycle	2nd Cycle	3rd Cycle
Public Polytechnic	6	–	–	8	2	–
Public University	5	3	3	11	7	3
Private Polytechnic	4	–	–	2	1	–
Private University	8	–	–	13	5	1
Σ	23	3	3	34	15	4

Table 2: evolution of the number of Journalism 1st Cycle Education Programs' available places (1996–2007).

	1996/1997	2007/2008
Public Polytechnic	185	394
Public University	282	669
Private Polytechnic	285	90
Private University	900	755
Σ	1655	1908

all of them at universities (thirteen). These data are testimony to a process of transference from private to public sector, since, according to data from 1996 (Mesquita and Ponte 1997), there was an equilibrium in terms of programmes (eleven public and twelve private), but a very substantial difference in terms of available places: in 1996, there were 467 available places in the public sector and 1185 places available in private universities as polytechnics; in 2007, there were 1063 places in public schools and 845 in private ones.[5] From this data, it is possible to identify a shift from the private to the public sector (especially public universities), which is consistent with the development of higher education in general in Portugal (Pinto 2004; Pinto and Sousa 2003).

In terms of postgraduate studies, in 2007 fifteen 2nd cycle journalism programmes (equivalent to a master's degree) and three 'post graduations' (this type of programme is a specialization and does not involve a master's degree) were found. As for the 3rd cycle, there were four Ph.D. programmes in Communication Sciences, with a specific field of Journalism.

The traditional areas of affiliation (Faculties and Schools) of journalism education programmes are still Social Sciences and Humanities, with the exception of public polytechnics, where Journalism and Communication programmes belong to Education schools. This was, however, a political and not scientific decision. As for the programmes themselves, there is a mixed system, of Communication and Journalism Studies. The most common model is 'Communication Sciences', and only two programmes called specifically-and-only 'Journalism' were found (a third is called 'Journalism and Communication'). This mixed model has always been a reference for journalism higher education in Portugal (Pinto and Sousa 2003; Mesquita and Ponte 1997), with a subtle alteration: the title of programmes. The most common used to be 'Social Communication' and now is 'Communication Sciences'.

This mixed system is based on a specialization logic: there is a common set of courses ('hard courses' like Semiotics, Sociology, Methodology, History, Economics, Psychology, Languages, etc.) that all students must attend, and then, according to their area of choice (in most cases Journalism, Advertising, PR, Organizational Communication, Marketing), they will take specific courses. So, it is very common to see PR and Advertising in the same curriculum as Journalism, but they are actually separated, according to students' options in terms of specialization. As for programmes designed for specific fields or according to medium, that is not a common situation at all. Once more, in terms of medium, specific courses for each media were found in the curricula, but there were no programmes centered on television, press, radio or internet. At best, two 'post graduations' in television studies were found. The same goes for journalism fields. It is possible to identify compulsory and elective courses on subjects such as international journalism, environment, scientific journalism, cultural journalism and other, but not specific programmes on these topics.

The impact of new media on the content of journalism curricula is evident, by the number of compulsory and elective courses. But, we feel the need to go deeper in our analysis, by looking at syllabi, technical resources and available equipments. Only then, when considering real functioning conditions, as well as students' production, can we really evaluate how new media have been taken into account by journalism education programmes.

As for faculty, we have mostly academics, but there is an increasing number of on-the-job journalists participating as teachers in laboratories and practical courses. There are also former journalists, that have decided do go back to university and get their Ph.D., becoming members of the staff. This has been a relevant contribution to overcome the traditional divide between academia and the newsroom. Despite this effort, this is still an issue that needs to be addressed by journalists and teachers, especially through the encouragement of exchanges, debates and promoting research on newsrooms and with journalists as subjects.

Faculty members have very different backgrounds, but the most common are the areas of humanities and social sciences, although there is a growing number of teachers with degrees in journalism and communication sciences. We believe this can be explained by two main factors: on one hand, the fact that communication sciences and journalism are, as we have demonstrated, very recent courses in Portugal; on the other hand, traditional curricula structure had a strong emphasis on social sciences and broad communications issues (Pinto and Sousa 2003), which required staff from those specific backgrounds.

When it comes to students, they are mostly applicants from Portuguese high schools, but there are also some professionals seeking to expand their academic knowledge. We can witness this at all levels of education: initial (1st cycle) and postgraduate studies (2nd and 3rd cycles). Women are, in several cases by far, the majority of students attending journalism higher education and even if we only have data for the public sector, there is no reason to believe that private schools follow a different pattern. To illustrate this tendency, it can be pointed out that the programme with fewer women still has a percentage of 58%, and the programme with the highest proportion of women shows a percentage of 84%. The average value for the public sector is 74%.

The debate over theory vs. practice has existed since the very beginning of journalism education in Portugal. It has traditionally opposed academics and professionals, but, also, within academia, has been a focus for discussion between universities and polytechnics (Pinto and Sousa 2003). Also, it has been an issue for students who have often said that communication/journalism programmes are 'very theoretical'. Even though it is far from being solved we believe a path has been initiated in the last few years in order to narrow the gap that divides this two universes (Pinto 2004), especially by means of the collaboration of professionals in teaching activities, through progresses in research and joint participation in debates. Another explanation can come from the fact that newsrooms are increasingly composed by professionals with higher education degrees, especially in communication/journalism.

Nevertheless, the issue stands and needs to be addressed in a new context. In fact, it is possible to observe that the Bologna Process has caused some changes at this level, particularly on the distinction between polytechnics and universities, being the first traditionally associated to a more practical education. At present, all programmes (universities and polytechnics) are three-year programmes and data from research conducted by one of the authors of this chapter leaves us to believe that no major differences exist between curricula, when it comes to the ratio of theory: practice. Of course, this is an analysis based on online available curricula. For a clearer understanding, we should look at syllabi, but mostly at real, functioning conditions of the so called 'practices' and 'laboratories'. So, there is a differentiated reality that goes from highly practice-oriented curricula to more theoretical ones, but, from this analysis, we cannot really evaluate if there are sufficient resources (human and technical) to implement curricula. For sure, there has been an increase in practical courses.

The same could be said of the proportion of journalism courses vs. general education. Since Communication Sciences with specialization in Journalism is the typical model for journalism education in Portugal, it is not surprising that general education and communication courses have a great relevance in curricula. Still, the scenery here is also very diverse: we have programmes very much oriented to Journalism where journalism courses play an important role and then we can find self-characterized Journalism programmes that have only one or two journalism courses. It is, therefore, difficult to establish a pattern that is valid for the general situation. Once more, it would also be important to look at syllabi to have a better idea of real curricula content.

We believe that this issue is closely related to accreditation: there is not a national board to do the accreditation of journalism education programmes. It is done generally by the Government (Cabinet in charge) for all higher education sectors. When a programme is proposed there must be conformity to legal standards for higher education, but there are no specific criteria for journalism education. As for the evaluation of the quality of programmes, it is, at this moment, a suspended process.[6]

Connection to industry is not a tradition for Communication/Journalism higher education programmes. It is not done in terms of funding,[7] mutual accreditation or involvement in hiring practices. Internships have been the most relevant and persistent connection to the media industry. In fact they have worked as an informal hiring practice for newsrooms (Fidalgo 2004), and many journalism programs had internships as courses. With the Bologna Process and the cutback on semesters (from ten or eight to six) and the need to reduce courses, internships ended up disappearing from many 1st cycle university curricula (in some cases they were transferred to 2nd cycle programmes). On this specific issue polytechnic curricula do make a difference, since most of them kept internships, at the end of their last semester.

Journalism higher education in Portugal is still an area of some tension and debate, a work in progress, especially in the changing scenery that journalism itself is immersed in. Nevertheless, we can identify relevant progresses, especially during the last decade, in curricula, faculty and recognition from the profession.

Other players in journalism education: Continuing and in-house training

Although, as we have established, higher education is, without doubt, the most relevant paradigm for journalism education in Portugal, this is a system constituted by other players, more or less relevant. We can organize the involvement of these institutions in three distinct models: (1) on one hand, there is what could de classified as 'protocol training', a type of instruction with a degree of formalization and consistence in time and in terms of offer; (2) there are a number of organizations that provide different initiatives, but do it sporadically; (3) there are entities that provide grants to be applied in journalism education, but do not develop programmes themselves.

As for the first model, 'protocol training', it is represented by CENJOR – Protocol Centre for Journalists' Professional Education (Centro Protocolar para a Formação Profissional de Jornalistas), the most representative institution when it comes to continuing training. CENJOR initiated its activities in 1987, as a result of a formal protocol between IEFP – Institute for Employment and Professional Training (Instituto do Emprego e Formação Profissional); GMCS – Social Communication Media Cabinet (Gabinete para os Meios de Comunicação Social), both public organizations; SJ – Journalists' Union (Sindicato dos Jornalistas); AID – Daily Press Association (Associação de Imprensa Diária); and APIMPRENSA – Portuguese Press Association (Associação Portuguesa de Imprensa).

CENJOR's goal is to 'contribute to the improvement of information quality, national, regional or local, and the enhancement of the sector's entrepreneurial activities', through the enrichment and qualification of professionals and regular collaborators; the adaptation to new areas of social communication; the acquisition of broader professional skills; and the updating and development of media companies.

CENJOR offers practical training is several areas: television, radio, press, photojournalism, digital journalism, design and multimedia and journalistic companies' management. These activities are organized in three different levels: initial training, for people who want to enter the job; continuing training, for journalists who want to perfect their skills; and professional training, as a complement for graduates from journalism and communication sciences degrees.

To carry out its programmes, CENJOR has a non-permanent staff (instructors) of more than 100 professionals. They are academics, journalists and technicians from diverse areas, whose curricula and relevant experience ensure the demanded quality level of training.

Students that successfully conclude General Training (Formação Geral) and Continuing Training (Formação em Exercício) Programs receive diplomas; the ones that attend other programmes are given Participation Certificates.

CENJOR is a member of European Journalism Training Association – EJTA (Associação Europeia de Formação em Jornalismo – AEJF, and was part of its executive board between 1998 and 2000. Since 1988, CEJOR has contributed to journalism training (for journalists and other professionals working in the media) in Angola, Cape Verde, Guinea Bissau, Mozambique e S. Tomé e Princípe. According to cooperation protocols, the Centre receives trainees from PALOP (Portuguese Speaking African Countries) or sends trainers to those countries.

The second model for journalism training, as we defined it above, is the case of organizations that provide different initiatives, but do it sporadically. Here, we can group diverse institutions, including in-house training, a union or even an observatory.

The Press Observatory (Observatório da Imprensa) defines itself as an 'Advanced Journalism Studies Centre'. It is a private and non-profit institution, created in 1994 by a number of professionals working in the area of journalism, with the general goal of improving the quality of journalism in Portugal. Based in Lisbon, it has developed activities in journalism training, by organizing programmes, seminars, meetings and congresses, in different parts of the country, but mainly in Lisbon (the capital).

The Observatory has collaborated with Lusophone University (Lisbon) for the development of two postgraduation programmes (from January to July 2001): Judiciary Journalism and Economic Journalism; it has organized programmes on 'New Technologies and New Communication Languages' (Santarém) and 'Great Principles and Genres for the Written Press' (Lisboa); it has been promoting seminars on specialized fields of journalism, such as health (biomedical research, clinical innovation, pharmaceutical industry, media coverage of health), political journalism, territorial planning and EU policies. Press Observatory has also developed, in 2004–05, the programme 'Press and Regional Development at Vale do Tejo' and, in 2007, the project 'On-line Information and Communication and Regional Development'.

The Law Communication Institute (Instituto Jurídico da Comunicação), at Coimbra University (Law School), has been offering, for more than ten years, the Communication Law programme (Curso de Direito da Comunicação). This is a one-year postgraduation (two semesters), opened to journalists aiming at 'providing specialized training in juridical communication issues'. Students that successfully complete the programme are given a certificate. Applicants should have a Law degree, or another suitable degree (Journalism or Communication, for instance). Exceptionally, media and journalism professionals can be admitted, regardless of their academic achievements, as long as they regularly attended high school and their curriculum gives evidence of their skills. Classes are undertaken on Fridays (late afternoons) and Saturday mornings (i.e. out of work hours).

The Oporto Journalism School (Escola de Jornalismo do Porto) organizes training programmes for journalists, on subjects such as: 'Discourse Construction and Public

Speaking', 'Communication and Sports', 'Communication Services' and 'Documental Cinema: Image and Signification'.

As for the National Journalists' Union (Sindicato Nacional dos Jornalistas), it sporadically organizes, along with other institutions, specific training initiatives such as 'Justice and Judiciary Journalism' or a programme on 'Safety and Defense for Journalists'.

When it comes to in-house training, it is fair to say that some main Portuguese media companies develop training plans for their employees. But the case of RTP's Training Centre (Centro de Formação da Rádio e Televisão de Portugal) should be highlighted, because this is the only media company that has a specific department to deal with in-house training. This Centre was created in 2004, when Portuguese public radio and television were merged in one single broadcasting company. It inherited the rich and long going experience from both public operators' training centres, which gave a fundamental contribution to the training of professionals for radio and television, especially from the 1960s to the 1980s. This centre trains not only journalists, but also other professionals, such as producers, light and sound technicians or anchors. Training programmes are mostly practical, but supported by cooperative and critical methodologies. When it comes to the specific area of journalism, training schemes employed in recent years are based on the constitution of small teams, up to fifteen people, that work together for several days, on seven different areas: Voice Techniques, News, Portuguese Language, How to Communicate, How to Write, Set and Visualization.

Last, there is Luso-American Foundation for Development (Fundação Luso-Americana para o Desenvolvimento), that represents the third model that was considered: entities that provide grants to be applied in journalism education, but do not develop programmes themselves. This foundation establishes, on a regular basis, grants for on the job journalists, which imply going abroad, to the United States, to attend education and training programmes in prestigious American organizations.

Finally, the role of the Church, as an institution that provides journalism education and training, should also be mentioned. On one hand, there is the Portuguese Catholic University, with higher education programmes (all three cycles), in Lisbon, Oporto and Braga. On the other hand, as an owner of a media group, the Portuguese Catholic Church ends up also playing a role in providing in-house training for its employees.

Concluding Remarks

If there is, as Berger (2000) claims, an 'organic and intrinsic relationship between journalism and democracy', one might say, for sure, that, in Portugal, Journalism Education is the offspring of democracy. Journalism existed (and resisted) the dictatorship that lasted almost half of the twentieth century in Portugal – in some cases by going along with it, in other cases subjugated by it and, still, trying to resist it, many times in ways that could be considered creative and courageous. But Salazar's regime never allowed any education project is this area, despite some – not many – attempts that were made in this direction. Nevertheless, it would not be fair to state that before April's Revolution there was not journalism higher education in Portugal exclusively as an imposition from the dictatorship. Other factors may have influenced this political attitude, namely the renitence to this idea, that still existed among an important segment in the profession (Sobreira 2003; Sousa et al. 2007).

This observation allows us to highlight an issue mentioned at the start of this chapter: the fact that journalism higher education is still recent makes it very difficult to have enough critical reflection on this subject. The launching of postgraduate programs – master and Ph.D. – from the mid-1980s onwards – was an opportunity to develop research and to the growth, especially in the 1990s and in the first years of the twenty-first century, of a relevant editorial production, through the regular publication of scientific journals and several book series, by different editors. At the same time an association was created (SOPCOM), gathering most of Communication Sciences' faculty and researchers. This allowed the establishment of a permanent scientific structure concerned with journalism education and research, which is one of the sections that gathers most interest and participation in its congress. Also, Portuguese researchers have been increasingly participating in international associations (IAMCR, ECREA, ICA, AEJMC), including LUSOCOM – Communication Sciences' Lusophone Association (Associação Lusófona de Ciências da Comunicação), which gathers researchers from Portugal, Brazil, Galicia and Portuguese-speaking African countries.

The all-encompassing framework presented here brings up some critical observations, which should be further questioned by concerned actors and participants in the process, as well as to other countries and their experiences. Unfortunately this an area where research and production are still very scarce.

These are some issues worth highlighting for debate:

- **A favourable climate:** it is our understanding – from contacting education and training institutions and professionals – that the idea of the importance of academic education has been spreading and it has become, if not consensual, at least widely accepted. We may say that things have changed if we compare it to what was the feeling a few years ago (Pinto and Sousa 2003). As possible explanations, we would point out journalists' growing participation in journalism higher education, as teachers; the fact that many journalists have been attending advanced programmes and postgraduations; and the fact that newsrooms are increasingly being filled with newly-graduated journalists.
- **Theory vs. practice:** despite the fact that some still believe this is an unavoidable and unsolvable tension, our knowledge of the field leads us to believe that a curricular separation of theory and practice still exists. This situation compromises the critical reflexivity that should characterize each one of these dimensions. This issue is strictly related to the need for more interaction between academics and professionals, a subject that will be addressed next.

- **University/Polytechnic:** at a legislative level, projects and goals for each one of these higher education subsystems are clearly defined and, whether we like it or not, have their own logic. Truth is, once the Bologna Process reform was undertaken, when looking at curricula (1st cycle) it seems that differences between those two different types of teaching/ learning are blurring. This also represents a change in relation to what was the tendency some years ago (Pinto and Sousa 2003). The question is, then, pertinent: if differences are becoming irrelevant, should such a distinction be maintained, especially when it represents diverse working conditions, in terms of research, staff statute and funding?
- **Education, research and labour market:** despite efforts made during the last two decades, it is important to ensure that journalism teaching/learning is supported by research. It is also fundamental to continue to develop and strengthen bonds between academia and professionals. Internships at newsrooms represent an opportunity for recent graduates, as well as a chance to identify talents for future hiring. It should also be promoting a more regular and systematic exchange between teachers and researchers, on one hand, and professionals, editors and managers, on the other hand.
- **A programme certification system:** such as it exists, the process for creating new higher education programmes implies the acceptance and registry of a programme at the official organization (Government), as long as it gathers the formal conditions required by law. It would be important to have an independent and recognized organization in charge of programme certification, in order to evaluate a set of very important conditions, such as: real functioning conditions; quality of faculty and resources; and quality of teaching, according to the programme's specifics; and assurance in terms of evaluating if graduates' skills and capacities are suitable for being a journalist. Without this process of certification, it can always happen that 'a single course makes a programme'. This aspect is strongly related to the following one.
- **The (re)organization of the education network:** this is a debate undertaken by some and an issue that has been on the political agenda for some time. The main argument, for many, has to do with the unbalanced relationship between the growing number of programmes for journalism education and the also growing numbers of unemployed.[8] According to this point of view – based on an understanding of the way universities should look at the market when proposing their projects, which is also criticized – there is no need for so many programmes, even if they do not lack applicants, and the journalism education network should therefore be reduced, according to a set of quality criteria. The task of identifying and applying those criteria should fall to a certification system, such as the one previously mentioned. Some research has been made on the subject of unemployment and integration on the market among journalism graduates (Figueira and Granado 2004; Graça 2007; Marinho and Silva 2007; Marinho 2007a; Marinho 2008; Sousa 2007) and some of them show a tendency for growing unemployment. Nevertheless, this is a very sensitive issue that demands more data to be clearly understood, in order to take measures.
- **Coordination between institutions:** each schools', department's or programme's own investment to consolidate their journalism education projects could explain the lack of

interaction between programme managers and even between courses. The fact that each programme is relatively free to define its curricula and courses and teachers can define their own syllabi is positive, but, because it is done in a rather 'autistic' way it prevents people from learning with the experience of others and from defining common reference patterns. This is a field for work and discussion that should be pursued, taking advantage of international networks and funded programmes for common initiatives. At the national level we have already argued (Marinho 2006; Marinho 2007b) that it is crucial to promote a large debate on the subject of journalism education, with the contribution of all actors involved. Bologna Process could have been an opportunity to do it, but, as far as we are concerned it was a lost opportunity, reduced mainly to political and administrative debates.

If journalism is contextual and profoundly intertwined in each society's social and political fabric, the same goes for education. But the contextual dimension does not contradict values, models and relevant common aspects that come from experience. Digital technology, new actors of the journalistic field, new types of learning associated to digital and multimedia and old and, yet, always new ethical and deontological issues make it urgent to rethink journalism and, necessarily, journalism education. A greater citizens' involvement, at different levels, in the process of news production and even at the leadership of new programmes – even if, at this point, we do not have a clear knowledge about the consistency and continuity of some current phenomena – creates challenges for education and training organizations, forcing them to rethink their offer and to take on new responsibilities when capacitating new actors.

The Authors

Manuel Pinto, associate professor at Minho University – Portugal (Communication Sciences Department); director of the Communication and Society Research Centre (research interests: Journalism studies; Media literacy and citizenship).

Sandra Marinho, lecturer at Minho University – Portugal (Communication Sciences Department); researcher at the Communication and Society Research Centre; ongoing Ph.D. on Journalism Education.

Notes

1. The 4th International Press Conference gathered in Lisbon, in 1898, 343 journalists from eighteen countries (France alone was represented by 102) and from different political ideologies (Sousa et al. 2007).
2. The National Union of Journalists was founded in 1934, during Salazar's authoritarian regime, to represent journalists, namely at the Câmara Corporativa – a second Câmara, dedicated to represent business men and workers from different segments, but entirely submitted do political power.

Before this, a number of professional associations had existed, considering journalists whether 'writers' whether 'print workers', a relevant fact to the analysis of the constitution of journalism as a profession in Portugal (Valente 1998).

3. There is some information available at the Higher Education Access Site (General-Directorate for Higher Education), especially regarding available places, enrollments and applicants' characteristics. But most of these data concern only state universities and polytechnics (http: //www.dges.mctes. pt/DGES/pt. Accessed on 17 August 2008).

4. To classify a programme as a journalism programme we used as a criterion the fact that the programmes themselves officially consider 'journalist' as at least one of their graduate profiles. This was done by consulting their internet sites.

5. Our analysis is based on available places and not on enrolments, because we only have available data for enrolments on the public sector. Although enrolments are the best and most accurate indicator, we had to use available places, in order to compare both public and private sectors.

6. This task was attributed to CNAVES – National Council for the Evaluation of Higher Education (Conselho Nacional para a Avaliação do Ensino Superior), but recent reforms suspended its activities. Now, a new agency has been created, Accreditation and Evaluation Agency to Ensure Quality in Higher Education (Agência de Avaliação e Acreditação para a Garantia da Qualidade do Ensino Superior). It is still not functioning, but has already been regulated ("Despacho que regula o Sistema de Avaliação de Qualidade para o Ensino Superior,").

7. Public programmes are funded by the State's General Budget and private programmes, as far as we know, are not funded by the media industry (some of them are associated to private Foundations).

8. According to data provide by Employment and Professional Training Observatory (Observatório do Emprego e Formação Profissional), in April 2007 there were 722 unemployed journalists enrolled at Employment Centers in Portugal. 68% of them had a higher education degree.

References

Berger, Guy (2000), 'Brave New World? Democratic Journalism Enters the Global Twenty First Century', *Journalism Studies*, 1(1), pp. 81–99.

Correia, F. and Baptista, C. (2005), 'O ensino e a valorização profissional do Jornalismo em Portugal (1940/1974)', *Cultura*, 21, pp. 233–256.

Cunha, A. (1941), 'Jornalismo Nacional: das malogradas Associações de Imprensa à alvitrada Ordem dos Jornalistas Portugueses', *Boletim do Sindicato dos Jornalistas Portugueses*, 2, pp. 7–39.

Ferreira, V. (2005), 'Formação em Jornalismo, um tempo para aprender', *Jornalismo & Jornalistas*, 21, pp. 20–23.

Fidalgo, J. (2004), 'Jornalistas: um perfil socioprofissional em mudança', *Comunicação e Sociedade*, 5, pp. 63–74.

Figueira, J. and Granado, A. (2004), 'Quem são, onde estão e o que pensam os licenciados em Jornalismo por Coimbra', *III SOPCOM*, Covilhã, 22–23 April.

Graça, S. M. (2007), 'Os problemas-chave de ingresso no jornalismo em Portugal', *Congresso Internacional Premium – A Integração Profissional dos Licenciados em Jornalismo/Ciências da Comunicação*, Jorge Marinho e Salomé Pinto da Silva, Porto, pp. 111–131.

Marinho, S. (2008), 'O Percurso Profissional dos Licenciados em Jornalismo num Contexto de Mudança: o caso da Universidade do Minho', *Comunicação e Cidadania – Actas do 5º Congresso* da *Associação Portuguesa de Ciências da Comunicação*, Moisés de Lemos Martins e Manuel Pinto, Braga, Universidade do Minho, pp. 428–440.

Marinho, J. and Silva, S.P. (2007), 'Integração dos licenciados em Jornalismo/Ciências da Comunicação nos mass media do Grande Porto', *Congresso Internacional Premium – A Integração Profissional dos Licenciados em Jornalismo/Ciências da Comunicação*, Jorge Marinho e Salomé Pinto da Silva, Porto, pp. 149–179.

Marinho, S. (2007a), 'Integração profissional e formação em jornalismo e comunicação: o caso da Universidade do Minho', *Congresso Internacional Premium – A Integração Profissional dos Licenciados em Jornalismo/Ciências da Comunicação*, Jorge Marinho e Salomé Pinto da Silva, Porto, pp. 13–33.

Marinho, S. (2007b), 'A Formação em Jornalismo: sinais e problemas de um debate latente', Manuel Pinto e Sandra Marinho (ed.), *Os media em Portugal nos primeiros cinco anos do séc. XXI – Cronologia e olhares sectoriais*, Porto: Campo das Letras, pp. 129–142.

Marinho, S. (2006), 'Reflexão sobre a necessidade de novo um paradigma para o ensino do Jornalismo: o caso da Universidade de Columbia', *II Seminário Internacional Media, Jornalismo e Democracia – Jornalismo e Actos de Democracia*, Escola Superior de Comunicação Social – Instituto Politécnico de Lisboa, 13 November.

Mesquita, M. (1995), 'L'enseignement du journalisme au Portugal – le miracle de la multiplication des cours', *Sigma – Communication Sciences Meeting*, Siena, 22–23 September 1995.

Ministério da Ciência Tecnologia e Ensino Superior (2006), 'Despacho que regula o Sistema de Avaliação de Qualidade para o Ensino Superior', Despacho 484 (2.a série), *Diário da República*, pp. 331–339.

Pinto, M. (2004), 'O ensino e a formação na área do jornalismo em Portugal: crise de crescimento e notas programáticas', *Comunicação e Sociedade*, 5, pp. 49–62.

Pinto, M. and Sousa, H. (2003), 'Journalism Education at Universities and Journalism Schools in Portugal', In Romy Fröhlich and Christina Holtz-Bacha (eds), *Journalism Education in Europe and North America*, New Jersey: Hampton Press, pp. 169–186.

Sobreira, R.M. (2003), 'O ensino do jornalismo e a profissionalização dos jornalistas em Portugal (1933–1974)', *Media & Jornalismo*, 3, pp. 67–87.

Sousa, J.P. et al. (2007), 'Indicadores de produção bibliográfica portuguesa sobre jornalismo até à Revolução de 25 de Abril de 1974' (on-line: http: //teoriadojornalismo.ufp.pt/conteudos/indicadores.pdf. Accessed 20 September 2008.

Sousa, L.N. (2007), 'Processo(s) de transição ao trabalho: o caso dos diplomados em Comunicação da Escola Superior de Educação de Viseu', *Congresso Internacional Premium – A Integração Profissional dos Licenciados em Jornalismo/Ciências da Comunicação*, Jorge Marinho e Salomé Pinto da Silva, Porto, pp. 34–59.

Valente, J.C. (1998), *Elementos para a história do sindicalismo dos jornalistas portugueses – Parte I (1834–1934)*, Lisboa: Sindicato dos Jornalistas.

The Spanish Journalism Education Landscape

Ramón Salaverría and Carlos Barrera

Introduction

The School of Journalism of *El Debate*, in 1926, was the first one to offer training courses for journalists in Spain. Promoted by the catholic newspaper of that same name, it worked uninterruptedly over ten years until the outbreak of the Spanish civil war (1936–1939). Regarding its teaching methodology, it was directly influenced by the journalism schools of the United States, which were visited by the new School's promoters before its foundation with the purpose of gathering experiences to undertake their task. After the civil war, in 1941, the Escuela Oficial de Periodismo (Official School of Journalism) was created. This school was highly politicized, since it depended on the dictatorship government of Franco (1939–1975). It served to control access to the profession, because it granted the journalist accreditation card, either through its regular courses or through special intensive courses for the qualification of working journalists. With the passage of time, the political control on the Official School of Journalism slightly tempered regarding content as well as organization matters. In addition, the government allowed the creation of some private education establishments led by the Catholic Church.

The first university institution for the education of journalists was Instituto de Periodismo (Journalism Institute) of the University of Navarra, bound to the Opus Dei, a personal prelature of the Catholic Church. From 1958 to 1971 it was, as a matter of fact, a University School, although it was not legally established, because the Spanish legislation did not allow it. The students attended courses in Navarra, but their studies had to be confirmed by the Official School of Journalism, in order to get the journalist card by means of an examination that they had to take at the end of their studies. In 1960, another School of Journalism of the Church started to work in Madrid, with a similar validation system for its studies.

The studies of the Official School of Journalism started with a three-year programme, but then become four-years long with the reform of 1967, to which the two above mentioned private institutions adapted too. As of 1971, the government promoted the studies of Journalism, Broadcasting, and Advertising and Public Relations in university studies of a higher level. In accordance with those new regulations, during the academic year 1971–72 three new Schools of Communication started up in Madrid, Barcelona and Navarra, with study programmes lasting five years. The first two involved the disappearance of the Official School, which had offices in both cities, whereas in Navarra the transformation of the Journalism Institute was less complicated due to the university tradition that it had had since the beginning. Doctorate studies began in 1976, and in 1978 the first doctoral thesis in Communication was read at the University of Navarra by Ángel Faus.

In 1981, the School of Communication of the Basque Country started to work. The boom of the new Schools of Communication took place in the late-1980s and early-1990s: some of them were of catholic inspiration, such as Cardenal Herrera-CEU in Valencia and the Universidad Pontificia in Salamanca and others had a public character such as those of Seville, Santiago, Málaga, Vigo, etc. The number of universities with degrees in Communication – that is, Journalism, Broadcasting, Advertising and Public Relations – rose from 23 in 1999 to 40 in 2004, although not all them were offering the Journalism degree.

In many cases, the School that offers some of the three Communication degrees includes other knowledge disciplines (mainly Social Sciences and Humanities), and therefore offers degrees in different areas other than Communication. To be more precise, around 2004 there were only thirteen Schools which were specifically Schools of Communication, against the 27 that could be considered as 'mixed'. This is due to the young character of Communication Studies as well as to the fact that a good number of these new degrees have had their origin within other departments or university Schools, but do not have enough entity to make a specific School of Communication by themselves.

However, after five decades of university studies of communication in Spain, there is a case for saying that there is a well-grounded, if young, academic tradition. At the beginning it was difficult to find and train journalism professors, both in the pioneering experience of the Journalism Institute of Navarra of 1958, as well as since 1971 in the recently-created Schools of Communication in Madrid and Barcelona. Up until the implementation of doctorate studies at the end of the 1970s, the professors who constituted the initial faculty members came mainly from other disciplines such as Law, History, Philosophy, Sociology, Philology, etc. In addition, there were many cases of journalists that left their professional field in favour of education – starting doctorate studies in Communication or other areas where it was possible to enrol. Since the 1980s, and more especially in the 1990s, the trend in the model of recruitment of professors has changed and nowadays the Schools of Communication are mainly fed by people trained in Communication degrees.

From a numerical point of view, the increase of the teaching staff has been significant: the initial 139 professors of the academic year of 1972–73 rose to 1,205 during the academic year of 1993–94. Therefore, in twenty years, its number was multiplied by ten, increasing in the same way as the number of students. The problems arose in other scopes – logically due to the youth of the studies, such as subjects that were roughly consolidated in terms of contents – such as a lack of manuals and the lack of economic resources to cover the necessary teaching staff and to build the adequate facilities.

The flexibility of the hiring formulas for teaching staff and the particular specificity of Communication Studies, with remarkably practical aspects, allow the collaboration of professionals of mass media, advertising agencies and public relations firms as part-time associated professors. This formula is even more used in master's degrees, where specialization and practical aspects are more emphasized than in graduate studies.

The university Schools of Communication, therefore, present a double profile: at the same time as they are the usual place where the future professionals are prepared, they are also the academic environment where research in communication is carried out, within the context of the departments. Together with the increase of the number of students in Schools of Communication, there has been a rise in the scientific production both at a national and international level. Thus, Spanish professors have reached, for instance, the presidency of important associations of research in communication such as Manuel Parés i Maicas and the IAMCR (International Association for Media and Communication Research) between 1996 and 2000, and Esteban López-Escobar at the WAPOR (World Association for Public Opinion Research) between 2005 and 2006.

On the other hand, there are diverse national associations of professors and researchers in Communication. The main one, with several hundred members, is indeed the most recent one: Asociación Española de Investigación de la Comunicación, AE–IC, (Spanish Association of Research in Communication), founded in February 2008 with the aim to foster research in communication, to promote cooperation between researchers and to create research networks of investigators, and to establish a cooperation policy with other international research associations. The national scene of academic associations on Communication is completed with the Asociación de Historiadores de la Comunicación, AHC, (Association of Communication Historians), created in 1992, and Asociación Internacional de Jóvenes Investigadores en Comunicación, AIJIC, (International Association of Young Researchers in Communication), founded in 1997. In addition there is an academic association exclusively focused on journalism: Sociedad Española de Periodística, SEP, (Spanish Journalism Society), founded in 1989. All of them organize annual or biennial meetings, and publish their own proceedings.

It is also worth mentioning the educational work that the unions of journalists and professional associations of the press carry out, mainly organizing congresses, seminars and workshops for the continuous education of their members. Besides, many of those organizations also promote research around the journalistic profession, through the publication of magazines and annual reports, with the collaboration of both professional journalists and university professors. Nevertheless, the level of associationism of Spanish journalists remains quite low. In 2008, there were seven unions of journalists in Spain which gathered a little more than 2000 professionals. In addition, there were around 50 press associations in a number of cities throughout the country, all of them integrated in the Federación de Asociaciones de la Prensa de España (Federation of Press Associations of Spain; FAPE).

Back to the academic field, throughout these fifty years of university journalism and communications education, the contents have little-by-little become richer thanks to the increasing maturity and stability of the Schools, especially of those with greater tradition. Although there have been and there still are variants as far as the educational approaches of each institution are concerned, university education in journalism in Spain has generally tried to keep a balance between subjects on (1) the fundamentals of social sciences and humanities, (2) those referring to communication studies from diverse viewpoints (law, ethics, history, sociology, public opinion, business, etc.), and (3) the practical courses aimed at training the students in the basic skills and know-how of each profession or specialization. The second and third groups are the most characteristic of the School, where the specific teaching staff is necessary to develop an education of quality based on the particular theoretical foundations that distinguish communication in general and, more particularly, journalism from other scientific disciplines.

In the beginning, the need to differentiate communication studies from surrounding areas led to the shaping of a new field with a strong theoretical focus. Moreover, the practical subjects were limited due to the lack of technological facilities and by the difficulty of providing personal attention to all students. Over the years, however, these defects have been progressively corrected. Nowadays there is a fairer balance between cultural background, communication theory and professional training in schools, and students enjoy a wider range of facilities.

Since its establishment as a university School in 1971, Communication Studies were divided into three fields, as referred to above. These fields were initially called 'sections' and later, with the 1991 reform, became 'degrees': Journalism, Broadcasting, and Advertising and Public Relations. 'Journalism' mostly included the studies aimed at training professionals for the press; 'Broadcasting' embraced those aspiring to prepare practitioners for radio, television and cinema; whereas 'Advertising and Public Relations' provided the necessary knowledge to develop a career in all these fields, including the communication departments of companies and all kind of organizations. In recent years a new trend has emerged to also group under the Journalism degree those studies that give qualification to inform, regardless of the platform (press, radio, television, Internet), leaving to Broadcasting the responsibility for the education of professionals focused on fiction genres: cinema, television and other audio-visual new formats.

There is no unanimity as far as the itineraries of education in each one of the three degrees is concerned. Some universities opt for offering one or two years common to the three degrees, and a second period where each degree has its own subjects. Other teaching models prefer to distribute the students according to their degrees from the very beginning. Therefore, the primary specialization level is determined by the three official degrees that can be offered. A subsequent level of specialization is optional to the Schools, should they want to offer their own specific degrees or diplomas derived from the selection of certain subjects on the part of the student all along the four, or five, years of the degree. The recent approval of the master's as official postgraduate studies has turned them into the most suitable way to offer specializations that enable for specific professional tasks in communication.

The legal reform of the curricula in 1991 was based on: (1) the reduction from five to four years in the majority of the undergraduate studies, (2) the increasing autonomy of the Schools to organize their own curricula, and (3) a wider disposal of optional subjects and the number of credits awarded for extracurricular activities and for the accomplishment of professional internships during the summer. At the same time, the beginning of exchange programmes with European Union countries through the Erasmus and Socrates programmes promoted the geographic mobility of students and professors, thanks to the numerous agreements signed between the Spanish Schools and those of other countries.

While awaiting the indepth reform that will bring about the new European Space for Higher Education in 2010, the Spanish university system structures its knowledge and education around five main sections: Humanities, Social Sciences and Law, Experimental Sciences, Technical Sciences and Health Sciences. Journalism studies are part of the 31 degrees assigned to the category of the Social Sciences and Law, the most popular branch of all, which attracted 46% of university students during the academic year 2004/2005. In this section, which is integrated by other degrees such as Law, Sociology or Political Sciences, Journalism Studies have reached, in recent years, a high level of popularity among students, along with other related degrees such as Broadcasting and Advertising and Public Relations.

According to the report *La Universidad española en cifras/ The Spanish University in numbers* (2006), published by the Conference of Presidents of the Spanish Universities with data from the academic year 2004/2005, Spain had a total of 1,191,201 university students, out of which 17,232 were enrolled in Journalism degree (1.45% of all Spanish students). The number of students registered in any of the three degrees in Communication, including that of Journalism, was 43,827 (3.68% of the total).

Both the absolute figures as well as the relative percentages of Journalism students have increased in recent years. During the academic year 2000–01, 15,980 students registered in some of the courses offered by the Journalism degree. Five years later, during the academic year 2005–2006, the number amounted to 17,122. This growth is especially significant if we consider that, between 2002–07, the population of under-30s in Spain underwent a fall of 5.12%, resulting in a general decrease of the registration in university studies.

One of the factors that explain this high demand of Journalism studies has much to do, undoubtedly, with the increasing feminisation of the University in Spain. Already during the academic year 1984–85 there were more women than men registered in the Schools of Journalism. In recent years the percentage of female students has steadily grown, especially in certain areas such as Social Sciences and Law, but at a lesser extent in the Technical and Experimental degrees. As a consequence, according to the *Informe Anual de la Profesión periodística/ Annual Report of the Journalistic Profession*, during the academic year 2006–07 nearly 70% of the graduates in Journalism were women. Another obvious result is the fact that 60% of the new affiliations to professional organizations of journalists correspond to women as well. However, such a high proportion of college students is not parallel to the number of women journalists in active-duty, since this profession still remains mostly masculine in Spain; 57% of journalists in active-duty are men.

In 2008, a total of 33 Spanish universities were offering the degree in Journalism, out of which 45% were public and 55% private. Nevertheless, although there were more private than public centres, the latter were those who had a higher number of students: during the academic year 2003–04 the students registered in the first year of Journalism in public universities were 3,597, whereas those registered in private universities came to 1,017. In any case, during the last decade there has been a noticeable transfer of students from public towards private universities.

As for the geographic distribution of the graduates in Journalism, Spain presents a remarkable centralism: a little more than a third (more precisely, 36.5% during 2004) belongs to one of the universities in Madrid. The rest of the Journalism graduates studied at public or private universities from other regions of the country, notably from Catalonia with 8.4% of Journalism students. Out of the seventeen autonomous communities into which Spain is divided, only four of them – Asturias, Cantabria, La Rioja and Extremadura – lack a University with Journalism Studies.

By 2008, all the courses in Journalism required compulsory attendance. It is not possible to graduate through online courses. Some universities, especially in Catalonia, offered only the two last courses of the Journalism degree, with an open access for students from other degrees. The average registration fee for the first year of Journalism was €611 in public universities and €5,668 in private centres.

Along with the progression of Journalism studies, over the last decade there has been a proliferation of postgraduate courses, mostly with a more professional than academic nature.

Regarding academic postgraduate degrees, several universities have doctorate programmes in Journalism or, more often, Communication. Among them, only the University of Navarra and Universidad Complutense have, since the academic year 2007–2008, their own Doctorate programme acknowledged with the Quality Accreditation of the Ministry of Education and Science. This Quality Accreditation, among other privileges, allows them to receive public aid for the mobility of students and professors.

The offer of professional postgraduate courses is now even wider. According to the *Informe Anual de la Profesión Periodística/ Annual Report of Journalism Profession* 2007, there were 90 master's programmes in Spain that year. Since they usually have between fifteen and twenty five students, the total number of students of professional postgraduate courses in journalism can be estimated at between 1,500 and 2,000.

As a general rule, they are one-year courses and are taken by young university graduates of any major. In addition, they usually offer either a kind of thematic specialization –politics, economy, sports, fashion, etc. – or specialization by media – press, radio, television, agencies or Internet. Their cost is quite varied and goes somewhere between €1,500 and €12,000, depending on the specialty, the centre and the modality (personal attendance or online courses).

Many of these programmes are nowadays organized by media companies. The first one of those master's degrees started up in 1986 thanks to the initiative of the newspaper of largest circulation, *El País*, under the name of Escuela de Periodismo. Following the trail of this postgraduate programme many other master's have arisen around the main Spanish newspapers, such as *ABC*, *El Correo*, *La Voz de Galicia* and *El Mundo*; the radio networks, such as Radio Nacional de España and COPE; and, even, the news agencies (Agencia EFE).

In order to give more prestige to their studies, these media have looked for university partnerships: Universidad Autónoma de Madrid in the case of *El País*, Universidad Complutense with *ABC*, the University of the Basque Country with *El Correo*, the University San Pablo-CEU with COPE, etc. Those programmes always include an internship period in media pertaining the group that organizes the master's. This way, the media companies have a group of young journalists ready to be hired by their own publications each and every year, although the hiring rates of these students are far from being high.

Aside from these master's offered by journalistic companies, the professional postgraduate programmes might be classified in three categories: (1) master's exclusively offered by universities, independently of media companies of any kind, (2) professional programmes offered by schools and non-university educational institutions, and (3) journalistic training programmes organized by foundations. Just like the doctorate programmes, the professional master's that meet certain academic requirements may also, since 2006, obtain the recognition as an Official Master by the Ministry of Education and Science and, in fact, several programmes have already received this accreditation. The adaptation of all the university careers to the new European Space for Higher Education is causing an academic reinforcement of the professional master's, because those students who aspire to enrol in a doctorate programme must have previously studied an Official Master's programme.

The processes of quality accreditation have been consolidated in the Spanish university system in recent years. In 2002, the Agencia Nacional de Evaluación de la Calidad y Acreditación, ANECA, (National Agency for Quality Evaluation and Accreditation) was set up. This public Agency supervises the quality of Spanish universities, by means of processes of certification and accreditation oriented to promote their integration in the European Space for Higher Education. These filters of quality are applied to university schools and departments, to syllabi and even to professors.

Graduate and postgraduate studies in Journalism offer professional versatility that qualify those who take the courses to carry out very diverse job positions, including those not related to journalism. Nevertheless, in spite of that versatility, the huge number of graduates in journalism that leave university every year make it difficult to achieve full employment in the labour market. Thus, according to the registry of the Instituto Nacional de Empleo, INEM, (National Employment Institute), 3,473 Journalism graduates were unemployed in Spain at the end of 2006. This number might certainly seem quite high, however it is necessary to consider that, according to the *Informe Anual de la Profesión Periodística/ Annual Report of Journalism Profession* 2007, the total number of Journalism graduates between 1976 – the year in which the first promotion accessed the labour market – and 2007 is near 64,000. Out of that total figure of graduates, around 26,000 worked professionally as journalists in 2008, that is to say, hardly 41%. Another statistic that helps to put this number into context comes from *Informe del Mercado de Trabajo de los Jóvenes (Young Labour Market Report) 2008*, according to which, Journalism is not amongst the twenty five graduate programmes that generate the highest employment rates for young people.

Concluding Remarks

In spite of the difficulties to access the labour market, the truth is that, in barely four decades, Journalism university studies have consolidated as the main way to access the profession. Although after the end of Franco's dictatorship in 1975, the journalist accreditation card was not mandatory and access to profession remains free in theory, media companies usually choose, in a high percentage, journalists trained at the Faculties to build their teams. This is certainly a sign of the recognition that professionals grant to the education developed by the Schools.

The brief history of these studies shows, nevertheless, how there has not been a unique model equally shared neither throughout time nor by all the universities. The curriculum reforms have been relatively numerous due to several reasons: the non-existence of a previously solid tradition in this field, the development of the academic and scientific structure for journalism and communication, the changes in the professional habits that have led to new demands in the labour market, and the challenges that new media and technologies have brought to our field.

The educational model in journalism has been changing, according to the different schools, between giving priority to common and mandatory subjects in order to provide a solid and homogenous background, or rather focusing on the different thematic or media specializations. Supporters of the first model emphasise the need for a solid scientific knowledge of communication, its processes and its effects on the part of journalists, whereas those that support the second model, consider that Schools should connect the students as much as possible to the real world that they will live in after their passage through the classrooms. Evidently, between these two poles there are intermediate visions that try to make both models compatible or to reach a balance of priorities. The high margin of autonomy that Schools enjoy regarding the design of their study programmes makes possible this disparity of models. However, all the new programmes, adapted to the demands of Bologna, need to be submitted to the approval of ANECA, who may put a stop to the excessively theoretical or practical-professional approaches.

As a result of these evaluations, ANECA published a report with some recommendations to the Schools of Journalism in 2006. Along with some organizational weaknesses, the report emphasised four main challenges for university curricula:

1. Lack of coordination among the departments involved in the teaching of the graduate subjects.
2. Insufficient manpower to face the new educational needs raised by the European convergence.
3. Scarce supervision of the internships that students carry on in the companies.
4. Disregard for the results of graduates, in order to improve and review the curricula.

In short, on the one hand, this report raises the concern about internal logistic problems at the universities, reminding the need to adopt a training model that suitably combines theoretical knowledge and professional skills. On the other hand, it also points out the necessity of tuning up the educational offer of the Faculties with the professional demands of the journalistic companies. In fact, the Spanish media companies have been, for years, demanding from the Faculties of Journalism a training programme that meets the professional needs of the market. However, it should also be remembered that those same companies often give little help to the necessary professional training on the part of the students and recent graduates. Not in vain, many of those companies do not consider their interns as students in a training process, but rather as totally trained journalists who, temporarily, take the place of journalists on their staff in exchange for harder labour conditions and a much lower salary.

While these problems are solved, a new trend that has recently started and that will probably continue is the specialized education provided by university master's programmes. The initiatives from the professional or associative spheres have focused indeed in programmes of specialization through master's – often in collaboration with universities and especially aimed at young graduates – and courses or seminars for practitioners. However, the amount of economic resources that the Spanish journalism companies devote to the continuous education of their journalists remains quite low.

In summary, there is a growing trend towards the rapprochement between the academic and the professional world, either through the presence of professionals as associated professors or guests in activities of the Schools of Communication, or by means of the close relationships that journalism professors try to maintain with practitioners and their companies. Time will tell if this process ends with a robust educational system for young journalists which, at the same time, meets the changing demands of the professional world.

The Authors

Ramón Salaverría is director of Journalism Projects Department at the School of Communication, University of Navarra (Pamplona, Spain), where he is senior lecturer of Journalism.

Carlos Barrera is lecturer of Journalism and director of the Master degree in Political and Corporate Communication at the School of Communication, University of Navarra (Pamplona, Spain).

References

ANECA (2006), *Libro Blanco. Títulos de Grado en Comunicación*, Madrid: Agencia Nacional de Evaluación de la Calidad y Acreditación (ANECA).

Barrera, C. and Vaz, A. (2003), 'The Spanish Case: A Recent Academic Tradition', In R. Fröhlich, and C. Holtz-Bacha (eds.), *Journalism Education in Europe and North America*, Cresskill, NJ: Hampton Press, pp. 21–48.

Barrera, C. (2009), *Historia de la Facultad de Comunicación de la Universidad de Navarra. Medio siglo de enseñanza e investigación (1958–2008)*, Pamplona: EUNSA.

Canel, M.J.; Rodríguez Andrés, R. and Sánchez Aranda, J.J. (2000), *Periodistas al descubierto. Retrato de los profesionales de la información*, Madrid: Centro de Investigaciones Sociológicas.

Farias Batlle, P. (dir.) (2008), *Informe Anual de la Profesión Periodística, 2007*, Madrid: Asociación de la Prensa de Madrid.

Hernández Armenteros, J. (dir.) (2006), *La Universidad española en cifras*, Madrid: Conferencia de Rectores de las Universidades Españolas (CRUE).

INEM (2008), *Informe del Mercado de Trabajo de los Jóvenes 2008*, Madrid: Instituto Nacional de Empleo (INEM).

Martínez Nicolás, M.A. (2006), 'Masa (en situación) crítica. La investigación sobre el periodismo en España: comunidad científica e intereses de conocimiento', *Anàlisi: Quaderns de comunicació i cultura*, 33, pp. 135–170.

Murciano, M. (2005), 'La enseñanza del periodismo, nuevos desafíos internos y externos', *Cuadernos de Periodistas*, December, pp. 89–100.

Salaverría, R. (2007), 'Spanish Media Landscape', In G. Terzis (ed.), *European Media Governance*, Bristol: Intellect Books Ltd, pp. 277–288.

Tejedor, S. (2007), *La enseñanza del ciberperiodismo*, Seville: Comunicación Social Ediciones y Publicaciones.

Vigil y Vázquez, M. (1987), *El periodismo enseñado*, Barcelona: Mitre.

The Turkish Journalism Education Landscape

L. Doğan Tılıç

Introduction

The first press law of republican Turkey (made in 1931) established certain conditions regarding the education of journalists. According to the law at the time, journalists had to have secondary school or high school degrees. This law led to discussions about opening a journalism school. However, when the mentioned educational prerequisites for journalism were lifted in 1933, the first attempts of founding a journalism school in Istanbul died along with it (Alemdar 1981: 2–3).

The first initiative for journalism education in Turkey goes back to 1947. Sedat Simavi, who was then the chairman of the Journalists Society and who a year later founded the country's leading daily *The Hurriyet*, wrote a letter to Istanbul University and demanded the establishment of an institute for providing journalism education. The demand was welcomed and the Senate of the University decided on the establishment of an Institute of Journalism in the Faculty of Economy on 24 November 1949. The two-year Institute began its lectures with 479 students in 1950. The interest was high since many journalists who were lacking a university degree saw it as an opportunity to get a university diploma. However, this first attempt was not a success due to the lack of qualified lecturers and most students left the programme after a while. The first lecturers were senior journalists of the time and the lack of journalism professors turned the Institute into a school where general social and cultural courses became dominant. Later, the Institute was transformed into the Istanbul Journalism and Communications School, which then became a prestigious school of journalism (Topuz 2003: 375–6).

In fact in 1966, before the establishment of the Institute, the Istanbul Private Journalism School had started giving journalism education as the first school in this field. The length of the education was three years (after three years secondary school graduation) and one year (after a six-year [three plus three] stint at high school). Courses such as Turkish Language and Literature, Sociology, Psychology, Philosophy, Logic, History, Geography, Commercial Mathematics, Algebra, Statistics, Finance, Economy, Foreign Language, National Defense, Composition Writing, Stenography, Journalism and its Techniques, Newspaper Administration, Seminars on Journalism, Turkish Press Law, Turkish and World Press History, Press Techniques and Photography were taught in the School. The School, which was opened in 1948 and closed in 1963, was the very first journalism school of the country (Altun 1995: 105–6).

The curriculum of this first school was a combination of technical and practical knowledge of journalism and of general science courses. In general, this tendency, which in the following years took the form of theoretical and practical courses, continued in Turkish journalism schools even until today.

The establishment of the Journalism and Communications Higher School in Ankara was also an initiative of journalists, who in June 1962 applied to the UN Office in the Turkish capital for assistance. Turkish communications expert and journalist Dr. Hıfzı Topuz, who was then working as the Chief of the Free Circulation of Information Section in the UNESCO centre in Paris, was sent to Ankara to study this project. The rector of Ankara University accepted the suggestion and proposed the foundation of a department within the Faculty of Political Sciences. On 26 June 1962, the University approved the foundation of the department. UNESCO supported the department with equipment, experts and scholarships and sent Professor Roger Clausse of the Social Communications Department of the University of Brussels to Ankara to prepare the programme of the new department, where journalism education began in the academic year of 1965–66. The French journalist from the state broadcasting corporation ORTF Georges Pitoleff lectured in Ankara and four young students, who were sent abroad with UNESCO scholarships, later served as leading academics in the field (Topuz: 376).

The Journalism and Communications Higher School in Ankara became a leading model for the public journalism schools which were later opened in other cities.

In the second half of the 1960s, a private journalism schools period began in Turkey with the opening of three schools; in Istanbul (1966), Ankara (1967) and Izmir (1968). They had two forms of education as either daytime or evening classes; both lasting for three years. As a consequence of the general reaction to all private schools, which were accused of 'diploma trading', those journalism schools, along with the others, were also connected to public universities in 1971 (Altun: 110–1). Private journalism schools did not play a significant role in the Turkish journalism education until private foundation universities began to be opened in the 1990s.

Besides the Journalism and Communications Higher School of Ankara University, the Communications Higher School of Anadolu University in the central Anatolian city Eskisehir has a special place in the journalism education of the country. The foundation of the school began in the early 1970s along with the project of setting up a television station of the university in the town. With the technical support of Germany, an educational television channel had been established in 1972 and was later transformed into the Higher School for Cinema and Television in 1975. It was then changed into the Faculty of Education with Television in 1979 (Altun: 111–2). Since its foundation, Anadolu University has played a major role especially in giving technical/practical education for TV journalists.

The 12 September 1980 military coup also had a great impact on the universities of the country. A Higher Education Council was founded and all universities were centralized under it. The Journalism and Communications Higher Schools were all connected to the presidencies of the universities and in 1992 those schools were all transformed into Communications Faculties (Altun: 112–3). In the 1992–93 academic year, the Communications Faculties had a total of 5955 students and the number of those who received graduate-level diplomas in journalism had reached 792 (Topuz: 792).

Communications Faculties today

The number of students studying in four-year programmes of Turkish Communications Faculties has exceeded 8000 in the year 2008. Even though official data is not available 60 per cent of their students are estimated to be male and 40 per cent female (Geray 2008).

Communications Faculties usually had departments such as Journalism, Radio and Television and Public Relations and Advertizement. This classical division within the Communications Faculties continued mostly as it is until today. In recent years some faculties opened departments such as Visual Communications Design, Information and Documents Administration, Visual Arts and Communication Design, Photography and Video, Journalism and Internet Journalism.

There were five university-level journalism schools, all public, in 1982. The boom in the 1990s raised the number of Communications Faculties to twenty six today, excluding the five Communications Faculties giving education abroad (Northern Cyprus and Kyrgyzstan where many students from Turkey are studying registered under the Turkish Higher Education Board) and the Middle East Technical University in Ankara which does not have a faculty but a graduate level 'Media and Cultural Studies Programme' within the Social Sciences Institute. The Joint Platform of Communication Faculties, which draws together the faculties in the country for joint academic activities and to exchange their experiences, has 31 members including the universities in northern Cyprus and Kyrgyzstan. This number may soon reach 40. The present Turkish government has a policy of opening universities in all Turkish provinces and the decision to open eighteen new universities in various Anatolian towns was passed by Parliament early in 2008. Several of those universities will definitely have Communications Faculties.

It should also be mentioned that the communication education given in Turkey is not restricted to the twenty six Communications Faculties. An increasing number of Fine Arts Faculties include units of communication education and even Faculties of Business Administration (e.g. Atılım University in Ankara) and Faculties of Arts and Sciences (e.g. Dogus University in Istanbul) have departments related to communication education (A.U. ILEF 2007: 36).

The twenty six Communication Faculties of the country, all of which are accredited by the Higher Education Council as is required, can be categorized under three titles. Such a categorization will enable us to see which of the faculties belong to state or private universities and where they are located: (1) Faculties of the Public Universities in three major cities (Istanbul, Ankara and Izmir); (2) Faculties of the Public Universities in Anatolian cities; (3) Faculties of the Private/Foundation Universities (Yılmaz 2008: 12).

The table below lists the Communications Faculties giving journalism education and their location. It can be said that Anatolian universities have less access to foreign language and literature and follow a more traditional curriculum in their education, whereas private/ foundation universities, some of which use English or French as their language of instruction,

Table 1: Turkish Universities with Communication Faculties.

Istanbul – Ankara – Izmir	Anatolian Cities	Private-Foundations
Istanbul University	Ataturk University (Erzurum)	Bahçeşehir Uni. (Ist.)
Marmara University (Ist.)	Erciyes University (Kayseri)	Bilgi Uni. (Ist)
Galatasaray University (Ist.)	Fırat University (Elazığ)	Istanbul Commerce Uni.
Ankara University	Karadeniz Teknik Uni. (Trabzon)	Maltepe Uni. (Ist)
Hacettepe University (Ank.)*	Mersin University (Mersin)	Yeditepe Uni. (Ist)
Gazi University (Ank.)	Selçuk University (Konya)	Izmir Economy Uni.
Aegean Uni. (Izmir)	Mediterranean Uni. (Antalya)	Yaşar Uni. (Izmir)
	Anadolu Uni. (Eskişehir)	Kadir Has Uni. (Bolu)
	Kocaeli University (Izmit)	Başkent Uni. (Ankara)
	Cumhuriyet Uni. (Sivas)	

* has only graduate students

and significant universities of the three major cities more closely follow the developments in western universities and in the field.

As seen from Table 1, journalism education is mainly given by state universities. The private/foundation universities, which are relatively new, still require some time to compete with state universities.

Most of the faculty instructors are the academics who are holding degrees in their respective fields. Although there are professional journalists teaching in various faculties, it cannot be said that the Turkish communication education has a tradition of teaching by professional journalists. Professional journalists usually teach only courses such as 'News writing and reporting' and 'Media ethics'.

Deans of the Communication Faculties often stress the need for having senior journalists to teach more courses and admit that the journalism education in Turkey very much lacks in incorporating the experiences of the sector. However, they also stress as a problem that senior journalists have very weak ties to academic disciplines and the faculties have almost no connection to the sector (A.U. ILEF 2007: 26). Some senior journalists, increasingly in the recent years – probably also due to job cuts in the sector – have shown an interest in coming to the academy for MA or Ph.D. degrees. In the long run, this turn of events may fill the gap.

Communication Faculties become a part of the Bologna process once their universities join it. Most Turkish universities mentioned in the above table, which happen to be all of the significant universities of the country, are a part of the Bologna process, the Erasmus programme and European Credit Transfer System (ECTS). However, the formation of contacts and the accreditation with Erasmus universities is not as easy for Communications Faculties as it is for example for Engineering or Medicine Faculties. Some faculties have overcome those problems and the Communications Faculty of the Ankara University has agreements with two faculties; one in Poland and one in the Netherlands. It has also sent five of its students to foreign institutions for internships within the frame of the Erasmus programme in 2008 (Geray 2008).

In Turkey, journalism education is offered almost only in state and private/foundation universities. There are not many alternatives to them. The private Erol Simavi Communication and Education Center could be mentioned as an exception. The Center, which no longer exists, was established in 1990 and belonged to The Hurriyet Foundation. It used to accept students, with an examination, from the graduates of Communication Faculties and other social science departments. It also used to give scholarships to the students, who were lectured by professors of various universities, senior journalists and by statespersons, politicians and leading business people who contributed to the programme with conferences. Although it did not give job guarantees to its graduates, several successful graduates of the Center were later employed in the sector. Simavi sold *The Hurriyet* to Aydin Dogan in 1994 who then closed down the centre. Dogan later established The Communications High School within the frame of the Ministry of Education.

The UM: AG, Ugur Mumcu Investigative Journalism Foundation, was founded in memory of the prominent journalist Ugur Mumcu who was assassinated on 24 January 1993, by a car bomb. Since 1996, UM: AG gives 2.5-month long journalism seminars to interested persons, mostly graduates of Communications Faculties. From the year it was founded until the end of 2007, a total number of 1800 people had participated in the seminars. However, those seminars cannot be considered as journalism education compared with the education given in faculties.

Since 1995, Academy Istanbul, a private foundation school, has had a two-year programme running in journalism, radio and TV and advertising.

The last thing to be mentioned within this perspective can be the short term trainings given to journalists, especially to local journalists, by some NGOs and journalist organizations. In this context the long-running cooperation of the Turkish Journalists Society (TGC) and Konrad Adenauer Foundation is worth mentioning.

An ongoing debate on the curriculum: theory or practice

Professor Oya Tokgöz (2006) underlines that The Journalism Institute of Istanbul University (the first) mostly aimed at educating 'professionals' contrary to the Journalism and Communication Higher School of Ankara University which had a greater emphasis on 'social sciences'. This is indeed a reference to the first split in the theory and practice of Turkish journalism education.

Turkish Communications Faculties, all of which have four-years of education, seek to combine both theory and practice. However, the weight of theory or practice changes from one faculty to the other. While the students of the Communications Faculty of the Anadolu University become more familiar with practice, especially in radio and TV journalism;

students of the Communications Faculty of Ankara University have more theory courses than practical ones during their education.

As mentioned before, Communications Faculties traditionally have the departments of Journalism, Radio–Television, and Public Relations and Advertisement. Recently, Communications Design, Cinema, Video and Photography, Information and Document Management were added to those departments either separately or by joining one of the traditional departments.

During the first year, courses such as Turkish language, Turkish history and Principles of Kemalism[1] are given in most of the faculties. Then courses from social science disciplines ranging from sociology, psychology, economy, cultural anthropology, political sciences, international relations, philosophy, and law to contemporary literature are taught. In addition to these, incredibly practical courses such as newspaper design, TV programming, news writing and reporting, web design, documentary cinema, journal publication, Internet journalism, radio journalism, photojournalism, using Mac programmes, etc. are also included in the curriculum of faculties.

Radio, TV, newspaper, internet journalism, PR and advertising are the major fields concerning specialization. Specialization in science and technology, environment, war and conflict reporting, sports journalism, etc. depends only on the interest of students and can be developed by taking elective courses from other faculties.

It can be held that there is pressure both from the students and from the sector for increasing the weight of practical courses in the curriculum. There is also a resistance to those pressures from the faculty who tend to consider communication as an interdisciplinary research field.

The technical language spectrum of the Communications Faculties cannot be reduced to how the newspaper pages will be designed or how the camera will be used. Cleary, these two technical uses necessitate knowledge, writing skill and an understanding about what you want to see from the camera. (Özbek 1993)

Mutlu (1998) points out the tense relationship between the media industry and the qualifications of the graduates of the Communications Faculties and underlines that this tension is due to giving priority to theoretical problematic questions in the foundation of Communications Faculties despite being found as a result of practical needs and demands. He proposes a 'third way that combines the theory and practice' but also stresses that although the proposal sounds good, it is the most difficult thing to achieve.

In an interview for this article, Professor Haluk Geray, the Dean of the Communications Faculty of Ankara University, declared that there was no data about the percentage of the courses which were theoretical/social or practical in general. On the basis of his observations he estimated that on average 70% of the courses given in Turkish Communications Faculties were theoretical/social and 30% were practical. He added:

However, for my own faculty, I can say that 60% is theoretical/social and 40% is practical. Indeed, students also have a chance for practice out of their courses. Especially in the fields of advertising, short film and documentary, radio, photography, journalism (there is the school newspaper) they can practice outside the courses and the highly motivated students can easily increase the ratio of practice to 50%.

Internships are of course another chance for journalism students to practice. However, they do not have a formal graded 'course' status in any of the Communications Faculties. Students are motivated to undertake internships and some try really hard, both to learn more about the profession and to have some access to their future working institutions. Internships are on a voluntary basis for students during their summer holidays. Most graduates of Communications Faculties criticize the fact that they have graduated with a lack of information about the practical dimension of the profession because internships were not obligatory in their schools.

The relationship between the media industry and the faculty

The relationship between the media industry and the faculty begins first of all with the voluntary internship process of students. Students suffer a lot as a result of this first contact with their profession due to difficulties of finding places ready to accept them as interns. Media institutions and the professionals already holding a job in a TV channel, radio station or newspaper office often consider the interns as an encumbrance and as troublemakers. Interns are kept away from the direct news production and mostly are used to do the footwork.

Representatives of the media industry often complain about the education given in the Communications faculties. Graduates and interns are often blamed for being incapable of doing the ordinary professional work and for having worldviews not fit for the market. Ertugrul Ozkok, editor-in-chief of the mainstream daily *The Hurriyet*, has once expressed his feelings about the faculties saying 'Communications faculties graduate enemies to the media.' (Ozkok 2001).

Journalism schools and Communications Faculties were originally established to meet the demands of the media sector. A.U. ILEF Report (2007) stresses that the complaints of the sector were reproducing the division of theoretical/professional knowledge and the general structure and the functioning of the sector needs to be analysed to understand the real meaning of the complaints.

However, the report also points out that the uneasy relationship between the sector and the faculties could be tried to be solved by working on three specific topics: (1) Employment possibilities, (2) Internship possibilities and (3) Research possibilities.

Both the faculties and the sector have the consensus on the first topic that the market is saturated. It has been proposed several times that the number of Communications Faculties should be restricted and new faculties should not be opened. Unfortunately, neither the faculties nor the sector has much to say on this issue which is determined by government policies. As mentioned earlier, the current public policy regarding universities is to open universities in all provinces of the country despite the lack of the necessary infrastructure such as buildings and academic staff.

Educating and providing the academics who would educate future journalists both at a theoretical and a practical level is a matter of time and also the education of educators. It cannot compete with the rapid expansion of communication education. Professor Tokgöz (2006), while questioning if a real need existed for the large number of faculties, also pointed out that the high education strategies beginning from the early 1990s has contributed to having young academics who could teach in Communications Faculties. In the beginning of the 1990s the Higher Education Board opened the way for master's and Ph.D. degrees abroad. Private/foundation universities which were opened after 1997 started graduate programmes such as the ones state universities already had running. Those who got their Ph.D. degrees from such programmes started teaching and that, to an extent, fulfilled the need for educators.

Professor Tokgöz stresses that undergraduate-level communication education, which began half a century ago in order to meet the demands of the media sector has already become institutionalized. Having said that, the institutionalization of graduate level education is still in need of time.

Profile of Turkish journalism students

It is not possible to talk with scientific certainty about the profile of Turkish journalism students on the basis of a general study which had around 8000 students of the Communications Faculties of the country as its subject. By observation, it can be said that the students of the private/foundation universities are better off compared to the students of the state universities. It may also be said that students in the private/foundation universities initially chose to study journalism with lesser interest than the state university students.

The data about the profile of Turkish journalism students can be found in a study of the Communications Faculty of the Ankara University which studied its own students in 2006. The data is from all faculty students including those who studied public relations and advertising, radio-TV and journalism. One can assume that there are some differences between the students of these separate departments. Still, the study of the A.U. Communications Faculty, which is one of the two leading faculties in the country, can give an idea about the profile of journalism students in Turkey.

The poll shows that 27% of their students come from the city of Ankara, 21% come from other big cities, 19% from smaller provincial centers and 33% come from small towns and villages. In 2006, when the official minimum wage was 380.46 TL (€200), almost half of the families of the students (44%) had a monthly income of 500 to 1000 TL (€290 – €580). 21% of the families had a monthly income of €580 – €1160, 10% with €1160 – €2320, only 2 per cent had more than €2320 and 21 per cent had less than €290 a-month. It can be concluded that most journalism students come from lower middle class and lower class families and the poorest are those who come from the small towns of the countryside. Most of the students share a rented house with several friends (42 per cent) and 31 per cent live in state dormitories.

Fifty per cent of the students chose to study in the Communications Faculty to work in the communications sector and 42% came to university expecting that a university degree would make it easier for them to find a job in general. This means that half of the students do not have an interest in working as journalists and applied to the faculty just because their grades in the university entrance examination put them into that field by chance.

Regardless of the fact that A.U. Communications Faculty is among the top faculties in journalism education, students' responses to the poll indicate that they were not satisfied with the academic atmosphere of the faculty and the means offered to support their education. The biggest dissatisfaction appears to be in the foreign language education given to them. Two other major dissatisfactions were expressed when they were asked whether the courses were preparing them for working life and whether they were good enough to help them in their future professional practice. However, the students expressed their satisfaction with the theory courses.

It can be understood that students' main complaints were the lack of practice and the heavy weight of theory in their curriculum, a view which was not shared by their teachers.

Concluding Remarks

Professor Suat Gezgin (2007) the dean of the Communications Faculty of Istanbul University, stresses that having too many communication faculties and the very high students quota given to those faculties were the main problems of communication education.

The point Gezgin made is confirmed by the developments within the media sector during recent years. Since the year 2000, thousands of journalists lost their jobs and are waiting to get jobs in the media sector. New graduates join those more experienced journalists each year in the growing unemployed journalists' pool hoping to get a seat in the media institutions which do not have many vacant posts.

The demand factor in the rapidly increasing number of communications faculties must also be mentioned. With the opening of private radios and televisions and emergence of 'media stars' who got astronomic salaries in the 1990s, the young generations started considering journalism as a short cut to fame and money. Hoping to become well-to-do celebrities, very much contradictory to the motivation of the previous generation, has motivated the new generation to study journalism. Besides, the debates on globalization and that the global world was a world of communications, a world of a network society in which 'communicators' would be highly valued and demanded was another push factor into communication studies. The fact that journalism turned into one of the most distrusted professions and social prestige in general was very low, were omitted under the influence of shining images of media stars.

Technological developments in the field of communication, the transformation of ownership structure from traditional journalist families to conglomerates and the concentration of the media in just a few hands have led to massive job cuts in the sector. On the other hand, such developments have also forced a change in the qualifications of a journalist demanded by the sector. 'Multi-skilled' individuals, who can produce news pieces for different media, who can make videos and take photos while writing a story, have become more demanded than journalists specialized in a single field. This tendency is very much likely to grow. Since the sector has an impact on communication and journalism schools, we can expect a re-formation of the curricula, accordingly. Indeed, several communication faculties have started working on projects to adopt themselves to such developments.

Such developments and the new media will be an opportunity and advantage for the young generation journalists, especially in underdeveloped and developing countries. Turkey can be listed among those countries, where young journalists may have a chance in this sense.

The use of the internet is rapidly growing in Turkey. While in the year 2005 the percentage of the population who hadn't used the internet was 82.4%, this ratio decreased within two-years to 70.1%. The data indicates that 55–65 per cent of the urban households will have internet access within the next 10 years. On the basis of such developments, journalism education needs to be reconsidered in each faculty, especially at the practical level.

Under existing conditions of having so many communication faculties, graduates of which are likely to fall into the unemployed pool, one may argue that radical steps such as closing some of the existing ones, contrary to opening new ones, need to be made in journalism education. Having a four-year journalism education programme also needs to be debated. Students who hold degrees in various fields such as sociology, psychology, economy, politics, international relations, etc. may get journalistic skills with a one- or two-year study on that background (Tılıç 2001).

In reality, some of the Turkish Communications Faculties are very well aware of the fact that the traditional organizational structure of communications education has been changing. Curricula and departments of communications faculties are differentiating and in some places university education in journalism has left its place to seminars, courses, projects and flexible programs (A.U. ILEF 2007: 18–19). Considering both the global developments and the developments in the communications field in Turkey, Turkish communication faculties have started to discuss the need for a new vision, new strategic targets and how to produce a new education model.

The Author

L. Doğan Tılıç is Assoc. Prof. at the Middle East Technical University (METU) Media and Cultural Studies Programme. Currently reports for the Spanish News Agency EFE and writes a column in Turkish daily *BirGün*.

Notes

1. The founding state ideology of Turkish Republic promoted by its founder Mustafa Kemal Ataturk. It marks a radical split from the traditional institutions of the Ottoman Empire and stresses secularizm. The six basic principles of Kemalism are listed as Republicanism, Secularism, Nationalism, Populism, Revolutionism and Etatism.

References

Alemdar, K. (1981), 'Cumhuriyet Döneminde Gazetecilik Eğitimi Konusunda İlk Girişimler, *İletişim*, AITIA Gazetecilik ve Halkla İlişkiler Y.O. Yayın Organı, 3.

Altun, A. (1995), *Türkiye'de Gazetecilik ve Gazeteciler*, Ankara: CGD Yayını.

A.U. ILEF. (2007), 'İletişim alanında ve eğitiminde durum saptaması, Summary Report, Unpublished.

A.U. ILEF. (2008), '2020 Vision and Strategic Targets', http: //www.ilef.ankara.edu.tr/visionandtargets. php. Accessed 21 June 2008.

Geray, H. (2008), Interview for this article on 4 August 2008.

Gezgin, S. (2007), 'Türkiye'de gazetecilik egitimi, http: //www.konrad.org.tr/Medya%20tr/10suat.pdf . Accessed 20 June 2008.

Mutlu, E. (1998), 'Tartısma: İletisim egitimi, *Kültür ve Iletisim*, 1(2), pp. 16–27.

Özbek, M. (1993), 'İletisim egitimi üzerine', *A.Ü. İletisim Ankara Üniversitesi ILEF Yıllık 92*, Ankara, pp. 307–328.

Özkök, E. (2001), 'Bir kokteylin perde arkası', The Hürriyet Daily, 24 May.

Tokgöz, O. (2006), 'Türkiye'de iletisim fakültelerinde egitim kadrosunun konumu: Elestirel bir bakıs ile degerlendirme', *Kültür ve İletisim*, 9(1), pp. 33–70.

Topuz, H. (2003), *Türk Basın Tarihi*, İstanbul: Remzi Kiatabevi.

Tılıç, L. D. (2001), *2000'ler Türkiyesinde Gazetecilik ve Medyayı Anlamak*, İstanbul: Su Yayınları.

Yılmaz, B. (2008), 'Ethics courses in Turkish Communications Faculties', METU: Media and Cultural Studies Program, Unpublished paper.

Part IV

The Eastern European/Post-Communist Media Model Countries

Introduction

Karol Jakubowicz

H allin and Mancini (forthcoming) note that political change in Central and Eastern Europe 'has implied the adoption of the most typical features of what has always been defined the liberal or Anglo-American professional journalism.' In part, they continue, this has meant a major autonomy of the journalists from political power, but, at the same time, very often, this took place in absence of a clear and strong professional identity able to defend reporters from all the risks that the sudden commercialization posed. Hence, they conclude, among the principal challenges facing CEE media systems, is 'a poor professional education, together with all the mirages offered by the new commercial system and a habit of subordination to the needs of the ownership.'

In the present volume, this view is echoed to some extent by Alexandru-Bradut Ulmanu's comment that the most evident challenges for Romanian journalism in general consist in the need to overcome lack of professionalism and know-how (which translates into low professional and ethical standards), lack of resources and corruption (as often media outlets around the country are being used by their owners as tools to gain political influence and economic advantage).

Though he paints an oversimplified picture, we may in general agree with Gross (1999: 149) that under the Communist system, 'journalism education was defined as political education and coupled with propagandistic techniques to be applied both in print and broadcast media." Any degree of liberalization of the regime created more openings for 'system-indifferent,' and – in very rare cases – 'system-challenging' journalistic content, but the more totalitarian or authoritarian a Communist country was, the less room there was in the media for anything but 'system-supporting', i.e. propagandistic content (Jakubowicz 2007). This does not mean that there was no good journalism, at least in the more liberal Communist countries. Paradoxically, there may, at least in some cases, have been more of a sense of community among many media practitioners and determination to protect, to the extent possible, journalistic autonomy in those times than today.

Dissident, underground or oppositional media, where they existed, did not, as a rule, favour 'liberal or Anglo-American professional journalism': rather, a very combative and politically-engaged form of reporting.

After the fall of Communism, the media and journalists found themselves, as Lauk (2008: 193) puts it, in a certain 'normative vacuum', and there was 'confusion as to how to behave in the changing public sphere where the old patterns did not work and new ones were yet to be introduced or adapted.' There was, says Lauk, no consensus among journalists as to how the newly achieved press freedom was to be used or what guidelines to follow, though it was clear that both the functions and roles of journalists as professionals and the media system as such in the changing society needed to be redefined and reshaped.

That, it would appear, created an ideal opportunity for journalism education to step in, fill that vacuum and help shape a new understanding of the professional role and definition of journalism. Of course, local schools and universities were not alone in this:

hundreds of Americans rushed to Eastern Europe and the former Soviet republics to spread the gospel of democracy. Among them were some of America's most altruistic journalists, who hoped to midwife a newly independent press. Since the collapse of Communism, the US government and private agencies have spent more than $600 million on media development [worldwide]. (Hume 2004: 9; see also Hume 2007).

Western Europe and the EU pitched in, too, of course.

Yet, years later

editors still [spoke] of the difficulty of getting some of the former reporters to break away from the one-note reporting of opposition to the former totalitarian regime, and to adopt the professional standards of general, nonpartisan, well-rounded reporters able to report all sides of the story, fully and fairly. (Aumente 1999: 75)

If so, then perhaps this form of journalism has been honoured more in the breach than in the observance, and its adoption may have been more declaratory than real.

The limited impact of the model of 'liberal or Anglo-American professional journalism' may be due to the fact that it is by no means universally practiced or accepted and is actually a vanishing quantity even in the countries where it is supposed to be practiced. It may perhaps be preserved in some enclaves of the quality press, but certainly not in the kind of journalism that Tony Blair (2007) described in one of his farewell addresses as 'hunting in a pack [...] it is like a feral beast, just tearing people and reputations to bits.' He concluded that the relationship between public life and media is now damaged in a manner that requires repair: 'The damage saps the country's confidence and self-belief; it undermines its assessment of itself, its institutions; and above all, it reduces our capacity to take the right decisions, in the right spirit for our future.'

No wonder, therefore, that the credibility and impact of all these altruistic journalists and teachers have been limited. In her contribution to this book, Nada Zgrabljić Rotar of Croatia goes further and says that 'it seems that American and French "romantic journalism" is history.' Why? Contemporary times, she explains, require technologically literate journalists, with knowledge of media management and understanding of market forces influencing the media industry. Therefore, in her opinion, there is a need for new educational curricula in journalism, as it morphs into public relations, marketing, etc.

The question, as one reads contributions to this book by authors from the region, is whether journalism education actually has indeed contributed to shaping a new understanding of the professional role and definition of journalism, and to raising the professional skills of journalists. Two supplementary questions suggest themselves. First: has journalism education actually been capable of making such a contribution? And second: even if it has, would its impact alone have been enough to achieve this effect?

Regarding the first of these supplementary questions, many pointers could be sought in information provided by the authors on who provides journalism education, by whom it is taught, and what is actually taught. If courses are offered by universities and schools which have undergone little change since before 1989, or by entities with no interest in a new professional journalistic culture (e.g. employers' associations or private media companies), then chances for its development are minimized. The same would be true if teachers continued to teach in the same way as under the previous regime and if the content of education was unchanged. Also, if journalism education concentrated on teaching practical skills, without much concern for a necessarily much-changed normative basis of journalistic professionalism, compared to Communist times. Connections with the industry are another factor: while very important in terms of practical, hands-on training, they may also inhibit efforts to teach students norms and standards different from those prevailing in the industry and serving the owners and publishers, rather than the public interest.

The second question goes beyond the scope of this book and requires consideration of the totality of factors which help shape the way journalism is practiced. One consideration, of course, is that, as noted by Péter Bajomi-Lázár in this volume, not all of the journalism students intend to work in the media afterwards, limiting the potential impact of journalism education. Also, journalism is an open profession and publishers or editors can employ anyone they like. As pointed out by Alexandru-Bradut Ulmanu, 'journalism education' is a phrase which still makes some Romanian journalists nervous. They are always quick to argue that many brilliant journalists have never been to journalism school, whereas quite a few of those who have were never really successful in this profession. He argues that journalists who hold this view are 'on the verge of extinction' in Romania. Perhaps so, but is that true of the region as a whole?

More importantly, however, journalism culture and professionalism are not abstract constructs, but a reflection of the societal situation in which the media operate. Epp Lauk is right when she says in her contribution to this volume that 'Journalism and journalism education are shaded by political systems where ever they exist. They perform different roles and functions in diverse regimes and are dependent on the degree of freedom at their disposal.'

Eckstein (2001) notes that highly discontinuous social change (rapid change, broad in scale) generally has pathological consequences. It is difficult to imagine a more discontinuous and conflict-generating process of social change than the all-embracing transition of post-Communist countries. Also, that certain highly consequential political issues generate especially intense conflicts. Democratic development and consolidation which has produced three types of regimes in the region – democratic, semi-democratic and autocratic (Ekiert, Kubik and Vachudova 2007) – certainly has that effect. Consequently, it would be difficult to imagine an environment that is less conducive to dispassionate, aloof, fact-centred 'Anglo-American' journalism than what has been happening in Central and Eastern Europe over the past two decades. This is hinted at by Lauk:

> Although journalists were generally aware of the principles of 'good journalistic practice' and ethically responsible reporting, the legal and/or conventional framework that would have motivated them to follow these principles was still missing [...] journalists and other media professionals also faced emerging generation tensions, pressures from the new political elites, media owners and investors, and the uncertainty of employment conditions [...] market concentration, (hyper)commercialization, fragmentation of channels and audiences, and drastic newsroom cutbacks. (2008: passim)

All this has influenced the development of journalism cultures in all post-Communist countries.

Not insignificant in this connection has been the 'messianic' vision of the role of journalists, shared by many of them in Central and Eastern European countries, and reflecting the traditional role of the intelligentsia in the region. This has resulted in a type of journalism which is conviction-driven, giving rise to a partisan, advocacy-oriented and campaigning style of writing, bordering at times on propaganda. This is why, as has been found in Russia,

> commitment to a serving role in the public interest and restriction to mere facts are often regarded as a devaluation of [Russian journalists'] professional status [...] journalists who adapt to western standards of objectivity are often regarded as 'robots' by their more traditionally oriented colleagues. (Voltmer 2000: 478)

As one reads contributions by authors from the region, it is obvious that journalism education and training has been a growth industry in the past two decades. Also, that it is, perhaps unavoidably and in a way evident also in other regions of the world, a field of education and research that is still in search of its identity. That is natural at a time of fast change in the media landscape, creating new challenges for the media and new requirements for journalists. However, journalism education also seems to sit uneasily between practical training for future working journalists and more theoretically-oriented media studies. With reference to the situation in the Czech Republic, Jan Jirák and Barbara Köpplová highlight 'intense discussions' about the suitable content of journalism education, vacillating between general education courses (in political science, history, literature, linguistics, etc), an intellectual background enabling journalists to think about their job critically (journalism or media history, media sociology, etc.), and vocational training (technologies ranging from the early stages of photography to more recent online journalism). Also Péter Bajomi-Lázár of Hungary voices a recurrent theme in many chapters, when he says that the approach applied in journalism training is either theory-oriented (as with scientists) or practice-oriented (as with media and marketing professionals). Whereas the former think in terms of the social, cultural and political implication of journalism, the latter in terms of market needs. In fact, he adds, most institutions offer a mixture of these two approaches, but this shotgun marriage makes for strange bedfellows.

What further complicates matters is that journalism education is offered by a variety of schools and courses, also outside academia. To give just one example of many to be found in the various chapters: in Poland, there are numerous centres that organize educational classes intended for secondary school graduates who are interested in practical preparation for jobs. Among them there are education centres and schools of journalism run by different mass media institutions, especially by press syndicates operating in Poland (e.g. Passauer Neue Presse, Axel Springer, Bauer Group or newspaper and magazine editorial offices or public TV and radio). Courses and training programmes for journalists are also run by three professional associations of journalists in Poland: the Associations of Polish Journalists, the Association of the Journalists of the Republic of Poland and the Association of the Journalists of the Catholic Press.

Commenting on a similar situation in Croatia, Nada Zgrabljić Rotar notes that such a variety of educational programmes gives prospective students a choice between different schools, but on the other hand fragments the profession and hinders the development of a commonly shared self-definition of journalism.

Lucyna Szot of Poland differentiates between teaching staff educating students in the fields of journalism and social communication in main academic centres in Poland and others. They are, she says, 'steeped in tradition and well-prepared for the job.' By contrast, she adds, outside academic centres with long years of tradition, there is a shortage of properly trained teaching staff. That is why provincial higher schools (especially non-public ones) hire young teachers or journalists working for the local press who teach students in their spare time.

'Steeped in tradition'; 'academic centres with long years of tradition' – one wonders if that is an advantage or disadvantage in the specific situation of a post-Communist country. Naturally, it all depends what traditions are at play. Péter Bajomi-Lázár notes, for example, that Hungarian journalism teachers 'despise the tabloid press and commercial broadcasters.' So, journalism education focuses on 'quality' journalism, despite the fact that, since the political transformation, quality newspapers and public service broadcasters have lost most of their audiences. Consequently, students of journalism are taught to follow the 'social responsibility' model of journalism, which cannot always, according to Bajomi-Lázár, be applied to the actual expectations of the mainstream audiences. He calls this a highly normative approach, contrasting popular culture as expressed by the mainstream of the mass media on the one hand, and 'high culture' as delivered by some outlets and the classic arts on the other. And he seems to suggest that a better way is to adopt an interpretative approach, seeking to understand why and how the contemporary press and media operate and to place the press and the media in a societal, economic, and political context.

Many authors point out that the expectation in their countries is that more practical subjects than theoretical ones should be taught. Yet they also note that, as in Poland, universities have little contact with the media industry. In some cases, both sides are to blame. In Slovenia, owners and managers still believe that journalists do not need professional education, and so refuse to allow their journalists and editors to attend workshops, seminars or postgraduate study.

Journalism education, as it appears from contributions to the book, is facing many challenges and these will not go away any time soon. As the field changes, so journalism education will need to adjust.

Jan Jirák and Barbara Köpplová note that the concept of journalism itself is becoming increasingly mixed with advertising, public relations, promotion, lobbying, consumers' services, etc.: 'This is the result of merciless pressure from commercialized media, a lack of professional identity of working journalists (including the weak position of journalistic union), and rapid changes in technology which have made programs in journalism education quite expensive.'

Therefore, as Auksė Balčytienė of Lithuania points out, the old definition of the journalist (based primarily on roles associated with the process of gathering and disseminating information) no longer applies. Journalists are becoming guides or interpreters rather than just providers of information. Yet, she believes that independent and professional journalistic discourse should be preserved (especially in the era of homogenization of media content, commercialization and further trends towards hybrid content production).

What, then, can be done to preserve the journalistic discourse in the midst of all the changes (media convergence and concentration, increasing power of political and economic news sources, professionalization of political communication) that are posing dangers to it?

This collection does not provide an answer to this crucial question, but then, it was not intended to. What it does show is, as Epp Lauk puts it, that after twenty years of press freedom and construction of civil society on the one hand, and the growing pressures of the capitalist market on the other hand, it has become obvious that 'free market journalism is not the same as free journalism.' The professional choices and decisions of journalists depend increasingly on the interests of their employers. This, she says, 'is reflected in the growing degree of self-censorship.' Journalism has become more of a production than a creation, and as a consequence, journalists often treat their sources not as individuals but simply as material for a story.

Any hope for journalism education, then? Epp Lauk accepts that educators cannot change the environment, but believes they can provide young journalists with the necessary knowledge and skills to be able to meet the challenges of their profession at any time and place, and most important of all under any circumstances. Auksė Balčytienė has a higher ambition: professional journalistic culture may, in her view, have the ability to withstand economic and political pressures and to fulfil the mission of providing critical independent analysis. In this context, she believes, it remains of crucial importance for journalists to be able to define (through education) and to preserve (through professional practice) an independent, critical journalistic discourse. In an avalanche of texts and messages reaching citizens via all the distribution technologies, it is important that they should be able to recognize those produced thanks to professional journalism and distinguish them from all the others. Formal training and academic reflection on media performance are crucially important for the formation of professional identity which should then translate into high-quality journalistic product – so necessary when disintermediation allows everyone to disseminate messages to everyone else.

Above, we asked one main question and two complementary ones. Time for preliminary answers at least: journalism education actually has made some, but limited contribution to shaping a new understanding of the professional role and definition of journalism, and to raising the professional skills of journalists. It has not actually been capable of fulfilling this task adequately because there is still too much confusion as to what is really needed, and a clear axiological and normative foundation for this new understanding and definition is still missing. Also, its impact alone would not have been enough to achieve this effect, given that journalism and the media are largely shaped by the societal context in which they operate. That context is itself still in a state of upheaval, producing many contradictory pressures on the media.

'Watch this space' – this is how journalists often signal that a story is still developing and new developments should be expected. One is tempted to conclude this brief introduction in precisely this way. Journalism and journalism education in Central and Eastern Europe have come a long way, but still have a long way to go in dealing with issues resulting partly from the legacy of the past, and partly from the challenges of the future.

The Author

Karol Jakubowicz is Chairman of the Intergovernmental Council, Information for All Programme (UNESCO).

References

Aumente, J. (1999), 'The Role and Effects of Journalism and *Samizdat* Leading up to 1989', In J. Aumente; P. Gross; R. Hiebert; O.V. Johnson and D. Mills (eds), *Eastern European Journalism Before, During and After Communism*. Cresskill, N.J.: Hampton Press, pp. 41–78.

Blair, Tony (2007), 'On Public Life', Lecture by the Prime Minister The Right Honourable Tony Blair MP, Reuters, Canary Wharf, London, http: //image.guardian.co.uk/sys-files/Politics/documents/2007/06/12/BlairReustersSpeech.pdf. Accessed 7 September 2009.

Eckstein, H. (2001), 'Lessons for the »Third Wave« from the First: An Essay on Democratization', http: //repositories.cdlib.org/cgi/viewcontent.cgi?article=1112&context=csd. Accessed 7 September 2009.

Ekiert, G.; Kubik, J. and Vachudova, M. A. (2007), 'Democracy in the Post-Communist World: An Unending Quest?', *East European Politics and Societies*, 21(1), pp. 7–30.

Gross, P. (1999), 'Before, During and After: Journalism Education', In J. Aumente; P. Gross; R. Hiebert; O.V. Johnson and D. Mills (eds), *Eastern European Journalism Before, During and After Communism*, Cresskill, N.J.: Hampton Press, pp. 147–184.

Hallin, D. and Mancini, P. (forthcoming), 'Introduction', In B. Dobek-Ostrowska; M. Głowacki; K. Jakubowicz and M. Sükösd (2008) (eds), *Media Systems East and West: How Different, How Similar?* Budapest: Central European University Press.

Hume, E. (2004), *The Media Missionaries. American Support for International Journalism*. Miami, Fla., http: //www.knightfdn.org/publications. Accessed 12 August 2009.

Hume, E. (2007), *University Journalism Education: A Global Challenge*, Washington: Center for International Media Assistance, http: //www.ned.org/cima/CIMA-University_ Journalism_ Education-Report.pdf. Accessed 11 August 2009.

Jakubowicz, K. (2007), *Rude Awakening: Social And Media Change in Central and Eastern Europe*, Cresskill, N.J.: Hampton Press, Inc.

Lauk, E. (2008), 'How will it all unfold? Media systems and journalism cultures in post-Communist countries', In K. Jakubowicz and M. Sükösd (eds), *Finding the Right Place on the Map: Central and Eastern European Media Change in a Global Perspective*, Bristol: Intellect Books, pp. 193–212.

Voltmer, K. (2000), 'Constructing Political Reality in Russia. Izvestya – Between Old and New Journalistic Practices', *European Journal of Communication*, 15(4), pp. 469–500.

The Bulgarian Journalism Education Landscape

Manuela Manliherova, Minka Zlateva and Teodora Petrova

Introduction

There are two periods of journalism education in Bulgaria:

1. Pre-academic journalism education (1894–1952)
2. University education in journalism (since 1952/1953 academic year in the University of Sofia 'St. Kliment Ohridski' till now).

Pre-academic journalism education

One of the hardest periods in Bulgarian history, which is over 1300 years old, is the Ottoman rule (1396–1878). This period impeded the cultural and public life of Bulgaria for 500 years. This is the reason why the Bulgarian journalism issues started much later than in the other European countries and why both of the first Bulgarian periodicals were founded outside of the country. The first Bulgarian periodical – the magazine named *Lyuboslovie/Philology* was issued in 1844 by Konstantin Fotinov in Smirna (now Izmir in Turkey) and the first Bulgarian newspaper *Bulgarski orel /Bulgarian Eagle* was published by Dr. Ivan Bogorov in Leipzig, Germany in 1846. From the first start of Bulgarian journalism, the journalists and people who edited and issued the Bulgarian periodicals had adopted, as a pattern, the European way of writing.

After the Liberation of Bulgaria from Ottoman rule (1878) most of the authors in the Bulgarian press were intellectual and writers and had no special journalism education. The aim of the press was to educate the people in Bulgarian and to raise their national identity. In 1894, on the fiftieth anniversary of the launch of the first Bulgarian periodical, the Organized Journalism Professional Movement was founded. One of the aims of this movement was the education and the professional development of the young generation of journalists in the Bulgarian press.

The first period of journalism education in Bulgaria can be called 'the pre-academic training in Journalism' (1894–1952). The main role for the training of Bulgarian journalists during that pre-academic period was played by the professional organizations: 'the Society of journalists from the capital' (founded in 1907) and the 'Union of the professional country journalists' (founded in 1924). The forms in which the professional training was carried out included seminars, language courses, tours, competitions for the best reports and articles, meetings with foreign journalists. There were even some funds for scholarships in London, Paris, Berlin, and Rome for the best trainees.[1]

University education in journalism

The first academic course of journalism in Bulgaria was established at the Philological Faculty of Sofia University 'St. Kliment Ohridski' for the 1952–1953 academic year. The university is the oldest and most honoured academic educational institution in Bulgaria and marked its 120th anniversary in 2008 as Alma Mater of all Bulgarian universities. The name of its patron, St Kliment, is deeply connected with educational tradition – he is the founder of the first educational school in the country.

The second period of Journalism Education or so called University education in Journalism can be divided into two parts.

The first part covers the years from the academic year 1952–1953 until 1989. It is the period of academic education in Journalism before the transition period of the country to democracy.

After World War II Bulgaria became a part of the Soviet share of influence and the patterns of academic courses of Journalism in Sofia University were designed after the curriculums of the faculties of Journalism in the Soviet union – Lomonosov Moscow State university and Leningrad State University (now Sankt Petersburg State University). At the beginning the courses of Journalism were situated in a separate Chair of Journalism, established at the Philological Faculty of Sofia University 'St. Kliment Ohridski'. The first university lecturers in Journalism had a long professional experience in press and radio. Three of them were academically-educated in Vienna.[2] They had to teach practical skills. Even from its beginning the Journalism education was connected with media practice. The Chair of Journalism had good exchange experience with the Faculty of Journalism at the University of Leipzig in DDR. The curriculum for the MA of Journalism (5-year educational course) was discussed and designed following meetings with lecturers from other East European countries.

In 1974 the Chair of Journalism became a Faculty of Journalism at Sofia University and it was the only faculty of Journalism in Bulgaria. Most of the journalists in Bulgaria had a university diploma of this faculty. It was the only faculty of Journalism within the frame of the university education in journalism.

The second part of the second period in Journalism University education or so called period of Journalism education from 1989 until now is the time after the transition of the country to democracy. The Faculty of Journalism of Sofia University was still the only faculty for media studies. The name of the Faculty of Journalism was changed in 1991. It was called the 'Faculty of Journalism and Mass Communication'. In the 1990s the Faculty council changed its curriculum and most of the ideological lectures were removed. Many courses on public communication, media management and social studies were introduced instead.

In 1995 a new Chair was established – the UNESCO Chair 'Communication and Public Relations'. It was the first place in the country where PR and communication studies were started as a university degree. University education in the field of PR and advertising was established in three degree programmes – BA, MA and Ph.D. It was founded under a project, managed by Mr. Pierre Andre Hervo, President of the International Public Relations Association (IPRA) at the time, as per the initiative of the Faculty of Journalism and Mass Communication of Sofia University, and with the support of Mr. Alain Modoux, Director of the UNESCO Communications department and of the National UNESCO commission for Bulgaria at the time. It was the main direction in the university preparation of public relations (PR) specialists. The communication was to be perceived as a power building confidence between the people, building the democratic society – and this was set as an aim of the educational programme of PR. It represents the active result of this project, the development of which is guided by the recommendations of the IPRA and the Ministry of Education and Science in Bulgaria. The Chair not only educates professionals in the fields of advertising and PR but also became a cornerstone in the foundation of the PR professional community.

In 1997 a new course in Book Publishing started at the Faculty of Journalism and Mass Communication of Sofia University. It was the only Chair in Sofia University. There was a Chair of Librarian Information Studies at the Faculty of Philosophy. Book Publishing is also studied in the University of Veliko Turnovo. In Sofia there is also a University for Librarian studies and Information technologies.

In 2004 and in 2008 the Faculty of Journalism at Sofia University changed the educational curriculums according to the Bologna Process and ECTS. Other Bulgarian universities where media studies existed also made efforts to cooperate with the changes of the common European educational space.

The university education in Journalism, PR and Book Publishing is in Bachelor, Master and Doctoral programmes.

Current trends in academic education and training in journalism

In Bulgaria generally there are two ways in the teaching of Journalism:

- University journalism education;
- Journalism training offered by other media organizations. We can also list here individual training or in-house training by media organizations, professional organizations and NGOs.

There are several universities that offer university education in the fields of Journalism, PR and Book Publishing. The oldest one is the Faculty of Journalism and Mass Communication at Sofia University. In the 1990s there were other private and state universities that offered BA and MA programmes in Journalism and PR. The journalism education has a blooming process at state universities – Sofia University 'St. Kliment Ohridski' and the University of National and International Economics, where Journalism was started as a separate Chair of Economical Journalism but years after it was settled as Journalism. Journalism is studied as complimentary study in the Philology Faculty in Shumen State University. The same is true in South-West University 'St Neofit Rilski' in Blagoevgrad. Technical University in Sofia and the National Sports Academy also offer special courses in Journalism and PR. The private universities that teach Journalism and PR are New Bulgarian University, American University in Blagoevgrad, Bourgas Free University, and Varna Free University.

The Journalism departments and faculties are specialized on Journalism and Mass Communication university education. Different types of courses – journalistic skills such as reporting, writing for the news, etc., or specialized topic training such as economic journalism, media management, PR etc. are offered.

Other training courses are offered by media organizations. Some media organizations offer in-house training as new products are introduced in the media. Universities also offer some specialized training for working journalists. Many of the journalists gain their training when starting work in different media organizations. They either have personal training on their own or they are trained in-house if the media organizations which have special software, as is the case with Balkan News Corporation TV, the first private national TV station. Westdeutsche Allgemeine Zeitung which is the owner of one of the most circulated newspapers *Trud*, and of others such as *24hours* and other weekly newspapers and magazines, train the people in the headquarters as well as in the regional offices. The situation is the same in the media organizations of the Union of Newspaper Publishers and other media, radio and TV organizations.

Different NGO organizations such as the Association of Private Broadcast Radio and TV organizations (ABBRO), Media Development Center (MDC), ProMedia IREX, and others offer different kinds of journalism training – acquiring journalistic skills, computer editing, investigative journalism, Integration European processes and others. The other Bulgarian training institutions are Bulgarian Union of Journalists and Union of Journalists 'Podkrepa'.

The teachers

The lectures in the departments and faculties of journalism and mass communication are provided by academic staff – professors, associate professors, Ph.D. students, academic visitors, and teaching associates. Guest lecturers are invited from EU and other universities. Lecturers and researchers are also invited as guest lecturers in the frame of the Socrates/ERASMUS programme, Fulbright, Open Society and Alexander von Humboldt programmes.

Some of the faculties like Faculty of Journalism and Mass Communication at Sofia University invite professional journalists, including editors of many major national newspapers, magazines and broadcasters. They regularly visit the departments as guest speakers, external examiners or specialist lecturers; they also participate in workshops. Tutors are invited as guest lecturers and project managers in the universities to teach practical courses in press, radio, TV and online journalism, PR and advertising.

The curricula

The universities like Sofia University 'St. Kliment Ohridski', New Bulgarian University, and University of National and International Economics provide education in different forms and at different levels in educational qualification degrees Bachelor, Master and the educational and scientific Ph.D. degree. The BA takes four years while MA programmes last one to two years depending on the field of study.

Journalism and PR training is also offered by cooperations between universities, media and other organizations including NGOs. The Journalism Faculty of Sofia University also has cooperations with the BBC, Bulgarian national radio, Bulgarian National TV and courses and links with universities in the EU.

The Bachelor degree courses in Journalism, Public Relations and Book Publishing are aimed at integration of theory and practice. In the Faculty of Journalism and Mass Communication in Sofia University the training is carried out in TV and Radio studios (there are Radio 'Alma mater' and TV 'Alma mater'), the photo laboratory, and the newspaper publishing computer centre where student publications are processed. Universities print students newspapers, have students radio stations and broadcast TV programmes. The curriculum is aimed to combined theory and practice and to teach the students professional practical skills, communication and social studies.

The students in Journalism are mainly divided into print, radio and TV journalism. They also specialize in thematic areas such as economics, culture and politics. Students in PR study advertising and media. Students in Book Publishing study book editing and book marketing.

Many journalism departments and faculties in Bulgaria provide training in print, audio-visual journalism and public relations. In the content of the education of Journalism, the students are specialized in training in media – radio, television and print journalism. The students develop proficiency in the history of journalism (Bulgarian, European and US journalism), media law, media ethics and foreign languages. They take courses in investigative journalism, European integration processes, international communication, intercultural communication, media education, sociology, media deontology, radio and TV programming, producing, media management, and sports journalism.

In journalism and mass communication studies, some courses in online journalism and Web-managing skills are offered as part of the MA programmes. Those or similar courses are included in journalism MA programmes in the curriculum of Sofia University 'St. Kliment Ohridski' and of the New Bulgarian University. The state Sofia University offers MA courses. The Faculty of Journalism and Mass Communication is specialized also in MA courses – 'Electronic media', 'Print media', 'Public Relations', 'Public Communication'.

Each of the universities teaching media strives to have permanent contacts with universities and colleges in Europe and North America, with a number of leading scholarly and public foundations in the country and abroad. There is a current exchange of lecturers and researchers, of literature and syllabi; joint scientific projects are carried out within international programmes as TEMPUS, Leonardo da Vinci, Socrates/ERASMUS and ERASMUS-Mundus programmes, British Council, Friedrich Ebert Foundation, Konrad Adenauer Foundation, French culture institute and abroad with organizations such as the BBC, Mitteldeutsche Rundfunk (MDR), and Iowa state university in the United States. Media faculties regularly organize seminars and conferences with participation of their students. Students and lecturers have the opportunity to spend a semester with the students' and lecturers' exchange Socrates/ ERASMUS programme. Students and lecturers from the Faculty of Journalism and Mass Communication at Sofia University can spend a semester studying or teaching abroad though the EU exchange programme Socrates/ ERASMUS in Austria, Germany, the Netherlands, Belgium, Spain, Poland, Lithuania, Estonia, Finland, Italy, Portugal or Greece.

For example within the frame of the annual international conferences of UNESCO Chair 'Communication and PR' at the FJMC of Sofia University there was a students' workshop featuring the papers and presentations of Bulgarian and international students. The PR students from Sofia University worked together with students from Ganesville University and Iowa State University (United States). Together they prepared the first Bulgarian-American book collection *John Atanasoff and the new civilization*[3] on the occasion of the hundredth anniversary of the birth of the 'father of the computer' John Atanasoff – the great American scientist with Bulgarian origin. The MA students from the Faculty of Journalism and Mass Communication at Sofia University had the opportunity to work on a project and produce a multimedia product on Balkan image, for a special module ' The image of Europe in Bulgarian children's websites.[4]

The mid-career Media Development Centre offers online courses, classes in PR and journalism – print design and web-design, audio-visual training and summer courses for practitioners. The training sessions are during working hours and last from a few days to three weeks. The other Bulgarian training institutions such as the Bulgarian Union of Journalists and Union of Journalists 'Podkrepa' design training programmes also last for several days.

Continuing education

Continuing education is offered by different institutions: universities, training centres, and professional organizations.

- **Universities** offer one, or one and a half, year MA programmes for journalists and PR specialists both full-time and part-time. The programmes are in different field of media studies. Faculty of Journalism and Mass Communication at Sofia University offers MA programmes for part-time students: Journalism and media, Electronic media, Media economics and other programmes. The New Bulgarian University offers programmes in Multimedia, Computer graphics and Animation, Management of mass communication and PR, Film and TV art. The university opened its own centre for continuing education and offers programmes in Marketing and Advertising, and Public speech for radio and TV. Programmes mainly in the field of Marketing are offered in the University of National and International Economics. One of specific specialties in media education is 'Economics of Communications' in the Economics and Management of Communications department at the Faculty of Economics of Infrastructure, University of National and International Economics . MA programmes in the field of Journalism are offered also in the American University in Blagoevgrad, and th Universities of Shoumen, of Plovdiv, of Veliko Turnovo, Varna Free, and Bourges Free University.[5]

Training centres

Licensed training centres offer training courses in the field of Journalism. 'Center for development of media' offers distance-learning courses on a pattern of BBC distance learning, Diversity Bulgaria and radio journalism with the help of MATRA programme. The Matra Programme (the Dutch Ministry of Foreign Affairs) http: //www.bearr.org/en/node/1921

- They offer courses on Election campaigns, English for Journalists, Media management, and Radio management (3–7 days) on different topics. Some of the courses are organized for journalists of South-East Europe because the centre is a member of SEENPM. 'Media center Pro Media' also organizes professional training in Radio and TV Journalism, Ethnicity and diversity, Investigative Journalism and other courses.
- **Indoor training sessions:** WAZ group, Economedia, ReTV, Bulgarian National TV, BTV, National Radio and others organize short-term in-door training.
- **Short-term training sessions:** Union of Journalists and other professional and media organizations offer two to three day seminars and training programmes. Some of those seminars are organized by the professional organizations, others in cooperation with other institutions or foreign foundations. EU Institutions, World Bank, Bulbank and other national and international institutions also organize short-term training for journalists covering specific fields.

Accreditation

The BA, MA and Ph.D. programmes in the field of Journalism, Public Relations and Book Publishing at Sofia University 'St. Kliment Ohridski' are accredited by the National

Evaluation and Accreditation Agency, which is a statutory body for evaluation, accreditation and monitoring of the quality in higher education institutions and scientific organizations. All other BA and MA programmes of universities that offer media and communication studies have to be accredited and evaluated by the National Evaluation and Accreditation Agency.

Training institutions issue diplomas for BA and MA programmes, Ph.D. diplomas are issued by High State Attestation Commission. Universities are the educating institutions. Certificates are issued by universities for specialized training over one year courses.

BA and MA programmes of the universities are accredited according to the ECTS. Bulgarian universities coordinate their teaching programmes with the Bologna process. The national coordinating body for Bologna process and accrediting of Higher Education Diplomas is the Ministry of Education and Science.

Associations

Media teaching schools are members of international bodies. Faculty of Journalism and 'Mass Communication and Media Development center' are members of the EJTA. EJTA is the European Association of Schools and training organizations of Journalism. UNESCO Chair on Communication and Public Relations of Faculty of Journalism and Mass Communication of Sofia University is a member of ORBICOM – the world net of UNESCO Chairs on Communication and Public Relations and is a member of EUPRERA – European PR Education and Research Association.

Since 1997, UNESCO Chair 'Communication and PR' at the Faculty of Journalism and Mass communication of Sofia University has organized annual international scientific conferences to cover most actual topics in public communication. These have been attended by university lecturers, journalists, PR experts, doctoral students and undergraduates from more than 30 countries across Europe, the United States, Australia and New Zealand. 2009 saw the twelfth international scientific conference take place on the topic 'Communication and Civilizations', organized together with UNDP – Bulgaria and EJTA and dedicated to the UN global initiative 'Alliance of civilizations' (16–17 May).

In 2004, under a Phare project on technical assistance for improving professional standards of journalism, an Ethical Code of Bulgarian Media was drafted with the participation of EU experts and approved by various organizations and media.

Concluding Remarks

The main characteristics of the media landscape can be summarized shortly like this: most existing dailies are addressed to a broad readership. In terms of content, they can be described as specific hybrids that have the characteristics of information papers and yellow press. Tabloids, both dailies and weeklies, have dominated the print media market. Most regional and local newspapers are published weekly or two to three times per week, except some twenty regional ones which are issued daily in the bigger regional centres. The biggest owner on the Bulgarian newspaper market is the German media group Westdeutsche Allgemeine Zeitung (WAZ).

The media landscape is changing and the media economy shows enlargement of foreign media group's capitals in the country. German, American, Norwegian and Irish capitals are already in the media market. A strong wave of digital change in the audiovisual industry can be seen. Media organizations signed a Code of Ethical Standards in Media which they try to comply with.

Statistics from Media Development Center's 2002 survey of Bulgarian media offers a revealing insight into the make-up of the workforce. The journalistic community is almost equally divided between men (48%) and women (52%).

The academic education of Journalism in Bulgaria tries to be part of the Common European academic space and to be part of the Bologna educational process to introduce high standards of university education. The Bulgarian university education also tries to introduce new ways of flexible learning such as distance learning and lifelong learning. The universities try to improve their work with the Alumni Associations' and to be in touch in university network associations. They strive to be aware of new methods of university management and of the product the universities offer to the education market.

The Authors

Manuela Manliherova is a lecturer of Radio Journalism in Faculty of Journalism and Mass Communication of Sofia University.

Minka Zlateva is a lecturer of Media and PR, Communication Skills, Reporting and Media Education in Faculty of Journalism and Mass Communication of Sofia University.

Theodora Petrova is a lecturer of TV journalism and New Media in Faculty of Journalism and Mass Communication of Sofia University.

Notes

1. Zlateva, Minka (2006), 'From newspapers schools to the academic diploma. The role of professional societies for the development of the pre-academic journalism education in Bulgaria', in Konstantinova, Zdravka & Minka Zlateva (eds). *Professionalism and traditions. 110 years of organized journalism movement in Bulgaria*, Sofia: University Publishing House 'St. Kliment Ohridski', pp. 117–131.
2. Zlateva, Minka (2008), 'Die akademische Journalistenausbildung in Bulgarien und der Beitrag von Wiener Studenten zu ihrer Entwicklung', in Peter Bachmaier, Andreas Schwarcz und AntoanetaTcholakova (2008), *Österreich und Bulgarien (1878–2008).Geschichte und Gegenwart. Wien : Verein" Freunde des Hauses Wittgenstein", S. 217–234.*

3. Zlateva, Minka (ed.) (2005), *John Atanasoff and the new civilization. First Bulgarian-American students summary*, Sofia: University Publishing House 'St. Klimet Ohridski'.
4. The students made special module "The Image of Europe in Bulgarian children's websites within the framework of the Project European Commenius 2.1. EMECE 226642-CP-I-FR-C.2.1 'Media education for European citizenship' (2007–09) and took part in the National research project against violence in the schools (2009).
5. Petrova, Teodora and Manliherova, Manuela (2006) in Hans Paukens, Sandra Uebbing and Verlag Reinhard Fisher (eds), *Journalism, Its Education, Training and Development in Bulgaria, Tri-Medial Working in European Local Journalism*, Munich, pp. 105–108.

References

Ilchev, Ivan et al. (2008), *University of Sofia St. Kliment Ohridski. The first 120 years*, Sofia: University Publishing House 'St.Kliment Ohridski'.

Petrova, Teodora and Manliherova, Manuela (2006) Journalism Education in Bulgaria In Hans Paukens, Sandra Uebbing (eds), , *Tri-Medial Working in European Local Journalism*, pp.105–108, http: // www.update.dk/cfje/Kildebase.nsf/ID/KB01074653/$file/Documentation%20Trimedial.pdf?Open Element accessed September 28, 2009.

Zlateva, Minka (ed.) (2005), *John Atanasoff and the new civilization. First Bulgarian-American students summary*, Sofia: University Publishing House 'St. Kliment Ohridski'.

Zlateva, Minka (2006), 'From newspapers schools to the academic diploma. The role of professional societies for the development of the pre-academic journalism education in Bulgaria, In Konstantinova, Zdravka & Minka Zlateva (eds.) *Professionalism and traditions.110 years of organized journalism movement in Bulgaria*, Sofia: University Publishing House 'St. Kliment Ohridski', pp. 117–131.

Zlateva, Minka (2008), 'Die akademische Journalistenausbildung in Bulgarien und der Beitrag von Wiener Studenten zu ihrer Entwicklung', In Peter Bachmaier, Andreas Schwarcz and Antoaneta Tcholakova, *Österreich und Bulgarien (1878–2008).Geschichte und Gegenwart*. Wien: Verein 'Freunde des Hauses Wittgenstein', pp. 217–234.

The Croatian Journalism Education Landscape

Nada Zgrabljić Rotar and Djurdja Vrljević Šarić

Introduction

The first newspaper ever published in Croatia was *Ephemerides Zagrabienses*. It was published in Zagreb (the capital) in 1771, however, not in Croatian but in Latin language. This fact is not surprising, considering that Croatia is a country whose development was defined by the political circumstances in which the territory inhabited by one nation had been divided and ruled by several different governments through several centuries thus allowing foreign languages such to dominate over Croatian. In 1806 a bilingual newspaper, printed in Italian and Croatian, by the name of *Il Regio Dalmata – Kraglski Dalmatin* was published in Zadar. The first newspaper in the native language was issued in 1835 by the name of *Novine Horvacke* (Horvat 2003). Its publishing represents the beginning of the development of Croatian journalism. The fact that *Novine Horvacke* is still being published proves how significant and successful the newspaper was in its efforts to unite the nation, culturally and linguistically. Today it is called *Narodne novine* and is the official newspaper of the Republic of Croatia. *Novine Horvacke* opened a path for dozens of others dailies, weeklies and monthlies published by different social groups in the following decades. But the development of journalism – the growing variety of publishers and newspapers – would not immediately lead towards the institutionally organized education of journalists.

Beginnings of journalism education in the mid-twentieth century

The first, 'Higher journalistic school' ('Viša novinarska škola') in Zagreb was founded by the socialist Croatian government in 1950. At the time Croatia was one of Yugoslavia's Republics. The aim of the government was educating its 'cadre' (Malović 2002), supporters of the regime who would spread the 'pro-socialist propaganda' among the people. Therefore, the curricula as well as the Head of the school were approved and appointed directly by the Ministry of science and culture. The school had a two-year programme in which only gymnasium graduates could have enrolled. But only one generation of 'regime journalists' (51 people) finished the programme – because the government decided to close the school in 1952. For the next twelve years Croatian journalists would be educated in similar 'regime schools', but in other Yugoslav Republics. However, the publishers also started to realize the importance of journalism education and as a result – the biggest national publisher at the time, *Vjesnik*, started its own 'School for journalists' ('Škola za novinare') in 1964. The school was a great success and during its existence (1964–1970) it educated numerous journalists, who were later gladly hired by various Croatian and Yugoslavian media, because the programme had 'armed' the students with practical, vocational knowledge.

In 1971 the Study of journalism started at the Faculty of Political Sciences at the University of Zagreb (Fakultet političkih znanosti Sveučilišta u Zagrebu), one of the oldest universities in Europe. It started also as a two-year programme, but by 1986 it developed into an independent four-year study after which the students were called Bachelors of journalism. The programme was based almost exclusively on theory and therefore did not meet the expectations of the professional journalists' organizations, publishers or broadcasters until, three decades later, it was changed – and the new curricula included theory and practice.

In the early 1990s, after Croatia became an independent country, a new era in journalism education started. The awareness of the importance of scientific, cultural and technological institutions for high education had grown and the attempts began to adjust the Croatian educational system with the systems of other European countries as well as the contemporary principles of market economy. The changes were not easy to make since Croatia was, at that point, in the middle of the Fatherland war, and there was still a lack of democratic experience among the political leadership. 'Democratic changes in the nineties and establishment of a new Croatian state, had a negative reflection on the state of Croatian journalism. The new government also introduced a certain kind of journalists suitability' (Malović, 2002: 62).

The first serious changes in the field of media studies and journalism education began in 1992 when Croatian Studies (Hrvatski Studiji) were started as an independent faculty at the University of Zagreb, formed by the leading party, without any knowledge on the side of the Senate of University. The Croatian Studies was assumed at the beginning as a two-semester university programme, but it soon became a parallel faculty of social sciences and humanities. This was a reason why the study of journalism at Croatian Studies (seen as a parallel to the study of journalism at the Faculty of political sciences of the same University) was almost shut down by the Senate. This did not happen, due to the vast support of the public as well as repeated protests of the students from Croatian Studies.

The Law on High Education in 1994 introduced two separate directions in high education: scientific and specialist. However, the first real changes in the sphere of academic education of journalists in Croatia – the system and the methods as they are today – were regulated in the Law on science and high education in 2003. The aims of the law include organizing the system of scientific action and high education and defining new rules and criteria on the formation of universities, polytechnics and schools, or in other words the freedom of scientific action and work. The Law based on the rules of the Bologna Process obligated universities to reform higher education with the aim of setting up a unique European space for high education in the year of 2010.

Present: Variety of educational programmes

Contemporary Croatian journalism education is developing in three main frames – as a high education scientific and specialist study programme at public universities and private schools, as a study programme for postsecondary education and in the form of vocational training for both young and professional journalists, organized by their employers or by professional associations.

High education study programmes

Based on the Law on science and high education, in the past few years several new universities and schools which include the studies of journalism have been formed. Private and state faculties have made new plans and programmes – for Bachelor (three-year) studies and Master studies which last for five years (3+2) – based on the principles of respect for the amount of new information the students must receive, giving students the possibility of choosing the optional subjects, allowing the mobility of teachers and students and cooperation with related universities as well as other criteria of the European Transfer Credit System (ECTS).

The reform according to the Bologna Process enables students who did not obtain a Bachelor degree in journalism to enter Master studies in that field. Ph.D. studies in the fields of journalism and communication sciences have not yet been started. The programmes for doctoral studies in these fields are still to be finished and evaluated by the Ministry of science, education and sports.

Despite of the fact that the university studies of journalism in Croatia have existed for more than 30 years, the lack of competent highly-educated experts in the field is one of the key problems of successful and complete realization of programmes for high education in all existing journalism and media studies courses. There are several reasons for this: poor personnel policy during socialism, material circumstances of the educational institutions, and the poor social and political situation during the Fatherland War and the increased demand for a highly educated staff which is typical for the Bologna Process. Because of that for journalism and media studies programmes in different faculties and universities the key subjects are often being taught by the same professors. As a consequence, the differences among mutually and formally different study programmes are decreasing.[1]

Today, high education in the field of journalism can be acquired in four separate study programmes in three Croatian Universities[2] and as specialist studies at two private schools for high education – High Journalistic School (Visoka novinarska škola) in Zagreb and High Multimedia and Communications Technology School (Visoka škola multimedijskih i komunikacijskih tehnologija), also called TV-Academy in Split.

The Faculty of Political Sciences of the University in Zagreb (Fakultet političkih znanosti Sveučilišta u Zagrebu)[3] performs Bachelor and Master programmes of journalism since

2005. Finishing the programme, students are called a Bachelor or Master of journalism. The BA programme curricula consists of obligatory subjects through which students gain theoretical knowledge (introduction and history of journalism, mass communication theory, research methods in journalism etc.), as well as general (foreign languages, Croatian and the EU political system etc.) and practical knowledge (printed/radio/television/ agency journalism, journalistic genres etc.). Students must also take some of the offered elective subjects (sociology, political sciences, new media, online journalism etc.). Graduate programmes also consist of obligatory and elective subjects. The Faculty has a rich library, a computer laboratory for students and teachers, and a modern radio and television studio. Students have an opportunity to learn from professors from foreign universities (such as University of Tennessee, Queens College New York, and University of New Mexico) through different workshops, or visits to foreign television productions.[4] The Faculty is the home of Student Radio, where students practice radio journalism, and of *Plus* magazine which has been printed there since 1994. 'The Center for Media Research' and 'Center for Life-long Education' have also been established. Study's deficiency is the inadequate, scanty space in the Faculty buildings, unfamiliar with modern requirements.[5]

Since 2005, Croatian Studies of the University in Zagreb (Hrvatski studiji Sveučilišta u Zagrebu)[6] runs BA and MA study programmes in communication science for obtaining the academic title of Bachelors/Masters of Communication science. The Study of Communication science at Croatian Studies was made in reference with the Institut für Kommunikationswissenschaft in Salzburg (Austria) and College of Journalism and Communications University of Florida (United States). Various international study programmes in the field have also been taken into consideration while forming the curricula (Freie Universitaet Berlin, Universitaet Muenchen, London University, Universita del Sacro Cuore – Milano, Universita della Santa Croce – Roma, Pontificia Universita Salesiana) with the aim to achieve the ideal combination of theoretical, general and professional knowledge courses. The BA study programme provides students with basic qualifications for media and public communications practice. MA study gives a wider spectrum of knowledge and skills necessary for leading positions and critical performance in public communications. Study consists of thirteen major courses. Some are focused on journalism practice and public relations (agency/print/radio/television communicating, PR), some on scientific research of media and the public (theory of mass communication and media, mass communication research methods etc.) and others are general knowledge courses (foreign languages and rhetoric). The programme is conducted in a new, very modern environment, appropriate for up-to-date study.

The Department of Communication Science at the University of Dubrovnik (Odjel za komunikologiju Sveučilišta u Dubrovniku)[7] founded in 2003, has offered an undergraduate study of 'Media and Society Culture' since 2005. As of 2007 the Department also teaches two MA study programmes – 'Public Relations' and 'Media'. These are intended for anyone planning to work in the media and public relations, such as journalists, corporate managers, PR and marketing experts, organizers in government and public departments, political parties, local administration and different companies. Obligatory courses are more theoretical (mass media theory, media research methods, communication aspects of media etc.) and the elective subjects give professional journalistic knowledge (students learn local media, crisis reporting, online production, media reporting about elections, media and children etc.) which is rounded with practical work in the 'project of the year', also evaluated according to ECTS credits. From the year 2007, the University publishes its own journal called *Medianale*, for expert and scientific papers in the field of media, journalism and PR. The plan of the University is to establish cooperation with all universities in the country and with the University in Ljubljana (Slovenia). Collaboration with the University of Wienna (Austria) and the University of Stirling (Scotland) has also been mentioned. This ambitious programme is, like all others, limited by lack of educational experience and tradition and insufficient numbers of experts in the educational system.

The Department for Information and Communication Sciences of the University in Zadar (Odjel za informatologiju i komunikologiju Sveučilišta u Zadru)[8] performs Bachelor degree study in 'Culture and Tourism' – finishing this undergraduate study students obtain the title Bachelor of communication science. In the academic year 2008/2009, the Department also launched a Master degree programme called 'Journalism and Public Relations'. New international doctoral studies with a Ph.D. programme in journalism are still in formation. The University of Zadar is the oldest Croatian university founded in 1396, and renewed in 2002 in independent Croatia. Today it consists of 23 departments, participates in Tempus projects and different international university organizations. MA study of journalism in Zadar is important because of the town's long tradition in journalism.[9] It is a multinational city with a multinational population, but also an important tourist destination for people from all over the world, cherishing in that way cosmopolitism and multiculturalism. In such an environment, the need for young educated experts becomes evident, so the purpose of the study is to educate journalists and communication experts in tourism for successful public communication. Studies are based on the principles of the Bologna Process, taking into consideration students' and professors' mobility, and with adequate ECTS crediting.

High Journalistic School (Visoka novinarska škola)[10] in Zagreb was established and started working in the academic year 2007/2008. The first private high school of journalism in the country provides a three-year journalism programme called 'Professional Journalism Study'. The school was established by NCL Media Group which publishes, among various other newspapers, one of the most influential political weeklies in Croatia – *Nacional*. The study programme is based on programmes of respectable European universities and schools such as Hochschule für Künste Bremen, Homeschool Umbrella, Kunsthochschule für Medien Köln, Hochschule der Medien Stuttgart and Filozofická Fakulta u Ružomberoku with an emphasis on the experience of the first and most famous journalism study in the United States at the Missouri School of Journalism. The schools' innovation is the distinct directionality towards practical work and students are encouraged to start working in journalism during their schooling. Practical knowledge courses, workshops and seminars combine to make up two-thirds of the curricula. Theoretical courses in the field of information and communication sciences make up the other third of the programme. Finishing the study programme, students get the degree of Bachelors of journalism. Classes are taught in Croatian, by teachers who are professors from other faculties in Croatia or respectable journalists.

Since 2007, High Multimedia and Communications Technology School (TV-Academy)[11] in Split (Dalmatia) has had the permit to perform three specialist Bachelor study programmes: Multimedia Technologies (with sub-specializations in TV technologies and communications, montage, filming and direction), Multimedia Creation (sub-specializations in coverage, animation, the making of TV scenarios and anchoring) and Multimedia Production and Marketing (TV production and propaganda). In the academic year 2008/2009 the first students were enrolled in the school's programmes and studied in small groups. The scholarship is more expensive than in any other journalism school in the country, and students must bring their own equipment. Teachers are experts in television production and film-making, as well as experienced TV journalists. The school has contacts with foreign universities (such as Mercy College – specializing in Journalism, Radio/Television Production and Film/Culture, American University in Bulgaria – Journalism and Mass Communication etc.) with the aim of entering their exchange programmes for students and professors.

Postsecondary journalism education

The only school which is currently performing postsecondary study programmes in journalism – as well as in public relations and media management – is a private media academy called Studia Intermedia[12] in Zagreb. The programme of the school is verified by the Ministry of Science, Education and Sports.[13]

Journalism study lasts for two semesters. The first semester is more theoretically-based and provides students with the knowledge in media research, media communication, media ethics and legislation, media literacy, entrepreneurship and management, visual communication, European integrations, Croatian law-system and political institutions. The second semester is more practically-oriented. During it students get introduced to the basics of journalism, visit media houses, learn about particular forms of journalism – research, agency, printed, radio, television, and web journalism and attend parallel practical workshops. The educators at the media academy are media experts, college professors and scientists as well as professional journalists. Finishing the programme, students get the vocational diploma of 'assistant journalists'.[14]

Professional associations and in-house organized vocational training

The Croatian journalists' association (Hrvatsko novinarsko društvo – HND) has a long tradition of organizing various mid-career as well as beginners' vocational trainings and educational programmes with the aim of promoting journalistic knowledge and skills.[15] The main reasons for starting these alternative forms of education were down to political pressures on journalists and the incapability of young and poorly-educated journalists to stand up against those as well as the other pressures of their employers. Since the 1990s, HND started, co-organized (with other professional organizations) and supported various programmes, workshops, seminars and conferences. Mid-career training programmes are organized through a series of specialist seminars for professional journalists who specialize in finance, politics, or environment reporting etc., while young journalists are being vocationally educated through Journalistic Workshop (Novinarska radionica).

Journalistic Workshop was started in 1997 and intended for young journalists (twenty five to 35 years of age). The workshops were sponsored by international media institutions such as Press Now, Open society Croatia (Otvoreno društvo Hrvatska), EU, IREX ProMedia, The Freedom Forum, as well as German and French Embassies in Croatia. The teachers were selected among the established Croatian and foreign journalists, law and media experts. The essence of the programme was learning ways to get the information, researching, news and story writing, interviewing, editing and information selecting, the use of the Internet, journalism ethics, legislation and relating with the authorities. The international financial aid was not a constant, but workshops still continue and are held in cycles, two or three times a year.

'International Center for Education of Journalists' – ICEJ (Međunarodni centar za obrazovanje novinara Hrvatska)[16] was founded in 1998 by the Croatian journalists' association, Open society Institute Croatia, and the town of Opatija (in Istria), as an independent, non-government and non-profit organization. Its mission is educating journalists and promoting journalism. So far, ICEJ has hosted over 200 international seminars with over 5500 participants from over 40 countries. Workshops, conferences and trainings are focused on different aspects of journalism, media and social phenomena. Besides organizing seminars for young journalists, ICEJ had turned to mid-training of professional journalists offering expert courses for the promotion of their professional knowledge, like researching, applying new technologies in their work, digital photography etc. The educators are foreign and national experts, scientists and accomplished journalists. Also, ICEJ organizes international assemblies on the key issues in journalism like ethics, freedom of the media, media-state relations, war reporting, media and science etc.

Trade Union of Croatian Journalists (Sindikat novinara Hrvatske – SNH), founded in 1990, has permanent cooperation with trade unions and associations in European countries. In cooperation with IFJ, SNH has organized a series of very successful union seminars in Croatia, Bosnia and Herzegovina, Macedonia, Serbia and Monte Negro in order to help journalists in these counties to organize effective trade unions with the goal of protecting union members form 'social dumping'. SNH is the regional coordinator of the 'IFJ CARDS Program for the media'. The Union is planning to start a regional pilot-centre for the union education of journalists and is already coordinating all such regional IFJ programmes.[17]

Major publishers and broadcasters in Croatia also organize their own in-house vocational training courses for their young journalists – beginners. Such occasional workshops and seminars are usually run by their own experienced and educated journalists whose mission is to teach the basics of the 'craft': news writing or reporting, 5W, story writing, dealing with sources of information, checking and double-checking of information, basic professional standards etc. Today, major media houses (both private and public) like *EuropaPress Holding* – EPH,[18] national Croatian television (Hrvatska televizija) and Croatian Radio (Hrvatski radio) perform in-house vocational training courses for their young journalists.

New demands on journalists demand new educational programmes in journalism

Although the tradition of journalism education in Croatia is almost 60 years old, principles of modern media studies in Croatia are very young. Their development begun after Croatian independence, when, together with democracy and free market development, the awareness on the importance of free media and independent journalism became bigger. The idea was to separate the media from the government and political influence and form public media – national reporting agency, radio and television. The social component of journalism was emphasized (there was still the belief in the journalist as watchdog and champion of freedom), it was believed that a journalist works in public interests, controls the government and in due time, truly and accurately informs the public on most important social topics and events. In that way, s/he enables the public (deliberative public) to contemplate and participate in democratic process. The question of autonomy was in the focus of professional interest.

Transition brought deregulation and media privatization through the entrance of foreign capital and foreign holders which speeded up the commercialization of media content and the degradation of ethical and professional standards. Media politics was dealing with maintaining the balance between public and commercial media, and the profession was contemplating questions of ethics and self-control. The role and importance of the education of journalists became more evident. It has been shown that Croatia lacks relevant scientific research institutions, modern schools for journalism, and also teachers. When other public and private studies and schools for journalism, besides Faculty of Journalism at the Faculty for Political Studies in Zagreb, were established, the biggest problem was an insufficient number of scientists who specialized in media and journalism. The same problem occurred in the neighbouring countries. In other words, competition, labour market and the Bologna Process increased the need for quality experts and teachers specialized in media and journalism.

Today, modern trends like media concentration and corporative management impose new, different demands on journalists. Journalism, as a profession, demands new skills and knowledge. It seems that American and French 'romantic journalism' is history, corporative systems ask for technologically literate journalists, mobile and independent. The knowledge in media management that understands market laws influencing the media industry is important. In such circumstances, there is a need for new educational programmes in journalism. Journalism became closer to public relations, marketing, and other occupations, why in practice journalists often violate basic principles of ethics and professionalism which leads to identity crisis as well as a crisis in the educational system. Pluralism of educational programmes in Croatia assures a choice between different schools, but on the other hand fragments and undermines the profession.

Education is under the control of media trends, social events, financial situation and political circumstances. The media impose the imperative of speed, which then backfires making the education seem like something quick, easy and simple. Journalism is very popular among young people, but the idea of what and how much needs to be learned to become a good journalist is different for everyone. It depends not only on the precognition and desires of the student, but on objective historical circumstances in each country. The evidence can be found in empirical research on the principles of education for the journalist of the twenty-first century, conducted by Splichal and Sparks in the 1990s (1994). The complexity of the question was pointed out by Len Masterman (1985) in his book *Teaching for media*, who noticed that the need for education in media domain grows in step with its consumption in the society, and that young generations are more interested in understanding modern communication technologies and their ideology.

However, as the studies for journalists are being developed, it would be necessary to develop the system of media education on all levels, from pre-school to students and the public, as recommended by the media politics of the European Union, UNESCO and other international groups. Learning about the media is necessary for everyone, and it is important to expand them from high education to secondary and primary education. Media are important for the development of political culture, social and personal success. If media literacy and media education were pursued as carefully as educational systems for journalists, studies would enrol students with good precognition on media theory and practice, and people would share the ethical responsibility and contribute to the efforts of the profession to serve the public, social interests and democracy.

The Authors

Nada Zgrabljić Rotar is Assistant Professor and a Deputy Head at the Department of Information and Communication Studies, University of Zadar. She also teaches at University of Maribor and has extensive cooperation with University of Ljubljana.

Djurdja Vrljević Šarić works in journalism – as a radio and newspaper journalist and co-editor. She is currently employed on a regional political weekly *Šibenski list*.

Notes

1. Taking into account the already mentioned fact that there is a lack of university professors in the field of communication sciences, some universities are cooperating among themselves as well as with other, mainly foreign, universities in order to accomplish the number of teachers required for the realization of Ph.D. studies, which are important because they will enable continuity in the educational process.

2. In the academic year 2007/2008 the first generation of Bachelors of journalism or communication science according to the Bologna Process have finished their studies at the Faculty of Political Sciences at the University of Zagreb (Fakultet političkih znanosti Sveučilišta u Zagrebu), Croatian Studies at the University of Zagreb (Hrvatski studiji Sveučilišta u Zagrebu), University of Zadar (Sveučilište u Zadru) as well as the University of Dubrovnik (Sveučilište u Dubrovniku).

3. All information about the Faculty on http: //www.fakultet.fpzg.hr/

4. In 2005 they visited Swedish media SVT and TV4, and also University of Stockholm. The same year, students have also visited BBC in London. Unfortunately, visits to foreign television productions are not an obligatory part of the study programme, but an occasional one.

5. Since the foundation of the Faculty, the number of study programs and students has continuously been growing making the Faculty building in the city centre overcrowded. Efforts are being made to dislocate the Faculty.

6. Further information about the Faculty accessible at http: //www.hrstud.hr/

7. Website address http: //www.unidu.hr/

8. More information about the Faculty on http: //www.unizd.hr/

9. The First newspaper published in Croatian language (simultaneously with the Italian version) called *Kraglski Dalmatin* was published in Zadar in 1806.

10. Website address http: //www.nclstudij.com/

11. Website address http: //www.tv-akademija.hr/

12. Website address http: //www.studiaintermedia.hr/

13. More information about the process of the verification of study programs and other activities of the Ministry in the field of higher education on http: //public.mzos.hr/Default.aspx?sec=2510 (accessed on 21 March 2009)

14. Searching the Internet, we also found other institutions which offer 'crash-courses' in journalism, but without the valid certificate. Since finishing such programmes is not a guarantee of professional knowledge, nor does it supply a person with the vocational diploma of 'journalist', the programmes are not mentioned in this paper.

15. Croatian Journalists' Association is also one of the few organizations which constantly keep track of the educational structure of their members. The latest information dates to November 2008 and, according to the annual report of the Commission for HND Membership, the association has 3235 members, among which 1318 are women (40.7 %). In the educational structure of the membership – over 60% of the membership has Bachelor, Master or even Ph. D. degrees (21 members). The numbers show that considering all the problems the journalism education system has struggled with in the past decades – current educational structure is better than would be expected.

16. Website address http: //www.icej.hr/

17. SNH's efforts are mainly directed towards signing collective work contracts with publishers and broadcasters. So far, the Union has been able to sign such contracts with ten major media houses, private and public, in the country. The Union has also prepared the Proposition of Collective work contract which should be signed on the state level and protect all Croatian journalist and media-employees. In order to improve the educational structure of journalists, SNH's Proposition includes the obligation on employers not to, when hiring young journalists, employ candidates without a BA degree.

18. *EuropaPress Holding*, the biggest private publisher in Croatia which owns several of the most-read newspapers, started its own school 'Journalists' Academy' in 2001 to ensure that young educated journalists are in the making. The school's three-month programme was based partly on the educational training given by Journalistic Workshop and ICEJ courses. The programme

had a theoretical part (practical journalism knowledge taught by experienced journalists, EPH employees) and practical part – constant writing and rewriting of the text. After creating a few generations of young EPH journalists 'Journalists' Academy' ceased working. The publisher has announced the re-starting of a similar school, but so far it is only an idea.

References

Horvat, J. (2003), *Povijest novinstva Hrvatske 1771–1939,* Zagreb: Golden Marketing.

Malović, S. (2002) 'Croatia s bitter-sweet experiences: Education of journalists in Croatia', In *Education of Journalists in South-East Europe: A Step Closer to Professionalism*, Sarajevo: Media Online selections, pp. 59–75.

Masterman, L. (1985), *Teaching the media.* New York: Routledge.

Medijsko zakonodavstvo RH (2003), *Ministarstvo kulture RH*: Zagreb.

Mihovilović, Maroje (2007), 'Nova škola žurnalizma – koncepcija studija: Praksa je temelj novinarskog obrazovanja' (16 July), *Nacional.*

Potter, W. J. (2001), *Media Literacy*, London: SAGE Publications.

Barbarić, Diana (2008), 'U splitskom predgrađu TV-akademija za 123 tisuće kuna' (18 May), *Slobodna Dalmacija.*

Splichal, S. and Spark, C. (1994), *Journalists for the 21st Century,* New Jersey: Ablex Publishing Corporation.

Zgrabljić, N. (2003), 'Media Policy and the Public Broadcasting Services in Croatia', *Medijska istraživanja/Media Research*, 9(1), pp. 59–77.

References

The Czech Journalism Education Landscape

Jan Jirák and Barbara Köpplová

Introduction

The basis of contemporary journalism education in the Czech Republic was established in the early 1990s, following the end of the cold war. During the transformation process of society and its institutions – including public communication – the media and press have shifted from the role of a state (and 'ruling' party) propaganda tool to a more liberal, market-driven system. These changes were accompanied by a redevelopment of journalism education, very broadly inspired by international context.

Beyond the influential factors of international context, other characteristic features are typical for journalism education in the Czech Republic (and former Czechoslovakia):

1. The involvement of union(s) of journalists in the development process of journalism education from the beginning until the end of the 1980s (but not after).
2. Tension between the demand for 'better educated' journalists articulated by politicians, intellectuals and the general public and the lack of interest in further education expressed by journalists themselves.
3. The struggle to establish journalism education within a university framework.
4. Intensive discussions about the suitable content of journalism education, vacillating between general education courses (in political science, history, literature, linguistics, etc.), an intellectual background enabling journalists to think about their job critically (journalism or media history, media sociology, etc.), and vocational training (technologies ranging from the early stages of photography to more recent online journalism).

All these four traits can be tracked in the historical path of journalism education in Czech society (Jirák and Köpplová 1996).

A historical outline of Czech journalism education

The development of Czech journalism education can be divided into three distinct periods:

1. The earliest attempts to establish more systematic journalism education can be found in the first period (from the second decade of the twentieth century until the beginning of the World War II). Of course, the very first occasional courses were organized in late 1880s.

It is mostly designed as 'mid-career training' aimed at working journalists and supported by the journalistic union. In the academic year 1912–13, a regular set of political science courses offered by České učení pro politické vědy (Czech School of Politics) was enriched by elective courses designed for working journalists. The courses were focused on the legal framework of the journalistic vocations, journalism history, journalistic techniques and newspaper management, including administration, promotion and advertising.

The struggle to establish journalism education continued after World War I, mostly thanks to the developments in Leipzig, Germany, where the regular study programme was already established. For the academic year 1921–22, a two-year study programme for journalists was prepared at Charles University but never became a reality. In the academic year 1928–29, the Svobodná škola politických nauk (Free School of Political Studies) was founded in Prague as the first institution designed specifically for educating journalists. By definition, the school was a mid-career centre aimed at educating working journalists. The curriculum was informed by 'novinověda' ('newspaper science'), a sort of journalism sociology mixed with social and cultural history, developed by social and humanity scholars inspired by German Zeitungswissenschaft.

The courses were offered until the beginning of World War II but were suspended under the Nazi occupation. After 1945, the courses were revitalized, but without institutional support, and the school itself was replaced by Vysoká škola politická a sociální (College of Political and Social Studies). During the entire period, established political parties published periodicals and organized courses for 'their' journalists, as well. (Jirák and Köpplová 2006)

2. The second period (from the end of World War II until 1989) was very dynamic both socially and politically. In 1948 the Communist Party became the ruling party, and the 1960s – particularly the remarkable year 1968 and Prague Spring – in the middle were a definite breaking point. For journalism education, it marks a period of development from occasional mid-career courses towards systematic 'pre-career' journalism education, organized predominantly within the framework of a university environment.

The inspiration of organized Soviet journalistic education had been apparent since the 1950s, as well as the perceived necessity to control and influence media professionals. However, the first steps towards university journalism education had been taken before the former Czechoslovakia became part of the Soviet bloc. In 1946 and 1947, the first positions for journalism lecturers were filled at Charles University in Prague and Palacký University in Olomouc, respectively. Both types of journalism education – mid-career training and pre-career university courses – were developing during this whole period, dominated by the educational tenets of university journalism. After 1948, when the Czechoslovak media adopted a Soviet-like model, journalism education changed accordingly. Pre-1948 journalism education was replaced (the Vysoká škola politická a sociální was closed at the beginning of the 1949–50 academic year) and a new system of mid-career courses and university education was established afterwards, both strongly supported by the Union of Czechoslovak Journalists, the journalistic organization established after World War II.

University journalism education began at the Philosophical Faculty of Charles University in Prague at the beginning of the academic year 1953–1954. In 1960, at the Institut osvěty a novinářství (Institute of Further Education and Journalism) –the continuing development of journalism education could be seen as an emancipation process within the academic environment (at Charles University in Prague and Comenius University in Bratislava). Journalism education struggled to establish its own department, and later its own faculty, especially at Charles University (a faculty of journalism has never been founded in Bratislava, the capitol of the modern Slovak Republic).

This effort culminated in the establishment of the Fakulta sociálních věd a publicistiky (Faculty of Social Sciences and Journalism) in 1968. The word 'publicistika', inspired by the German *publizistik* is a synonym for 'journalism', but its meaning is slightly shifted towards the more cultural and literary tradition of journalism. The faculty was terminated in the early 1970s, as an effect of the changes after 1968, and the Faculty of Journalism was established in 1972. What looks like a peak of the emancipation process was in fact evidence of more strict control of the media and journalists. The Faculty of Journalism was operating in close cooperation with the Communist Party and the organization of journalists. The curriculum offered by the Faculty of Journalism was a mixture of academic courses and vocational training. To the academic background of lectures in the theory of propaganda, Czech language and style and the history of journalism was added an obligatory set of courses in Marxism-Leninism. The programme offered courses in print journalism, in radio and television journalism and in promotion and advertising – so-called 'socialistická propagace' or 'socialistic promotion'. The intellectual background of the journalism education was the 'teorie žurnalistiky' ('theory of journalism'), an applied Marxist-Leninist theory of the role of journalism in socialistic society blended with a criticism of Western journalistic concepts (see also Jirák and Köpplová 1998).

3. The third period (from 1990 to present) of journalism education can be characterized as a shift from a party and state controlled paradigm to a liberal, democratic one. In 1990, the Faculty of Journalism in Prague was cancelled and journalism education at Charles University became part of a newly established body – the Fakulta sociálních věd (Faculty of Social Sciences).

The concept of journalistic education has been transformed under the supervision of EJTA (European Journalism Training Association) with support of the Tempus project. The fundamental features of this change were (a) focus on vocational training (practical courses, connection with experienced journalists and 'real' media, not just school media designed for exercises and training and lecturers who are very loosely connected with the professional practice) and (b) clear distinction between journalism training and any kind of 'academic' background. Media studies and communication in the mass media were determined as a necessary academic background for journalism education at Charles University, and the Department of Mass Communication (later renamed Department of Media Studies) and the Department of Journalism were founded in 1993.

Simultaneously, new types of journalism education appeared in the 1990s. In addition to Charles University in Prague, journalism study programmes were established at other public universities: Masaryk University in Brno from 1995, originally within the study programme of sociology; Palacký University in Olomouc as of 1992; and the Technical University in Ostrava from 2006 – as well as in private universities and non-university schools of higher education. Likewise, attempts to institutionalize the 'in-house' journalism education conducted by publishers or broadcasters can be witnessed during this period.

Contemporary Czech journalism education

At present, Czech journalism education is developing in four different frameworks:

a. As a study programme organized by public universities – at Charles University in Prague within its Faculty of Social Sciences, at Masaryk University in Brno within its Faculty of Social Studies, at Palacký University in Olomouc within its Philosophical Faculty (Faculty of Arts) and at the Technical University of Ostrava within its Faculty of Economics. The first three of these universities offer Bachelor and Master degrees in Journalism, while the fourth offers a Bachelor programme in Economic Journalism. The Prague Faculty of Social Sciences is arguably the most 'traditional' school of journalism education, as this was the institution responsible for restructuring the discipline in 1990 after the pre-1989 Faculty of Journalism was dissolved.

b. As a non-university study programme organized by schools of higher (post-secondary school) education. The most important among these was founded in 1997 as a non-bachelor degree in journalism at the Vyšší odborná škola publicistiky (Higher Professional School of Journalism), which is affiliated with the Catholic Church.

c. As in-house vocational training courses organized by publishers and broadcasters (both private and public). Passauer Neue Presse, the Bavarian publisher and owner of several Czech regional dailies, operating in the Czech Republic as VLP (Vltava-Labe-Press), has organized courses for journalists just entering the profession since the 1990s, and from the late 1990s in cooperation with Charles University in Prague. In 2005 they approached Masaryk University in Brno and established a vocational training centre called Institut regionální žurnalistiky (The Institute of Regional Journalism) in cooperation with the Faculty of Social Studies. Other media also organize courses for beginners, mostly centered around basic information on production standards, computer systems, working with technical equipment, etc. For instance, the Czech Press Agency (ČTK) offers a 10-day course for newcomers covering such traditional bases as the principles of agency journalism, basic professional standards, journalistic skills (how to check sources, preparing for events, etc.), Czech language/composition, and so on. Likewise, some elements of journalism education can be tracked down in public service radio (Český rozhlas, Czech Radio) and television (Česká televize, Czech Television).

d. As a set of courses in journalism, creative writing, film and television editing or online production organized by private universities and non-university schools under a variety of headings. In these settings, 'journalism' is apparently not a sufficiently 'catchy' word for promoting a programme that students are required to pay for. For instance, the Literární akademie Josefa Škvoreckého (Josef Škvorecký Literary Academy) in Prague offers such courses within the programmes called Komunikace v médiích (Communication in Media), Redakční práce (Editing), Tvůrčí psaní (Creative Writing) and Tvůrčí psaní a publicistika (Creative Writing and Journalism). Univerzita Jana Ámose Komenského (Jan Amos Komensky Universit), a private university in Prague, offers some journalism courses under the auspices of Sociální a masová komunikace (Social and Mass Communication).

National unions of journalists and employer associations are not well established in the Czech Republic and do not run or supervize courses in journalism education. Syndikát novinářů České republiky (The Syndicate of Journalists of the Czech Republic), the main union of journalists in the country, has not won a strong position among Czech journalists, and many of them – including leading 'celebrities' of the profession – have not applied for membership. Employers associations are very rare, are not supported by private publishers and broadcasters (Czech public television is one of few exceptions), and serve mostly as trade unions for their members and other employees.

What journalism education means in the Czech Republic

The duality of training vs. education can be found in the content of journalism education in respected institutions throughout the Czech Republic. Generally, study programmes are developed upon a presumption that there should be (a) a theoretical background for journalists, (b) a set of courses covering professional training and (c) some courses of general education.

Regarding (a), the theoretical background, all programmes mentioned above accept media studies/mass communications/new media theory as a 'theoretical' background or a framework of journalistic studies. Some of them are more 'media sociology' orientated (Fakulta sociálních studií, Masaryk University), while others are more focused on 'media history/media studies' (Fakulta sociálních věd, Charles University, Filozofická fakulta, Olomouc). The weak point of theoretical background in these programmes is a lack of genuine media and journalism research analyzing the Czech situation and a subsequent heavy dependence on foreign (mainly Anglo-American) literature.

Regarding (b), the vocational training is usually a combination of academic coursework and journalism projects on one side and internships in newsrooms or broadcast stations on the other side. School courses can be divided into two groups: lectures/courses about journalism as a profession (media law, journalism ethics, journalism genres, etc.) and programmes/projects based upon work-study or 'learning-by-doing' (school newsroom, school radio and/or TV studio, etc.). There is a strong tradition in Czech journalism education to teach 'genres' (news, commentaries, columns, features, etc.), which developed most notably in the 1970s and 1980s into the so-called 'theory of genres'. The main focus of this perspective is on teaching how to write/record/edit a proper piece of journalistic work. In all schools, this is the basis of practical journalistic training (accompanied by some courses on work with sources, online journalism and electives in various branches of journalism – sports journalism, literary or film criticism, etc.).

A wide diversity can be witnessed within (c), the courses of general education. Some schools stick to the tradition of 'journalist as a writer and educator' and focus on language and linguistics, the history of literature and cultural history, aesthetics, etc. (this is true for Vyšší škola publicistiky, Literární akademie and partly Fakulta sociálních věd, Charles University). Some schools rely more heavily on courses offered by other departments of the same school, and ask students of journalism to enrol for instance in introductions to various social sciences (this is true for Fakulta sociálních studií, Masaryk University, and partly for Fakulta sociálních věd, Charles University). In the case of Economic Journalism in Ostrava, the general education is replaced by a groundwork in economic courses. As we note later, some programmes at public universities are organized as 'major only', and some as 'major and minor' in combination with some other programme. In the latter, the courses of the second programme serve as an educational background for students of journalism. Clearly, the concept of 'educated' journalism is far from being stabilized or unanimous.

In the programmes mentioned above one can find three types of instructors/lecturers. First, there are lecturers with academic backgrounds overseeing coursework in what each of these institutions feels is an appropriate academic background for future or working journalists. These lecturers are typically specialized in media studies, sociology of media, media history, linguistics and media semiotics, media law, and so on. As a second type, there are full-time instructors (in many cases former journalists, sometimes graduates of journalism at public universities with some journalistic experience) teaching introductory courses in journalism and organizing internships. And finally, there are working journalists, professionals, who work as part-time instructors or guest teachers. Not coincidentally, there is scepticism and ambivalent attitudes regarding the existence of journalism education among Czech journalists, and many of them are not willing to participate in journalism education (Volek; Jirák 2006). The typology of lecturers/instructors reflects the duality of thinking about journalists and their requisite education: on one hand there is tendency to 'train' journalists in basic skills, new technologies, professional standards, etc., while on the other hand there is a tendency to 'educate' journalists in some more general academic field (media studies, history, philology, political science, etc.).

How journalism education is organized and accredited

The process of organization and accreditation of journalism studies differs for universities and colleges (both public and private) and for non-university schools.

Universities have widely accepted the ECTS and restructured the journalism education programme according to the Bologna Process. The typical structure – which can be found in Fakulta sociálních studií, Brno, Filozofická fakulta, Olomouc as well as in Fakulta sociálních věd Prague – is a three-year programme for a Bachelor degree and a further two-year programme for a Master degree (in Prague, this system was established in 1993, far before the Bologna Process started). In Brno and Olomouc, there is a 'major and minor' system for Bachelor degrees, and students of journalism can combine journalism education with other academic disciplines. In Prague, there is a 'major only' system at the Bachelor level and students focus on journalism study exclusively.

In both Brno and Prague there is a quite well developed structure of specializations. In Brno, students are encouraged to specialize in journalism, media theory or multimedia after passing the introductory set of journalistic courses in the first year and a half. In Prague, students are encouraged to choose between print/photo journalism and broadcast journalism after the same period of time. In Brno, Olomouc and Prague, the Master programme is more theoretical, focusing on media studies/mass communications, and students who already hold a Bachelor degree in journalism education are encouraged to follow this track (but students from other fields are accepted). In addition, in Prague there is a special two-year programme of journalism designed for Bachelor graduates from other fields without restrictions (but not graduates of Bachelor journalism education). In Prague, there is also a three-year post-graduate doctoral programme (Ph.D.) in media studies, which is also open for graduates of journalism education.

Non-university programmes are three-year programmes at the bachelor's level (Literární akademie). Vyšší škola publicistiky requires three years but is not allowed to graduate their students as Bachelor's diploma holders, which means they are only certificated and cannot apply for Master's programmes. Any Bachelor's or Master's programme must be accredited by the Ministry of Education of the Czech Republic and its Accreditation Council. There is no involvement of journalistic unions, publishing or broadcasting organizations or any other self-regulating body.

Concluding Remarks

Both public and private schools in the Czech Republic are developing media-related programmes, especially as of the late 1990s. There are many programmes focused on media studies/mass communications, marketing communication, advertising, multimedia and new media, visual communication, creative writing and so forth. Such schools know that 'media sells', but believe that 'journalism does not sell', and in most of them some element of journalism education is incorporated, but not many are willing to open and run a full programme dedicated to journalism education (however courses in news writing and editing and creative writing are included in their curricula). Only public universities declare the mission to educate future journalists as such.

The possible reason for this situation is that journalism itself is less and less clear in its boundaries and is becoming increasingly mixed with advertising, public relations, promotion, lobbying, consumers' services, etc. This is the result of merciless pressure from commercialized media, a lack of professional identity of working journalists (including the weak position of journalistic union and fuzzy concept of professional standards), and rapid changes in technology which have made programmes in journalism education quite expensive.

Last but not least, there are some 'human factors' within the schools themselves to be considered. For instance, there is an ambivalent attitude towards journalism education among actual students of journalism. Many more young people apply for journalism studies than can be accepted by the public schools, which is one reason private schools are so eager to incorporate some elements of journalistic education into their curricula. Yet many of those who are accepted do not plan to ultimately work as journalists and prefer to accept jobs as spokespersons, copywriters in advertising agencies, etc. This sort of ambivalence is the reason behind many private schools choosing not to advertize their programmes as 'journalism education'.

The changing media environment, as well as the melting boundaries of the journalistic profession and the weak position of the journalistic union (and consequently undeveloped professional standards) will probably influence the future development of journalism education in the Czech Republic and lead to a true 'post-journalistic' era in mass media. Journalistic education will be mixing with pre-career education of advertising, public relations and other media professions (as it does in media production itself).

The Authors

Barbara Köpplová, media studies associate professor, a chairperson of the Department of Media Studies and chairperson of the Center for Media Studies CEMES, Faculty of Social Sciences, Charles University, Prague.

Jan Jirák, media studies professor, a member of the Department of Media Studies and founding member of the Center for Media Studies CEMES, Faculty of Social Sciences, Charles University, Prague.

References

Jirák, J. and Köpplová, B. (1998), 'Fakulta sociálních věd', In *Dějiny Univerzity Karlovy IV*, Praha: Karolinum, pp. 533–542.

Jirák, J. and Köpplová, B. (1996), 'Kontury vývoje vzdělávání českých novinářů', *Dějiny a společnost*, 5, pp. 10–14.

Jirák, J. and Köpplová, B. (2006), 'K vývoji novinářského povolání', In *Acta Musei Nationalis Pragae, Řada C – Literární historie*, LI (1–4), pp. 19–27.

Volek, J. and Jirák, J. (2006), *Vybrané atributy profesního sebepojetí českých novinářů*, Mediální studia I/2006, pp. 21–38.

The Estonian Journalism Education Landscape

Epp Lauk

The Estonian Journalism Education Landscape

Introduction

The story of journalism education in Estonia is also a story about journalism and the profession of journalism. All three are survival stories that reflect the historical reality of Estonia as a country and as a nation. Journalism and journalism education are shaded by political systems wherever they exist. They perform different roles and functions in diverse regimes and are dependent on the degree of freedom at their disposal. Journalism in Estonia dates back for over 300 hundred years but in that time there has been freedom of press for less than 30 of those years. This is because Estonia has been ruled by a succession of foreign powers throughout its history (cf. Misiunas and Taagepera 1993: 13–25; O'Konnor 2003).

The role of journalism and journalists in nineteenth century Estonia, a province of the Russian Empire at the time, was to become the 'voice for Estonians by Estonians'. The emerging national press, stressing and propagating cultural and national values and uniting Estonian people around these values rapidly became an important means of 'nation-building' and, later on, national survival. The second half of the 19th century was also a period of strictest censorship when the 'camouflage' strategy 'reading and writing between the lines' began to develop (Høyer, Lauk and Vihalemm 1993).

By the late 1930s, journalism in the independent Estonian Republic (1918–1940) had gained several characteristics of a profession: a professional organization – the Estonian Journalists Union (EJU) with a membership of 100–120 was established to safeguard professional values, ethics and journalists' integrity, and to protect journalists' interests in relation with their employers. The EJU also maintained contacts with many journalist organizations in Europe. Although there was a lively discussion in the Estonian press during the inter-war years on the quality of journalistic production and journalist training, no attempt was made to establish any kind of formal professional education for nascent journalists (Lauk 1993). Journalists had various educational backgrounds and gained their professional skills in the newsrooms. The EJU occasionally arranged courses for reporters and editors, and gave scholarships for studying abroad.

The Soviet take-over of Estonia in June 1940 and the remaining years of World War II oversaw the complete destruction of both the profession of journalism and the free press. In the first six months of the Soviet rule, 32 journalists were executed. Several hundreds were arrested and sent to Siberian labour camps in the deportations of 1941 and 1949, and only a few succeeded in escaping abroad at the end of the WW II. Out of nearly 700 journalists who worked in the Estonian press in early 1940, only a few continued their careers after the restoration of the Soviet regime in 1944. There is still no information concerning the 211 journalists who disappeared during 1940–46.

The time of birth

The imposition of the Soviet model of journalism after World War II in Estonia was relatively smooth as there were no more bearers of the continuity of old traditions and values. The Soviet regime made journalism the most important tool of brainwashing the population. Freedom of speech was constitutionally guaranteed for the exclusive purpose of securing the Socialist order and serving the interests of the Communist Party. An overwhelming censorship mechanism was developed and maintained in order to supervise and control the content and performance of the media (cf. Lauk 1999).

For ten years after the war, journalists for the Estonian Communist press were trained in the Journalism Schools and Faculties of the Communist Party Colleges according to the Soviet journalist doctrine. These studies consisted of courses lasting from between two to three weeks up to twelve months. More important than professional skills and knowledge was loyalty to the Communist authorities. Most of the post-war journalists, however, had no journalism training whatsoever. It is hardly surprising then, that as a consequence the 'wooden language' style and propagandistic content, characteristic to the Soviet press, developed in the Estonian print media.

Journalism education in most of the former Communist countries in Central and Eastern Europe is a post-World War II phenomenon and almost always developed in literature departments at universities (Johnson 1999: 34). Estonia is not an exception.

Journalism education in the Estonian language at Tartu University began in 1954 as a direct result of an error of judgement by the ideological overseers in 1952. The Faculty of Humanities, in 1952, had applied to establish a Department of Journalism with twenty five students. The Faculty, had in the applications, stated that a key factor in the need for the

---

The Soviet journalist doctrine

It is the party that guarantees the journalist the necessary freedom of action [...]. In using the freedom of activity, offered by the party, the journalist must see to it that this freedom is realized to the fullest extent in the interests of society. The party has the right to demand from the journalist ideological clarity, definite views and a principled manner.

In case when the activity of a journalist does not correspond to the demands of the party, it is empowered to deprive him of the right to speak in its name or may choose other means of influence over him. (Tepljuk 1989)

Department was the rising propaganda importance of the press coupled with the shortage of professional journalists. The authorities felt that supervising an entire department was a lot more difficult than a 'specialist' section in philological studies. Consequently, the Ministry of education allowed 'journalism' to be included as a specialist course in the curriculum of Estonian language and literature in the academic year of 1954. The error of judgement lay in underestimating the power of Estonia's mother tongue to act as a unifying factor in the survival of the nation and as an opposition factor against the Soviet authorities.

In 1954, the first eight students were enrolled. For the next 40 years, the University of Tartu remained the only institution in Estonia that provided journalism education. During the first two decades, 1954–1976, journalism was offered as a specialty at the Department of Estonian Philology to small groups of seven to ten students. In 1976, a separate five-year long journalism curriculum was launched and twenty five students enrolled. Two years later, the independent Department of Journalism was established with six teachers on the staff.

The 'founding father'

As a rule, institutions and ideological movements require an innovator to have the idea and then to nurture the concept through its formative years till it can survive on its own. Fortunately for Estonian Journalism Education there was a 'founding father'. Juhan Peegel (1919–2007), a young, newly qualified teacher was employed as a researcher in Estonian language and folklore. Crucially he had had experience working as a journalist for the free press during the pre-War years as well as for a Soviet newspaper during his time as a student at the University. Peegel was instrumental in the Faculty's plan to create the Department of Journalism.

Given the responsibility of compiling the curriculum, Peegel modelled the existing officially-accepted curriculum of Estonian philology to suit the needs of teaching journalism. He managed to avoid teaching propaganda journalism by building up journalism courses on linguistics, the mother tongue, the history of Estonian language and culture and the traditions of the national press; and subsequently became the only full-time teacher of journalism. Furthermore, with the help of his students, Peegel also initiated a lasting research into Estonian journalism history that remained the only field of journalism research for the next ten years.

Walking at the edge of abyss

Tartu University was one of the strongest centres of the silent resistance and opposition to the ruling regime throughout the fifty years of Soviet occupation. The brief method employed by Professor Peegel to explain to his students the concept of a freedom of choice fairly reflects the subversive teaching atmosphere in the University: 'God said to Adam:

Please, choose yourself a wife! – And he gave him Eve'. His advice to students who began their careers as journalists was dangerously heretical: 'If you are asked to publish something that you feel you cannot do, find a way to say no'.

At the beginning of the 1970s, the Communist Party launched a major campaign aimed at 'the strengthening of the ideological work of the masses'. As a direct consequence the existence of Journalism education in Estonian language at the University of Tartu came under serious threat. The Communist Party Colleges, which were specialists in training the 'Party soldiers' using Russian as the language of instruction had already taken over journalism training in Latvia and Lithuania (Gross 1999: 151). Fortunately the Head of the Propaganda Department of the Central Committee of the Communist Party in Estonia, at that time, was a former journalism student. His intervention ensured that the courses in journalism continued in Estonian at Tartu.

The Communist Party was all too aware that the media was a double-edged sword. Consequently anyone involved in the field of journalism education, be they students or teachers came under continuous surveillance from the KGB and Communist Party officials. The KGB was seldom successful in their numerous attempts to recruit voluntary informers among journalism students and teachers. More successful was the strategy of blackmailing and intimidation. In some cases, for example, students were trapped by the KGB when caught by the militia for minor public disturbances, and under the threat of being expelled from the University, they were then released by the KGB on the condition of the agreement of cooperation. There were cases where such students came to their professors and told them what had happened.

Institutions that came under such close scrutiny had two choices: either they ceased any activity the scrutinizers deemed subversive or devised a 'camouflage' strategy that disguised all intentional activity. In the Department of Journalism, a 'hidden curriculum' strategy was introduced.

The Communist authorities demanded that teaching in journalism must follow the official All-Soviet Union curriculum created in Moscow. The standard curriculum in Tartu was, however, fulfilled with a largely different content. For example, under the title of 'Criticism of the theory and practice of bourgeois journalism' the Department taught 'Mass Communication Theory'. In much the same manner, those subjects that were strictly off-limits in the All-Soviet model, such as the journalism of the Independence period and the journalism of the Estonian Diaspora, were included in the 'history of Estonian journalism' course. Methods of sociological research were also introduced to students when they wrote their research papers. This, of course, was not reflected in the curricula and syllabi, written in Russian, for those who kept their eye on the Department.

A small section of the All-Soviet curriculum was allowed to be fulfilled with local content. This enabled teaching the history of Estonian journalism and Estonian literature, literary and theatre criticism, environmental issues etc. that were all taught in a national context, without following official dogmas and interpretations.

The Code of Ethics adopted by the students of journalism in 1980 was a superb piece of camouflage. This was outwardly very dangerous for its position was contradictory to the Communist Party's view of the duties of a Soviet journalist – the 'daily concern about the strengthening of ideological influence over the masses' (Tepljuk 1989: 122). The Code stressed the common human values and stated, for example, that journalists should not work for the authorities but for the Estonian people; that they should defend transparency and truth, and not propagate values that they personally do not accept; and they should respect another's right for personal opinion as much as their own. Every student who signed the code, made a promise to follow it in their journalistic work.

A copy of the Code soon reached the KGB. However, in stressing human and professional values and taking a non-confrontational tone – the loyalty of students and teachers did not become an issue. Instead, the wording of the Code was condemned, as it did not use the compulsory ideological vocabulary of the Communist Party. The Code of Ethics remained unchanged from 1980–1997. It also remained the only Code of Conduct for Estonian journalists until 1997, when a new Code was adopted.

Naturally the pressure of working in such a strict ideological environment forced journalists to regularly make compromises in balancing their convictions with expressions of loyalty to the 'paymaster'. Those who had graduated from Tartu University had benefited from the atmosphere of a small, tightly knit, academic community where they had been taught to appreciate national and cultural values, a code of ethics, and ideas of serving their nation. Few became true collaborators. A survey among Estonian journalists in 1988 indicated that the most highly appreciated professional values of the Soviet time were integrity, devotion to serving their readers and a creative attitude towards their work.

A new beginning for journalism education

The mass media played a significant role in demolishing the Communist regimes in East and Central Europe and in the reconstruction of democracy and the free market economy. In the process of restructuring the media systems, these countries experienced a short period of a huge expansion of the press that brought thousands of inexperienced newcomers to journalism jobs. In Estonia, 51 per cent of journalists started their careers between 1990 and 1995 and most of them did not have any journalism training whatsoever (Lauk 1996).

New forms of journalism and mass media emerged, which did not always meet the needs of democratic publicity, but did meet consumer and business expectations. 'Much was done simply to make a profit in a new marketplace, regardless of ethical concerns, and sensationalizing media content was often the easiest way to make money' (Hiebert 1999: 81). The newcomers had only a vague idea about the principles of good journalistic practice, about the media's role in developing democracy and civic society and their own professional responsibilities.

Journalists and journalism educators in Estonia faced the same difficulties as the other post-Communist societies in re-defining the role of journalists and journalism in the new circumstances. Re-conceptualizing journalism education was a part of the challenges of the rapidly changing times. A number of practical problems also needed to be solved: lack of textbooks and manuals, lack of appropriate technical equipment and facilities and computers, lack of competent teachers and researchers, scarcity of resources etc.

The immediate bonus of independence in the transition period was that new avenues and opportunities to learn opened up for both the teachers and the students. Contacts with universities abroad were quickly established. This aided the rapid re-orientation of the curricula and the upgrading of the content. Already at the dawn of independence, in the summer of 1990, the first cooperation agreement between the journalism Department of Tartu University and the Department of Journalism and Mass Communication of the University of Tampere, Finland, was launched. Soon after the first visit of a delegation from Tampere, the journalism Department in Tartu received several shipments of books from Finland. These initiated the foundation of the library that today has over 5000 titles and 132 journals, and is the best and the largest library of media and communication literature in Estonia.

A major change in the Department occurred in 1992. Up to that point journalism was taught within the Faculty of Humanities. The Department has since become part of the Faculty of Social Sciences. This change was a reflection of the movement in the perspective of the whole profession, where the spirit of resistance was no longer necessary as journalists adapted to the key elements of the free market economy – mutually beneficial alliances with sources of revenue.

The curriculum had started to change as early as 1989, when the proportion of practical training and internships was dramatically increased. This was basically an immediate response to the high demand of the time for journalists and reporters caused by the rapid diversification and expansion of the Estonian media. So great was the demand that many students left the Department after just one or two years of studies to go into well paid work in the press, television and commercial radio. Within a few years, however, it became obvious that the potential of academic education was not so much in providing students with good practical skills, but in developing their analytical skills and expanding their knowledge of media and society and their interaction.

In 1990, just prior to Estonian independence, a major curriculum reform occurred at the University of Tartu – the requirement to follow official Soviet curricula was abolished. A new structure of studies was introduced that included a 4-year Bachelor's programme of 240 study units of the European Credit Transfer System (ECTS), a 2-year Master's programme (120 ECTS) and a 4-year Doctoral programme (240 ECTS). Postgraduate study programmes in Journalism, as well as in Mass Communication, were established in 1992. Since 1996, the Department also started teaching Public Relations (PR) at the Bachelor's level. PR is taught in the contexts of organizational and marketing communication, political communication and knowledge management. Master's and Doctoral programmes in Media and Communication were established in the year 2000. As the number and scope of the programmes taught in the Department had become much broader than just journalism, the name of the Department was changed to the Department of Journalism and Communication in 2000.

Study programmes in journalism[1]

The curriculum of journalism was essentially restructured and revised again in 2001, when the University of Tartu introduced the principles of the Bologna Process (3-year Bachelor's, 2-year Master's and 4-year Doctoral programmes). As a result, in the autumn of 2002, students were for the first time admitted to the Journalism and Public Relations programme at the BA level. By the autumn of 2005, admission was opened to three Master's level programmes: Journalism, Media and Communication, and Communication Management. The BA programme aims at giving a basic education in journalism and communication, elementary knowledge and skills for doing research in journalism and communication, and skills for working as a reporter or public relations officer. The first year studies, therefore, mostly contain general introductory courses in social sciences. In the second year students can choose specialization courses on public relations or journalism or a combination of both, and in the third year, more specific courses in journalism, communication and public relations. It is possible to graduate from the BA programme either by writing and defending a thesis (demonstrating the ability of using theoretical and methodological knowledge obtained during the studies by solving a specific empirical or practical problem) or passing a BA exam.

The 2-year Master's programme in journalism qualifies students to work as an editor in the press or electronic media. It is also possible to join the Master's programme after the successful conclusion of Bachelor's studies in some other discipline, so long as certain subjects from the journalism curriculum have been taken as optional courses. The Master's level programme provides students with the theoretical knowledge necessary for critical assessment and understanding the developments of the media and society. The students also obtain the knowledge and skills for independently solving the problems related to information analysis, text production and teamwork. The initial supervisory experience allows them to critically reflect both their own and others' professional performance. The programme offers intensive teaching and training of various methods of research and journalistic practice and prepares the students for work as editors in the press, broadcasting or online media. The experience of academic research allows continuation of studies at Ph.D. level. Optional courses in Media Literacy give the students an option to work as a media teacher in primary or secondary schools.

During the Master's studies, the students spend 14 weeks (in two periods) in media organizations completing various tasks. During their internships, the students have a mentor in the news organization and also have close contact with a supervising teacher. Graduation from the MA programme is possible either by submitting a research thesis or passing an exam. A Master's thesis in journalism is an original piece of research, which contains an overview of respective literature, a methodological and theoretical chapter, description of empirical data and data analysis, and results of the research. The thesis must contain elements of problem setting and solution, and offer new aspects for understanding the object of the study.

Table 1: The number of students at the Institute of Journalism and Communication 2002–2007.

	2002	2003	2004	2005	2006	2007
All BA and MA programmes	262	304	345	374	401	422
(number of graduates)	n.a.	n.a.	(36)	(91)	(80)	(101)
Doctoral programmes	13	17	24	28	29	36
Total	275	321	369	401	430	458

The Doctoral programme of the Institute of Journalism and Communication[2] is in Media and Communication, but theses can also be written on journalism issues. Doctoral students are involved in the research projects of the Institute and they must also publish their results in international journals.

In general, instruction in the Institute of Journalism and Communication is in Estonian, but the Institute also provides teaching in English in the format of a non-degree programme for international students (24 ECTS).

The study programmes of the Institute of Journalism and Communication successfully passed international accreditation in the spring of 2008.[3]

Research

A specific difference between university education and vocational education is that the former is supported by research and based on research results. Therefore, all university teachers – and also the students – are involved in research.

During the Soviet time, all research into mass communication and journalism was limited and strictly controlled. As a result, so many taboos and sensitive issues existed that the publication of sociological research data was next to impossible. Deliverance from ideological supervision enabled the Institute to enlarge and diversify both the scope and the methods of research and to join the international academic community.

Since Estonia's independence, research into Estonian journalism has developed from historical descriptions to analyses and comparisons; and includes issues such as development of journalism as a profession, sociology of news, various text and document analyses, discourses of censorship, changes in journalistic culture, journalism ethics, media policy, media literacy etc.

The first comparative historical-sociological study (in English) about the development of the media in all three Baltic countries (*Towards a Civic Society: The Baltic Media's Long Road to Freedom* by Høyer, S. Lauk, E. and Vihalemm, P.) was published as early as 1993, as a result of the joint efforts of journalism and media researchers from Vilnius, Tartu, Riga and Oslo.

The focus of the sociological media research shifted from limited audience studies and content analysis of newspapers and radio broadcasts to issues of societal and political

Table 2: The number and qualifications of employees in the Institute of Journalism and Communication in 2008.

	Staff	Doctoral degree	Master's degree
Professors	3	3	
Senior lecturers	4	4	
Lecturers	3	1	2
Researchers	8	3	6
Assistants	6		6
Total	24	11	13

transition and the media in the 1990s. Changing values and identities, political culture and political communication, issues of the integration of non-Estonians, development of social space etc. are some of the current fields of research (see more: Vihalemm 2001). From 2000 onwards, the new media and development of the 'information society' in Estonia has become increasingly relevant.

A young, well-educated and qualified generation of researchers is developing (see Table 2). Prior to 1997, there was just one academic in Journalism holding a Doctoral degree and two holding a Candidate degree of the Soviet period (which was later deemed to be on a par with a Ph.D.). Between 1997 and 2008, nine Doctoral degrees have been obtained by young scholars of whom one defended in Norway and three in Finland.

International contacts

The Institute of Journalism joined the European Community higher education programme ERASMUS in the academic year 1999/2000 and is collaborating today with universities and colleges in twelve countries (with twenty bilateral agreements for students and teaching staff exchange in the academic year 2007/2008). In the framework of the ERASMUS programme, the longest and closest cooperation partners have been the Danish School of Media and Journalism in Århus, the University of Oslo, the Swedish School of Social Sciences of the University of Helsinki, the University of Jyväskylä, the University of Tampere and Hanze University Gröningen. During the years 2005–2007, twenty three students have had the opportunity to study in partner universities and twenty six foreign students have been studying in the Institute of Journalism.

The Institute is also a member of the European Journalism Training Association (since 1995). The research and teaching staff of the Institute is also an institutional member of the International Association of Media and Communication Research (IAMCR). The institutional membership in international professional organizations includes the European Public Relations Education and Research Association (EUPRERA), the International

Communication Association (ICA), the European Communication Research and Education Association (ECREA) and the Baltic Association for Media Research (BAMR).

The Institute has organized four European Media and Communication Doctoral Summer schools in Tartu during 2005–08. The first summer school was mainly organized using the resources of the Institute, but the second received funding from the European Commission with the project named 'Intensive Programme in Media and Communication – enlarging Europe, enlarging communication'. In 2007, the summer school project successfully applied for three continuous years of funding and for the period of 2007–09 the project is called European Media and Communication Doctoral Summer School. The 2007 application included eighteen partner universities.

The objectives of the Summer School for 2007–09 include: (1) to provide an intercultural and multilateral dialogue between academics of new and old EU member states, focusing on an enlarged Europe, its democracies, its people, its ethnicities and the role of media and journalism; (2) to provide mutual support for Doctoral studies in Media and Communication in the expanding network of the partner universities, supported by ECREA; (3) to further expand the collaboration to those universities not yet members of the network; (4) to create a respectful but critical dialogue between academic researchers, governments, civil society and media industries (Self-Evaluation Report 2007: 65).

Other journalism and communication programmes in Estonia

In addition to Tartu's journalism programmes, some alternative curricula have existed in journalism, media and communication studies in Estonia since 1995. During 1995–1998, advertising and media, film and video production courses were taught in Tallinn Pedagogical University, and media and public relations at Concordia International University Estonia (CIUE, a private institution). In recent years, these curricula have been united under the auspices of Tallinn University, CIUE no longer exists and Tallinn Pedagogical University has been reorganized into Tallinn University. Tallinn University's Baltic Film and Media School (BFM) offers programmes in English in television and cinema production, audio-visual media and PR at Bachelor's level (three years); Communication management and the Art of Film and Video at Master's level (two years). The Film Department also teaches film-making in Estonian both at BA and MA level. BFM is orientated to teaching practical skills and artistic vision and preparing high quality specialists in the media production field. Therefore, there is no emphasis on academic research. Due to some problems in the curriculum design, the curricula of BFM were conditionally accredited in 2008 for three years.

Since 2007/2008, Tallinn University has taught a journalism programme in Russian (Institute of Slavonic Languages and Cultures) at BA level. The aim of this programme is to provide students with basic skills and knowledge necessary for starting a career in journalism and prepare for continuing studies in the field of media. The emphasis is on

Russian culture and journalism. At the Master's level, Tallinn University offers a programme for editors-translators. The purpose of this programme is to educate bilingual professionals able to work as translators and editors both in Estonian and Russian language media. The Institute of Estonian Language and Culture of the University of Tallinn also offers a Master's programme for Estonian language editors, trained in editing specific texts of various fields of life (e.g., law, public administration), including the media. This programme does not contain journalistic subjects, such as for example, news writing.

Tallinn University also teaches Communication, Information science and information management, but these programmes are not related to journalism.

Academy Nord, a private institution in Tallinn, offers a Marketing and Advertising programme in Estonian and Russian at BA level and a Psychology, Marketing and Communication programme at MA level.

The Estonian Journalists Union and Estonian Newspaper Association do not provide regular teaching, but arrange occasional workshops, seminars and courses for journalists.

Concluding Remarks

Within the last 50 years, journalism education and research in Estonia have expanded from a single specialist course into a wide and varied curriculum that, while maintaining its roots deep in the national culture and conscience, has successfully reached across international borders into other languages and cultures.

The development of journalism education and research in Estonia could be, in retrospect, characterized by three distinct periods facing remarkably different challenges – the Soviet period 1954–1990, the post-Soviet Transition 1990–1998 and EU Accession and Membership period 1999–2009.

The key challenges of journalism education and research during the Soviet period and the post-Soviet Transition period were largely 'inwards' – Juhan Peegel and his colleagues' creation of Journalism courses that reflected Estonian values and Estonian resistance to Communist ideology, and latterly an attempt to rein in the lack of societal responsibility and professional ethics displayed by the media during the rapid transition from a command economy to free-market economics. A further challenge during the Transition period was posed by the Government's 'internetization' programmes by which Estonia would not play catch up with Western Europe in the use of Internet, but would put in place an innovative Wi-Fi technology enabling the entire population to have Internet access by the end of the first decade of the twenty-first century. Digitalization and the Internet era have, in a short period of time, brought about substantial changes in the nature of journalistic work, but also in its values and standards. It is fair to say that Estonia is an 'Internet society', and it is also developing rapidly as an 'information society'. A great deal of teaching already happens in a 'virtual environment' and the Web has become an element of both the study and research environment. The study programmes should be able to prepare journalists to meet the demands of the rapid development of communication and information technologies in the best way. The educators, therefore, face a task of updating and revising curricula and teaching methods, that makes Curriculum Development a vital component of journalism education today. As a relatively new field, Media Literacy has also become an increasingly important sphere of teaching and research at the Institute of Journalism and Communication.

Two other phrases are relevant to the three periods – proactive and reactive. Journalism education and research during the Soviet period was proactive. During the Transition period, the pace of change within the media industry was rapid and chaotic and far quicker than any changes in the teaching and research of media and mass communications. During the EU period, Journalism education and research remains reactive in order to provide young journalists with high quality education and training to be able to meet the challenges of their working environment within globalizing and commercializing media industry. Journalists' professional choices and decisions depend increasingly on the interests of their employers, and this is reflected in the growing degree of self-censorship. An important aspect in academic journalism education is and will remain the adoption of professional consciousness, values and standards by the students.

The key challenge in the EU Accession and Membership period may be described as 'outward' looking in the need to meet international requirements not only at the educational level ('Bologna system') but also research levels which increasingly require membership of, and compliance with, international organizations and projects.

The 'division of labour' among Estonian higher education institutions that provide journalism, media and communication programmes will most probably change in future. Since the late 1990s, the university city of Tartu has had no mainstream media outlets. The majority of the media (and consequently, the jobs for media specialists and journalists) are concentrated in the capital of Tallinn. Tallinn University has a good potential to broaden the scope of journalism programmes and focus on practical training, while the Institute of Journalism and Communication at Tartu University will continue to be a centre of high quality research and journalism pedagogy.

Acknowledgement

Research for this article has been supported by a research grant No 7547 'Changing Journalism Cultures: A Comparative Perspective' by Estonian Science Foundation.

The Author

Epp Lauk, Professor in Journalism, Department of Communication, University of Jyväskylä, Finland.

Notes

1. Description of the study programmes of the Institute of Journalism and Communication is based on *Self-Evaluation Report 2007*.
2. In September 2007, in connection with the University structure reform, the Department was named the Institute of Journalism and Communication.
3. See more about the study programmes and requirements at: http: //mail.jrnl.ut.ee/webpage/18. Accessed 5 March 2009.

References

Gross, P. (1999), 'Before, during and after: Journalism education', In J. Aumente; P. Gross; R. Hiebert; O.V. Johnson and D. Mills (eds), *Eastern European journalism: before, during and after Communism*, Cresskill, NJ: Hampton Press, Inc., pp. 147–184.

Hiebert, R. (1999), 'Transition: from the end of the old regime to 1996', in J. Aumente; P. Gross; R. Hiebert; O.V. Johnson and D. Mills (eds), *Eastern European journalism: before, during and after Communism*, Cresskill, NJ: Hampton Press, Inc., pp. 79–123.

Høyer, S.; Lauk, E. and Vihalemm, P. (eds) (1993), *Towards a civic society. The Baltic media's long road to freedom. Perspectives on history, ethnicity and journalism*, Tartu: Baltic Association for Media Research/Nota Baltica Ltd.

Johnson, O.V. (1999), 'The roots of journalism in Central and Eastern Europe', in J. Aumente; P. Gross; R. Hiebert; O.V. Johnson and D. Mills (eds), *Eastern European journalism: before, during and after Communism*, Cresskill, NJ: Hampton Press, Inc., pp. 5–40.

Lauk, E. (1993), 'Journalism in the Republic of Estonia during the 1920s and 1930s', In Høyer, S.; Lauk, E. and Vihalemm, P. (eds) (1993), *Towards a civic society. The Baltic media's long road to freedom. Perspectives on history, ethnicity and journalism*, Tartu: Baltic Association for Media Research/Nota Baltica Ltd. pp. 119–141.

Lauk, E. (1996), 'Estonian journalists in search of new professional identity', *Javnost/The Public*, 3(4), pp. 93–106.

Lauk, E. (1999), 'Practice of Soviet censorship in the press. The case of Estonia', *Nordicom Information*, 21 (3), pp. 27–39.

Misiunas, J. and Taagepera, R. (eds) (1993), *The Baltic States: years of dependence 1940–1990*, Berkeley, Los Angeles: University of California Press.

O'Konnor, K. (2003), *The history of the Baltic states*, Westport (Conn.), London: Greenwood Press.

Self-Evaluation Report (2007), *Self-Evaluation Report of the Accreditation of Curricula,* The University of Tartu, Institute of Journalism and Communication, Tartu: Manuscript.

Tepljuk, V. M. (1989), 'The Soviet Union: Professional responsibility in mass media', In T.W. Cooper (general ed.) with C. G. Christians; F.F. Plude and R. A. White, *Communication ethics and global change*, New York: Longman, pp. 109–123.

Vihalemm, P. (2001), 'Development of media research in Estonia', *Nordicom Review*, 2, pp. 79–85.

References

The F.Y.R.O. Macedonia Journalism Education Landscape

Dona Kolar-Panov and Jana Ivanovska

Introduction

The beginnings of journalism education in Macedonia can be traced back to 1977 when at the Ss. Cyril and Methodius University, Skopje, an interdisciplinary journalism study programme, hosted by the Faculty of Law, the Faculty of Economics and the Faculty of Philology, was established. Until then Macedonian journalists were mainly educated at the universities in Ljubljana, Slovenia, and in Belgrade, Serbia (both in the former Socialist Republic of Yugoslavia) at their Faculties of Political Sciences. In 1988 Journalism Studies were upgraded to a separate major at the Faculty of Law at the Ss. Cyril and Methodius University.

In the early 1990's, after the Macedonian independence from former Yugoslavia and the start of democratization of the country, the international donors were only interested in the democratization of the media in Macedonia and channelled funds into helping the development of independent media (Kolar-Panov 1999). However, with the introduction of over 200 print and electronic media outlets and the noticeable poor quality of journalism practiced by them, the focus has shifted towards reform in journalism education (Sopar 2001: 2). At first, international organizations like IREX Pro Media, OSCE, Press Now and others organized short training courses for the practising journalists (OSCE 2002, 2003a, 2003b, 2006). Later, as result of an increased pressure from the international community, and due to the Macedonian aspirations for European integration, the first reforms in higher education were introduced, including reforms in journalism education. As the state university Ss. Cyril and Methodius University offered studies in Journalism and Communication only in the Macedonian language in a country with a multi-ethnic and multilingual population, where 25.1 per cent of the population speaks Albanian (Republic of Macedonia, State Statistical Office, 2002),[1] one of the priorities was to establish journalism studies in the Albanian language. When the first (private) Albanian-speaking University in Macedonia, the South East European University (SEEU) in Tetovo, was established in 2001, its Faculty for Communication Sciences and Technologies offered a Bachelor's degree in Communication Sciences, which included studies in journalism, communication and media. The same study programme was offered until the academic year 2007/2008, when SEEU restructured the Faculty for Communication Sciences and Technologies into the Faculty of Languages, Cultures and Communications, and currently offers a three-year Bachelor's degree in Communication Sciences, and also offers second-cycle studies, leading to an MA degree in Communications.

The only vocational (non-academic) training for journalists was offered for four years, from 2003 to 2008, by the Macedonian Institute for Media (MIM), in the form of a One Year Diploma Programme in Journalism. In 2008 MIM founded the School for Journalism and Public Relations which is offering two study programmes – for journalism, and for public relations and corporate communications.

There are three other private universities offering studies in journalism and communication: European University and New York University Skopje, both in Skopje, and the FON University in Skopje and Struga. However, the European University transformed its Faculty of Communication and Media into Faculty of Political Sciences in 2007, and the first and the only generation of graduates with BA in Communication and Media will graduate this year (2009).

Two other universities announced studies in journalism, communication, and public relations: the state Tetovo University in Tetovo, and the private University for Tourism and Management in Skopje. Their study programmes are not yet available.

Historical and socio-cultural context

Macedonia is a small landlocked country in the south of the Balkan Peninsula and is one of the seven newly formed states (including Kosovo) that were established after the disintegration of the Socialist Federal Republic of Yugoslavia. Macedonia gained its independence peacefully from Yugoslavia in 1991.

The unfavourable historical conditions caused by the domination of foreign powers in the last ten centuries – the Byzantine, Bulgarian, Serbian and the Ottoman Empire – influenced the development of Macedonian language and culture as it was repeatedly disputed, banned and persecuted by the regimes in power. Following the establishment of the Macedonian state inside the Yugoslav Federation in 1944, Macedonian language was finally encoded, and the first newspaper in literary Macedonian language, *Nova Makedonija*, was published on 29 October 1994. It is important to mention here, that in recognition of the multicultural composition of the Macedonian society, newspapers in Turkish and Albanian languages were published soon after the publication of *Nova Makedonija* (*Birlik* in Turkish in 1944 and *Flaka* in Albanian in 1945). However, journalism education did not follow that trend and the majority of journalists from Macedonia were educated in Serbo-Croatian at the large university centres in Yugoslavia until 1977, when the first interdisciplinary study programme in Macedonian language was established as 'Interdisciplinary Studies in Journalism' at the Ss. Cyril and Methodius University in Skopje. Albanian language programmes in journalism and communications were introduced much later, in 2001, by the South East European University (SEEU) which, as mentioned above, is the first accredited university in Macedonia to offer higher education in Albanian language.

At the time of its independence in September 1991, Macedonia was the least developed of the former Yugoslav republics and remains the second poorest country in Europe. The growth of the Macedonian economy has been low since democratization, the foreign direct investments are incidental, and the standard of living is falling. As good education and qualified human resources are considered to be the key for progress today, this is an area where Macedonia seriously lags behind. For example, in 2006 as much as 53% the population over 15 years of age in Macedonia had only elementary education, incomplete elementary education or no education at all, and 37% had high-school education. Only 10% have completed higher education, 0.2% have completed MA studies, and only 0.1% have completed a Ph.D.. Furthermore, Macedonian students do not graduate on time, and until recently over 80% graduated after the designated deadline (Center for Research and Policy Making 2006: 5–6).

The transition from socialism to capitalism brought political and economic instability to Macedonia, which has impacted the development of the country on all levels. The emerging social stratification, similar to that which has arisen in the other post-communist countries, has not allowed fair distribution of the state wealth, and the shaky political pluralism does not reflect social division in the society. There is a widespread corruption which also includes education institutions, the media sector and the journalists (Bosnjakovski 2005: 9).

When Macedonia was granted the status of candidate country for membership in the EU by the European Commission in 2005 (Government of the Republic of Macedonia, Secretariat for European Affairs, 2005a), an emphasis was put on the need for the harmonization of Macedonian laws and policies with the EU ones. Reforms in education are one of the priority areas, and among others they call for improvement in media professionalism and further development and reforms in journalism education (Government of the Republic of Macedonia, Secretariat for European Affairs, 2005b).

The overall economic and socio-cultural conditions in the country are reflected by an eclectic and overcrowded media market with a large number of media outlets, both print and electronic (there are over 200 media organizations in Macedonia and their number changes on a daily basis). The existence of the large number of media, instead of resulting in competition for journalistic excellence, has led to the employment of often untrained and unqualified journalists, thus pushing the already poor journalistic standards to an even lower level.

There is also a degree of unpredictability to the changes in journalism education landscape in Macedonia which only mirrors the instability and unsettledness of the country's education system as a whole (see Center for Research and Policy Making 2006). Because of that, the description of the higher education institutions offering courses in journalism and/or communication and media that is presented below should be treated only as snapshot frozen in time – in April 2009.

State University: Ss. Cyril and Methodius University, Skopje

Faculty of Law 'Iustinianus Primus'

The Journalism study programme at the Faculty of Law 'Iustinianus Primus' at Ss. Cyril and Methodius University, Skopje was established in 1977. It started as an interdisciplinary study programme (Interdisciplinary Studies in Journalism) hosted by the Faculty of Law, the Faculty of Economics and the Faculty of Philology. In 1988, Journalism Studies became, and still is a separate major at the Faculty of Law, together with the majors in Law and Political Science. Since the establishment of the degree in journalism at the state university, more than 2500 students have enrolled, more than 900 have graduated, and 800 are still considered active students. On average, 30 students enrol at the Journalism programme each year at the Faculty, which is located in the urban area in the capital city of Skopje.

From 1988 until 2004, the Faculty of Law offered a four-year Bachelor's degree in Journalism. The courses offered were mandatory and were derived from the studies in law and political science, together with a number of courses from the Faculty of Philosophy. Students were taught approximately two journalism/communication courses in each academic year, however, there was no requirement for practice or internships.

Under increased pressure from the international community and with the help of international organizations, the first steps were taken towards reform of journalism education in the Republic of Macedonia in 2001. The Department of Journalism at the Faculty of Law, through cooperation with the Dutch organization Press Now and financial support from the OSCE, organized the first Summer School in Journalism. The Summer School was held for four years and was attended by young journalists and journalism students, including communication students from SEE University. In 2004, the Summer School was renamed and reorganized into a Journalism Laboratory, with the aim to fulfil the practical gap that existed in regular studies, and at the same time offer the students a possibility to gain credit towards their degree.

In the academic year 2005/2006, the Faculty of Law began to offer a reformed curriculum in journalism studies, based on the Bologna Declaration Principles and applying the European Credit Transfer System (ECTS). The new study programme was accredited by the Ministry of Education's National Accreditation Board. Students could now obtain a three-year Bachelor degree in Journalism, followed by a two-year Master's degree. The study programme of these two years enables the student to choose a specialization either in Journalism or in Media and Communications.

After completing the third year of studies, each student needs to complete a mandatory month-long internship at a media outlet. Practical courses, as well as a dissertation are planned for the last semester of the Master studies. The specialization in Media and Communication offers courses in advertising and marketing, as well as in political and business communication.

The Journalism Department at the Faculty of Law is also the only institution in Macedonia offering a doctoral degree in journalism. The doctoral studies consist of a six semesters of course work, after which a doctoral dissertation is prepared and defended. After successfully defending the dissertation students are awarded the degree of Doctor of Journalism and Communicology.

However, there are problems with the new curriculum which is supposed to be taught according to Bologna Principles and the ECTS, and one of the problems is that these rules are not always followed in the actual teaching process. The studies are poorly organized, not enough attention is paid to the students, and there are too many students for the teaching space available. In addition, the majority of the courses offered by the Journalism Programme are taught by lecturers from other faculties, who have no or very little background needed for the specialized courses that are offered by the new curriculum. The teaching staff includes fourteen professors from the Faculty of Law, five professors from the Faculty of Philosophy, three professors from the Faculty of Philology, seven junior teaching assistants and four part-time lecturers invited to teach specialized courses.

Institute for Sociological, Political and Juridical Research

The Institute for Sociological, Political and Juridical Research is a part of Ss. Cyril and Methodius University and was the first academic institution in Macedonia to offer Postgraduate Studies in Communication at MA level starting in 1995. It is a two-year course, consisting of three semesters of coursework with the fourth semester reserved for preparation of the master's thesis. After successfully defending the thesis students are awarded an MA degree in Communications. The Studies are accredited by the Ministry of Education's National Accreditation Board and since 2005 the Institute participates in the Bologna Process and has adopted European Credit Transfer System.

The Institute, being a research institution, has an advantage of actively including students into research projects and training them as future researchers in the fields of communication and media and culture. However, the Institute enrols only a small number of students each academic year (between twenty and thirty) and has a high dropout rate. The study programme offers a high level of specialization by offering a large choice of elective courses, however, it is theoretically based and does not offer practical courses and internships. The courses offered consist of core courses in communication and media theory and social research methods, while the list of electives consists of a range of specialized courses in communication, media and culture, television studies, political communication, public relations, advertising and new media.

Most of the teaching staff is engaged on a part-time basis and mainly comes from the faculties and other institutes of Ss. Cyril and Methodius University. Foreign visiting lecturers teach specialized elective courses when there are no experts available in Macedonia. The Institute has no official affiliations to the industry, however the graduates are highly regarded by the labour market in Macedonia, and the majority of graduates hold senior communication and media-related positions in local and international organizations, while a smaller number are employed as members of junior teaching staff at universities (both state and private) in Macedonia.

Private universities

South East European University (SEEU)

The South East European University (SEEU) was established in 2001 as a private-public not-for-profit higher education institution, and is located in the town of Tetovo. It was the first accredited university in Macedonia to offer higher education in Albanian language, and now also offers courses in Macedonian and English language. The SEEU faculties are accredited by the Ministry of Education's National Accreditation Board and have adopted the ECTS according to the Bologna Declaration Principles.

Concluding with the academic year 2007/2008, SEEU's Faculty for Communication Sciences and Technologies offered a Bachelor's degree in Communication Sciences which included Studies in Journalism, Communication and Media. The Faculty also offered a three-semester Master's degree in Communication, with two areas of concentration: Corporate Communication and Media Strategy.

The 2008/2009 academic year saw the introduction of the Faculty of Languages, Cultures and Communications. The newly formed Faculty now offers a three-year Bachelor's degree in Communication Sciences, including interdisciplinary courses from the areas of journalism, media, public relations, organizational communication and marketing. The Faculty also offers second-cycle studies in three streams: Media Studies, Public Relations and Marketing Communication, as well as Corporate Communications, all leading to an MA degree in Communications.

The majority of the teaching staff comes from the ranks of SEEU lecturers, at the Ph.D. and MA levels. In addition, there are a number of part-time lecturers and visiting professors from the affiliated organizations, institutions and universities from Albania, France, Kosovo, The Netherlands, Denmark, United States, etc.

New York University Skopje (NYUS)

New York University Skopje (NYUS) has received its accreditation as a private higher education institution from the National Accreditation Board in 2006. It offers courses in English and Macedonian language, based on a combination of European and American study programmes. NYUS conducts its study programmes according to the Bologna Principles and has adopted the ECTS. In addition, the NYUS study programmes are also compatible with the American Credit Transfer System (ACTS), which allows for easier student mobility.

The Faculty of Communication and Media Studies at NYUS offers a three-year Bachelor of Arts degree in Communication and Media. The first year of studies is dedicated to general education courses and to introductory courses in communications and media, while the second and the third year include a combination of communication, new media, journalism and public relations mandatory and elective courses.

After completing the Bachelor degree, students can enrol at the two-year Master of Arts degree in Communication Studies, Public Relations or Communication and New Media. Each student needs to complete an internship at a relevant professional organization as a core course at the second year of the postgraduate studies.

Teaching staff at the Faculty of Communication and Media Studies at NYUS include internationally-educated junior and senior academic staff, as well as visiting lecturers invited on the basis of their professional expertise in the relevant area.

FON University

The FON University was initially established in 2003 as the first private higher education institution in Macedonia, under the name Faculty of Social Studies (Факултет за општествени науки- ФОН -FON). The University was accredited by the National Accreditation Board at the Ministry of Education as FON University in 2007, and implements the principles of the Bologna Declaration and the European Credit Transfer System.

FON University offers a three-year Bachelor's degree in Journalism and Public Communication as one of the programmes at the Faculty of Political Sciences. It also offers relevant courses on postgraduate level, and after completing the fourth year of studies, students obtain a Specialist degree in Political Science, stream in Journalism and Public Communication. After completing the fifth year, students are awarded a Master's degree in Political Science, with a major in Journalism and Public Communication.

The three years of the undergraduate studies mostly include courses in the political science, with only the basic introductory journalism and communication modules. The fourth and the fifth year offer more specialized courses in journalism, as well as public relations, marketing and international communication courses. There are no practical courses or mandatory internship at any study levels.

The instructors at Faculty of Political Sciences teaching the courses in Journalism and Public Communication predominantly come from the ranks of FON lecturers, at Ph.D. and MA level, and often do not have a background in journalism and/or communications. The study and training facilities of FON University are located in the urban area of both Skopje, the capital of Macedonia, and Struga, a town in the southern part of the country. FON University offers courses in Macedonian and Albanian language.

The School for Journalism and Public Relations

The School for Journalism and Public Relations is a higher education institution accredited by the Ministry of Education's National Accreditation Board in 2008. It was founded by Macedonian Institute for Media (MIM) which until 2008 offered the One Year Diploma Program in Journalism. This programme was offered from 2003 to 2008 and has provided professional practical training in journalistic skills for those who had already graduated in either journalism or other social science disciplines. Out of 96 enrolled students (24 per year), 93 students graduated (41 male and 52 female).

MIM also organized a six-month journalism training programme for Roma journalists from 2005 to 2008. The programme was funded by the Open Society Institute, Budapest, and the Balkan Trust for Democracy. In three years, a total of 36 students graduated, out of which 12 were female and 24 were male.

The newly established School for Journalism and Public Relations programme offers a three-year undergraduate degree and a one-year postgraduate specialist degree. Students obtain a diploma in either Journalism or in Corporate Communications and Public Relations in three years, and a postgraduate specialist degree after completing the fourth year, in either Journalism or in Corporate Communications and Public Relations. The study programmes are based on the Bologna Principles and apply the European Credit Transfer System.

Fifty students are enrolled within the first academic year – 23 studying journalism and 27 Corporate Communications and Public Relations – 25 are female and 25 are male. Lecturers at the School include local academic staff from the fields of journalism, communications and the other relevant academic disciplines. Students are also taught by visiting professors from the two partner universities – the Danish School of Media and Journalism and the Windesheim University of Applied Sciences in Netherlands, as well as by experienced journalists and public relations experts and practitioners from Macedonia and abroad.

The School is currently developing new MA programmes in partnership with other high education institution in Europe and in the region, and is planning on organizing summer schools for journalism and PR, distance-learning courses and other professional training sessions for media and PR professionals.

The School's parent organization, MIM, is a non-governmental and non-profit organization established in 2001 to support the progress of the Macedonian media sector towards professionalism through specialized forms of training and further education of journalists and media professionals. MIM is part of the Network for Professionalization of the Media from South Eastern Europe (SEENPM), the Organization of Media in South Eastern Europe (SEEMO), as well as of the Reporting Diversity Network (RDN).

Concluding Remarks

There are five higher education institutions (four universities and one high professional school) in Macedonia that currently offer education in journalism, communications and public relations. They are all accredited by the Ministry of Education and Science's National Accreditation Board, and all have introduced the European Credit Transfer System.

However, the majority of institutions have a number of weaknesses which include: too broad and eclectic study programmes, lack of specialization in specific areas, lack of practical courses, lack of appropriate teaching staff, lack of teaching equipment, etc. The main weakness of the curricula is lack of teaching staff with journalistic experience and a lack of practical courses and internships on undergraduate level. There are also very weak links to media organizations and to the labour market, as well as a lack of insight into the competencies sought by the national labour market. The autocratic leadership styles and 'ex cathedra' teaching, unwieldy and inefficient administration and a labyrinth of bureaucratic procedures are specific to the state Ss. Cyril and Methodius University, while too much influence from the owners and their desire to make a profit at any cost, even at the expense of the quality of studies, are typical for private universities.

The newly established School of Journalism and Public Relations (by the Macedonian Institute of Media) is introducing the more vocationally-oriented journalism education, and promises to bring different standards into journalism education in Macedonia. Given their past achievements in journalism education and training (including the success of the One Year Diploma in Journalism), other higher education institutions involved in journalism education in Macedonia will have to take notice and introduce changes in their curricula in order to stay competitive. In addition to this, it seems that the continuation of the positive trends from the perspective of the European integration of the country, education reform will have to be continued and even accelerated in order to bring the education standards closer to Europe, which in turn will bring demands for further improvements in journalism education.

The Authors

Dr. Dona Kolar-Panov, Professor of Communication Studies and Dean of the Faculty of Communication and Media Studies at New York University Skopje.

Jana Ivanovska, MA, Teaching Assistant at the Faculty of Communication and Media Studies at New York University Skopje.

Note

1. Macedonia has the following ethnic structure: Macedonian 64.2%, Albanian 25.2%, Turkish 3.9%, Roma (Gypsy) 2.7%, Serb 1.8% and other 2.2%; and the following linguistic structure: Macedonian 66.5%, Albanian 25.1%, Turkish 3.5%, Roma 1.9%, Serbian 1.2% and other 1.8% (Republic of Macedonia, State Statistical Office, 2004).

References

Bosnjakovski, M. (2005), *Etika i novinarstvoto vo jugoistocna Evropa – Makedonija/Ethics and Journalism in Southeastern Europe – Macedonia*, Skopje: Makedonski Institut za Mediumi, http://mim.org.mk/mim/pages/common/database/comertials/etika.pdf. Accessed 28 April 2008.

Center for Research and Policy Making (2006), *Private or Public Education: Is There Fair Competition? Accreditation of Private Universities in Macedonia*, Skopje, September 2006, http://www.pasos.org/www-pasosmembers-org/publications/private-or-public-education-is-there-fair-competition-accreditation-of-private-universities-in-macedonia-in-english-and-macedonian. Accessed 27 April 2008.

FON University, http//www.fon.edu.mk. Accessed 4 September 2009.

Government of the Republic of Macedonia, Secretariat for European Affairs (2005a), 'Extract from the Presidency Conclusions of the Brussels European Council', in *Granting the Republic of Macedonia Status of an EU Candidate Country*, Brussels, 17 December, http://www.sei.gov.mk/Documents/eip/conclusions_en.pdf. Accessed 28 April 2008.

Government of the Republic of Macedonia, Secretariat for European Affairs (2005b), 'Analytical Report for the Opinion on the application from the Republic of Macedonia for EU membership SEC (2005)', 1425COM (2005), 562 final, http://www.sei.gov.mk/documents/eip/ANALYTICAL_REPORT_COM_(2005)562.pdf. Accessed 28 April 2008.

Kolar-Panov, D. (1999), 'Broadcasting in Macedonia: Between the State and the Market', *Media Development*, London: World Association for Christian Communication, pp. 33–39.

New York University Skopje, http//www.nyus.edu.mk . Accessed 4 September 2009.

OSCE (2002), 'OSCE launches media management and marketing courses in Skopje', Press Release, 26 November, http://www.osce.org/item/7149.html. Accessed 31 May 2008.

OSCE (2003a), 'OSCE Skopje Mission trains journalists on computer assisted research', Press Release, 30 June, http://www.osce.org/item/7617.html. Accessed 31 May 2008.

OSCE (2003b), 'Journalist training on media freedom and responsible reporting starts in Skopje', Press Release, 12 September, http://www.osce.org/item/7756.html. Accessed 31 May 2008.

OSCE (2006), 'OSCE Mission in Skopje supports course to improve access to information', Press Release, 28 August, http://www.osce.org/item/20185.html. Accessed 31 May 2008.

Republic of Macedonia, State Statistical Office (2004), 'Census Data 2002', Skopje: State Statistical Office, http://www.stat.gov.mk/pdf/kniga_13.pdf. Accessed 28 April 2008.

School of Journalism and Public Relations, http//www.vs.edu.mk. Accessed 4 September 2009.

SEE University, http//www.seeu.edu.mk. Accessed 4 September 2009.

Sopar, V. (2001), 'Education of journalists in the Republic of Macedonia', *Media Online*, 7 December, http://www.mediaonline.ba/en/?ID=159. Accessed 20 April 2008.

Ss. Cyril and Methodius Unuversity, Skopje, htpp//www.ukim.edu.mk. Accessed 4 September 2009.

The Hungarian Journalism Education Landscape

Péter Bajomi-Lázár

Introduction

The political transformation in 1989–90 triggered the privatization of the newspaper and the broadcasting industries – and that of journalism education. Since then, communication and media schools mushroomed all over Hungary in both the public and the private sectors. The content of journalism education has undergone fundamental changes; students of journalism, once taught to be the 'soldiers of the party', are now trained to be the 'watchdogs of democracy'. Education today is based upon the Anglo-Saxon standards of neutrally objective, fair and impartial journalism, which, however, does not imply that active journalists too would always abide by the very same standards. There are some 66 institutions of education for future media professionals in Hungary, of which eighteen are hosted by universities and university colleges. Each year, over 2500 students are admitted to the communication and media departments of the various higher educational institutions. Communication and media education in Hungary today meets the Bologna Criteria. Institutions offering a BA degree provide students with practice-oriented education, while MA and Ph.D. level studies focus upon theory. While most of the audiences now use commercial broadcasters and the popular press to meet their needs rather than the public service media and the quality newspapers, many of the journalism schools continue to teach the theory and practice of quality journalism, and fail to provide students with practical knowledge applicable in a market marked with tabloid journalism.

General context

Hungary is a post-communist democracy that joined the North Atlantic Treaty Organization in 1997 and the European Union in 2004. Since the early 1990s, the economy has been largely privatized, and multinational, mostly Western European, investors have purchased the major industries and services, albeit some key areas – such as public transportation and the health care system, for example – are still under state control. The per capita GDP in 2007 was HUF 2,523,000, i.e., approximately EUR 10,092 (KSH 2008). Hungary has a population of nearly 10,000,000.

Since the political transformation in 1989–90, Hungary's multi-party parliamentary system with general elections held every four years had been relatively – i.e., compared to other post-communist countries in the region – stable until recently. Since 2006, however, economic problems and political conflicts have repeatedly shaken the country, and triggered the split of the incumbent socialist-liberal coalition government in April 2008. Currently, a minority government of socialist stance runs the country.

The deep ideological cleavages dividing the political elites are also reflected in the news press and media: most outlets are explicitly or implicitly associated with the various political parties. In a way similar to Poland for example, analysts use the metaphor of 'media war' when describing the Hungarian press and media landscapes. This bloodless conflict, which began in 1990 and has, with varying intensity, persisted to this day, has been fought for political control over the press and the media. The political elites of both the left and the right, convinced that the press and the media are capable of shaping public opinion and voting behaviour, have pursued various strategies to exert pressure upon journalists in an attempt to use them for the purpose of political propaganda (Bajomi-Lázár and Sükösd 2008). Despite such attempts, however, the Freedom House has been qualifying the Hungarian press and media as 'free' since 1998; in 2007, the country scored 21 points (Bajomi-Lázár 2008).[1]

Since the political transformation, the press and media in Hungary have undergone fundamental changes. The major trends of change are as follows:

- the privatization of the newspaper market;
- the proliferation of the newspaper market with hundreds of new titles, including political dailies, weeklies and other periodicals;
- the tabloidization of the entire newspaper market, including some of the quality newspapers;
- the privatization of the broadcast media;
- the proliferation of private radio stations and television channels;
- the commercialization of the broadcast media, including public service broadcasters;
- the proliferation of the online media (Bajomi-Lázár 2005).

On the eve of the political transformation, there were a total of 1720 print publications, four nationwide radio stations and two nationwide television channels, and a few dozens of local cable television channels (Seregélyesi 1998). By contrast, in 2007 there were an estimated 3000 print publications (Levendel 2007). As regards terrestrial and satellite broadcasters, there currently are four nationwide public service television channels, two nationwide commercial television channels, 43 local television channels, three nationwide public service radio stations, and three nationwide private radio stations (two run by commercial enterprises and one by the Catholic Church), as well as 168 local terrestrial radio stations. There also are 534 cable television channels, including teletext providers, and five cable radio stations, not counting internet radio (ORTT 2008a, 2008b).

The number of broadcasters is expected to grow further with the introduction of digital broadcasting in 2011 at the latest. This significant growth in the number of broadcasters, print and online publications has created a growing demand for journalists and, consequently, has been coupled with the proliferation of schools providing journalism education.

Table 1: University or college degrees of journalists by educational field in 2006.

Education	%
Media and communication studies	32
Humanities	35
Natural sciences	2
Legal studies	3
Technological studies	5
Economics	8
Agrarian studies	2
Arts	1
Other	12
Total	100

Source: Vásárhelyi (2007: 25).

There are an estimated 10,000 journalists in Hungary and in the neighbouring countries' Hungarian-inhabited areas (Zöldi 2002). According to a representative survey conducted by sociologist Mária Vásárhelyi among 940 journalists in 2006, 31 per cent of them are under the age of 30, and 27 per cent are aged 31–40 years; the average age is 39 years. The journalism community is getting younger: in 1997, the average age was 44 years as yet (Vásárhelyi 2007). This implies that, since the political transformation, a generation change has been started: nearly 60 per cent of the now active journalists began their career in the new, democratic, regime, i.e., were not trained in the spirit of the 'agitation and propaganda' model of the late party state.

Currently, 83 per cent of all journalists have a university or a college degree; their educational background is displayed in Table 1 above.

History of journalism education

Prior to the political transformation of 1989–90, journalism education was largely lacking in Hungary. Under the state socialist regime, journalists were selected on the basis of political, rather than professional, criteria. Loyalty to the party state and its official ideology, Marxism-Leninism, was a major criterion qualifying those fit to fill key positions – the so-called nomenclature – of the news press and media.

The media policy of the state socialist regime was based on a number of monopolies, including the monopolistic distribution of information by the Hungarian Wireless Agency, the monopolistic provision of printing paper by the Paper Company, the broadcasting hegemony of Hungarian Radio and Hungarian Television – and the monopoly in journalism education of the school of the Hungarian Journalists Association (Magyar Újságírók Országos

Szövetsége – MÚOSZ), the only professional organization at the time (Bernáth 2004). The only university department providing journalism education, which had been hosted by Eötvös Lóránd University in Budapest, was closed down in 1957 because of the activities of some of its professors and students in the 1956 revolution (Zöldi 2002). Under the party state, entry to the MÚOSZ school, a must for all beginners of the profession, was conditional upon the successful passing of a test on ideological questions. Furthermore, representatives of the Agitation and Propaganda Department of the Hungarian Socialist Workers Party – i.e., the late communist party – held seminars to students of journalism on current political and ideological issues on a regular basis (Sükösd 2000). In 30 years, thousands of students have completed this school (Zöldi 2002). Despite the state socialist regime's attempts at controlling the press and the media, however, prominent members of the journalism community were busy destroying former taboos in the late 1980s, and thus accelerated the fall of the party state and the rise of an ideologically pluralist society (Sükösd 1997/98).

The political transformation in 1989–90 triggered the privatization of the newspaper and the broadcasting industries – and that of journalism education. Since then, communication and media schools mushroomed all over the country in both the public and the private sectors. The content of journalism education has, of course, undergone fundamental changes; students of journalism, once taught to be the 'soldiers of the party', are now trained to be the 'watchdogs of democracy'. Education today is based upon the Anglo-Saxon standards of neutrally objective, fair and impartial journalism – which, however, does not imply that active journalists too would abide by the same standards. In fact, as regards practice, European style engaged journalism seems to be the main rule, and objectivity the exception (Sipos and Takács 2005).

Current status of journalism education

Institutions

'Journalism studies' as such do not exist in Hungary, albeit some minor institutions offer specifically designed short-term courses to future journalists. Most institutions provide journalism courses as part of 'communication and media studies', the curriculum also including media sociology and psychology, media policy, history of communication, theories of political communication and the like. Some of them – such as the Communication Department of Kodolányi University College for example – focus upon the training of journalists, whereas others offer some classes related to journalism but, typically, concentrate upon other aspects of communication and the media. As a general rule, however, most institutions seek to cover all areas of journalism from the print press via radio and television until the internet.

Currently, there are some 66 institutions that offer courses on communication and the media, including classes on journalism.[2] Of these, eighteen are hosted by a university or a university college, and offer courses that have been accredited by the state (OFIK 2008, for a list, see the appendices).

The higher educational institutions providing graduate students with a diploma that testifies their completion of communication and media studies at some level or another can be classified like this:

1. **Accredited higher level training** as provided by a higher educational institution to students graduating from high school; the training takes two years and has been accredited by the National Educational List.
2. **Bachelor of Arts**, or BA, in a higher educational institution to students graduating from high school; the training takes three years and has been accredited by the Hungarian Accreditation Commission.
3. **Master of Arts,** or MA, in a higher educational institution to students with a BA degree; the training takes two years and has been accredited by the Hungarian Accreditation Commission.
4. **Postgraduate training** provided by a higher education institution to students with a BA or an MA degree; the training takes two years on average.
5. **Philosophiae Doctor,** or Ph.D., provided by universities to students with an MA degree; the training takes three years.

Of these, BA level education, which today meets the European Union's Bologna Criteria, attracts the highest number of students (see below). Institutions offering a BA degree provide students with a practice-oriented education; most of them have their own radio and television studio, as well as online, and frequently print, publications. By contrast, MA and Ph.D. level education focuses upon theory.

In addition to higher-level institutions, there are a number of other schools in the field, most of which provide practical training for future journalists. These are

- either hosted by journalism associations (like, for example, the György Bálint Academy of Journalism of the Hungarian Journalists Association),
- or by publishing houses and broadcasting companies (like the Népszabadság–Ringier Education and Training Institute),
- or by private companies (such as Teleschola School of Television Journalism),
- or by private foundations (such as the Center for Independent Journalism, CIJ).

Most of these institutions are located in Budapest, the capital city (Kovács 2007a).

It needs to be noted that currently CIJ is the only one that offers courses designed specifically for the future journalists of Hungary's largest ethnic minority, the Romany community. CIJ's Roma Mainstream Media Internship Program was launched in 1998, and has trained 95 journalists of Roma-origin to date.[3] In addition to this, the Minority and Ethnic Rights Foundation has also offered some journalism courses to Roma and disabled youth in recent years.

Students

Communication and media studies are quite popular with students; they ranked number four on the list of the most wanted BA and MA studies in 2007 among high-school graduates. In that year, 2694 students applied to study communication and the media at the various universities and colleges; the rate of applicants, however, displayed a 25 per cent decline compared to 2006 (Fábry 2007).

In the public (i.e., state-owned) sector, the first diploma can be obtained free of charge, whereas private institutions impose a fee upon most of their students.

The leading institutions of communication and media studies are displayed in Table 2. below.

It needs to be noted that communication and media departments prepare students for a number of professions related to communication (such as spokespersons, marketing and public relations managers, and the like), of which journalism is but one. The question, however, remains whether the press and media markets will be able to employ such a high number of journalists in the forthcoming years.

There is no data available on the motivations of those choosing communication and media studies. It is, however, most likely that the popularity of such studies lies in the fact that they allow students to find employment in a variety of areas, ranging from the press and media through private enterprises to public administration, because, since the privatization of the economy and the transformation of state into public administration, a high number of institutions have been seeking communication and media experts. Also, they enable those interested to continue their studies on an MA and, possibly, Ph.D. level.

To this, analysts add that, as a general rule, journalists are better paid than the average intellectual, and the profession offers more chances to be 'close to the fire', which also may be attractive to the young (Kóczián 2001). Furthermore, communication and media studies are particularly popular with those who, when completing secondary school at the age of 18, have no specific plans for their future, and expect this kind of education to give them some

Table 2: Leading institutions of media and communication studies in 2007.

The highest number of applicants to communication and media studies

Budapest College of Communication (BKF)	2200 applicants
János Kodolányi College (KJF)	1921 applicants
Budapest Business School (BGF)	1179 applicants
The highest number of students admitted	
Budapest College of Communication	525 students
János Kodolányi College (KJF)	350 students
King Sigismund College (ZSKF)	249 students

Source: Kovács (2007b)

time to make up their minds. In addition to this, 'moving picture and media studies' have been, since 1995, a part of the primary and secondary school curriculum from the age of 13 onwards (Szíjártó 2001), and may have raised interest in many secondary school students (Zöldi 2002).

Instructors

Because communication and media studies were non-existent prior to the political transformation, those educating future journalists have typically no specific qualification or degree. Most of them are

- either academics from the social sciences (such as political science, sociology, social-psychology),
- or academics from the humanities (such as literature, history).
- or professional journalists with decades-old practical experience in the field,
- or professionals of marketing and public relations.

As a result, the approach that they apply is either theory-oriented (as with academics) or practice-oriented (as with media and marketing professionals); in fact, most institutions offer a mixture of these two approaches. Whereas the former think in terms of the social, cultural and political implication of journalism, the latter in terms of market needs (Kitta 2005).

Curriculum

Analysts argue that there are two marked approaches to communication and media studies. Some try to draw students' attention to the 'dangers' imposed by the media, such as the assumed impact of tabloidization, media violence, and pornography, which is believed to have grown with the proliferation of the tabloid press and commercial broadcasters. This is a highly normative approach, contrasting popular culture as expressed by the mainstream of the mass media on the one hand, and 'high culture' as delivered by some outlets and the classic arts on the other. Others seek to understand why and how the contemporary press and media operate. This is an interpretative approach that seeks to place the press and the media in a societal, economic, and political context (Császi 2003).

In fact, the majority of Hungarian intellectuals, including many media educators, tend to display an anti-tabloid attitude (or, to use Ian Ang's terminology, 'the ideology of mass culture') as regards the mass media. They despise the tabloid press and commercial broadcasters, and oppose them to 'quality' newspapers and public service broadcasters. This misunderstanding of tabloidization, of the public, and, consequently, of the societal role of journalism in contemporary societies, has the result that, frequently, journalism education focuses on 'quality' journalism, despite the fact that, since the political transformation, quality newspapers and public service broadcasters have lost most of their audiences. Consequently, students of journalism do get acquainted with the 'social responsibility' model of journalism, which, however, cannot always be applied to the actual expectations of the mainstream audiences.

In the first few years after the political transformation, literature in the Hungarian language on communication and media studies, and especially on journalism, was barely available for students. Since then, some of the major works – such as William L. Rivers' and Cleve Mathews' *Ethics for the Media* (1988 [1993]) or Hugo de Burgh's *Investigative Journalism* (2000 [2005]) – have been translated, and are now available at an affordable price or through public libraries. Since about the year 2000, a growing number of books have been published by Hungarian authors that provide a theoretical background to journalism education, including several book series such as *New Membran Books* (Új Membrán Könyvek – Új Mandátum Publishing House, series editor: Miklós Sükösd, 1998–2005), the *Mediabook* series (Médiakönyv – ENAMIKÉ, series editor: Mihály Enyedi Nagy, 1998–2003), and *Antenna Books* (Antenna Könyvek – PrintXBudavár ZRt., series editor: Zsolt Kozma, 2006–present). There also are some readers in the Hungarian language that offer a collection of the most frequently cited research studies of the Anglo-Saxon world. Some communication and media research periodicals, such as *Jel-Kép* (Symbol, established 1994) and *Médiakutató* (The Media Researcher, established 2000), that offer readings to students on a regular basis, are now also available for students.

Concluding Remarks

Before the political transformation in 1989–90, journalism education was monopolized by the party state and was part of the 'agitation and propaganda' machinery. The changes triggered the privatization and proliferation of the press and media and, along with them, of communication and media education. Public and private institutions offering training for future media professionals mushroomed all over the country, and have been highly popular with students. Currently, they offer a wide range of levels, forms, and contents of education. Communication and media studies have become an industry with a variety of institutions – private schools, NGOs, universities and university colleges, as well as communication and media research workshops and publishing houses – engaged in the field.

Over the past decade, a generation change has occurred among Hungarian journalists, with the average age of active media professionals declining. This change has certainly been fostered by the rise of commercial radio and television and their hunger for young journalists who meet the tastes of their mainly young audiences.

Despite the fact that most of the audiences to date use commercial broadcasters and the tabloid press to meet their needs rather than the public service media and the quality newspapers, many of the schools of journalism continue to teach the theory and practice of quality journalism. For this reason, many of the young generation of journalists acquire the actual practices and daily routines of the profession only after they leave school and find employment with a media company which, as a general rule, is owned by multinational Western European media conglomerates.

The Author

Péter Bajomi-Lázár is senior research fellow at the Department of Politics and International Relations at the University of Oxford, and professor of communication at the Social Communication Department of the Budapest Business School.

Notes

1. One to 30 points qualifies a country as 'free', 31–60 points as 'partly free', and 61–100 points as 'not free'.
2. This paper was completed in May 2008.
3. For details, see the webpage of the organization at http: //www.cij.hu/index.php/articles/c36/ (last accessed 4 May 2008).

References

Bajomi-Lázár, Péter (2005), 'Hungary', In Marius Dragomir et al. (eds), *Television across Europe: regulation, policy and independence*, Budapest and New York: Open Society Institute, 2, pp. 789–864.

Bajomi-Lázár, Péter (2008), 'The consolidation of media freedom in post-communist countries', In Karel Jakubowicz and Miklós Sükösd (eds), *Finding the Right Place on the Map. Central and Eastern European Media Change in a Global Perspective*, Chicago: The University of Chicago Press, pp. 73–84.

Bajomi-Lázár, Péter and Sükösd, Miklós (2008), 'Media Policies and Media Politics in East Central Europe: Issues and Trends 1989–2008', In Isabel Fernández Alonso and Miquel de Moragas (eds), *Communications and Cultural Policies in Europe*, Barcelona: Generalitat de Catalunya, pp. 249–269.

Balázs Sipos and Róbert Takács (2005), 'Újságírói normák', In Péter Bajomi-Lázár (ed.), *Magyar médiatörténet a késő Kádár-kortól az ezredfordulóig*, Budapest: Akadémiai Kiadó, pp. 53–88.

Bernáth, László (2004), 'A MÚOSZ iskolája. Képzés a káosztól a rendig', In *Médiafüzetek/Médiaoktatás*, 2, pp. 55–60.

Császi, Lajos (2003), 'Médiaoktatás ma és holnap'/'Media education today and tomorrow', http: //www.sulinova.hu/letoltes.php?sess=&fid=36. Accessed 7 May 2008.

Fábri, István (2007), 'A legkeresettebb szakok 2007-ben', http: //www.felvi.hu/index.ofi?mfa_id=445&hir_id=8262&oldal=1. Accessed 7 May 2008.

Kitta, Gergely (2005), 'Média és oktatás', In Zsolt Antal and Tibor Gazsó (eds), *Magyar médiahelyzet*, Budapest: Századvég Kiadó, pp. 83–98.

Kóczián, Péter (2001), 'Média és oktatás', In Csermely Ákos (ed.) *A média jövője 2001*, Budapest: Média Hungária, pp. 103–106.

Kovács, Bálint (2007a), 'Újságíróképzés: számos helyre jelentkezhetnek még a diákok', http: //emasa. hu/cikk.php?page=sajto&id=2892. Accessed 7 May 2008.

Kovács, Bálint (2007b), '2631 kommunikáció szakos gólya kezdi meg tanulmányait ősszel', http: // emasa.hu/cikk.php?id=2878. Accessed 7 May 2008.

KSH [Központi Statisztikai Hivatal – Central Statisztical Office] (2008), 'Bruttó hazai termék 2007. I–IV. Negyedév', http: //vg.hu/lapokkepek/fileok/0/185_gdn20712.pdf. Accessed 7 May 2008.

Levendel, Ádám (2007), 'Az internet a sajtó halála?', In László Bellai (ed.), MÚOSZ Évkönyv 2007, Budapest: MÚOSZ, pp. 77–80.

OFIK (Országos Felsőoktatási Információs Központ – Hungarian Higher Education Information Center) (2008), 'Szakkereső/kommunikáció- és médiatudomány', http: //www.felvi.hu/ft8/ talalatok.ofi?mfa_id=1&oldal=0&int_id=-1&szer_id=-1&nev=Kommunik%E1ci%F3. Accessed 7 May 2008.

ORTT (Országos Rádió és Televízió Testület – Hungarian Radio and Television Board) (2008a), 'Vezetékes műsorszolgáltatók', http: //www.ortt.hu/nyilvantartasok/1206716809vezetekes_mszolg_ 20080328.xls. Accessed 7 May 2008.

ORTT (Országos Rádió és Televízió Testület – Hungarian Radio and Television Board) (2008b), 'Földfelszíni sugárzású helyi és körzeti műsorszolgáltatók', http: //www.ortt.hu/nyilvantartasok/ 1207589121helyi_korzeti_mszolg_20080407.xls. Accessed 7 May 2008.

Seregélyesi, János (1998), 'A nyomtatott sajtó helyzete', In Gabriella Cseh and Mihály Enyedi Nagy and Tibor Solténszky (eds), Médiakönyv 1998, Budapest: ENAMIKÉ, pp. 191–196.

Sükösd, Miklós (1997/98), 'Media and Democratic Transition in Hungary', Oxford International Review, winter, pp. 11–21.

Sükösd, Miklós (2000), 'Democratic Transition and the Mass Media in Hungary: From Stalinism to Democratic Consolidation', In Richard Gunther and Anthony Mugham (eds), Democary and the Media. A Comparative Perspective, Cambridge: Cambridge University Press, pp. 122–164.

Szíjártó, Imre (2001), 'A média tantárgy a magyar közoktatásban', Médiakutató, winter, pp. 113–128.

Vásárhelyi, Mária (2007), 'Foglalkozása: újságíró', Budapest: Magyar Újságírók Országos Szövetsége.

Zöldi, László (2002), 'Utánképzés a nyilvánosságiparhoz', In Mihály Enyedi Nagy, Gábor Polyák and Ildikó Sarkady (eds), Médiakönyv 2002, Budapest: ENAMIKÉ, pp. 61–78.

Zöldi, László (2004), 'A médiaoktatás ellentmondásai', Médiafüzetek/Médiaoktatás, 2, pp. 11–18.

The Latvian Journalism Education Landscape

Elita Plokste

Journalism studies in Latvia today are not valued and accepted in a unified way. Students, lecturers and industry representatives differ regarding the value of practical skills and fundamental, theoretical knowledge in journalism education. Some value the development of basic skills: some emphasize the need for competence, wide scope and the ability to analyse and work in the short term.

This article will review journalism education in Latvia and its development since Soviet times. Current journalism opportunities in Latvian higher education will be analysed. Professional organizations and associations, private media companies and their contribution to journalism education will also be evaluated.

Looking back – a history of journalism education

Latvia was dominated by other countries from the late twelfth century; newspapers circulated in Latvia from the seventeenth century, predominantly in German and Russian, as a direct result of the political and social issues in the territory. It was not until 1919, after WWI, that the opportunity arose to establish an independent Republic of Latvia and to subsequently develop a considerable Latvian media market.

The first notable precursor to traditional journalism education in Latvia came in 1917 when Latvian authors and journalists established a labour union. Later this was transformed into the Latvian Press Association and dealt with the professional aspects of media work.

In the nineteenth century, according to studies of Vita Zelče, press workers came from a variety of professions. Most newspaper editors in the first half of the century had received a theological education. By the second half of the century, many lawyers had become editors of newspapers and magazines. Press workers and journalists mostly came from the circles of authors, poets, teachers and low-level civil servants. A similar situation existed during the period between the two world wars. The largest and most influential newspaper of the era, *Jaunākās Ziņas* (published since 1911 with a circulation of 90,000), was published by Antons Benjamiņš, an elementary school teacher. He felt that teachers were the very best journalists, because they were disciplined, had a sense of responsibility, and had good and calligraphic penmanship. There were a few journalists who had received professional training abroad, but they did not play any major role in the business. The dominant view in the 1920s was that a journalist is born, not made, and could not be trained at an educational institution.

In the latter half of the 1930s, the Latvian Press Association began to discuss problems related to the professional capacities of journalists, focusing also on experience that had been gained abroad. These debates were reflected in the association's monthly journal, *Vārds*. One of the theorists of the Latvian media world, Arturs Kroders, supported the establishment of a school of journalism. Starting in 1938 Kroders examined the prevailing situation and took into account the experience of journalism schools and institutes in Germany, France, Belgium, Poland and the United States. The Institute of Journalism was ready to begin its work in the autumn of 1940. The plans were discarded, however, as a result of the Soviet occupation of Latvia, which took place in June of that year (Zelče 2005).

The onslaught of WWII and the establishment resulting from Soviet occupation meant that Latvian journalism culture was destroyed – journalism became official and controlled; media owners and most intellectuals were arrested, executed or deported to Siberia, and many journalists had been replaced.

Journalism education in Soviet times

After WWII Latvia remained occupied as part of the Soviet Union. During the Soviet regime, journalism was a tool of governance and propaganda. Therefore, even journalism education was strictly governed and controlled, with the primary journalism task of that time to train and organize the working people in ideological and political terms, according to Communist philosophy.

In the Soviet Union, journalism studies were possible only in the Communist Party Colleges. However, in Latvia's case, journalism education was used as a representation of achievements in the field of culture of the new Soviet Republic of Latvia. The main role for the journalism education foundation of the time was played by executives who helped the Soviet regime show those achievements of culture and politics in Soviet Latvia. New dean of the Faculty of Philology at the State University of Latvia, Andrejs Upīts, was a writer turned professor during Soviet times, and he became active in this way. Upīts also believed that philological education must necessarily cover a vast spectrum – the need for journalism education was clear from this perspective as well. Also of noteworthy mention for his role in the foundation of journalism education was Roberts Pelše, both literary critic and professor of the theories of Marxism and Leninism.

In 1945 the Faculty of Philology (as of then not yet officially registered) took over the journalism study programme from the School of the Communist Party Central Committee, whose main goal was to train party, Soviet and ideological activists. The curriculum was supplemented with a few courses from the field of philology and then journalism studies began. Most instructors were graduates from the University of Marxism-Leninism in Moscow or Leningrad. In 1947, when the State University of Latvia prepared to graduate its first group of journalism students, the process was legalized, and the Department of

Journalism and Editing was established. The first specialists trained in the field of journalism were graduated from the State University of Latvia in 1949.

Journalists were considered to be political figures, and party schools felt that they should have a monopoly in training them. Therefore tension between universities and party schools arose. In 1951, it was decided that there was no point in training journalists at the State University of Latvia, and no more students were admitted to the programme. The last graduation took place in 1955. Remarkably, this process was accompanied by the retirement of Andrejs Upīts. During the first period of journalism studies, some 140 people had completed journalism education in this programme.

Due to those journalism studies in the State University of Latvia (which took place directly after WWII), journalism education was subject to a rapid revival. Perhaps for this reason it was possible for students of the State University of Latvia to express their initiative and generate an effort to stimulate a return of journalism education to Latvia's education system. In 1958 students were admitted to a correspondence course in journalism in the Faculty of Philology.

In 1969 the Journalism Department was reopened. The Department had new instructors, all of whom had an academic education. In comparison to the situation immediately after World War II, the curriculum was considerably less ideological in content, and there were more practical activities. Still, it remained under the directorship of Moscow State University, and only a few courses could be replaced with local issues and initiatives. These new courses in the programme could only be replaced after intense discussion and fierce debate with the administration.

In the long run, due to requests from Russian language writing newspapers and the Central Committee, full-time Russian- and Latvian-speaking students were enrolled in turns, on alternate years. As for part-time students, both language groups were still enrolled simultaneously every academic year. Considering the imposed bilingualism of public life, education in one's native language was not deemed important at that time – everyone who was able could study in either the Latvian- or Russian- language group.

Overall, in Soviet times 'The Department of Journalism' graduated approximately 963 students. Unfortunately, we may only say 'approximately' as no precise data for the 1949–55 graduates exists.

Journalism studies during Soviet times may be characterized by an explicit orientation towards government demand, with an orientation towards the Soviet Party's doctrine of journalism education more or less modified according to the political leanings of the exact time. Any studying within this period was featured in order of the ideological importance of its subject matter. A study plan was developed by Moscow University and became mandatory for all Soviet Union's Universities. According to this plan, only Russian philology courses could be replaced based on the particularities of the republic. Considering the imposed bilingualism of those times, only part of Russian philology courses could be replaced with Latvian philology and other courses. Yet, even in those instances the replacement became the centre of great debate in the Department of Journalism and with the University's administration. Therefore, journalism studies were possible only with a great significance upon the philological education in the programme. For students of those times, Latvian (or Russian) philology was essential in their education programme. Ascension to copy-editor or journalist professions was possible only as a collateral profession.

Still, the second period of journalism education in Soviet times may be marked by its orientation towards professional study. Students had four internship courses held in regional and urban media over five years of study. Additionally, several courses were conducted involving practicing professionals – journalists from differing media. In the 1970s and 1980s, the journalism programme was among the favourites at the University of Latvia, and there was substantial competition for study places. The programme brought together strong and creative personalities.

Nowadays

With the time of *Glasnostj* and Awakening, we can speak about the end of the Soviet period in journalism education in Latvia. In 1988, State University of Latvia could dispose of the unitary education plans developed by Moscow University. From that point on, the programme was developed on the spot, reacting to local needs and realities.

This time of change was fulfilled by the regained independence of the Republic of Latvia in 1991. Latvia State University regained its pre-occupation name – University of Latvia. In the academic year 1991/92, students began to study the Communication Science Bachelor programme, which was seen as the first step towards a comprehensive communication science education. In the academic year 1992/93 Department of Journalism was renamed as Department of Communication and Journalism, accordingly validating the tendency and novelty of those new times – including the need to teach public relations (PR) and advertising, as communication spheres supplementary/ competitive to journalism. In 2000, the new faculty of Social Science was established, at once unifying all 'new' science departments, which during Soviet regime were taught under strict control and in different faculties. Therefore, journalism was no longer taught in the Faculty of Philology and gained its legal place in the family of social science.

After regaining independence and introducing a free market the media industry rose remarkably along with other industries requiring PR and advertising specialists. In response to these changes in society, the number of available education programmes in communication science was significantly increased. At present, after graduating school, there are three options for the study of journalism, three programmes for advertising and nine possibilities in PR education. The current number of programme attendants and graduates shows that journalism has lost its front-runner position in favour of PR and advertisement.

Current possibilities in journalism education

Journalism studies in Latvia at the moment are available at three levels – bachelor, master's and doctoral.

The Bachelor degree is available in two variations – a professional Bachelor degree offered by Vidzeme University College for media and journalism studies and an academic Bachelor degree offered by the University of Latvia, under the study programme 'Communication Science' and Riga Stradiņš University, under the study programme 'Journalism'.

To continue their studies, students can choose the Master's study programme at the University of Latvia ('Communication Science') and at Riga Stradiņš University ('Communication'). University of Latvia also provides Doctoral studies for Communication Science.

There are three schools that provide journalism education in Latvia and before comparing them it is important to acknowledge that they differ greatly in experience and their resource bases. A couple of years ago it was the University of Latvia who played the main role in journalism education because of its history and the number of students who graduated

Table 1: Journalism study possibilities in Latvia.

	LU	*RSU*	*VUC*
Level: Bachelor degree			
Programme	Communication Studies	Journalism	Media Studies and Journalism
Specialization	Communication Science (Journalism module)	Journalism	Journalism
ECTS	180	180	240
Study mode	Full-time – 3 years, Part-time – 4 years	Full-time – 3 years	Full-time – 4 years
Level: Master degree			
Programme	Communication Science	Communication	
Specialization	Journalism	Academic research	
ECTS	120	120	
Study mode	Full-time – 2 years, Part-time – 3 years	Full-time – 2 years	
Level: Doctoral degree			
Programme	Communication Science		
Specialization	Journalism		
ECTS	210		
Study mode	Full-time – 3 years, Part-time – 4 years		

from their study programmes during that time. Nowadays Riga Stradiņš University is also competing in the field of academic journalism education by offering different programmes and studies without modules – with a narrower focus on journalism. In 2007 (licensed until 2010) one more player joined the competition – Vidzeme University College – which developed the newest programme for journalism studies; offering the only possibility to focus studies on journalism, with students gaining a professional Bachelor degree after graduation.

Journalism study programmes at University of Latvia have a remarkably high capacity due to the institution's experience and resources – there are around 100–150 first year Bachelor-level students in full-time studies and 100–150 students in part-time studies as well. Riga Stradiņš University gathers groups of around 50 students, but Vidzeme University College only admits 30 students, approximately, each year.

There are State-budget funded places at the University of Latvia (twenty five at BA level, twenty at MA level) and in Vidzeme University College (ten). At Riga Stradiņš University students can only study journalism using their own funds.

Vidzeme University College and Riga Stradiņš University offer full-time courses only. At the University of Latvia students can study part-time – with lectures taking place on Saturdays. Online courses and other materials are made available for these students to allow them to gain an education as good as those who study there full-time. This is an important indication that journalism studies are available not only to high school graduates but also to professional journalists who cannot manage to study full-time or afford to move to the city where the university is located.

Comparing academic staff, University of Latvia is a convenient leader considering the number of lecturers and professionals involved in teaching, as well as the number of teaching professors, associated professors and doctors.

All schools cooperate with universities worldwide through the ERASMUS students exchange programme:

- Vidzeme University College: nineteen universities in eleven countries (Austria, Belgium, Estonia, Italy, Iceland, Germany, Great Britain, Norway, Portugal, Sweden and Turkey);
- Riga Stradiņš University: thirteen universities in nine countries (Finland, Denmark, France, Germany, Iceland, Lithuania, Norway, Slovakia and Turkey);
- University of Latvia: fourteen universities in ten countries (Denmark, Estonia, Finland, Germany, Italy, Lithuania, Malta, Norway, Poland and Spain).

All programmes cooperate with industry – mostly through guest lectures and student internships, as well as during practical tasks within lecture courses and course papers.

Journalism at Bachelor level

University of Latvia and Riga Stradiņš University saw transformation of their Bachelor programmes in the academic year 2007/08 according to the Bologna declaration; reducing the length of their courses from four years to three. As a result both academic Bachelor programmes now count as 180 study units in the European Credit Transfer System (ECTS). The professional Bachelor programme at Vidzeme University College takes four years to complete and counts for 240 ECTS.

In spotting differences between these programmes, Vidzeme University College is the only one which offers students the opportunity to study journalism in one of the regions of Latvia, as both the University of Latvia and Riga Stradiņš University are settled in the capital of Latvia – Riga.

There are differences in the teaching of the programmes and their approaches to journalism education. In Latvia all programmes are divided into three parts, that are differentiated not as major and minor, but as: compulsory sections for all students (A part); limited choice courses according to students' professional choice and interests (B part); and as open choice courses according to students interests (C part). The main differences between journalism programmes can be seen in the courses offered and in their division between those parts of the programme.

University of Latvia, unlike Vidzeme University College and Riga Stradiņš University, realizes its programme in modules. For the first three terms all students of the 'Communication Science' Bachelor programme take compulsory (communication and related science) course modules to gain a better understanding of the issues dealt with by communication science and, of course, for a more general academic education. It is only after studying and realizing all professional possibilities available to communication science – i.e. after graduating from introduction courses in journalism, PR and advertising – that students have to make their final choice of profession which will then be applied through professional orientation modules taught in small groups. Considering the current climate, this is a very handy approach to journalism studies – students can be sure of their career choice as it is based on their knowledge and experience in different fields of communication, not only an idea and feeling for their future profession. Module programmes give students a better understanding of what is happening within the competitive fields of communication and increases their communication literacy. This study approach also makes it easier for students to change their profession if there will be such a need in the future.

Vidzeme University College also evaluates the rapidly changing situation that students can face in the industry – several introduction courses in advertisement and PR are also included in the mandatory course parts offered by Vidzeme University College.

The main differences between journalism study programmes can be found in their organizational structure; at Vidzeme University College, the professional Bachelor programme has 83% of professional study courses – meaningful emphasis is placed on communication theory and media studies, a compulsory part of the programme. This

Table 2: Journalism BA programmes – organizational structure.

Programme	A PART – compulsory courses			B PART – limited choice courses		C PART
	General education	Internship	Final Thesis	Professional specialization	Internship	Open choice
VUC Media Studies and Journalism	General education courses (30 ECTS), Professional theory courses (54 ECTS), Professional specialization courses (66 ECTS)	4 Internships (39 ECTS)	18 ECTS	Professional orientation (24 ECTS)	–	9 ECTS
	86.25%			10%		3.75%
RSU Journalism	General education courses (18 ECTS), Social science courses (40.5 ECTS), Research methods in social science (19.5 ECTS), Language courses (24 ECTS)	Internship (3 ECTS)	15 ECTS	Professional orientation (55.5 ECTS)	4.5 ECTS	
	66.70%			30.8%		2.5%
LU Communication Studies	General education courses (21 ECTS), Professional theory and practice courses (57 ECTS)		15 ECTS	Professional specialization – journalism module (63 ECTS), Social science (12 ECTS)	Internship – compulsory (9 ECTS)	3 ECTS
	51.6%			48.8%		1.7%

course also leaves 14% of the study modules to individual choice, most of which is meant to give students an opportunity to specialize more – according to different media. The rest of the programme is designed to create an equal level of knowledge and skills for all students. Compared to the other journalism study programmes, Vidzeme University College is remarkable for its practical orientation: 16.25% of the programme is devoted to internships (four of which are held in a different kind of media). The duration of internships rises accordingly to year of study – four weeks in the first year, six weeks in the second and third years, and ten weeks before the diploma ends, in the last year of study. At the moment there are no further journalism education possibilities in Vidzeme University College.

Riga Stradiņš University offer an academic Bachelor programme in journalism. It has strict demands with literature and day-to-day studies – students gain their knowledge through theoretical summary writing and analytical work. The journalism education programme at Riga Stradiņš University is therefore beneficial for its academic education and narrowed focus to journalism and media studies, and uses a theoretical and academic approach to analyse certain journalistic issues. It is possible to continue journalism studies in Riga Stradiņš University in order to gain a Master's degree in 'Communication'. This master's programme is academically orientated, with the main focus on research.

The study programme at the University of Latvia offers its students the possibility of examining their decision to become a journalist. Due to the study plan of the programme students can take their time in evaluating the other options of specialization – PR and advertising; once they have chosen, their studies are focused strictly on their chosen specialization. The programme provides a remarkable amount of base knowledge to every student; this can help graduates to orientate themselves and be more flexible in today's rapidly changing media environment. The other half of the study programme is devoted to journalism studies and individual projects according to students' interests. The journalism module of the programme is made up of theoretical courses that develop students' analytical skills as well as several practical courses according to students' interests and media orientation.

The Master's programme in 'Communication Science' at the University of Latvia is also modular: one module is dedicated to journalism with a focus on media management and research. The Doctoral programme in 'Communication Science' is aimed at preparing highly qualified science personnel with internationally comparable competences in the field of communication science and an internationally-equalized Doctoral degree.

Professional associations and journalism education

At the moment journalism programmes at university are the only way to develop and acquire journalism education in Latvia. Working journalists currently cannot really increase their level of professional knowledge in any other way. This was different during the first years of regained independence when Latvia's journalists were offered different opportunities to enhance their professionalism. Many lecturers visited Latvia for seminars and conferences that were organized by the Journalist Union of Latvia. Also some of the journalists had the opportunity to go on an 'experience exchange' abroad. Scandinavia, Baltic Sea countries and European journalism organizations cooperated to very great extent at that time. This cooperation was at its peak in the middle of the 1990s. But when the first wave of exaltation passed, and Latvia was not a new democratic country any more, this support and cooperation vanished. Latvia's Journalist Union lost its position and value in society and among its members – now the issue of professional journalism education is in the hands of journalists themselves, or media organizations with their own priorities and interests.

Concluding Remarks

Journalism has been one of the most popular disciplines in recent decades, both in education and as a profession. Journalism education developed rapidly according to facilities and growing developments. Considering the developments of previous years, journalism education in Latvia could be at its golden age within just a few years – the media market has developed to a great extent, with different kinds of media channels and interplay, and education programmes could be tailored to the needs and interests of students and the industry. But due to the economic crisis this will not be the case. Tension in the media market is growing each week. Before the crisis, all of the main printed media, as well as some TV and radio programmes developed their online versions using the newest technologies, channels (such as online TV) and social networking (Twitter, http: //www.twitter.com). Today it is a question of survival – with such hard times in the state's economy it is not just state and advertising market funds that are shrinking, but also the audience's ability to consume those media products. At the very beginning of the crisis many journalists experienced wage cuts and changes to their payment system that were more convenient for the media employer and less profitable for the employee. But now there is the question of who has the staying power to be able to remain until the renewal. The current conditions are not helping working journalists' education and improvement of their professionalism. Due to an increasing workload and decreasing salary, good practice is diminishing. At the same time this crisis can be used as an opportunity to acquire something previously unapproachable – for example – if a job is lost, studies can be approached or renewed.

The Author

Elita Plokste is Ph.D. candidate and lecturer in University of Latvia, Communication Science Department. Fields of interests – organizational communication, corporate culture, integrated marketing communication.

References

Aumente, Jerome; Gross, Peter; Hiebert, Ray; Johnson, Owen V. and Mills, Dean (1999), *Eastern European Journalism: Before, During and After Communism*, Cresskill: Hampton Press, INC.

Higher Education Quality Examination Center of Latvia (HEQEC), homepage http: //www.aiknc.lv. Accessed 21 May 2008.

Høyer, S.; Lauk, E. and Vihalemm, P. (eds) (1993), *Towards a civic society. The Baltic media's long road to freedom. Perspectives on history, ethnicity and journalism*, Tartu: Baltic Association for Media Research/Nota Baltica Ltd.

Lapiņa, Laura (2006), *Journalism and communication studies in University of Latvia*, Rīga, LU Akadēmiskais apgāds.

Plokste, Elita (2008), 'Communication Science study possibilities in Latvia', In *66th Conference of the University of Latvia*, Riga, Latvia, February 14 – 15, 2008, University of Latvia.

Riga Stradiņš University homepage, http: //www.rsu.lv. Accessed 21 May 2008.

Self-Evaluation Report (2008a), 'Riga Stradiņš University Communication science Bachelor program self-evaluation report', HEQEC homepage, http: //www.aiknc.lv/lv/prog_view.php?id=5657. Accessed 23 May 2008.

Self-Evaluation Report (2008b), 'University of Latvia, Communication science Bachelor program self-evaluation report', HEQEC homepage, http: //www.aiknc.lv/lv/prog_view.php?id=5351. Accessed 23 May 2008.

Self-Evaluation Report (2008c), 'University of Latvia, Communication science Master program self-evaluation report', http: //www.aiknc.lv/lv/prog_view.php?id=4743. Accessed 23 May 2008.

Univeristy of Latvia homepage, http: //www.lu.lv. Accessed 21 May 2008.

Vidzeme University College homepage, http: //www.va.lv. Accessed 21 May 2008.

Zelče, Vita (1994), 'Research of Latvian Press in the 19th Century', *Journal of the Institute of Latvian History*, 2, pp. 27–39.

Zelče, Vita. (2000), 'Latvian press in the 19th century's 50's and 60's', Bērziņš, Jānis (eds), *Latvia in the 19th century. Reflections of History*, Riga: Latvijas vēstures institūta apgāds.

Zelče, Vita, (2005), 'The Field of Communications Studies and Education in Latvia. An Historical Review', First European Communication Conference: *50 Years of Communication Research: past & future*, Amsterdam, November 24–26.

The Lithuanian Journalism Education Landscape

Auksė Balčytienė, Audronė Nugaraitė and Kristina Juraitė

Introduction

During the twentieth century, the media's structures, genres and styles followed the overall changes in the socio-political systems that shaped modern Lithuania. For instance, literary genres played a significant role in setting the course for the development of Lithuanian journalism in the first half of the twentieth century, including the two decades of the First Republic (1918–40). Then later, during the years of Soviet occupation and communist rule (in 1940–41 and from 1945 until 1990), the cultural sphere acquired a political role: the cultural and literary press created an alternative public sphere and acted as a channel for public participation (Balčytienė 2006). In recent times, the settled situation in the media field is once again shocked with new challenges, such as structural and organizational reforms, ongoing marketization and commercialization of journalism, increasing media concentration and overabundance of hybrid media.

In Lithuania, the history of journalism training and academic research dates back to about one hundred years ago. It started with the intensification of the national consciousness and public movements associated with it. Indeed, an important quality of the historical turning point was the 'right timing': in 1904, the right to publish in the Lithuanian alphabet was regained after four decades of prohibition (since 1864), the critical intellectual thought intensified and the ideas of statehood establishment started to spread out.[1]

Since the early twentieth century those Lithuanian activists involved in journalism activities emphasized the need for professional competences for editors and press leaders. The very first steps taken in the field of the professionalization of journalism were special correspondence courses organized on a voluntary basis since the early 1920s (Gudaitis 2001). These initiatives were developed by people involved in book publishing as well as general education. Quite a few early press workers had received journalism training in other countries (the United States, Germany and France), however, most professionals had no possibility to study abroad and could only develop their competences and skills through self-education, namely, exchanging printed lectures and other learning materials published in periodicals. This, however, did not meet the desirable standards of professionalism: learning materials were poorly translated and based only on limited sources.

The role of the Catholic intelligentsia in promoting journalism in Lithuania can be seen in different ways: first, lectures in journalism were introduced at the Faculty of Theology and Philosophy of Vytautas Magnus University (VMU) in Kaunas back in 1925–26, and in 1939–40, Juozas Eretas, the public intellectual, offered lectures open to students of the entire university; second, by promoting the circulation of some publications, the conservative clergy hampered the periodical's neutral nature.

Briefly, it took quite some time (about two decades) until the full institutionalization of the profession (university structures to educate journalists and press workers) took place. It wasn't until 1941, when the Department of Sociology and Journalism at Vytautas Magnus University in Kaunas (at that time Kaunas was a provisional capital of Lithuania) was established, that the profession acquired an institutional status. This was the only place in three Baltic States at that time, where journalism was included into the academic curriculum (Juraitė et al. 2008). The lifespan of journalism training at university level, however, was very short. In 1943 Nazi Germany shut down the whole university.

Vytautas Magnus University was re-opened soon after the war but operated for only a few years until 1950 when it was closed down following the decision of the Soviet government. Gradually, the intellectual thought and academic life in humanities and social sciences in Kaunas came to a standstill. Vytautas Magnus University was re-established in 1989, in the milieu of national revival and the ideas which stemmed from sentiments to the pre-war Lithuania, the need of the humanization of science and the desire to open up to the world.

In the Soviet period, journalism was taught only in Vilnius University. At that time, the studies lasted for five years. Apart from the lectures in journalism and practical training, a significant time was devoted to learning the proper usage of the native language, studying Lithuanian and foreign literature, philosophy, logics, Lithuanian and world history and other similar subjects. With the exception of studies of the language and partially the studies of literature, the studies of history, philosophy, economics and journalistic subjects were carried out in compliance with the dominating Marxist methodology of those times.[2]

Present times: changes in media field and scope and character of journalism training

Indeed, a common understanding in media studies is that convergence of media systems and homogenization of journalism is becoming a worldwide trend. At the same time, the widely discussed commercialization of the media is, in fact, strongly related to the social changes: a mass audience has now shape-shifted into new audiences with personalized interests and needs, thus, media reorients itself towards producing news and information as a 'saleable product'.

Still, in spite of all contemporary challenges that journalism is facing (market-led reforms, commercialization and commodification of content) professional journalistic culture may have the power to withstand economic and political pressures and to fulfil the mission of critical independent analyst. In this context it remains of crucial importance for journalists to be able to define (through academic trainings and education) and to preserve (through professional practice) journalistic discourse so that citizens would be able to recognize certain signs of professional journalism and distinguish these from other texts (Balčytienė

No.	School and year of establishment (reorganization)	Type of studies, no of ECTS	Size: approx. no of admitted students	Programme characteristics	No. of faculty; Expertise and research interests
1.	Institute of Journalism (Faculty of Communication, Vilnius University) 1949–90; 1991; 1995–	BA (240 ECTS), MA (120 ECTS), Ph.D. (normally, 4 years)	40 (BA), 12–20 (MA), 1–2 (Ph.D.)	The most comprehensive structure of journalism studies (3 levels: BA, MA and Ph.D.); the programmes provide theoretical and practical tools to facilitate orientation in today's fast changing media environment and analyse journalism events, their consequences and reasons; focusing on practical skills training	Faculty: 11 Research interests: journalism history, broadcast journalism, print and Internet media transformations, modern communication theory and practice
2.	Department of Public Communications (Faculty of Political Science and Diplomacy, Vytautas Magnus University, Kaunas) 1941–43; 1998–	MA (120 ECTS)	15–25 (MA)	The only school in Lithuania which offers only MA level studies (it was a so called 'pragmatic' decision); the programme offers complete set of both real-media and academic analysis experiences; graduates work in all media (conventional and online) as publishers, editors, reporters, producers, and writers; programme is offered as daytime studies	Faculty: 7 Research interests: comparative media studies, journalism cultures, European news reporting, European public sphere, sociology of journalism, political communication, generic analysis, risk and science communication
3.	Department of Communication (Faculty of Social Science, Klaipėda University) 2000–	BA (240 ECTS)	20 (BA)	Focusing on regional media needs; studies organized both as daytime and part-time	Faculty: 5 Research interests: journalism history, journalism ethics and media law
4.	Šiauliai University	Professional BA (60 ECTS)	11 (professional BA degree)	Professional skills training oriented part-time studies	Faculty: n.a. Research interests: practical skills training

and Harro-Loit 2007). In other words, formal training and academic reflection on media performance are crucially important for the formation of professional identity.

In Lithuania, at present, journalism training is mainly provided by universities; there are only some exceptions such as short-term professional training courses organized by the media industry itself, the Lithuanian Journalists' Union, as well as some NGOs (such as the Lithuanian Journalism Centre). Media in-house training is gaining popularity albeit slowly. Another popular form of organizing trainings is through bilateral agreements between media and journalism schools.

Each of the four universities where journalism education is provided has its own profile which differentiates the logic of training across different schools geographically located in the four largest Lithuanian cities (Vilnius, Kaunas, Klaipėda and Šiauliai) (see Table 1).

Journalism specialization is a common format in all journalism schools except for the Department of Public Communications at Vytautas Magnus University in Kaunas (VMU) where cross-media training has been promoted in journalism education and an academic media research tradition has been set up.

Traditionally, BA level studies concentrate on basic skills training such as reporting and editing skills while MA level studies offer further specialization into higher level education in the field (training of editorial and managerial professional competences as well as skills of reflection and academic research). In all schools, international cooperation is realized through bilateral agreements for student and staff exchange programmes, academic research partnerships, professional networks and local, national and international internships and job placements.

Geography of journalism schools: Traditions, type and character of studies

At present, university degrees of both bachelor (BA) and master's (MA) in journalism are offered only in the Institute of Journalism (based in the Faculty of Communication) of Vilnius University. The Department of Public Communications at the Faculty of Political Science and Diplomacy at Vytautas Magnus University in Kaunas offers only postgraduate (MA) studies, while the Department of Communication in the University of Klaipėda organizes only bachelor level studies. Šiauliai University offers professional education in journalism.

Vilnius University has the longest tradition of admitting students to study journalism, while the oldest school where journalism education and scholarship has started is Vytautas Magnus University in Kaunas.

In Vilnius University, journalism education (as a five-year programme) started in the Faculty of History and Philology and the first group of twenty five journalism students was admitted in 1949. In the period from 1940s–60s journalism studies were a concurrent part of the Lithuanian language and literature studies. At that time, none of the teachers in journalism[3] had academic degrees and the first lecturer to defend thesis for their doctoral degree was Jonas Bulota (in 1964). Correspondence courses were started in 1954 with six years of studies. As expected at that time, journalism training programmes were ideologically focused; moreover, the programmes were identical in the schools of higher education all over the Soviet Union.

In the period of 1961–66 university level training of journalism was suspended under the claim of inadequate ideology (or to put it more precise, as not fitting the requirements of the communist party and Marxist ideology). As a result of ongoing requests from the journalists' union to restart university education, the trainings were launched anew and each year 20 students were admitted to study journalism. Since 1986, when the Faculty of History and Philology was reorganized into two autonomous academic units (faculties), studies of journalism were organized in the Faculty of History.

Since 1975, students could choose one of the three tracks of specialization in print, broadcast and photo journalism. Gradually and with a growing need to train more journalists for the rapidly developing broadcasting sector, each year 40 students were admitted. In 1985 two new departments were established in the same faculty – the Department of Print Media and the Department of Broadcast Media.

After the political breakthrough of the 1990s, independence was re-established in Lithuania (and with that the freedom of expression and the press) which became a new impetus for the profession to formally institutionalize democratic performance ideals for the media. In this context, and on the basis of two departments, an Institute of Journalism was formed. Fifteen teachers and three researchers were working there at that time with a major goal to modernize journalism studies. Different initiatives and projects were initiated to fund the formation of different types of education: training labs, libraries and seminar rooms were established in cooperation with the Open Society Fund Lithuania, the Freedom Forum foundation and the others.

In 1995, the Faculty of Communication was established and two different levels of journalism education were launched with a BA programme of four academic years and a MA programme of two academic years. These changes[4] were a sign of the altered perspective towards the whole profession. Indeed, in a few years the focus in education has changed from the preservation of cultural traditions and critical self-expression in complicated literary forms (a practice nourished in the education programmes of soviet time) towards development of professional standards such as studying the role and functions of media for democracy, analysis of political and economical trends and comprehensive surveillance of domestic and international events.

Journalism training in Kaunas – the second largest city in Lithuania with a population of about 400,000 – has taken a different path since the very beginning of re-establishment of journalism education at Vytautas Magnus University. To continue a pre-war tradition of journalism education in Kaunas, the Department of Journalism was established in 1998 providing one graduate programme in Journalism. In 2006, the MA-level programme in Integrated Communications was launched thus the department was renamed into the Department of Public Communications where two graduate programmes are taught – 'Journalism' and 'Integrated Communications'.

In Vytautas Magnus University, the decision to launch journalism training only on a postgraduate level was intentional. It was based on the belief that aside to professional skills training, prior subject-matter knowledge (gained during undergraduate studies, for example, in political science, history, philosophy, arts or philology), analytical and critical thinking skills and research experience are of particular importance for a future journalist.

Each year fifteen students are admitted to study journalism in Kaunas; many of the students have practical experience and reporting skills. The programme is committed to the mission of high quality training in the art and science of journalism; it is also theoretically- as well as practically-oriented and aims to educate media professionals for different spheres of media and communications, including mainstream, as well as online media journalists, editors and designers. The Journalism Master's level study programme includes eight compulsory study subjects (each worth 6 ECTS), five elective courses have to be chosen out of ten during one and a half year period (three semesters). Journalism students have also to complete two research projects, an internship (each equals 6 ECTS) and the final thesis (30 ECTS).[5]

The Department of Communication at Klaipėda University was established in 2000. Their Professional BA programme has tracks in print and broadcast media while this school has a strong focus to training professionals for regional media. Journalism as a specialization is also offered at Šiauliai University, but its specificity is professional skills training orientation and part-time studying mode.

To conclude, in Lithuania, Bachelor level studies are designed to be completed in four years or eight semesters, while a Master's study programme in Journalism continues for two years or four semesters. The duration of a semester is fifteen weeks.

Obtaining a Bachelor's degree requires a completion of 240 ECTS and Master's degree requires 120 ECTS programme; each credit representing 40 hours of work in different forms, including lectures, practical assignments (training of reporting and editing skills, analysis of radio, TV, press and Internet specifics), course papers, homework, independent study, etc. In MA studies, by their fourth and final semester, the students have completed the fundamentals of the study programme and they follow academic writing courses and prepare their Master's theses. The Journalism programme is completed with the public defence of the Master's thesis.

Traditionally, each school has its own history and practice to organize professional trainings, developing international relations and investing in academic research. At present, in all schools internationalization of studies (development of integrated study modules, international internships and joint degree programmes) is one of the core objectives of journalism education through student and teacher mobility and other international experiences. International summer schools are another option for to updating and strengthening studies, while there are also plans to introduce new study modes and modules, build international contacts and initiate joint research and academic networking projects.

Gender imbalance has lately been observed among all journalism schools students and graduates. Apparently, more women are admitted into studying journalism than men. In all schools more than half (in some courses about 75 per cent) of students in journalism are females.

Another observation apparent in this profession in Lithuania is its strong reliance on practical skills training (with exceptions in journalism training at a master's level where programmes involve close integration of journalism and media, political science and sociology matters as a basis of their studies, thus academic research, media performance analysis and critical reflection are the competences educated jointly with practical vocational techniques).

From theory to practice

Journalism training schools have direct connections to the media industry either through student internships or other forms of cooperation such as agreements to organize joint courses, seminars and professional trainings. At BA level there is a requirement that at least a 15 ECTS-credited course in professional practice related matters has to be passed during the BA studies; at MA level (VMU practice), an internship is organized in the summer semester and lasts a minimum of six weeks (6 ECTS credits).

At VMU, students are trained in professional skills while producing breaking news, features, commentaries and visual news reports for the different kinds of news portals that are professionally designed and maintained to reach the university community (students and professors), as well as the broader audience from the city and the region. VMU hosts a modern newsroom where students may do their internships in the university newspaper *Universitas Vytauti Magni*. Employees of the Public Communications Office, alumni in Journalism and Integrated Communications are also involved in different activities (project implementation, seminar and summer school organization). In Vilnius university, students produce the university newspaper *Universiteto žurnalistas*, online media project 'Info Jazz', and the radio channel START FM.

There are two professional organizations of journalists in Lithuania. Lietuvos žurnalistų sąjunga (the Lithuanian Journalists' Union, LJU) is the oldest one;[6] at present it has around 1000 members (the number of journalism professionals in the country totals at around 3000). Žurnalistų draugija (Society of Journalists) was established in the early 1990s when the first independent newspapers appeared in Lithuania and it has about 100 active members.

Both organizations are represented in media self-regulation commissions and committees (Ethics Commission of Journalists and Publishers) and take an active part in organizing professional training seminars and courses. The Lithuanian Journalists' Union regularly organizes trainings on the basis of the needs expressed by the professionals. Over recent years, the biggest attention has been paid to the media in the regions and training programmes were offered in election reporting, EU news reporting, online reporting and editing, newsroom management and journalism ethics. In the media industry, professional training is carried out on an irregular basis; a somewhat more structured and regular training programme is offered by the public service broadcaster (the Lithuanian National radio and Television, LRT) and the Lithuanian Journalism Center, which is an NGO and organizes courses in investigative journalism training, elections reporting, etc.

Briefly, there is no regular practice to organize professional training sessions in the media industry, but this is certainly done occasionally. The frequency of such seminars is usually several times a year. In addition to various professional seminars, higher education may also play a significant role for the qualification of journalists. For example, in a research study which was performed in Lithuania within the framework of research project Media Democracy Monitor (MDM)where leading news media representatives were interviewed on the media role in democracy, half of media professionals from Lithuania described journalistic education as an unimportant criterion in the selection of new journalists (D'Haenens et al. 2009). It was only the chief editor of regional daily *Kauno diena* who considered journalistic education to be an important criterion and underlined its positive effect on employee's professional responsibility and ability to find relevant information. But despite the low value that the respondents attribute to journalistic education, the percentage of journalists who are educated in this field is quite high. In four out of nine of the selected leading news media organizations such journalists form 75–100% of all newsroom journalists (Kaunas' city paper *Kauno diena*, online-only news portal *Delfi* and radio and TV newsrooms of the public service broadcaster); in two organizations it comprises about a half of the journalists (TV3 television station and radio station Žinių radijas) and in the last three organizations such journalists form a much smaller part of the staff – from 10–30% (free daily *15min*, , online-only news portal *Bernardinai* and tabloid daily *Vakaro žinios*).

It is interesting to note that many representatives of the selected news media contrasted professional education with experience or innate talents. The majority of them concluded that practical skills for a good journalist are more important than special education, even though there was no such intention in the question to make such comparisons (D'Haenens et al. 2009). A gap between the normative and real world perceptions of journalism and journalism education has also been illustrated by a pilot research study (Mažylytė 2008), aimed at comparing opinions of journalism educators and professionals regarding the quality of journalism education in Lithuania. The research showed that despite regularly updated curricula, journalism schools have failed to build more solid bridges between the academia and the media industries (thus, also to prepare journalism graduates for a more successful entry into a job-market). Critical rhetoric towards journalism education usually originating from the media professionals' circle has been increasing together with other factors challenging the identities of journalism professionals such as the tabloidization and popularization of media, growth of user-generated content online, etc.

As to academic organization and professional networking, media scholars and journalism students in Lithuania are active members of the Baltic Association for Media Research (BAMR), which holds annual meetings to review media development and changes in the three Baltic countries.

BAMR was established in 1993 in Estonia as an NGO and the main centres of joint activity are the Institute of Journalism and Communication at University of Tartu, the Department of Communication Studies at University of Latvia, the Institute of Journalism at Vilnius University and the Department of Public Communications at Vytautas Magnus University. At present, there are 73 BAMR members (among them twenty five from Estonia, twenty four from Latvia, twenty one from Lithuania, two from Norway and one from Finland).

The organization holds annual meetings for scholars and professionals and offers varied activities, yet the scope of activities could be improved to assess challenges in journalism training organization in the three countries. Some of the initiatives are on the way, for example an attempt to develop integrated international Ph.D. programmes in Estonia, Latvia and Lithuania to overcome certain drawbacks related to the lack of critical mass of journalism professors and experienced and internationally known researchers in each country.

Discussion and outlook: Challenging the profession

Significant changes have taken place in Lithuanian mass media in the past two decades. The current picture of media landscape creates a diverse impression: the news media environment is crowded with rich media formats and diverse niche audience groups. This creates new challenges both to news producers and receivers. In a multi-channel society, the news organizations are gradually losing their role as the only gatekeepers and agenda-setters. With growing availability of new communication technologies, the audiences themselves become effective news finders.

All the ongoing changes in the media sector pose further questions and concerns to the journalism profession. Old responses to the question of who is a journalist (based primarily on the roles associated with the process of gathering and disseminating information) do no apply to the present situation. In a crowded news environment, where both external and internal diversity of media is found, the function of journalism is dramatically changing. Journalists are becoming guiders, interpreters or even sense-makers, rather than just providers of information.

On the assumption that independent and professional journalistic discourse is worth preserving (especially in the era of homogenization of media content, commercialization and further trends towards hybrid content production) one should ask about the possible means to counterbalance the disappearance of journalism. A crucial question emerges: What must be done and by whom (and how, if possible) to preserve the journalistic discourse in the midst of all the changes (media convergence and concentration, technological diffusion, increasing power of political and economic news sources, professionalization of political communication) that are posing dangers to it?

Our assumption is that, in such a context, university education should develop critical thinking, and provide future journalists with the analytical methods and vocabulary necessary for the deconstruction of social and political processes that influence journalistic performance. As discussed elsewhere, the academic context and critical media analysis courses organized to perform media discourse analysis, to discuss such concepts as 'intertextuality', 'hybrid media', 'promotional writing', etc. make the phenomena of mixed discourses of journalism and promotional writing as well as advertising more apparent (Balčytienė and Harro-Loit 2007; Harro-Loit and Ugur 2008).

Another argument in this direction is the fact that, in 2006, the European Journalism Training Association (EJTA) accepted the standards of journalism education (Tartu Declaration, EJTA competence profile). The assumption of EJTA is that liberal and market-oriented vocational training in professional journalism is not sufficient to counterbalance the pressures of the market. Competence goals listed in the Tartu Declaration refer to a journalism graduate's ability to critically assess media democratic performance and to discuss journalism's public role in the context of political, economic and socio-cultural developments.

At the same time, small nations (such as the Baltic States), are facing particular pressures in how media and journalism education and research is organized. In Lithuania, for example, one crucial problem with journalism training is that the number of students at MA levels is relatively low; in addition, many of the students have full-time jobs before they graduate from the university. Thus, despite the facts that MA programmes fit the training standards supported by EJTA (having courses of self-reflection, media research methods, critical analysis and internship) this professional and academic knowledge does not really infuse among the media professionals. In short, there is a gap between the available knowledge at academia and practice that is actually spread among the journalistic professional community. In addition, many critical concepts for media analysis are not adequately popularized and remain understandable only in the context of academic scholarship; moreover, this knowledge is not accessible to other interested audience groups.

Generally, low levels of media literacy and a limited audience understanding of how the media operates affects both the openness of the journalistic profession towards criticism from outside actors (public intellectuals, scholars, general public), and the development of research practices and traditions in media scholarship. With regard to journalism theory, it is worth mentioning that there is a strong interrelationship between the media research tradition (i.e., how journalism is described and assessed) and the journalistic culture.

In Lithuania, journalism textbooks lean on the approach taken from historiography, which, in fact, is a result of four decades of journalism training in the Faculty of History and Philology in Vilnius University. Judging from journalism textbooks, rather often the trainers tend to follow the philosophy of the Anglo-American so-called professional model and argue on what the journalistic genre should be (fact-centred, neutral, balanced) rather than to analyze the forms that are used in the Lithuanian mass media in reality. In addition, there is a lack of empirical studies examining the development of Lithuanian journalism and depicting it as a social phenomenon.

In small countries such as the Baltic States, the number of scholars is limited, too. In this respect, the situation across the Baltic countries seems to be most favourable in Estonia, where the number of journalism and communication academics per capita of total population is larger than in Latvia and Lithuania.

Until now, the higher education reform in the Baltic countries and the system of ranking of academic publications did not motivate scholars to write in their national languages and to popularize media matters. In this respect, media performance and journalism quality analysis to increase informed public and academic debates about media performance is of major significance.

Widening public, as well as academic, discourse on media matters and media performance opens up new themes and issues and involves new actors in the debate. Thus the role of media literacy becomes crucial in increasing public awareness on critical concepts of journalism; an informed public also plays a role in helping journalists to find balance between autonomy and freedom, on the one hand, and accountability, on the other.

As already discussed, changes in the media environment require certain skills from both producers and the audiences (information receivers). For producers, journalistic education must provide critical reflection on the professional ideology and competences necessary for a critical analyst. The role of training and education of journalists seems to be of particular significance in bringing training of student journalists as close to practice as possible at the same time allowing analysis and reflection that is necessary for journalism professionals to fully understand both – the methods involved in news reporting and writing and the social repercussions of proliferating market journalism. At the same time, audiences must be equipped with necessary competences to make informed choices and assess the information accessed.

Concluding Remarks

To conclude, journalism training in Lithuania faces both challenges and certain drawbacks.

The major strengths of the journalism study programmes in all schools offering higher education courses include the following. First, the compulsory courses, which are oriented to the journalism theory and practice, are well matched and are appropriately supplemented by the electives. Second, active faculty involvement in academic research activities, their publications, participation in the research projects, initiation and involvement in national and international research projects, and active membership of faculty members in the international organizations (ICA, IAMCR, ECREA, YECREA, EJTA, and BAMR) should be emphasized. Journalism students are being involved in the research activities, particularly through the national and international projects; interdisciplinary and international study contexts strengthened by keeping close contacts with other master's level programmes (with political science and sociology) and projects at university level, as well as through the international exchange programmes. This is another advantage of journalism study programmes. Finally, the popularity of the programmes is rising among the Lithuanian students and there is a good record of alumni employment increasing within media-related organizations.

Weaknesses of the programmes include the following: decreasing motivation to study particularly at MA level (many students try to combine studies and work); no specializations of the programmes prepared yet although planned to include such specializations as investigative environmental journalism, risk communication, health journalism, sports journalism, visual journalism, citizen journalism; limited possibilities to study on Ph.D. level;[7] study programmes in English – although studying in foreign language guarantees international experience and broadens students' knowledge and understanding of journalism and media cultures, many students perceive it as a challenge because of a lack of previous experience of studying the subjects of journalism in the native (Lithuanian) language.

Taking into consideration global media changes, as well as national particularities of journalism culture, we envisage the following perspectives for journalism training and education in Lithuania: further internationalization of journalism education through joint study programmes at both MA and Ph.D. levels (for e.g., further design and development of online modules and virtual teaching exchanges); stronger emphasis on hands-on learning to empower young graduates with an extensive background in professional journalism and the technical skills needed for the job market; better integration of journalism professionals into the university curricula via teaching (internships, joint projects and curriculum development); higher flexibility in study forms provided by the universities, including correspondence courses, part-time curricula, life-long learning programmes, distance learning programmes; promotion of media literacy and critical media discourse among the general public.

These changes are necessary to strengthen quality journalism to withstand market-driven challenges. Otherwise, the role of journalism education at university level comes into question.

The Authors

Auksė Balčytienė is Professor of Journalism at the Department of Public Communications at Vytautas Magnus University in Kaunas.

Audronė Nugaraitė is an Associate Professor at the Institute of Journalism at Vilnius University.

Kristina Juraitė is an Associate Professor at the Department of Public Communications at Vytautas Magnus University in Kaunas.

Notes

1. After the national uprisings against the Russian Empire in 1830–31 and 1863–64, Tsarist authorities banned any publication in the Lithuanian language in 1864. Early development of the Lithuanian press and publishing era had commenced outside the mainland in nineteenth century. The first Lithuanian newspaper *Gazieta Lietuviszka* (The Lithuanian Newspaper) was published weekly in the USA in 1879–82. To support local Lithuanian newspapers' contributors, the first Lithuanian professional organization 'The Writing Society' was also founded in the USA in 1892. A few years later the Society published the first professional textbook *The Press and Culture* which was translated from German into Lithuanian and dealt with the journalism professional standards and identity (Bulota 1992).
2. At that time, journalism programmes were designed according to one standard to fit all the countries of the Soviet Union; each university could change only 25% of the programme to adjust it to the local (national) needs.
3. Different courses in Journalism curricula were taught by professors in history, Lithuanian philology and philosophy.
4. A number of significant reforms were implemented: first, the organization of journalim training and education was assigned to the sphere of social sciences (previously it was humanities), and second – two types of levels (BA and MA) of studies were introduced and journalism programs were shaped accordingly, i.e. focusing on the basics of media functioning and professional skills training (BA level) or media academic analysis and research (MA level).
5. Compulsory study subjects include Theories of Mass and Public Communication, Journalism Theory and Practice, Media Research Methods, Media Organization Management, Discourse Types and Genres, Creative Online Writing, Media Law and Ethics, Visual Communication. The programme's elective courses include both specific journalism issues oriented courses like Investigative Journalism, Fundamentals in News Reporting, Radio and TV Journalism, Communication Cultures, Press History as well as expansive subjects such as European Integration and Diversity Management, Communicating Politics, Media Innovations (a special course designed to deepen one's knowledge in media, society, culture, technologies and/or business).
6. The first professional association for journalists was established in 1922 as the Union of Lithuanian Writers and Journalists, later reorganized into Lithuanian Journalists' Union (LJU). Its membership had reached up to 208 by 1940, when the Soviet authorities closed down the organization. It was reopened in 1989.
7. Ph.D. studies in the field of Communication and Information are organized only in Vilnius; graduates of Vytautas Magnus University study at the doctoral study programme in Political Science offered at VMU. In Autumn of 2008, a new joint project of Tallinn University, Latvia University and Vytautas Magnus University – Baltic Graduate School for Social Sciences and Humanities – was launched with an aim to develop joint doctoral programmes in the fields of humanities and social sciences in the Baltic countries.

References

Balčytienė, A. and Harro-Loit, H. (2007), 'How to Preserve Journalism?', In International Conference *Comparing Media Systems: West Meets East*, 22–25 April, Poland: University of Wrocław.

Balčytienė, A. (2006), *Mass Media in Lithuania: Changes, Development and Journalism Culture*, Berlin: Vistas.

Bulota, J. (1992), 'Periodinės spaudos raida Lietuvoje', In V. Užtupas (ed.), *Žurnalisto žinynas*, Kaunas: Vilius.

D'Haenens, L., Marcinkowski, F., Donk, A., Maniglio, T., Trappel, J., Fidalgo, J., Balčytienė, A., Naprytė, E. (2009), 'The media and democracy monitor applied to five countries: a selection of indicators and their measurement', *Communications: The European Journal of Communication Research*, 34, pp. 203–220.

Gudaitis, L. (2001), *Žurnalistikos mokslas ir mokymas Lietuvoje*, Kaunas: Vytauto Didžiojo universiteto leidykla.

Harro-Loit, H. and Ugur, K. (2008), 'Media education as a part of higher education curriculum', *Informacijos mokslai/Information Sciences*, 47, pp. 78–87.

Juraitė, K., Lauk, E. and Zelce, V. (2008), 'The Early Development of the Baltic Journalists' Associations: A Comparative Perspective', in IAMCR World Congress *Media and Global Divides*, 20–25 July, University of Stockholm: Sweden.

Mažylytė, A. (2008), 'Žurnalisto profesinės vertybės: normatyvinis ir praktinis požiūriai', MA Thesis (unpublished), Kaunas: Vytautas Magnus University.

The Polish Journalism Education Landscape

Lucyna Szot

Introduction

2007 marked the ninetieth anniversary of the first form of vocational education for journalists in Poland. It was one of the first countries in Europe to educate journalists as the development of journalism education in the United States and Europe began after World War I. Poland has had a long Press tradition. The First polish periodical newspaper *Polish Merkurius* appeared in 1661 on the initiative of the Royal Court.

In 1917 a journalism course was launched in Warsaw by the Scientific Courses Association (Which later became the Free University). Soon after, the Faculty of Journalism was opened at the School of Political Science in Warsaw (Hanusz 1946: 109). Both educational establishments concentrated on teaching practical skills devoting a lot less time to theoretical knowledge. Hence, vocational training rather than systematic university study, however both establishments were keen to be recognized as university education providers.

A few years' later attempts were made in Krakow and Poznan to create educational establishments which would provide journalists with a more systematic education. However, this was only possible in Poznan and the Poznan Higher School of Economics was opened on 12 October 1926. It was a private school that ran three-year courses. In the 1930s, apart from its typical teaching activities the school ran, amongst others, an evening Journalism Course.

As time went on the formation of a narrow professional profile was becoming more and more evident. That is why in 1927, through the endeavours of many milieus, the Higher School of Journalism with a three-year curriculum was brought into being in Warsaw. Its aim was to hoist journalism training to university studies. The Higher School of Journalism was in operation from 1927 to 1939.

In the interwar period a lot of educators and practitioners of journalism were teaching journalists. After World War II, journalism started to be taught at universities. The first attempts to resume the education of journalists were made as early as 1945. In 1946 the Higher School of Journalism was opened in Warsaw. In 1947 the School merged with the Academy of Political Science and became one of its faculties. In 1949 another change was made – the faculty became an independent, interdepartmental College of Journalism within the Academy of Political Science.

An awareness of the need to educate journalists or of extending their education was growing in other academic centres throughout the country. In Poznan a course on Press issues began in 1946 at Poznan University Faculty of Sociology (Kafel 1966: 71). In the same year (1946) the Faculty of Journalism was opened in the Higher education School of Social Sciences in Krakow.

1950 marked the beginning of journalism university study because it was when Journalism units were set up at Warsaw and Jagiellonian Universities. Students required three years to complete their studies. In 1952 the Faculty of Journalism at Warsaw University was created. Studies at the Faculty of Journalism lasted four years and provided students with both theoretical knowledge and practical skills.

In 1965–1975 extramural studies – both graduate and postgraduate – were organized for journalists and editors. In 1970 as result of transformation the Institute of Journalism in Warsaw was set up.

At the beginning of the 1980s the basic type of journalism studies (five-year graduate studies) was reintroduced. Since 1972 higher education has been an indispensable condition for people interested in working as journalists while journalists occupying executive positions were obliged to complete their higher grade education.

By the 1980s most journalists had completed their university studies. In most cases they had a degree in the humanities as they had studied either the Polish language or history. There were fewer cases of journalists who had studied sociology, psychology, law or economics. Hardly any journalists had a degree in agriculture, medicine or any technical science. Taking such an educational structure into consideration, one should not be surprised that both in the printed press and radio and TV there were too many people willing to practice cultural journalism and not many well-educated journalists interested in economic issues. Despite the above-mentioned emphasis on higher education in journalism, in 1978 one in five journalists in Poland still only had a secondary education (Pisarek 1978: 190).

Until 1975 the only established Journalism school in Poland was the Institute of Journalism at Warsaw University, which in 1975 was transformed into the Faculty of Journalism and Political Science, existing in this form to the present day. Graduates with different disciplines from all over Poland could enrol on a two-year journalism course, which would provide each student with a good socio-political grounding, theoretical knowledge and practical skills. Graduates from the Warsaw Institute of Journalism often continued living in Warsaw after completing their studies; this is the reason why extramural postgraduate courses were established in Krakow, Katowice, Wroclaw and Poznan in the 1970s. Their aim was to prepare journalistic staff to work in the local press, radio and TV editorial offices and, most of all, to contribute in developing qualifications for young journalists who had not studied journalism.

The rules concerning the education of journalistic staff and for anyone interested in furthering their education in Poland had changed.

1975 saw further change. According to a new system, anybody who wanted to become a journalist had to complete their resident studies. Applicants to study journalism were chosen from political science students after completing their second year. Thus, journalism study formally became a specialist area within the field of political studies.

The Institute of Journalism at Warsaw University, as part of the Faculty, also ran extramural courses (both first and second degree) for journalists who had not received a higher education and who wanted to, or needed to in order to satisfy an employment requirement. Therefore, regardless of resident studies, these were postgraduate extramural courses intended mainly for working journalists. The journalism profession was still a calling open to anybody who had a higher education and the relevant skills and could cooperate with editorial offices.

The profession had a political nature and as a result many of its fraternity belonged to the Polish Communist Party (PZPR) or other political factions. In 1978 almost every other journalist was a Party member; this meant that, as far as the number of Party members was concerned, journalists as a professional body took up one of the top positions in Poland (Pisarek 1978: 190).

Apart from the traditional educational centres for journalists in Warsaw, Krakow, Wroclaw, Poznan and Katowice, new ones started to appear (also becoming part of the university structures) in Gdansk and Lublin, amongst others.

Fundamental for the freedom of the Press were the Round Table talks, which took place in Gdansk in 1989, where Lech Wałęsa participated. The fight of 'Solidarity' for freedom of speech had an impact on the law and practice. In 1990, on a statutory basis, The Censorship Department was closed down and the long process of transformation and privatization of the Press has started. After 1990, a generation change in the media had been initiated. These circumstances had an influence on the impressive development of higher education for journalism.

Since the 1990s higher education has undergone crucial changes. These were started when a higher education bill that regulated the functioning of schools for higher education was passed on 12 September 1990. Non-state (non-public) higher education schools were set up and developed. The graduate study system was differentiated by the introduction of a two-step system of education. At most universities and vocational higher education establishments three-year study courses were introduced, running within the structures of faculties of languages or political sciences.

1997 was a crucial year because, after attempting it for a few years, journalism finally regained its right to be a distinctive field of study, which seems to affirm its high social status. Aside from that, university courses run by non-university scientific institutions (the Polish Academy of Sciences) were created. Within the framework of the existing study structures, some universities regularly gave lectures (classes, seminars, etc.) in a foreign language.

Since 1998, by virtue of the higher vocational education schools act (26 June 1997), higher vocational education schools have been established. Their aim was to prepare students to do specific jobs, but these courses only led to a BA degree.

On 27 July 2005 The Higher Education Act (2005) came into force. It aids the alignment of the Polish education system to global, mainly European, standards and also helps regulate higher education in Poland.

Thus, from 2001 to 2006 journalism students and graduates constituted no more than 0.9% of all students at Polish universities.

Which entities run journalistic education?

Journalistic education in Poland is run by state and non-state higher education establishments.

State schools

Universities (there are sixteen in total) educate journalists mainly in journalism and social communication fields (first degree (undergraduate study), second degree study, uniform graduate study, third degree and postgraduate study): Warsaw University, the Jagiellonian University, Wroclaw University, Adam Mickiewicz University in Poznan, Gdansk University, the University of Silesia, Maria Curie-Sklodowska University in Lublin, the Catholic University of Lublin, Opole University, Szczecin University, Cardinal Stefan Wyszynski University in Warsaw, Lodz University, Nicolaus Copernicus University in Torun, University in Bydgos, University in Rzeszow, University in Bialystok.

Higher education vocational schools

At the moment there are 35 State Higher education Vocational Schools, which do not educate journalists as a rule.

Non-State schools

Non-public schools deserve special attention as far as the education of journalists is concerned. There are 348 non-state schools in Poland. Amongst them, are the following ones that educate future journalists within the journalism and social communication field. (nowadays there are 31).

Non-university scientific organizations also run journalist courses (e.g. The Polish Academy of Sciences). These courses supply basic journalism skills and knowledge, further developed in practice.

Moreover, there are other numerous centres nowadays that organize educational classes intended for secondary school graduates who are interested in practical job preparation. Amongst them are journalism education centres and schools run by different mass media institutions, particularly by the Press Syndicates operating in Poland (e.g. Passauer Neue Presse, Axel Springer, Bauer Group, Bertelsmann, Regional Media, Agora or newspaper and magazine editorial offices or public TV and radio). Large media concerns run training programmes for editors, directors, sales managers and journalists in a company development strategy framework. Journalists from these concerns take part in large scale training programmes, which gather the most important aspects and issues within the profession – from information editing methods, reportage and interviewing to law relevant to a journalist's day-to-day work.

Courses and journalism training are also run by the three professional journalist associations in Poland: the Association of Polish Journalists, the Association of Journalists of the Republic of Poland and the Association of Journalists of the Catholic Press. Associations in frames of members' courses concentrate on: workshop training for journalists beginning their practice and the status of the profession and its ethical rules. Training programmes concern such matters as: modern local newspaper, article parts and plans, journalism styles, editing methods, interview, literary and news reportage.

Teaching staff

In the main academic centres in Poland there is a long tradition of educating students in journalism and social communication where the teaching staff is well-prepared. However, in academic centres without such long standing, teaching staff are not always so well-prepared for such a task. In fact, this is why higher education schools (especially non-state ones) employ local press journalists as teachers or unqualified people who are still gaining knowledge and teaching experience.

Students and teachers on residential courses

The professional education of journalists in Poland has been quick to develop since 2000 and gained impetus in the 2002/3 academic year. It is symptomatic that between 2004 and 2005 the total number of the state and non-state higher education school journalism and social communication graduates in Poland at the Faculty of Social Sciences was 429 (including 322 women). Additionally, 198 students (including 149 women) completed residential undergraduate studies and 231 students (including 173 women) finished extramural undergraduate studies. According to statistics from 30 November 2005, there were 15,004 students in general (including 10,373 women) at state and non-state higher education schools in Poland offering journalism and social communication at the Faculty of Social Sciences, Out of a total of 15,004 students there were 6890 (including 4840 women) on residential programmes, 681 students (including 430 women) on evening courses and 7381 students (including 5077 women) on extramural ones. The data shows that 3944 students were in their first year – 1850 of them were on residential courses, 218 were participating in the evening and 1876 were on extramural courses (Chojnicka, Franecka, Ulatowska 2006: 37). The above are current growing trends.

Educational standards in the field of journalism and social communication

Universities have widely accepted the ECTS and have restructured their journalism education programme according to the Bologna Process.

1. **First degree studies**
   General requirements: First degree study lasts at least six terms (semesters).
2. **Second degree studies**
   General requirements: Second degree study lasts at least four terms (semesters). The number of classes should not be lower than 1000 hours. The number of ECTS (European Credit Transfer System) points should not be lower than 120.

   The graduate's qualifications: A graduate has the expertise to run and manage media institutions, both smaller units (editorial offices) and larger organizational institutions. A graduate has an awareness and understanding of the developing tendencies of contemporary media and their role in different aspects of the functioning of a modern information society. A graduate can fulfil the role of a journalist in a profession the public have confidence in. A graduate has the capacity and skill to make decisions under pressure and also solve difficult professional issues. A graduate is ready to start a third degree (doctorate).
3. **Third degree studies**
   Doctoral studies for students with an MA degree or equivalent, enables students to attain advanced knowledge in a given field or discipline. This prepares them for unassisted research and leads to a Ph.D. degree and lasts eight terms.
4. **Postgraduate studies**
   A form of education different from higher educational studies or doctoral studies, it is designed for people with an MA diploma and lasts two terms.

Relationship with industry

At the present time the relationship between tertiary level journalism and social communication and industry are almost non-existent. The most active in fields of internship organization are press concerns, professional journalist societies and journalists' trade unions. The press concerns run journalism institutes (e.g. Journalism Institute Polskapresse), which with radio and television editorial offices hold journalism workshops, concerning for example struggles with crisis, ecology and social attitude. Internships, practices and training programmes for students are also offered by internet portals, as well as editorial offices. To gain experience students accomplish ordered assignments and at the end of each they get a proper certificate.

Societies

Among others, universities and schools are part of the following international societies/ organizations: European Communication Research and Education Association (ECREA), European Public Relations Education and Research Association (EUPRERA), International Association for Media and Communication Research (IAMCR), International Communication Association (ICA).

Poland also takes part in international EU education programmes, for example: SOCRATES, Leonardo da Vinci, TEMPUS, ERASMUS which are coordinated by the Polish Ministry of Science and Higher Education.

Concluding Remarks

Journalism and social communication are very attractive educational areas for young people. Community journalism enjoys a lot of respect from people. However, journalistic professionalism in Poland needs systemic change.

Presently, the dynamics of the development of higher journalistic education in Poland is influenced by:

- A considerable demand for journalists,
- The fact that mass media regained public confidence as an institution after 1989, which created social support for their activities and an increased interest in the journalistic profession.
- The opinion that members of the profession enjoy a high social and material status.
- The opinion about the growing significance of higher education for its future existence, which means that an MA diploma is more and more often regarded as an indispensable element in the so-called 'personal career'.
- Demographic factors which make the wave of the so-called 'population explosion' move from lower level schools to academic educational centres.

Journalism is an open profession and is also an option for people who do not have any journalistic education. Therefore, it is similar to other professions such as acting. This feature must be retained. The idea of so-called 'talentism' (the view that no journalistic education is necessary) has been present since the beginning of journalistic education.

Despite many controversies over the validity and usefulness of specialist journalism schools, journalistic professionalism continued to gain respect and in the 1970s and 1980s journalistic higher education was universally accepted in Poland. Provisions in Collective Labour Agreement for Journalists employed in RSW 13 July 1989 resulted from the opinions and aspirations of the journalistic environment. In article 7 section 1 of this agreement it is stated that 'a journalist should have a higher education and training leading to an examination'.

Currently the above regulations are not in force. Higher education is not a prerequisite for a young journalist's employment. There are different paths leading to a career in journalism – it is an accessible profession. At the moment, out of all the intellectual professions in Poland, only journalism and literary occupations can be described as such – others require a university degree.

The accessibility of the profession is derived from the variety of functions fulfilled by the press as a political, social and cultural institution. In fact the recruitment criterion for the profession is not defined by any formal requirements. It seems, however, that contrary to liberal opinion, the profession is not open to everybody. It is difficult to apply only one rule in the selection of candidates (administratively accepted or scientifically developed). Without journalists with such diverse characters and personalities no editorial office would be able boast of such well–edited newspapers or magazines.

It is difficult to support the stereotypical view that a journalist is an amateur with an encyclopedic mind, who has to know something about everything in order to do his job efficiently. According to this notion therefore, a journalism study course should follow a pattern of 'general' education: only the basic elements of sociology, economics, politics (dependent on the economic situation), history of the press, grammar, and stylistics should be taught.

Advocates of such ideas claim that journalism courses are useless, because, the most important thing is to be able to write a note correctly or simple press information, proof read a dispatch and to be familiar with editorial technique. We can partly agree with this opinion because basic editorial skills are essential for a trainee or a young journalist. In the latter stages of the professional 'initiation' a grasp of how an editorial office functions or some other basic skills are not enough. A journalist should have a substantive knowledge and be in command of such mastery whilst being a creator and not just a mere imitator.

One should not forget about the social role of the profession and its responsibility for the word – duties that can only be fulfilled by professional journalists. The editorial experience of this chapter shows that over 80 per cent of corrections suitable for publication concern the press material by journalists who are under 30 years old. What is more, since 1995 the number of corrections sent to editorial offices has been increasing.

At present, despite much contention (as discussed above) over the validity and usefulness of special journalism schools, journalistic professionalism continues to gain in esteem and significance. In addition, more practical subjects are expected to be taught as well as theoretical.

Increasingly publishers employ well-educated journalists, specialists in advertising, marketing, and promotion all too well aware of the huge competitiveness in the media marketplace.

Theoretically, individual school and university programmes that run journalism courses are doing quite well. The Ministry of Education, in its minimum programme in journalism and social communication, wrote in characteristics of grades that

[…] the purpose of these studies is for the student's comprehensive preparation for the journalist profession and for other professions related not only to press, radio and television but also related to widely comprehended fields of social communication – public relations, publicity, advertising, promotion and institutions which run media education courses. (Resolution 591/99 from 25 November 1999)

However, what does it look like in practice? Workshops are often held by experienced journalists. Training students can be an additional source of income although it must be remembered that working in a press office often means they have to be available at all times, therefore they sometimes cancel classes. Former journalists employed by schools and universities, although having lots of experience, often cannot find their feet in modern journalism, which makes them a poor choice as teachers. They recall 'the good old days' and are not up to date with the latest editorial trends or practical journalism.

In search of saving money, universities frequently reduce the number of workshops and provide students with more lectures instead. Consequently, majors such as Methods of Media Research or Local Media are presented in such a way. During workshops students could be introduced to media 'from within' (e.g. focus group interviews), they could edit their own newspaper, etc. This is not without its problems – there is not enough good equipment, there are too many students in every group – which leads to a lack of proper infrastructure (Bratkowski 2001).

Generally students must complete at least one month of training in all majors. But this is often not enough. Students are left to their own devices to find placements and training courses. They need to complete their learning in workshops (which are expensive but the most efficient) in marketing, organization and media economics.

All of this is confirmed in interviews with working editors. In the general media marketplace there are not enough specialist marketing and press managers. Often these positions are mostly filled by people who have finished study or training in Warsaw

How people are selected onto journalism courses is also very important. Journalism is a very particular vocation; often requiring journalists' to sacrifice their personal life. The way journalists are recruited needs to change. Essentially, it does not matter how well someone can write or gather information or even make new contacts. During the recruitment efficiency of entrants must be taken under consideration. It must be emphasized that longer training in an editorial office (for more than one month) is very important. Journalism is a very dynamic profession, requiring work under the pressure of time, and 90% of what has been written is usually shorter or longer news. Unfortunately, graduates of journalistic studies often do not have the basic abilities necessary to practice journalism.

Graduates have only a theoretical basis which can't be transferred into practice. Over several years training in editorial office was practically unuseful.

Journalism course syllabi are no different to any other majors at universities, with several journalism-related subjects just added. At this point we must ask, 'what is it that actually provides one with a journalistic diploma?' Unfortunately, not much. For what reason then, is there is so much interest in studying journalism? It seems that most people who work in the media are aware that sooner or later guidelines for proper professional training will be instituted. The proposed changes presented by B. Michalski (1989: 49). received lukewarm interest from the journalist fraternity. However elemental mistakes are often made by journalists in their work and the lack of press law knowledge caused discussion over obligatory major education in journalism. However, elementary mistakes made by reporters and their lack of Media Law knowledge have led to debate regarding compulsory journalism education.

Today, there is a tendency toward media studies 3+2 (Bachelor's Degree + Master's Degree) or 5+2 (Master's Degree + postgraduate training). In these instances graduates become experts in a particular field, and studying journalism makes it easier to enter the profession.

It is possible to become a journalist even if journalism is not read as a major – some editors-in-chief even prefer graduates who did not major in journalism (Olędzki 1989). On the other hand, a modern media employee must specialize in nearly all disciplines. Narrow specialization is slowly being replaced by broader accomplishment. Therefore, the tendency is to perhaps create majors, that include not only journalism but also the wider comprehensive field of social communication with stronger growth potential.

On average, only 10–20% of journalism graduates work in the profession (Szot 2003) each year. Other graduates, though they try to work in the media, often leave to enter different occupations. Some of them find employment in organizations related to journalism (e.g. public relations, press offices). In smaller towns, where employment opportunities for journalists are scarce, finding a full-time job as a journalist is rather impossible.

Journalism, as a profession, can be undertaken by those with only a secondary education or who finished Art school. Even though journalists may lack a Master's degree it seems that due to creativity and strong personalities they win through to achieve success in this revered institution.

In spite of numerous controversies about running technical journalists' schools, professionalism has increased in value. In the 1970s and 1980s in Poland there were many followers of higher education in journalism and professional specialization.

Currently above-mentioned regulations are not in force. Higher education is not required in employing a young journalist. Different paths lead to the journalistic profession – it is an open occupation. Among all intellectual occupations only journalistic and literary professions are open – other occupations require university degrees. It is hard to follow the stereotype that a journalist should be a dilettante who has only general knowledge – then he will not be able to work efficiently. We mustn't forget about the responsibility and the social role of this occupation. There might be a helpful classification on actual journalistic professionalism, with technical skills and journalism in wider sense, which also contains norms and ethic. More and more complicated techniques and media, greater competition and harder work conditions favour the progressing specialization and professionalism of hired employees (journalists). Media occupations and specializations are slowly being separated, i.e. authors (creators) and executors (journalists), technical aids, administration, managers, etc. Although professionalism in media and journalism is required more and more, especially in larger institutions, access to these institutions is not excluded from talented writers and journalists without a proper education. In that sense this occupation is and will be open for gifted press reporters, regardless of their education. Nevertheless a combination of talent and knowledge gives the best guarantee of success, or at least promotion, at work. Those who come to work in media, because of their skills or predispositions, usually extend their knowledge in a particular domain before reaching proper qualifications.

Explaining journalistic calling as a 'community and country service' makes it an appealing career for the idealistic and young people. Undoubtedly all dilemmas connected with this occupation, which differ depending on publisher, editor or press owner, are disregarded; the significance of those dilemmas is not noticed until the practice. Contradictions inside the press offices divide the journalistic environment. Commercial and marketing success requires press managers to be skilful and make cold calculations, but it also requires disciplined business actions along with artistic imaginations or even journalistic fantasy. Every journalist works in a different field of expectations, and has different criteria by which to evaluate their work and make choices.

In large media institutions the basic contradictions can be seen between:

- criticism with creativity requirements and specialization and routine at work
- owner's interests and the citizen's right to freedom of speech
- salary for effectiveness of work or product and for labour time.

All these contradictions are in publishing activity itself, which always combines elements of prototypes and serial production. The commercialization phenomenon and economic conditions in which these processes are undertaken effect on the deterioration of journalism in Poland. Poor activity of creative societies causes this situation. Journalistic associations are weak and divided. They are not able to represent matters of journalistic environments in parliament efficiently. Currently they are not a very influential group, and would not be able to present journalists' ventures properly. Regulations do not provide occupational rights and protection for freelancers. This group has limited rights for information though.

The journalists should stay impartial, but not indifferent to vital social aspects and interests of their readers. To avoid partiality of relations, the journalists are prohibited to accept gratifications and free services of any kind. The Journalist Code of Conduct shows binding laws of differentiation between information and opinion, contains bans of direct comments to politicians' and social activists' opinions and forbids the abuse of emotional terms in informational messages. It also orders the protection of personal rights for informers and third persons who trust in the journalist (Michalski 1998: 33).

Almost all of the bans and orders of particular behaviour are not also regulation laws and moral codes. Expression of the kind of compromise between limitation of press liberty and the need of press responsibility is represented by idea that the behavioural norms of journalists, editors and publishers should come from self-limitation of press authors, so they should be settled by themselves (Kononiuk, Michalski 1998: 96). Nowadays that idea is acknowledged more and more widely. It is confirmed by the Resolution 1003 of the Parliamentary Assembly of the Council of Europe from 1993: '[...] media have to undertake to develop ethical norms that can guarantee freedom of speech and fundamental right of the citizens to receive true information and reliable opinions'.

That Resolution determines that the goal of the media is a kind of intermediary role – to serve as information services. Freedoms also have to be protected within the media itself, in case of external pressure. Thus publishers and journalists have to cooperate with the idea in mind, that founded observance of ideological orientation of publishers and owners is restricted by absolute requirement of true information and ethical opinions.

The influence of ethical codes on journalist practice in Poland is limited. They have the standard proposals character. The document of press deontology in Poland is the Ethical Card of Media accepted in 1995 by all journalist societies and also some broadcaster organizations. The card includes seven rules: rule of truth, objectivism, separation of information and comments, honesty, respect and tolerance, priority of receiver's welfare, and freedom and responsibility for relay content and form. As for contravention of law, one can be summoned – for the malfeasance of rules of the social norms code one can appear before the journalist court, and for the abuse of Ethical Card of Media one can be called up before the Ethical Card of Media Council. The effectiveness of this liability rule should not be overestimated. The essential matter is still diminishing role of ethical codes of journalists and journalist jurisdiction in Poland.

Human resources policy in editorial offices, low incomes and bad working conditions are causing experienced journalists to quit their jobs. Often people become a journalist by accident; there is a lack of people who are devoted to journalism not only as a way to make money. Media exaggerates news, which contributes to a regression of journalism standards. Though external cases should be penalized by the legal norms, civil mechanisms – like consumer rights and market rights – turn out to be the most effective. Also the financial arguments are more convincing than law orders and prohibitions. There is no way to settle the journalist's professional dilemmas in an indubitable way. And those dilemmas are the source of never-ending dispute over the sense of the journalist's practice. In principle – the conscience of the journalist decides.

Most of the media occupations are characterized by low professionalism, i.e. lack of clearly-defined qualifications and 'rules of actions' appointing standards of professionalism, which in connection with the cult of individualism and talent, favours the development of different ideologies (Mrozowski 2001: 242). Besides that, every journalist works in different fields of expectations, has different evaluations of his/her own work, and what is more – different criteria for success and work. A journalist must make his/her own choice and define his/her own work directions.

In principle, the above mentioned dilemma can't be arbitrated, and those issues are starting endless disputes about the meaning of work.

The Author

Lucyna Szot is lecturer at the Institute of Politics of the University of Wrocław.

References

Barta, J., Dobosz, I. (1989), *Press Law and Copyrigh*, Cracow: Jagiellonian University Press.

Bratkowski, S. (2001), 'Can we educate journalists?', *Journalists Forum*, 6, Warsaw.

Chojnicka, M., Franecka, A. and Ulatowska, M. (2006), *Higher education schools and their finances in 2005. Information and statistic studies*, Warsaw: Central Statistical Office, pp. 23–28.

Dobek-Ostrowska, B. (1998), *Modern communication systems*, Wroclaw: Wrocław University Press.

Dyoniziak, R. (1997), *Opinion polls and society manipulation*, Cracow: Uniwersitas.

Hanusz, Z. (1946), *Journalism*, Warsaw: Polish Scientific Publishers PWN, pp. 109–111.

Heath, R. (2006), *The Hidden Power of Advertising*, Gdansk: Gdansk Psychology Publishers.

Kafel, M. (1966), *Press studies. Introduction to key problems*, Warsaw: Polish Scientific Publishers PWN.

Kobylińska, Z. and Grabowski, D. (1996), *Journalistic ethos*, Olsztyn: Lux Mundi.

Kononiuk, T.; Michalski, B. (1998), *Legal issues of journalistic profession*, Warsaw: Publishing House Elipsa.

Michalski, B. (1989), 'We discuss about the model', *Zeszyty Prasoznawcze*, 2, pp. 49–53.

Michalski, B. (1998), *Fundamental issues of press law*, Warsaw: Publishing House Elipsa.

Mrozowski, M. (2001), *Massmedia. Power, entertainment and business*, Warsaw: Publishing House Aspra.

Olędzki, J. (1989), *Professionalism in journalism*, Warsaw: Polish Scientific Publishers PWN.

Pisarek, W. (1978), *Press – our daily bread*, Wroclaw: Ossolineum Publishing House.

Pisarek, W. (1988), *Journalistic rethoric*, Cracow: Press Research Centre RSW.

Pratkanis, A. and Aronson, E. (2005), *Age of propaganda*, Warsaw: Polish Scientific Publishers PWN.

Sobczak, J. (1998), *Polish press law*, Poznan: Publishing House Book Service.

Szot, L. (2003), *Journalists freedom in polish legal system*, Wroclaw: Publishing House Atla 2.

The Romanian Journalism Education Landscape

Alexandru-Bradut Ulmanu

Introduction

'Journalism education' is a phrase that still makes some Romanian journalists nervous. Journalism, such journalists say, does not need education. You are born a journalist, you do not go to school to become one. They are always quick to argue that many brilliant journalists have never been to journalism school, whereas quite a few of those who have do not really make it in this profession. And they often talk of journalism schools as places where you can learn theory, but not the real thing. However, those journalists, a few years ago quite numerous, are now on the verge of extinction. As the number of Romanian media outlets grows, especially in Bucharest, journalism school students and graduates are becoming the most obvious choice for employers.

A brief history

The reason for this reluctance against journalism education in the ranks of some of the more seasoned Romanian journalists has its roots back in the communist times, when journalism was a closed profession to almost all but those with impeccable dossiers – read 'healthy' working class origins, communist party membership and other such credentials.

After 1989 there came a sudden liberalization of the profession; people with the most varied backgrounds, such as engineers, doctors, professors or persons who didn't have any academic training at all could become journalists. And many did.

During communism, there was seldom any journalism training at an academic level, as the profession was practically reserved for the promoters of the communist ideology. A department of journalism functioned between 1956 and 1959 within the School of Law and Philosophy, and from 1961 until 1966 at the College of Literature, within the University of Bucharest (Coman 2007). From 1971 until 1989 there was only one school officially training journalists: a one-year graduate journalism programme within the communist party school formally known as the 'Stefan Gheorghiu' Academy of Political Sciences. Although admission to the school was usually reserved for party followers and activists (you had to be a member of the Communist Youth Union or the Romanian Communist Party, and also to have been employed for a certain time by a journalism outlet), the school did produce some journalists who were later regarded as good professionals. One alumni of the school became one of the best-known dissidents of the communist regime: the poet Mircea Dinescu. In its first years of existence, the school registered about 70 students per year, but in the 1980s it only counted about 20 students per year (Coman 2003, Petcu 2004).

The first post-communist journalism school appeared in 1990, through the government's decision, within the University of Bucharest. The school, which later was named the School of Journalism and Mass Communication Studies, is widely regarded as the leader among journalism schools in the nation, its curricula having been duplicated by other journalism academic institutions throughout the country. Since very early after its inception, the school developed relations with journalism schools in the Western world, especially France and the United States. Its curriculum has been developed stemming from the model of journalism schools in Western Europe and the United States.

For a few years after the fall of the communist regime, that is, in the first half of the 1990s, Bucharest's two main journalism schools at academic level where the said School of Journalism and Mass Communication Studies within the University of Bucharest and The Superior School of Journalism, founded by the Association of Romanian Journalists. While the former put emphasis on the academic formation of its faculty, which included practitioners as well as theoreticians, the latter employed mostly working journalists who brought to the school their own experience. The Superior School of Journalism, however, ceased to exist in 2002.

Types of journalism education

The number of journalism schools around the country reflects the great number of media outlets in Romania. There are several types of journalism training and formation in place in the country: academic schools (self-standing departments or journalism sections or classes integrated in other departments, such as Literature, Social Sciences or Philosophy); vocational schools such as independent training centres; on the job training; project-based training (shorter programmes devised by various non-governmental organisations, usually with funding from European and international institutions such as the European Union or the UN).

Academic journalism education

There are twenty-five higher education journalism schools legally functioning in Romania (Coman 2007), either as self-standing colleges within private or state universities, or as departments within Political Science, Sociology or Literature colleges. There are ten journalism schools belonging to state universities, and fifteen within private universities.

According to the Romanian law of academic evaluation and accreditation, higher education schools need to be evaluated by a commission of experts in order to receive a functioning licence. In the journalism field, of the twenty-five schools functioning, three schools in Bucharest, two in Timisoara and one each in Cluj, Iasi, Sibiu and Arad are the only ones accredited. The others have received a provisional authorization and are yet to complete a series of academic criteria in order to be fully licenced. Half of the state schools and one-third of the private schools had received accreditation by 2007 (Coman 2007).

Vocational journalism education

The Center for Independent Journalism (CIJ) in Bucharest, established in the early 1990s by the New York City-based Independent Journalism Foundation, but now functioning as an independent, self-run NGO, is the most important training centre for journalists and the single such institution offering training courses on a permanent basis. The Center offers paid semester-long courses for working journalists and students, and allows free access to its journalism library, formerly known as the Freedom Forum library, as it was started up as part of the network of the Freedom Forum foundation in the United States. CIJ is actively involved in advocacy activities on behalf of Romanian journalists, and is running a series of projects, funded by various institutions, aimed at the journalism community but also at other areas of Romanian society.

In the 1990s, the BBC School was the training facility where mid-career or beginner journalists could learn radio and TV journalism in an intensive, hands-on ten-week course taught by BBC professionals. About 150 people were trained by the BBC School in Bucharest, which produced some of today's best-known and respected journalists in Romania.

On the job training and coaching

Most Romanian media outlets do not have especially designed on the job training or training departments. Newcomers to the newsroom are usually coached by their more experienced colleagues and supervisors and are generally expected to learn the craft by doing the job.

In early 1992, the newly launched daily *Evenimentul zilei*, which later became one of the best-selling newspapers in the country, was training its new staffers in the so-called 'Evenimentul zilei Press School'. It was no proper school, but rather a coaching operation run by its director, experienced journalist Ion Cristoiu, who believed in on-the-job training.

Starting in the mid-2000s, however, due to the shortage of good journalists whereas the number of media outlets was growing, some companies have started to pay more attention to their training needs and to plan training and coaching activities more thoroughly. Several dozen local publishers, grouped under an umbrella organisation called The Association of Local Publishers, are commissioning trainers for short training sessions at the newspapers' premises. Acting in association helps pay the training costs. Such training sessions are seldom, however.

Another example of in-house training was press agency NewsIn, based in Bucharest, which ran a comprehensive training and recruitment programme when it started its operation, in 2006. Although thought up as a permanent programme, it was later discontinued.

Project-based training

One of the most common ways to provide journalism skills and knowledge to journalists was through training projects run by various non-governmental organizations and funded by American and European institutions.

Aimed usually at working journalists, such projects generally consist of short-term workshops and seminars, or a series of such venues bringing together journalists from various media outlets in the same place. They receive training in such areas as reporting, editing, photojournalism, investigative reporting or more particular disciplines like business reporting, community journalism, blogs etc.

The effectiveness of such workshops and trainers is sometimes low due to newsroom inertia: once back at their work place, many journalists who took part in training sessions tend to go back to the old habits their news operation had been embracing. This is the reason why some of the more recent training projects have started to pay more attention to in-house training and to the development of newsroom tools that could ensure the sustainability of the training effort.

One such project included a series of in-house training weeks, where trainers travelled to the newsrooms and worked with the journalists there without removing them from their day-to-day news production effort. The same project, funded by the Dutch MATRA programme and run in the period 2006 through 2008 by Bucharest-based StartMedia and FreeVoice in the Netherlands, with the participation of the Center for Independent Journalism in Bucharest, encouraged participating newspapers to develop their own style guides, codes of conduct and workflow routine so that both old and new staffers could observe written documents on the rules of the newsroom.

Journalism instructors and teachers

When journalism education was established in the early 1990s, one of the most important problems having to be faced by the new educational institutions was the lack of specialized educators. Who should teach journalism? On one hand, there were those experienced journalists whose expertise was limited to the type of press they had been forced to practice during communism – that is, heavily controlled by the communist regime, which used the media outlets for propaganda. On the other hand, just like many people from very varied professional backgrounds started to work in the press after the fall of communism, journalism academic education was soon to be populated by teachers who had experience in other disciplines such as social sciences, political studies, literature, foreign languages, or even computer science. It was a natural evolution since journalism had practically been a closed field beforehand.

This resulted in two types of approaches for the nascent journalism schools: on one hand, the University of Bucharest's school of journalism decided to compose its faculty of professionals from related fields whose disciplines were anyway part of the curriculum. The school's dean was Mihai Coman, who was an anthropologist, but also had experience as a journalist with the daily *Scînteia tineretului/The Youth's Spark,* which after the fall of communism became *Tineretul liber/The Free Youth* and other publications. He hired teachers who did not necessarily have experience in journalism, or, if they did work in the press, did not necessarily hold senior positions, but had expertise in grammar, literature, foreign languages, semiotics, sociology, political science etc. The school sent these staffers to be trained at journalism schools from Western countries such as France and the United States.

For more practical courses, the school chose to invite guest lecturers who held positions in the press. Also, students visited newsrooms and had a mandatory internship period each school year, when they were required to work in a media outlet.

On the other hand, the Superior School of Journalism, which benefited from close links to Bucharest-based publishers, recruited its teachers mainly from the ranks of well-known working journalists.

There were pros and cons for both approaches. The journalism school's curriculum at the University of Bucharest was well structured and quite similar to those of many Western journalism education institutions, but some critics said it favoured theory over practice. The Superior School of Journalism's working staffers were closer to the profession, but sometimes lacked the necessary academic skills or even the journalism standards required in West-European and American journalism outlets.

At that time, students and their schools benefited a great deal from the input of international teachers, scholars and journalists. At the University of Bucharest, but also in other newly established journalism schools across the country, some of the courses were being taught by British, French or American journalists who had been brought to the country through such programmes as Knight or Fulbright, or through the efforts of their countries' governments, which established partnerships with the Romanian Ministry of Education. Other sponsors included the Open Society / Soros foundations or the European Union.

As time has passed, journalism schools have started to hire their own alumni, some of whom had had time to build their own careers in journalism, thus bringing to the school both academic standards and professional expertise.

Over the years, journalism schools have started to show a preoccupation to involve journalism professionals in the teaching process, either as guest lecturers, or as permanent staffers. Journalists themselves have started to view teaching as a prestige-enhancement tool, and so are often happy to cooperate with journalism schools.

Content

There is no universal model for the specializations within Romanian journalism schools. Some, like the School of Journalism of the private 'Tibiscus' university in Timisoara, offer just a specialization in journalism. Others, like the School of Journalism and Mass Communication Studies within the University of Bucharest, offer a journalism track, as well as Advertising and PR tracks (in this case, students have to opt for one of the tracks after the first three semesters).

Basic journalism classes include, in general, news writing, news gathering, investigative techniques, ethics etc., and courses dedicated to print, wire services, radio, TV, design, multimedia and the Internet. In the past years some schools such as the University of Bucharest's journalism school or the 'Al. I. Cuza' University's school of journalism in Iasi have introduced online journalism classes, to respond to the growing needs of the profession, with soaring Internet audiences. However, online journalism is not yet an important part of the journalism curriculum. At the School of Journalism and Mass Communication Studies, University of Bucharest, students only attend the online journalism class in their last semester, although they do start classes dedicated to the Internet much sooner.

There is not a great deal of specialization into fields, such as science journalism, sports journalism, international news etc. Mostly students go through news journalism classes of a more general nature, but are able to take classes dedicated to a particular medium (print, agency, radio, TV, online), as well as laboratories dealing with technical specializations such as DTP, multimedia production or design.

Journalism schools' policy towards the profession and their curricula vary greatly from one institution to another. What working journalists and journalism institutions tend to dislike about most Romanian academic schools teaching journalism is the low level of adaptability to the profession's needs, that is, poor contacts with the media outlets, and too few practical, skills-based courses and laboratories.

> Schools of journalism are not equal, either with regard to curriculum design, or regarding the equipment quality and amount, or in terms of the faculty staff competency, [...] Very few have resorted to designing an educational pattern exclusively based on the development of abilities, professional culture, and critical thinking specific to journalism. (Coman 2007)

Indeed, looking at course plans from different schools there are visible differences in the ratio between theoretical and practical courses.

But even for the more theory-oriented journalism schools, the requirement for students to work at news outlets on internships is regarded as an important part of the curriculum. Internships are also a means for students to get a job, as some of them are invited to stay and work for the media outlets where they served as interns. Internships are a great way for the students to get a taste of the real life and access future jobs, and a good chance for the schools to have positive integration with and insertion within the profession. At the same time, internships are a marvellous recruitment opportunity for employers.

But the lack of a good relationship and understanding between journalism schools and media outlets on the subject of internships often leads to a situation where all parties, but especially the students are at a loss: as students start working for money, they choose to skip classes, and thus miss some of the fundamental academic activities which could allow them to become better professionals in their future careers. At the same time, media outlets are using the labour, but complain about the newcomers' skills and knowledge on the field. It is a catch-22 situation which could be resolved if both educators and professionals would sit down and work out a better arrangement. The situation is especially visible in the capital Bucharest, where there are a great number of media outlets and personnel needs seem to be ever-growing. (The global economic crisis, however, has forced many publications to cut costs by reducing wages and/or firing journalists, so the need for new personnel has dwindled as of late).

Journalism schools usually offer a Bachelor's Degree and a Master's Degree, according to the Bologna model, with three years of study for the Bachelor's and an additional two years for the Master's. The University of Bucharest also offers a Ph.D. programme.

Most universities in big university centres such as Bucharest, Iasi, Timisoara and Cluj have sound international programmes, with the students and teachers being able to take part in exchanges such as those facilitated by the ERASMUS, Socrates-ERASMUS or Leonardo da Vinci European programmes, and also bilateral agreements with other foreign universities.

Students and trainees

There are no official statistics regarding the number of students enrolled in journalism schools every year, or that of journalists taking part in training programmes.

The number of students accepted by each school varies considerably. The University of Bucharest, for example, takes 250 undergraduate students each year for the regular courses and an extra 200 for distance learning courses. The "Al. I. Cuza" University of Iasi has 238 places for the regular courses in communication and PR, and an extra 100 places for distance learning, and the 'Hyperion' University in Bucharest has 300 places for the regular programme and 200 for the reduced-frequency programme. Overall, we can estimate the total number of journalism, PR and advertising students currently enrolled in Romanian schools at 10–15,000.

Most of those who want to become undergraduate students are fresh high school graduates. In the past years, an increasing number of working journalists have taken up graduate courses or post-university specialization courses. In other countries, many people may become journalism students after getting a Bachelor's Degree in another field, but in Romania there is not a big trend in this direction at the time being.

No statistics are available regarding the ratio of male and female students, but from empiric observation one can deduce that women have a comfortable majority in journalism schools. Roughly, 60–80 per cent of journalism and communication students are female.

Accreditation

In Romania, higher education schools have to be evaluated by a commission of experts in order to receive authorization and accreditation. Upon completing a series of criteria, schools can be authorized for a limited time, after which they can receive final accreditation. Until recently, the body in charge with the evaluation of higher education institutions was the National Council for Academic Evaluation and Accreditation. Its role has been taken over by ARACIS – the Romanian Agency for Quality Assurance in Higher Education, established in 2006.

Romanian law makes it mandatory for higher education institutions to observe the Bologna Process and to take part in the European Transfer Credit System.

However, journalism in itself is a free profession and no board or professional organization has the power to recognize or deny any person the right to consider him or herself a journalist, or to work in the media. A university degree is not necessary, nor sufficient for a person to practice the profession. In other words, having a journalism degree usually does not offer any advantages when seeking a job as a journalist. However, journalism graduates do tend to get most of the journalism jobs, as those who went to journalism schools (or are still students in one) make the majority of the job seekers in the field.

Connection with the industry

As already explained, cooperation between journalism schools and the industry is rather poor. Some schools, such as the School of Journalism and Mass Communication Studies within the University of Bucharest, have internship agreements with news outlets, which bind the media companies receiving students as interns to produce written evaluations of their work during the internship.

Industry professionals cooperate with journalism schools, as guest lecturers or even staff teachers, but rather on an individual basis, as usually there are no formal institutional relations. Funding by the industry is limited (in the entire country there are just one or two laboratories equipped with computers donated by a media group), and there is no mutual accreditation or hiring agreement in place.

The industry and the schools often act as two divergent parties. The former usually complains that the journalism schools are too oriented toward theory and do not prepare their students for real life and real journalism, whereas the latter criticize media outlets for their low professional and ethical standards.

Associations

There have been several attempts at creating a national association of journalism schools over the years. Although there have been workshops, seminars and conferences where educators have come together to discuss the various aspects of their work and the ways in which they should cooperate, there is no formal cooperation at the level of the journalism schools.

However, the end of 2007 saw the start of AFCOM – the Association of Journalism and Communication Educators, which has over 100 individual members from communication schools as well as from the communication industry.

There is a Romanian Association of Press History, which has co-organized, in April 2009, an International Congress of Press History. The congress marked the 180th anniversary since the first newspapers appeared in Romania.

Concluding Remarks

Any professional with a good understanding of the values and principles of journalism who takes a look at the Romanian media can see why journalism education is vital. In spite of the tremendous progress made by the Romanian press in the past years, many media outlets in this country are yet to become the credible institutions that should give citizens living in a democracy access to relevant information and the opportunity to have a voice in society.

The most evident challenges for Romanian journalism in general consist in the need to overcome lack of professionalism and know-how (which translates into low professional and ethical standards and the incapacity to find solutions to capture or recapture audiences), lack of resources, and corruption (as often media outlets around the country are being used by their owners as tools to gain political influence and economic advantages). In addition to being prone to political manipulation, many publications and radio or TV stations turn to tabloidization and sensationalism, seen as the last resort in the fight to keep the public.

But good journalism and innovative approaches are much better answers to the challenges facing the journalistic community. Only, you need good journalists to practice good journalism and innovation. 'Good journalists? I'd be happy if they knew how to spell right,' a Bucharest-based editor told the author of this chapter recently, echoing similar exclamations from a good number of other senior journalists. Until the start of the global economic crisis, a large part of the Romanian media outlets had experienced a human resources crisis. As media expert Iulian Comanescu noticed, the number of media outlets kept increasing, whereas the nucleus of good, reliable journalists has stayed the same, which means the number of good journalists per media outlet diminished. And this is likely to translate into lower circulation figures (Comanescu 2006).

Under these circumstances, and taking into consideration the fact that, with Romania's EU accession, the funds for training projects received from international institutions have reduced considerably, the industry needs to realize it has to regard training as a fundamental component of its activity. Media outlets need to start investing in training programmes; they could either develop such programmes in-house, or they could start working closer with training and education institutions such as vocational training centres and university schools.

At the same time, journalism schools need to adapt themselves better to the market, offering more hands-on training and closing the ties with the industry, to the benefit of both parties, but mainly to the benefit of the students. Also, they should realize their role is not only to fulfil the jobs demand, but also to help strengthen democracy by moulding professionals with deep knowledge of the field and with high ethical standards, who could shift Romanian journalism toward the type of responsible, relevant media needed by a young democracy.

The Author

Alexandru-Bradut Ulmanu is a journalist and an international trainer specialized in print and online journalism. He writes for Esquire magazine (Romanian edition), and is an adjunct professor at the University of Bucharest.

References

Coman, Mihai (2007), 'Patterns and Experience: Journalism Education in Romania', In Hans Bohrmann; Elisabeth Klaus and Marcel Machill (eds), *Media Industry, Journalism Culture and Communication Policies in Europe*, Vistas: Berlin.

Coman Mihai (2003), *Mass media in Romania post-comunista/ The Media in Post-Communist Romania*, Polirom: Iasi.

Comanescu, Iulian (2006), 'Human Resources Crisis on the Romanian Media Market', *Romanian Media Explained*, 9 November, http: //www.comanescu.ro/2006/11/09/human-resources-crisis-in-romanian-media-market.

Petcu, Marian (2004), 'Invatamantul jurnalistic romanesc: schita istorica', *Jurnalism & Comunicare*, 3(8), pp. 94–111.

The Slovakian Journalism Education Landscape

Jozef Vatrál

Introduction

Today's democratic Slovakia, which became a member of the European Union in 2004, has gone through a few state formations in the era of 'Gutenberg Galaxy'. At the beginning of this era, Slovak territory was a part of multicultural Hungarian kingdom. After the Battle of Mohacs in 1526 where forces of the Ottoman Empire won, Ferdinand I. Habsburg became the new king of Hungary. He was elected the king by the Hungarian chamber in Bratislava (at that time in Slovak, German and Hungarian languages known as Prešporok – Pressburg – Poszony) which was a capital city of the Kingdom of Hungary until 1784.

The first leaflet newspaper *Zwo Wahrhaftige Newe Zeytung/Two Truthful News* was printed in German language in 1594. The first information in the leaflet was on the fights with the Ottoman Empire and the second news story informed people about a comet above Constantinopolis.

The first newspaper with irregular periodicity *Mercurius Hungaricus/Hungarian Courier,* aka *Mercurius veridicus ex Hungaria/Veracious Courier from Hungaria* was published in Latin during the period of 1705–11 in cities of Levoča, Košice and Bardejov as a part of an anti-Habsburg resistance service under the leadership of Francis II. Rakoczi. Foundation of the first weekly newspaper printed in Latin, *Nova Posoniensia/New Pressbourgh* (1721–22), was initiated by an important contemporary polymath Matej Bel. The first newspapers in the German language *Pressburger Zeitung/Pressbourgh News* (1764–1929), in the Hungarian language *Magyár Hírmondó/Magyar News* (1780–88) and in the Slovak language *Presspůrské noviny/Pressbourgh News* (1783–87) were founded.

The beginnings of modern Slovak political journalism were represented by *Slovenské národné noviny/Slovak National News* (1845–48). The second political newspaper of the Slovak nation *Pešťbudínske vedomosti/Budapest Knowledge* (1861–70) and *Slovenské noviny/ Slovak News* (1868–75) as well as the first daily newspaper *Slovenské noviny/Slovak News* (1900–01 and 1910–15) were published in Budapest. Another newspaper *Národné noviny/ National News* (1871–1948) was published in the city of Martin.

After the Austro-Hungarian Compromise of 1867, under which the Austrian Habsburgs agreed to share power with a separate Hungarian government, the Slovak nation was under even more intense pressure of Hungarization. Hungarian offices closed down Slovak grammar secondary schools and the all-nation cultural establishment 'Matica slovenská'.

The Slovak nation did not have any grammar secondary or higher education schools in operation again until the formation of Czechoslovakia in 1918.

The sovereign state of Czechs and Slovaks (1918–92; with a continuity break during World War II) literally saved the Slovak nation from a complete Hungarization and allowed them to develop their own social, cultural, and scholastic institutions and complex media system. Electronic media in the former Czechoslovakia were founded – public radio broadcasting in Prague (1923) and television (1953). Similar services were established in Bratislava – public radio (1926) and television (1956).

Where we came from

The beginnings of journalism education in former Czechoslovakia, where Slovakia was a part of this state formation between the years 1918 and 1992, are connected with the foundation of Slobodná škola politických náuk/the Independent School of Political Science in Prague in 1928. In Prague, between 1928 and 1931, the first magazine for journalists *Duch novin/ Spirit of Newspaper* was issued. The Faculty of Journalism was located at the Vysoká škola politická a sociálna/College of Political and Social Science in Prague between the years 1946 and 1950. Specialized study of Journalism was later opened at the Department of Journalism Faculty of Arts, Comenius University in Bratislava in 1952 (Šefčák 2002: 252) and from September 1953 was also offered at Charles University in Prague.

The Faculty of Journalism at Charles University was founded in Prague in 1972. In 1975 at Comenius University in Bratislava three departments and a research cabinet were opened: Department of theory and history of journalism, Department of periodical press and news agency journalism, Department of radio and television journalism and Cabinet of theory and history of journalism.

The content of the study in the 1950s was closely connected to a study of Slovak language and literature. A qualitative change was brought in the 1960s – more importance was put on education in journalistic subjects. Theory of journalism was developed, predominantly thanks to Professor Mieroslav Hysko, and a variety of specializations were introduced – print, radio, TV and other branches of journalism – national and international politics, economics, culture and sport.

After a military occupation of Czechoslovakia by armies of the Warsaw Pact in August 1968 our School of Journalism was labelled as contrarevolutionary. Five out of eleven teachers had to leave the University and another four were forced to stop their professional career at school. The content of the study programme was in line with the normalization era – there were many new courses of applied Marxist-Leninist theory in journalism, theory of propaganda and agitation, contemporary politics of the Communist Party of Czechoslovakia (KSČ) and Czechoslovak Socialist Republic (ČSSR), party leadership of mass media tools and propaganda, criticism of theory and praxis of bourgeois journalism, and manipulation by means of linguistics in bourgeois mass media. The role of a journalist was identified with the role of a political employee of the Communist Party.

Where are we heading to?

After November 1989 all study programmes were revised and adjusted in line with prominent European and American journalistic schools at universities. Katedra žurnalistiky/ Department of Journalism at the Faculty of Arts, Comenius University was founded in 1992 by a merging of three former Departments. The content of journalism education has been dramatically changed in the 1990s and became more comparable to the journalistic studies at other European and overseas universities, e.g. in Vienna, Bern and the University of Missouri. The Department effectively cooperated with the American Center of Independent Journalism (1993–2004). Transformation of the study programme was positively evaluated by Ami Lönnroth (1997) in a book titled *Journalism Training in Europe*.

The conditions of the small mass media market in Slovakia demand a universal journalist. Along with journalism graduates there are many graduates of other universities as well as journalists without a university degree working in editorial offices today.

Journalism or (mass)media communication was gradually taught from mid 1990s at the Department of Journalism, Faculty of Arts, Constantine the Philosopher University in Nitra; at the Faculty of Mass Media Communication, University of St. Cyril and Methodius in Trnava; at the Department of Slovak Language and Literature at Faculty of Humanities, Matej Bel University in Banská Bystrica; at Faculty of Arts, University of Prešov in Prešov; at the Catholic University in Ružomberok; at the Faculty of Mass Media at the private Bratislava School of Law and lately at the Department of Slovak Studies, Slavonic Philologies and Communication at Faculty of Arts, Pavol Jozef Šafárik Univesity in Košice. Two non-governmental organizations – Academy of Media Bratislava and School of Communication and Media in Bratislava – also started their journalism education activities in 2008.

Based on local conditions, journalistic schools cooperate with media and non-media organizations and seek material and financial support. In certain cases this cooperation is based on a contract. Media (private and public) are interested in providing internships in editorial offices, giving lectures or judging media products. Schools invite members of editorial offices for discussion meetings with students. The Department of Journalism in Bratislava has very good work-study relationships with Ringier Slovakia, Slovak Radio, Penta Foundation and Slovak Syndicate of Journalists.

The Department of Journalism at Faculty of Arts, Comenius University has been the only school in Slovakia, so far, to become a member of European Journalism Training Association – EJTA (1992). Students of the Department have been regularly attending the international project Euroreporter since 1994.

Novinársky študijný ústav/Institute of Journalism Studies was founded in 1955 at a journalistic organisation that dedicated its work to scientific research. Institutionalized media research was also held by the Institute of Journalism Studies in the 1990s and by its successor, the National Centre of Media Communication, which then ceased its activities in the year 2000. The Institute started with issuing a year-book *Otázky novinárstva/Problems of Journalism* in 1958 which has continued under the name *Otázky žurnalistiky/Problems of Journalism* since 1962 as a quarterly. Since 2002 this journal for theory, research and practice of mass media communication is issued by the Association Mass-Media-Science at the Department of Journalism, Faculty of Arts, Comenius University in Bratislava generally as two double-issues per year.

Three levels of higher education

Content of higher education study programmes in the area of Journalism and Mass Media Studies must follow the criteria defined by the Accreditation Commission, the advisory body of the Slovak Republic Government. The Accreditation Commission carries out regular complex accreditation of all higher education institutions in six-year intervals. Beside other attributes, the following ones are evaluated: level of research or artistic activities, material, technical, IT equipment and personnel security.

Slovak universities have adopted a three-level (Bachelor's, Master's and Doctoral degree) education system and implemented credit system (ECTS) according to the terms of the Bologna Process. As an example, we will describe the contents of Journalism study programmes.

Dominant themes of knowledge in Bachelor's study programmes, which take three years to complete, are bound with a genesis of journalism activities and the basics of the communication process in practice. The core programme consists of the following courses: Contemporary Slovak Language and Stylistics, Introduction to Journalism Studies, Genres of Journalism, History of Journalism, Creative Writing, Theory of Editing and Mass Communication Media Law. Other dominant themes include: Media specialization (periodical press, radio, television, news and marketing agency, new media), Psychological and sociological aspects of the journalism profession and New information technologies (the Internet). It is recommended that credit value of these courses reach at least 3–5 ECTS credits for the whole study programme. The completion of bachelor study consists of completing a final written thesis (8,500–15,000 words), the defence of the thesis and oral state exam. The graduates of the Bachelor's level study are awarded by the academic degree of 'Bakalár' or 'Bc.'

Graduates of successive second-level study programmes in journalism (which takes two years) gain knowledge from other areas applicable to journalism study – philosophy, psychology, sociology, politology, macro-economics, international relations, cultural studies, fundamentals of the theory of state and law, press and author law, information policy, ethics of journalism, media management and public relations. Students study one of the basic branches of journalism (domestic politics, foreign politics, economics, culture, sports or photojournalism). They are able to carry out media research. The completion of the Master's study programme consists of completing a diploma thesis (15,000–23,000 words), the defence of the thesis and an oral exam. The graduates receive a diploma and are awarded by the academic degree of 'Magister' or 'Mgr.'

An important part of both levels of the study programmes is the practical journalism performance of the students in school print, electronic and internet media and internships in private and public media and news agencies.

Higher education graduates of journalism who were awarded by the academic degree 'Mgr.' can carry out a rigorous exam, part of which is a defence of the rigorosa thesis (23,000–28,000 words). The graduates are then awarded by the academic degree 'Doctor of Philosophy' or 'PhDr.'

The Ph.D. study programme is a third level study and is ongoing according to an individual study plan under the supervision of a tutor. The standard length for pursuing a Ph.D. study programme is three years in a daily form and five years in an external form of study. The study part consists first of all from lectures, seminars and the individual study of special literature. The scientific part consists of an individual research project. The completion of Ph.D. study consists of completing a dissertation examination and the defence of the dissertation (23,000–35,000 words). Graduates of the Ph.D. study programme are awarded by the academic degree of 'Philosophiae Doctor' or 'Ph.D.'

International mobility of students within Socrates/ERASMUS programmes in the area of mass media science and journalism is not common enough despite the fact that, for example, the Faculty of Arts at Comenius University has joined the credit system of study (ECTS) since the year 2000. ECTS have been accepted by all schools of journalism in Slovakia. The Bachelor's study programme in journalism or mass media communication (180 ECTS) in daily or distance form usually takes three years. The Master's study programme (120 ECTS) takes two years and the Ph.D. study programme (180 ECTS) takes three years in a daily form and five years in an external form of study.

Feminisation of journalistic profession

Since the number of applications and thus the number of students interested in the study of journalism is above the capacity of journalism schools, each school organizes entrance exams. The content of entrance exams is not standardized nationwide. The majority of schools would agree that the results of entrance exams should take into consideration results from grammar secondary schools, talent and interpersonal skills important for journalism as a profession and also knowledge that are all measured via tests.

The Faculty of Mass Media Communication University of St. Cyril and Methodius in Trnava admitted the most students among all Slovak universities in the academic year 2008 accepting 200 for mass media communication and 300 for marketing communication. Four other universities (Comenius University in Bratislava, Constantine the Philosopher

University in Nitra, The Catholic University in Ružomberok and University of Prešov in Prešov) and the Faculty of Mass Media at Bratislava School of Law will each year admit approximately 300 students of journalism and mass media communication in total.

There is no such data available on the course gender splits, however, based on the statistics of the Department of Journalism at Faculty of Arts, Comenius University, we can presume that the trend of the feminisation of the journalistic profession continues. 70 per cent of all the students are women. According to a simplified and humorous interpretation of research on the journalistic profession in Slovakia which was carried out in 2005 by Samuel Brečka "a typical Slovak journalist is a women with higher education, age 40, divorced" (Brečka 2005: 17–26).

Concluding Remarks

Journalistic education, after the Velvet Revolution in 1989 and after the formation of an independent Slovak Republic in 1993, has been gradually transformed in a way that it corresponds with requirements of independent democratic society (Droppa 1997: 33–40). At the same time it quickly responded to a quantitative boom in the mass media area by the foundation of new schools aimed not only at mass media communication but also at marketing communication. It is a question though if Slovakia, a relatively small country, needs so many journalistic schools in a situation where financial resources for the university education do not allow them good personnel or technical and IT space and equipment. The most important challenges for journalism education in Slovakia were formed at the Conference Perspective from Retrospective in 2007 by Samuel Brečka:

1. Wider differentiation and specialization of Slovak media education;
2. Subordination of personnel politics to conceptional objectives of schools;
3. Intensifying and enhancement of research and scientific activities;
4. Increased number of qualified pedagogic staff;
5. Redesign of study programmes with the aim to bring more variety and be able to react onto current requirements of practice.

The Author

Jozef Vatrál Ph.D., Associate Professor, head of Department of Journalism at Faculty of Arts, Comenius University (2000–2007), chairman of Association Mass-Media-Science (2001–), editor-in-chief of *Otázky žurnalistiky/Problems of Journalism* magazine (2002–2008), member of Supervisory board of Slovak Syndicate of Journalists, and chairman of Commision for Education (2004–2007).

References

Brečka, S. (2005), *Novinárska profesia na Slovensku v roku 2005/Journalism as a Profession in Slovakia in 2005*, http://www.ssn.sk/source/document/000005.doc. Accessed 30 June 2008.

Droppa, B., Vatrál, J. and Vojtek, J. (1997), 'Proposed Changes to the Study Program of the School of Journalism, Faculty of Arts, Comenius University', *Zborník FiF UK Žurnalistika*, XXIII–XXIV, pp. 33–40.

Lönnroth, A. (1997), *Journalism Training in Europe*, EJTA/AEFJ, 1997, p. 207.

Šefčák, L., Vatrál, J. and Vojtek, J. (2002), 'Katedra žurnalistiky Filozofickej fakulty Univerzity Komenského 1952–2002/Department of Journalism Faculty of Arts Comenius University 1952–2002', *Otázky žurnalistiky*, 45, pp. 252–264.

The Slovenian Journalism Education Landscape

Marko Milosavljevic

Introduction

The history of professional journalism education in Slovenia is relatively short. Many of the Slovenian journalists and editors from eighteenth and nineteenth century were, like in Western and Central European countries, (also) writers, novelists and intellectuals with very different backgrounds and education. Most of them became journalists through practice and lacked organized knowledge and systematic journalistic epistemology and methodology. Even more, Slovenia didn't have a university education in the Slovenian language until after the fall of the Austro-Hungarian Empire, which it was a part of, in 1918. Therefore Slovenian writers, journalists and editors were mainly educated in Austrian universities, particularly in Vienna, in German.

Organized journalism education in Slovenia occurred only after World War II, in 1964, with the first course on journalism at the newly renamed High School of Sociology, Political Sciences and Journalism (formerly High School of Political Sciences). France Vreg, who established the study of journalism in Slovenia, studied comparative literature, however he was an editor of a partisan newspaper during the German occupation of Slovenia in Word War II and he later realized that journalists and editors need professional and organized education.

At that time, in 1964 when the first journalism courses were organized, the journalism study programme was part of the Faculty of Sociology, Political Sciences and Journalism, a faculty that was also important in the education of (communistic) politicians and was therefore often perceived as a political institution. Journalists in Yugoslavia (of which Slovenia was part of at that time) were officially defined as socio-political workers. However the Department of Journalism, even then, managed to develop a relatively independent programme, where many Western European and American professors and journalists came as guest lecturers, both in the area of applied knowledge and in the area of communication theory. The literature referred to at journalistic courses was predominantly American and Western European, most often available to the students in the original form through books and texts. In 1970 the school became part of the University of Ljubljana and was renamed again, as the 'Faculty of Sociology, Political Sciences and Journalism'.

In the end of 1980s, the socialistic federal system in Yugoslavia started to fall apart and journalists were one of the key elements in the spreading of more democratic and pluralistic views and demands in the society. A number of journalists and editors were jailed or prosecuted, and a number of dailies and weeklies were confiscated and their distribution prohibited. However all these attempts to stop or prevent the media and journalists from publishing critical articles were unsuccessful.

The journalism education programme at the University of Ljubljana, which was already very open in the 1980s, didn't have problems with following the social and political developments, since it was in many aspects actually the starting point for many young journalists and editors who started and promoted democratic and pluralistic views and processes. In the 1990s therefore, the study of Journalism became even more international, with guest professors from the United States, France and elsewhere coming on a regular basis, as well as with domestic Slovenian professors regularly visiting European, North American and other universities and research centres, as guest professors, researchers and other participants in the education and research of journalism and media.

The faculty became the 'Faculty of Social Sciences' in 1991 and remains so also today. The Faculty of Social Sciences also quickly became part of the Bologna Process and the European Transfer Credit System (ETCS) and was, in many aspects, actually the pioneer of these changes at the University of Ljubljana and in Slovenia as a whole.

Programmes

At present, Slovenian journalism education is developing in four different frameworks:

1. As a study organized by public universities – there are three main public universities in Slovenia and each is now offering or starting to offer courses on journalism or journalism studies. The Faculty of Social Sciences (Fakulteta za družbene vede – FDV), which is part of the oldest university in Slovenia, the University of Ljubljana, is today still the strongest provider of journalism education. The programme of journalism education is run by the Department of Journalism. There are also programmes of marketing and public relations, and theoretical media studies, run by the Department of Marketing and the Department of Media Studies, respectively.

   Two other state universities, University of Maribor and Primorska University, have recently started teaching media studies programmes (Media Communication at the Faculty of electro-techniques, computers and informatics; Media Studies, respectively), or they are preparing to; however they do not provide pure journalism courses or programmes.

   The Roman Catholic Church is establishing its own university with three faculties. These will not contain journalism programmes, however they also have plans to form and provide new journalists.

2. As a non-university study programme organized by schools of higher (post-secondary school) education – a number of newly established private faculties and polytechnics are preparing programmes, connected with journalism education; however these programmes haven't started yet. They include a two-year programme on Photography

(which includes some lectures on photojournalism) starting in Sežana, and Media Studies at the private Faculty of Media.

3. As in-house vocational training courses organized by publishers and broadcasters. Public broadcaster RTV Slovenia has established an Educational Centre which provides vocational training for their cameramen and women, voice training for radio and television speakers and hosts, etc. The largest newspaper publishing company Delo also provided their newly-employed journalists with in-house training; however this training is not as defined and planned as it used to be.

4. As a professional training programme organized by associations or non-governmental organizations (NGOs). The Union of Slovenian Journalists (Sindikat novinarjev Slovenije), employers associations and other organizations do not organize regular journalism courses and education. The only exception is the Peace Institute (Mirovni inštitut), an NGO that was part of the Open Society Institute and that occasionally organizes workshops on various media topics, particularly coverage of different minorities and for different minorities (such as Roma).

University journalism education is regulated by the general demands of university education in Slovenia. One of its main demands says that the courses must be run by academic professors and researchers with Ph.D. and other academic references. This is also the case with the Faculty of Social Sciences (FDV) main provider of journalism education in Slovenia which is part of University of Ljubljana (UL): the main part of its teaching staff in the Department of Journalism consists of academic professors and researchers. However most of them also have previous journalistic experience as journalists or editors. The Department also has a tradition of professional journalists teaching, and because of this tradition (and as an exception to the general rule of the University), a number of courses have been run by high-ranking and esteemed journalists and editors from television, radio and print media. These courses included Radio, Television, Editors Work, and similar.

Study of Journalism at the University of Ljubljana, which remains the only university programme on Journalism, offers different levels of degrees: Bachelor's, Master's and Ph.D. It is part of the Bologna Process and the European Transfer Credit System (ECTS). Its undergraduate programme lasts for four years, while its postgraduate master's programme lasts for one year. Students of Journalism are part of the wider section of Communication studies, which also includes Marketing and Public Relations, and Theoretical Media Studies. The Journalism programme is therefore concentrated on journalism studies and courses. All programmes and courses at the University of Ljubljana, as well as at other universities and polytechnics, must be approved by the National Board for Higher Education. A Ph.D. study of Journalism is also planned and will start in the next few years.

The concept of Journalism Studies

The main concept of Journalism Studies at the Faculty of Social Sciences has for decades been a quadruple combination:

1. General courses relevant for general knowledge and education.
2. Media theory and journalism theory courses.
3. A set of courses covering professional training.
4. A range of free courses, chosen by students according to their preferences.

Ad. 1. A number of general courses are offered to the students, on the presumption that journalists need good knowledge of some of the main aspects of society such as the courses on Economy and Law.

Ad. 2. A number of courses on general communication and media theory are also offered, such as Communication Methodology, and Theory of Mass Communication and Public Opinion. These courses should offer the journalists the key knowledge on media theory and effects.

Ad. 3. A third important segment of courses are those on general journalism issues, such as Journalism Ethics, Media Law, Stylistics, and on specific journalistic topics, such as News Reporting, News Writing, Radio, Television, News Editing. A course on new media is being prepared, and in the meantime some of the aspects of new media are already offered at the course Media Practicum. Specialized topics, such as science, sports, or international journalism, are also covered within this course. Science, sports or international television and radio journalism are covered within two other courses, Radio Practicum and Television Practicum. Both of them consist of different lectures by different professionals from the media who are experienced in these topics. Journalism education courses altogether represent approximately 50 per cent of their curricula.

Ad. 4. Since the study of journalism at the Faculty of Social Sciences is part of the Bologna system, students can choose a large number of courses according to their preferences and interests. These courses represent the fourth part of the curriculum where students choose courses that will help them to gain knowledge in the areas if their main (professional) interests and that should help them to gain more knowledge and expertise in the topics that they would like to cover as professional journalists.

International relations and relationships with the industry

The Faculty of Social Sciences at the University of Ljubljana is part of a number of exchange programmes with other institutions. These include institutions within the European Union

(EU), the United States and countries from Europe who are not members of the EU yet. More than 90 agreements are signed with different European faculties and universities, either bilaterally or through participation in the EU, ERASMUS and ERASMUS Mundus. In 2007/08, approximately 190 students of FDV studied abroad through these exchanges of students, and approximately 200 foreign students studied at FDV. A number of courses are offered in the English language, including News Reporting and News Editing, and almost 30 foreign students participated in this course. A number of professors from the European Union and the region visit the faculty every year and provide the students with guest lectures, adding the international aspect also to the courses and lectures. In addition to that, guest professors from the United States visit the faculty every couple of years, staying for one semester or a whole year and enhancing this international approach to journalism education even more.

All students of Journalism at FDV have to take an internship at one of the main Slovenian media companies. The Department of Journalism has signed special contracts or treaties with each of these main media companies, regulating the students' obligations and work during their internship. The internship takes place in the third year of studies and lasts for three weeks.

Approximately 50 students enrol each year into the Journalism programme at FDV. More than 80 per cent of these students are female.

The study of Journalism has been closely connected with the media industry ever since the 1960s. The first fund for scholarships, foreign guest lecturers and media equipment was already established by the then-Head of Department, the late Professor France Vreg, who also played a key role in establishing journalism and media studies in other Yugoslav republics, such as Croatia, Bosnia and Herzegovina, and Serbia. Direct connections with the industry remain alive ever since, as media companies participate in the organization of internships, but also with providing guest lecturers, professionals, as well as occasionally with funding and hiring practices. The Department of Journalism regularly interacts with media companies, managers and editors, informing students of different job positions, working opportunities, awards and other developments.

General situation of journalism education in Slovenia

One of the main problems of Slovenia in general is its small size which poses a number of limitations in economy, but in media, education and academia as well. Journalism education is thus facing a problem with finding an adequate number and quality of people who are educated well (for academia) and who are able or willing to participate as instructors (for professionals). The University of Maribor is, to overcome this problem, importing professors from Croatia and Austria; however this is still not a perfect solution as these professors do not speak the domestic, Slovenian language. As the number of institutions offering journalism and media education increases, the problem of an adequate faculty with educated and experienced staff will only increase in future years. Already fears of a lowered or inadequate quality of staff and programmes have been expressed.

The teaching staff can be divided into two groups: academic professors and researchers; and professionals. There are problems with both groups.

With the academics, there is a problem regarding adequate numbers and quality:

- As mentioned, because of the small population (2 million), there is a relatively small number of academics who hold Ph.D. and tenure, which enables them to hold courses at the university programmes. This was not a problem until recently, however due to the increase of education institutions it has lately become more of an issue.
- There is however also a problem regarding quality, or rather whether these academics are appropriate for journalistic education. Because of the rise in the number of journalistic education programmes available, and because of the increasing demand for the lecturers in this subject area, a number of lecturers have 'diverted' into the media field, particularly people from sociology and political studies, who often did not find adequate jobs or positions in their own areas of expertise. They have now become lecturers/academics in the media/journalism field however there is a problem with their expertise in this field, particularly with their practical knowledge and insight into journalism: its values, genres, history etc.

Regarding professional journalists and editors, who also contribute to the education process, there is no lack of them. However there are specific problems with their inclusion as well:

- There is a question of their pedagogical skills of transferring the knowledge and presenting it in an adequate way to the students/listeners. A senior position in journalism and years, even decades of experience in writing or editing does not automatically transfer into the pedagogical skill.
- There is a problem with their professional schedules. Top editors and journalists usually do not have enough time to lecture regularly on a weekly basis, and even if they agree to lecture regularly, often have problems with preparations and other obligations.
- There is also a problem of the transfer of old practices and in-house professional values from the companies and media where they come from. The reproduction of old patterns in the ways of journalistic behaviour, decisions and values can be problematic when it comes to the question of journalistic ethics, quality and responsibility. Since many of existing media and journalists lack a number of these qualities, there is a problem of whether the employment of professional journalists will lead also to the reproduction of these old problems and patterns.

A further problem with journalism education is related to the history of Slovenian journalism. 'Professionalism', as it is being defined and taught in Western Europe and the United States, is defined in terms of the history of their journalism, particularly in the United States, where impartiality and objectivity play a great role, reflecting also in the division between reporters and editorial writers. Slovenian journalism, on the other hand, was always closely related to politics and culture, not just in the period after World War II and socialism, but also before World War II, dating back to nineteenth century and divisions between liberals and clericals, so-called Young Slovenes and Old Slovenes. Socialism continued with this political influence on journalism; in spite of the fact that Slovenia was part of Yugoslavia where media censorship and repression was softer than in the countries of the Warsaw Pact, journalists were still considered to be 'social and political workers', as they were defined at that time by the Yugoslav Communist Party. This strong political (and partly also cultural and intellectual) role of journalists continues from after the fall of socialism in 1990 until today, as a number of them are closely connected to different political parties and pursue their own political agendas.

A further problem is presented by politicians, who often perceive journalists as either their promoters or their secretaries, who should write down just what the politician said at press conference or speech. Critical writing, reporting, discoveries of corruption and other wrongdoing are therefore often attacked by politicians as being biased or un-appropriate. Some of the new programmes of journalistic education are believed to be a result of some politicians and parties, who would like to educate future journalists according to their perceptions and to pursue their agendas and views, and to therefore shape the future media and journalism in Slovenia also through the education itself.

This political problem is related to the financial 'problem'. Namely the study of journalism has, in spite of all the obstacles, remained very popular and attracts a large number of applicants every year. This is also one of the reasons for the introduction of a number of new programmes in the last few years, since other universities and institutions saw financially attractive additions that would bring an increase of their revenue, which is falling in many other areas of education. However, as mentioned before, this financial motivation is not appropriately reflected in the quality of the study and of the personnel. Therefore, we could talk about the increasing 'tycoonization' of journalistic education.

Finally, there is a question of adequate journalistic educations per se. Since journalism is not a profession in the way law or medicine is, there is a long and consistent dilemma about what the appropriate education is for a journalist: is it a specialized university study? Or is it any university study 'enhanced' with professional training and workshops? Or is education actually irrelevant and anybody with good skills in writing and performing and with talent can become just as good or even a better journalist? This dilemma is particularly relevant for the Slovenian situation, since a large number of older journalists do not have (any) university education (or at least have not finished it with a diploma). According to some estimates by the Slovene Association of Journalists, there are approximately 40 per cent of such journalists.

The Education Centre of RTV Slovenia has, in the spring of 2009, started an initiative together with the Faculty of Social Sciences to find a solution for these journalists and to find a way for how they could finish their studies, keeping in mind their years of professional work experience, and similarly to some other professions, establishing a shorter education programme that would enable these journalists to finish their studying and gain an appropriate education.

However, because of this situation and the relative lack of formal education among Slovenian journalists, journalistic education programmes still face a number of problems or at least ignorance on behalf of many journalists and editors. They believe that any education programme is irrelevant and that only experiences count. Therefore they do not attend workshops, seminars and other forms of additional education, which can then often be relatively unsuccessful, with a low turnout; at the same time very few journalists decide to attend the Master's Programme in journalism/media or other areas of education as well. Only in the last few years is the situation slowly starting to change, since some of Slovenian newspapers and broadcasters have appointed editors who have a Master's Degree or Ph.D. This could lead to a change in the attitude of their media toward journalistic education, particularly on a postgraduate level.

Concluding Remarks

Because of the slow privatization of the media in Slovenia and the still important role of the state and the government in the functioning of the media and journalism (including for example the expansion of the controversial right of reply in all of the media), journalism is today still facing a number of dilemmas and unsolved problems, particularly regarding professionalization, professional education and the relevance of constant education of professional journalists. Many owners and managers still believe that journalists do not need professional education, and do not provide their journalists and editors with possibilities of attending workshops, seminars or postgraduate study. The future of journalism education in Slovenia is therefore closely connected with the development of media itself; this includes political culture, management culture and the development of society as a whole and the recognition of the importance of education, innovation and professionalization.

The Author

Marko Milosavljevič is Head of Department of Journalism at University of Ljubljana, Slovenia, and Chairman of The Committee for The Media at Slovenian Ministry of Culture.

References

Archive of Faculty of Social Sciences, internal documents, (1970, 1975, 1980, 1995).
Melita Poler Kovačič and Monika Kalin Golob (eds), *Poti slovenskega novinarstva – danes in jutri*, Media: Ljubljana, pp. 279–284.
Melita, Poler Kovačič and Monika, Kalin Golob (eds) (2004), *Poti slovenskega novinarstva – danes in jutri*, Media: Ljubljana.
Milosavljević, Marko (2004), 'Razvoj demokracije v Sloveniji: vloga in položaj množičnih medijev', In *Pogovori o prihodnosti Slovenije – Razvoj demokracije v Sloveniji*, Urad Predsednika Republike Slovenije: Ljubljana, pp. 90–99.

Conclusions

Soul-searching at the Crossroads of European Journalism Education

Kaarle Nordenstreng

The preceding 33 national accounts and the four regional overviews provide the reader with quite a panorama of journalism education in Europe. It is a truly diverse and rich landscape, to put it positively. But the landscape can also be characterized less favorably by borrowing the terms of some of the authors of this volume when referring to their respective countries: 'vagueness, immaturity, irrationality' (Siomos/Greece), 'anarchical, controversial, fragmented' (Le Bohec/France), 'disarray' (Bromley/UK). The title of this conclusion uses a neutral term – 'mosaic' (picked up from Siomos/Greece).

Reading the European mosaic is no easy matter, not only because the national accounts do not follow a standardized format but more fundamentally because the situation of journalism education seems to be quite specific to each country. The overall landscape emerging from these national stories is far from clear and does not follow the simple division into three proposed by Hallin and Mancini – not even complemented by a fourth sub-region of the post-Communist countries in Eastern Europe. All the same, the mosaic of these diverse national elements leads the reader to seek commonalities behind national peculiarities, and such a reading of the mosaic is indeed inspiring. It serves as a reminder of some of the basic characteristics of the European media landscape. For this reader, the mosaic immediately opens up five perspectives.

First, **history**. Early journalists used to be highly educated, as noted in the chapter on Germany: in the middle of the nineteenth century nine out of ten journalists had studied in a university. This was general academic education and not professionally oriented education. The idea of journalism as a profession evolved only towards the end of the nineteenth century and in the first decades of the twentieth century along with the growth of the press. Paradoxically, when the number of journalists grew and they began to identify themselves with a profession, their general educational level fell – an elite profession, now that of salaried workers. And this process of professionalization included from the very beginning journalism education as an idea if not yet an established practice, as noted for example by the Organized Journalism Professional Movement founded in Bulgaria in 1894 and by the International Press Conference of 1898 in Lisbon (documented in the chapter on Portugal).

Second, **growth**. The number of journalists has increased throughout the twentieth century, particularly after World War II, along with the expansion of the media industries, and this development occasioned the growth of journalism education since the 1960s. The growth in the media field has been significant in all respects – economic, political, cultural, and educational – and even if we disregard the hype customarily associated with the media among laymen, we can speak about a sunrise industry. Journalism education, regardless of its diverse and even 'anarchical' forms, constitutes an integral part of this growth story. The United Kingdom provides a good example with over 100 organizations currently offering journalism education or training and with the new disciplinary field of media studies having attained academic status. Germany lists nearly 200 institutions engaged in some kind of journalism education. Of other large European countries France lists 60 journalism schools and Poland 80 institutions of various types. Spain has 'only' 30 journalism schools – all university faculties or departments – but the volumes are impressive: over 17.000 students enrolled on journalism programmes, in addition to which over 26,000 were enrolled on other communication programmes in broadcasting, advertizing and public relations (figures for the academic year 2004/05). However, these are just a mere fraction of all the university students in Spain, who number over a million. The same growth trend is discernible in all the countries, although most of them list fewer than a dozen schools of journalism education.

Third, **integration**. Journalism is integrated not only with other disciplines in the humanities and social sciences but it cannot be strictly separated from the related media and communication studies, such as organizational communication, marketing communication, speech communication and visual communication. Technological developments dissolve the boundaries between different media as well as between media and the rest of the culture and economy. The keyword is *convergence*, whereby the media are integrating, not only within the media and journalists' workplaces but also throughout the whole media ownership system with its vertical and horizontal structures. Another keyword is *ubiquitous,* whereby the information and communication technologies become so central an element of life that they no longer appear as a big issue. As happened with electricity over the last century, ICT is becoming so important, so salient that it ceases to be special. And journalism education is part and parcel of this megatrend of introducing a new mindset. So far we have been monomedia-oriented with newspapers, radio, television, etc., each in its own pigeonhole, but this way of thinking is becoming increasingly outdated and replaced by the 'multimedia mindset'. This does not only mean mastering the skills of various media but is a fundamentally different paradigm of working and thinking.

Fourth, **journalism**. The educational landscape does not support the idea of an end of journalism in this time of digital abundance. Online news and user-generated social media do not render obsolete the gatekeepers and storytellers known as journalists. Quite the reverse, processing raw materials and packaging them into user-friendly forms demands more, rather than less, journalistic input and therefore journalism and its education are needed more than ever. Moreover, despite the popularity of tabloid materials and various kinds of reality television, there is a thirst for information – not only on matters of conflict and terrorism but also on matters of economy, ecology and so on. And this thirst is not satisfied solely by the digitally facilitated supply of information with countless new sources, online and other. What people need for their worldview is not just encyclopaedic material but also overview and comment – both objective information from trusted sources and enlightening information from stimulating sources. This is journalism in its purest form and there is little reason to believe that it has had its day. Consequently it is logical also to believe that journalism education has a firm existential foundation. True, pressures of tabloidization, infotainment, corporate management, etc. are strongly felt, as shown for example in the chapters on Denmark and Croatia, but nevertheless the mosaic suggests that the prevailing mode of schools of journalism is to 'continue to teach the theory and practice of quality journalism' (as put in the chapter on Hungary).

Fifth, **professionalism**. Finally, this reader is touched by the question posed by Bromley in his introduction: 'Education can either uphold journalism as a relatively autonomous activity, or disempower it in the interests of the state or media institutions.' Indeed, professionalism not only brings about good for journalism as it is typically understood but also gives rise to serious problems for democracy. The more competent and powerful you are as a professional, the more you become a prisoner of your own professional thinking at risk of alienation from so-called ordinary people. It is the dilemma of elitism and alienation from social realities which is not good for democracy – something that can be called the 'fortress journalism syndrome' of an exessively self-centred profession. Civic or public journalism are well known remedies for this syndrome, but the problem is more fundamental and poses a constant challenge for journalism education.

These five perspectives are accompanied by other aspects which no reader can escape:

- Journalism is an **open profession** – although France and Italy have a sort of closed shop tradition – and many journalists continue to be recruited from outside the journalism schools. The share of those journalists in the field having got a professional education is growing, but in most countries it is still just about half of the total number. Meanwhile, the share of those with a university education in any field (including journalism) is in many countries as high as 80 per cent. Journalists belong to the higher-educated professionals.
- Journalism education has grown in most countries to have **too many students** and schools turn out too many graduates. The field has evolved rather anarchically without rigorous educational policies as far as the volume is concerned. For example, in Finland the number of graduates was first set to fill about half of what is needed by the industry, leaving the other half to an open market, but with the advent of new polytechnics the supply of graduates from journalism schools has suddenly filled and even exceeded the demands of the job market.
- Despite an oversupply the graduates seem to be relatively **well employed** although the current economic crisis obviously depletes the labour force of the media industries. With their educational background the graduates enjoy fairly good employment prospects, also outside of journalism itself. On the other hand, Spain for example, reports that hardly 41 per cent of all graduates of the past 30 years are working professionally as journalists and that journalism is not among the twenty-five degree programmes with the highest employment rates for young people.
- The number of women students has grown as part of the **feminization** of the profession. The majority of journalism students are women, which is positive for balancing a

traditionally male profession. However, it is no longer good for the field if eight out of ten students are women.

- The **theory-practice division** is the most pervasive issue regarding the content of journalism education. It persists but seems to be diminishing with the gradual realization that both are vital for successful education in this field. However, the competition between universities and polytechnics has given it a new dimension.

For reflections on these and other pertinent aspects, the regional overviews and the national chapters – notably on Lithuania and Portugal – provide much food for thought.

With all this stimulation from the mosaic, the present reader is led to reflect upon the megatrends surrounding the media, the journalistic profession and indeed journalism education (see Nordenstreng 2008). In this context we can say that while journalism is not doomed, future journalists will typically work in a multimedia environment. Converging digital media structures lead to the diversification of journalistic skills propelling the profession in different directions.

One of these directions is online information seekers and processors in a corporate centre serving several media simultaneously, while another trend is to have specialists at each media end to edit the products for local users. Moreover, blogs and other forms of social media have created a plethora of grassroots communication. These developments will not render superfluous the need for profound knowledge of various areas of life and society; rather there is a growing need for substantial competence to promote serious and 'elite' journalism.

Then there is the well-known trend towards tabloidization, whereby serious news and information are accompanied by human interest and entertainment material, leading to 'infotainment'. Also, fact and fiction are mixed contrary to the conventional wisdom of journalism, leading to 'faction'. These are challenges to be taken seriously, but it is very shortsighted to use them as arguments to predict the demise of journalism. On the contrary, in these days of global economic crises one may paradoxically see the future of journalism in an optimistic light.

This reasoning is based on people's existential need to become genuinely interested in what is happening in the world – both far and near – which naturally whets the appetite to know and to understand how all these events relate to their own life situation. Such a hunger renders support to quality journalism: a compelling need for reliable information on economy, environment and society. This forecast suggests that we are approaching a new age of realism where people want to know, and journalism meets this burning need. Accordingly, we see on the horizon a renaissance for good old quality journalism (Nordenstreng 2009).

Consequently, the overall thesis of this reader is that the so-called 'information society' will not render journalism obsolete, but that it poses challenges and creates uncertainties. Some call them 'cyber revolutions' while others take them as conventional evolution, and in both camps there are those who approach them with enthusiasm and optimism as well as those whose approach is pessimistic or cynical. The real roots of the challenge go deeper than the mere technical surface of digitalization. Unfortunately the academic and political field is deficient in analytical understanding about what is really going on.

After these prospects it is logical to reflect on journalism ethics, media performance and the tasks which media are supposed to fulfil in society – in short, the normative roles of media and journalism. This area of professional debate and scholarship has not been buried under new technologies and globalization. Quite the reverse, it has been revived with projects which are effectively rewriting the now outdated four theories of the press (see Christians et al. 2009).

The Author

Kaarle Nordenstreng is Professor Emeritus at the University of Tampere in Finland, the site of Scandinavia's oldest institution of journalism education. He has headed the professional education section of the International Association for Mass Communication Research (IAMCR) and currently presides the Global Network for Professional Education in Journalism and Media (JourNet).

References

Christians, Clifford, Theodore L. Glasser, Denis McQuail, Kaarle Nordenstreng and Robert A. White (2009), *Normative Theories of the Media: Journalism in Democratic Societies,* Urbana and Chicago: University of Illinois Press.

Nordenstreng, Kaarle (2008), 'Soul-searching at the Crossroads of Journalism Education', *Media Development*, 55 (3), pp. 38–42.

Nordenstreng, Kaarle (2009), 'A Renaissance on the Horizon!' *Journalism: Theory, Practice and Criticism*, 10 (3), pp. 356–357.

Epilogue

Back into the Future? Re-inventing Journalism Education in the Age of Globalization

Jan Servaes

'In an exact sense the present crisis of western democracy is a crisis in journalism'

Walter Lippmann

Walter Lippmann, the beacon of American journalism, wrote these famous lines not in 2007, when the book from which I quote got reprinted, but in 1920, almost a century ago. He continued:

> All that the sharpest critics of democracy have alleged is true, if there is no steady supply of trustworthy and relevant news. Incompetence and aimlessness, corruption and disloyalty, panic and ultimate disaster, must come to any people who is denied an assured access to the facts. (Lippmann 1920/2007: 6)

Not much seems to have changed since... Although, today, in societies saturated with infotainment, 'sound-bites' and 'headlines', 'spin-doctoring', 'news-hypes' and 24/7 news circles we may need to do more to get our 'facts' right.

Traditionally, in communication sciences one used to refer to the book by Siebert, Peterson and Schramm (1956) for a positioning of the relationship between media and society, or, the so-called 'normative mediatheories'. Siebert, Peterson and Schramm started from the assumption that 'the press always takes on the coloration of the social and political structures within which it operates. Especially it reflects the system of social control whereby the relations of individuals and institutions are adjusted' (Siebert et al. 1956: 1–2). The four models they identified have become critiqued since for being too Western-centric and for making unrealistic universalistic claims. Additions such as the 'development model' and the 'democratic-participatory model' were added (for an overview see Hachten 1996, 2007; Merrill 1974, 1979, 1989; McQuail 2005; Nerone 1995; or Servaes 1989). However, Siebert's starting thesis was never questioned. The above mentioned authors also think that, as summarized by John Merrill (1979),

> media systems are, of course, closely related to the kinds of governments in which they operate; they are, in essence, reflective and supportive of the governmental philosophy. When viewed in this way, it is possible to say that all press systems are enslaved – tied to their respective governmental philosophies and forced to operate within certain national ideological parameters. (Merrill 1979: 153)

Two of the more recent contributions to the tradition of comparative media theories and systems are the work by Christians, Glasser, McQuail, Nordenstreng, and White (2009), and the overview presented by Daniel Hallin and Paolo Mancini (2004).

Several authors (and the editor of the book you are reading) have adopted the comparative overview presented by Hallin and Mancini (2004) as the framework for their analysis of European Journalism Education. The 'North Atlantic or Liberal Model' (which includes Britain, United States, Canada and Ireland) is presented by Hallin and Mancini as one of the three models. Walter Lippmann could be considered a clear-cut representative, if not the founding father of this model. The other two models are the 'Northern European or Democratic Corporatist Model' (Austria, Belgium, Denmark, Finland, Germany, Netherlands, Norway, Sweden and Switzerland) and the 'Mediterranean or Polarized Pluralist Model' (France, Greece, Italy, Portugal and Spain). As this book also incorporates the 'Eastern European or Post-Communist' countries (Bulgaria, Croatia, Czech Republic, Estonia, Macedonia, Hungary, Latvia, Lithuania, Poland, Romania, Slovakia and Slovenia) a fourth Model has been added. Karol Jakubowicz, who summarizes the Eastern European overview, quoting Hallin and Mancini once again, argues that, since the falling apart of the former Communist bloc, Central and Eastern European journalism education has embraced the liberal or Anglo-American version of professional journalism. While many local people (including journalists) initially welcomed the 'spreading of the gospel of democracy' (especially the financial benefits which accompanied it) into their world, this new love-affair has lost some of its glance lately, especially since the 2008–09 global financial meltdown has had a sobering ripple effect on all sectors of society, including the post-Communist version of journalism with its blind belief in unbridled individual freedom and free market principles. However, because of the strong historic role of the state, 'the Democratic Corporatist Model, we suspect, will have particularly strong relevance for the analysis of those parts of Eastern and Central Europe that share much of the same historical development' (Hallin and Mancini 2004: 305).

In view of the recent economic crisis, the far too optimistic hint by Hallin and Mancini (2004: 301) that 'there is [...] a clear tendency of convergence toward the Liberal system' against the two other models may need to be reassessed. Hallin and Mancini warn against simplistic generalizations – there are important differences among and within the media systems they grouped together – and plead for more comparative historical and ethnographic research on the subject. They also make an effort to assess how the three models 'might relate to other systems' in the so-called 'developing world':

Even though the Liberal Model has dominated media studies and has served as the principal normative model against which other media systems have traditionally been measured, it is probably the Polarized Pluralist Model, more than the other two, that is most widely applicable to other systems as an empirical model of the relation between media and political systems. We suspect that scholars working on many parts of the world – Eastern Europe and the former Soviet Union, Latin America, the Middle East and all of the Mediterranean region, Africa, and most of Asia will find much that is relevant in our analysis of Southern Europe, including the role of clientelism, the strong role of the state, the role of media as an instrument of political struggle, the limited development of mass circulation press, and the relative weakness of common professional norms.' (Hallin and Mancini 2004: 306)

Hallin and Mancini's comparative analysis, which has been adopted in this book, still overemphasizes political, technological and economic conditions, and implicitly disregards, apart from the proverbial lip-service, the importance of cultural dimensions in media systems and societies. By collapsing almost all non-Western countries and regions under one category, they do injustice to the complexity, specificity and richness of local, national and socio-cultural systems. For instance, in the African context, the anthropological analysis of the African political and media system by Francis Nyamnjoh (2005, 2007) or the philosophical observations by people like Kwame Appiah (2005, 2006) and Molefi Kete Asante (2007), are far more sophisticated and multifaceted than the Polarized Pluralist Model may make us believe. Already in the eighties (see Servaes 1982, 1989, 1992) I have argued in favour of a 'triple and dialectically integrated framework' for the study of the so-called normative media theories: at a philosophical, a political-economic, and a culturalist-anthropological level [Christians et al. (2009: 16) use a more or less similar typology: a philosophical level focusing on normative traditions; a political one assessing models of democracy; and the different roles the media can play. We consider the role of the media part of the culture at large.] The critique was that the classic models are based on, on the one hand, a too restricted (Western) description of concepts like 'freedom', 'democracy', 'objectivity' and so on, which allow little or no generalizations; and that, on the other hand, reality often doesn't comply to the principles defined in philosophical terms.

Traditional principles like the freedom of the press and professional journalism practices, I contended, need a radical rethinking in order to become an integral aspect of the process of democratization in both media and society.

The basic idea is that the manufacturing of information is conditioned generally by the political, economic and cultural conditions, as well as by the actual situation, in which the selection, production, transmission, distribution and consumption of information takes place. Firstly, news should never be looked at as only a series of facts or a window through which we look at the external world, but rather as a 'cultural product' produced within a specific interpretative framework. One should analyse the culture and structure in which news (or media content in general) is produced in both intentional and unintended ways. Secondly, news is an 'organizational product', generated by routine occupational practices in an institutional setting with specific performance demands and limits of time and resources. These organizational and institutional factors (private versus public, profit versus not-for-profit, commercial versus public service, hierarchical versus democratic-participatory etc.) also shape the structure in which news is being produced. Thirdly, news is being 'manufactured by journalists and citizens' who – often unconsciously – select and interpret a number of facts, based on an 'unclear vision on society'. Hence, as Golding and Middleton (1992: 112) state, 'we should never forget that news production, like all other social activities, involves real people doing real jobs about which they are able to reflect and over whose content they have considerable autonomy'.

News production has a lot in common with other social practices which are carried out on a routine basis in a formalized institutional context. It is at this point that the concept of 'professionalization' comes into play. On the one hand journalists and media workers in general use a specific paradigm of reality to cover events in the world; on the other hand professionalism also provides newsmakers with a set of 'implicit' practices of production routines (further elaborated upon in Servaes 1982, 1992).

Let me expand the above arguments in a number of ways: (1) on the need for more non-Western cultural perspectives to understand how communication and information principles have been interpreted and implemented in distinct cultural settings; (2) media and governance in general, (3) the implications of all this for journalism education; and (4) more specifically for the competencies journalists and knowledge workers need to acquire in order to be prepared for the knowledge society of the future.

Shifts in rights and responsibilities

The concepts 'freedom of information' and 'free flow of information' are of a relatively recent date. However, the ideas on which they are based are very old. In fact they go back to the old Western principles of 'freedom of opinion', 'freedom of expression' and 'freedom of the press'. For centuries, these principles have been at the base of the Western way of thinking (Barendt 2005; Dakroury 2009; Kierulf and Ronning 2009). They, among other things, were explicitly referred to in the American Constitution of 1776 and during the French Revolution. Article 12 of the 'American Bill of Rights' states that 'the freedom of the press is one of the great bulwarks of liberty and can never be restrained but by despotic government.' In the French *Les Droits de l'Homme et du Citoyen* of 1789 it is stated that 'the free expression of ideas and opinions is one of the most precious human rights; every citizen should be able to speak, write, and print freely; this freedom can only be restricted in those cases determined by law' (my translation, JS). Though the freedom of word and expression have always been subject to fundamental restrictions, they nevertheless are part of the European and American ways of thinking, which led to freedom of printing, a free press, the 'fourth estate' and the role of journalists as the 'watchdogs' of the system.

One can observe a 'double evolution' over the past half-century. Whereas originally the active right of the so-called sender-communicator to supply information without externally imposed restrictions was emphasized; the passive as well as active right of the receiver to be informed and to inform has gradually received more attention.

Therefore the principle of the 'right to communicate' was introduced as it contained both the passive and active right of the receiver to inform and be informed. This principle first appeared in 1969 in an article by Jean D'Arcy, the then director of the UN information bureau in New York. D'Arcy (1969: 14) wrote that 'the time will come when the Universal Declaration of Human Rights will have to encompass a more extensive right than man's right to inform, first laid down twenty-one years ago in Article 19. This is the right of man to communicate'. Only in 1974, this principle made its entrance in the UNESCO. Both individual and social rights and duties are included in this right to communicate. This right has become basic in the future search for a 'public or user oriented view on communication issues'.

As a fundamental human right, the right to communicate clearly indicates that another communication model necessitates democratization and thus a redistribution of the power on all levels (Fischer and Harms 1983; Lee 2004). The point of departure is not an elitist position, but development from the grass-roots. The so-called MacBride Report suggests that the right to communicate 'promises to advance the democratization of communication on all levels – international, national, local, individual' (MacBride 1980: 171).

Fundamental here is the other vision of the role of the authorities in processes of social change (Braman 1995; Held 1993, 1995, 2007). Unlike the confidence in and respect for the 'role of the state', which is characteristic of the traditional perspectives, this position takes a rather reserved attitude toward the authorities. At the same time, there is another and related shift taking place in the discussions on communication rights and responsibilities; that is, from the so-called maintenance duty of the government towards the media to the emphasis on the 'government's duty' to take care of and to create the conditions and infrastructure in which the freedom of communication can be realized and stimulated as a fundamental social right (Dakroury 2009; Dakroury, Eid and Kamalipour 2009).

Policies should be built on more 'selective participation strategies of dissociation and association' (Hamelink 1994; Servaes 1999) and communication rights closely related to 'human rights' (Galtung 1994; Hamelink 2004; UNDP 2004). As Nobel Prize winner Amartya Sen (2004: 20) argues: 'The deciding issue, ultimately, has to be one of democracy. An overarching value must be the need for participatory decision-making on the kind of society people want to live in, based on open discussion, with adequate opportunity for the expression of minority positions.'

The practical application of these liberties has escaped the national level and international agreements are needed. This shift can partly be explained as a result of 'changing power' factors, partly also through 'culturally defined interpretation' problems. For international agreements and declarations also the 'non-binding' character of many of these agreements is a crucial factor.

Examples of these shortcomings are readily available in the literature (see Sparks 2007). The interpretation of communication principles, the seventies debate on the MacBride Report (1980) and the New International Information Order (Boyd-Barrett 1977, 1982), or the current dispute about Western versus Non-Western definitions of 'objectivity' or 'bias in the news' is linked to power shifts on political and/or economic levels, as well as to the questioning of their universal validity (Thissu 2008).

In addition, in most cultures, there is a difference between the rules of the 'written and unwritten culture'. While many (non-Western) governments, in their official declarations and documents, underwrite the Universal Declarations issued by the United Nations, which for a number of historical reasons are mainly based on Western ideas, in reality they don't pay much attention to their implementation. This is often due to – again – reasons which have to do with power and culture. In Asia, for instance, a number of values and norms, which the West considers very important, like equality of men and women or democracy, are considered less important in reality. Other values, like respect for the elderly or loyalty to the group, on the other hand, are in the East considered much more important than in the West (Hsiung 1985; Hofstede and Hofstede 2005). This also counts for the interpretation of concepts like cultural and press freedom in, for instance, the post-Communist world (Casmir 1995; De Smaele 1999; Jakubowicz 2007), Asia (Iyer 2001), Latin America (Beltran 1993; Fox 1988) or the Muslim society (Hussain 2006), a discussion on journalism ethics and universal versus particular values (Christians and Traber 1997; Karikari 1996; Preston 2007; Ukpabi 2001), journalism in a Buddhist (Dissanayake 2006; Gunaratne 2007) or Confusian/ Chinese (Chen 2004; Gunaratne 2005) tradition; or deontological codes and practices in different parts of the world (Mendel 2008; Pigeat and Huteau 2000).

This brief overview of the rights discussion indicates that the communication and information systems have two key responsibilities. At the 'production' level, they should be able to utilize the possible diversity of provision and the mechanisms for expression. At the level of 'consumption', they should ensure universal access to services that can guarantee the exercise of full citizenship regardless of class, race, gender, income or area of residence. Therefore, the citizens' access to full participation has more and more been understood to be an obligation of governments. However, it needs to be emphasised that, even the best laws, policies and regulations may not work if they do not go hand in hand with an environment where a government has regard for these laws. In other words, 'laws and policies do not exist in a vacuum' – their success or failure depends on the political, social and cultural environment.

Independent journalism and good governance

It is generally assumed that communication provides the foundation necessary for the facilitation of good governance, through promotion of effective government, accountability, and the active engagement of participants in civil society.

'Governance' may be defined as (a) the process by which governments are selected, monitored and replaced, (b) the capacity of the government to formulate and implement sound policies effectively, (c) the respect of citizens and the state for the institutions that govern economic, political, and social interactions among them, and (d) the capacity for active and informed economic, social, and political dialogue among citizens within a public sphere.

Communication plays a pivotal role in improving governance and enhancing 'public participation'. Participation and monitoring mechanisms may be situated in national efforts to improve public sector performance, increase transparency and reduce corruption. Governance also incorporates attention to the 'public sphere', in which informed citizens actively engage in dialogue on political, economic and cultural matters of concern. Communication enhances the potential for civil society to hold governmental authorities accountable as well as to engage in political decision-making. Empowering citizens to demand accountability and participation in decision-making is critical to good governance. However, the argument goes, participatory communication can only foster in an environment of freedom from political, economic, and social pressures (Servaes 2007b, 2009a).

Issues to promote governmental transparency and to engage civil society are relevant to all media systems, not only 'print and broadcasting' but also for ICTs and the Internet (Hudson 2006). Discussions of relevant media systems must take into account the expectations and aspirations of the communities involved. For the media to provide a useful public sphere for political dialogue, the technological systems, content, and language need to be accessible by local communities. In addition, although most of this discourse tends to focus on the importance of news and information systems, the critical role of popular culture in political socialization should not be overlooked.

Therefore, the media have a 'dual role to play'. For instance, in the case of anti-corruption efforts they not only raise public awareness about corruption, its causes, consequences and possible remedies, they also investigate and report incidences of corruption. Hence, the effectiveness of the media depends on access to information and freedom of expression, a professional and ethical cadre of investigative journalists, and the availability of regular updates via short- or long-term training and education (Berger and Matras 2007). By the same token, in an environment of free speech and a free press, the media perform a watchdog function and expose social injustices wherever they occur.

Therefore, Norris and Zinnbauer (2002) argue that independent journalism, as a potential check on the abuse of power, is a necessary but not sufficient means of strengthening good governance and promoting human development. They suggest that these goals are achieved most effectively under 'two further conditions'. Firstly, in societies where channels of mass communications are 'free and independent' of established interests; and secondly, where there is widespread 'access' to these media. In 2005 UNESCO devoted its World Press Freedom Day theme to press freedom and governance. The Final Declaration of the global conference stressed that 'independent and pluralistic media are essential for ensuring transparency, accountability and participation as fundamental elements of good governance and human-rights based development'. It also called on UNESCO's Member States to 'respect the function of the news media as an essential factor in good governance, vital to increasing both transparency and accountability in decision-making processes and to communicating the principles of good governance to society'. (http://portal.unesco.org/ci/en/ev.php-URL_ID=18816&URL_DO=DO_TOPIC&URL_SECTION=201.html, 2005, accessed on 25 April 2007)

However, Puddenphatt argues that

the absence of state intervention on its own is no guarantee of a rich media environment. On the contrary: to promote a media environment characterized by pluralism and diversity, state intervention is necessary. To guarantee pluralism requires provisions for public broadcasting, commercial broadcast and print media and community-based broadcast and print media. (2008: 3)

Furthermore, Davis (2006: 89–93) observes that 'we are presently unable to measure and determine objectively media's influence within societies and specifically its relationship to governance and overall development, country to country'. Davis proposes the development of a Media-Governance Index which directly relates to the six dimensions of governance as defined by the World Bank (2009). Such an index would be capable of measuring negative as well as positive impacts of media activity, where media behaviour is working against governance or even promoting conflict.

A group of researchers under the guidance of Professor Anne-Sophie Novel (Guseva et al. 2008) studied the correlations between press freedom and different dimensions of development, poverty, governance and peace. They concluded that 'no conclusion can be reached as to the existence of causality between freedom of the press and the different variables explored, all the findings confirm the importance of the press for development' (Guseva 2008: 5). The three most important conclusions were:

(a) Press freedom tends to expand participation in the political decision-making process beyond a small inner circle, extending it to the whole population; (b) press freedom provides access to a whole variety of different ideas, opinions and information; and (c) press freedom makes governments more accountable to the population and allows policy implementation and the practices of those in power (corruption, for example) to be monitored. (Guseva 2008: 109)

All this leads Puddenphatt (2008: 10) to conclude that 'At the moment therefore I am not aware of research that conclusively shows the connection between media and governance'.

In search of media performance indicators

Puddephatt (2007) presents a comprehensive overview of the available diagnostic tools and performance indicators in the field of communication for development, especially the media's impact upon democracy and governance. He concludes that the indicators developed for UNESCO may be able to avoid some of the pitfalls identified in other assessment systems. He presents five principal categories of media indicators, which provide an organizing framework that can be adapted to the needs of media development initiatives in any given national context. 'The assumption is that to have a media environment that is supportive of democracy and good governance, all five categories will be positive' (Puddenphatt 2008: 10–11):

- **Category 1: A system of regulation and control conducive to freedom of expression, pluralism and diversity of the media:** Existence of a legal, policy and regulatory framework which protects and promotes freedom of expression and information, based on international best practice standards and developed in participation with civil society.
- **Category 2: Plurality and diversity of media, a level economic playing field and transparency of ownership:** The state actively promotes the development of the media sector in a manner which prevents undue concentration of ownership and ensures plurality and transparency of ownership and content across public, private and community media.
- **Category 3: Media as a platform for democratic discourse:** The media, within a prevailing climate of self-regulation and respect for the journalistic profession, reflects and represents the diversity of views and interests in society, including those of marginalized groups. There is a high level of information and media literacy.
- **Category 4: Professional capacity building and supporting institutions that underpins freedom of expression, pluralism and diversity:** Media workers have access to professional training and development, both vocational and academic, at all stages of their career, and the media sector as a whole is both monitored and supported by professional associations and civil society organizations.
- **Category 5: Infrastructural capacity is sufficient to support independent and pluralistic media:** The media sector is characterized by high or rising levels of public access, including among marginalized groups, and efficient use of technology to gather and distribute news and information, appropriate to the local context.

Journalism education: where to go from here?

What's the future of journalism education in all of this? As this book has documented, and as we have argued in Servaes (2009c), most journalism programmes are still struggling to find the right balance between vocational versus university education for journalists (and, if either, at what level: undergraduate or postgraduate?), the discussion continues on nature versus nurture, art versus craft, specialist versus general education, practice versus theory, production versus reflection, etc. Both in the United States and Europe, though conditioned and coloured by country-specific circumstances, much of this balancing seems to have been settled in favour of the latter options (Carpentier et al. 2008; Lavender, Tufte and Lemish 2004; Leung, Kenny and Lee 2007; Terzis 2007; Triandafyllidou, Wodak and Krzyanowski 2009).

On both sides of the Atlantic, gradually and slowly one starts noticing common trends and enduring issues in journalism education. A survey of the European Journalism Centre (Bierhoff and Schmidt 1997; Terzis 2007) and a 2001 symposium on the state of journalism and mass communication education at US colleges and universities (Brynildssen 2002; Cohen 2001) arrived at common issues, which could be summarized as follows:

(a) The need to focus on 'service to the public', not the industry;
(b) The need to address 'challenges posed by new economic, technological, cultural and social realities'; and
(c) The need to make journalism education 'diverse, inclusive, and glocal'.

The first theme focuses on which 'master' journalism education should serve. Instead of 'following the industry' and, at times, 'leading the industry', many scholars turn the pyramid upside-down and want to start at the level of the public, the citizens, the 'consumers' of journalistic products. The choice between a reactive and a pro-active attitude towards the industry has been replaced by a need for more qualitative audience and contextual research.

Journalists have to break away from the pep-advice provided by marketing and PR spinners in order to return to 'the core values of journalism' as practice. However, the core values have shifted quite a bit. Media concentration has created a 'corporate colonization' of many newsrooms and a worrying trend toward 'infotainment'. If this trend continues journalism educators' debates about core knowledge won't matter much because 'the democratic system will be without a Fourth Estate' (Cohen 2001: 20).

Journalists have to start re-inventing their role and place in the 'knowledge society' of the future (Breit and Servaes 2005; Hassan 2008). Knowledge is more than information. Knowledge is the sense that people make of information. Meaning is not something that is delivered to people; people create/interpret it themselves. Multiple sources and forms of knowledge are needed to know more about the nature of the problem in order to be able to examine alternatives and make choices. That requires people to have access to information on the issues that affect their lives, and the capacity to make their own contributions to change. Preferably, 'change we can believe in'. Understanding the context in which knowledge moves – factors of control, selection, purpose, power, and capacity – is essential for understanding how we as both journalists and citizens can become better able to learn, generate and facilitate change (Servaes 1999, 2008).

In addition, journalism education has to break out of its national carcass and 'internationalize'. One of the central questions is 'how do we escape national stereotypes in journalism education. How do we break the mould of a nationally biased understanding of media and news?' (Holm 1997: 48). More multicultural and international 'authentic' learning experiences, more innovative and critical reflection, more problem solving, social negotiation of information and knowledge, and collaboration are the challenges for journalism educators of the future. This will have a tremendous impact on teaching and learning: 'The teaching methods concerned change the role of the teacher from a disseminator of information to a learning facilitator, helping students as they actively engage with information and materials to construct their own understanding' (Blurton 1999: 49). UNESCO has made an interesting and hopefully useful contribution in this regard when it published a number of model curricula for journalism education for developing countries and emerging democracies, which could be adopted and adapted to assist journalism educators in different parts of the world (see Berger and Matras 2007; UNESCO 2007).

Journalistic competencies

Christians et al. (2009) identify four distinct yet overlapping roles for the media: the 'monitorial role' of a vigilant informer collecting and publishing information of potential interest to the public; the 'facilitative role' that not only reports on but also seeks to support and strengthen civil society; the 'radical role' that challenges authority and voices support for reform; and the 'collaborative role' that creates partnerships between journalists and centres of power in society, notably the state, to advance mutually acceptable interests.

Each role could be associated with a specific 'set of competencies' which the journalist or knowledge worker of the future need to acquire in order to perform adequately. In other words, competencies are characteristics that individuals have and use in appropriate, consistent ways in order to achieve desired performance. These characteristics include knowledge, skills, aspects of self-image, social motives, thought patterns, mindsets, and ways of thinking, feeling and acting (Dubois and Rothwell 2004; Irigoin et al. 2002). A competency is measured by identifying the behaviours or tangible results (outcomes) produced by their use in the context of the work performed.

The journalistic competencies needed to operate in today's complex world are manifold and are almost impossible to acquire during a regular journalism programme. They range from 'core or generic competencies' (e.g., communication, teamwork) to 'managerial competencies' (e.g., empowering others, decision-making) and 'technical or specialist competencies' related to specific jobs within the journalism profession.

To illustrate the complexity involved in today's journalism we provide a comparative overview of the competencies needed for only two of the several roles many journalists have to perform on a daily basis: radio broadcasting and internet journalism (adopted from Unesco 2007b).

Radio Broadcasting Competencies

Competency	Behavioural description
Radio Production	
Planning	Decide subject of programme. Research background information and issues. Use research to prepare key points and questions
Understanding of audience	Define the audience for the programme (e.g., farmers, high school students, factory workers etc.)
Interviewing	[see notes on radio interviewing]
Scripting	[see notes on radio scriptwriting]
Programme preparation	Engage personnel. Book and prepare studio. Assemble voice, music and sound recordings. Complete paperwork. Prepare yourself for the production task. Manage personnel and researchers. Pre-record as required
Programme production	Rehearse production. Record and mix actuality, voice, music, effects and other material. Ensure production and presentation quality by re-recording where necessary. Produce approximately to time [exactly to time in a live broadcast]
Presentation	[See notes on radio presentation]
Post-production	Edit for quality and time. Integrate all programme elements (speech, music, offline material etc.). Monitor segues between programming. Seek feedback and modify content accordingly
Monitoring	Review the programme to improve future production. Monitor audience and other feedback
Radio Presentation	
Competency	Behavioural description
Programme preparation	Undertake research and preparation prior to each programme to ensure it is topical, informative and entertaining
Communication style	Use tone of voice and choice of words to engage the listeners in presentation. Vary these as appropriate to suit specific audiences and subject matter, but always maintain your own natural personality
Knowledge	Keep up-to-date about current affairs, trends in music, local events and other material used in programmes
Operational efficiency	Integrate all programme elements (speech, music, offline material, other recorded material). Maintain exact timing of programmes and other material. Operate equipment skilfully to present a smooth programme
Radio Copywriting	
Competency	Behavioural description
Writing	Plan and write creative radio advertizements that meet the requirements of advertizers
Style	Write in a conversational style using the language of everyday speech.
Timing	Write advertizements that run exactly to the agreed time limit (e.g., 30 seconds, 60 seconds)

Competency	Behavioural description
Knowledge of regulations	Understand and apply relevant regulations, standards and rules
Music and sound effects	Choose appropriate music and sound effects to enhance the appeal and realism of advertizements
Studio direction	Select appropriate people (talent) to voice advertizements. Direct talent to gain the best performance in recording
Teamwork	Work harmoniously with the sound engineer and other personnel to produce effective advertizements. Deal effectively with the client

Radio Scriptwriting

Competency	Behavioural description
Planning	Design programme structure. Undertake research. Target appropriate audience (school kids, village people, young adults etc.). Decide programme type (drama, documentary, illustrated narrative etc). Decide style (formal, comic, conversational etc.). Create characters
Writing	Write draft script according to pre-determined factors [see Planning above]. Strive for creativity and flair. Choose appropriate music and sound effects to enhance the appeal and realism of script. Include clear production directions. Write script to correct duration
Editing	Work with producer to improve script prior to recording

Radio News and Current Affairs Production

Competency	Behavioural description
Preparation and planning	Keep up-to-date with public affairs and issues, monitor other media, contact sources. Undertake research and preparation prior to working on story to ensure topical, informative and newsworthy content and to check technology
Relationship building	Foster good relationships with sources. Keep sources confidential and know and comply with the code of ethics
Communications style	Use open questioning techniques in interviews, professional tone of voice to engage the talent and secure content for the deadline
Interviewing	[See notes on radio interviewing]
Writing	[See notes on radio scriptwriting]
Recording	Know your equipment and be able to troubleshoot and improvise if it malfunctions. Operate equipment skilfully. Record quality audio. Use editorial judgement to edit grabs. Meet deadlines
Editing	Sub-edit your own and colleagues' copy
Teamwork	Help colleagues with difficult stories, technology, personnel and content to meet deadlines and improve quality of output

Internet Competencies

Competency	Behavioural description
Website Design	
Planning site requirements	Determine site purpose, functionality and format with reference to client specifications. Negotiate alterations to ensure website meets appropriate technical protocols and standards
Understanding the audience	Gain an understanding of the content needs of the proposed audience and the level of their technical capabilities
Knowledge of software	Understand and be able to source applicable templates, style guides, software and IT tools and be able to analyse and compare characteristics, limitations and usage
Understanding of design impact	Manage design elements (e.g. visual composition, fonts, colours, etc.) in order to heighten the impact of the website and promote effective communication with the intended audience
Designing a multimedia product	Plan and design website architecture taking into consideration
	Web design and usability (e.g. finding a balance between visual impact elements and speed of downloads)
	Content features such as clarity, ease of viewing (e.g. how much scrolling is required to view the site), readability and how intuitive or logical the navigation is from one content detail to the next
	The functions and features of micro-content elements (e.g. headings, highlighted words, link text)
	Relationship between content and site design (e.g. giving the website a look in harmony with a particular corporate style)
	Functions and features of style guides (e.g. using cascading style sheets)
Understanding site functionality	Ensure the website is easy to update and, if appropriate, contains functionalities for accessing feedback and comments from site visitors
Web Writing	
Competency	Behavioural description
Content development	Identify content that is relevant to audience needs and that is aligned with website information architecture, design and functionality
Content writing	Generate content in accordance with audience needs and client requirements. Write in a concise and logical manner expressing complex and comprehensive information in short, easy-to-read sentences. Hyperlink to documents or articles where more extensive content is required. Ensure content is supported with appropriate visual and graphical material
Editing content	Edit content with reference to audience needs, site functionality and client requirements. Ensure that content is readily accessible and that information is clear, understandable, flows smoothly and is grouped logically
Creativity	Creatively and effectively blend words, images and other multimedia content
Cultural awareness	Due to the global reach of the Internet, ensure content is appropriate to and understandable by an international audience
Knowledge of regulations	Keep up-to-date with relevant copyright and intellectual property legislation and application principles

Concluding Remarks

The increasing multiplicity and convergence of ICTs, the Internet and social networks, the deregulation of media markets, and the cultural globalization/localization of media products and services forces a reassessment of existing journalism programmes and competencies. Multi-tasking on different media platforms and the 24/7 news circles challenge journalists not only in technical ways, but force them to reconsider classic notions of balance, objectivity and bias. Especially those working for mainstream media seem to have a hard time adjusting to the new reality of information overload and continuing inequality.

In order to promote participation, it is important to reinforce independent and pluralistic media. For media to be able to offer a critical view of government, political and economic systems must enable the media to operate in as open a public sphere as possible. Press freedom is never guaranteed, particularly when media industries are commercialized, even in a democracy. Apart from creating the appropriate political and economic environments for an independent media system, it is crucial to educate journalists to the highest ethical and professional standards possible.

How to deal with a permanent overload of information will be the key challenge for journalists and citizens alike, and how to regulate this in a democratic way will be the challenge for public authorities. For both 'journalists and citizens' the capacity and speed to access, retrieve, select and reproduce information and turn it into knowledge will determine power and facilitate change in the age of globalization.

The Author

Jan Servaes is Director of the SBS Center 'Communication for Sustainable Social Change' (CSSC), The University of Massachusetts at Amherst, USA, and Researcher at the 'Brussels Center for Journalism Studies' (BCJS), Belgium.

References

Appiah, K.A. (2006), *Cosmopolitanism. Ethics in a World of Strangers*, London: Allen Lane.
Appiah, Kwame Anthony (2005), *The Ethics of Identity*, Princeton NJ.: Princeton University Press.
Asante, M.K. (2007), *An Afrocentric manifesto*, Cambridge: Polity.
Barendt, E. (2005), *Freedom of Speech*, New York: Oxford University Press.
Beltran L.R. (1993), 'Communication for development in Latin America: A forty years appraisal', In D. Nostbakken and C. Morrow (eds), *Cultural Expression in the Global Village*, Penang: Southbound.
Berger, Guy and Matras, Corinne (2007), *Criteria and Indicators for Quality Journalism Training Institutions & Identifying Potential Centres of Excellence in Journalism Training in Africa*, Paris: Unesco.
Berting J. et al. (1990), *Human Rights in a Pluralist World*, Westport: Meckler Inc.

Bierhoff, Jan and Schmidt, Mogens (eds) (1997), *European Journalism Training in Transition. The inside view*, Maastricht: European Journalism Centre.

Blurton, Craig (1999), 'New Directions in education', In M. Tawfik (ed.), *World Communication and Information Report 1999–2000*, Paris: UNESCO.

Boyd-Barrett O. (1977), 'Media imperialism : towards an international framework for the analysis of media systems', In J. Curran, M. Gurevitch and J. Woollacott (eds), *Mass communication and society*, London: Arnold.

Boyd-Barrett O. (1982), 'Cultural dependency and the mass media', In M. Gurevitch, T. Bennett, J. Curran and J. Woollacott (eds), *Culture, society and the media*, London: Methuen.

Braman S. (ed.) (1995), 'Horizons of the State: Information Policy and Power', *Journal of Communication*, 45 (4), pp. 4–159.

Breit, Rhonda and Servaes, Jan (eds) (2005), *Information society or Knowledge societies? UNESCO in the Smart State*, Penang: Southbound.

Brynildssen, Shawna (2002), 'A Review of Trends in Journalism Education', ERIC Digest, http: //www.ericdigests.org/2003–4/journalism.html. Accessed 17 June 2006.

Carpentier, Nico; Pruulmann-Vengerfeldt, Pille; Nordenstreng, Kaarle; Hartmann, Maren; Vihalemm, Peeter; Cammaerts, Bart; Nieminen, Hannu and Olsson, Tobias (eds) (2008), *Democracy, Journalism and Technology: New Developments in an Enlarged Europe*, Tartu: Tartu University Press.

Casmir, Fred (ed.) (1995), *Communication in Eastern Europe. The Role of History, Culture, and Media in Contemporary Conflicts*, Mahwah: Lawrence Erlbaum Associates.

Chen, G.-M. (2004), 'The two faces of Chinese Communication', *Human Communication: A Journal of the Pacific and Asian Communication Association*, 7(1), pp. 25–36.

Christians, C. and Traber, M. (eds) (1997), *Communication ethics and universal values*, Thousand Oaks CA: Sage.

Christians, Clifford G.; Glasser, Theodore L.; McQuail, Denis; Nordenstreng, Kaarle and White, Robert A. (2009), *Normative Theories of the Media. Journalism in democratic societies*, Champaign IL.: University of Illinois Press.

Cohen, Jeremy (2001), 'Symposium: Journalism and mass communication education at the crossroads', *Journalism & Mass Communication Educator*, 56(3), pp. 4–27.

D'Arcy J. (1969), 'Direct broadcast satellites and the right to communicate', *EBU-Review*, p. 118.

Dakroury, Aliaa; Eid, Mahmoud and Yahya, Kamalipour (eds) (2009), *The Right to Communicate. Historical hopes, global debates, and future premises*, Dubuque IA.: Kendall Hunt.

Dakroury. A. (2009), *Communication and Human Rights*, Dubuque IA.: Kendall Hunt.

Daorueng, P. (2004), *Thai Civil Society and Government Control: a Cyber Struggle? Asian Cyberactivism: Freedom of Expression and Media Censorship*, Friedrich Naumann Foundation, Bonn.

Davis, Alan (2006), 'A road map for Monitoring and Evaluation in the Media Development Sector', in M. Harvey (ed.) (2005), *Media Matters: Perspectives on Advancing Governance and Development from the Global Forum for Media Development*, London: Internews Europe.

De Smaele, H. (1999), 'The applicability of Western Models on the Russian Media System', *European Journal of Communication*, 14 (2), pp. 173–90.

Dissanayake, Wimal (2006), 'Postcolonial Theory and Asian Communication Theory: Towards a Creative Dialogue', *China Media Research*, 2(4), pp. 1–8.

Dubois, David and Rothwell, William J. (2004), *Competency-Based Human Resource Management*, Palo Alto: Davies-Black Publishing.

Eide, A. et al. (1993), *The Universal Declaration of Human Rights. A Commentary*, Oslo: Scandinavian University Press.

Fischer, D. and Harms, L.S. (eds) (1983), *The right to communicate. A new human right*, Dublin: Boole Press.

Fox, E. (1988), *Media and politics in Latin America. The struggle for democracy*, London: Sage.

Galtung, J. (1994), *Human rights in another key*, Cambridge: Polity Press.

Golding, P. and Middleton, S. (1982), *Images of welfare: press and public attitudes to poverty*, Oxford: Martin Robertson.

Gunaratne, Shelton (2005), *The Dao of the Press. A Humanocentric Theory*, Cresskill (NJ): Hampton Press.

Gunaratne, Shelton (2007), 'A Buddhist view of journalism: emphasis on mutual causality', *Communication for Development and Social Change*, 1(3), pp. 197–210.

Guseva, Marina; Mounira, Nakaa; Novel, Anne-Sophie; Pekkala, Kirsis; Souberou, Bachir and Stouli, Sami (2008), *Press freedom and development. An analysis of correlations between freedom of the press and the different dimensions of development, poverty, governance and peace*, Paris: UNESCO.

Hachten, William (1996), *The world news prism. Changing media of international communication*, Ames: Iowa State University Press.

Hachten, William and Scotton, James (2007), *The world news prism. Global information in a satellite age (7th ed.)*, Malden, MA: Blackwell.

Hallin, D. and Mancini, P. (2004), *Comparing media systems. Three models of media and politics*, Cambridge MA.: Cambridge University Press.

Hamelink C. (1994a), *Trends in World Communication. On disempowerment and self-empowerment*, Penang: Southbound.

Hamelink, C. (1994b), *The Politics of World Communication. A Human Rights Perspective*, London: Sage.

Hamelink, C. (2004), *Human Rights for Communicators*, Cresskill: Hampton Press.

Handley, P. (2006), *The King Never Smiles. A biography of Thailand's Bhumibol Adulyadej*, New Haven: Yale University Press.

Hassan, Robert (2008), *The Information Society*, Cambridge: Polity Press.

Held, David and McGrew, Anthony (eds) (2007), *Globalization/Anti-globalization. Beyond the great divide*, Cambridge: Polity.

Held, D. (1995), *Democracy and the Global Order. From the Modern State to Cosmopolitan Governance*, Cambridge: Polity.

Held, D. (ed.) (1993), *Prospects for Democracy*, Cambridge: Polity.

Held, D. (1987), *Models of democracy*, Los Angeles: Stanford University Press.

Hofstede, G. and Hofstede G.J. (2005), *Cultures and organizations. Software of the mind*, London: McGraw Hill.

Holm, Hans-Hendrik (1997), 'Educating journalists for a new Europe', In Jan Bierhoff and Mogens Schmidt (eds) (1997), *European Journalism Training in Transition. The inside view*, Maastricht: European Journalism Centre, pp. 47–50.

Hsiung, J. (ed.) (1985), *Human Rights in East Asia. A Cultural Perspective*, New York: Paragon House.

Hudson, H.E. (2006), *From Rural Village to Global Village: Telecommunications for Development in the Information Age*, Mahwah, NJ.: Lawrence Erlbaum Associates.

Hussain, M. Y. (ed.) (2006), *Media and Muslim society*, Kuala Lumpur: International Islamic University Malaysia.

Irigoin, M.E.; Tarnapol Whitacre, P.; Faulkner, D. and Coe, G. (eds) (2002), *Mapping Competencies for Communication for Development and Social Change: Turning Knowledge, Skills, and Attitudes Into Action*, AED, Washington DC: The Change Project.

Iyer, V. (ed.) (2001), *Freedom of information. An Asian survey*, Singapore: AMIC.

Jakubowicz, K. (2007), *Rude awakening: Social and media change in Central and Eastern Europe*, Cresskill NJ.: Hampton Press.

Karikari, K. (ed.) (1996), *Ethics in journalism. Case studies of practice in West Africa*, London: Panos.

Kierulf, Anine and Helge, Ronning (eds) (2009), *Freedom of speech abridged? Cultural, legal and philosophical challenges*, Goteborg: Nordicom.

Komin S. (1988), 'Thai Value System and its Implication for Development in Thailand', In D. Sinha and H. Kao (eds), *Social Values and Development. Asian Perspectives*, New Delhi: Sage.

Komin S. (1991), *Psychology of the Thai People. Values and Behavioral Patterns*, Bangkok: National Institute of Development Administration.

Lavender, Tony; Tufte, Birgitte and Lemish, Dafna (eds) (2003), *Global Trends in Media Education. Policies and Practices*, Creskill, N.J.: Hampton Press.

Lee, P. (ed.) (2004), *Many Voices, One Vision. The Right to Communicate in Practice*, WACC-London: Southbound-Penang.

Leung, K.W.Y.; Kenny, J. and Lee, P.S.N. (eds) (2007), *Global Trends in Communication Research and Education*, Cresskill, N.J.: Hampton Press.

Lippmann, Walter (1920/2007), *Liberty and the News, 1920/2007*, US: Princeton University Press.

MacBride, S. (ed.) (1980), *Many Voices, One World: Communication and Society. Today and Tomorrow*, Paris: UNESCO.

McQuail, D. (2005), *McQuails Mass Comunication Theory (5th edition)*, London: Sage.

Merrill, J. (1974), *The imperative of freedom. A Philosophy of Journalistic Autonomy*, New York: Hastings.

Merrill, J. (1989), *The dialectic of journalism. Towards a responsible use of press freedom*, Baton Rouge: Louisiana State University Press.

Merrill, John (1979), *Media, messages and men. New perspectives in communication*, New York: Longman.

Nerone, J. (1995), *Last rights. Revisiting Four Theories of the Press*, Urbana: University of Illinois Press.

Norris, Pippa and Zinnbauer, Dieter (2002), *Giving Voice to the Voiceless: Good governance, Human Development and Mass Communications*, New York: UNDP Human Development Report Office.

Nyamnjoh, Francis (2005), *Africa's Media, Democracy and the Politics of Belonging*, London: Zed Books.

Nyamnjoh, Francis (2007), 'Africa in the New Millennium: Interrogating Barbie Democracy', *Communication for Development and Social Change*, 1(2), pp. 105–111.

Phongpaichit, P. and Baker, C. (1998), *Thailand's Boom and Bust*, Bangkok: Silkworm books.

Pigeat, H. and Huteau, J. (2000), *Deontologie des medias. Institutions, pratiques et nouvelles approaches dans le monde*, Paris: Unesco.

Preston, N. (ed.) (2007), 'Global ethics', special issue of *Social Alternatives*, 26(3).

Puddenphatt, Andrew (2007), *Defining Indicators for Media Development. A background paper*, Paris: Unesco.

Puddephatt, Andrew (2008), 'Diagnostic tools and performance indicators', Paper Harvard-World Bank Workshop on The Role of the News Media in the Governance Reform Agenda, JFK School, Cambridge, Boston, 29–31 May 2008.

Sen, A. (2004), 'Cultural liberty and human development', In S. Fukuda-Parr (ed.), *Human development report: Cultural liberty in today's diverse world*, New York: United Nations Development Programme (UNDP).

Servaes, J. (1982), *De nieuwsmakers,* Kapellen: De Nederlandsche Boekhandel.

Servaes J. (1989), 'Beyond the four theories of the press', *Communicatio Socialis Yearbook*, 8.

Servaes, Jan and Tonnaer, Clement (1992), *De nieuwsmarkt. Vorm en inhoud van de internationale berichtgeving*, Groningen: Wolters-Noordhoff.

Servaes, J. (1999), *Communication for Development. One World, Multiple Cultures*, (Foreword by Jan Pronk), Cresskill: Hampton Press.

Servaes, J. and Liu, S. (eds) (2007a), *Moving Targets. Mapping the paths between communication, technology and social change incommunities*, Penang: Southbound.

Servaes, Jan (ed.) (2007b), *Communication for Development. Making a Difference, Background paper for the World Congress on Communication for Development (Rome, 25–27 October 2006)*, World Bank-FAO-Communication Initiative, Washington DC.

Servaes, Jan (ed.) (2008), *Communication for Development and Social Change*, Los Angeles-London-New Delhi-Singapore: Sage.

Servaes, J (2009a), 'Communication Policies, Good Governance and Development Journalism', *Communicatio. South African Journal for Communication Theory and Research*, 35 (1), pp. 50–80.

Servaes, J.; Malikhao, P. and Pinprayong, T. (2009b), 'Communication Rights are Human Rights. A Case Study of Thailand's Media', In Aliaa Dakroury; Mahmoud Eid and Yahya Kamalipour (eds), *The Right to Communicate: Historical Hopes, Global Debates, and Future Premises*, Dubuque: Kendall Hunt Publishers, pp. 227–254.

Servaes, J. (2009c), 'We are all journalists now', *Journalism*, 10(3), pp. 371–374.

Siebert, F., Peterson, T. and Schramm, W. (1956), *Four theories of the press*, Urbana: University of Illinois Press.

Sparks, Colin (2007), *Globalization, Development and the Mass Media*, Los Angeles-London-New Delhi-Singapore: Sage.

Tehranian, Majid (2007), *Rethinking Civilization. Resolving conflict in the human family*, London: Routledge.

Terzis, Georgios (ed.) (2007), *European Media Governance. National and regional dimensions*, Bristol: Intellect.

Terzis, Georgios (ed.) (2008), *European Media Governance. The Brussels Dimension*, Bristol: Intellect.

Thussu, Daya Kishan (2008), *News as entertainment. The rise of global infotainment*, London: Sage.

Triandafyllidou, Anna; Wodak, Ruth and Krzyanowski, Micha (eds) (2009), *The European Public Sphere and the Media: Europe In Crisis*, Basingstoke: Palgrave Macmillan.

Ukpabi, C. (ed.) (2001), *Handbook on journalism ethics. African case studies*, Windhoek: Media Institute of Southern Africa.

UNESCO (2004), *Education makes news! An EFA media training resource kit*, Paris: Unesco.

UNESCO (2005), *Media and Good Governance*, http: //portal.unesco.org/ci/en/ev.php-URL_ID=18816&URL_DO=DO_TOPIC&URL_SECTION=201.html.

UNESCO (2007a), *Model Curricula for Journalism Education for Developing Countries & Emerging Democracies*, Paris: Unesco.

UNESCO (2007b), *My media trainer. A self-instructional training of trainers program*, Paris: Unesco (DVD).

World Bank (2009), *Governance matters 2009. Worldwide governance indicators 1996–2008*, Washington DC, http: //info.worldbank.org/governance/wgi/index.asp. Accessed 17 June 2009.